First published in 2016
by Ally
peter@allypress.co.uk

Distributed in the UK by
Central Books
99 Wallis Road
London E9 5LN

Text © Luke Thompson
Front cover image © Estate of Lionel Miskin
Rear cover image: drawing by Heather Spears

ISBN: 978-0-9934734-9-4

Printed in England by SRP

Luke Thompson

Clay Phoenix
A biography of Jack Clemo

ALLY

Acknowledgements

The Arts and Humanities Research Council funded my research. Without their support none of the uncollected poems, published in *Archipelago, PN Review* and in *Clay Phoenix*, would have emerged. Nor would the forgotten dialect tales, published as *A Proper Mizz-Maze* by Francis Boutle. Equally, I would not have had the chance to edit the *Selected Poems* of Jack Clemo, which was published by Enitharmon in 2015 and introduced by Rowan Williams.

During the writing of this biography, Tim Kendall and Nick Groom were especially helpful, with editorial suggestions and guidance through the study of Clemo I presented for my PhD. Christine Faunch, Angela Mandrioli, Gemma Poulton and Sue Inskip of the Special Collections Library at the University of Exeter, and Jo Moore of Wheal Martyn Country Park and Museum, all helped in so many ways that it would be impossible to list them. The largest collection of archival material relating to Clemo is held at the University of Exeter, so I relied on their help and generosity throughout my research, including for permission to reproduce extracts from Clemo's diaries and correspondence.

I am grateful to many people for a variety of reasons. Some shared their memories and stories of the Clemos, others shared their correspondence and personal collections. Thanks are owed to the following: Father Benedict Ramsden, Sophie Bateman, Sara Ramsden, Pat Moyer, Norman Stone and 1A Productions, Sally Magnusson, Paul Hyland, Louis Hemmings, Cliff Moorhouse and the Manchester Academy of Fine Art, Stan Dobbin, Dennis Hall of Inky Parrot Press, Kim Cooper at the Cornish Studies Library, James Whetter and The Cornish Banner, Donald Rawe, Michael Williams, Malcolm Gould, Derek Giles, Ivor Bowditch, Bodmin Library, Alan Kent, Heather Martin, Heather Spears, Michael Spinks, Peter Woodward and the Sterts Theatre, John Hurst, Gemma Goodman, Emma Mason, Andrew Symons, Charles Thomas, Alan and Margaret Sanders, Frances and Ray Brown, Grace Gribble, Preston Gribble, Jennifer Pursall, Barbara Luke, Shirley Ball, Maria Willcox, Tony Jasper, Alwyn Marriage, Eileen Mitson, June Trethewey, Margaret Brearley, David Mabey of the London School of Hygiene and Tropical Medicine, Felicity Warner, *Resurgence* magazine, Trevor Vacher Dean and the *Dorset Year Book*, Tony Martin, Len Barnett, David Stark, Romer Mynne and the Savage family, Jean Rafferty, Michael Hanke, Rachelle Lerner, Esther and Roger Race, and L. Michael Kaas of the Mining History Association, Colorado.

Letters from Cecil Day Lewis to Jack Clemo, and the extract from the poem 'Emily Brontë' are printed by permission of Peters Fraser & Dunlop on behalf of the Estate of C. Day Lewis. Frances Bellerby's letters and Charles Causley's letters, as well as 'Homage to Jack Clemo' and the unpublished wedding poem, appear by kind permission of Bruce Hunter. Daphne du Maurier's letter appears with thanks to Kits Browning and the Estate of Daphne du Maurier. The letters from A.L. Rowse appear courtesy of the Royal Institute of Cornwall. The extracts from Sir Arthur Quiller Couch's letter to Clemo appear with kind permission of Gerry Hones, and those from E.W. Martin appear thanks to Derek Scantlebury. I am grateful to Craig Raine and Peter Jay for allowing me to publish their letters to Clemo, and to the estates of George MacBeth and Derek Savage. I am very grateful to John Miskin and the Lionel Miskin Estate for permission to reproduce the fascinating correspondence between Miskin and Clemo, as well as the cover image.

Most of the images used appear to have been taken by Eveline and Ruth Clemo or by Bella Peaty, Ruth's sister. Some, however, were taken by unacknowledged studios, while others were taken on site by professional photographers. I am grateful to the Cornwall Centre Collection at the Cornish Studies Library for permission to reproduce the wedding images taken by GWF Ellis, and to Ricky Knight for permission to use the striking RL Knight portrait of Clemo. Thanks to Paul Broadhurst, Tricia Porter and Ander Gunn for permission to use their terrific work. Unfortunately, I have not had any luck tracing photographers John Chard or David Hills. I thought I had almost tracked Mr Hills, after speaking to other writers and publishers who had dealt with him, but the trail ran suddenly cold. Apologies to all the photographers named John Chard whom I contacted in error.

Two people who helped in different ways have sadly died over the three years taken to complete *Clay Phoenix*: Paul Newman and Brenda Angilley. Paul was a writer who helped with initial thoughts and ideas while I was putting together proposals for the project. He produced many works relevant to my subject, including *The Man Who Unleashed The Birds*, reviewing Frank Baker and the artistic circle surrounding him in mid-twentieth century Cornwall. Brenda Angilley died the same year, 2014. Brenda appeared on the documentary film *Roots of my Story*, having known Clemo as a girl. She appears throughout Clemo's writing and was a significant influence on *Confession of a Rebel* and *The Clay Verge*, two of Clemo's most remarkable works. My meetings, interviews and conversations with Brenda were invaluable to my attempt to reconstruct the wartime and immediately postwar periods of Clemo's life. Among Brenda's treasured possessions was a flood-damaged copy of *Confession of a Rebel*, given to her by Clemo and meticulously inscribed with the numbers of every page on which she is mentioned.

CONTENTS

Acknowledgements	4
Note on the text	10
Introduction	11
Clay	21
'put forth thine hand'	43
Twilight Where God Dwells	73
'Teach me, Only Teach Love'	107
Travail	143
War Comes to Goonamarris	177
Wilding Graft	197
Confession of a Rebel	229
The Clay Verge	247
A Mystical-Erotic Quest	267
'Beneath the ashes'	299
The Invading Gospel	323
The Map of Clay	355
Cactus on Carmel	377
Ruth and the 'Dorset Pull'	401
The Echoing Tip and Broad Autumn	423
The Marriage of a Rebel and The Bouncing Hills	465
A Different Drummer and The Shadowed Bed	485
Greeting the Unseen	515
Postscript	543
Bibliography	552
Endnotes	571
Index	589
List of illustrations	608

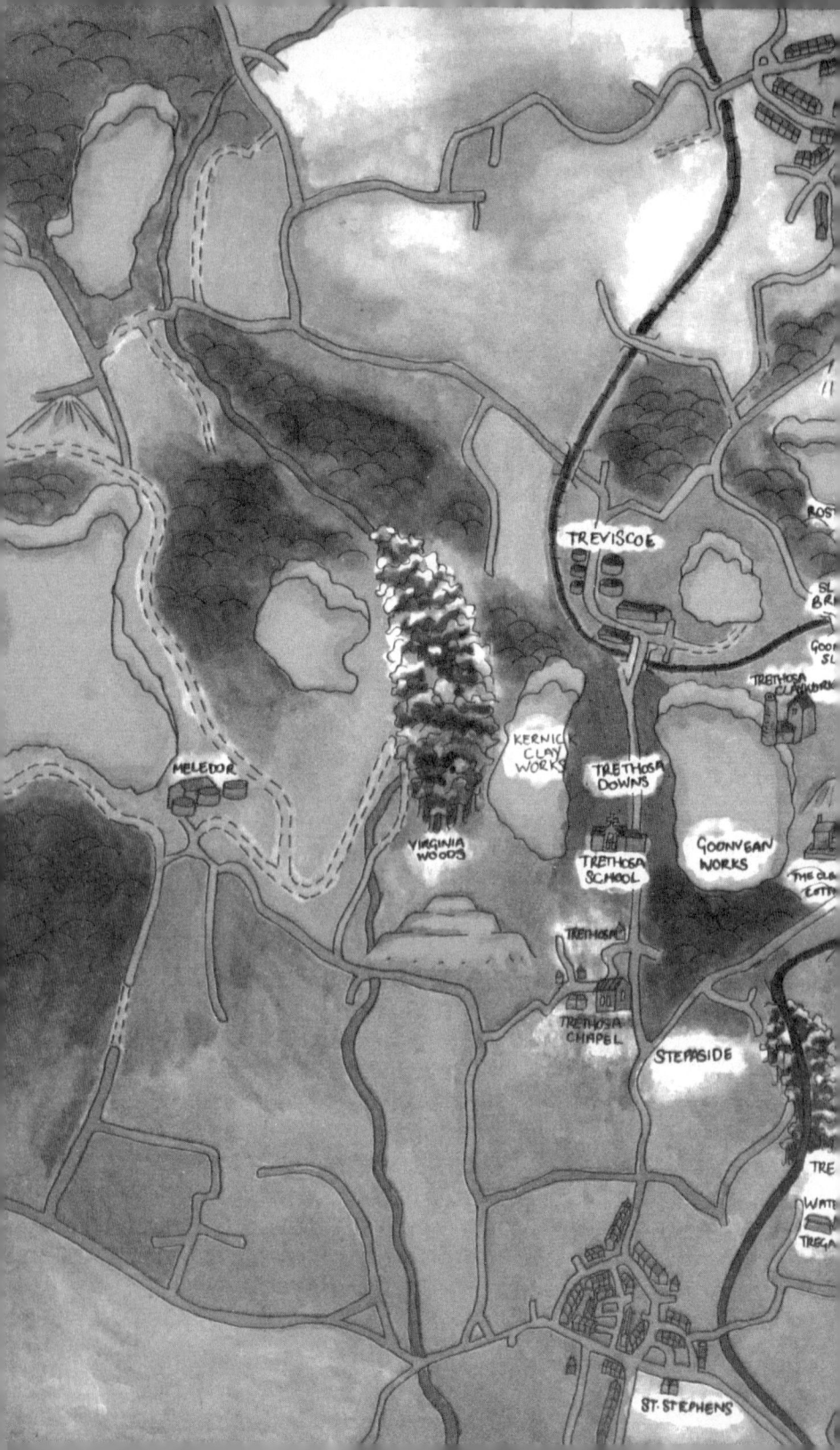

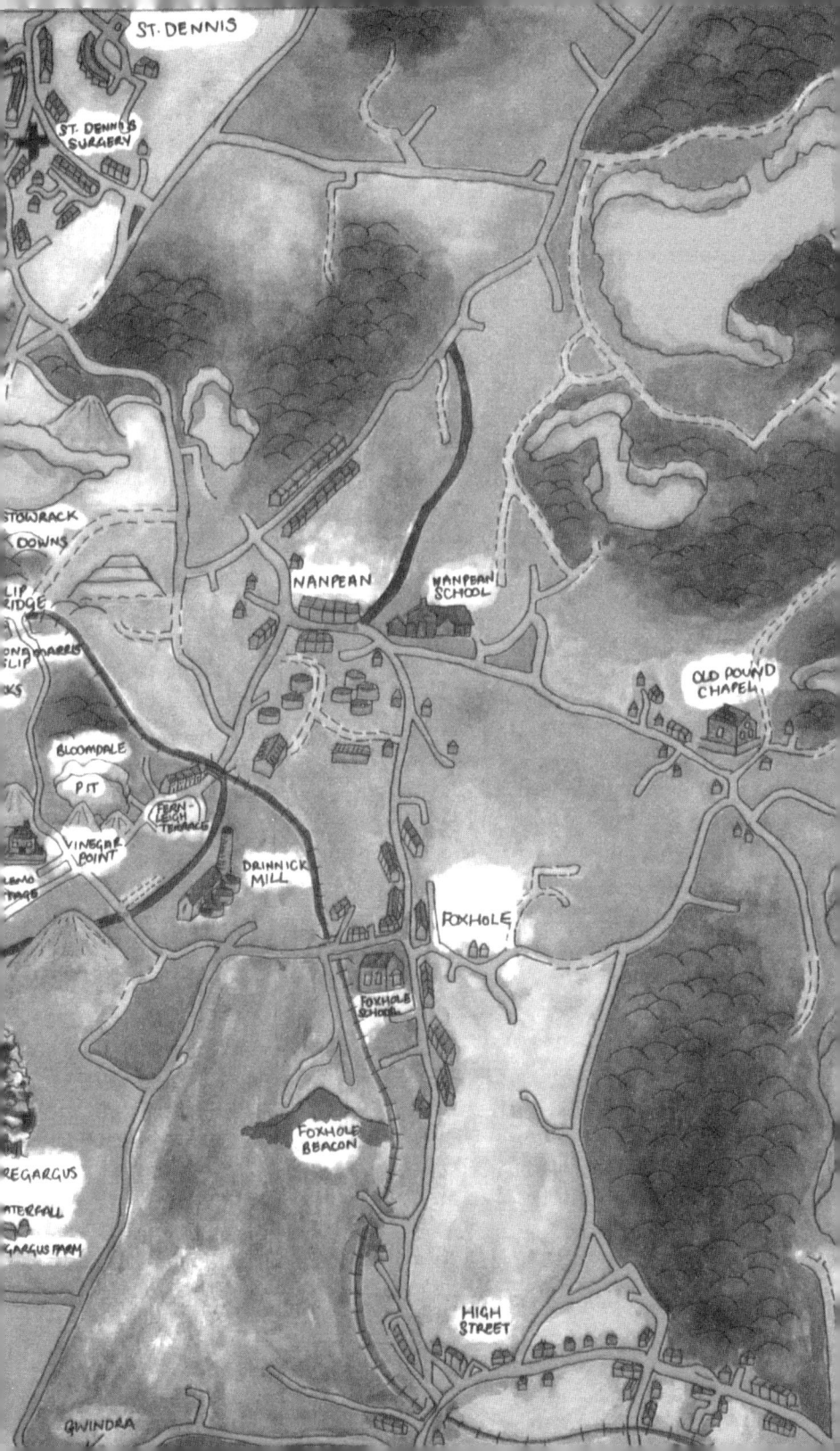

Note on the Text

Jack Clemo's handwriting is difficult to read, so much so that his diaries have been used by the University of Exeter to illustrate the problems that can face people working with archive materials. Over the three years of reading Clemo's handwriting, I have come to decipher it relatively easily, but occasionally a word has eluded me. When I have been unable to interpret a word completely, I have marked it with question marks in square brackets: [??]. When I believe I have deciphered a word, but am not completely certain, I have put the word in square brackets with question marks either side of it: [?example?].

It may be noticed that the text includes ellipses both with and without square brackets, either . . . or [...]. This is to differentiate between the ellipses used by Clemo himself and those employed by me. The ellipses without squared brackets are Clemo's, the ellipses within squared brackets are mine.

At the beginning of chapters, I have often used Biblical quotations. They tend to be favourite passages of Clemo's, referenced in the diaries of the period and usually written out in full at the front, as 'Mottos' for the year or pertaining to Clemo's state of mind or health. Clemo quoted from the King James Bible in his diaries and publications, a practice I have followed throughout *Clay Phoenix*.

Lastly, I have tried to preserve the 'voices' of the writers and correspondents quoted. For example, Clemo's mother's writing has a good deal of character, which I feel is better preserved without marking irregularities with [*sic*] notes. I have treated others the same, including the youthful Clemo, his wife Ruth, and the artist Lionel Miskin, the latter of which seems to have adopted a number of unconventional spellings deliberately.

SEPTEMBER, 1936.

INTRODUCTION

Since last December 31 I have travelled far, and been taught much in the school of life. I have suffered, and sinned, and wondered, and lost faith, and regained it [...]. What I now see clearest is that I must trust God more, be more childlike in my faith, and less ready to doubt at least appearance of evil. I must fight with more energy against the sins which I am too prone to love and harbour – lust, with its pleasure, its thrills and its delusions; pride and insincerity in thought and word.

As a teenager, Jack Clemo would begin each New Year by writing a summary of the previous twelve months. He would list failings and successes, spiritual ambitions, romantic and literary hopes, and often write a poem. These moments brought a sense of occasion to the end of the year. They tidied away the past, created order, and announced new beginnings. The above entry is taken from Clemo's earliest surviving diary, from 1934, when he was eighteen years old. Sixty years later, in 1994, the year in which he would die, Clemo could no longer see the diary in front of him. He had been blind for forty years, and deaf for almost sixty. His writing was a laborious scrawl of infrequent entries, only a sentence or two in length. To indicate where each diary day began and ended, notches were made along the side of the page, across which Clemo would run his finger, feeling for where to write. The only way of conversing with him was by writing in capital letters into the palm of his hand with one's index finger.

As a very young man, fully sighted and sound of hearing, every one of Jack's diary entries would be crammed with hundreds of small, tight, hurrying words. These are unrestrained documents of delight or despair, resisting confinement to the page. Perhaps surprisingly, the early diary entries, written in such ebullient haste, are more difficult to read than the slower script written in blindness and old age.

The final diary is sombre reading, sparse and increasingly a record of suffering and confusion. Photographs from the year show Jack to be a tiny, wasted figure, always hunched or curled up, as though withered. His body had been assaulted by disease since childhood, undermining his senses, bones, nerves and heart. This he survived, almost miraculously, and it was cancer that overwhelmed him. Cancer crushed the man, and not only physically. In 1994 Clemo had a vague feeling of disappointment and loss. He was aware that his fame had waned from the fullness of the fifties, sixties and seventies, when he was featuring alongside or sometimes headlining over writers such as Seamus Heaney, Anne Stevenson, Geoffrey Hill and John Updike; but more than that, Jack seemed weary. The sleeplessness, discomfort, the uncertainty of hospital tests, and the spreading cancer impeded his joy, the feeling of God's presence in his life. Even then he did not submit to despair, and when there was nothing to report besides the pain, Clemo did not write at all. The following is a typical entry: 'Ruth phoned to Gwen about my stomach pains yesterday then bought tablets Gwen recommended. I felt the spiritual uplift of her prayers'.[1] The backstory is one of pain, but it is only recorded because of the attendant 'spiritual uplift'. Knowing that he only wrote to record positive news, this diary is poignantly sparse.

Attentiveness to joy was hard-earned and practised – a more mature form of the relentlessly optimistic expectation of God's promises being realized, of Jack's personal covenant satisfied. In spite of the deep poverty into which he was born, the tragedies of his heredity, the loss of family, the physical and social decline that began in young childhood, and the grim prospect of his future, it is one of Clemo's most exceptional qualities that he remained hopeful, with faith in God's favour and grace, always on the cusp of fulfilment or regeneration.

The writing of Clemo's life offers some specific challenges. His disabilities precluded him from conversation, so there are no iconic anecdotes of sparkling badinage at social gatherings, no Johnsonian witticisms or one-liners, no illuminating pronouncements. There is almost no dialogue at all. On the other hand, this inability to engage conversationally led to an abundance of correspondence. Had A.L. Rowse been admitted to the Clemo cottage as he had desired, we might not know what interests they shared, but as they could only converse through correspondence, their relationship has survived and is held in the archives of the University of Exeter's Special Collections Library.

Clemo's archive shows the route he travelled to attain peace and satisfaction, and no document reveals the writer's emotional, spiritual, intellectual and physical development as completely as the diaries. Beginning in 1934, we have every diary until the year of Clemo's death in 1994, with only 1939 and 1940 missing (apparently burned by Clemo during a period of desperate loneliness and misery). The diaries are supported by an extensive collection of letters, scrapbooks, manuscripts, financial documents and photographs, as well as a few artefacts and Clemo's personal library, many volumes of which are heavily annotated or contain letters from literary figures such as Sir Arthur Quiller-Couch, T.F. Powys and Joseph Hocking. It is an impressively complete collection, and one of the most extraordinary things about it is that, before now, it has not been fully worked through. Supporting this archive are other, smaller collections. Wheal Martyn has the second largest collection after Exeter, with manuscripts, artefacts, photographs and various papers, augmented in 2013 by their acquisition of the Jack Clemo Memorial Room collection held at Trethosa Chapel. Most of the Clemo material was saved. However, the chapel documents with their record of baptisms, weddings, expenses and minutes, have disappeared. Happily, Clemo's writing desk was rescued, and conservation work was undertaken in 2014 to replace hinges and handles and cure it of woodworm. It now squats in the museum on permanent display. Another invaluable resource is the *Cornish Guardian* microfilm archive in Bodmin Library, which shows Clemo's earliest attempts to gain an audience with his controversial correspondence and poetry.

In spite of all of this freely available material, little in-depth work has been done on Clemo. There has been only one lengthy publication, written by the presenter Sally Magnusson and entitled *Clemo: A Love Story*. This is a brief history of the role of Providence in Clemo's romance, and the book was so heavily controlled by Jack and his wife Ruth that Magnusson was prevented from adding anything new to the mythology already established in Clemo's autobiographies, *Confession of a Rebel* and *The Marriage of a Rebel*.

In recent years, the study of Clemo has been reduced to Cornish interest and Christian journals, despite which, Clemo's relevance might be greater now than ever. A self-proclaimed rebel, Clemo led his rebellion to the fields of ecoliterature, theology and even to poetics. In correspondence, the poet Toby Martinez de las Rivas, who has written on Clemo, highlighted the poetic aspect of Clemo's rebellion:

> [Jack Clemo's] wilful refusal to be roped into anything which might constitute poetic fashion led him in some very strange and difficult directions. Many poets considered radical today use techniques (and underpin these techniques philosophically) with literary ideas which are the height of fashion – deconstructionism, non-procedural grammar, syntactic confusion etc. But Clemo, like another great literary hero of mine, Barry MacSweeney, is recognisably different in his lone adherence to ideas which served more or less to isolate him.

Within ecopoetics, Clemo can be grimly antagonistic. Popular writing about the 'natural world' can imply a kind of Golden Age pastoralism, either lamenting the loss of a connection to nature or suggesting that progress or wellbeing depend on establishing or re-establishing the relationship, returning to the 'wild'. But Clemo's was not the voice of rustic bliss or romantic elegy. He condemns the 'paganism' of Wordsworth and Keats, and it is a condemnation he might have levelled at contemporary nature writers, too. For Clemo, man and 'Nature' are born together, both fallen. Instead of encouraging their connection, Clemo's poetry and post-Calvinistic approach demand that we sever the bond between man and the world and submit to God. Indeed, in his best-known poems Clemo assaults natural beauty, delighting in the industrial destruction of the fallen world, and using the boundary as a metaphor for God's assault of his own body and senses. For example, in 'The Excavator', one of Clemo's strongest early clayscape poems, published in both *The Clay Verge* and *The Map of Clay*, the excavator-poet talks about the 'delicate aesthetes', the nature poets:

> I cannot speak their language; I am one
>   Who feels the doggerel of Heaven
> Purge earth of poetry; God's foolishness
> Laugh through the web man's ripening wisdom spun;
>   The world's whole culture riven
> By moody excavations Love shall bless.
> All staining rhythms of Art and Nature break
> Within my mind, turn grey, grow truth
> Rigid and ominous as this engine's tooth.
>   And so I am awake:
>   No more a man who sees
> Colour in flowers or hears from birds a song,
>   Or dares to worship where the throng
> Seek Beauty and its old idolatries.
> No altar soils my vision with a lax
>   Adult appeal to sense,
> Or festering harmonies' magniloquence.
>   My faith and symbol shall be stark.
> My hand upon these caterpillar-tracks
>   Bogged in the mud and clay,
>   I find it easier to pray:
> 'Keep far from me all loveliness, O God,
>   And let me laud
>   Thy meaner moods, so long unprized;
>   The motions of that twisted, dark,
>   Deliberate crucial Will
>   I feel deep-grinding still
> Under the dripping clay with which I am baptized.'

In these clayscape poems we find another way in which Clemo's poetry remains of interest. Here is a technical and functional mining language developed and used for industry by working men, being employed for a completely different and subversive purpose. Clemo is in the unique position of being born an insider, with an insider's geography and insight, but Clemo held an alien set of values and ambitions. His work is the only literary account of the clay country in the mid-twentieth century, of the industrial language, landscape, culture and dialect. Yet Clemo is not regionally containable, not *merely* of local interest. He is connecting with the ageless and infinite, with God, sex and suffering, in an extraordinarily unguided and isolated fashion. He is an anomaly. As his good friend Derek Savage said, Jack is 'a unicorn, phoenix and hippogriff'.[2]

In recent years, interest in Clemo's work appears to have grown, largely owing to contemporary discourses on regionalism, ecopoetics, identity and place, and popular books in the 'new nature' bracket, such as Philip Marsden's *Rising Ground*. At Warwick University, Gemma Goodman has been working on Clemo's novels, while Emma Mason has worked on the unusually personal and hybrid theology. At Principia College, Illinois, Heather Martin has written and spoken on the poetry from a Christian perspective, while at Falmouth Kym Martindale continues to work on a monograph of Frances Bellerby and Clemo. The sole full-length study to have used the archive is Heather Martin's thesis, which still used just a handful of files from the three hundred available at Exeter.

Clay Phoenix draws from the complete Clemo archive, as well as those of many other writers, including A.L. Rowse, Charles Causley, Derek Savage and Ernest Martin. It also relies on personal interviews with Clemo's friends and family, and people from the surrounding villages, with contributions from some of Jack's early love interests, cousins, and his foster-sister Frances Brown (née Allen). During interviews with Clemo's more recent friends, I found frequent discrepancies and disagreements. It was as though each had projected their own needs onto Jack: the need for a sympathetic believer, for a father-figure, or for someone genuinely connected to God. Clemo's oddness, elusiveness and silence offered a blank canvas, or malleable clay. It is probably significant that there is no one alive who knew

Clemo before he lost his hearing and sight. Most of his remaining close contacts did not see the man of passion, the internal workings, the fears, doubts, or dynamism. They only knew the married man, the celebrated poet, the 'fulfilled believer'. They saw feathers and flight but none of the fire and ash. Perhaps this highlights the importance of rooting a biography in Clemo's personal papers and private diaries.

These are the richest resource. By revealing events as they were being experienced, they avoid the distortion of hindsight. This is especially relevant to the Jack Clemo story, owing to what I call his apophenic impulse. Throughout his life, Clemo observed dates, numbers, literary biographies, wildlife, and even the weather, in search of patterns that might shed light on his destiny. These patterns, he believed, were established by God and should be considered revelatory and mystical, and he used them to structure his autobiographies, informing his faith and expectations of the world. What the archives offer – the diaries in particular – is the raw material or data; the events as they happened, prior to their selective arrangement into these patterns.

But the diaries are more than a remedial resource. After Clemo died, his widow read through them and attempted to sanitise the story. Working two mornings a week, she took scissors, Tipp-Ex and a black marker to the pages, destroying or obscuring statements and suggestions she did not like, often tearing out whole weeks of entries at a time. Sometimes Ruth even rewrote events, an act that goes beyond expurgation and enters wilful dishonesty. The most significant act of this sort was performed on the account of how she and Jack were introduced, corresponded and married, a narrative reclaimed in *Clay Phoenix*. However, her editorial attempts were often incomplete, and the subjects of missing passages can still be determined by careful cross-referencing of the diaries and letters. This reveals that Ruth tried especially hard to edit sections relating to Jack's early romantic feelings, the real occasion of their meeting, and his lifelong medical condition. Among these revelations, one was frequently and awkwardly mooted in interviews and correspondence. This was the query hanging over Clemo's sexual attraction to children. The subject is a difficult and sensitive one, and this biography is the first to attempt any sort of negotiation of the material. Even so, I have had to rely almost exclusively on Clemo's own interpretation of events as they are presented in the remaining diary entries, and this is not at all satisfactory. One relationship in particular, with a girl named Barbara, is clearly sexually exploitative. Even basing our judgement entirely on Clemo's account of the relationship, he was an adult and she was a child, and there was certainly an abuse of power.

There were many other girls of various ages whom Clemo knew, some of them described in his writings in erotic terms. It is worth noting that those whom I have been able to interview have denied that they experienced inappropriate attention. However, this is one area which I am unable to investigate beyond Clemo's own account. I have presented the available evidence as it appears in the diaries, which remain the most illuminating resource available to the researcher, offering Clemo's immediate impressions and emotional responses to events which would be reinterpreted and stylised later, when he came to write his autobiographical works.

These diaries were given to Exeter in 2007, the year that Ruth Clemo died, by which time Clemo's public appeal was at a low ebb. They were the final donations of a process that had begun in 1980, when Jack negotiated the sale of some of his literary manuscripts with the poet and Exeter academic Ron Tamplin.

The story that emerges from all of this previously unanalysed material differs from the 'official' biography of Clemo's construction. Clemo established a mystic narrative, writing and rewriting his life, exposing himself confessionally, but on his own terms and mythopoeically. This remarkable bird has been colouring himself in. In spite of which, beneath the dripping paint, the plumage of the Clay Phoenix is no less strange.

Trethosa Pit, with Goonvean incline, Dry and Engine House (courtesy of the China Clay History Society).

I
Clay

O Lord, thou art our father; we are the clay, and thou our potter; and we all are the work of thy hand.

Isaiah 64:8

Cornwall's cultural shifts in the twentieth and twenty-first centuries have moved slower inland. Industry dominates the landscape, with excavated moorlands, pits and dumps, office buildings, drys, trucks and rail tracks. Though only a few miles distant, this is a long way from the Arthurian coast or the Cornish Riviera, 'the bland, beauty-haunted domain of Cornwall's popular novelists'.[3] The roughly defined clay area remains in cold contrast to those coastal regions. It is not a tourist destination – not an easy space to sell to the visitor – and the Eden Project squats uncomfortably on its fringes, hidden from the brutal gaze of the clays in its exhausted pit.

The shape of the land derives from an eighteenth-century desire to make fine porcelain. This porcelain is said to have been first brought from China to Europe by Marco Polo, but it was the East India Trading Companies in the seventeenth century that popularised it in Britain, turning it into a valuable import and its production into a potentially useful investment. There was a race to discover and patent the recipe, which the Devon-born Quaker and chemist William Cookworthy won. In 1745 he was shown materials from Virginia by the American Andrew Duché, along with an example of the porcelain made from them. The minerals required for the process were china clay (or kaolin) and china stone, both types of decomposed feldspar found in granite. For the manufacture to be practical, Cookworthy needed a source of both minerals in Britain, and it was in the granite spine of the Cornubian batholith that runs across the southwest, protruding prominently at Dartmoor, Bodmin Moor, St Austell, in the far West of Cornwall and on the

Isles of Scilly, that he found them. The first deposit discovered was of an inferior quality at Tregonning Hill near Helston, but on a later trip 'in the neighbourhood of the parish of St Stephens, in Cornwall', Cookworthy found 'immense quantities of both'.[4]

Cookworthy's partner, Richard Champion, took over the company from its founder, and was given the patent for Cookworthy's hard porcelain. Champion tried to renew the patent, but was met with serious opposition by the Staffordshire potters, particularly by the influential and celebrated Josiah Wedgwood. Renewal of the patent was successful, but Champion was now being pressured on one side by Wedgwood's opposition and on the other by the amounts he was paying to the landowner Thomas Pitt and to the heirs of Cookworthy. Wedgwood and the Staffordshire potters moved in, looking to lease workable land, aware that Champion was financially vulnerable and that he would soon have to sell the patent. The collection of potters who took it on became known as the New Hall Company.

Through the nineteenth century the original large clayworks were sold off to new prospectors, many of them local. Farmland was leased, quarries were dug and drained, and small conical waste tips were raised on the edge of each concern. Before long, dozens of these white pyramids blistered on the gutted belly of mid-Cornwall, dominating the skyline and landscape. Redundant now, the pyramids are growing green with resilient wild plants, rhododendrons and buddleia. The spring, river and drainage water that was once pumped out of the bottoms of the pits has been left to flood them, making deep lakes and pools, turquoise from the kaolin particles. Some of these, like Lansalson, near Ruddlemoor, with its rhododendron woodlands covering the peak and running down the slope to hang over pale blue waters and clay-bleached shore sands, look more like tropical oases than derelict industrial sites.

The principle of the mining has not really changed since the nineteenth century. A warning horn sounds and the rock is blasted with explosives, exposing a new face in the pit. Powerful water cannons are fired at the pit face, washing away the kaolin particles and leaving only waste rock, which is removed and transported to the tip, or burrow. In the early days, the unwanted rock refuse was carted up on rails by horse, or by engines discarded by the tin and copper mines, and emptied at the top by a sky-tip worker. This was the job Clemo once told his head-teacher he would like to do when he grew up, 'yearning for the sense of freedom, elevation and remoteness that must be felt up there on the ridge'.[5]

Down below, the clay washed away by the water cannons is left to settle, then filtered, and the slurry carried away to dry. In the earlier days the drying was done naturally, by barrowing the clay into pans and then simply leaving it, a method that took many months. As demand increased this came to be considered a cumbersome and inefficient process and the dry kilns were developed. These were long stone buildings with porous floors, over which wet clay would be poured and raked flat. At one end of the building was a fire, and at the opposite end was a chimney stack, the ends connected by a flue that ran beneath the porous floor, so that the room was heated and hot air drawn under the levelled clay. Instead of the drying taking much of the year, this process reduced the time to a couple of days. When Clemo's father worked the clay, before Jack was born, he laboured in one of these hot, oppressive, steam-filled drys.

Clay-mining did not only change inland Cornwall, but the need to transport the kaolin and other minerals led to coastal developments, such as the quays of Pentewan and Par. Charles Rashleigh began expanding a harbour at West Polmear in the late eighteenth century, for clay and copper exportation. The population rose from just nine people to nine hundred over fewer than ten years, and West Polmear changed its name to Charlestown, now a popular tourist destination. Similarly, Christopher Hawkins in the early nineteenth century developed Pentewan, and Joseph Treffry completely altered Par, which was still exporting enormous amounts of clay at the beginning of the twenty-first century. At Par there remains a large industrial plant, much of it abandoned, although some of the buildings are working drys, receiving clay slurry through pipelines and transporting it to Fowey Harbour along private roads.

The clay country is culturally unique in Cornwall. The communities do not change as quickly as the coastal towns, and you find the same family names in the phonebook as you do in the graveyards. Through the twentieth century many traditions have died out, but

Tea Treats and feast days, brass bands and male voice choirs could hardly be called things of the past, and the story is still told of the time Treviscoe Male Voice Choir brought home first prize from the International Eisteddfod at Llangollen in 1956.[6]

One tradition quickly diminishing in the clays is Methodism. This was the foundation of Clemo's Christianity. The impressive, thick-set chapel at Trethosa, where the Clemos worshipped and where Jack's mother taught the Sunday School, was built by the Bible Christians in 1876, Methodists having previously met in a makeshift chapel on Trethosa Farm.[7] The Bible Christian movement was a splinter Methodist group founded by William Bryant, who was born a few miles to the north-east of the clay country, at Gunwen, near Luxulyan. They placed firmer emphasis on the Bible as the source of all statements about faith, but did not really deviate from Wesleyan Methodism. Bryant himself did not defect from Wesleyanism, but was expelled from the Church, seemingly for his maverick egoism and 'inability to work with others'.[8] His own Church was a great success in Devon and Cornwall, entering the few areas hardly touched by the tireless Wesley.

Wesley himself did visit the area once, in 1757. He mentions preaching there in his journal:

> At two I preached in St Stephen's (in-Branwell), near a lone house on the side of a barren mountain; but neither the house nor the court could contain the people; so we went into a meadow, where all might kneel (which they generally do in Cornwall), as well as stand and hear. And they did hear, and sing, and pray.[9]

In 1907 the Bible Christian group joined two other Methodist factions to form the United Methodist Church, which in turn merged with another two larger Methodist groups in 1932, the Primitive and the Wesleyan Methodist Churches, forming the Methodist Church of Great Britain. This is the reason why maps from the 1930s show chapels previously labelled as 'Bible Christian' being relabelled 'Methodist'. It did not mark an ideological or spiritual development, but a practical alliance.

The new and living activism of Methodism and the Bible Christian movement was central to Clemo's faith. It was a taste he never outgrew, a present vitalism, immediate and urgent, with preachers fierce and earnest. The God of Clemo's clay-pits did not care for Latin and ritual, but for faith and living souls. Methodism is known as a working-class faith, largely because of the missions made by Wesley and his followers, who did not value the souls of the wealthy over those of the poor. It appeared a more inclusive and down-to-earth sect. Not only did it show greater equality among the classes, but the Bible Christians enlisted equal numbers of men and women as preachers in the early days (as well as a disproportionate quantity of wrestlers).

Almost everyone in the villages went to chapel on a Sunday, most of them twice, and some of them three times if they were helping or attending the Sunday school: men and women, adults and children, captains and labourers, farmers and clay-workers. It was the social focus of the week for many. There were a few pubs in the area, of course – the Grenville Arms in Nanpean, the Queen's Head and King's Arms at St Stephen – but a large proportion of the congregation supported the temperance movements, and Trethosa Chapel hosted their meetings.

Other than Sunday services, villagers met labouring at the clayworks or in the fields, at band practice or at choir on Thursdays. It would have been both men and women going to work in the pits in the early days, the women doing lighter work like scrubbing sand from the sun-dried blocks of clay, but this changed with the new drys, and in the early twentieth century women would have been more likely to meet at the shop or on the daily visits to one another's homes.

It was at choir that Jack Clemo's parents met, the fifteen year-old Eveline Polmounter and the eighteen year-old Reginald Clemo. Eveline was born and raised on Goonvean Farm, in a devout household. Her father John was an illiterate clay labourer and farm worker. Her mother, Elizabeth Jane Bullen, known as Jane, was from a family of 'some local distinction', Clemo said, being better educated and from a tin mining background. The tinners were considered harder working and tougher than the clay miners, enduring greater risks and worse conditions. Jane lost her father Joseph at Dowgas mine, the tin and copper works between St Stephen and Sticker, which meant that her brother, George, had to support the family, working at the same mine in which his father had died. On the 1861 census, when George was fourteen, he appears to have been the main earner in the household. By the 1871 census his mother is no longer there, having gone into service as a cook at St Erme, and George is head of the household, with two of his younger sisters, Jane and Sarah, working with him at the mine and living in the family home at Resugga Lane End.

This George Bullen, Clemo's great uncle, was the most distinguished of the family in Clemo's eyes, having been raised in such grim circumstances and having gone on to become a respected Methodist minister. Bullen went to Yorkshire to study at Joseph Lawrence's East Keswick training college, where impoverished young men desiring to perform missionary work could be trained. As a result, Bullen is found in the late nineteenth century in a remote community on the east coast of Newfoundland, called Wesleyville, where in 1884 he became the first minister of the Methodist circuit. Before long, Bullen was pushing farther up the coast with his family to the even more remote Twillingate and then Notre Dame Bay. In 1889, he moved to Michigan, serving at Shepardsville, Potterville, Hastings, Carson City and Reed City, until settling at Muskegon Heights on Lake Michigan with his wife Selina, where he died in 1917. In *Confession of a Rebel* Jack used George Bullen to represent the polar opposite of the Clemos, specifically his father, who, he writes, had gone to America 'to entangle himself in the grosser roots of materialism'.

George's sister, Elizabeth Jane, married John Polmounter in 1871. They had twelve children together, although only six survived – a high infant mortality rate, even then. Of the survivors, the eldest, Frederick, went to America in a ship full of Cornishmen and women when he was eighteen and settled in Pennsylvania; Alfred married Anna and stayed in the area; Lucy married Richard Grigg, who inherited Penrose Veor Farm in St Dennis, close to Annie who married Wilfred Greenslade; Bertha was born prematurely and did not develop well, but was looked after until her death by Eveline, the last child and Jack's mother, who was born on 9 January 1894.

Clemo describes the uncertainty of farm life around the clayworks, where buildings could be quickly knocked down as quarries deepened, and the rest of the land was suffocated with waste sand as the burrows spilled over. He does not offer a vision of rustic simplicity and a salubrious pastoral existence: 'The carts rattling about under puffing stacks were filled as often with coal and clay as with farm produce, manure or fodder. Nature's role was reduced to a minor one, and her hold was precarious.' The industrial destruction of the Polmounter farm when Clemo was a child is mentioned in the poem 'Goonvean Claywork Farm', published in *The Map of Clay* and addressed to his mother. Here, the tearing down of the building is a preparation of the landscape of their faith:

> Near the white gashed cliff where the orchard
> Held its brave menaced fruit
> You crouched and were tortured
> By the clang on the thrusting rails,
> Watching the iron lines encroach,
> Hearing the clash of the buffers
> That signalled my fate's approach,
> The grimy burdens rumbling through the clay.

The chapel at Trethosa was not even twenty years old when Jack's parents, Reggie Clemo and Eveline Polmounter, were born. It was there that Eveline felt her personal call to God. She was already a Christian and a Methodist in 1906, but she experienced the evangelical 'rebirth' – one's personal commitment to Christ, beyond church or chapel affiliations, more often called a 'conversion'. She writes in her pamphlet *I Proved Thee at the Waters*: 'At the early age of twelve, in an evangelistic service at our Bethel Chapel, I dedicated my life to Jesus Christ, and this experience gave me a mystical love for devotional reading.' Note the use of the word 'mystical' here. This is a different mysticism from the more familiar High Church experience. Eveline's mysticism, like Jack's, was more subtle and quotidian, an everyday observation of God's personal influence in her life.

Eveline was a devout child in a loving household, with respected parents and a missioning Uncle George. Some of these traits Clemo believed he inherited, and the importance of bloodlines and hereditary characteristics becomes a key feature of his sense of identity and place in the world as he nurtured his compulsion for patterns. In *Confession*, he quotes a Michigan obituary praising Bullen for his 'Celtic temperament' and theological mind, his 'exquisite sensitiveness', 'shyness' and his 'strong and subtle intellect':

> Some of these qualities I inherited, with a similar endowment from the Hocking family, and had not the Clemos been such a rough lot I should probably have become a clever man of the conventional sort, perhaps a writer of genial stories like the Hockings'; I might even have entered the ministry.

The Hockings were popular novelists of their day. There were three of them who wrote, two brothers and a sister, but Clemo refers only to the brothers Joseph and Silas. Clemo's inheritance from the Hockings is mentioned both in *Confession* and in a short essay published in Denys Val Baker's *Cornish Review*. In the autobiography, it is 'the romantic narrative talent I had derived from the Hockings', and in the *Cornish Review*, their kinship proposes 'the probable derivation of my talent'.[10]

Clemo claims in *Confession* that he did not read much by the Hockings, and in the diaries he records having read just one book, Silas's autobiography *My Book of Memory*, which was damned as 'shallow, disconnected stuff', a 'mere string of anecdotes and stories about the famous people he met'.[11] He called them 'fashionable' and 'naïve' superficial writers and was so passionately critical of them in an early draft of *Confession of a Rebel* that Cecil Day Lewis had to ask Clemo to tone it down for fear of libel. Clemo is not arguing that he received his talent from reading their work, but that something was passed on as though through the blood.

The Hockings were not close relations. They were first cousins twice removed: Jack's father's mother's mother's father was also Silas, Joseph and Salome Hocking's father's father. Yet the blood of those distant cousins, carrying their narrative talent, was somehow passed to Clemo. The logical fallacy of Clemo's belief here is an important one, because the 'blood' claim is an irrational pattern-seeking behaviour – the apophenic impulse – that will be seen throughout his life, in his relationships with women and with other writers, and in his interpretation of the world and God. Clemo's concern for bloodlines and inheritance is indicative of probably the most important narrative detail of his life story, relating to his father Reggie and to Clemo's disabilities.

Eveline would live with and care for Jack until her death, when he was sixty-one. She made a promise not to die before she saw him married; a promise she kept against the odds. Her devotion was vocational, assiduous and dogged. Reggie's significance was equally but very differently vital, and although he died when Jack was an infant, his influence is an immediately recognisable feature of Clemo's life.

Reggie was born on 5 November 1890 at High Street, a mile south of Foxhole, but the family settled on Trethosa Downs, bordering the Polmounter farm at Goonvean. Clemo described their cottage on the Downs as

> one of a block of three squalid dwellings almost encircled by the towering white rubble from Trethosa clay-pit. Outside the garden wall was a railway siding flanked by a long line of drying-kilns with their grim stone pillars, wooden awnings and corrugated-iron roofs. The air was foul with clay-dust and the grime of coal trucks coming in from Cardiff.[12]

Reggie was one of eight children, all of whom survived: Anne, Ellen, Lucy, Hettie, John, Fanny, Reggie and Horatio. Horatio alone is presented generously by Clemo, 'the single wholesome exception in a family of raw pagans.'[13] He was an excellent singer who appeared regularly in the local newspapers and taught Jack music in the 1920s. Of the other siblings, 'few of them turned out well', Clemo wrote in *Confession*. One 'became a nymphomaniac in her teens and was removed to Bodmin asylum', while another 'drifted to London and had a son by a German lover'.[14] Their mother, Esther Clemo (née Trudgian), was 'a tall, vigorous old woman, scornful of men, cynical in her view of marriage' with a 'sharp, almost witchlike face'. She was a 'shrivelled, rasping old grandmother',[15] on whom Clemo would base the brothel madam Sal in his debut novel *Wilding Graft*. Similarly, her husband John Clemo was 'a drunken lout from the Mitchell area', a cruel, abusive man, ferocious with his wife and children:

> I had heard a little of those nights when John Clemo, returning from St Stephen's pub in drunken fury, would drive his wife and children outdoors and on to the sand-dump, where they often remained till morning.

John is the template for Zachary Kruse, the father of the hero Joel in Clemo's posthumously published novel, *The Clay Kiln*. Joel is a fusion of Clemo's father and himself, and is said to have

> hidden from his father, waiting with childish, impotent rage as he watched Zachary stagger past, shouting, peering into the empty wagons, pushing open the unlocked doors of the cuddies […]. Sometimes Joel had been caught and thrown upon the sand and beaten or had been forced to stay for hours, late into the night cowering upon a ledge along the side of the chasm.

There is a sense that Jack comes to terms with his family history quite late in life, and his treatment of the Clemos is one way of gauging this. In the 1949 *Confession*, for example, he dismissed his name on the first page, writing: 'The name Clemo […] is, I believe, rarely found outside the Duchy, though I am not curious enough about etymology to know anything of its derivations. I have never bothered to trace the family further back than my grandfather'. He adds that since he has turned away from his 'natural fate' in favour of his 'Divine predestination', any 'atavistic tendencies' would have been chipped off. This allows Clemo the belief that only the inherited tendencies that are of benefit to God and to Clemo's divine destiny remained in him. In other words, it is the useful blood of both families that flowed through Jack's veins. In *The Marriage of a Rebel*, thirty years later, Clemo observed the paradox in this sentiment and went back further in his history to find out more about his blood:

> The Cornish Clemos are descendants of a French family called Clement who escaped from France to Cornwall soon after the massacre of St Bartholomew's Day in 1572. The young male Clements married Cornish girls [...]. The French are supposed to be clear, logical thinkers and they are supposed to understand sex. The Celts are alleged to be primitive, full of wild mystical intuitions, so that they become melancholy dreamers when their more ferocious tendencies are not being provoked. I possess the characteristics of both groups.

Clemo is better at ease talking about the past in *Marriage*, when the storm and stress of his hope and despair have been soothed by belief in a promise kept and by his resignation to this 'inheritance'.

It may be seen in this passage that Clemo had a tendency to simplify and polarise people and facts. He did this with his parents from an early age. On the one side there are the dark and sordid Clemos, and on the other the devout and loving Polmounters, the Ahura-Mazda and Ahriman of his personal pantheon. Exaggerating qualities in this way might be a useful trait for a novelist, a recognition and development of clear tensions, but it is also a simplification of the world, a tidying-up of messy issues, and should be considered an aspect of Clemo's pattern-seeking behaviour. The tendency to perceive events in terms of polarities is inherent in the devil-versus-Christ construct and in good-versus-evil, and it is also in the Nature-Divinity polarity of the early clay poems and in the novel *The Shadowed Bed*.

In his biography, Clemo is seeing a prenatal pattern which makes not only spiritual but scientific claims. Attributing specific talents and inclinations to distant cousins or a vaguely assumed Gallic ancestry, he is expressing the belief that concepts and behaviours

Reggie Clemo (left) and his brother John, in Butte, Montana, c. 1910

Reggie Clemo (left) and friend 'on a ranch', 1911.

pass in an almost fully schematised way from one member of the family to another. The example of the two families, the Clemos and the Polmounters, of which Jack is the composite, is a good one. Clemo is hard on his father's side, impressing on the reader that his own nature embodies a primal conflict between their bad pagan depravity and the good simple Christianity of the Polmounters. This he saw as the conflict of his character, the blend of deviant and Christian blood warring in his veins. Clemo is a battlefield, a frontier.

The importance of blood and heredity has at least three sources. First is the Bible, in which God visits 'the iniquity of the fathers upon the children' (Exodus 34:7) and will not allow a 'bastard', 'Ammonite or Moabite', 'into the congregation of the Lord; even to their tenth generation' (Deuteronomy 23:2-3). It is also implicit in dozens of references to 'sons' throughout the Bible, and most obviously in punishment of the original sin. Secondly, the Methodist hymns use the word 'blood' prominently. Clemo grew up with these and played them at home, along with the hymns of Ira Sankey, on their little pump organ. In later years, when deaf and blind, he would still sing or hum those old tunes to himself. Thirdly, Clemo's personal condition – his physical inheritance – led him to analyse its cause, which he will have seen perfectly paralleled in the Exodus passage on the 'iniquity of the fathers'. Clemo alludes to this inheritance in his poetry, often pointing towards America, though never explicitly stating his meaning:

> I heard the rock blasted the day I was born,
> But the ignition, the rocking fervours that flayed
> My Cornish harvest – for these
> You must search the bleared West, its forensic night:
> Prairies and headstocks, reeling streets.

In this unpublished poem of 1961, entitled 'Inheritance', Clemo is writing about where his real roots – 'The clues to a life so torn' – might be discovered:

> Cornwall cannot speak alone
> For this poet she calls her son.
> Manhattan has marked me too. Anaconda
> Farther back [...]

A.L. Rowse, a contemporary of Clemo's from the St Austell area, writes in his autobiography: 'There was no money for anybody of the working class to travel [...] unless it were abroad to America, from which it was expected that you came home "made".' Eveline Clemo also writes of this expectation with regard to her husband, explaining that 'we decided [Reggie] should go to America for a few years, as wages were much higher in the States than in the clay industry, then he would return home and our youthful dreams would become a reality.' In 1909, Reggie embarked on his *wanderjahr*, heading for the Wild West of wealthy gold, silver and copper mines, for adventure and fortune, and it is there that he would gather Jack's 'inheritance'.

There is a slightly surprising element to Reggie's decision to leave at the beginning of 1909. Eveline Clemo wrote that she fell in love with Reggie 'at the early age of fifteen'. She turned fifteen in January 1909. So, at most, they could only have been in love for a few weeks before 'we' decided that Reggie should disappear alone for a number of years. It is not the usual behaviour of newly besotted lovers. Clemo states it differently, and somewhat more plausibly, in *Confession of a Rebel*, implying that Reggie wanted to escape the squalor of home for the promise of glamour and adventure in America.

On 17 March 1909, Reggie left Southampton aboard The White Star's *Adriatic*, landing in New York just over a week later. From New York, he intended to go on to Michigan, as he wrote in the ship's register. It was quite common for miners working at Michigan to move west to Montana, where the lively immigrant communities were gathering in Butte, and by 1910 Reggie can be found living with his older brother John and his sister Fanny at 413 West Boardman Street. Fanny had travelled out to join them on 9 October 1909, aboard the St Louis, and on the passenger list she wrote that she was heading straight for Butte. John Clemo, who had already been in America for five years, was working at Mountain View Mine, known as 'Saffron Bun' for the number of Cornish working it, and Reggie was probably working alongside him.

Boardman Street was a colourful area of Centerville, which itself was an immigrant community of mostly Cornish and Irish miners. Indeed, the whole of Butte developed around the mines, originally gold and silver before the growing demand for electricity increased the value of copper. Centerville was close enough to the copper mines for the miners to walk to work, with Mountain View out to the South. But the Clemo household was also just ten minutes' walk from an enormous bustling red light district covering many blocks and targeting the swollen population of miners, many of them single young men a long way from home. A few years before Reggie arrived, the brothels sprawled over the streets of Mercury, Park, Main and Arizona. By 1909 the area was being 'cleaned up' and the wooden shack 'cribs' made way for new brick buildings. Trade hardly suffered, and the business behind the sturdy brick walls remained the same. Of particular note was 'Venus Alley', the red-paved shadowy lane between Mercury and Galena. As well as this, along East Mercury, with several doors opening onto Venus Alley, was a brothel now renowned as 'America's longest running house of ill repute', the Dumas, active from 1890 until 1982 and now a museum.

'He was an extrovert,' Eveline wrote of her husband, 'loving the world and the gaiety of life'. Jack puts it differently: 'He went to America and was there betrayed by the quality of his ideals'. In Sally Magnusson's book the story becomes even more explicit: 'he seems to have found it hard to resist the frontier spirit, where the work was hard but the drinks and the girls were easy'.[16]

Reggie returned to Cornwall in 1911, but did not stay long and left Southampton for New York a second time on 27 July that same year, this time aboard the *Majestic*.[17] By now, Reggie and Eveline were engaged, Reggie having sent her a ring just after her sixteenth birthday, in 1910. The ring has survived, a showy gold piece with six rose-cut rubies flanking a row of five small pearls, and it appears to have been resized at some stage. Reggie also sent photographs of himself, about which Jack wrote in *Confession*:

In the many studio portraits of himself which he gave my mother, his clothes are fashionable, the shirt-cuffs, bow tie and hat being arranged with the meticulous care of a young dandy who wants to be admired or flattered. This trait of swagger was probably a reaction against the squalid slovenliness of his home.

Reggie returned home again late in 1912 to bury his father. He reignited his relationship with young Eveline very quickly and she became pregnant around February 1913 so that their marriage had to be rushed.[18] Neither Jack nor Eveline tells this full story, but each gives a different half of it. Clemo writes: 'On July 5th, 1913, the pair were married at St Austell. Within a year their first child was born'. In Eveline's book we learn that 'on the 26th November, our first child was born – a little girl – she lived only five weeks. This was the first cloud to darken my life.' The poor child died in a particularly disturbing way, 'with pus coming out of her ears and eyes', as one of Eveline Clemo's cousins, Maria Willcox, put it. By stating that Eveline and Reggie were married in July, but only remarking that the girl was born 'within a year' of their marriage, Clemo is obfuscating the fact that she was conceived out of wedlock. Similarly, Eveline Clemo only tells that she was married in 1913, without giving the wedding date, while stating that the child arrived in November. Pre-marital sex was disapproved of by both Jack and Eveline, and is quite inconsistent with Eveline's later, more puritanical, moral resolve.

Reggie and Eveline had only been together for a few weeks of romance in 1909 and for two months at the beginning of 1913 before she was pregnant and they had to marry. They hardly knew one another at all. By the time of their wedding day, Reggie had started back at Trethosa clayworks. In fact, he returned just in time to take part in the infamous strikes of 1913. Demands were being made for better pay and a working day shortened to eight hours, with longer lunch breaks and wages every fortnight instead of monthly. The strikes led to violence, with strikers attacking both the police and their own neighbours. The house of a shift boss was dynamited at Nanpean, and a local policeman was shot. A brutal force was brought down from Bristol and Glamorgan constabularies, which had experience of striking miners, but by this time the loss of wages had caused many to sell their belongings and others to doubt the purpose of their actions. In October the same year the workers returned to the pits and Reggie, briefly, to the dry.

The couple were living at the time with Eveline's parents, John and Jane Polmounter, at Goonvean Farm. Eveline's sister Bertha was there, too, as was a man named Richard Best, who was the farm's resident eccentric. It was a religious household, where Eveline said she 'first saw the reality of Christian love and principles put into everyday living.' Her mother had always been deeply religious, and her father became a preacher, speaking at the local chapels, although he had not been a Christian when they married. Stephen Lane, in his 1989 thesis, plausibly suggests that one of Eveline's hopes in marrying Reggie was that she would be able to convert him from his lack of faith in the same way that her mother, Jane, had converted John Polmounter. Clemo writes that 'within a few months of her marriage John was kneeling beside her' in prayer: 'He had been broken down by the sight of Jane kneeling twice a day at his bedside, calling on God to have mercy on him.'[19] This would not be the case for Eveline, and her kind idealism caused her to suffer. Speaking much later with her son, when Jack told her how 'wonderful is the blood of the two' parents in him for their combination of sensuality and spirituality, Eveline replied with stoic reflection: 'Then – if that was necessary – I didn't make a mistake in marrying your father.'[20]

When John Polmounter was ill and unable to rise, Reggie helped at the farm. Eveline's parents worried about her marrying Reggie, but Polmounter and his son-in-law appear to have got along, and it was John's encouragement of Reggie to stick up for himself against the volatile Richard Best, nicknamed 'Master', that caused one of very few fond moments shown by Jack in his imagining of his father. When Reggie moved in, Best was in his mid-seventies, 'a semi-lunatic [...] with no taste for women,' Clemo wrote. Best had been born on the farm, and when Polmounter inherited it Best refused to leave, so he was kept on as a farmhand. He is described as a 'grotesque' figure, filthy and malicious, albeit occasionally helpful. Best did not like Reggie even before he was living at the farm, and in Clemo's first autobiography he tells how on those mornings when Reggie helped out, Best would sabotage him:

> At first Reginald let him have his way, but John told him he 'mus'n give in to Maaster' […]. Thereafter Reginald stood firm; and the picture of those two – the old, half-crazed man and the young dare-devil – bickering childishly over the sacks of grain amid the morning shadows of Goonvean barn, has a touch of fantastic comedy about it.

Jack also recounts a story from the same period, when his father agreed to shoot an 'old and diseased' farm dog, leading it out to the field with a gun. 'He returned to the house, looking shame-faced, the dog trotting at his heels.' This inability to 'kill a dog in cold blood' is evidence of 'a weak, vacillating character' to Clemo, who adds that in spite of Reggie's unwillingness to kill an animal, 'he could have killed his best friend in hot blood.'

All of this was happening in the wake of the tragedy of Eveline and Reggie's daughter's death, but instead of having time to mourn and adjust, Eveline's history of suffering was just beginning. Seven months after her child died – a year into their marriage – war started, and Reggie had no intention of joining it. To avoid conscription he found work at the Royal Arsenal munitions factory in Woolwich and left his new wife behind at the farm with her parents. 'This was not an easy parting', writes Eveline Clemo, 'coming so quickly after the loss of our baby.' Reggie only rarely came home.

There is a remarkable silence about Reggie's time in London, considering the fact that he was there longer than he was with his wife. The Royal Arsenal records were not kept and neither Eveline nor Jack wrote about it. He was there for at least a year, probably two. Eveline tells the story as though he remained in London until 'the end of 1916', while Jack says that after only 'a year at Woolwich Arsenal' he was 'transferred to Devonport Dockyard', where 'he led an exemplary moral life'.[21] On other occasions when the accounts of mother and son conflict, it is usually Eveline who proves more reliable.

At any rate, on one of her husband's infrequent visits in June 1915, Eveline became pregnant a second time. Her hardships were now gathering pace, and a few months into her pregnancy, her own father died. The farm changed hands and the rest of the family were forced to move. Richard Best remained, but the pregnant Eveline and her absent husband Reggie, her disabled sister Bertha, and their elderly mother Jane, moved from Goonvean Farm to a two-bedroomed clayworkers' cottage on Goonamarris Slip, at a corner known locally as Vinegar Point, owned by Goonvean and Rostowrack China Clay Company. The cottage, with its identical attached neighbour, stood alone on the slip in the shadow of the clay dumps:

> When I looked out of the back bedroom window I could see nothing beyond our garden hedge but the grim smoke-belching stacks around Goonvean pit-head and the mountainous heaps of white rubble thrown up from Bloomdale, Goonvean and Trethosa pits. When I looked out of the front bedroom window I could see nothing but the fields of Goonamarris farm slanting steeply down to a coppice, the more wild and rugged gorge of Tregargus carrying the stream between thicker belts of woodland to the south-west, and southward the green dome of Foxhole Beacon topping a broad flank of heath.[22]

A white gate opened onto the road, and a granite path led up to the solid wooden front door. Inside, the cottage was dark, each of the four rooms having a single window. Downstairs and overlooking fields was the front room, which would hold a settee, a pump organ on which Eveline would give lessons, and later a small writing bureau by the window. There was a fireplace for heating, and beneath the stairs was the spense, a close space used for washing, and later used as a dark room for developing Eveline's photographs. Beyond this was the kitchen with an old Cornish cloam oven, which, said Eveline in a 1976 interview, gave pasties 'a different flavour from what we have on our electric cookers.'[23] To avoid wasting milk, she made clotted cream on the range, which was then added to most meals.

The staircase was darker still, leading up to the two bedrooms, one to the front and one to the back, where husband, wife, sister, mother and the soon due newborn would all sleep.

Outside, looming over the cottage, was the Bloomdale sand burrow, 'a long curving dump which frequently, in rainy weather, spilled over into the lane outside our garden'. The spilling sand was a constant reminder that nothing in this landscape was permanent, and it is an image to which Clemo returned in his dialect tales and again in the 1951 short story, 'The Clay Dump'. In time, Goonvean Farm would be devoured by the works, the lanes would close, the burrows would swell, the pits would be expanded or flooded, and the cottage too would disappear.

Yet this was the sole time that Eveline would move house. The rest of her life's sufferings were all enacted within those four unyielding granite walls. And this was Jack's birthplace. It is where he would write all his novels, stories, dialect tales, his autobiographies, theological works and most of his poetry. It is where he would live his first sixty-eight years, cramped in those tight, hard rooms, playing in the garden, or wandering on the dumps and clay paths, alone except for his dog and his Bible.

II
'put forth thine hand'

Sing, O barren, thou that didst not bear; break forth into singing, and cry aloud, thou that didst not travail with child: for more are the children of the desolate than the children of the married wife, saith the Lord.

Isaiah 54:1

'It was a fitting birthplace for me,' Jack wrote, 'being dwarfed under Bloomdale clay-dump, solitary, grim-looking, with no drainage, no water or electricity supply, and no back door'.[24] In her own, more ceremonial, account of Jack's birth, written in the 1970s, Eveline Clemo announces his arrival with heightened phrasing which lends a prophetic tone: 'On March 11th, 1916, our second child was born, a little boy who was to become the Cornish writer and poet, Jack Clemo.' This is the tone of a proud mother, whose son is the centre of her world. Eveline's commitment to her child, and her faith in him, was not deterred by the strain of her circumstances. Already she had lost a baby, a parent and a home in fairly swift succession. She had gained a husband who showed little desire to be with her, and she had effectively become the head of a household comprising her ageing mother and disabled sister, while she herself nursed her newborn boy. Yet, still, this was only the beginning of the suffering that would lead her to the brink of despair.

After the horror of her daughter's death there was anxiety for the boy christened Reginald John Clemo, and terrific relief when he appeared healthy. In the 1980 BBC dramatization of Clemo's life, *A Different Drummer*, Reggie is depicted as being present at Jack's birth, rushing in to inspect the child. In *Confession*, Jack simply writes: 'My father is said to have been satisfied with me'. The family were close to finding an unhappy kind of stability, though within months even this was threatened.

The war caught up with Reggie and he was called into the Navy. Jack says this was in early 1917, while Eveline dates it as late 1916.

Eveline, Reggie and the baby Jack, 1917.

The military records show that Eveline is correct and that Reggie was engaged at Plymouth on the training base HMS Vivid II from 1 December. The records also describe Reggie as 5'6", of sallow complexion with brown eyes and black hair, of very good character and satisfactory ability. Eveline did not want Reggie to leave for war and prayed for it to end before he was deployed. In the meantime, Reggie's 'daredevil spirit' expressed itself in a way that suggested he too was now eager to be at home, in 'one of the few incidents in my father's life that make me feel proud of him':

> At week-ends the dockyard workers were allowed to visit friends and relatives who lived within ten miles of the port; longer journeys were strictly forbidden. The ten-mile limit enabled my father to cross the Tamar and proceed as far as St Germans, where it was supposed he stayed. But, unknown to the dockyard officials, he always borrowed a bicycle there and rode thirty miles westwards through Cornwall to Goonamarris. He would arrive home on the Saturday night and return the next day to report, quite truly, that he had been to St Germans![25]

In this account, Clemo believes that his father had been transferred from the Woolwich munitions factory to work at Devonport Dockyard and it was from this job that he cycled back to Goonamarris. Eveline's version of Reggie's weekend visits has him cycling from the naval barracks as a serving recruit in training, rather than a dockyard worker:

> At the end of 1916, my husband was called from the munition factory to serve in the Navy and he remained at the Royal Naval Barracks at Devonport until October 1917, often daring enough to break the rules of the Barracks not to travel over ten miles unless permission was given.

On 30 October 1917, Reggie was called to action to serve on HMS

Tornado, one of the new R class destroyers built for the Great War. Reggie would be one of many second class stokers shovelling coal into the three boilers in the belly of the ship. On a winter night not quite two months later, on 22 December, HMS Tornado was on escort duty with a group of other destroyers in the thick fog of the North Sea. They were near the Maas lightship at the mouth of the river running through Rotterdam when flotilla leader HMS Valkyrie hit a mine. The Valkyrie survived, but a few hours later another destroyer, HMS Torrent, was hit. HMS Surprise went to help the sinking Torrent, but was also struck. With Torrent and Surprise going down quickly, Tornado turned to get clear, but in trying to escape it too was hit. Two hundred and fifty two men were killed, and in the bowels of the ship Reggie had no hope. He would have either drowned or been boiled alive.[26]

The ship sank in the dark early morning of the 23rd and the telegram arrived at Goonamarris on the 27th, two days after Christmas. Again, Eveline proves herself the more reliable narrator, as Jack mistakes all of these details. By his account, Reggie was at sea in the summer, rather than late October; his ship was torpedoed rather than mined; and the telegram arrived on Christmas Day rather than two days after. Clemo's version is more dramatic; the embellishments, perhaps, of a young novelist.

Reggie's tale is not told with sadness in *Confession*, and Clemo offers a jocular addendum:

> Some years later a brother of [Reggie's], a spiritualist, attended a séance in America at which, he declared, my father's spirit materialized [...]. According to this spiritualist account Reginald was not drowned but had his limbs blown off by the explosion and died instantly. I do not give much credence to the statement, because my uncle was not the kind of man to whom spirits are likely to tell the truth.

A funeral card from Reggie's service has survived in their family papers, reading 'In loving Memory of Reginald, The Dearly-beloved Husband of Eveline Clemo and dear Father of Reginald John Clemo,

Who lost his life on H.M.S. Tornado, Dec 23rd, 1917, Aged 27 years'. The irony of these platitudes would have been understood by the villagers who turned out for the funeral, but always Eveline remained loyal to Reggie and regretful of their tragic history, arranging for her own gravestone to read:

> In Loving Memory
> of
> Eveline Clemo
> Who died at Goonamarris
> 4 June 1977 Aged 83
> And her Beloved Husband Reginald Clemo
> Who died at sea
> 23 Dec 1917 Aged 27
> Heavenly Love Abiding

In 1918, Eveline had to learn to cope without even the rough security of a bad marriage. Jack reported that after suffering the 'first shock and prostration' of mourning, his mother 'yielded everything' to Christ, surrendering herself to 'His purpose', whatever it might be. She gave up

> her hope of remarriage, with all the pleasures and social contacts that make life bearable to the average woman. She renounced every human narcotic, choosing to suffer an unmitigated spiritual stress so that its creative power might have free access to my personality.[27]

There is some ambiguity in these words. The phrase is written as though there is only one aim in Eveline's renunciation, but really Clemo gives two. The first is 'co-operating' with Christ's purpose, while the second is for the 'creative power' to have access to Jack's 'personality'. The assumption is that God's sole purpose for Eveline now is to raise Clemo.

Perhaps this is so. And perhaps the death of Eveline's own mother in 1919, as Eveline was yet recovering from the death of her husband, was also a divine facilitation of her servitude. Jane Polmounter was

The spliced family photo

Eveline and Jack, 1920

Jack, 1926

bedridden and suffering from dementia. By the time of her death Eveline was exhausted and overwhelmed. Jack writes that she was ordered to stay in Newquay for recuperation, but within a month had witnessed the wrecking of a ship off the Newquay coast.[28] She watched as the lifeboats were launched to rescue it, while the sinking ship vividly recalled her husband's death, and her misery deepened. Jack and his mother removed themselves inland again to their little cottage.

At this time, Jack is said to have been 'a winsome, intelligent and brilliant child', precocious, able to recite the Lord's Prayer and nursery rhymes by the age of eighteen months. 'You'll never rear him, Mrs Clemo – he's too good for this world!' one neighbour told her.[29] Others said "E'll suffer for it' and "E's too forward 'e is – no 'ealthy sign, Mrs Clema.'[30] So eager was Jack to learn, we are told, that he would collect up the greasy scraps of paper thrown out of passing clay trucks, wrapping the workers' pasties, to find more reading material. Photographs of the infant Jack are few, but those that exist are of a healthy, solid child. There is one in which he appears to have been photographed with both his father and mother, Reggie in naval uniform and Jack in a white suit. On second glance, however, the infant is too old for Reggie to still be alive, and for some reason the father's hand is transparent. It has been spliced, a fantasy photo imagining what the family might have looked like had Reggie survived the war.

Another photograph, from 1920, shows Jack and his mother in a studio shot, Jack standing on a chair beside her, with one arm around her shoulder. He looks perplexed and distant. Eveline is wearing black. It was not the fashion to smile in photographs, and exposures were longer, so Eveline's expression is relaxed. Her eyes have fallen gently sad, but her mouth has a curve in the corners as though readying to smile. Soon after this was taken, when Eveline and Jack were settling back into the cottage, a new threat emerged. Jack was still four, with a few days before his fifth birthday, when he felt a pain in his eyes. Lamplight or sunlight were unbearable, and Eveline noticed as they sat down to breakfast that a film had formed over his right eye. She took him to the doctor at St Dennis, who said it was iritis and referred them to Truro. Jack was prescribed 'tonic' and eyedrops and told to avoid the light. For now, he had to be kept in a darkened room, and if he needed to go out then his eyes must be bandaged. 'Only this drastic treatment could save me from permanent blindness', he wrote in the early 1940s.

Jack recalled the first trip to hospital, the bus from St Stephen and the smell of the building, as well as the waiting room full of other children with eye problems, 'some blindfolded, some wearing dark glasses, others celluloid shades: all tense and unnatural.'[31]

This was a devastating period of development for a child to be sick and locked away in the dark. He would never be the same again, and his mother knew it. She saw in the clouding of his eye the same disease that took her daughter, and she fell into a suicidal despair:

> I have never forgotten the stress I went through at this time. It seemed as if all my hopes had been dashed to the ground. I felt I could not face life with a blind child and with no husband to help to carry the burden. My human weakness gave way under the strain. One day, in an agony of spirit, I went to my bedroom and, taking my Bible in my hand, I knelt by my bedside praying to God for light in the darkness.[32]

The world was breaking her, devouring her home, parents, husband and children. With this pain, guilt and fear, this feeling of abject defeat, Eveline reached for her Bible, and it fell open at Isaiah 54:

> Fear not; for thou shalt not be ashamed: neither be thou confounded; for thou shalt not be put to shame: for thou shalt forget the shame of thy youth, and shalt not remember the reproach of thy widowhood any more.
>
> For thy Maker is thine husband; the Lord of hosts is his name; and thy Redeemer the Holy One of Israel; The God of the whole earth shall he be called.
>
> For the Lord hath called thee as a woman forsaken and grieved in spirit, and a wife of youth, when thou wast refused, saith thy God.
>
> For a small moment have I forsaken thee; but with

great mercies will I gather thee. [...]

O thou afflicted, tossed with tempest, and not comforted, behold, I will lay thy stones with fair colours, and lay thy foundations with sapphires.

And I will make thy windows of agates, and thy gates of carbuncles, and all thy borders of pleasant stones.

And all thy children shall be taught of the Lord; and great shall be the peace of thy children.

The aptness of the wording – the shame, the abandonment, the children – struck her immediately. This was God talking to her. It was God making a promise, a personal covenant – a bargain even – faith in which was the marrow of the Clemos' hope, and remained with them throughout their lives. Always, Eveline would recall this promise, though it was condensed in her memory. When asked in a 1971 television interview to recite the passage, she muddled it together:

Fear not, I have called thee as a woman forsaken and grieved, a wife of youth when thou wast refused, saith thy God. For a small moment have I forgotten thee, but with great mercies will I gather thee. Thy maker is thine husband. Thy children shall be taught of the Lord.

Eveline's mixture of word-perfect accuracy and rearrangement is suggestive of the points most salient to her condition. But what is the nature of the 'shame' that she omits?

The answer is the key to Clemo's work and life. When Reggie returned from America in 1912, he did not bring back his fortune. There was no money, no wealth, nothing saved or invested for the future, nothing to give his wife and family. Nothing, that is, except syphilis, contracted in the brothels of Butte. Congenital syphilis killed their daughter, and now it threatened their son with blindness. It is a fact suggested in both published and unpublished poems, autobiographies and even in the novels, knowledge of which adds greater texture, meaning and tension to Clemo's senses of inheritance, invasion, the need to redeem sexuality, his connection between marriage and healing, the repeated metaphor of leprosy, of degradation, as well as his fascination with America. Reggie's activities in Montana defined Jack in a profound and inestimable way.

The symptoms shown by both the baby and then Jack were classic of congenital syphilis. The girl died of an early form, with typical discharges of catarrh and rhinitis, the symptoms Maria Willcox described so frankly. Jack's syphilis was 'late stage', first revealing itself when he was almost five. Weeping eyes and painful photophobia would be expected, with inflammation of the cornea, and when the symptoms persisted, iritis might occur, lasting for weeks or months. A second bout of eye troubles could be expected around puberty, often affecting one eye before the other, as in Clemo's case. Meanwhile, sensorineural deafness may occur at any time, along with headaches, heart trouble, joint pains and insomnia. Jack should expect the bony parts of his nose to collapse and his brow and lower jaw to protrude, while his teeth become notched. The disease would quarry into his face and senses, leaving a landscape of painful white wherever he looked.

Syphilis is never *directly* referred to in Clemo's work, and even the later diaries have been edited so that the word is either blacked out with a marker pen or torn out and destroyed, though it is alluded to often and powerfully; no moreso than in the unpublished 1962 poem, 'Montana Shade'. 'Montana Shade' was later overhauled to become 'Bunyan's Daughter', a poem purporting to be about John Bunyan's eldest child, Mary. In this way, Clemo disguised the biographical content. In the original version, the mature poet is directly addressing the diseased prostitute his father visited – the deep root of his narrative.

> If I could kneel at that grave –
> In Butte, I suppose, but I shall never know –
> Where you lie, once harlot and slave,
> Mother of all my sorrow –
> Would the western sky yield a narcotic,
> Or burn me bare to the debt,
> Almost too poignant to be spoken,
> Where our life-currents met?

The Rockies, cattle-range and copper seam,
The Indian encampments – these would be less exotic
Than the bond between us: fused in a bad dream
Before I was born. You gave me the shameful token.

Your practised hand did the routine work,
Pressed the thorns and spear
Into the blind hereditary stream
Which foamed on through the murk
Till a cry from Cornwall made the target clear.
The small boy was stabbed in the dark;
The youth cringed at the world's disdain,
Grovelling alone on the clay-bed
In spectral silence, fighting to keep sane.
I owe to you all the leprous scars,
Peeled back to slime which spat at the cross:
Fumes from the sunken furnace;
Ice on the prison bars,
As I staggered from loss to loss,
Crying all night because you had made me one
Whom other women would shun.

The world asks questions I do not ask;
Saints fumble with the seals;
And if I meet you at the golden gate
All heaven will be looking on
To learn what an innocent victim feels,
Caught in the mesh of fate.

I would forestall eternity
And let men overhear
While still on earth, what I have whispered
So often through my tears,
And would whisper again if I knelt where you lie.
I have reached out to you
With the caress of Christ in my soul these thirty years:
Never a condemning thought;

Nor in the end would I undo
All the agony you brought.
I would not insult you with mere forgiveness:
I penetrate the unseen,
Find something so massive, something so playful,
Mere forgiveness would fall between.

You need not even be shy,
Montana Magdalene,
Much less ashamed if we come face to face:
We are just fellow sinners,
Liberated by His grace.[33]

Eveline's 'shame' is both religious and humane. 'Know ye not that the unrighteous shall not inherit the kingdom of God? Neither fornicators, nor idolaters, nor adulterers, nor effeminate, nor abusers of themselves', wrote the apostle Paul in 1 Corinthians 6:9. In the Old Testament, in Exodus 22:16, the rule was that if a man 'entice a maid that is not betrothed, and lie with her, he shall surely endow her to be his wife'. There was a similar expectation in the clay villages: when a woman became pregnant the couple were to marry. But the cost of fornication was not only to bind Eveline to a man unsuited; it also bound her to the shame of knowing that her son's sickness and her daughter's death were given from her own sin and her own body.

To a secular reader, regardless of their views on marriage, it is difficult to blame Eveline for the infection. It was Reggie's carelessness that led to his contraction of syphilis, and he passed it on to his young fiancée. It is not known whether Reggie was aware of the infection, or at what stage a correct diagnosis of either Reggie or Eveline might have been made. At the time of their daughter's death it would have been possible for the couple to have been tested for the 'Wassermann reaction', and to have been treated with Salvarsan, a new arsenic-based drug administered by a laborious course of injections. Neither test nor treatment was reliable, and there is no evidence that Reggie or Eveline undertook either. Eveline's family had a history of infant mortality, and the couple may have believed that the girl's death was consistent with this. It seems unlikely that Eveline would have risked a second child had she believed herself syphilitic, though her despair and apparent sense of shame when Jack's eye trouble began suggest that by this point she knew something. The most consistent guess would seem to be that a diagnosis was made following the death of her firstborn, and that she and Reggie were then tested and/or treated. Eveline would have believed that all was well and that her son was healthy. Jack's iritis destroyed this hope, and threatened the only good thing she had left.

The eye trouble lasted nine months, with daily treatments given up at St Dennis surgery that meant Eveline had to wheel her son almost two and a half miles to the village in his old pram.

> Before the blindness came I was a plump, jolly, pink-faced little fellow, very lively, chattering and laughing all day long. Those few months of isolation, with the mental nightmare of inarticulate terrors and panics […] had changed me into a thin, pasty-faced brat, dull-eyed, silent and morbid.[34]

This is how Jack entered school at six years old, sickly and remote. For nominal catchment reasons he was expected to attend Foxhole, though his attendance lasted only one day. Clemo writes that the headmaster thought he was a dunce and refused to accept him. Instead, he would have to attend the school at Trethosa, half a mile due west of the cottage, a 'rather stupid decision', Clemo thought. Trethosa School was a little nearer than Foxhole as the crow flies, but between the cottage and the school were the clayworks of Goonvean, which the child would have to walk through by an exposed track:

> The journey to Trethosa School […] led us usually, through Goonvean clay works, around the edge of the enormous unfenced pit, in which blasting was frequently in operation. An alternative course led around the southern end of Trethosa sand-dump, along the gravelly ridges where a false step might send one hurtling into a disused quarry full of slimy green water.[35]

Predictably, Jack was not suited for school, and *Confession* was intended in part to be a condemnation of contemporaneous schooling, a condemnation also found in his letters to the *Cornish Guardian* through the 1930s. Modern schooling did not accommodate exceptional children, Clemo thought, but only normal people: the 'sympathetic nurture of my abilities was impossible in any Council school'.[36] There appears to have been a tension at school, of which Jack would have been at the frontier. Education was increasingly secular, with faith expected but liberal, and this was not in harmony with Jack's upbringing, where faith was primary and primitive.

The child was weak, sickly, under-developed and not especially bright, in spite of his precocious infancy. He was not fit to play sports and physical games with the other children, nor clever enough to stand out in class. His body was at odds, his faith at odds, and for the boy to survive he would have to make a virtue of being at odds. It is remembered as village talk the way in which Jack stood alone in the playground, away from other children, leaning against a wall. He did not join in the play and he did not have friends, so when he walked home he usually walked alone across the moor, marsh and quarry.

The teachers encouraged this alienation: 'The headmaster nicknamed me "Jean" because of my supposed effeminacy – a nickname that stuck to me throughout my later schooldays'. Clemo was in all possible ways a misfit, a fact which simultaneously crippled and fortified his character, leading him to become more remote, but to see in that remoteness a glory, a pattern, and a confirmation of extraordinariness. In his youth we find the beginnings of the apophenia that becomes more imposing in adult life. In looking to survive overwhelming weaknesses, young Jack instinctively sought to reinterpret them as strengths, increasingly invoking Biblical bases and the design of the ultimate authority. This reframing of his own idiosyncrasies often emerged in subtle ways, especially in the tensions between Clemo's personal experience of God's approval and intentions for him, and his Biblical, dogmatic faith. More crudely, we see it in Clemo's rejection of cleanliness when he was sixteen, which he put down to his mother 'revealing the squalid story of the Clemos and my father's tragic disharmonies'.[37] An 'anti-social bias had been a part of my nature since childhood […]. If I was told that any particular habit was beneath my dignity I would be all the more inclined to practise it.' He broadened his accent and began using dialect words picked up from books:

> Often for days on end I wouldn't wash my face or comb my hair; I refused to bother about shaving [...]. I seldom laced my shoes until the afternoon, never troubled to fit my neck with a collar and tie and when my mother fitted these on so that I might be 'presentable' to pay some visit, I would keep them on until the end of the week, wearing them in bed, too lazy to remove them before sleeping. [...] I knew now that I had sprung from a family that had produced more than its share of moral degenerates, and only when my habits and appearance conformed to this degradation did I feel at ease, self-contained, not divided.[38]

This seems to be the same instinct that drove the apparent candour of Clemo's autobiography and caused him to write it as a 'confession'. It is the desire to create a context for his shame, to be punished and absolved. At the same time, it is a clear and typically teenage attempt to understand himself, although Clemo had little chance of maturing in an ordinary fashion, given his atypical circumstances.

Jack's profound unordinariness and sickliness led him to avoid school when he could, and he notes that the school only tolerated his common absence from the 'belief that I could not survive into adolescence'.[39] This suggests that the school knew of Clemo's syphilis, which meant the whole village knew.

Clemo hated school, hated the institutional prescriptive aspect of it, and condemned the nascent decadence and frivolity of his peers. The only part he enjoyed was the brief service in the morning, with its hymns, prayers and Bible study. He found it impossible to keep up with the other children in class, a fact worsened by his absences, and although he enjoyed reading, he claims to have had no academic talent at all. In truth, the school does not sound very much to blame for Clemo's failures, excepting the headmaster's nicknaming, and *Confession* sneers a little too eagerly at the 'system' even when it is supporting him. For example, 'Miss Sarah' helped Clemo to win several prizes for his writing, yet he says: 'my only clear memory of the period is of Miss Sarah's habit of snapping out at me during times of quiet study: "Don't frown so, Clemo!"'.

His mother proudly recalled his writing talent:

> I remember the infant teacher telling me how impressed she was with the first composition he wrote and how she took it to the Headmaster, who read it to the upper class saying, 'I should think you'd be ashamed to write another composition after hearing this one written by a boy of six.'[40]

This story has not survived, but in a later interview Eveline mentioned that it had been about a mouse.

The prizes Jack won for his writing included copies of Harriet Beecher Stowe's *Uncle Tom's Cabin* and Hall Caine's *The Christian*. (Caine's melodramas would be an important, if detrimental, influence on Clemo's early novel drafts.) Some of these prizes were sponsored by outside groups, such as the National Canine Defence League, who presented Clemo with a copy of Charles R. Johns' novel about a Scottish Terrier, *Aberdeen Mac*, for an essay he had written on dogs.

Aside from these moments, school was a miserable and hostile place where Jack's otherness was exaggerated. He was an only child, adored and sheltered by his mother, without any male role model, and with the legion adversaries of his syphilis and personal tragedy. 'I was apart, left to live my own life; not of their world', he wrote in *Confession*. The full experience was summed up in a short paragraph in an even more distantly retrospective feature for *Cornish Magazine*:

> My formal education consisted of spasmodic attendance at Trethosa Council School between the ages of six and thirteen. The only things I liked at school were the girls and the Bible. I was fascinated by the sentimental feminine appeal, and I loved the scripture lessons,

but the prosaic items of the curriculum bored me and I refused to respond to any of my teachers. Even before adolescence I seemed to be one of those who can come alive only under the stimulus of religion and sex.[41]

Both Jack and Eveline recalled the headmaster, Mr W.S. Pellymounter, with some fondness, and two notable stories are offered. The first is when Pellymounter asked Jack what he wanted to be when he grew up, to which 'I replied frankly and unhesitatingly that I meant to be a sky-tip worker'.[42] The second story is from a 'Parents' Day' at the school, in what would be Jack's last year. It is detailed with pride by both Eveline and Jack, as a moment when the headmaster was saying something positive about the boy: 'Mrs. Clemo, your son is a born philosopher', Pellymounter told her, on which Clemo commented: 'I suppose that in some sense he was right'.

It has to be acknowledged that Clemo had an agenda when he recorded this in *Confession of a Rebel*. He derogates the school system as he derogates the villagers, other writers who he feels have not helped him enough, old girlfriends and family members. The repeated condemnation of others and simultaneous elevation of himself can be unappealing and seem ungenerous. The work was said to have an evangelical purpose, but the self-concern and the personal attacks sometimes obscure this effect. In the short chapter on school, it is not only schooling itself that is sneered at, but individuals. There is even some contempt in that begrudging admission, 'I suppose that in some sense he was right.' His criticism of the syllabus as such was that, 'My taste and temperament were never consulted'. And there is more than a little arrogance in his disbelief when it was suggested that he ought to do some homework, as though 'homework, with special attention to arithmetic, would help the mind that was to make a synthesis of Calvinist dogma and sex mysticism!' At the root of all this is the revolt of an indulged only child.

Covering the 1920s and Jack's period of schooling, the only sustained account we have comes from *Confession*, so we rely unsatisfactorily on this narrative for the majority of his first fourteen years, and to a lesser extent his first twenty years. Having said this, there are many surviving photographs to consider. Jack's mother was ever ready with her camera on family visits, special occasions and trips to the seaside. The importance of the photographic evidence is easily demonstrated by an image of Jack's father. Both in *Confession* and in magazine articles, Clemo wrote about his father being a cowboy working on a ranch in Montana, which he apparently did while still at the Butte mines, and how 'I still like to think of my father as a cowboy rather than a clay-worker'. He says that they own a photograph of Reggie with a revolver working on a ranch, and he uses this as evidence of his father's 'latent violence'. This photograph has survived in an early album, and is labelled 'Reg on a ranch near Butte: 1911 (with revolver).' But the photo is not what Clemo claims; it is a studio shot, a fake, and the 'ranch' is a prop, with a backboard painted to resemble a log cabin and 'Ranch No 1' written on it. The gun, too, is a prop, the finishing touch to the elaborate cowboy outfits both Reggie and his friend are posing in, with woolly chaps and lassos.

There are several school photos of Clemo, the earliest being from 1922, in which all the children are looking soberly at the camera. Except, that is, for Jack, who is looking off somewhere to the left of the photographer and grinning mischievously. There are others of him in later years, including a group photo from Miss Sarah's class, but mostly the pictures are taken on daytrips to the beach, at Porthpean, Portholland, Sennen Cove, Porth, St Ives or Land's End, or near the cottage with his Pomeranian dog Gyp, in all of which Jack contrarily appears as a flourishing outdoorsy type of boy, with a carefree slouch accentuated by posing with his hands buried deep in his pockets, wearing a flat cap and baggy slacks. Physically, Jack is skinny, though not exceptionally so, and no moreso than several other children in the school. When he is not wearing a cap, his dark hair is parted roughly to the side. It is quickly apparent that in all these photographs there is little evidence of friends. There is one boy who appears unlabelled in the pictures, and the pair seem close, photographed on the beach or reclining together, either a relative or possibly the boy mentioned in *Confession*, named Brian, Jack's only male friend, who was 'one of my fellow-actors in the negro sketch' they performed. Of the few other children living nearby at this time, Jack recalls kissing a village girl 'behind gorse bushes on the Slip', though apparently these fellow children had all moved away by the time Jack was seven.

The photos do not give the impression of a 'pasty-faced brat', as Clemo described himself, and the only feature at all suggestive of his condition is his walleye. Jack's right eye – the one that Eveline had observed covered with a white film – is turned outwards and slightly up, which it does not appear to have been before the first bout of eye trouble. In most of them Eveline is present, either in the picture itself or behind the camera. She and her son, now as ever, are inseparable. Indeed, 10 June 1942 was 'the first time in my life that I've been separated from her', Jack wrote in his diary, and this was due to a serious illness, when Eveline was admitted to Devonport Hospital for an operation. Jack was twenty-six.

An equally pervasive presence throughout these years is Aunt Bertha, though she is scarcely mentioned in the books. For some years, when evacuee and foster-children were brought to the cottage, the three adults – Jack, Eveline and Bertha – shared the large front bedroom. Bertha was Eveline's older sister, born in 1891, and she had moved with Eveline and their mother into the cottage, where she lived the rest of her life. Yet Clemo mentions his dog more frequently and with more tenderness than he speaks of her. From the autobiographies it might be imagined that Bertha was almost always absent from the cottage. She is a ghost in the household, an insubstantial figure, unobserved, discounted – except in the photographic record. Here Bertha is present at all the events she is omitted from in *Confession*, on holidays and daytrips, picnics and walks, with Eveline and Jack and myriad cousins. She has a great shock of wisping black and grey hair that grew up and outwards in curls, adding five or six inches to her height. She is extraordinarily small, at around four feet, so these few added inches are exaggerated. In the photos she has a broad neck, heavy, square face and thick round glasses. Her figure varies considerably, though most often she is stout, with her shoulders rounded forwards. She was born prematurely, according to Clemo,

> because a workman was killed at Goonvean clay-pit at the end of August 1891. Another labourer had come

banging on the door of Goonvean farmhouse and panted out the ghastly news. My grandmother, Jane Polmounter, who was expecting a child in the late autumn, was so upset that she was soon in premature labour.

Bertha was a tiny baby, and as an adult 'used to tell people with evident pride: "When I wiz born they could put me in a milk-joog"'.[43] Grace Gribble of St Stephen recalls Bertha, Eveline and Jack visiting the house, and Bertha joking about an aircraft during the war that 'flew so low it nearly touched my head!' She would also collect money for charities. This is remembered by many villagers, as well as in the Trethosa Chapel 'Statement of Accounts' for the Sunday School.[44] Year after year, Bertha's collection and donation to the Sunday School is entered, and there appears to have been competitiveness between Bertha and a certain Miss Harris, another charity collector who performed marginally better than Bertha by around sixpence every year after the First World War. On top of the frustrating annual loss to Miss Harris, in 1925 one Mrs Keast joined the list and thrashed them both by a whopping £4. Determined never to suffer this ignominy again, the following two years suggest a fresh resolve, and for 1926 and 1927 Bertha is on record as the chief charity collector at the Chapel. Reading through year after year of these records, it is hard not to share in her triumph.

Bertha was not a healthy individual either. As well as her stunted size and short-sightedness, she was also diabetic, had learning disabilities and heart troubles. Yet Clemo shows little sympathy. In *Confession* she is ignored, in the diaries she is mocked, and in *Marriage* she is pitied. Her death was written about churlishly, and Clemo did not attend the funeral. Even the death itself was uninteresting to him. In the 1949 diary Clemo marks it: 'Bertha is really ill, obviously dying – and no word from E.' The illness is a matter of immediate inescapable fact, but the problem of this brief love interest 'E.', or Eileen, not replying to his letter was the real concern.[45] And he was correct, Bertha *was* dying. She died the following morning, 13 March 1949, but again Clemo does not show any emotion aside from irritation that the house is full of other people, 'shadowy figures', as he puts it. When Eveline had married, Bertha had attended; when her first daughter was born, she was at the farm; when their father John Polmounter had died, Bertha was there; at the birth of Jack, she was present; at the death of Reggie they were all at the cottage; when the mother, Jane, died, Bertha was again there. But she is not mentioned, her feelings are unrecorded, her concerns are not Jack's.

Eveline's appearance in the photograph albums, on the other hand, is appropriate to her presence in Clemo's life and writing. She appears on every page of the diaries, at length in the autobiographies, and later, when Jack was blind and deaf, Eveline was the filter through which the world was forced to pass, communicating with her son by spelling out words in capital letters on the palm of his hand with her index finger. She describes herself as 'introvert, sensitive, meditative, mystical and somewhat solitary'.[46] Clemo describes her as 'superior in character and taste to her three sisters' and theologically 'not without talent'.[47] Physically, he describes her as 'dark, tight-lipped, with her sad, probing black eyes'.[48] In *The Marriage of a Rebel* this description of her eyes is repeated: 'her large black eyes probed' through 'horn-rimmed spectacles'. Clemo cannot talk of his mother's eyes without noting their penetrative black gaze. The quality of her eyes is remarkable in the photographs, too, where they appear harder or sadder than her mouth. Clemo's description continues:

> Her sallow face, which had never been softened by cosmetics, was deeply lined with suffering, and the big nose and determined jaw suggested that strength of character had developed in her at the expense of superficial charm. But there was no bitterness in her expression.

This description matches all accounts of her, as a strong but kindly authority, dour but not cruel. 'You wouldn't throw your last snowball at her, put it that way', Preston Gribble told me.

'Never did she try to scold me into goodness', wrote Clemo, 'nor did she confuse me with talk about the Christian ethic. She lived that ethic as no one else I had known ever lived it [...]. Her purity and unselfishness impressed me as they impressed others in their daily contacts with her'.[49] Alan Sanders, born at Stepaside, remembers Eveline very well from his childhood, and describes her as a generous woman, 'who would give anything', an example of which was shown in her treatment of the Solomon family. The Clemos themselves were a poor household. Bertha was disabled, Eveline widowed, and Jack a syphilitic schoolchild. Yet, when a family appeared in even worse trouble than they were, she gave what she had to help. The Solomons were thrown out of their Foxhole home, having failed to pay rent. They had wandered over, now homeless, to Goonvean, where the father built a stone hut with a corrugated iron roof for them. The Clemos were the nearest household and when Eveline heard of their trouble she began to give them food, cook their meals and give the children cocoa in the morning. She did this until the council intervened, sending the family to the workhouse in St Austell.

Through these years, as many others, Eveline was supporting the family on her War Widow's pension and sometimes helping out at other homes or giving lessons on the organ. To make the coal stretch further, Eveline and Jack would take their zinc bath and buckets to collect discarded cinders, known as 'cherks', from the claywork engine houses, or Jack would be sent up the Slip with a wheelbarrow gathering 'smutties' left from gorse swaling, a chore that found its way into a 1936 dialect tale, 'Charlie, the Smutties, an' the Baaby'. A memory from one of these moments impressed itself especially on Clemo:

> I would sometimes climb fifty feet up to reach the newest layers, crouching ankle deep in the black ash, glancing down at mother as she waited beside the bath among the shadowy bushes, the stacks of Goonvean growing dim across the fields behind her, the clay-pit remote and melancholy. The beauty of the scene was an enrichment that prevented me from ever feeling humiliated or degraded while thus grubbing amid the dirt.[50]

They grew their own cabbages and potatoes, went blackberrying in the autumn, and collected milk from Goonamarris Farm. There was no shop in Goonamarris itself, but there was a Co-op up at Nanpean that delivered to the cottage. In 1926 and 1927, Jack was allowed to ride on the horse-drawn Co-op van, because the driver, Harry Phillips, was courting one of Eveline's nieces, Elizabeth Viney Grigg, daughter of Lucy. 'Some of my happiest recollections of childhood are of those long rides with Harry in the creaking van, around St Stephen, Coombe and Trelyon, past the uranium mine at Terras', Clemo wrote.[51] Either Eveline or Jack would collect the milk, which again is a quotidian event that held great significance for Clemo later, as it became a common theme in his early novel drafts, and those trips with Harry went on to facilitate a youthful romance. Among the choking kaolin dust and cold granite, there lay a few glittering gems.[52] The most radiant of these was Eveline Clemo's commitment to her son, which put in place a faith-based framework capable of subsuming the adversary that pursued them.

The syphilis, the poison of Eveline's disgrace, had only been waiting for the catalyst of puberty. This came at the end of 1928, and the world changed again for Jack as his eyes swelled and the pain recommenced. He began New Year 1929 blind, but the Clemos devised a way of easing at least some of the discomfort:

> After some discussion an alternative method was found, freeing my eyes from bandages while ensuring that no light reached them. We had an old square board which was pushed out above the stairway when mother papered the inner walls of the landing. This was placed in the recess about ten feet above the bottom of the stairs and became my perch from nine o'clock in the morning until bedtime [...]. Beside me on the board was a small cup of boracic lotion and the wad of cotton wool with which I occasionally bathed my eyes to ease their smarting. When I looked over the edge of the board I could see a faint blur of light on the stairs below. But I seldom glanced down.[53]

He now enters an important transformational phase. The syphilis had reignited and Clemo would not return to school. He did not want to and he was not able to, having performed so poorly in his exams. In most families it would be expected that the boy would find work, but Jack was not at all inclined to it, and in *Confession* he searches for reasons why he could not even take a 'soft job at Treviscoe Co-operative'. His eyesight wasn't very good, and anyway the walk would be hazardous in the winter, passing the clay-pit and tanks. Besides,'I knew that I should find such work uncongenial'. It was 'effeminate', he said, and he did not like the idea of staying in all day. In *Marriage* he continues to give excusive reasons: 'I could not face the daily proximity of rough, insensitive labourers who read nothing but newspapers and talked about nothing but sport and the "bloody Government"'.

Jack was a spoiled child, his mother indulging him with the urgency that came of believing that he might not survive childhood. He had no father and no peers whatever to share or contrast the progression into adolescence. He had already sufficient reason to consider himself exceptional, and there was no one to refute this. Puberty and sexual arousal, for instance, were met without any guidance, and without any friend experiencing the same, or male relative to empathise or explain what was happening. Sex education was to be performed by Eveline Clemo, Jack's devout puritanical Bible Christian mother, who knew very little about pubescent males. She considered masturbation and nocturnal emissions sinful and believed Clemo's normal nascent sexuality to be evidence of a genetic sexual obsession and deviance inherited from his father. So, what might usually be considered normal male teenage urges and experiences seemed to Eveline proof of Jack's sexual aberration. It was in the blood.

Jack's sexuality was inspired during this spell of pubescent blindness by a girl called Evelyn. The occasion of their meeting was the marriage of Harry the Co-op driver to Viney Grigg, on 27 April. Jack went with his mother to Penrose Veor, the Grigg family farm in St Dennis, where Viney was getting ready. When the party left for the chapel, Jack stayed behind, 'and those who remained at the farm were too busy preparing for the reception to take much notice of me. All except one – Harry's sister Evelyn'.[54] She was a little more than a year younger than Clemo, but considerably more mature. Clemo describes the interest she seemed to take in him, stroking his hair and arms, and leading him around. The simple interest excited an obsessive, fantastical desire for her that lasted throughout the 1930s. In *Confession*, Clemo writes that he adored her for six years only, but even in later diaries he is questioning whether Evelyn has really made the right choice by getting married to someone else, or whether she has been deceived away from God's will that she and Jack were meant to marry.

By 1930, Jack had left school, stopped attending chapel, and started attending to girls. He refers to this as his pantheistic phase, though this is not a very precisely used term and the processes and expectations of God (for example, in prayer and appeal) remained the same, with moments of exhilaration and sexual excitement still considered Providential. Clemo had a basically fundamentalist Methodist leaning – eschewing entertainment, dancing, sport, film and drink – with a taste for extremism and a God who acted dynamically. In *Confession*, he briefly describes his 'pantheism':

> It was not that I felt any Shelleyan or Wordsworthian rapture in Nature – that was still beyond my temperamental range; but I could not recognise the chapel God in the Power that had restored my sight. God had become to me more cloudy, diffused, a vague Spirit of the universe, mystical and, of course, non-moral.

Other than the questionable morality of Clemo's God during this period, the self-accusation does not tally with unpublished contemporaneous documents, but seems to have been developed in considerable hindsight. For instance, Jack's favourite reading at the time was the popular fiery sermonising of Talmage and Spurgeon. So there is little *practical* difference between this 'pantheistic Spirit' and Clemo's later faith. Rather, Clemo's dismissal of the village faith was rebellious and aesthetic. In *The Invading Gospel*, Clemo's 'spiritual autobiography', he acknowledged what he more frequently suggested in his private diary:

> I did not doubt Christianity – I merely disliked it; or rather, I disliked its façade, while being conscious that behind the façade was some tremendous secret which I could not get at but which was the only thing that could satisfy me.

What did change were Clemo's focus and the language of his belief. He began to understand more, to read and study a diverse literature that showed conflicting perspectives and differing tastes. If there was a vague sense of worldly rapture to some of Clemo's early expressions of faith, this was not 'pantheistic' or 'pagan' in any recognisable form, and his beliefs did not alter as radically as has been suggested. Rather, we see in this sense of having emerged from a dark past into a newly enlightened present or brightening future, a trend that will be perceived throughout Clemo's life and work. He is the constantly regenerating 'clay phoenix', ever-optimistic, ever-hopeful, and ever-apophenic. The tidy compartmentalization of his past is a part of the retrospective imposition of patterns on his life, and a way of separating painful events of the past from his present and future. But it also had the effect of mythopoeically simplifying his life, creating an illusion that greater changes were constantly occurring. This simplification and myth-making has informed the majority of studies on Clemo, so that the narrative established and repeated is often misled and misleading.

We have a fair idea of what Clemo was thinking at this time because of another development that sprung from his 1929 blindness and his defection from school. There still hung over Jack the question of what he was to do with his life. How was he to survive? How was he to help his mother and pay his way? She had encouraged him to get an office job at the works and in the mid-1930s she sent him up to Goonvean to see how he would get on there, though he did not take the hint and in his diary wrote:

> In the evening I went to Goonvean claywork to see some fellow my mother saw yesterday, who'd asked her to send me down, as he wanted to see me. Spent a pleasant half-hour there in the rude cuddy by the

mica – a fire burning – a very bare place. Talked with the old clay-worker about my writing, about the cinema, about Mussolini – all sorts of subjects, quite homely and natural it was.[55]

Jack had thoroughly rationalized his unwillingness to work, and partly perhaps as a further defence against his sense of inferiority and distaste or fear of others, Clemo comes on a decision that allows him to stay at home with his mother in the house and not have to engage with other people except on his own terms: 'What about if I was to write stories like – like they 'Ockings?'[56]

Jack with novel MS, 1935

III
Twilight Where God Dwells

And, behold, I am with thee, and will keep thee in all places whither thou goest, and will bring thee again into this land; for I will not leave thee, until I have done that which I have spoken to thee of.

Genesis 28:15

Eveline would have preferred her son 'to stand in our pulpits and preach, not to write novels',[57] but in the 1930s Jack entered a new period of his life and began an outpouring of experimentation in form, style, religion and ideas. His literary ambitions ensured that the period is well documented. The diaries begin in 1934, and Clemo also began writing provocative letters, poetry and opinion pieces for the *Cornish Guardian* on an almost weekly basis, beginning in 1930. There are short stories, dialect tales, early poems, correspondence and drafts of novels, all documenting Clemo's self-propulsion into the world, with his new ambition and sexual awareness both awoken by the pubescent bout of blindness. Clemo's sense of abnormality was nurtured by his isolation, while his awareness of his body and sexuality came mostly from D.H. Lawrence novels, outdated books on sexual biology, and the public's response to his histrionic pronouncements in the local paper.

There is, then, at the beginning of the 1930s, a further leap into the atypical. His life was already anomalous. He was a contrary syphilitic drop-out living on the edge of a clay-pit with his mother and aunt, physically enfeebled and ill-equipped to cope with his burden. To evade despair he reinterpreted his situation. The natural choices for a young man finding his way might be to shun others, to shun normality, to embrace his individuality, and we see Jack, at this critical stage, doing all of these things, wedging himself deeper and more irrevocably into the role of misfit and rebel. His development would now depend largely on himself, his own direction, imagination and reactionary individualism. He did not know what other boys were going through, or which of his urges were natural, peculiar or divine. It is no wonder that he became fixated with experience and with his own biography, when he was working on understanding all of this so completely in the dark. And it seems inevitable that many of his life experiments and attempts to drag himself towards maturity were blundering and dismal disappointments, none more so than his earliest attempts at love-making and understanding sex.

These began in the 1930s with romantic infatuations. The first was Evelyn Phillips, beginning in 1929, and the second was Barbara Rowse, who was a young child at the time. The relationship with Barbara was inappropriate and it might be uncomfortable to read.

Clemo's affections were by no means exclusive to one girl or the other, although his spiritual ideal was. So, in the same year that he would describe his ideology for 'But one Book, one God, one girl',[58] meaning Evelyn, he would also write: 'B. is all I want, because in her I find what I sought in Evelyn, what I've prayed for for years.'[59] 'B.' was Jack's abbreviation for Barbara, which would be changed to 'Ba', when the 'Browning pattern' was observed later in the decade. This 'Browning pattern' was a perception of similarities between Clemo's own romantic life and that of Robert and Elizabeth Barrett Browning. 'Ba' was the affectionate abbreviation Browning used for Elizabeth Barrett in their correspondence. There were still other love interests, which erupted excitably, though they tended to be briefer and less space is given to them in the diaries and autobiographies. One of these others was a girl named Violet from Foxhole. In the 1934 diary Violet, or 'V.', as he refers to her, is considered an alternative to Evelyn, and Jack is uncertain which one is destined to be his wife:

> Is she at Foxhole – V? or at St Austell – my Evelyn that used to be? Or perhaps – I don't hope – she is in the ways of sin and prostitution, crying out for me to understand her suffering and her hunger. I DO – I DO! I would go now if I knew where she was; I would fall with her that we might rise together from a common level.[60]

The desperation and drama are important to the understanding of Jack's early development. The romance is largely fantastic, nourished in a dark corner of the cottage, where he worked and brooded at a cramped bureau. There is no outlet or social suppuration of this bulging emotional pustule. It swells fanatically and awkwardly. Clemo's sensitive, creative and active brain was confined in the cottage as in a crucible, and all the violence of adolescence and maturation were intensified.

The obsessive theme of finding a wife, also in the above diary entry, will be the most frequently recurring theme of Clemo's biography. The only extraordinary aspect of the quotation is that it does not refer to God's role in the procurement of a lover, as the entries usually did. Otherwise, it is quite typical. For example, there is the impression given that it does not really matter whom Jack marries; it could be Evelyn, could be Violet, or could be some prostitute he has not yet met. That final sentence is hyperbolic. Jack did not look for a partner among those 'in the ways of sin and prostitution', but the sense that he would marry anyone interested in him is consistent with coming years. So this early diary entry shows Clemo looking for marriage-as-such, rather than particularly concerned with individuals, but also it shows him as a fantasist. The dramatic fantasy of his relationships is not apparent from the autobiographies, but it is a key feature of his romantic development.

Both Evelyn and Barbara complained about the ways they were portrayed in Clemo's work. Evelyn was upset with *Confession* and Barbara much later with the 1980 television film *A Different Drummer*. Barbara had not read *Confession*, in spite of being given a copy by Jack, but she had seen the film, and she was so upset by it that her husband telephoned the Clemos to complain on her behalf. Nothing much is known about the complaint, but it was sufficient that Jack felt the urge to reply, and he composed a letter stating that he could not see what all the fuss was about, using Evelyn's response as justification: 'Evelyn and her husband were somewhat annoyed at first, thet soon got iver ut and Evelyn continued to be friendly with my mother'.[61] Aside from the typographic errors, there is an unconventional morality being suggested; it does not matter whether Barbara got upset or was misrepresented, because she would get over it eventually, just as Evelyn had. It is a dangerous and self-serving moral system.

Barbara and her husband were complaining, not only for the indiscretion, but for factual inaccuracies, and such complaints were becoming familiar to Clemo. Eileen Funston, mentioned in both autobiographies, and Mary Wiseman, to whom Clemo was engaged in the 1960s, both disputed the nature of their relationships as portrayed by Clemo. Brenda Angilley (née Snell) also disputed any sense of romance, and June Trethewey has given her own excellent account of their brief connection, which again differs from the published version.

It is not known what part of *Confession* offended Evelyn, but the description of her father might not have pleased her:

> A pathetic figure slumped at the table, sometimes fumbling with a Braille manual [...] warped by an uncongenial atmosphere both at home and in the Church. [...] And the warping process was completed by something like a monomania on the subject of smoking.[62]

Or perhaps she was annoyed for having been written about at all, when in her mind there had never been a relationship.

The story Clemo tells of the Evelyn romance begins with the wedding of Harry and Viney. After this, the teenagers did not see one another for a year, though Jack writes that his eyesight began to return immediately afterwards, connecting this romantic experience with his healing, as well as to his decision to become a writer. Love, healing and literature were all connected from this moment. The year of that wedding, Clemo submitted his first piece of writing to *Netherton's Almanack*, an annual publication based in Truro, containing 'much that is interesting and instructive, three copyright Cornish Tales, and a large amount of Local and General Information', as the cover informs us. The tale was entitled 'Benjy an' his Sweetheart' and would appear in the 1931 issue, published in December 1930. Around the same time, Clemo had received a wave of encouraging acceptances, in the *Cornish Guardian*, the *Christian Herald*, *Tail-Wagger Magazine*, and to a lesser extent with a music firm in London. It was following these that he became a regular presence at the Phillips household. To begin with, Jack was visiting the Phillipses when Harry Phillips, Evelyn's brother, lost his job as the Co-op cart driver and found new employment driving a milk van for a farm near Grampound:

> Harry offered to give me rides in the car as he had done in the old Co-op wagon before his marriage, and from the summer of 1931 until the spring of 1932, I walked on several mornings a week to Foxhole to meet the milk van as it came out from St Austell. I rode to Nanpean and thence back around Rostowrack to Goonamarris. Harry usually stopped at his parents' home for a cup of tea, and I too would be invited indoors. Thus I was seeing Evelyn nearly every day.[63]

It is for this connection to the farm and to the milk run that Evelyn 'usually appeared as a farmer's daughter' in Clemo's novel drafts during the period.[64] However, Jack's trips out with Harry were called to a halt when villagers complained that he might 'infect the milk'. Jack's malaise made him more vulnerable to colds and flu, and his coughing upset the clients, so he was no longer allowed to travel with Harry. If he wanted to see Evelyn, he would have to walk to the farm deliberately, without the excuse of passing by with Harry.

By all accounts Evelyn did not encourage Jack. He only really talked to Mr Phillips, while Evelyn sat aside from them, listening to the gramophone or knitting. When he had written a new story he would take it to Nanpean and read it out to the family, sometimes having to wait for 'some squabble' to die down before continuing. Clemo writes how alien 'these family matters' were to him, and they distressed him as such: 'they did not fit into my ideal world at all'.[65]

In his infatuation with Evelyn we see more of the apophenic tendencies, heightened by Jack's youthful passions. Mr Phillips had been blinded in 1931, which Clemo saw as a meaningful parallel to his recovered condition: 'That Evelyn's father [...] should lose his sight just as I had recovered mine, was surely proof of a fated attachment between us'.[66] It was also too much of a coincidence that his

Pomeranian had been born at Evelyn's own home and given to Jack by her brother Harry, and that it had arrived on Evelyn's birthday. 'Even the dog I regarded as a symbol, a pledge of destiny', he wrote.[67] Jack desired Evelyn profoundly. Later he would make two claims that seem counter-intuitive. The first was that he had not *erotically* desired Evelyn, and the second that 'Neither then nor later was I "in love" with her'.[68] He says that he was only 'obsessed'.[69] This statement that he was never 'in love' with her contradicts the diaries, and is the sort of claim that anyone looking back and re-evaluating their failed relationships might make. But certainly, he was 'obsessed'. At the time, Jack was so besotted that he fantasized about their future together, planning children and choosing toys in Woolworth's, like the couples he saw on his hospital trips to Plymouth. He slept with her photograph under his pillow, kissing it many times before placing it beneath a copy of the New Testament and going to sleep. And when he was simultaneously besotted with the child Barbara, he had an hallucination:

> I was in bed thinking about B. last night when suddenly a cry seemed to ring through my brain: 'Jack!' and I said, 'What is it, Evelyn?' – 'You're being untrue to me!' came the answer. It was strange, like Rochester's experience in Jane Eyre; it seemed so real, [...] I told myself it was only imagination.[70]

Jack had read *Jane Eyre* just over a year prior to this event, and he observed a likeness with his own love of Evelyn: 'Read "Jane Eyre" – oh, what a book! It rent my soul about – that prayer of Rochester and the [?mysterious?] answer which presaged Jane's return . . . Like Evelyn and I'.[71]

Jane Eyre made an impression on the young Clemo and became a strong influence, containing a number of resonant points of interest. To begin with, there is the representation of 'fate [...] or Providence',[72] which is shown through the many improbable connections and 'coincidences' of *Jane Eyre*. There is also the tendency towards melodrama, and the differentiation between a divinely approved and divinely disapproved marriage, illustrated by Brontë's treatment of the proposals made by Rochester and by Rivers. Although the proposal of Rivers is made in God's name, it is not the 'will of Heaven'. Rather, it has been determined by God that Jane and Rochester should be spiritually connected, and it is Heaven's will that they should at last come together.

In 1942, when writing *Wilding Graft*, Clemo read *Jane Eyre* again, observing in his diary: 'the copious style helps to correct my tendency to sketchiness. How that Rochester can talk!'[73] There is also a biographical parallel that Jack never acknowledged, as Rochester was blinded and 'a cripple' before his future wife at last came to him, vowing to look after him. This happened in Clemo's life, albeit thirty years later. Some time into their marriage, Rochester's sight began to improve, and Clemo, too, would expect his blindness to improve after marriage. Clemo even adopted Rochester's terms of endearment, calling his lovers 'elf', 'pixie' or 'fairy'. Jack's most common term of endearment for Ruth was 'pixie', but he also wrote the poem 'Clay Fairy' for a girl named Iris in 1946.

The other claim about Evelyn, that his love for her was not sexual, could be questioned. In a 1987 letter to the Irish poet and publisher Louis Hemmings, he writes:

> My feeling for Evelyn was virtually sexless. She was my ideal muse, mediating a divine mystery that inhibited the vulgar physical cravings of adolescence. And when this ethereal bubble was pricked it was replaced by Browning's vision:
> 'To live, and see her learn, and learn by her…
> Not by the grandeur, God – but the comfort, Christ.'[74]

Fifty years earlier, in 1937, Jack wrote about what went wrong with his attempt to woo Evelyn:

> I prayed and had faith, but I did nothing to make her love me, physically – the 'works' of a love-life. I'm so afraid of losing B. now I have reached the cause of past failure, that I feel some definite unforgettable physical bond must be forged between us.[75]

The problem was, he thought, that their relationship had not been physical, and here he seems to suggest that he will not make that mistake with Barbara. The sexual implication is fairly obvious, and is well supported by the writing produced from this period, in the novels, poetry and letters to the paper. Sex was very much on Clemo's mind when he was infatuated with Evelyn, and the fact that she was the object of his desires is clear from the poetry dedicated to her, and from moments of Clemo's idling recorded on the backs of old manuscript pages and notebooks where he plays with her name, in verses and acrostics. But Clemo's experiences and ideas of sex can be confusing. In his early *Cornish Guardian* correspondence, sex appears to be a possible mystical point of contact between a person or a soul and God. It is an idea which Clemo would develop. The majority of sources point to a conceptual grouping of Evelyn, God, sex and love. The 'relationship' between Evelyn and himself may not have been physical, but it is not true that his feelings were sexless.

However, Jack's understandings of 'sex' and 'mysticism' are not always straightforward. 'Sex', in his early years, was misunderstood, and mysticism appears to evolve as a concept. Writing much later, in preparation for a BBC interview, he thinks about Evelyn and 'the romantic vision she'd brought me. I floated around in a mystical cloud and couldn't come down to earth even to court the girl.' 'Mystical', in this instance, means something like 'magically obscure'. But Clemo uses 'mysticism' to mean many things, at times separating or hybridising historic usages, or embracing several meanings at once.

By Christmas 1933 the relationship between Jack and the Phillipses had become tense. Evelyn was fed up with Jack's attention and let him know: 'Evelyn was here – and a bloody devil she was [...] giving me hell to end the year with'.[76] The words 'hell', 'devil' and 'bloody' used as profanities are unique to this period of Jack's teenage years and are very soon discontinued. For the mid-1930s, however, they are liberally committed to the diaries.

The break in their meetings came at the beginning of 1934, when Jack was recovering from another bout of eye trouble that had begun at the end of the previous year, and in March Evelyn's mother brought all Jack's belongings left at the farm over to the cottage, now that he was no longer welcome. The tension had been building for some time, as Jack continued to pester Evelyn, and it is possible that the Phillipses were less tolerant or indulgent of his attention to Evelyn after the syphilitic symptoms re-emerged. They made it clear that Jack was no longer to try to see her and that he must leave her alone.

Jack did not completely heed their request. Instead of ceasing to bother her, he decided to follow her, and when he heard that she was due to be singing at Old Pound Chapel, a little bethel between Nanpean and Karslake, he set off to surprise her. Evelyn did not respond well:

> When I next visited Nanpean Mr. Phillips informed me very gravely that Evelyn had complained about my presence at Old Pound, that she resented my following her about in this fashion [...]. I was not surprised by the news; I had known for months that Evelyn was growing increasingly annoyed at the gossip that linked her name with mine. But I hung on and decided that I must see her alone and put the facts before her in the exulted manner of a Teufelsdrockh.[77]

Yes, he understood that she was upset. Yes, he expected it and accepted it. Yes, he could appreciate that he should leave her alone now. But if he could only see her one more time...

The evening at Old Pound Chapel had a significance independent of Evelyn. Being in that out-of-the-way bethel, hearing the Sankey hymns with their direct and simple message, and seeing the honest faith of these 'old-fashioned' working people, ignited his love for 'primitive Christianity':

> Had I perhaps, all along, been searching for the secret of Nonconformist Puritanism, aware that it might contain a revelation sufficient for my life and destiny if only I could view it by a sudden oblique light, as no one had ever viewed it before?[78]

This reverie is interpreted as a minor victory for dogma over idealism within his temperament, and suggests a place for Clemo in the chapel tradition. That place, of course, would have to be unique and original, and we see in this episode the sense in which Clemo is deliberately a misfit. Instead of observing the similarity of his primitivism to that of the congregation, he assumes that his own is categorically different, 'as no one had ever viewed it before'. It may be argued that the key difference between his faith and the congregation's is simply the assertion of his individuality, the sense that faith must find room for his idiosyncrasies and idealism. In other words, this is a kind of idolatry justified by a rule of exceptionalism; a rule such as election or mysticism, where one has a link to God that others do not. This is not stated yet, but becomes apparent as themes develop. It is a step beyond the personal conversion experience and covenant of Methodism and towards a more solipsistic view. The experience could not be simply personal. It had to be qualitatively different.

The 'relationship' with Evelyn was now over, but Jack's hopes were not. He had invested a good deal of thought and emotion into her, and he would not give up. For one thing, he had submitted his first collection of poetry to C.W. Daniel publishers, which was entitled 'Twilight Where God Dwells' and dedicated to Evelyn. The collection sees the narrator writing to and about his love, a girl named 'Brenigan', who represents Evelyn. The publisher rejected it, stating:

> There is ample evidence that you have had a big experience as a poet but it is not so clear that you have succeeded in transmuting it into poetry with the literary skill necessary for your work to be accepted as having outstanding merit.

They said they would reconsider publication if Clemo was able to raise 'half the costs of manufacture', which he was not. Only nine pages of this manuscript definitely still exist. The following, entitled 'Midnight Longing', is among them:

> To lie awake and to stretch tired, yearning arms
>   Where dim shapes flutter, white, in the dark room glide,
> Seeking a form among them, real, and expect some charm
>   Of shadow to make flesh, for a love unsatisfied.
>
> To whisper a name, soft, question the startled air,
>   And to answer, myself, as the voice so beloved would say,
> Loud, that the wind thro' the night in its course might bear
>   Echo, and stir one love wrapped in dreams. Sweet play.
>
> To curse at the hours, slow-moving, at languid time
>   That speeds not the year when the body withheld shall lie
> And be loved and receive speech due to itself in its prime,
>   And the voice speak, echoing mine in our one soul's cry.

Clemo returned to this poem more than ten years later, in 1945, retitling it 'Midnight of the Flesh' and changing it 'almost completely', as he said, to be compatible with his new faith.[79] The difference is remarkable. The 1945 version is rewritten to reflect his new fusion of sex and theology, and while it is not the best poem from the period, it certainly shows a touch of maturity. The new version reads:

> To lie awake and stretch tired, yearning arms
>   Where you, girl-phantom of my prison, glide,
> And try and make love's wanton, secret charms
>   Turn shade to flesh for seed unsatisfied.
>
> To call your name and woo the heedless air,
>   To speak, myself, what your ripe voice should say,
> And burrow to the craven help of prayer,
>   Imploring Him who sneers in this delay.
>
> Is He afraid earth-sparks would foul His lip
>   In that great hour when we together cling
> As I ascend the fountain steps to dip
>   My torch in waters whence the rainbows spring?

> Torch that now sears my vitals: Nature still
>   Glares with the greedy glint of lecherous fire.
> Your breasts are rounded into Calvary's hill,
>   And 'gainst the sky his Cross is on the pyre.

The reason for so few of the poems from 'Twilight' being left in these manuscripts is probably that many of them were used to compile the earliest version of *The Clay Verge*, which draft has around fifty poems, finally whittled down to seventeen.

Jack was also religiously invested in Evelyn. He had observed the auguries and concluded that they were destined to be together, to enter a relationship that included God, his mother, himself and her. He held the utmost conviction that it was God's intention for them to marry, a pattern repeated through all Clemo's romantic attachments. After the severance of their contact, this conviction wavered, and Clemo began to transfer his hopes onto Barbara. Still, through 1934, 1935 and 1936 Jack mourns the loss of Evelyn, adding an occasionally optimistic passage: 'God *can* convert a soul without the conscious will of that soul, making, compelling it to yield itself. So it was with me – so it shall be – *and is* – with Evelyn. Thank God! Oh, thank God!'[80] In 1936 he still kept her photograph under his pillow, and Evelyn was 'My dear girl, my Evelyn'.[81] Later that year, Mrs Clemo bumped into her in St Austell and discovered that she had a boyfriend. She tried to break the news to Jack carefully, but he did not react well:

> Very much upset. It has come suddenly – last evening mother spoke of Evelyn, and it seems that while I have been indifferent, hearing no word of her, she has gone down the road to sin and death. My God! I do not know how to bear this. Her character gone, her name a by-word […]. I could give her up to another man, but to give her up to the devil, to eternal death – oh, I can't and will not, if there be a God![82]

'If there be a God!' Clemo never doubted that there was a God. Indeed, Clemo believed in the reality of both God and the Devil consistently. But while he never disbelieved, he did, at times, *spite* God. Such moments are unique to the mid-1930s. They appear in no other period, and in no other format. Nor do they appear except in the context of romantic pain. In the following passage, Clemo confronts God directly:

> O God why need we quarrel so? [...] Last night my heart was broken about in the anguish of pleading. I cried for Evelyn – cried, cried to make it up with her [...]. How long, O Lord? You hide yourself and will not answer me, and then I grow bitter and curse you; and then when the dark mood passes I come with my bleeding heart and confess that I have sinned, I plead for you to forgive when all the while it is your fault because you do not answer me. How easy it would be for us to live always close to each other: but you are stubborn, just as I am, and will not give her to me; and then you blame me because I, too, grow sullen and resentful ... oh, it is so silly, so stupid, Lord, this endless fooling, this eternal folly and rising up to blame myself and crying to you, cry, cry, when always you mock me and make me fall again to repeat the silly thing all over [...] oh, my God![83]

The following day he continued:

> Hour by hour I sit and cry out for love – for love – not spiritual, not God-like, but love as men know it when it kills them and dooms them. The only joy I want is sensual [...] body with body oh, how good it is – a lie down in twilight where there is no God, to yield with pure nakedness and crying with the [?constancy?] of rhythm in blood and life-force. It is all the heaven a man should want, this intoxication of sense and warmth with lips pressed on lips, breast heaving, naked and soft beneath the straining of body to [??] with body as the life-seed quivers, awakes, thrills and rushes to

contact – . Bliss – bliss – till it is past – and then – Hell – hell of remorse – for what? God! What a mistake for man to have a soul! I'd give anything to get rid of mine, to live entirely in that sensuous straining – intoxication of forbidden fruit!

Entries for the following week have been torn out.

In the same vein, though more direct and disingenuous, is this passage from the end of 1934: 'I tell you there is no God. You are deceived. Religion is a myth – Christianity a lie, Christmas a fable. If it were true it would surely let a fellow be happy'. The idea that God will make one happy – or 'let' one be happy – in this world will be seen again. Later, after he has read C.S. Lewis, Clemo formally adopts Lewis's idea that suffering is essentially good for us, a part of a greater intention, although he continued to believe that the promise God made to unite him with Evelyn could not be broken. Jack expected God to make him happy, and he expected God to do what he asked. This is clear from the earlier diaries, and is justified in the 1949 correspondence with Eileen Funston, who queried this expectation of Clemo's. Jack replied with a shortened Bible quotation from John 14:14: 'If ye ask anything I will do it'.

Such passages illustrate the nearness of God in Clemo's worldview. Clemo talks to Him directly, shouting at Him like He is a frustrating parent in the next room, a plastic presence, a man he can insult and upset – challengeable, changeable. This conception of God as a real presence is central to Clemo's cosmology, and especially to his conception of 'mysticism'. At the moment this mysticism is a day-to-day immediate observation of God's presence, interest and intervention in his life. Clemo's theology will develop, but some basic assumptions about God's nature are already clear. He is present in the world at all times; He answers prayers; He has favourites; He intervenes; He is both present and transcendent; He ought to make Jack happy.

That God had no intention of making Jack happy yet is shown by a major development of the 1930s. At the same time as Evelyn Phillips was growing tired of Jack's attention, Eveline Clemo began to reveal the full story of his father:

> She did not disclose it all at once, but gradually, hint by hint, during our many discussions of marriage and morals. My views on these subjects were already becoming heterodox – I championed free love and would argue for hours about what I was pleased to call 'sanctified smut' – and it was partly as a warning to me that my mother forced herself to tell the ugly secrets which she had kept for nearly twenty years.[84]

The revelations probably included the story of the 'nymphomaniac' aunt and whoring father, possibly her own premarital sex, pregnancy, the death of her daughter and the contraction of syphilis. She introduced Jack to the guilt of sex and its awful presence in his own body and blood.

It was to these revelations that Clemo reacted with a deepening antisocialism and masochistic self-alienation. He writes that his mother's facts 'were to have a far-reaching effect for good upon my spiritual and literary growth; but their immediate result caused her to regret bitterly that she had burdened me with such knowledge'. The revelations 'plunged my whole life for a while into dark chaos', Clemo writes; 'I was aware only of the awakening of something malicious and cynical, a destructive force that had been biding its time'.[85] With this 'destructive force' he debased himself to appear slovenly, offensive and rougher, and it is while indulging this shabby sex-obsessed identity that his congenital syphilis progressed, requiring urgent treatment.

From the letters of local writer Frank Baron we know that Clemo had an operation in Plymouth in 1934, at the end of September or beginning of October, when he was 18. Details of it have been cut from the remaining diary fragments, although some mention of ear troubles may be found. We do know that Jack had his first course of injections in October 1934, however, from the two-year anniversary he marked in 1936. Following this course, the deafness improved and Jack was able to listen to his neighbour's gramophone again. But the new symptom was unyieldingly progressive, and the moments of reprieve were fleeting taunts, a test to his nerves. Throughout the 1930s, the disease was treated in Plymouth, and then in Truro through the wartime 1940s.

Weekly or fortnightly, Jack visited South Devon and East Cornwall Hospital in the Greenbank area of Plymouth, ten minutes' walk from the train station. These trips were painful, distressing and expensive, and the Clemos appealed to various charitable bodies for help. They were also Jack's only journeys outside of the county, so they were liberating and enlightening. He would travel on the train, walk through the large stores and bookshops, watching the girls of the city, hoping to catch one's eye or elicit a smile.[86] While wandering about the Barbican he saw the Blackshirts, Oswald Mosley's fascists, 'lounging around outside' their headquarters on Lockyer Street. He accidentally saw lovers when he looked over a wall on Plymouth Hoe – they were 'lying about in the grass … My God!' – and for the rest of the day, 'I could think of nothing but those lovers lying in the sunlight'.[87] Most weeks he would be given his arsenic injections of Salvarsan or Neosalvarsan, drugs with nausea and headaches among their side effects, with regular 'blood-lettings', as Clemo called the Wassermann reaction tests. The sensorineural deafness would come and go through the second half of this decade, giving Jack and his mother frequent false hopes of recovery. Deafness is an unpredictable syphilitic symptom, but the doctors would have known that it was very likely to remain and gradually worsen. Yet Jack would hope for and expect recovery, either medical or miraculous – or a combination of both – and several times it was announced that such a miracle had been worked. In 1934 his mother told him:

> If it hadn't been for my prayers you would never had heard again. The specialists at Plymouth didn't think you ever would. They told me only a miracle could ever bring back your hearing … that worked me into a fever, and I prayed – prayed – and God answered.[88]

Following another course of injections in 1935, the doctors are said to have agreed:

> To Plymouth – with mother today – the last trip of the course. There all day – first to S.D. Hospital, where I

> saw in the report book some interesting remarks about me. Left ear fixed, right opaque .... opacity at bottom corner of left eye. Nose healed, leaving perforation of [...] plate .... H'm. They report that I'm looking much better, which is a consolation, anyhow ..... [89]

As well as the hope that he might be improving, this second entry suggests the deterioration of his nose. It is unclear whether it refers to the caving in of the cartilage, or to his sense of smell. In an unpublished paper by Clemo's friend and correspondent, Helena Charles, Charles quotes Clemo: 'for nearly half my life three of my senses, sight, hearing and smell, have not been normal. These senses being dulled I was naturally stimulated to the defensive conviction that after all, I was not missing much'.[90] Jack and Helena met in 1949, so the reference to 'nearly half my life' would seem to date the loss of his sense of smell to this period in the mid-1930s.

In spite of believing himself to be improving, 1934 was the year which, in hindsight, Clemo would consider the first year of his deafness. If Eveline's prayers were answered at all, then the magic worked only briefly. Jack's hearing slowly worsened, and the reports of 'good' days grew fewer as the days of 'no improvement' or 'no change' increased. The emotional strain of this was considerable, for although the specialists may have told the Clemos that his hearing would probably never improve, Jack and Eveline both believed in the power of prayer and that God's will was for Jack to be happy and healthy. The ear troubles, as the earlier eye troubles, were God's 'strange testing', but if they kept their faith and continued to pray and to thank God, then 'What God has done for other "Uncurables" He can and will do for me'.[91] This last quotation comes from the 1949 diary, fifteen years after the onset of deafness. Over these years, as for many subsequent years, Jack would expect improvement, looking out for slight changes in his health or mood or for a sign. Ecstatically, he might observe a mild difference and hastily announce his imminent 'full recovery', only to be thrown back into dismal silence days later. Always expectant, overjoyed at the vaguest hints of health, fiercely disappointed at each relapse and regression, Jack was straining his damaged nerves, and it may be little wonder that his personality was at its most volatile over these years. The following entry from 1934 shows the passionate confusion typical of the period:

> By train again to Plymouth, in dull weather again. Girls in the 'bus – oh, my heart! It has come back – I do not know why, or how – but all day the old agony has been tearing me. I walked about Plymouth like one in torment, looking everywhere – everywhere, for a smile in some girl's eyes, for a love-glance, some food for my heart which is sinking and faint and tormented with all the mockery of hell. Through Spooners and Woolworths I went, pushing against the eager throngs of people, mad with rage and defeat. I was cursing them, cursing God, striving terribly to throw Evelyn out of my thought and find among this teeming crowd another – another for whose kisses, for whose love avowals and passion-hearings I did not have to wait and plead and spend my strength in praying for. Oh! it shakes me to the core . . . the old uncertainty, doubt, fear, hate and lust. The tears [?blinker?] my lids as I [??] myself through the unheeding crowd. What was I? Who cared – who knew? Defeat, defeat, and no Evelyn, no heart in God's whole world to share my suffering.[92]

This was a tense period. Jack's hopes for love were being thwarted, the syphilitic symptoms had returned and worsened, he was, as we will see, in continual press controversies in the letters pages of the *Cornish Guardian*, and the truth about his father was being gradually revealed. In other words, on top of the usual pains and pressures of adolescence, and as well as Clemo's circumstances and temperament having prevented any understanding of his young self through peers or parenting, the problems were heaped ever higher onto the boy, and the weight was unsustainable.

When considering the suggested cruelty of Evelyn in her rejection of Jack, it must be borne in mind that there is no evidence she ever encouraged him. All we have is a moment of kindness when she helped him at the wedding, and a walk they took home from chapel one day, the anniversary of which is kept in the diaries. Otherwise there is little sense of Jack and Evelyn interacting. Jack's affections were not reciprocated, but were an annoyance to the girl. Mrs Clemo observed this later, telling him, 'I don't believe Evelyn ever loved you – it was all on your side', to which Jack mused, 'But what – oh, what was on God's side? What did He, does He, feel?'[93]

Evelyn married in 1937, by which time Jack's affections had begun to turn to the young daughter of their next door neighbour, a three-year-old girl named Barbara Rowse. One of the most frequent entries of these early years is along the lines of 'Playing with B. all morning', and she is mentioned even then in a physically stimulating way:

> Barbara was so very loving today, as if to answer my craving for love-love-love. She kissed and kissed me and heaved her little body against mine; and I tried, tried to snatch out of it all something of the reality I seek. Pitiful – pitiful, my God – why should I be starved, [?wasted?] – like this?[94]

For the next few years Clemo is split between the physical presence of this girl and the more conventional love for Evelyn. At the same time, he was declaring himself in love with Violet.

Violet gets scant mention in the autobiographies, with little more than a note that he had been, for a short while, in love with her, and that Evelyn's teasing him about her had caused him to use bad language for the first time. He is rather downplaying the infatuation. Violet was a less frequent visitor to the Clemo cottage, but in the diaries he records dreaming of her often, and Barbara is sometimes spoken of as a stopgap until Violet sees sense or the 'real thing' comes along.

However, in *Confession*, Barbara is given the prominent role and said to have been 'leading me towards my true faith and work'. Her 'influence soothed and adjusted me for the grafting of the dogma in its true Christian form'. By the time he came to write *The Marriage of a Rebel* in the late 1970s, Clemo had begun to distance himself from this infatuation, misleadingly claiming: 'I knew that this friendship was only a slight foreshadowing of the real drama.' In the diaries, Jack continues to wonder whether Barbara might return to him as late as 1946, after most of *Confession* had been written.

Throughout these years, Clemo's relationship with Barbara is couched in romantic terms, and he records a number of experiences of sexual stimulation. The rest of this chapter will explore the available evidence, attempting to reconstruct the narrative and to reveal its significance to Clemo's writing.

In the earlier diaries Barbara provides 'relief' for Jack, her kisses and innocent affection turned into a fantasy of romantic love. On the backs of juvenile manuscripts one might occasionally find drafts of love letters fantastically discussing plans for their wedding and future together. The fantasy is not the real problem. The presence of any girl was a way of gaining experience of what girls were like, of what they wanted, of how one behaved towards them, how they differed, and so on, and preferring a younger girl might well have seemed a kind of self-preservation. When Evelyn outgrew Jack she mocked him, his naivety and immaturity, his childish outbursts and fancies. Barbara was still only a child, and her innocence had many years left. She would not mock Jack, reject him, challenge him or leave him, so long as he continued to amuse and please her. Actually, Jack was good with children, enjoying their games, their lack of inhibition, their simple honest pleasures, the absence of sophistication and self-consciousness. Children were easier for him to be around, and they gave him room to explore his own character, to try out personae, and even to enact the lover. He would remain in charge of the relationship he fancied, and he would not be hurt so easily. And Jack acted the role of lover with theatrical violence. He pined and raged and wept and prayed, cursed and blew kisses, poetized and sighed, climbed the clay peaks and gazed over at the villages and farms where the girls he loved lived.

But there are other ways in which Clemo's fixation on a child is more troubling. The love would always be one-sided, the power in the relationship all his own, and this one-sidedness indulged and grotesquely developed Clemo's tendency to solipsism. In the villages his dramatic expressions of love for children naturally caused controversy and were condemned. As a result, the innocence of the relationships is often overstated in *Confession* to counteract the gossip, which has persisted even years after his death. The village gossip was exacerbated by Clemo's condition and reputation. It developed over considerable time and it was, unfortunately, nurtured by Clemo. The rumours about his illness and his father's past were commonly shared, but his mother also suffered from gossip about his not attending chapel, apparently receiving anonymous letters of disapprobation. His press controversies did not help either, and one of his correspondents almost growled through the paper that the real Jack Clemo was not the all-knowing elected Lothario he claimed to be. Parents did not want their children associating with him, however they may have respected Mrs Clemo, and rumours of queerness in his behaviour towards the children were exaggerated by the more general distaste many already felt towards Jack. People had gossiped about the boy and his family ever since his syphilis had become common knowledge. They were wary of him, and several children recall being told to keep away from the Clemo household by their mothers. This sort of gossip would always find a role in Clemo's novels, a devil's discourse or fallen playmaker, and the villagers themselves are more often portrayed as despicable, scurrilous and cruel.

The attachment to Barbara is Clemo's most controversial. The villagers often thought the worst, while other writers have ignored it altogether and have encouraged biographers to do the same. Jack prevents this occlusion by talking about the 'relationship' at such length in *Confession*. Written so soon after the events, the autobiography gives Barbara a leading role, despite the immaturity of the relationship, as a result of which Clemo would need to justify himself later and revise the account. His wife added to the problem by editing the diaries and letters after his death. The effect on the reader is a deep suspicion, and it is probably the same suspicion that has led so many writers to avoid the question altogether.

Clemo did not necessarily find Barbara sexually attractive; she was conveniently present and innocently unreserved, affectionate, and her childishness gave Jack the opportunity to act the lover without mockery. He was able to dictate terms without contradiction, and this gave him space for experimentation and meditation. He considered Barbara his muse. Within this fantasy, Clemo recorded the kisses he shared with her as though the child's innocent kisses were a real lover's. He wrote of them holding hands, walking together, of her leaning back in his arms while she sat on his knee, and of playful 'romps' in front of the fire as though they were passionate embraces. And it seems he thought of them as such, as though he *was* in a relationship. He knew that his mother and Aunt Bertha did not approve, so he would disappear with Barbara into the back garden and hide by the wall or in the outhouse to receive her kisses and hold her in his arms. Sometimes these embraces had greater significance than others, as when Clemo was sexually aroused. But conclusions should be guarded. His naivety of expression with regard to sex in the newspapers has already been observed. He did not use the word in a correct way, and while he strongly implied that he had had personal experience of physical sex, all the evidence suggests that he had no experience whatsoever and that even masturbation was rarely, if ever, deliberately indulged. In *Confession* he implies that he avoided masturbation altogether, and this was also suggested by Father Benedict Ramsden, a good friend of Jack's later in life, although the erotic satisfaction Clemo occasionally derived from his contact with Barbara may be considered very close. The point is that Clemo's language of love and sex cannot be trusted, and his reflections on his relationships are reflections on one-sided fantasies. We have to be very careful to pick out facts from the often extravagant phrasing. For instance, Clemo often talks of a 'full expression' of love in the diaries, which he differentiates from kissing and which he intends to mean something physical. Had someone less sexually foolish written this we might conclude that they meant intercourse. But Clemo appears to mean nothing more than achieving sexual arousal.

Barbara would come in before or after school, as well as at weekends and during holidays. Often the two families would make daytrips to the coast, and several photographs remain of them all paddling and posing together. Jack called her 'B.', or sometimes 'Baby' or 'Barby', as in: 'Darling Baby – how she is mine now'.[95] This is all a part of the lover's role, and from 8 December 1937, Barbara would have a new and lasting pet name: 'Ba.' To make sense of this, it might be worth deviating a moment.

Through 1936 and 1937 Jack had become increasingly infatuated with the poetry and life of Robert Browning, and for Christmas 1937 his mother bought him *The Browning Love Letters*, a large volume containing letters exchanged between Elizabeth Barrett and Robert Browning from 1845-1846, beginning with the inspired declaration of love – 'I do, as I say, love these books with all my heart – and I love you too' – which Browning wrote in his very first introductory letter to Elizabeth Barrett. This impressed Clemo deeply, and these letters, along with A.R. Skemp's short biography and Rudolf Besier's play *The Barretts of Wimpole Street*, which Clemo read in 1935 when it was serialized by *John O'London's Weekly*, had an unexpectedly significant impact on Clemo's life. It was 'in the light of Besier's play', wrote Clemo, that he perceived the pattern for the solution to his own problems and desires: 'a love-life in which Christian mysticism and normal human feeling were ideally balanced'.[96] He read how two people could connect instantly, deeply and lastingly, and he saw his own hopes for a spiritual and physical love realized in their swift, dynamic marriage; the sickly Barrett being freed from her oppressive symptoms and confinement through Browning's optimistic devotion. Clemo, like Browning, could be 'priest and lover'. This was how love was meant to be, and how his own *had* to be.

The original picture of the lovers was taken from Besier and petrified in Clemo's mind by the letters. As with *Jane Eyre*, Clemo saw in the Besier play many parallels and 'promises'. The promise of predestination and spiritual connection is overtly present, but so is the promise of physical recovery:

> ELIZ. As I told you before, I am a dying woman.
> BROWNING. (*Passionately*) I refuse to believe it. For if that were so, God would be callous and I know that He's compassionate.[97]

The play is set within a single scene, Elizabeth Barrett's 'bed-sitting room' in the Barretts' 'melancholy house in Wimpole Street'.[98] When Barrett and Browning first meet they find themselves immediately intimate, excited, stimulated and understanding of one another. The impression is that they were made for each other, destined to be together, again like Rochester and Jane. Much is made of 'Providence' and of their special compatibility.

Clemo found this emphasized in Browning's poetry, too, initially in the conversion described in 'Pauline'. The merely human love for Pauline was surrendered to God, and, following conversion, there came 'the exultant declaration of a reborn, eternal love'.[99] This was the blueprint of Clemo's search for sexual, erotic or marital fulfilment on earth – 'an earthly search in the state of grace', as he called it. A phrase in Browning's 'Pauline' also serves to justify the apophenic impulse of Clemo, the narrator admitting the same pattern-seeking behaviour: 'and thence I date my trust in signs / And omens – for I saw God every where'.[100]

In short, everything Clemo desired – health, love, predestined happiness, God – were illustrated in the life and work of Browning. In the 'Wimpole Street Miracle', as he came to call it, Clemo recognised the template of his own life. Here was further evidence of the promise God made with his mother through the passage in Isaiah.

This is the 'Browning pattern', then, the observation of similarities between Jack's life, faith and expectations, and the biographies of Robert and Elizabeth Barrett Browning. From the observation of similarities, Clemo inferred the revelation of his own destiny and aspired to their perfection in faith and love. The 'Browning pattern' is possibly the best known eccentricity of Clemo's biography, and the most important and pervasive manifestation of the apophenic impulse. In Clemo's words, what he gained from it was the belief that 'the sort of faith towards which I had been groping, and which Browning had so perfectly expressed was sane and practical when rightly focused and integrated'.[101] At its root, the 'Browning pattern' is romantic, though the romanticism is so central to Clemo's self-identity that the 'pattern' imposes on all areas of his life. As well as informing predictions for 'Years of Destiny', such as 1945, the centenary of the Browning marriage, Clemo applied the pattern directly to his relationships, in the first instance to the one with Barbara:

Everything I could write to my Ba has been written already either by R.B. or his Ba. Have I not for years – yes, years! – thought of my love as a miracle 'ordained granted by God' – to make room for which my love was 'devastated'?[102]

Later: 'How I wish it could be here as at Wimpole St. – ostensibly a friendship, the love growing between Ba and me'.[103] And there were more mundane examples of the influence, as when Jack's pet Pomeranian Gyp died in 1935 and he was replaced with another Pomeranian, named after Elizabeth Barrett's dog, Flush, 'believing that he would live to see something similar to what his namesake had seen in the darkened room at Wimpole Street'.[104] (Here again, the vicissitudes of Providence reflected in a Pomeranian.)

Later, in his 1946 diary, Clemo would declare 12 September 'a special day of prayer and dedication. As that was the only way out for E.B.B., so I know that something similar is the only way out for me'. This was the date of the Browning wedding, and it would be used as an important sign in future relationships.

It is ridiculous that Clemo expected Barbara, aged six in 1937, to be his Elizabeth Barrett (or his Robert), and it surely illustrates the depth of unreality in this fantasy. And yet, the connection informs Jack's language and writing, so that we start to read entries like: 'Poverty, scorn, hatred I can bear gladly, only let Ba be on thy side, my side!' And we find poems 'dedicated to Ba aged 6'.[105]

In depictions of Barbara in Clemo's early fiction, the girl becomes conflated with and at times separated from the Evelyn characters, as the true love interest. She is his muse, and he believes he cannot write without her:

> I took Barby again, outdoors while mother was at St Dennis. It rained, and we went into the outhouse and loved – loved with all intensity. AB came out and almost saw, and then mother: and I know by her manner, the way she looked at me, that she understood, realised: but oh, God! there was no other way, if I am to live, if I am to write, if I am to grow and be strong for service.[106]

It is a striking diary entry for several reasons. The sense of Barbara as Clemo's muse might be noticed. Jack always believed that he wrote more and better when he was in love, a belief contrary to the facts, as will be seen again in the 1940s, when he repeatedly writes how he is lacking love and all inspiration while at the same time composing three of his most memorable books. The inspiration he drew from Barbara only helped him to produce a handful of domestic dialect tales and some immature, unpublishable novel drafts.

But there are some stronger and more troubling themes developing in this passage. The phrase 'loved with all intensity' is suggestive, although it might refer to their more usual kissing and holding. There is also the desire to evade Eveline and Aunt Bertha, and the sense that Jack considers his physical 'experience' with Barbara necessary to be of 'service' to God. The idea that Barbara is some sort of bolstering or training 'for service' is rare in the diaries, though God is certainly considered to be involved in what could be thought a dangerous way. We have seen that Clemo pursues patterns, in fate, destiny, predestiny and Providence. We know he believes in prayer and in the day-to-day involvement of God with human affairs. But here he runs the risk of full-blown narcissism. Events in the world are being interpreted not only *by* him, but also as *for* him. This is the case with the Barbara fantasy:

> Nothing can be more certain than that God over-rules it –: He has brought it about in answer to prayer; prayer has kept it a secret between Himself, B. and I – the more intimate sides of it, I mean – I do not fear. […] Her love came, not of my choosing: it was given. I did not seek it nor take but when it is offered.[107]

God has given Barbara to Jack, and she and subsequent girls are considered almost as commodities, or servants of Clemo's will. This is repeatedly observed through the 1930s. Because his mother has not found out the more intimate details, God is approving the relationship, directing it even. Because God is presenting Barbara to Jack, Jack has to 'take' what he is given. And because Clemo has prayed for Barbara to come round, that means that when Barbara *does* come round it is only in answer to prayer. This idea that God will change another human being's mind in response to Jack's desires is shockingly egocentric, and one might worry that if Clemo considers his sexual excitement and fulfilment divinely justified – not only *allowed* but also *given* by God – then he may have felt justified to go beyond the acts recorded. A religious reader might have further problems. One could be the question as to whether this relationship really was endorsed by God. If so, what implications does this have? Was Clemo being shown the preference of the elect in having his unconventional desires indulged? What evidence is there that it was God and not the Devil offering the child? If this last possibility ever crossed Jack's mind he did not mention it. Rather, he prayed daily for the deliverance of a girl, and when she came it was an answer to prayer:

> Last night B. playing with ink and got it over her dress, and her mother's [...] threatened to keep B. from coming in at all. I prayed passionately that God would defeat that aim, and today she's been in! Thank God![108]

Or, in a more volatile mood:

> This morning until 10 o'clock I was in a horrible mood of rebellion, cursing, vowing never to write another word for God [...] because B. hadn't come in. [...] I raved still more violently, and wanted to lay hands on something to kill and destroy. [...] Then, after I had come to my senses and prayed [...] God sent my B. in.[109]

When his prayers are not answered Jack has terrible outbursts, cursing everything in a childish tantrum. The same formula was applied to his literary success, as he waited for news of submitted stories and novels: 'This morning it was very hard for me to see the postman pass by with nothing for me after I had prayed, and I went wild with rebellion'.[110] It is this aspect of self-centredness that might make a Christian reader doubt the authenticity of Clemo's relationship with God. When Barbara laughs at him he will 'Curse her', or begin 'Raving like a demon': 'Life is too hellish to endure ... – wild thoughts of suicide – oh, I'm going mad: I *know* it's madness, and prayer can do nothing'.[111]

Again:

> B. in, and so good! Playing here with me, playing wheelbarrow race, and rolling on the floor, and sitting close, and then making models from comics, [??] she stood close to me and I felt her warm body and her hair caressing my face. Went out full of [??], to pick blackberries – so thankful for the 'little nurse' – hoping that it would lead me to a fullness of praise. But d-n it, God is so utterly idiotic – when I came back, mother gone to shop, and AB not there; and I just asked her to sit on my lap – only that – and she sneered and said: 'I don't want to....' Everything crashed again, curses pounded in.[112]

This passage marks another development in the Barbara fantasy; a pleasure which followed from Barbara sitting on his lap, and which Clemo is sensitive to because nobody else approved, and it appears from the above quotation as though Barbara did not always enjoy it either. That nobody approved would make it seem self-satisfying to Clemo, an idea incompatible with his fantasy. He wanted to feel like a real 'lover' and 'mystic', not like a pervert, but several times Barbara is uncomfortable. In the above quotation, it upset Clemo and made him curse God, although it may be worth noting he did not attempt to force her into anything. Another time, Jack's honesty with himself about her feelings is clear, if padded with endearment: 'A little love with B. today: but she doesn't lead me outdoors now; afraid, I believe. Oh, dear girl!'[113]

Ruth attempted to edit the more salacious details, but her work was done inconsistently, as though by a tired or distracted mind, and the result is mixed. On first reading, one might believe that the missing passages would reveal something horrendous. However, on further study, by decoding the euphemisms and attending to the anniversaries and patterns marked out in the diaries, one would conclude that the handful of overlooked entries are of the same nature as those torn out. For example:

> Rejoice not against me, oh mine enemy: when I fall I shall rise! The devil has – or thinks he has – good cause to rejoice today, since I yielded myself to love again with B. and for nearly an hour gave myself up to an orgy of kissing and – other things. It was in the afternoon, mother being at Dorothy's, papering.
>
> Oh, God – God only understand the remorse, the shame, the sense of utter, utter frustration and weakness. ...
>
> I have prayed all evening for B. that God will not allow her to suffer for my weakness. If she went away I should feel, to my dying day, the agony of remorse, the shame of guilt, the fear that it was I – I – a son of God, redeemed by Christ – who had led her first into the evil path. Forbid, oh my God! Send Evelyn to satisfy and sanctify my yearnings![114]

More explicitly:

> Only one kiss because AB. would have heard, but in each other's caresses we found all that had been 'locked away since and lost awhile' – so much so that I had an orgasm. I lived [...] the day in a sort of dream, hardly daring to believe it had really happened. .... but if any man has ever known the presence of God I know it now.[115]

There are two aspects to be considered here. The first is that the orgasm is not at all usual, but a surprise to Jack, almost as though it has never happened before. So the phrase commonly used, of a 'full expression' of love, does not mean orgasm, and sexual gratification is not the object of Jack's 'sexual' 'experience'. (This should be remembered when we find Clemo calling himself a 'sex mystic' and using the sub-title '*A Mystical-Erotic Quest*' for his second autobiography.) A further aspect is that the orgasm is expressed as a mystical experience, as 'the presence of God'. God is not only complicit here, but facilitating and rewarding Jack's physical relationship with Barbara.

At no point, one might observe, is Barbara's enjoyment considered. Aside from the issue of her inability to give informed consent, Clemo's sole focus is on his own pleasure, and this is indicative of a more persistent character flaw. Consider the weakness of the following justification from 1936. Jack and Eveline have been discussing the inappropriate pressure he has been placing on Barbara. He reflects:

> I am really living only for B. now, humanly. […] I feel rather bitter towards mother because she so often keeps B.'s love from me. B. in again in day, playing dominoes. It's certainly not hurting her. I've never seen fear of shock or shame on her face because of my love.[116]

Jack appears to be writing that it is fine for him to continue as he has been, so long as Barbara does not express fear, shock or shame. It is utterly one-sided, only about Jack's pleasure and showing no consideration for Barbara's interests. There is more evidence of this in the manipulative techniques he would sometimes use when Barbara did not want to kiss him. He would sit in his chair with his face in his hands pretending to cry until the girl relented. Many nights Jack and his mother sat and talked through his prospects, butting heads over this affair:

> Talked with Mother last night about B. and I – still she will not believe that God is behind it – 'If He were, you wouldn't get such bad moods.' Oh, she won't see that the bad moods are present only when B. isn't – when the devil lies and dares to suggest that God has not fulfilled His pledge and supplied all my needs.[117]

Eveline also believed that Jack was destined to love and marry, and that his wife would be provided by God. She supported him in all aspects of the theory of love-making, and for this reason she seems to have found it difficult to argue with his convictions that first Evelyn, then Violet, then Barbara, were God's chosen mates for him. For long nights they argued in front of the fire, Bertha sitting quietly. 'Got talking with mother in the evening' is a common refrain, and for all of Jack's idiosyncrasies and tempers, these evenings reading and talking with his mother – listening to her, considering and respecting her opinion – are a constant and endearing presence. They are a part of daily routine in the cottage, and it was only on the subject of girls that they fell out. Sometimes, this was because instead of paying Jack attention, Barbara had gone to Eveline, or even to Aunt Bertha, as in this 1937 entry:

> B. on my knee [...] – felt the ardour and was glad. [...] And then – suddenly, unexpectedly – she kissed A.B. – damn the sight for ever! [...] The kiss I prayed for – given to another before my eyes! [...] I broke down and cried until we went to bed – cried and sobbed my heart out.[118]

He loathes when Barbara kisses his mother or aunt, and is even struck with jealousy when he sees her kissing her own mother.

In March 1938, the 'romance' is severed by circumstance. In February, Barbara's grandfather, Marshall Rowse, having moved to Trewoon to escape a family feud with the Angilleys, crashed his motorcycle and died. Barbara's parents decided to relocate to Trewoon to live with the widow, and they left within a few weeks.

Jack's initial response was dramatic:

> I must not – oh, I *must* not write much now – too horrible it is – I feel that I am dying, my life ebbing away in this grief, grief inconsolable. I can't bear to stay here [...] beyond all my understanding or my faith is this horror of darkness. Ba to leave, to go away! It can't be – oh, Lord, Lord, how I have prayed today.[119]

The following day he has calmed:

> trying to see God's hand even in this, working for me and Ba. Absence makes the heart grow fonder, they say […]. It is a terrible shock but I feel God upholding me.

Next day, the family left. Jack was devastated, and it is said that the 1939 and 1940 diaries were destroyed by him because of the desperate misery he suffered as a consequence. In 1938, however, his faith appeared healed almost immediately, within twenty-four hours. In later years, this period is looked back upon as the occasion of Clemo's 'conversion'. This is worthy of note, as it is central to his mature theology. In hindsight, Clemo writes that he experienced a 'gradual conversion', completed around 1937-38.[120] But it seems that the sense of this conversion's finality comes from it being punctuated by Barbara's move to another village, as well as the revelation that Evelyn had married. These facts gave the impression of the end of an era, which was further confirmed by the start of the Second World War and the arrival of evacuees. The event of the conversion, Clemo states, was sex. Contrarily, the diaries for the period show nothing emphatically different, no monumental change in outlook.

The moment, on 4 September 1937, where Clemo writes 'Surrender of everything to God', does not stand out in the diaries. It is one among many absolute statements of faith, change and conviction. A few days later, he writes about Barbara, 'She's a child and I must not forget it',[121] as though he is intending to change his treatment of her following his epiphany, but nothing changes. This was a period of heightened turmoil, with Clemo falling, repenting and falling again: 'Oh, it's all tears – tears when I sin, tears when I plead, tears when I doubt, tears when I trust – only tears!'[122] One week: 'I feel so different this week – free not only from sin but from the desire to sin'.[123] The following week he is marking 'love' and 'kisses' in emphatic red crayon. He was arguably at his lowest point to date, intellectually aware of the sin, emotionally certain of the correctness of his love, physically tempted, and unable to repair the rift.

It was at this point that the world around him changed, almost as though he was unable to live a good Christian life without outside help. As the rift appeared to grow, seeming irreconcilable, the miracle came. God intervened and removed temptation. Barbara left, Evelyn married, and Christ drew nearer. This appears to be the root of Clemo's conversion experience and the mark of his new life. Now, in the diaries, it will be more frequent to read of his suffering in terms of frustration and dullness, rather than the 'demonic raving' of these earliest years.

Before looking at Clemo's literary output during the 1930s, it ought to be noted that there was a peculiar and pronounced interaction between his biography and his writing. He famously wrote in *Confession*: 'I am one of those writers whose creative work cannot be fully understood without reference to certain broken boundaries in their private lives'. So, what were these 'broken boundaries'? Sex? Girls? Syphilis? Faith? In the 1930s, Jack's differences had become more pronounced and strained. His interest in sex naturally developed, and his relationships with girls were enthusiastically announced. The syphilis progressed, enveloping him in deafness and dulling his sight. He was testing personae, trying voices and personalities. He was the lover, the elect, the prophet, the poet. His life and body were a battleground between warring forces: on the one side despair, disease and solitude; on the other hope, love, promise, faith. In the midst of these dramatic and damaging developments, Clemo determined to become a writer, and inevitably these diverse straining boundaries spilled into his work. Theoretically and experimentally, they entered the inflammatory newspaper letters in the *Cornish Guardian*. Defensively, they entered the dialect tales, 'throwing off the stagnant gloom'.[124] Ideologically, the boundaries were intimated and overcome in the narratives of novels. The following chapter will be looking at the early boundaries, these uncertain years of self-discovery and experimentation as Clemo reached out to a general public.

IV
Teach Me, Only Teach Love

Lord Jesus, Thou seest I patiently wait;
Come now and within me a new heart create;
To those who have sought Thee Thou never said'st 'No' –
Now wash me, and I shall be whiter than snow.

James Nicholson, 1872

Clemo's influences at this point are diverse and conflicting, and his literary output reflects this. The quantity of material from the 1930s shows how the ambitious young man approached his audiences, in the *Cornish Guardian* newspaper, the dialect tales, the poetry, and the published music lyrics. It was a time of experimentation in life, ideas and styles, and as well as a number of false starts and aberrations, we will find here the origins of the celebrated writer.

The best record of Clemo's early ideas has been collected in the archive of the *Cornish Guardian*. These are the most extensive and illuminating of Clemo's publications in the 1930s, in particular for the emergent literary voice that would mature into the autobiographical voice of *Confession of a Rebel*. There were, however, a handful of false starts. The one that immediately stands out is '"Gyp" and the Cats', published by *Tail-Wagger Magazine* in January 1931, around the same time as 'Benjy an' his Sweetheart' was published in *Netherton's Almanack*. '"Gyp" and the Cats' was a sentimental piece of nonsensical anthropomorphism, written from the point of view of Jack's Pomeranian. The intended effect of the narrative voice is similar to that of the contemporary fleeting online trend of 'lolcat': 'To hold pen hurts paw-paw and not much more I can write'. Happily, the voice was not given a second outing. The contemporaneous dialect tale is of greater value, as it is one of the only literary accounts of domesticity and of regional perceptions of the inter-war period in the quickly changing china clay region, and it is an intimate record of a now almost unspoken language form. In terms of publishing history, the dialect tale marks Clemo's first narrative success and it led to the publication of around twenty similar pieces through the 1930s, a handful of which were returned to in the 1980s and reproduced for a children's book, *The Bouncing Hills*. The tales have only recently been collected together and published as *A Proper Mizz-Maze*. But the dialect tale and the *Tail-Wagger* piece are similar in one way. They are both light-hearted attempts to write in an unnatural voice. Jack does not know how he is meant to write yet and he experiments with voices distant from his natural idiom.

Elsewhere, at the same time, Clemo was experimenting with verse. His earliest poems are dramatic Cornish renderings and death-obsessed reveries, metaphysical love poems and symbolist landscapes. The following was published in a Plymouth annual in 1932 and is entitled 'The Legend of the Doom Bar'. It is a dramatic adaptation of a folktale accounting for the notorious ship-wrecking sandbar at the mouth of the Camel River:

> On the strand the mermaid lay,
>   Basking idly in the sun:
> Came a man with deadly spear,
>   And the deed was swiftly done.
> Too late he found out his mistake –
>   'Twas a seal he'd meant to take –
> For while life was ebbing fast,
>   With the breath that was her last,
> She reached out, and in her hand
>   Took some pebbles from the sand,
> And threw them with a curse
>   Into the bay.
> Then the man in terror fled.
>   But ere he the news could spread,
> Night came down before its time
>   Upon the day.
> For upon the western sky
>   Came a cloud of awful gloom;
> Swift it spread across the heav'ns,
>   Like a wingèd horse of doom.

'Mid the darkness rose a cry,
  Scarce above a quiv'ring sigh –
Wraught with horror, dread and fear
  As the people watch'd it near –
Watch'd and trembled with affright,
  As th' untimely shroud of night,
Fell in shuddering silence over
  Land and sea.
Then each turn'd with bated breath,
  And each face was gray as death
"Tis the end!' the whisper echoed
  Shudderingly.

For three days and nights the gloom
  Was unpierced by any light;
Land and sea lay dead beneath
  A canopy more black than night.
When at length the darkness fled
  And the sun its wan light shed
Thro' the gloom,
  At the entrance to the bay
There a mighty sand-bank lay,
  Now called, alas! but aptly
    'Bar of Doom.'

These poems found their way into the *Cornish Guardian*, *Doidge's Annual* and *Christian Herald*, while other verses were sent to London in Clemo's early flirtation with the music business, when he wrote to 'one of the fee-snatching music publishers, inviting lyrics' with some slushy pieces inspired by Evelyn.[127]

Clemo was a lifelong lover of music, and musicality came easily and naturally to him. His mother played the organ and gave lessons, and both his parents had been in the chapel choir. Indeed, in *Confession*,

> the picture that remains most compellingly in my mind is that of mother seated at the organ, absorbed and remote in the pale light of the oil lamp, playing and

singing hymns out of a tattered, red-backed copy of Sankey's *Sacred Songs and Solos*.

Their neighbours, the Trevertons, owned a record player, and Mr Treverton would invite Jack over, 'to sit on the bench while he played his gramophone to me'. Publishing music, then, was attractive, as well as being a money-making scheme. The manuscripts for all three songs have survived: 'Dreams of Yesterday' and 'Flower of the Vale' from 1931, then 'Heaven Number Eight' from 1935. The tunes are catchy 'popular' pieces for voice and piano, probably best described as parlour music. In 1937, Jack was invited to submit further lyrics, 'but God overruled wisely, and has taught me not to write that kind of thing again'.[128] The process seems to have been that one sent one's lyric away with a fee and the publisher had a composer set it to music. The contributors were told that they would receive a percentage of any profits after costs. The company, having received Jack's lyrics, assured him that his work would be a tremendous success and all he had to do was send them £15. Eveline Clemo had managed to scrape together £20 of life-savings over the years, and, in faith, she gave it to Jack for his music. She lost every penny:

> No money, no money from anywhere. M. almost breaking down under the weight of this – feels she's at the end of things – no money for rent, which is a week overdue already – and there's debt to pay back. Think of it. £1.8.0 a week – that's all she gets, to keep herself and I in everything – food, clothes – and to pay rent and rates out of! I don't know how she does it.[129]

The music of these pieces does not bear any relation to the lyrics. Clemo's first submission, 'Dreams of Yesterday', was a melancholy poem with the refrain 'I know it's no good wishin' for what can never be, but I just can't help a'thinkin' o' those happy days wi' thee', though the piano music is cheery and ends with a triumphant chord sequence. The opposite happened to 'Flower of the Vale', Clemo's second submission. This time, the romantic sugariness of the lyric – 'Flower of my heart! sweet flow'r of the vale! None can excel thee, nay, none can compare' – is set to a dark and melancholy tune. 'Dreams of Yesterday' sold just eight copies. 'Heaven Number Eight' did not fare any better, but at least the music was more appropriate; a bouncy tune that could almost be the theme music for a sitcom. Jack left six copies in the shop at St Dennis, and none of them sold. Not long after, the music company wrote to Clemo:

> I am rather disappointed to have to report that so far there has been no demand whatsoever for this song, and our efforts to date, to popularize the number have proved singularly unsuccessful.[130]

Clemo did not attempt another, but the story is given a postscript in the 1941 diary: 'I see in the paper that the publisher of my last song, which ruined us financially, has been sent to prison for such pursuits'.[131]

More encouraging were Clemo's experiments in the local paper. The *Cornish Guardian* put Clemo in contact with the world beyond the surrounding villages. He could talk about the arts, education, religion, sex and culture, and expect a response. It was an unconventional social education, but such unconventionality would be typical of Clemo. This newspaper archive is important for several reasons. Biographically, it is through the papers that Clemo developed relationships, particularly with older men. Frank Baron, S.E. Burrow and John Rowland were all first encountered in the *Cornish Guardian*, and these volatile and ambivalent connections were the closest Clemo came to friendships. We can also follow Clemo's development of thought through them, as he tried out new ideas and was forced to explain himself, to debate and adapt. Clemo's writing in the papers is often hyperbolic, contradictory and poorly expressed, but the roots of his later thoughts and convictions are to be found here, allowing us to trace a definite progression.

The first of these progressions is the literary voice. Clemo is shocking, dismissive, peremptory, at times exposed and vulnerable, usually self-important and provocative. The effect he is trying to achieve is of a formal, authoritative register, precocious and impressive. He wants to impose himself as an exciting, rebellious individual, transcending the soppily pious establishment. This is the juvenile voice of *Confession of a Rebel*, the self-educated genius. In the local newspaper we observe the voice undergoing a brutal maturation process. Jack was stuck in a frustrating, friendless world, a life lived at his desk in the corner, or wandering over the sand dumps with his Bible. He reached out to the public with the same feelings of severance and impunity a young Facebook or Twitter user might today, toying with personalities and ideas, and to some extent the newspaper controversies were a kind of practical play.

By the time Jack was sending his inflammatory pieces, the paper was already established as a cultural and theological battleground, with a handful of regular contributors dominating the field. One approached these men expecting an argument, and Clemo provoked many of the most striking and violent disputes of the decade. His first letter was about books for boys and was published in October 1930. The writing is unnaturally heightened and indulgent, and is as melodramatic as his novel drafts from the period: 'I think there are far too many "thrillers" read today by the younger generation', he says, adding in an optimistic timbre that, as the youth matures, his manhood will pull him 'upward' and 'the books he despised he will love, those he loved he will despise. [...] Wait; the voice of the man is calling, and it shall not call in vain. Ere long it will burst its upward way despite every handicap. Then he will see his mistake.'[132] Jack was fourteen when he wrote this, so he had not experienced this 'growing up', but the ebullience of overwritten enthusiasm reflects an unevenly developing teenager, immature but ambitious, inexperienced but more than competent. The overall message of the piece is leave the boy alone and he'll come good in the end, which is almost reminiscent of Isaiah's 'Fear not'. It is a liberal message, and it will often be observed that Jack can be both stridently liberal and stridently conservative in his outlook. Also, that first letter shows the familiar anti-establishment position. Clemo is responding to two conventions: that boys read lots of thrillers, and that people condemn boys for reading too many thrillers. And he contradicts both: boys should read fewer thrillers and people should just leave them alone. Clemo's cynicism towards the establishment and established wisdom is a predictable personality trait. He was both a teenager and largely self-educated.

In the next series of letters, his liberal anti-establishment ideas again emerge. The view was expressed in the *Cornish Guardian* that belief in Father Christmas should be discouraged in children. Clemo disagreed, arguing that children should be allowed to enjoy the magic of Father Christmas: 'When at length the truth comes, the old memories will alleviate the blow and the child will thank its parents for having been allowed the joys of childhood's illusion.'[133] It was a mild disagreement, and some might think it hardly worth writing in to the paper, but Clemo was trying to pick a gentle fight, and he was clearly disappointed with the limpness of responses. Still, it did not take him long to learn how to properly upset his audience, and the following Christmas he really threw down the gauntlet: 'I believe [...] that until a child knows the full facts of sex, it cannot grasp the full significance and therefore the full enjoyment, of Christmas.' This is a more confident Clemo. He has settled into the newspaper and is pleased with his ability to engage, shock and upset his readers and interlocutors. He ends the letter with a telling narcissistic uncertainty: 'This letter may reveal me to your readers in a new light.'[134] Such a conclusion was unnecessary, drawing attention away from the argument and turning it to himself. Clemo is inviting feedback, not just on ideas, but on himself personally. He is reaching out to the readers and correspondents, inviting them to look at him and to consider him. The inappropriateness stands out on the page, and predictably the readers and correspondents were hostile and derisive, instigating a long sequence of defensively defiant letters.

Clemo's most prolific combatant in the paper was S.E. Burrow (1855-1939), an elderly vicar and novelist who responded to Clemo's outbursts with well-aimed mockery. Firstly, he noted Jack's repetition of the word 'full' in his letter on sex and Christmas:

> Kindly note the 'full facts,' 'full significance' and 'full enjoyment'! Master Jack was evidently 'full' to overflowing at the time of penning this revealing communication [...]. He has evidently heard or read something about 'human contact' until he has become obsessed by it, and places it high on a three-legged pedestal before which we are to bow! [...] I am more disposed to regard

him as a priggish, self-inflated dogmatist, who has tried
to look clever by putting on his grandmother's spectacles. This is bad for the sight – things get blurred![135]

Wounded, Clemo replied:

> Sir – Mr Burrow's letter is puerile in the extreme – a
> meaningless jumble of quotations and comments – an
> anaemic apology for criticism, since he evidently had
> none of the real thing to offer.[136]

Clemo then explains what he meant by 'sex', which was, simply, the physical birth of Christ. That is, Jack wanted children to understand that Jesus was born in the usual way. These are his 'full facts of sex'. It is possible that Jack is disingenuously back-tracking here, but more likely he has misunderstood the common context of the word 'sex'. For Jack, the concept of sex is inevitably linked with childbirth, so that he could be referring to anything from intercourse to parturition.

In the wake of this argument, Jack attacked popular culture, particularly the movies. In 1928 he had gone to the cinema with his mother, probably to The Savoy on Truro Road in St Austell, and he later wrote to the paper:[137]

> Not so very long since, I saw my first film – and most
> likely my last. It was a wanton, glamorous affair. It dealt
> with marriage problems, seduction, divorce – all that
> much of immorality without which the cinema would
> cease to exist.

He claims that while it disgusted him at first, soon 'I was fascinated, thrilled. I desired to see more like it. Thank God I did not!' It may be assumed that the seductive element of his criticism is fabricated, to allow the indignant conclusion: 'Youth to-day, taken in the mass, is a victim of the films. I repeat, a victim.'[138]

It cannot be known what film he might have seen that was at once so immoral, repellent and hauntingly seductive, though it is tempting to look through the 1928 cinema advertisements and guess. The Savoy had a weekly choice of films, mostly two or three years old, and in 1928 they showed a 1926 Rin Tin Tin movie, *The Night Cry*, as well as Betty Balfour's *Blinkeyes* and Fay Compton's *London Love*. Charlie Chaplin's *The Gold Rush* was also playing, and though it does not cover the listed topics, Clemo did sustain a hatred of Chaplin, which emerged several times, as in this 1944 diary entry:

> Charlie Chaplin's been arrested for selling a girl to the brothels. What a vile lot these film stars are – as bad as the Nazis – yet the crowds go on idolizing them. Better bomb Hollywood than Berlin if we want a moral clean-up.[139]

This was untrue. Clemo was listening to the salacious scandalising he usually condemned. Chaplin had been arrested after an actress and mistress claimed that he was the father of her child. He was not, as it turned out, but the scandal gained momentum, and the case that went to court was a charge of human trafficking, related to the vaguely-worded Mann Act, of which he was acquitted. He did not sell a girl to a brothel, but the news suited Clemo's disgust in this 'perverse jazz-born culture largely imported from America', as he wrote in the paper.[140]

As well as the movies, Clemo could never abide dancing. It was worldly and, essentially, a flirtation. Jack was influenced by his chapel childhood, and possibly by his father's American history, but the fierce hatred persisted. He condemned Barbara for her involvement in dances in the 1940s, and used it as a narrative device in early novel drafts, where dances were held in clay-drys. He would also demand that any future wife should never go to a dance after they marry, and it will be seen how Jack despairs when a marital prospect is said to enjoy dancing.

The combatant in the above exchange, the Reverend Samuel Edwin Burrow, became a correspondent outside the paper as well. He was one of the *Cornish Guardian*'s most frequent contributors, writing articles and letters, as well as a weekly feature in Cornish dialect under his alter-ego Ebenezer Trewiggen, or Eb. Though born in St Columb, Burrow was living in Bournemouth. The above exchange was by no means the most vitriolic between the teenager and septuagenarian. Disagreements would begin in the letters pages until they became unsustainably personal and offensive, at which point either the editors would refuse to publish any more, or Burrow would switch to the voice of Eb and continue to mock Jack in dialect, to which Jack gamely responded. Outside of the paper they wrote to one another with perfunctory politesse, offering birthday greetings and compliments on publications. Inevitably, however, the correspondence turned sour and Burrow would frequently use passages from their private exchanges to attack Jack in the newspaper.

In terms of Jack's maturation, being able to argue with his elders was an important part of clawing his way to adulthood, although it all happened in a very teenage way, Jack at once enjoying the compliment of being taken seriously while also trying to dismiss everyone else as fools and charlatans. Burrow found Clemo's posturing self-importance ridiculous, but he recognized that Jack was extraordinary. The boy was objectionable and arrogant, but he was also talented. Part of Burrow's disbelief in Clemo's swaggering conviction was that Jack had not had any experience of the world beyond his cottage. Here was a young teenager telling grown men, reverends and war veterans what the world was really like, what love, sex, God, battle, politics and people were about, when he knew few people beyond the clay country. This was a common criticism of Clemo, and we see it again when Cecil Day Lewis questions a number of generalizations in the submitted draft of *Confession of a Rebel*.

The following letter from Burrow reveals their relationship:

> Dear Jack R!
>
> Many thanks for your kind congratulations on attaining my 80th and for your good wishes.
>
> Frankly, I had not intended writing you again – your wild effusion in the Guardian, replying to Mr Slater & myself, in which you politely said we might 'go to the devil and nobody be the worse for it', seemed more than usually offensive from your pen. I wrote what I thought was a fitting reply, but the Editor did *not* print it!

But I should have learnt better by this time than to take serious notice of anything you write – you are yet young, and in the raw. I *hope* you will mature & ripen into decent citizenship by & by.

I notice that you renew your invitation to visit you when in Cornwall, and you add – 'call and tell me just *what you think of me*'! Now, in that request you give yourself away. You are absorbed in *Self*! You have very exalted & extravagant ideas concerning yourself – your wisdom, so profound and so wise that you need no other teachers! Your religious opinions so vastly superior to the orthodox and generally accepted that you can't waste time in listening to others preach! You see from this that I am not waiting to visit Cornwall to tell you what I think of you! I think you are clever – and you have gifts which if sanely cultivated might mean much to yourself & others. But you have already arrived and there is nothing more to learn!

My dear Jack. Go to school again, and first of all learn *how to write* so that others can decipher what your pen is meant to say! It is not a sign of superlative wisdom & learning to write in hieroglyphics which call for the services of an expert with a magnifying glass! It is rather an insult to your correspondents! I see you purpose resuming your Self effusions! Don't! Decent people are ashamed of you, & most laugh at you. Is that what you desire? It is time you pulled yourself together and played the man & not the fool! Yours sincerely
  SE Burrow.[141]

There is an uneven mix of propriety and insolence in Jack's having written to Burrow as he seems to have done. He has pretended to be polite and respectful by writing on Burrow's birthday, but then used it as a way of continuing an argument. He wants Burrow to approve of him, as a child might, but he also wants Burrow to appreciate his 'genius'. In Burrow's reply we see the same perfunctory courtesy used as a veil for the assault that follows.

Burrow's letter offers a strong sense of what Jack had written to him. There is mention of Clemo's philosophy of experience, an idea that litters manuscripts, newspaper correspondence and personal letters. This philosophy, Clemo says, is derived from his reading of Galsworthy's *Forsyte Saga*, and for Clemo it is the root of mysticism; it is the touch of God by a special sort of grace. In his next letter to Burrow, Clemo has explained that 'experience' is not about going into the world and finding adventure or observing different cultures. Jack can experience humanity by looking closely at himself. Burrow does not quite understand Jack, and writes in reply: 'you admit ignorance of anything but Self. You ask what you can do under such circumstances and answer your own question by deciding that the only course is to use your self material in the realm of "fiction"!'[142]

Burrow's observation of the selfishness of Clemo's solution is valid, but it could not seem so to Clemo. Jack was alone and self-involved by both circumstance and determination. According to his philosophy, he had been put into this position by God and it was his own to cope with. It was this 'experience' which Jack thought he had to understand and interpret. Experience is primary, but it is the experience of God in one's life, rather than the 'worldly' and 'extrovert' experiences of travel or adventure. Those extrovert experiences Clemo called 'Natural', 'Nature' being the force opposed to God. Burrow did not know the history of suffering, sickness, alienation and poverty in Jack's life, and did not fully comprehend him, partly owing to Burrow's character and partly to Jack's confused elucidation.

In his reply to the above letter, in which Burrow calls Jack a laughing-stock, Clemo wrote that he did indeed want to be laughed at. It has been noted how he affected a thicker accent and dialect to alienate himself from the villagers who had already outcast him, and how he refused to change his clothes and wash. When personal circumstances and disease were forcing him into defensive isolation, he chose to take control of them, to determine the conditions of detachment, to make of them a decision, strength and virtue instead of a weakness and victimhood. In his paradoxical programme of self-alienation, Clemo wanted to be laughed at and despised, but for his own actions rather than for the things he could not help.

In the newspaper, debate usually swung around Clemo's unpredictable and violent expressions of faith. The vehemence of his outbursts is reminiscent of the firebrand preachers he loved, such as Billy Bray and his own grandfather John Polmounter. The difference is that Clemo, at this time, was not referring his congregation back to the Bible as the Wesleyans were, but inverting the formula and directing people into the world and experience. In 1932 he wrote to the paper: 'Of God we must learn from life, not from the monotonous routine of so-called "religious instruction" in a schoolroom.'[143] Similarly, three years later: 'Experience is always a sacred thing'.[144] And in 1936, in *John O'London*, he adds: 'A faith that is worth having must be the product of experience, and must remain plastic, moulded by circumstance'.[145] God is not in the church, then, but in the world around, and the 'true' Christian experiences Him directly. This is the extent of Clemo's pantheism, but it is also consistent with his later idea of a 'divine covenant' between God and the individual, and of God's role in the life of the 'elect'. That is not to say that Clemo's later theology can be unearthed fully formed in the 1930s. We find ideas he would later retract, such as: 'Creed is for the nominal believer; the real Christian gambles with God',[146] and 'dogma blunders against the fact that Christianity is indefinable'. Note the difference between his derision of dogma in 1936 and his strong taste for it in the 1940s, as expressed in the poem 'A Calvinist in Love', from *The Clay Verge*: 'Our love is full-grown dogma's offspring'. This is the final poem of the sequence, and is meant to show the lovers who have abandoned 'Nature' for Christ and have redeemed their physical love by submitting their wills to Him, 'Making the wild heats of our blood an offering'.

Not long after this private correspondence there was a useful public exchange between Jack and another newspaper combatant, Peter Dartnell. Jack had made a grand statement in favour of experience and against Tolstoy and Carlyle, to which both the Reverend Parkyn (a regular opponent) and Dartnell responded. Parkyn was rude, largely because in his previous letter Clemo had claimed that the clergy did not believe half of what they said, but Dartnell was quite constructive. In the same piece to which Parkyn had replied, Clemo said that the teachings of Christ were of 'no more value to mankind than the teachings of Plato, than the guesses of Euripides, than the code of Mohammed.'[147] He was becoming obscure, and Dartnell responded that if he does not believe in the Creed or dogma, nor place any special value on the teachings of Christ, what does he believe? He questioned Clemo systematically, and Clemo leapt at the chance to explain himself.

Firstly, Dartnell asked, what does Clemo mean by the 'Revelation of God in life'? Clemo replied: 'Suffering any evil, the workings of "coincidence," the rhythms of change – these are revelations of God, and should be studied'. Evil, here, is either done or allowed by God, and 'coincidences' are patterns to be interpreted. This is one of the most striking of Clemo's beliefs, and its role in his life becomes increasingly prominent.

Secondly, Dartnell asked whether Clemo considered the Bible to be the word of God, to which he replied: 'Yes, I accept the Bible as the inspired word of God, though secondary to the revelation of experience.' Potentially, this too could be problematic, since the interpretation of these experiential revelations depends on the mind, of which Clemo writes:

> I do not regard the mind of man as God's greatest work. In fact, I regard it as being today God's greatest handicap. Men will accept as religion only what they can 'explain,' and so they never touch religious experience at all. The mind can only serve God while it is the servant of emotion, religious instinct, passion, impulse.

But is the mind that divines God's intention from 'coincidences' a 'servant of emotion'? It could be, in the sense of La Rochefoucauld's aphorism: 'The mind is always the dupe of the heart'. The desire to find patterns is the 'heart' or passion aspect, while the search itself is of the 'mind' or reason. But this is simply the formula of all problem-solving. The sentiment behind Clemo's unusual statement, of course, is pure D.H. Lawrence, and risks the same solipsistic and perverse self-justification. Recall Lawrence's outburst in *Fantasia of the Unconscious*:

> If a child makes you so that you really want to spank it soundly, then soundly spank the brat […]. Never be ashamed of it, and never surpass it […]. The only rule is, do what you really, impulsively, wish to do.[148]

The risks on a humanistic level are dangerous enough, but Clemo had the intensifier of God's approval. In spite of these dangers, the sense is fairly clear: feeling is primary, and the purpose of the mind is to find the best way of indulging one's desires. In doing this, one is serving God.

Clemo states that the Bible is secondary to the 'revelation of experience', though it is still the Word of God, assuming that the two will not contradict one another. That is, the Bible and 'experience' are both valid ways of approaching God, and they should reveal the same message, though 'experience' goes further by revealing one's own personal journey and covenant with God.

Clemo skips quickly over the third of Dartnell's questions, on whether he is Catholic or Protestant ('I have no intention of associating myself with either the Protestant or the Catholic Church, but shall remain simply a Christian'), and then gives a more important answer to the fourth enquiry as to whether man himself is evil:

> While not declaring that man is 'evil and rotten to the core,' I do believe that, of his own efforts, he will never realise his own ideal, much less Christ's. We have to insist more and more on the impotence of man. History about us, philosophy behind us, urge this truth. What is the sum of human philosophy but a commentary on the self-frustration of man? […] Man is obviously by nature at the mercy of unknown influences.[149]

Let us take from this sentiment only that man cannot 'realise his own ideal' alone. This is Clemo's response to humanism, and the implication is that man needs to submit to God and to Christ. But how can he know what he is submitting to? How does he know it is God? Clemo would argue that he knows by the revelation of experience. But if experience is primary to belief, then what is it about this experience that is so explicitly Christian? That is, it rather seems to be the case that Clemo's 'experience' of God is predicated on a Biblical understanding of God and Christ prior to experience.

Practically speaking, too, there is a problem. Clemo's conclusions from the 'patterns' he observes, and from the passions he feels, are consistently thwarted. We have seen in the case of the child Barbara how Clemo said that she 'must' come round, because his passions are telling him so. Most of the time she does *not* come round when she is supposed to, but when she *does* the essentially randomised reinforcement is imagined to be a great triumph of the divine pattern. Further, in his diaries Clemo makes very firm predictions, including the years in which important events will take place, particularly with regard to his marriage. 1939 was a key date of romantic destiny. It was intended to be the year when circumstances were arranged for Jack and Evelyn to marry, though when the year came Evelyn had already been married for two years to another man.

Clemo's direct answers to Dartnell may have opened more questions for the reader, but they were a useful exercise, as well as an informative statement of his progression. They comprise the most mature of his public utterances up to this point; more mature since they contradicted some of the violent statements from previous weeks. For example, the teachings of Christ are no longer of as little use as Plato, Euripides or Mohammed, but of a significance second only to direct experience of God.[150]

In *Confession* we see better how Clemo is using the word 'experience', putting pressure on a common understanding. His 'experience' is an internal response to stimuli, which we see several times in *Confession*, such as when he writes of the Browning love letters that they 'gave me just the imaginative poise I needed, balancing the "childishness" of my actual experience, broadening its significance and rooting it in a sense of spiritual maturity'. His 'actual experience' is maintained, but it is increased by further reflection. In normal formulations of 'experience' there is implied a variety of external stimuli being internalized usefully. Clemo's formulation reduces the external stimuli and emphasizes the importance of thoughts and feelings.

The philosophy of experience also informed Clemo's reading. The Browning love letters were an influence, but before them Clemo was looking urgently for other writers and artists in a situation similar to his own. Of course, he was reading for enjoyment, to observe style and to show off in the paper, but he was also looking for a writer who had suffered and succeeded, or had similar faith and ideas. He was acutely aware of D.H. Lawrence as a teenager, and was bound to be attracted by the biography and work of that miner's son writing so dynamically and directly about sexuality and sexual liberation as an uncompromising individualist at odds with the world. Mostly, though, Jack read biographies and biographical sketches in the papers, and clippings from these filled his scrapbooks. In search of people in similar circumstances, Clemo looked especially closely at syphilitic authors, such as James Joyce and Alphonse Daudet, however unlikely they were to appeal. (As a matter of fact, he hated both Joyce and Daudet, and the closest he came to syphilitic sympathy was Van Gogh.) Jack wanted to find a connection, a pattern, a model; clues to his own mess and uncertainty. In 1935 he read a biography of Hall Caine and declared it,

> A fine book, amazing me with the likeness of H.C.'s youth and outlook with mine. He almost became a sceptic in early manhood – like me. His interest was in humanity, the […] lost, outcast as is mine. Great man![151]

Clemo's enthusiasm for having found a writer in some ways like him led him to pronounce Caine 'Great', though he fell from grace as Clemo matured, and by 1941 he had been relegated from Clemo's list of writers among his 'Elect' down to 'Minor Influences', with G.K. Chesterton for company. Chesterton could not be one of the 'Elect', Clemo wrote, because he seems not to have reported any answer to prayer or to have experienced any personal communion with or guidance from God.[152] There were six men (no women) considered of Clemo's elect: Browning, Spurgeon, Galsworthy, C.T. Studd, Thomas Hardy and T.F. Powys. The only unexpected inclusion might be Galsworthy, a writer not often associated with Clemo.

He was recommended by Gordon Meggy, a writing coach engaged to help Clemo in the 1930s. Both Galsworthy's *The Forsyte Saga* and Charlotte Brontë's *Jane Eyre* are strong and largely unexamined influences on Clemo's prose in the 1930s and early 1940s, when all his novels were written.

By discovering similarities to the celebrated, Clemo was looking to show his own extraordinariness. It did not especially matter what the similarity was, and could be any triviality or chronological coordination. In the *Cornish Guardian*, his youthful desire to be considered a 'genius' got Jack in trouble after he compared himself to a number of celebrated men, including Epstein, Tolstoy, Carlyle and Hardy. It was an ambitious comparison for an unpublished teenager to make, though the aspects of their personalities he observed in himself were not especially flattering, and included 'hypochondria' and 'eccentricity'.[153] To infer any meaningful similarity between a great writer and an opinionated boy from such qualities was absurd, and naturally his old sparring partner S.E. Burrow responded, as 'Eb': '"Like Epstein", Jack R. Clemo does not care what people think or say about him! That's fine, that is – "Like Epstein"!'[154] Burrow's mockery ruffled Clemo, and the young man responded, but blundered into the same mistake, this time comparing his 'justifiable self-confidence' with that of Chatterton, Pitt and Hugo. Burrow's criticism stood; there was no reason for Clemo to invoke these names to describe his character unless he was intending to infer that he was like them in another way too. He must not, he declares, be dismissed as 'a mere scribbler of letters'. Pardoning himself if he seemed immodest sometimes, he wrote: 'the knowledge that one's mind has given birth to something like 700,000 words – which mine has done during the past three years […] well, it brings a sense of achievement […] which, I admit, is at times liable to break down the barrier of prudence.' He adds that his novel, at this time entitled 'Gwinbren', 'has been passed as up to publication by a famous London literary institution'.[155]

Clemo was posturing as a genius and comparing his flaws with the flaws of established writers to suggest that he deserves to be considered among them. He continued to show off in this vein, making wilder claims to genius and sexual experience as the year progressed. 'For several months', he writes, 'I studied embryology', though it 'makes one regard child-bearing as mere cold, hard biological fact'.[156] Clemo did not study embryology, certainly not in the way implied, and he makes similar claims when talking about Freud. On 23 June 1934 he pompously wrote how 'disgusting' Freud's libidinal link between God and 'Nature' relating to one's parents was, and the blasphemy of God being described as 'nothing but an exalted father'. The attack was so vicious that any psychoanalyst reading the piece might have found it stimulatingly deflective and defensive. When questioned, it turned out that Jack had only read a fragment of a single essay of Freud's, 'The Economic Problem of Masochism', and a biographical sketch that he had cut out for his scrapbook. Not only was there no special insight, but there was a lack of basic understanding. This might well have been the result of arguing with men older than himself. To keep up with them intellectually, Jack took shortcuts, relying on summaries from his scrapbook cutouts and his copy of Arthur Mee's *Children's Encyclopedia*, given to him in 1926. Clemo's literary education was similarly piecemeal. On a hospital trip to Plymouth he bought *The International Library of Famous Literature*, a twenty-volume collection of poetry and prose collated by Richard Garnett and first published in 1898. The collection contains a vast range of recent and historical world literature (including Garnett's own work), from Classical Greek to the present day. Entries were short, the prose being only a single story or chapter from a longer work; sufficient to get some sense of a writer and sufficient to claim familiarity in the *Cornish Guardian*. Clemo later reduced these twenty volumes, as he did not have enough bookshelving in the cottage. He cut out the bits he liked and fixed them together into just two volumes. He then rewrote the contents page, carefully glued the pages in and saved himself around three feet of book space. The salvaged works show his preferences and professional interests. The presence of Elizabeth Barrett Browning, Carlyle, the Romantics, Hugo, Donne and Blake is not surprising, though others, such as Pierre Loti and Pasquale Villari, are more so. The selection also included several theologians, and it was here that Clemo first read Calvin, specifically the exciting though unilluminating 'Prefatory Address' of his *Institutes of the Christian Religion*. It is likely that this is the only work of Calvin's that Clemo ever read, which is remarkable considering that almost all commentaries and reviews call him a Calvinist, and Clemo identified himself as a Calvinist or sometimes 'Neo-Calvinist'. The emphasis on Calvinism was toned down when it became the most frequent context of criticism, but Clemo's 'Calvinism' was never the Calvinism of Calvin. It was an agreement with specific foci viewed through the filters of, to begin with, the immensely popular Charles Spurgeon (arguably Clemo's greatest theological influence) and, after 1943, Reinhold Niebuhr and Karl Barth.

In 1934, following this protracted debate on sex, Clemo received a putdown in the newspaper that cut deeply. The letter hurt Jack so much that he tore up the paper and burned it. It came from a new young novelist who had received some recent attention. Daphne du Maurier, writing here as Daphne Browning, had published three novels and was living in Surrey, with a second home at Bodinnick, the opposite side of the river from Fowey. Her father was more famous than she was at this time, and the headline of the letter is 'From the Late Sir Gerald Du Maurier's Daughter':

> Sir, As a great lover of Cornwall and its inhabitants, though forced by necessity to live many months away from both, a weekly link and reminder comes with the 'Guardian,' which is sent me with unfailing regularity by one of the truest and most genuine of Cornishwomen.
>
> In the name of those who like myself wish to breathe something of the very air of Cornwall with our weekly paper, may I protest against the inevitable and wearisome exchange of personalities between Mr Hawken, the Rev. Parkyn, Mr. Clemo and Ebenezer Trewiggen, which is threatening to spoil, if it has not done so already, the tone of your paper.
>
> Let these gentlemen settle their differences privately in correspondence, but not before our eyes in print. We are not interested in their views, religious, political or sexual, and we object to valuable space, which might have been given to descriptions of Cornish people and

> their towns and villages, being filled with unpleasant discussions tainted with malice, serving no purpose whatsoever and verbose to the point of imbecility, not only worthless but irritating, and ugly to the eye.
>
> The tendency appears to spread, others are following their example, and surely it would be happier for all of us if you closed your Correspondence Column, rather than let it be monopolised by people who, at our expense, thus gratify their lamentable desire of seeing their names in print.
>
> Daphne Browning.[157]

The editors appear to have been impressed by the letter, apologising immediately and assuring du Maurier and the public that the 'correspondence is now irrevocably closed'. Jack never forgave du Maurier. When he read *Rebecca* a few years later he could only say it was 'merely a gripping story',[158] and in *Confession* he recounts the letter in a somewhat dismissive way. He does not have it to hand, of course, having burnt it, so he quotes from memory and the only phrase he recalls with complete accuracy is 'ugly to the eye'. This phrase, he remarks, 'suggests that even fashionable lady novelists can lose their sense of humour when trying to suppress something they do not happen to like'. More revealing in the account in *Confession* is that Clemo tells the reader that du Maurier's attack was levelled at him. He misquotes her as having written: 'We are not interested in *his* views, religious, political or sexual, and if *he* wishes to express them let *him* do so in private correspondence and not before our eyes in print' (my italics). Clemo has imagined that du Maurier singled him out personally for attack, when really she criticised all the men involved. He continues that it hurt especially because she was 'one of the class who should have recognised my talent and encouraged me'. The obligation of du Maurier's 'class' is repeated as Clemo criticises Sir Arthur Quiller-Couch for not championing the working-class boy when, later in the decade, Jack sent him one of his early novel drafts. Q wrote a kind and encouraging letter in response, with suggestions on what worked and what did not, but this was a great disappointment to Jack, who had expected Q to launch his career.

It would have seemed more valid for Clemo to have criticised du Maurier's suggestion that the correspondence pages be scrapped in favour of 'descriptions of Cornish people and their towns and villages'. She appears to have wanted to read of a romanticised, simplistic rurality; a patronising reduction and containment of the region. Clemo, Parkyn, Burrow and Hawken *were* Cornish, and questions about God, sex, art and politics *were* the concerns of a *Cornish Guardian* readership. Her letter highlights a key difference between the two writers and their perceived positions within Cornwall. Clemo felt no need to promote or reinforce any prescribed regional identity. He would not become any more or less a son of Cornwall or of the clay. He was writing from a particular place and region, but he was not a writer of reductive local concerns. He wrote from his native landscape out into the world. The idea of du Maurier's that the *Cornish Guardian* should ignore the underlying humanity and politics of its readers when it reached beyond village concerns, and only showcase common desires when they subscribe to her picture of an isolated and romantic localisation is deplorably naïve. Very likely, du Maurier's outburst was exacerbated by her personal circumstances. In the summer of 1934, she was in mourning for her father and had accepted a traumatic commission from Victor Gollancz to write Gerald du Maurier's biography. She wrote it quickly over the summer and it was published the same year. She was also living the life of an officer's wife in Surrey, a place she did not want to be, with duties she did not want to perform. Du Maurier felt trapped and disconnected, longing to be back in Bodinnick, a place she associated with personal freedom and distance from the real world. The Cornwall Daphne du Maurier felt she needed at this time of heightened stress and misery must have seemed a long way from the Cornwall represented in this protracted debate between Jack and his combatants.

The closest Clemo himself came to the appearance of regional reductiveness was also his chief literary success of the decade: the short farcical dialect tales with their gentle humour and homely themes. These easily escape the prescriptive accusation. They are not imposing any containing values, but reflecting everyday scenarios in a locally specific idiom. For example, there are stories about painting a window frame, fetching 'smutties', losing a fire poker, and doing the washing. The humour of the pieces does not lie in the scenes themselves, but in the language used. It is a self-aware and ironizing humour. An established dialect writer, Frank Baron, encouraged Clemo to continue writing these stories, helping him place them in journals and telling him not to waste his time on press controversies. In these early days Clemo leaned on Baron for help, and Baron did his limited best, putting the tales and poems in the hands of minor journals and publishers. One collection of stories was said to have been accepted by the publisher Jordan, but eventually the book fell through.

Dialect became the subject of a minor controversy in the *Cornish Guardian*, during which Clemo engaged with another writer, John Rowland. Rowland is a figure who appears occasionally throughout Clemo's life. In his own autobiography, *One Man's Mind*, Rowland describes himself as a novelist, scientist and criminologist. He says he began his career as an agnostic, rationalist and journalist, whose work included interviews with many of the major minds of the day, such as H.G. Wells, George Bernard Shaw and Julian Huxley. He also says that reading Clemo's first novel and autobiography helped him with his defection from rationalism to Christianity. Rowland was a writer of absurd yarns in awkward prose, and even in his autobiography he squeezes in a handful of pop-science howlers, particularly on Darwinism. As a criminologist, Rowland consciously wrote for the popular market, with titles such as *A Century of Murder*, which carried the tagline: 'A famous criminologist selects some of the most sensational crimes of the day.' His novels, too, were crimes, including the 1935 debut, *Bloodshed in Bayswater*, which would have been accepted for publication by the time of his press correspondence with Clemo. Later, in 1950, the novel *Time for Killing* was dedicated 'To Jack R. Clemo from one Cornishman to another'. Rowland possibly dedicated the book to Clemo because of Clemo's recent literary success. Jack would not have enjoyed Rowland's books, but Rowland is notable to Clemo as a Cornishman (living on Castle Hill in Bodmin), and as a published writer. More significantly, Rowland was the man who introduced Clemo to one of his biggest literary influences, the novelist T.F. Powys, when he sent him *Mr Weston's*

Good Wine. In the end, however, Clemo marked Rowland's 1984 death glibly: 'John Rowland has died – a likeable man, though superficial'.[159]

In their 1935 exchange in the paper, Rowland described his admiration for the swift progress of the Cornish language. Jack disagreed: 'The attempt to found a Cornish literature in the ancient tongue is patriotic folly run to seed [...]. I am convinced that it is more profitable at present to focus attention on the preservation of Cornish dialect'. Why, he is asking, is so much effort paid to an extinct language being flogged back to life while the live and spoken dialect is ignored? 'Ugly its words may appear in print,' Clemo said, 'but spoken dialect is one of the most refreshing sounds one can hear amid the roar and din of this mechanised age.'[160] It is suggested that the Cornish Celtic Revival Movement's promotion of language over dialect is an attempt to unify Cornwall's identity, homogenizing characteristics for the whole county, to define Cornwall in a more simplified way and to give the county a stronger sense of its identity and position within the wider Celtic diaspora.

Clemo's own use of dialect is almost contradictory. On the one hand in the tales he is exercising his understanding of domestic normality, while on the other in speech he uses it to offend those around him. 'I fought ["intelligence"] all along the line, even in speech, using the Cornish dialect, the rough slipshod English of the working people', Clemo writes in *Confession*. He is distinguishing himself from 'the working people' here, seemingly for the facts that he himself did not have a job and he had learnt better 'Standard English'. He continues:

> I read everything I could find about ancient Cornwall, and wrote poems about its legends, customs and prehistoric atmosphere. [...] I sprinkled my stories with Cornish phrases copied from the text-book, learnt the Cornish equivalent of many simple English phrases, and amused the Phillips's by repeating them at Nanpean. [...] I must have bored [Evelyn] with my talk of the Gorsedd, the Tyr ha Tavas (Land and Language) cult, the Old Cornwall Societies; and when I prophe-

sied that I would one day become a bard, standing amid some hut circle in my ceremonial robes, recognized by the crowd at last as a remote and mystic personage – well, she was sensible and refused to be interested.

In 1933 Jack wrote a glowing piece in the *Cornish Guardian* about the Bardic ceremony he had observed at Roche Rock, evidently enjoying himself: 'beneath the granite pile of the Rock, with the soft mists creeping, and the blue-robed bards and the chanted Cornish – there, for a little while, one could forget, and fold one's arms, and sleep, and dream…'[161] The same ceremony was dramatized in novel drafts of the period, and finally published in *The Clay Kiln*. The speaker in the following passage is one of the lead girls, Marvran:

> The summer after I left school, the day they held the Gorsedd here […]. There were crowds everywhere, filling the roadside and all the fields and downs between here and Roche school. Looked like a carnival, only a bit dull – all the bards were dressed alike in blue robes. The ceremony was boring, just jabber in Cornish, a foreign language to us moderns. We just ate ice-cream and pretended it was a fete or something. When it was nearly over some of us girls began climbing round the rock; and we found Joel Kruse sitting up there […] behind a pillar. All by himself glowering at the crowd as if he was the spirit of the place […]. All those modern bourgeoisie – pretending they're Druids or Bards.

Clemo's sense of Cornish-Celtic identity is strained, as it would continue to be. It was a party to which Clemo wanted to be invited, although he was not always sure whether he would accept the invitation. Three times in his life he was invited to become a bard, in 1961, 1966 and 1970. On the first invitation he wrote in his diary: 'This would fulfil my adolescent dream, but my tastes have changed since then, and my handicaps bar me anyhow'.[162] Next time, in 1966, he was in a turbulent relationship and did not want to accept unless his fiancée could be with him, which she could not. In 1970, Clemo was at last in a position where he felt he could accept the bardship, though we will see that this was still not a straightforward decision.

A second Cornish language disagreement developed in the *Cornish Guardian*, again in 1935, when Jack took on the driving force of the Cornish Celtic Revival movement, Robert Morton Nance. Nance was one of the key developers of the Cornish language, a founder member of the Gorsedh, a Grand Bard, and also founder of the Old Cornwall Societies. As such, he was one of the two most important figures in the history of the revivalist movement, along with Henry Jenner. Clemo's disagreement with Nance was about the Cornish prayer being spoken in a church, which Jack thought inappropriate:

> The Gorsedd prayer [...] is admitted to be equally suitable for Christians, Mohammedans or Jews. The movement therefore cannot be termed Christian, and it seems the height of irreverence to utilize Christianity as a medium for the revival of principles so obviously irrelevant.

He soon warms to his theme:

> I was at one time as ardent a Celt as any member of Tyr ha Tavas. [...] I dreamed of becoming, one day, a Bard of the Gorsedh, and wrote to Cornwall noble panegyrics, poems, eulogies. All that has fallen from me [...]. And now that I am no longer fanatically eager to establish Cornwall as a distinct nation, isolate it, glorify it at the expense of the great outside world – well, I do not regard myself as less truly a Cornishman.[163]

Note that Jack uses the word 'Cornishman'. He is arguing that he is no longer a nationalistic exclusionist, but also remarking that the Cornish are different from the non-Cornish. The implication is that one can be proud of one's Cornishness without excluding or denigrating others. This idea remained with Clemo, and is formed again in a 1980 interview for *The Observer*, when he says: 'I dislike nationalism of any sort as it weakens charity and creates racial prejudice'.¹⁶⁴ Clemo's argument against nationalism (and racism) is that it does not fit with Christian morality.

In the *Cornish Guardian*, Clemo adds that the purpose of his own writing in dialect is more appropriate than the Revivalist method; that he explores the beauty and 'mystery' of the land and people. Nance responded to say that the movement is 'an initiation into this very mystery, making one no longer a stranger in one's own land'. Overtly, Nance is talking of *reclaiming* Cornwall and its 'individuality'.¹⁶⁵ Jack responded softly, perhaps surprised by the interruption of such an eminent figure:

> My communication was not so much a wholesale condemnation of the Celtic Movement as a plea for some sense of proportion. The Movement is harmless and may even be beneficial, kept within limits, but in intruding itself upon definitely religious ground is it not rather over-stepping these limits?¹⁶⁶

With persuasive calm, Nance wrote that 'Cornish is very much at home in a church that was built and worshipped in by Cornish speakers'.¹⁶⁷

Anti-revivalist sentiment is expressed most strongly in *Confession*, though it was softened afterwards as other friendships developed. In *Confession* the Revivalist movement is referred to as the 'Cornish "national" movement' and described as 'misguided, futile and wasteful', then accused of 'pathetic pretentiousness'. Frank Baron, whose Cornish bardic name was 'Colon Len', meaning 'Faithful Heart', wrote to Clemo following the publication of *Confession* and referred to its vehement though brief anti-revivalist sentiments:

> I quite agree with your attitude towards the Cornish Gorseth. When I spoke at St Austell Old C[ornwall] Soc. recently I had a quiet jibe at the Cornish language as spoken by the Blue-robed dignitaries!
>
> It is rather fun to process in Bardic Robes and watch the picturesque ritual, but inwardly I regard it all just as I look upon Freemasonry which I have avoided.¹⁶⁸

This would be one of the last letters they exchanged.

There was one other unusual relationship in the late 1930s that developed through the *Cornish Guardian*. William Martin was a much older man, and in 1937, after their newspaper correspondence had led to private correspondence, he visited the Clemos at Goonamarris. Clemo describes 'the short muscular figure with the fresh-coloured, ravaged face and grey moustache'[169] of this 'Northumberland poet and socialist'.[170] His chief significance to the Clemo story is that he was the template for the 'atheist' character Mervyn Griffiths, in *Wilding Graft*. Martin was not an atheist himself, but Clemo did not always use the word conventionally. Certainly, both Martin and Griffiths disliked the Church, were desperately emotional, and had similar mining and marital backgrounds and similar political opinions.

Martin was writing from Castle Hill in Bodmin and sent Clemo 'the most extraordinary letters I have ever read [...] so full of contradictions that I was quite unable to tell from them what he really believed'.[171] A damaged veteran of both the 1899-1902 Boer War and the Great War, Martin presents himself to Clemo as a man of the world. He had worked for many years in the coal industry, travelled extensively, listing Borneo, Russia, Siam, France, Italy, Spain, India and China as places visited, and he was trained as a Wesleyan Minister. His tone in the letters is taut and heightened, often apocalyptic. He describes himself as a 'miner poet' and invites Clemo to treat him as a father:

> I like you Jack, I love you my Boy, as if you were my own Boy. Three years ago my own son (Dan) was killed in a motor accident, he was 23 years of age, he is gone from me, a fine great man 6ft 3 in height, so I pass my love on to you.[172]

He offers fatherly advice:

> Don't hate, don't discard, don't be moody when you think some would shun you, love comes to those that work for it, the clouds are only nature's blotting pad to

> ease the glare of the sun from the mental vision, so I do
> ask you, as a father to a son, do your best, keep a stiff
> lip, until the day breaks, and the shadows fly away.[173]

He tries to encourage Jack's writing in a fatherly way, saying that Jack was 'one who was looking into the far future, as a soul that had come down through the ages, as one who had drank of the wine of the farewell gathering, before the judicial murder that shook the world, and blackened the pages of the centuries.'[174] It is understandable that Clemo was bemused. The letters show an inconsistent and extreme character and even the biographical elements expressed in the letters are difficult to untangle.

This awkward relationship did not last long: 'The reason for the swift collapse of our friendship was that I was no longer the only or the chief object that drew his mind and heart to Goonamarris'.[175] Martin was trying to be too fatherly. He wanted to marry Eveline Clemo. Martin's confusing theology was not compatible with Eveline's, and when his intentions became clear his visits were discouraged.

The volatile veteran also disagreed with the Clemos politically. In one letter, Clemo wrote of the cruelty being displayed in Russia at the time, to which Martin replied that Jack had got it all wrong. Drawing on his extensive travel experience, Martin declared that the Russians only 'kill spys who try to make a hell of a peaceful nation. Spys that are sent by so called Christian England, Germany, land of hope and glory, Italy, the enemy of a true Christ.'[176] This was written in 1937, in the midst of Stalin's 'Great Purge'.

Clemo's interest in Russia was a new development, showing that world politics were imposing even on the remote and unworldly Clemo cottage. The threat of war, fascism, Germany, and the personalities of Mussolini and Hitler filled the correspondence pages of the *Cornish Guardian*, and while Clemo may be applauded for his perspicacity on the Russia situation, the same was not the case of his thoughts on the imminent war (or feminism):

> I entirely agree with 'H.J.W.' that 'the prospect of a
> continent under arms is an ugly monstrosity'; but then,

> many other cheerful things are ugly monstrosities –
> pigs, for instance, and ladies' trousers. And sabre-rattling and bomb-dropping are mere fashions that will
> pass away as surely as female trousers-wearing or any
> other form of destructive madness.[177]

In *Confession*, Clemo notes that the war seemed 'vague, distant and irrelevant' to him, and to an extent this was inevitable. Not too far away, just the other side of St Austell, A.L. Rowse was suggesting the same in his diaries: 'Sitting after breakfast at this familiar view again. War on, but there is hardly a sound, except the seagulls clamouring on the surface of the water'.[178] Clemo was certainly a good distance from the frontline, and when bombers did pass, when the roads were blocked, when Plymouth burned, he was still a passive observer. There was nothing he could do, and we might read in his enforced passivity the root of his bombast. In 1938 in the paper, under the heading 'Is Pacifism Enough?' he writes:

> I know people pretend that modern life is a nightmare
> because Mussolini and Hitler were born; but the actions
> of dictators could not disturb people unless they were
> spiritually unsound.

The stupidity of this is the implication that people would only care about their children and loved ones suffering and dying if they were bad Christians. If people were good Christians they would not care about their family members being shot or drowned, gassed or tortured. Clemo almost certainly did not mean to suggest this, but he is still showing more immaturity than might be expected of a man now in his twenties. He continued: 'If war comes to England it will be God's judgment on us, not merely because we were immoral, or ignored the church, or gambled, or got drunk, but because we were afraid.'[179] What he means to say is that a Christian should not fear death. If they fear death then they do not have faith. It is a position he would retain, expressing it in a better context in his poetic response to Dylan Thomas, entitled 'I Go Gentle', written in 1970:

> That terminal rage gets us nowhere
> Except in the wrong grave, the dead end.
> My day's light slackens gently
> Among these quiet, mystical white horns,
> Clay horns that sounded my entry
> And are silent only while the clues cohere
> For a fuller enactment. I touch a tip,
> Feel the echoes, feel the pictures blend
> In the bleached cone with no nudge of farewell.
> What need of anger as I await the dawn-swell
> Of each particle after the lean hour's dip?

In the same collection, *The Echoing* Tip, published in 1971, the idea is repeated in 'William Blake Notes a Demonstration' as the narrator declares: 'If men can't die praising God / They're not ripe for life'.

There has been some questioning of Clemo's apparent support of Mussolini during this time. In the *Cornish Guardian* he wrote:

> No one independent of Press tirades could share the common fanatical hatred of the Italian Dictator. He has made colossal mistakes because he is a colossus among men. A truly great man has been defined as one who 'commits immortal follies.' Mussolini is that. So was David, you may remember.[180]

Clemo was testing out his reading of Nietzsche here. In subsequent correspondence he retracts the impression he gave of Mussolini being 'great' and condemns the dictator's actions roundly. In *Confession* he returns to the theme to set out his meaning more clearly. Unfortunately, this led to further misinterpretation, culminating in the poet and critic Donald Davie writing an eccentric essay for the *PN Review* about what he considered to be Clemo's development from 'fascism' to 'monarchism'.[181] The quotation Davie used to establish that Clemo was a fascist was from *Confession*:

> The religious aspect of an enthusiasm was the only one that could grip me for long. Thus I should have

become a misfit even among the Fascists had I been able to join them. [...] The foundations of democracy were, in my view, undermined by its complete ignoring of theological truth. Its avowed purpose was to make life as agreeable for those who crucified Christ as for those who shared spiritually in His crucifixion, and this I knew must lead to moral apathy, religious impotence and chaos in all human relationships. I wanted, in short, a world run much as Calvin had run Geneva, a government that would not allow the proud and greedy and frivolous to persist in their illusion that they were on the winning side. If the Fascist and Nazi leaders were attempting something on these lines I entirely approved of their policy.

Davie took from this that Clemo supported the fascists, ignoring the big 'If'. *If* the fascists and Nazis promoted humility, generosity, sobriety and Christianity *then* Clemo would support them. They did not, so he did not. Clemo did not support violence, nationalism or any form of exclusionism, and it was as a result of Davie's article that Clemo felt he had to spell this out in his interview with *The Observer*.

There does remain an admiration of Mussolini in the newspaper correspondence, but it is not for what Davie claims. Quite simply, what Clemo admired was the force of his will, the personality cult, the idea of someone enormous, persuasive and magnetic. Clemo wanted a modern Calvin. It is a similar admiration to that Clemo would feel for Billy Graham in the 1950s.

Politically, what Clemo wanted was a Christian kind of philosopher king, a charismatic benign ruler chosen and supported by God, one of the 'elect'. This sense that he preferred the personality to the policy is borne out by both the 1936 newspaper correspondence and *Confession*:

> I had a vague but deep admiration for Mussolini and Hitler: the qualities in them which the cold English temperament derided as bombastic and theatrical

appealed irresistibly to me with my mystical bias towards epic vitalism and fanaticism.[182]

In the newspaper, the controversy raged and Clemo enjoyed being the provocateur. He began arguing that Britain had little cause for assuming the moral high ground over Italian war crimes:

> We are asked to condemn the Italians because they are using poison gas in an effort to obtain a colony by force. Yet, if poison gas had been available a few hundred years ago, Britain would have employed it to build up her 'great and glorious' Empire.[183]

Clemo knew that many of his readers would be veterans of some of the wars he invoked, including the Zulu and Boer wars, and he knew the response he would receive. One letter from a pacifist suggested that the comparison between Mussolini and Drake had little meaning, and that society had 'evolved' since then anyway. Clemo's response discloses a number of persistent beliefs. Four centuries of evolution, he writes,

> have doubtless put on another coat of whitewash to the 'sepulchre' called civilization, but the essential 'uncleanness' of human nature is, I doubt not, as prolific as ever inside. The Italians have allowed it to break out. They, at least, are honest, and know better to pretend, as Britons pretend, that an abstract evolutionary force has brought the human race to a more angelic condition.[184]

Human nature is bad, Clemo says, but it is better to express the badness. Moreover, Clemo's attack on 'social evolution' is a nascent attack on humanism, as he understood it. Clemo's understanding of humanism is relevant to all his work, as he so frequently denigrates it in his writing. Instead of the humanistic focus being on one's ability to improve oneself, Clemo thinks that humanists believe that special (as in, 'of species') perfection may be attained by a directedness of the collective will; a kind of self-determining evolution which in

Clemo's mind places man in the role of creator and in charge of destiny. The emphasis on man being in control or responsible for his own life is correctly attributed to humanism, but the implication of special perfection is not.

Another comment made on evolution and Darwin in the newspaper, in 1933, shows further scientific and philosophical naivety. Clemo argued that Darwin was an unhappy man, and that so were his followers, like H.G. Wells: 'So the evolutionary theory does not seem to have made anybody happy. That, in my opinion, is proof enough that there is something wrong with it.'[185] The scientific validity of a statement is determined by whether it makes one happy or sad. This is a very unsatisfying use of the word 'proof', and a facile mode of dismissal. But it is a mode of dismissal used in Clemo's books, too. In *The Invading Gospel* Clemo dismisses the perspective of the 'modern Church' that God and Christ were 'nice', by calling their position 'dull'.

A biographical response to Clemo's scientific methodology might be to ask whether Jack himself was happy. Had faith made him happy? Certainly, he was an optimist, but his diaries and letters suggest that his overwhelming emotions were disappointment and frustration. He is bitterly lonely and suffering from syphilis. He is also poor, which distresses him. So it cannot be the case that Clemo believes God makes us happy *now*; instead, it must be the case that God will make us happy in the future. But in so far as the reward is deferred, so too must the conclusion that God makes us happy. We do not yet know that God will make us happy. This is a matter of faith, and it is faith itself that we are trying to 'prove'. It will be seen later that Clemo uses the word proof in both an archaic theological sense and in the more conventional sense used here, meaning something like conclusive evidence.

Perhaps what he means is that we believe in God because *belief* makes us happy. But to say we believe because it makes us happy is still a weak statement and the same argument could be made by liberal Protestants, spiritualists, pantheists and pagans. This is clearly not Clemo's intention. Rather, he seems to be appealing to the reader's preference for feeling good and saying that the idea of God makes you feel better than the ideas of humanism and Darwinism.

In the press controversies, Clemo explored considerable literary, theological and political ground. He was buffeted, embarrassed and abused, sharing his opinions on sex, God, Darwinism, humanism, fascism, war, films and books, schooling, celebrity and genius. He constantly tried to write about himself, offering readers not only ideas but also biography and self-interpretation. This is the nascent voice of *Confession of a Rebel*'s narrator. It has been assumed all along that he is of the elect, a chosen one and a genius, and these are ideas that will be approached in later discussions of Clemo's theology, as well as in his relationships with women. We will see in *Confession* a stronger attempt to collect and frame the narrator's life, work and faith into a coherent structure. Clemo will return to reconstruct the period, and even though he will try to distance himself from the juvenile newspaper controversialist, the later ideas are clearly developed from these intellectual experiments. This is true in the non-fictional prose to a greater degree than the fictional. The earliest fiction was more influenced by a handful of unfashionable writers, so that Clemo's first novel drafts reflect a combination of juvenility, inexperience, ambition and a dated literary context. But the manuscripts of these earliest attempts are central to an understanding of Clemo's literary and biographical progression, and the professional critical work undertaken by Gordon Meggy was important to the evolution of his novelistic style. It is on this narrative talent that his reputation and career were founded, albeit the poetry on which his legacy depends.

V
Travail

I am the man that hath seen affliction by the rod of his wrath. He hath led me, and brought me into darkness, but not into light. Surely against me he is turned; he turneth his hand against me all the day. My flesh and my skin hath he made old; he hath broken my bones. He hath builded against me, and compassed me with gall and travail. He hath set me in dark places, as they that be dead of old.

Lamentations 3:1-6

In his lifetime, Clemo published only two novels, *Wilding Graft* in 1948 and *The Shadowed Bed* in 1986. A third novel, *The Clay Kiln*, was edited and published posthumously, in 2000. However, they were written in reverse order, the earliest novel draft that would be included in the composite *The Clay Kiln* having been written in 1930, the earliest version of *The Shadowed Bed* completed in 1938, and the earliest draft of *Wilding Graft* in 1943.

The histories of *The Shadowed Bed* and *Wilding Graft* are fairly straightforward. *Wilding Graft*, in particular, was much the same in published form as it was in its first good draft, with only the ending being completely rewritten. *The Clay Kiln*, on the other hand, is a composite novel, made up of over a dozen drafts and seven or eight other early novel attempts. By the end of the 1930s Clemo had written a million words towards these various novels, and although he is remembered now primarily for his poetry, he identified himself as a novelist for much of his life and always regretted the lack of attention paid to his fiction. Writing in *Confession of a Rebel*, Clemo put the failure of the early novels down to the onset of deafness:

> The tendency to patch and re-write old incidents instead of inventing new ones was increasingly characteristic of my method, and was probably due to my deafness, the inability to get in touch with active life that would supply fresh material. I expended tens of thousands of words in re-fashioning scenes so feeble in themselves that they should have been scrapped at the outset. My

writing was always haphazard, undisciplined, without conscious direction.

The idea that his deafness thwarted his ability to write novels is called into question by the fact that his most successful, *Wilding Graft*, was both conceived and completed when deaf, as was *The Shadowed Bed*, his other prose triumph. In a similar way, Clemo claimed in his 1941 diary that his writing suffered without a muse, though again this would be the year that he began both *Wilding Graft* and *Confession of a Rebel*. It appears he mistook what made him work well with what made him happy. Clemo might not have had hearing or a muse when he began *Wilding Graft* and *Confession*, but he did have experience, time and discipline, which proved to be of far greater value.

The Clay Kiln's history begins with a group of novels which I will collectively refer to as the 'Cuckoospit' sequence. This starts with the short novel, 'Travail'. 'Travail' was redrafted many times throughout the 1930s, and submitted to agents and publishers under at least ten different titles, the last of which was 'Cuckoospit'. Drafts varied in length from 30,000 words to 90,000, though they were all versions of the same story.

The book was begun when Clemo was just fourteen and he finished two versions extremely quickly, 'Travail' and 'The Heart of the Celt'. Fragments from four of the earliest drafts have survived, but they are difficult to read and the story is disjointed. However, there is sufficient to get an impression of the style. In the following passage, from a 1931-32 draft, the narrator is describing Jowan's love interest, Gwinbren:

> There appeared to be about her no alluring quality and one wondered whatever Jowan could see in her. She had not been a good scholar; she was not 'charming'; was not even pretty so people said.
>
> People took only that first glance. Jowan took a second, a third... then his eyes were dazzled by a great light and he fell on his knees and cried: 'Girl! Girl!' For the first time he realised what the word really meant.

The melodrama in these fragments is cringeworthy, but we find in this manuscript the embryonic themes of the Jack-like hero's exceptionalism, specifically his romantic or erotic exceptionalism, and of a providential sort of love. Gwinbren is described as unattractive to everyone except Jowan. It is as though they were made for one another. Notably, too, the story is of a first love. This is the narrator's first understanding of 'girl', and, indeed, Gwinbren was based on Clemo's own first love, Evelyn. This is unmistakably a youthful exercise, but it is possible to perceive in the juvenilia a number of key themes of Clemo's mature and published writing.

As with all of Jack's endeavours, his mother supported him wholeheartedly with his literary ambitions, and although she appears to have been surprised at his decision to leave school and become a novelist, once she had come to terms with it she applied herself to her son's success fullbloodedly. In the first instance, she wrote to Jack's distant cousin Joseph Hocking for advice. Hocking was ill when he received the letter and he had been ordered to lay aside all work. As a result, his response was brief and disappointing:

> With regard to the lad of whom you spoke, he, if he has the real stuff in him, will make his way. Editors and publishers are always on the look out for ability and the only way is for him to persist in doing his best and then sending his writings to what seems the right quarters until he succeeds.[186]

Eveline Clemo contacted the various church and council bodies asking for financial help. Particularly encouraging was Sam Jacobs, an old Labour politician from Trethosa. This is the same Sam Jacobs described by A.L. Rowse in *A Cornish Childhood*: 'a natural leader of men, firm as a rock, like a rock in physique, staunch and unbreakable; uneducated, but with a great respect for education, a touching humility towards the educated, as modest and shy with them as a child'.[187] When Jacobs heard of Clemo's eye troubles and ambitions, he determined to help and to get the boy appropriate writerly training, and after many frustrating rebuffs, Jacobs was asked to submit an example of Jack's writing to the Ministry of Pensions at

Plymouth. The only presentable piece early in 1931 was the dialect tale, 'Benjy an' his Sweetheart'. Jacobs must have been a persuasive man, because armed with just this simple Cornish tale he convinced the Ministry to pay for a correspondence course at Gordon Meggy's 'Premier School of Journalism'. This was a London-based firm occupying two floors of the large building at the end of Adam Street. It was an apparently popular service for budding writers looking to get published. Most of the correspondence from Meggy has survived, bound in an old manuscript of 'The Dreams of Yesterday' song. It covers the years 1931-33 and reveals much about Clemo's early literary development and first attempts at writing the novels that would later be chopped up, tossed about and re-forged into *The Clay Kiln*.

Meggy comes across as a generous man, and when funding ran out for Jack, he offered to keep the boy on as a student free of charge. It was Meggy who encouraged Clemo to cut articles out of the paper and keep them in scrapbooks, a habit he maintained throughout his life. Years later, these scrapbooks would be shown by the Clemos to students and interviewers working on the poet, and they constitute a bulky part of the Jack Clemo archive. Meggy also encouraged Clemo's philosophy of experience, defining the important sort of experience as 'not actual experience [...] but mental'.[188]

The correspondence course invited Clemo to post his writing off with a letter, to which Meggy would reply with detailed, forthright commentary and tasks for Clemo to undertake. The first adult story disappointed Meggy, and he told Clemo that if this was the best he could do then he should stick to writing for children. Clemo tried again, sending a second story that woke Meggy up to Jack's potential. The new story was 'so much better than anything I should have expected from one of your age'. Still, he said, it was 'not [...] a particularly strong story'.[189] A third was attempted, the dialect story 'Postman Treziz Vinds Out', which Meggy condemned for having no plot, no obstacle to overcome and an implausible relationship: 'I suggest therefore that you scrap it.'[190] Further discouragement came when Clemo posted Meggy the novel, 'Travail'. Before he had even read it, Meggy wrote: 'I must warn you that first novels are rarely more than a clearing of the mind for better work'.[191] Heaps of criticism landed with Clemo's post: 'The emotions described seem out of all proportion'; 'I find a certain pretentiousness in the writing which I would like you to try to eliminate from all future work';[192] 'Put this story in the wastepaper basket and make a resolve not to indulge in anything of the kind in future.'[193] He criticized the melodramatic elements: 'No normal healthy young man is going to lose his self-control and start trembling because he is asked to go to a party.'[194] (It is true that the characters 'tremble' and 'quiver' rather more than is common.) Clemo sent several drafts from the 'Cuckoospit' sequence, though none of them impressed Meggy. It was too short, and 'more hysterical than dramatic', he explained. 'If you keep the character emotionally exposed all the time it is like presenting something inside out – and just as unpleasing.'[195]

The effect of this relentless criticism was expressed in *Confession*, where Clemo wrote that Meggy was 'plainly disappointed and perplexed' by him, although it is clear from the letters that Meggy also thought well of his pupil. 'You are bringing to the job a good measure of original talent', he wrote, followed by: 'I know that you are going to succeed because with your spirit there is nothing that can stop you.'[196]

Nevertheless, Clemo was upset by Meggy's verdict on the novel, especially the way in which the love affair, based on his feelings for Evelyn, was damned:

> I see that you deal in the first part with a love affair between a boy and girl of fourteen or thereabouts. This is a great mistake, for you will never get a reader to take an affair between such youngsters seriously.[197]

This hints at the main point of conflict between Meggy and Clemo. Meggy was training his pupil for publication, while Clemo wanted greatness. This becomes plainer as we see Meggy repeatedly stressing the importance of the novel's length: 'it is not the slightest use submitting a novel that is under seventy thousand words'. Meggy wrote this in 1932, just as Aldous Huxley's *Brave New World* and Stella Gibbons's *Cold Comfort Farm* were released, two of the most memorable books of the year and both considerably below Meggy's magic word count. It was Meggy's job to make Clemo's writing as marketable as possible, not to make Jack the writer he wanted to be. Similarly, Meggy encouraged Clemo to write to the *Cornish Guardian*, because he considered any publication and engagement with an audience to be good.

Meggy's focus on marketability over artistry gave Clemo good reason to ignore some of his advice. Jack did not think that romances between teenagers were any less authentic than those between adults, and he was protective over criticism of the male lead in the novels, since each of these was based on Clemo himself. (It might be noted as one reads through Clemo's manuscripts that the hero ages in pace with the author.) Clemo also would not give up the idea that the majority of clay country villagers were trivial gossips, wicked sinners, fools or bullies, as they appear in these early manuscripts. He used his novels as both defence and vengeance against the gossip he himself had suffered. This portrayal seems to have been exaggerated by Clemo's reading of D.H. Lawrence, especially of *Kangaroo*, in which there is a chapter set in Cornwall, entitled 'Nightmare'. Lawrence's narrator describes the pettiness of locals and their persecution of the 'individual', and it is possible that Jack's second title for the 'Cuckoospit' sequence, 'The Heart of the Celt', was adapted from *Kangaroo*. Meggy observed this tendency to exaggerate the malevolence of the community and remarked that the love-interest's father is described as full of 'malice and venom', without the reader ever being shown these qualities. The narrator was imposing his own views of real people without showing their justification in the novel. This happens again in *Wilding Graft*, as the reader is continually told how awful the antagonist Griffiths is, without having been shown anything especially bad. A 1936 draft of the 'Cuckoospit' books verges on self parody with its one-word title, recalling perhaps the ultimate moment of persecution by the gathered hordes before Pontius Pilate: 'Crucify!'

In the diaries there are a number of entries concerning village gossip, such as this from 1937:

> Mother complaining that 'people who pass must think you're a child of sex – I bet they have fun over you,

playing all the time with a little girl like B.' I said: 'As if I cared about that!' and mother was silenced. Yes! What *do* I care? Let everybody laugh, and, if they care to make dirty guesses at what our relationship is when we're alone together – I care not a jot!'[198]

The cruelty of these gossiping villagers was observed by A.L. Rowse when he wrote to Clemo following the publication of his first novel. Rowse was born at nearby Tregonissey, now a part of St Austell, but he considered Clemo's area – the 'Higher Quarter', as he called it – to be almost a different world, a place of 'grinding poverty and stunted lives', as Philip Payton wrote in his life of Rowse. In his letter to Clemo, in 1948, Rowse enquired:

> You know so much more about the life of the people than I, *are they really like that?* You give a terrible portrait of them in the book […]. You must know pretty well what I have always, or for so long, felt about them: their hypocrisy, their narrowness and meanness […], their back-biting and ungenerosity, their love of doing some-one down […]. But are they really so appalling, do you think, as you see them?[199]

A counterpoint to Jack's dismissal of the people around him is his desire to write about himself. Not only did he fictionalise himself in the 'Cuckoospit' sequence as Jowan, in the same way that he fictionalized himself in subsequent books as Joel, Euan and Garth, but he also wrote long prefaces to his works. When Jack sent Meggy an updated draft in 1933, now entitled 'A Star Shall Lead', it appears that even then, at the age of seventeen, he had written about his literary achievements in a long biographical preface. Meggy discouraged this, saying that it is too dramatic and self-absorbed, 'too unwieldy and […] lays unnecessary stress upon the labour you have put in upon the book.'[200] But Jack submitted similar prefaces with most of his early work, and they were usually rejected. Clemo wanted to be read on his own terms, and always within the context of his personal 'travail'. He wanted to analyse his experience and hold himself out for either justification or approbation. His Methodist upbringing, being an only child, fatherless, an outsider at school, living outside the villages, his disease and disabilities, the heaping of ill-fortune and the temperament determined by these factors, all led to an intense introspection that made him susceptible to solipsism and narcissism. While immature, these would be his weaknesses, but later they would prove his strengths. Without the belief that God was personally and specially invested in Clemo's life, the constant hope and optimism that mark his work from this time forward would not be possible; the tension between warring faculties, and the painful juxtaposition of present suffering against promised relief would not exist. One of the first observations a reader will make of Clemo's novels is that they all have happy endings. None of them was written when Jack was stable and happy, but all when he was uncertain, alone and physically deteriorating, and it is this same basic optimism in the face of facts that unmistakably marks his poetry, prose, religiosity and personal outlook. Indeed, the absence of optimism was one of the strongest criticisms he had of his beloved Thomas Hardy, and late in life, in 1983, when reading a Braille copy of Hardy's *Desperate Remedies*, Jack notes what a relief it is to find a happy ending at last.

In spite of Clemo using himself as the model for his novels' heroes, it was the female characters that impressed Meggy. 'The girl is delightfully sketched', he wrote; 'I have very little fault to find with the way in which you have sketched her.' However, 'The boy Jowan is less happily sketched. It seems to me that his thoughts and his utterances are considerably at variance with the type he is supposed to be.' He 'appears somewhat effeminate', and is never with other men. Then there is the mysterious question: 'Why on earth should [Jowan] think of his dead sister when he is making love?' It is true that Clemo's male characters are uneasy in dialogue with other men. Even when they are workers, they do not converse convincingly, and rarely does a leading male have a friendship with another man. Meggy recognised that the characters were based on Jack, but he suggested that they suffered from a compromise between the autobiographical and the ideal, the temptation to put highbrow philosophical and theological ideas and poetic quotations in the mouth of an uneducated miner. This, Meggy considered, was the 'main defect'.[201]

There is one biographically intriguing comment from Meggy in these letters that is never explained: 'I do not think that you need worry about the fact that story incidents remain so vividly in your mind'.[202] We have no record of what Clemo had written to Meggy, or even whether he was haunted by his reading or by his writing, but it is tempting to imagine that the passage is suggestive of the force of Clemo's memory. He was able to reproduce dialogue and landscape in his writing long after he had lost the ability to hear and see them, and it has been remarked by friends and family that Jack's memory was astonishing. He composed poetry in his head, drafting and editing it before committing it to paper, and his memory impressed the American poet T.R. Hummer to such an extent that he came to exaggerate it in his essay on meeting Clemo, 'In the Palm of the Poet's Hand'.

Correspondence with Meggy dissolved gradually after the course finished, with Clemo understandably disappointed. Meggy had dismissed the majority of his writing, especially the novel, but the process had been useful as Clemo's first introduction to popular markets and editorial criticism. Some of the stories submitted to Meggy would be printed by the almanacks and small journals later in the decade, but mostly Clemo continued to work on 'Cuckoospit', the novel Meggy had recommended for abandonment. By the time Meggy's final letter arrived in 1933, 'Cuckoospit' had been through innumerable revisions and at least five titles: 'Travail', 'The Heart of the Celt', 'March Dawn', 'A Star Shall Lead', and 'Gwinbren'. Before long, it received five more: 'Shame of Thy Youth', 'Crucify!', 'The Halt and the Blind', 'Devil's Prize', and 'Cuckoospit'. Many of these show Biblical references. 'Travail', for example, is a word frequently used in the King James Bible, rendered as 'hardship' in more recent translations. 'A Star Shall Lead' seems to be a reference to the Gospel of Matthew, the only book of the Bible to describe a number of wise men with a star that 'went before them, till it came and stood over where the young child was'. The title in this instance parallels Clemo's pattern-seeking and 'revelation from experience'. By observing natural phenomena as revelations from God one may be drawn closer to Christ, as the wise men were. The phrase 'Shame of Thy Youth' is from Eveline's Isaiah passage, her promise from God that suffering was only a temporary state for her and Jack, and that they would be rewarded in the end. The two titles 'Devil's Prize' and 'Cuckoospit' suggest a freshly empowered stimulus. They date from 1937-38, when Jack was submitting to the influence of Robert Browning and 'Devil's Prize' is probably a reference to Browning's 'A Soul's Tragedy':

> I seem content
> With ruining myself, why so should they be,
> And so they are, and so be with his prize
> The devil

'Cuckoospit', too, may be a reference to Browning's metaphorical use of the word in 'Fifine at the Fair', one of Clemo's favourite poems. 'Cuckoospit' is used to represent the jealous spite of 'the elf': 'Then thrice the bulk, out blows / Our insect, does its kind, and cuckoospits some rose!' John T. Nettleship, a contemporary of Browning's, interprets the passage to mean that 'the touch of hate makes such a spiteful man do his best to poison the life of a real true man, as the aphis, according to his nature, tries to kill the rose by surrounding it with the poisonous foam'.[203] It is a title suggestive of the role of malicious gossip in the novels.

The life and works of Browning had become devotional Sunday reading, alongside the Bible and Spurgeon. Browning's optimism was seductive. Optimism was a personal ideal with which Clemo wrestled constantly, in the face of increasing solitude and hardship. 'This is the title I want to merit', he wrote in his diary: 'The Browning of fiction'.[204] The Browning influence further punctuated the sense of a new beginning and of the 'gradual conversion' of Clemo in 1937-38.

In spite of a more mature outlook, influenced by Browning, the next novel had exactly the same problems as 'Cuckoospit'. 'The Former Rain' was written as a sequel and finished in 1937. In the seven years that had passed since the first draft of 'Travail', this was Jack's first new idea for a novel. Before then, he could only tinker with the tired manuscript, rearranging chapters and making long lists of alternative titles ('Her that Halteth', 'Private Plot', 'Shallow Feet', 'Culled Thistles', 'Culled Briars', 'Serpent's Prey', 'Serpent's Home', 'Twine Amaranth'). He continued to send the failed novel to publishers for rejection, apparently receiving twenty-one for the 'Cuckoospit' sequence alone, including from his future publisher Methuen. Of these, the majority were standard printed slips, and only John Green offered anything like critical feedback: 'The general feeling is that it is far too sentimental and romantic, and makes much high-flown tragedy over nothing very dreadful'.[205] Among these rejections is a reference to a work that has disappeared completely, entitled 'Peace and Sex: Four Fantasies', the only record of which is the rejection slip sent by C.W. Daniel stating that the manuscript was too short for them to consider.

One literary agent, A.M. Heath, recognised sufficient promise in 'The Halt and the Blind' to tentatively take it on, writing: 'Quite frankly, we are taking this up on the strength of its promise, since we feel that the latter part of the story is rather weak and that we may have difficulty in placing the book.'[206] Although the novel failed, Heath asked Jack to give them first refusal on his second attempt, the plot of which Jack described in his diary:

> Thought of theme for next novel today – out of my own exp[erience] as in the first – the hero has a girl (Evelyn) […]. He is desirous to save another (V.B.) […]. Saves her thro' a 'criminal offence' (draw on relation with B here). All but a transcription from my personal experience – must write subjectively – nothing else has life.[207]

This was 'The Former Rain', a title taken from the Book of Jeremiah: 'Neither say they in their heart, Let us now fear the Lord our God, that giveth rain, both the former and the latter, in his season' (5:24). Charles Spurgeon makes sense of this passage in his expositions, writing that what is meant is rain being given at the correct time for growing and harvesting crops. He adds, characteristically, that the passage shows the day-to-day way in which God manages the world's affairs. Other suggested titles for the novel included 'Wide Compass', 'Marred Clay', 'Locusts have Eaten', 'Gourd of Jonah', 'Bloom for Locust', 'Private Snow', and 'Fished Murex', all references to the Bible, Spurgeon or Browning.

In theme, 'The Former Rain' is not very different from 'Cuckoospit'. It is an overwrought romance about a young man pursuing the wrong girl, and then pursuing the right girl. It was immediately rejected by Heath and both manuscripts were returned to Clemo as a result. Still, Jack was reluctant to give up on the two novels and only recognised them as failures much later. 'The Former Rain', he wrote in *Confession*, was 'drab and colourless, without a gleam of poetry or humour'. In the 1930s he did not see the faults so clearly, and instead of giving up two failed novels, he decided to work the best bits of both into other stories. He even tried to squeeze one phrase from an early 'Cuckoospit' draft into *Wilding Graft*. It was an ugly passage, describing the girl and the boy kissing, 'her mouth sucking at his as if it were a nipple'. It seems a childish and overtly Freudian projection, but Clemo thought it poignant. When he submitted *Wilding Graft*, the literary agent Raymond Savage, who would become a pivotally important champion of Clemo's writing, said the first thing Jack had to take out before he would consider the novel was that 'disgusting' description about the nipple.[208] The history of *Wilding Graft* will be considered fully in Chapter VII.

In 1937, then, there are two failed novels, 'Cuckoospit' and 'The Former Rain', both set within the same area and using the same characters. The next evolutionary step was 'Private Snow'. This was begun in 1937, using the best bits from 'The Former Rain'. Again, it was rejected. Harmony Press explained why:

> Characterisation has been carefully conceived, and the descriptions of the clay area and the work carried on there are especially commended.
>
> Drawbacks lie in the length of the work – 80, 000 words is more or less essential to the commercial publisher [...] and a doubt is expressed by the Reader as to whether the technique of the work is of sufficient excellence to command publication at a publisher's risk.[209]

It was 'Private Snow' that Clemo sent to Sir Arthur Quiller-Couch at the end of 1939 for his opinion, which, surprisingly, was given: 'There's a deal of power and promise in it and I think it should find a publisher', he began, although, 'You guess, I dare say, that it is not the kind of story I like at all.' The Clemos had hoped that sending the book to Q would be a shortcut to publication, success and celebrity. He was known to help young Cornish people, as he had A.L. Rowse – and who could be in more need of help than young Jack? It was an unreasonable expectation, considering the subject matter and the quality of the novel. Nevertheless, Q believed the work showed sufficient promise to offer four pages of criticism and encouragement. He, like Rowse later, queried the vileness of the characters: 'I know Roche pretty well, and its people [...] are a tribe – almost a race – apart. But I confess I hadn't realised their habits of dirt, open lust, and filthy talk, and hope your readers won't take this clan as representative of Cornish folk in general'. He continued to give helpful feedback, stating where the work was 'heavily over-written – especially in descriptions of scenery', with 'too much repetition of the Egdon Heath business'. He made note of places where the action of a scene had been spoiled by Clemo pausing to describe minuscule details of a character's facial expressions. The criticism was kindly, and the overall impression encouraging, with Q concluding: 'the story itself is well-knit and strong and in certain descriptions [...] quite in place and very good indeed.'[210]

'Mother and I were bitterly disappointed', wrote Clemo in *Confession of a Rebel*:

> We had hoped for much from Q., having heard of his generosity to talented Cornish boys, his determination to give working-class Cornish youngsters of promise an equal opportunity of educational advance. One point we had overlooked – the obvious fact that all these children were normal school products while I was a wild Ishmael of the moors, untouched by such refined institutions.[211]

Clemo's account of Q is not borne out by the letter itself. In *Confession* he states that Q had written that the 'Bloomsbury intellectuals would smack their lips over my work'. This is used as though a compliment, but the context is not given. Q had written:

> I know that the exposure of our common humanity 'without benefit of laundry like a rag on a clothes-line' is the vogue among novelists just now, and some Bloomsbury reviewers will smack their lips over Irene and Ann and even Marvran's slangy talk in places. But perhaps you won't resent a few technical hints, by observing which I think you will greatly improve the story.

In his diary, Clemo rewrote Q's reference to Hardy and the 'Egdon Heath business' in a similarly optimistic way:

> I feel my work will be the Christian counterpart of [Hardy's] – glanced thro' 'Tess' and 'Jude' and saw for the first time what 'Q' meant in saying that I'd put too much of the Egdon Heath business into P.S. It gave me a pleasant surprise that a keen critic like Sir Arthur should compare my first novel with one of Hardy's.[212]

When he came to write *Confession*, Clemo still had not come to terms with Q's lack of practical support, and he attacks the older man's novels, ideology and character. Clemo was inexperienced and likely unaware that Q would have been posted many novels from ambitious young writers. It was generous of him to have read it, let alone to have given it such critical attention. Q died in 1944, and it was not until 1949, when A.L. Rowse wrote a long defence of his friend, that Jack began to revise his opinion of the Fowey man.

'Private Snow' was redrafted through the Second World War, as Q had instructed, and retitled 'Roche Snow' because Jack knew too many other contemporary novels with the word 'Private' in the title. The replacement of 'Roche' would make it stand out in the 1943 Tom-Gallon Award, he thought. As it happened, the winning novel was *A Well Full of Leaves*, by Elizabeth Myers, whose husband, Littleton Powys, Jack would come to know. At the time of the award, however, Clemo wrote bitterly and suspiciously about Myers being awarded the prize when she was already an established writer and related to the Powys dynasty: 'there were a lot of strings pulled behind the scenes to get her the award'.[213] Meanwhile, Clemo was at work on yet another 'new' novel, 'Unsunned Tarn', using material recovered from the 'Cuckoospit' sequence. The title is again from Browning, this time from 'Paracelsus':

> Shall I sit beside
> Their dry wells, with a white lip and filmed eye,
> While in the distance heaven is blue above
> Mountains where sleep the unsunned tarns?

'Paracelsus' is being read by the scholarly hero Euan in a later, amalgamated typescript of 'Unsunned Tarn', as he considers his girlfriend, Lela. Lela will leave Euan for one of the debauched, worldly men of the novel, proving herself to have been merely a preparation for Euan's real love of Gwen. In the earliest draft, the hero was named Jowan, though as the novels were combined the name seemed too similar to the other hero, Joel, and was altered.

To be clear, then, 'Cuckoospit' has been butchered and blended into 'Unsunned Tarn', while 'The Former Rain' has been used for 'Roche Snow'. At the same time, there was an original work being drafted. The first version of this was completed in 1938 and entitled 'The Lamb of Carn Veor'. This will be considered in a later chapter, as it is the first draft of a novel unrelated to 'Cuckoospit' and published in 1986 as *The Shadowed Bed*.

'The Former Rain' and 'Roche Snow' were two of three component parts that together would become the posthumously published *The Clay Kiln*. The third was 'Sown Light', a novel beginning in the Scilly Isles, at Hugh Town, and leading back to Cornwall. The title has two references, one to Psalm 97:11 – 'Light is sown for the righteous, and gladness for the upright in heart' – the second to Spurgeon's sermon 'Sown Light'. The theme of the sermon, as of the novel, is of God's justness, his presence in the world, and predestination.

'Sown Light' uses the characters of 'Unsunned Tarn' and 'Roche Snow', so that Clemo now had a trilogy or village saga by the end of 1941. With this trilogy, its story ending at the outbreak of war, Clemo conceived an ambitious plan. He would publish the three novels as a sequence, collectively titled 'A Comedy of Clay', and would then begin a second trilogy of novels to span the duration of the war. At the end of 1941 Clemo had even begun work on the first volume of this second trilogy, *Wilding Graft*, and had mapped out notes for the following two, to be entitled 'The Hired Razor' and 'Mainmast'. At the time of planning this second trilogy, nobody knew how long the war was going to last, but Clemo always believed the end was imminent.

The manuscripts and typescripts of this original trilogy are patchy, but handily in his 1942 diary Jack summarises the 'theme' of each volume. 'Roche Snow', the first volume, is about the 'need for Christian ideal of love', and it was intended to introduce the 'germ of predestination idea'. Clemo's mature ideas on predestination were given in summary to Sara Ramsden, who wrote about Clemo in 1990. Clemo believed in 'a predestination to Heaven or Hell of those who choose or deny God through the assertion of their free will'. The picture parallels the two choices between 'fate' and 'predestiny', or 'Nature' and 'faith', already touched upon and developed in Clemo's poetry.

The second novel of the trilogy, 'Unsunned Tarn', is described in the diary as a 're-emphasis of Christian love-ideal' with greater 'stress on predestination, more philosophy through Euan Kella as a mouthpiece and very much a self-portrait. Much veiled autobiography in the shaping and essence of situation.' The third novel, 'Sown Light', was to include a 'deeper probing of essential Christian love, predestination theme fully developed and healthy mysticism infused through Bryn Vosper, another attempt at self-portraiture, stressing the more dully acquiescent side of my nature linked with vigorous and almost vulgar sections.' This final work was going to satirise 'the modern Church', and to have 'more use made of international background – as far as it serves to enforce my theme.'

As the 1940s progressed and the novels continued to be rejected, Clemo made the decision in 1945 to weave 'Roche Snow' into

'Unsunned Tarn'. Now, instead of having three related novels, he would have two, the original 'Sown Light' and this composite novel which retained the title 'Unsunned Tarn'. 'Unsunned Tarn' is at this point made up of the 'Cuckoospit' sequence, 'The Former Rain', the earlier 'Unsunned Tarn' and 'Roche Snow'.

In 1946, as Clemo prepared to submit the novels again, he made some final changes to 'Sown Light', retitling it 'Penance of the Seed', a quotation from Francis Thompson's 'Ode to Easter'. At this critical time, Jack had four works to show a publisher: the two novels that would at length be successful, 'The Lamb of Carn Veor' (*The Shadowed Bed*) and *Wilding Graft*, and two destined to fail in their current format, 'Penance of the Seed' and 'Unsunned Tarn'. The agent interested in Clemo, Raymond Savage, was impressed with all of these to begin with, writing that he thought 'Unsunned Tarn' as good as *Wilding Graft*. He sent the manuscript to the publisher Robert Hale, who replied in profound disagreement:

> The promise [shown in *Wilding Graft*] has not been fulfilled. [Clemo] has rectified none of his faults and has lost the freshness of touch that characterised his earlier work. He is a bad character drawer; the people in this book do not act or speak like live beings; there is not light and shade, and the bad characters are so naively portrayed, and with such hatred that they are almost funny. He has also a great liking for scandal and fills the book with bits of gossip about all sorts of quite irrelevant people. This is, in a way, very similar to his other book but is not as good. I would not recommend publication.[214]

Hale had been led to believe that 'Unsunned Tarn' was a new novel, and *Wilding Graft* a first attempt. The impression he must have had, then, was of Clemo getting worse, whereas the exact opposite was really the case. Savage invited Clemo to send the other novel, 'Penance of the Seed', but the agent was becoming wary:

> I can see what is really the whole trouble with regard to your work in these three books and I think I am right.

> You have got a huge canvas and you have got too many people coming and going in the picture. After all, each book is in some measure a repetition of the others, and I believe that by careful elimination of extraneous people and incidents you could compress the whole into one really first-class volume.[215]

Savage sent the manuscripts to be independently read by Osyth Leeston. Leeston came back with extensive suggestions for all three manuscripts – *Wilding Graft*, 'Unsunned Tarn' and 'Penance of the Seed' – adding that 'Unsunned Tarn' was, over all, the strongest. Then Savage was sent 'Lamb of Carn Veor' (then 'Lamb of the Green Bed') and he immediately told Jack that this was 'far and away the best thing you have written'. Savage's role in Clemo's literary development blossomed at this stage, although the only novelistic success he had with Clemo was *Wilding Graft*.

Following the interest shown in *Wilding Graft* by Chatto & Windus, the editor and future Poet Laureate Cecil Day Lewis offered his criticism of the 'Unsunned Tarn' and 'Penance of the Seed' manuscripts. In disagreement with Leeston, Day Lewis believed *Wilding Graft* to be considerably better:

> in these two novels more than in Wilding Graft, we become aware of the machinery by which he achieves his purpose: the 'message' is not deeply integrated with the action: the author is too obviously manipulating his characters to certain moral ends, indeed at times we feel he has invented them simply as vehicles for these ends and that he is not enough interested in them as human beings.

This criticism marks the beginning of Cecil Day Lewis's considerable impact on Clemo's career. Not only will he oversee the work to be undertaken on *Wilding Graft*, but he will also inform *Confession of a Rebel* and be responsible for the selection of poems collected as *The Clay Verge*. Day Lewis was frank and accurate in his criticism. He went on to write that the old novels appear 'tired and perfunctory' compared with *Wilding Graft*, and that the 'passion is too often stated rather than implied', that Clemo comes 'perilously near to melodrama [...] probably the inevitable result of flogging a tired theme', and that the 'most obvious defect' was the 'inability to handle sophisticated characters', stemming from Jack's lack of 'knowledge of the world'. Lastly, 'his "modern" girls, Joan in Unsunned Tarn, Lela in Penance of the Seed [...] are very crudely portrayed, and sometimes are indistinguishable from the stock bad-girl figures of Parish Magazine serials.'[216]

Clemo was devastated by the rejection. 'The blackest day of the year', he wrote in his diary.[217] But Day Lewis had added a strong compliment to his criticism, which should also be acknowledged:

> I have so firm a belief in this writer. There is much in these novels which is impressive: for instance, the village prostitute, Olive Buzza, is a really remarkable creation: his skill in first isolating a number of characters on the periphery of his story, and then drawing them together, holds out great hopes for his future: and his descriptive power, though the images it creates in these two novels are not so illuminating or essential on the whole as those of Wilding Graft, is evidently that of a born poetic novelist.

Tragically, the progress of Clemo's syphilis would render Day Lewis's prediction irrelevant. It would never be seen how good a novelist he might have become.

After this exchange, Clemo returned to Savage's suggestion that he should compress the other books into 'one really first-class volume'. Writing frankly to Clemo, Savage said:

> Let us summarise the position – you admit that your work has been turned down by 37 publishers, and we can only say that if you do not take the advice of experts you will go on having your work refused. We are fully aware of your circumstances, but it is penny wise and pound foolish to try and get a publisher to

accept three books which are not quite good enough than one which is really good.[218]

Now that *Wilding Graft* had been taken out of that equation, Jack had 'Unsunned Tarn' and 'Penance of the Seed' remaining. He understood Savage to mean that he should blend these stories together, a task begun in 1950 and finished in 1951. The new work was entitled 'The Dry Kiln'. The typescripts show that the version completed at this time was Clemo's final draft, ready for publication, and its history afterwards is easily documented. It was rejected in September 1951 by Chatto & Windus, and then set aside for forty-seven years.

In 1998, four years after Clemo's death, this over-worked and abandoned novel was given to the publisher Charles Thurlow of Cornish Hillside Publications. Two versions of the typescript exist, one in Exeter's Special Collections and the other at Wheal Martyn China Clay Museum. The Exeter typescript shows Clemo's intentions for the book before it was abandoned. The one in Wheal Martyn, on the other hand, shows the version edited by the Padstow writer and publisher Donald Rawe, on Charles Thurlow's request and with Ruth Clemo's permission. Rawe had been visiting and corresponding with the Clemos since around 1970, and was a natural choice. In his 'Editor's Note' to *The Clay Kiln*, Rawe explains that 'only where the writing appeared to our 21st century expectations difficult to interpret and, at times, jarringly unsubtle, have I dared to change the occasional epithet or phrase'. This is an understatement of the work carried out. The first and most obvious change Rawe made is to the title, discarding 'The Dry Kiln' and renaming it *The Clay Kiln*, which Rawe said 'may be better understood today'. It is one of a number of questionable amendments. It is questionable because a 'clay kiln' has no specific meaning to Cornish clay-mining, and might even be considered tautological. The correct phrase was, indeed, a 'Dry', and any reader familiar with Clemo's work would have been aware of the term. Decisions of this sort might suggest that the intended readership was not primarily those familiar with Clemo's work or those familiar with the clay region. It is valid, then, to ask who the intended readership might have been. The publisher is a well-considered Cornish-interest house, marketing within Cornwall and specifically within the St Austell area. They are publishing a St Austell writer out of favour at the time, except within Cornish and Christian literary markets. On top of this, *The Clay Kiln* is the weakest of Clemo's novels, and would be damaging to his popularity and future readership if taken as typical or representative of his mature output, rather than as juvenilia or as a failed work of academic interest. But if it was to be regarded as the juvenilia of an exceptional writer, it would have made more sense to have stuck with the author's intentions. Now, if the book was to be sold within Cornwall, but was not intended for people familiar to Clemo or the clay district, and not intended to be of academic value, the only obvious market remaining is that of the visitors and tourists. Yet this seems an unlikely market for Thurlow to target, especially with a Jack Clemo novel. It is possible that intentions were muddled or conflicting and never fully reconciled.

The Clay Kiln's real interest is as an academic or biographical piece, and the manuscript should have been published as Clemo intended it. Instead, a number of minor errors were introduced to the text, and a significant number of alterations were made, which ought to be acknowledged. Some of the changes are subtle, and others quite intrusive. Of the latter, new descriptive passages were inserted into the text, written by Rawe rather than by Clemo. For example, the passage describing Marvran's journey out of Falmouth is entirely Rawe's invention: 'dawn broke over Pendennis Point; she saw again the abandoned castle rising from the mist'. There were changes made to the dialogue and especially the dialect. The dialogue of 'The Dry Kiln' was intended to be relatively free from dialect, to make the work more readable, just as *Wilding Graft* had been. In Clemo's original dialogue a Cornish accent is implied, without being distracting. For example, an accent is evident in Clemo's sentence, 'I aren't going to bandy words', which is about as close to dialect as the writing gets in Clemo's version. Rawe changes this sentence to, 'I aren't going to bandy words with 'ee', which introduces a phonetic spelling, but also alters a localised derivative of the saying 'I'm not going to bandy words with you' into an anglicised formulation with Cornish pronunciation imposed, at the same time depriving the phrase of a regional characteristic and making it more awkward to read. Another small example is the phrase, 'Anyhow it soon brought him to boiling point', which was changed by Rawe to 'Anyhow it soon brought 'n to boiling point'. It is only slight, but such changes make the dialogue untidy and the Cornish voice imposed rather than implied.

From beginning to end the novel has been altered, and it is the ending that best shows how unnecessary the process became. In Clemo's version daybreak is described as it approaches Hugh Town in the Scilly Isles, where the lovers Joel and Lorraine are standing. The narrator follows the risen sun across Cornwall to the clay district, as the light 'fanned out over the grey roofs of clay-dries until its seaward flash from Land's End struck the tower like a sundering blade and dropped in broad warmth of peace upon the lonely watchers.' This is altered by Rawe for publication, so that the light 'struck the tower like a sundering blade, casting the broad warmth of peace upon the lonely watchers.'[219] Again, it is only a slight alteration, but it is to the detriment of the passage's purpose. The original phrase was not problematic, imprecise, difficult, archaic, or in any other way inappropriate. More importantly, the alteration muddles the metaphor of the dropping blade. In Rawe's version the blade reference is doing no work at all. In fact, it makes little sense for the 'blade' to be 'casting' warmth on the couple. Instead of a violent warmth dropping with the blade, the flash of light has become more like a blanket in Rawe's version.

The published book is, then, doubly flawed, an unsuccessful amalgamation of too many other works inappropriately edited. To understand the book's intentions better we should look at the unpublished versions – the final draft of 'The Dry Kiln' and its component parts, 'The Comedy of Clay'.

The 'Comedy of Clay' trilogy, as conceived in 1941, would have had three heroes: Joel in 'Private Snow', Jowan in 'Unsunned Tarn' and Bryn in 'Sown Light'. As the books merged, Joel remained the main hero, a tough, surly dry-worker from a bad family. Jowan became Euan, a bookish young man who finished school but decided he preferred employment in the clay industry. Bryn, meanwhile, was a slightly slow-witted character of primitive faith who, since leaving school, had read nothing but the Bible.

Each of the three characters is an idealized aspect of Jack himself: the social outsider, the bookish outsider, and the religious outsider. They are each strong and attractive young men with special talents who reject the triviality of everyday village life and are rejected themselves, in spite of which they all find perfect Christian love and marriage. One might almost see the act of writing these stories as a kind of repetitious prayer or meditation. Clemo introduced his problems, added the principles of his faith, and enforced a happy inevitable resolution. Much later, in 1990, he would explain this to a friend and correspondent, Felicity Warner: 'Every novel or short story I wrote had a happy ending – chiefly because I was its hero and I felt that if I meted out tragedy to this fictitious person I would suffer the same fate'.[220] This approach made for an unusual blend of realism and idealism. The industrial rural landscape and people are described excellently, if cruelly, with intimate awareness and attention to detail, but working behind them is the force of divine predestination, guiding elect Christians to a hybrid spiritual-worldly fulfilment. They are realist novels with a hidden but explicitly stated optimistic faith driving them to conclusion. A Christian Realism, perhaps.

When Clemo drew the three stories into a single volume, he was reluctant to reduce the number of characters, so that most of the fringe characters remained with no space to develop them. Bryn was edited out completely, while Joel's original lover, Marvran, was turned into a false start. All of the other novels had involved a failing relationship at the beginning, so this is not a problem in itself, but the writer appeared unwilling to reduce the importance of the Marvran character, and it is not until well into the second half of the book that we are introduced to the destined love interest, Lorraine. The many scenes of tension with Marvran have been a waste of time, an unresolved distraction.

The formula of the separated novels had been that a new heroine was introduced at the beginning and an old fringe character developed afterwards, and their drama would play within the established framework of the village and the villagers' chatter and sin. As the old characters reappear, the reader feels a comfortable sense of context which juxtaposes well against the excitement of the new protagonist and the exposition of a previously minor figure. Clemo did all of this very ably, structuring the stories with easy competence. The amalgamated novel lost almost all of the vigour and structure as the stories merged. When Day Lewis and Savage suggested that Clemo boil the stories down into one book, they had intended for Clemo to reduce the number of characters and to focus the novel on a single love story using the best features from previous attempts. Instead, Clemo kept practically all of the characters and ran parallel narratives. The trilogy's charms were lost, and a new set of problems introduced. Replacing the resolution of the trilogy, in which the three successful couples from each of the novels congregate in Joel and Marvran's house, 'The Dry Kiln' essentially has the Scilly Isle ending from 'Sown Light', in which Bryn (now Joel) and Lorraine return to Hugh Town for their honeymoon, meditating on Providence and predestiny. It becomes an unbalanced and underwhelming finale.

In spite of all this, a number of useful features remain. In its evolution we can see the effect of Jack's disabilities and biography on the story. We can trace his reading, as well as his theological and moral beliefs as they develop, and we may derive from the work a considerable commentary on the people and places of his native region. Firstly, there is the base melodrama, with characters quivering, gasping and anxiously gripping furniture, from Clemo's earliest reading, and the use of Providence, fate and God's romantic will, as he found in *Jane Eyre*. There is also the influence of T.F. Powys, which Savage asked Jack to tone down in 'Unsunned Tarn': 'three times during the book you refer to T.F. Powys. Don't you think it might be a good idea to cut this out, otherwise, you might be accused of being too influenced by him in your writing?'[221] Like Clemo, Powys set his stories in small rural communities, often with recurring characters and a clear allegorical purpose, and it was after reading Powys's *Goat Green* (sometimes called *The Better Gift*) that Clemo decided to make Joel a footballer, as he noted in his diary:

> The idea has been in my mind ever since I read Powys' *The Better Gift*. I'd thought reference to sport out of place in my mystical type of writing, but when I read Theodore using [...] the two so convincingly I changed my mind.[222]

The Clay Kiln's emphasis on divinely ascribed lovers, while not originally considered through Jack's reading of Robert Browning, was impressively bolstered by it. There are several mentions of Browning in the text, including an inscription from 'Ixion' and a reference to 'The Statue and the Bust'. The latter poem, Jack notes in his 1937 diary, was an inspiration for the novel sequence, which may be imagined in the love-at-first-sight scene between Joel and Lorraine in *The Clay Kiln*. In 'The Statue and the Bust' a young bride sees a duke passing and they fall immediately in love. It is this aspect and the apparent narrative sympathy with the socially condemned lovers which Clemo used. He, too, fell in love quickly and often, believing that God approved his love in spite of its tendency to head in forbidden directions.

The theology of *The Clay Kiln* is not as deliberately constructed as the mature works. Clemo is informed primarily by his personal beliefs, Bible studies, and his reading of Charles Spurgeon's sermons. Predestination is central to the story, and it might be worth outlining where Clemo's ideas on the doctrine derived. It was Calvin who emphasized the importance of predestination. Calvin's picture is of the 'predestination of some to salvation, and of others to destruction'.[223] For Calvin, those who would be saved and those who would be damned were predetermined from the very beginning by God and there is nothing anyone can do to change their fate. These are the elect and the non-elect, respectively. Clemo's impression of predestiny came from post-Calvinists like Spurgeon, whose position is neatly outlined in the sermon 'Predestination and Calling'. For Spurgeon, election is a call from God that has been answered by man:

> Many are called but few are chosen, because there are many kinds of call, but the true call, and that only, answers to the description of the text. It is 'an holy calling, not according to our works, but according to his own purpose and grace, which was given us in Christ Jesus before the world began.' This calling forbids all trust in our own doings and conducts us to Christ alone for salvation, but it afterwards purges us from dead works to serve the living and true God. If you are

> living in sin, you are not called; if you can still continue as you were before your pretended conversion, then it is no conversion at all; that man who is called in his drunkenness, will forsake his drunkenness; men may be called in the midst of sin, but they will not continue in it any longer.

The word 'chosen' seems odd here, as odd as it will seem in Clemo's own work. The picture Spurgeon very clearly outlines in his sermon is that many people hear the call to salvation, the call of and to God. This is their 'conversion' experience. However, for it to be considered a 'true' conversion, the called individual must respond, by aligning themself with God's will and teaching. If the individual continues in their debauchery and sin then it is not a 'true call' and they are not 'chosen'.

> If I be called I must have been elected, and I need not doubt that. God never tantalized a man by calling him by grace effectually, unless he had written that man's name in the Lamb's book of life. Oh, what a glorious doctrine is that of election, when a man can see himself to be elect.[224]

This is the 'Consolation' of Spurgeon's sermon, though is it really any such thing? 'If he hath called thee, nothing can divide thee from his love.' *If* he hath called thee. What if he hath not? This could only be considered a consolation to Spurgeon's audience if they had been called. Spurgeon seems to consider that anybody exposed to the Church or the Bible has, in a sense, been 'called', exposed to this great 'truth', and they may either respond by submission to it, or they may carry on with their lives as before. Both sorts of person might believe in God after the 'call', but only one is elect. Spurgeon's argument suggests that submission amounts to election. So the two groups of people comprising the non-elect are those who are never exposed to the 'call', and those who did not respond to it.

Spurgeon's position is a kind of compromise between the doctrine of election and that of free will. Many have been called, but only those who choose to submit are the elect. And who could complain of being excluded if they have chosen to ignore the call? Those who know of the doctrine are aware of the 'call', and those who have not heard of the doctrine or the call cannot care.

There is an uncomfortable playing with the idea of freedom here, and it is worth looking at since almost all of Clemo's beliefs are filtered through Spurgeon. In another sermon, Spurgeon says:

> But there are some who say, 'It is hard for God to choose some and leave others.' Now, I will ask you one question. Is there any of you here this morning who wishes to be holy, who wishes to be regenerate, to leave off sin and walk in holiness? 'Yes, there is,' says someone, 'I do.' Then God has elected you. But another says, 'No; I don't want to be holy; I don't want to give up my lusts and my vices.' Why should you grumble, then, that God has not elected you to it? For if you were elected you would not like it, according to your own confession.[225]

It is a circular sort of argument. If God had made you want to submit to Him then you would submit and you would be grateful. If God has made you so that you do *not* want to submit, then you do not want to submit and you have nothing to complain about. The obvious and unanswered problem here is that God could have made everyone want to submit. God has taken away this person's freedom by making it causally impossible for them to accept the 'call'. It appears as abjectly unfair as the original formulation of Calvin, even though it is a softening of the doctrine.

Clemo accepted a version of predestination in *The Clay Kiln*, though it is slightly different from the version we will see in *The Invading Gospel*. That later version is informed to a greater degree by Karl Barth, and is at once more forgiving and more personal than Spurgeon's picture. The predestiny in *The Clay Kiln* is very like the fatalism of Hardy, but instead of there being only one malign spirit, leading people irrevocably to their doom, there is a second, a benign God, who leads those that he favours through the same trials and suffering, but towards final satisfaction and gain. The malign spirit remains in Clemo's work, the guiding hand of 'Nature' towards one's fate, but the faithful force of predestiny can overrule it. Intriguingly, Clemo adds to this formula the possibility of fate still threatening the predestined pattern. In *The Clay Kiln* it is the Second World War that offers this possibility:

> Quietly they had discussed the possible effects of the war upon their marriage: inconvenience, separation, material uncertainty. Having conquered their personal fate they were confronted by a wider fate, with its monstrous threat to the predestined pattern of their lives.

There is Natural fate, Christian predestiny, and now there is another worldly force – a 'wider fate' – apparently made of some other quality. It is a more general fate. Here are at least three competing forces essential to causality, all of them defined by their certitude and none of them achieving certitude. One is 'fated' to Hell *unless* one submits to God, in which case one is 'destined' to Heaven, *unless* the 'wider fate' intervenes. It seems here that, far from solving the problem of Calvinistic predestiny, Clemo has reinstated both free will and contingency to chance. It is a very obscure way of arriving at a stance that to all appearances remains simply causal. By making the multiplicity of fates and predestinies potentially conflicting, Clemo seems to be undermining the quality of the Creator's forethought, or otherwise to be sacrificing the meaning of 'destiny'. If one can submit fully to God and so enter a route of divinely predestined fulfilment, and yet have this route blocked by an unforeseen fate – remembering that 'fate' has been evaded by the submission to Christ – then there is a problem.

The happy ending, too, introduces a claim about fate and destiny, this being Clemo's own promised, divinely approved and achieved marriage. That is, it seems to be the moral of the story that worldly pleasures are the expected reward for renouncing the world in favour of Christian devotion. Physical, passionate, erotic love – albeit along with spiritual companionship – is the reward for putting your faith in God. Clemo also believed personally that his disabilities would be healed, his hearing returned, and, later, his eyesight and sense of taste. Indeed, Clemo's personal situation really challenges the boundary between the spiritual and physical in a human being. He was forced to confront his faith and his God in a very personal and immediate way.

The questionable moral of this outlook is that the reward for escaping 'Natural fate' and worldly pleasure is in fact a worldly pleasure: marriage, sensuality and companionship. One gets what one desires most if one is a good Christian. This is a tension at the heart of Clemo's fusion of personal experiential mysticism and dogma. The depth of his desires, Clemo felt, could not be there for nothing. God would not nurture and excite these desires vainly after he had submitted wholeheartedly to Him. This belief accounts for the early attempt to sublimate sex, marriage and physical love. If they can be considered somehow a bridge between the spiritual and physical worlds then they are a divine gift, a point of mystical contact.

The Clay Kiln also reveals a number of biographical parallels between the work and life of Clemo. Marvran, for example, is Evelyn, and her changing role in the evolving narrative echoes Clemo's changing feelings towards the real-life girl. In 'Private Snow' and the earlier versions of 'Unsunned Tarn', Marvran is the destined lover, but when the novels are combined and in real life Evelyn has married someone else, the Marvran character becomes 'cheap' and 'worldly', a mere 'preparation' for the real thing. Euan is reading books on sex and D.H. Lawrence, just as Clemo read books on physiological aspects of sex by R.T. Trall and T.W. Standwell, loaned to him in 1934 by Frank Baron. There are many such details: Marvran's dog is named Flush, just as Jack's was; Joel's reprobate family was modelled on Esther and John Clemo; and Joel's awkwardness around women is similar to Clemo's, with the feeling that he is missing some subtle technique of flirtation which he would understand if he were a 'slick fellow'. The representation of women in the novel is characteristically conflicting. There are puritanical expectations, with virginity being more attractive, make-up being 'garish artificiality', and the repeated references to the sinful frivolity of dancing. These are inherited from the fundamental Methodist upbringing of Jack and his mother. But it is worth recalling that while Clemo is conservative on matters of sexual attraction and marital expectations, there is no expression of misogyny in his approach to women who are academics, theologians, artists or friends. This again may show the influence of the Bible Christians and chapel circuit, which used a greater number of women preachers than any other Methodist sect. Equally, his progressive attitude towards women could have been assumed by the strength of the cottage's matriarchy.

There remain in *The Clay Kiln* some of the solipsistic tendencies observed in other juvenilia. We are to infer, for example, that the villagers and God alike have an all-consuming investment in the progress of young lovers. However, there is also a reaching out towards a more mature expression. Clemo's descriptive writing begins to reveal the inspired and vigorous intimacy he had with his industrial environment:

> The 'dry' was some fifty yards in length, and low-roofed; its outer side was the storage linhay, closed by wooden shutters swung between stone pillars and hinged, not at the sides like a door, but to the timber beams supporting the roof. Most of these shutters were now hanging down, and as the building had no windows the kiln, some twelve feet above the storage area in which dried clay-cubes were stacked, was deeply shadowed. Through the fetid steam the slurry on the kiln-pan glinted, bubbling whitely up like a leprous skin.

A 'born poetic novelist', Cecil Day Lewis had said, and Clemo's descriptions are immediately evocative to anyone familiar with the industrialised moorland around St Austell. Jack wrote of the character Euan that he 'knew the idiom of the countryside, the bleak lyricism of the flowing sand', and he would have been aware that this applied to himself too.

The Clay Kiln is a juvenile work of the pre-war period, a grotesque composite beast, but Jack's talent is budding. The theology grounded in personal experience is a bold undercurrent of the novel, however unappealing it is to logic, and the use of malicious gossip to drive the plot is achieved very successfully.

The novel ends as Britain is due to enter the war, and this moment would mark a new chapter in Clemo's development. The first two years of the war diaries are missing and much is due to change. He is a young man in his mid-twenties, who is lonely and suffering from the strain of failed romance. He is deaf from the progression of his syphilis, the only real inheritance from his dead father, and he is poor, living with a crippled aunt and widowed mother in a workers' cottage. His teenage urges have been typical, but they have all been discovered in darkness, interpreted within a peculiar framework, and at times troublingly directed. The most wild and treacherous waters of youth have been navigated in an oarless dinghy. From the villagers, he received only taunts and the hurt of gossip about the shame of his father. Socially, Jack tried to 'confess' his shame by acting in a 'shameful' way – never washing, shaving or changing his clothes, and there was an 'incident' recalled in *Confession* when he seditiously ate a pasty in the street. Jack set a theological context for his solitude and individualism in order that he might resolve the tensions between his faith and circumstances. The confessional exhibitionism has not yet been outgrown, as records from the *Cornish Guardian* show, but it has matured and will continue to do so throughout the following decade, away from the controversial and towards reconciliation.

The extraordinary conditions in which Clemo grew up made him unevenly balanced in a unique way. The awakening of sexual awareness was given excessive significance, so much so that it had to be related to God. Indeed, Christianity seems to have been the only ideology strong enough to sustain the suffering. The death of his father, the syphilis, the poverty, the isolation, the novelty of sex – there *had* to be a reason. The recurrence of pain year after year, the relentless losses, these could not have been chance. So why choose Jack? What was so special? Was he the damned offspring of a sinner? He did not feel himself to be. Then perhaps the suffering was a purification process, a mystical favour gifted by God, preparing him to be received. In this way sex really could be Clemo's path to God, with the suffering of his inheritance and the ecstasy of orgasm perfectly poised.

Clemo's faith towards the end of the 1930s is more consistent, more self-aware and adoring. Less frequent are the violent rages spat at the Almighty, and less poisonous his letters to the paper. Reaching out to the *Cornish Guardian*, Clemo often made sensible points, though he made them in a perverse way, his maturity and intellect at different developmental stages. The following decade is a period of maturation and control. Politically and theologically Clemo becomes engaged, the quality of his prose improves markedly, and he moves gradually away from the timid sexuality of child romances. Yet the intensity and confusion of youth remain, and this duality of his nature – this rupturing tension – is reflected in the work; the potent clay-set romance of *Wilding Graft*, the sublimely uneven chronicle of *Confession of a Rebel*, and the brutal industrial metaphorical poetry that would constitute *The Clay Verge*.

Still Clemo has hardly set foot outside of the cottage and the sand dump, and his routines continue through the war. Thursdays he goes to Foxhole for the paper. Tuesdays he goes for his injections and his mother goes to choir practice in the evening, returning by 8:30pm – any later and Jack panics. In the mornings he lies in bed late reading the Bible, then sits at his writing bureau by the window of the front room, looking out at the hedge and the stone wall, and the road where clay trucks pass. There the Italian prisoners of war would wait for Harry's bus to take them out to the farms, peering in at Jack hunched over his desk, teasing and flattering the poet and his mother. The facts of the Second World War would remain remote to him, passing through the front door with the newspaper and the charming Italians, or with the evacuee children sent down from London. Jack kept his own dramas within the cottage, for which the war was an inconvenient but appropriate metaphor.

Evacuees playing outside the Clemo cottage, 1944

VI
War Comes to Goonamarris

'War's bound to knock out a industry like ours where so much depends on the exports. Germany was one of our biggest customers on that there continent o' Europe, and now, o' course, none of our clay isn't goin' there – though you'd think they'd need more clay instead o' less, considerin' the amount o' crockery Hitler must ha' smashed up in these tempers he'd get.'

Wilding Graft

The clay industry and villages suffered during wartime, with impeded exportation, difficulty replacing machinery parts and a severely diminished male work force. Many pits were forced to close, and even when the war ended the industry continued to suffer, with ill-maintained equipment and a shortage of coal. The works needed to maximise efficiency and minimise waste, which led to further machination and the development of aggregate companies able to use the discarded sand and rock. These waste products can be found everywhere, from road construction and mortar sand to bird feed and golf bunkers, and they define some of the new-build houses of the clay towns, which are rendered a storm-cloud grey by the aggregate. Even now the war's influence remains evident, as the pressure was felt most keenly by smaller concerns. There were forty-one companies mining china clay at the outbreak of war, but as they struggled and closed, the bigger companies took advantage, buying up the smaller concerns so that today there is a near-monopoly held by the French mineral-giant Imerys.

As well as industrial stress and anxiety, war brought new threats of attack to Cornwall. The coastline was always vulnerable to naval strikes, but the 1939 war brought with it the additional threat of attack by air, a threat realised as soon as France fell in 1940. The Germans set up bases along the Gallic coast, which meant that Cornwall had a tactical value and vulnerability. Attacking planes would pass over, and while the small fishing and mining villages might not seem natural targets, there were many unpredictable strikes from retreating German aircraft offloading their bombs before returning to France, having been unable to drop them on the targeted military bases, larger towns and ports. Around the clay area, Par, Pentewan, St Blazey and Goss Moor were hit in the 1942 raids, destroying homes, churches, harbours and livestock. In 1941 four bombs were dropped on Foxhole, an attack mentioned in Clemo's *Confession*, having come soon after Jack had given his first religious address at Trethosa Chapel, on Psalm 46. The Foxhole explosions could be heard from Goonamarris.

The fall of France and the threat of air strikes increased the urgency of evacuating children from London and the south-east into rural areas. Cornwall was still safer than London, and floods of evacuees arrived. Trains would take them to St Austell, and a coach would drive them out to Nanpean or Trethosa School to be billeted. In their cramped cottage, Eveline, Bertha and Jack took in two children, Pat and Doris Jauncey. Originally billeted elsewhere in the village, the Jaunceys came to the Clemo cottage following a death in the summer of 1940, soon before the London Blitz. They left again in 1942, when the threat was thought to have lessened, and Pat returned two years later with two of her younger siblings, David and Rita. They finally left in 1945, but would return to Cornwall sporadically for holidays.

Another evacuee, Irene, arrived with the Jauncey girls just before her eighth birthday in July 1940. Although billeted with the Kessells next door, Irene spent much of her time playing with the Jauncey sisters at the Clemo cottage. However, by 1941 a tension had arisen between the two neighbouring families. The Kessells were suspicious of Jack and thought his friendships with children – especially Irene – unhealthy. This was further fuelled by Clemo's turbulent infatuation with Barbara. Barbara herself still visited the cottage occasionally to see the London girls, and the manner in which she now ignored Jack hurt him, leading to a number of 'hysterical outbursts' overheard by the Kessells next door until they 'thought it prudent to keep Irene away from me as much as possible'.[226] The Clemos, on the other hand, believed Irene would be better off living with them and the other girls. 'Mother says I[rene]'s begged her time and again to take her away from Mrs. K., and now it shall be done', wrote Jack in 1941.[227] But the 'outbursts' had already damaged Jack's brittle reputation, and 'being unfamiliar with the latent peculiarities of my temperament these village folk took my violent behaviour very seriously'.[228] The Kessells reported Jack to the billeting officer, claiming that he was unstable and a threat to children, the result of which was that in October Jack 'had to endure a revolting psycho-analytical test by Dr Coleman of Bodmin Asylum[229] before they were satisfied that it was an innocent friendship. Perhaps they weren't *satisfied* even then'.[230] Following this test, Jack recorded his initial thoughts in his diary:

> Our Dr had reported what Mrs K said and I had to see the hospital psychoanalyst and go through a gruelling test while he probed for abnormalities. All in vain! [...] He told mother he was fully satisfied that there are no sexual aberrations in me – in ref to Irene, of course, but it applies to my whole outlook. The devil has received a crushing blow over this business, foiled and routed at every point. [...] And the dramatic sense of being 'on trial' – for he told me I was 'accused of assaulting an evacuee girl' – this will be a wonderful help to my writing – the real sensational touch which is always so fruitful for me.[231]

Writing in *Confession*, Clemo almost seems to implicate himself. When asked by Dr Coleman who his favourite writers were, he says he became flustered, mentioning 'Galsworthy and Hall Caine, both of whom had ceased to be my favourites years before. But it was probably just as well that I did not admit that my favourite author was T.F. Powys'. The sense is that had the doctor known the truth then his conclusions might have been different. Dr Coleman continued to question Jack:

> He did not refer to masochism or sadism, and I thought it unnecessary to mention these traits [...]. I was very relieved that he did not ask whether I had been in any way obsessed with other young girls. I was anxious that Barbara should be kept out of this, and that our old

spiritual attachment should not be dragged into this murky by-path. It would be very difficult to explain to a psychiatrist what she had done for me, and what I still felt about her.[232]

The approach here appears very similar to Jack's approach to the whole process of writing his autobiography. He does not want to tell a direct lie, but he will omit key information in order to construct an alternative narrative.

In the last part of Coleman's examination: 'I was quite calm and collected. I had read enough books on sex and psychology to give intelligent answers to the psychiatrist's questions. I knew what he was talking about, what he was trying to get at'.[233] The impression in all of this is that Clemo was getting away with something. It was not pleasant, but for Clemo it served two functions. Firstly, it exonerated him. He confessed the ignominious event in his diaries, letters and books, and the effect ought to have been freedom from or transcendence of public oppression. Secondly, Clemo used the event to exalt himself:

> My mind was unusual but sound and wholesome, with firm moral control. [Dr Coleman] added – and I mention this as a mere factual detail – that there was no doubt that I possessed the mentality of a genius and was likely to show a taste for extreme simplicity which would be misunderstood by average adults.[234]

The following page, he refers to this as 'the official confirmation of my "genius"'. This was unlikely to have been told to Jack himself, as he was deaf at the time of the visit, and it was not recorded in any accounts of the psychological analysis in his diaries or correspondence. The gentle, favourable distortion of events is a feature of confessional literature and it will be considered further in Chapter VIII.

With the doctor's absolution, Irene was able to move into the Clemo cottage within the week. This new girl knew how to make Jack happy, writing notes like 'I love God' or 'I love Jack' and handing them to him.

At the same time, in November 1941, only a month after Irene arrived at the cottage, Jack read Thomas Hardy's *Jude the Obscure* and *Tess of the D'Urbervilles* very quickly, finishing them both over two days, and in December he began thinking about some new work of his own – a novel, to be entitled *Wilding Graft*. This was a fruitful period for Jack. Both *Confession of a Rebel* and *Wilding Graft* were begun in 1941, the first 500 words of the former having been written back in June. *Wilding Graft* progressed swiftly, and within twelve months Clemo had written 75,000 words to it. By this time the situation in the house had changed. Pat and Doris had left in February, only four months after Irene had moved in, a sort of movement quite typical for evacuees, just as their return in 1944 would be, following the threat of the unmanned V-1 flying bombers, or Doodlebugs. After the Jauncey girls left, the cottage felt empty, and Eveline Clemo went looking for a new girl. She found Joan Slade, a ten-year-old from Dulwich, intended to be a playmate for Irene. Joan stayed with the Clemos until September 1944, but is mentioned only a handful of times. In his 1942 diary, Jack writes that he does not want her to come at all. He wanted the old evacuees back. He dislikes Joan before she has even arrived, and it is no surprise that he tries to find fault immediately, not even attempting to befriend her. In *Confession* she is dismissed as 'a pathetic little slum product', 'a silent, remote shadow', and in the diaries, when she leaves, Clemo remarks that he won't 'miss her at all'.[235]

Pat, Doris and Irene, on the other hand, appear disproportionately frequently in *Confession of a Rebel*, which gives an inflated sense of their importance to Clemo's biography. This is because the girls were all present while he was writing *Confession*, and there may be a sense in which they are important to Clemo's readers as a corrective to the earlier concerns over Jack's sexualising of the child Barbara. It appears as though Barbara was an exceptional infatuation that went too far. Clemo revelled in infatuations and enjoyed playing the lover. He also enjoyed the company of children immensely. But the case of Barbara was unusual, and although in his response to Dr Coleman there is the suggestion of some further fall with Irene, Jack does not appear to have responded to subsequent girls in the same way. He found Irene charming, particularly her artless simplicity:

> We've had Irene's school report, and the Master says she's backward […]. I know that's one of the chief reasons I like her so – I hate this cleverness which dries up all the human feeling in girls, makes them cold, aloof, competent. God give me a girl with a warm heart, simple and emotional, and I shan't care much what sort of mind she has.[236]

Clemo is delighted with Irene, but the diaries suggest that she is not desired in the way that Barbara was. He is not asking for Irene to love him, but praying for a more mature girl with her qualities to enter his life. In *Confession* it is suggested that Irene was almost as important to Jack as Barbara, and he even found a pattern to support a connection between the two girls, writing that the weather on the Saturday Irene arrived was 'oddly similar to that other fateful one on which Marshall Rowse had been killed'. That is to say, it was raining.

But the idea that Irene was of pivotal personal importance to Clemo is not evidenced outside of *Confession of a Rebel*, and it seems as though her textual presence is exaggerated there by her closeness at the time of writing, and by her leaving in June 1945. It is only in 1945, as she edges towards a more appropriate age for courting, that Jack wonders whether she was, after all, intended to be his wife.

By this time, Eveline Clemo was as committed to finding Jack a partner as he was. At the very least, she needed some help at home. Her health was not good, and in 1942 she had been critically ill and hospitalized. She worried about who would look after Jack when she was gone. It was a problem, as Jack was an awkward burden to inherit and there would be few people willing to bear him, with perhaps fewer still he would be willing to bear. Jack, too, felt this concern, and it would haunt him whenever his mother fell ill.

Two years after the war had finished, Eveline went to see the evacuees and was dismayed to find that Irene had a boyfriend her own age. She was not the least interested in returning to the dark, isolated cottage in the clay country. So Jack remained committed to Barbara, who was herself approaching a conventional age for courting:

> Cheered [...] by the news that thousands of girls are marrying at 16 or 17 – in 1941 over 30,000 English girls were married under the age of 18. It gives me such heart for Ba – oh, I do believe I shan't have to wait long.[237]

When 'Roche Snow' was finished and submitted again in 1944, Jack wanted the dedication to be for Barbara, and to read: 'remembering happy days at G. while this book was being written'.[238] Barbara's photograph remained above his writing desk, and he still believed they were destined to be together. In the opening few pages of the 1945 diary, this belief was expressed in his expectations for the year. We have noted Clemo's custom of announcing the start and the end of each year, summarizing what was past and planning what was to come. In this entry, the apophenic impulse informs him what to expect, and he notes: 'the coincidence of the numbers (14, 29) of the promise "when it is come to pass" fits the present year – if Ba is the right one'.[239] This is one of Jack's more elaborate patterns. What he means is that this year Barbara would be fourteen and Clemo would be twenty-nine, and that their ages signal a Biblical reference, to John, 14:29: 'I have told you before it come to pass, that, when it is come to pass, ye might believe'. Clemo goes on to observe that 1945 would be 'the seventh year since the old life ended with Ba's leaving here, so that, like Jacob, I've served 7 years for the promised blessing'. Jacob waited seven years to receive Rachel, just as Clemo expected to be given Barbara. Then, of course, he noted that 1945 was the centenary of 'the Wimpole Street miracle', when Robert Browning and Elizabeth Barrett met. These were all 'proofs' assuring Clemo of romantic success in 1945. It was the 'Year of Destiny'.

True to form, nothing romantic happened. In fact, Clemo later noted that 1945 was the darkest year he had had since 1939, when he had destroyed his diary. The past, one may note, was always desperately gloomy and pained, while the future was to be brilliant and fulfilled. The ash left behind, fiery new feathers before.

The war years, then, were a muddle of childish happiness and deep loneliness. There was no romantic physical love throughout the war, but only the hope of Barbara one day returning to him and the immediate playful affection of evacuee children. Still he maintained that he could not write without romantic love, simultaneously preparing his most powerful novel, most extraordinary autobiographical work, and his best-celebrated poetry. Jack's war was fruitful but solitary. His record of events during these years, in *Confession* and in the diaries, is a unique wartime document.

For much of the war the action remained distant to Clemo. He was not disturbed by night-raids and searchlights as his mother and the evacuee children were, because his deafness meant that he could not hear the bombs or aircraft: 'Jerry planes around here at 3am – mother heard bombs dropped and saw searchlights. [...] I slept thro' it all'.[240] Quite early on, the war tried to approach, when Jack was called up 'to be medically examined by the military authorities':

> Mother accompanied me and explained that I was deaf and had been blind, so after a quick glance at me the doctor filled in my exemption certificate declaring that I was 'suffering from complete blindness and deafness' – a statement that made me grin when presently I read it on Redruth station.[241]

On the way back he bumped into Evelyn with her baby in St Austell, apparently for the first time since storming out of the Phillips's farm: 'I knew from the complete absence of emotional turmoil that there was no possibility of my ever being ensnared again by the illusory values of an ideal world'.[242] Jack was ever 'starting again', confirming his faith, resolving to progress and never to return to a particular viewpoint or state of mind. And this one would last no longer than others. Clemo's love of resolutions was attached to his pattern-seeking and schematic manipulation of events. By processing events so consciously, and externalising them as though objectively, he separates himself from them and puts them behind him, so to speak. We see a similar attempt at self-analysis and objectivising through the graphs and charts Jack drew in his diaries, reductively plotting his emotional wellbeing between the perceived poles of happiness and misery. Elsewhere, Clemo delineates his religious development before 1955 into six tidy sections, or marks his reading out of a hundred. By ordering the world in this way, it is as though he is able to take control of it, to cordon it off and remove himself to a safe distance. If he can show that something misguided or humiliating is categorically distinct from how he is now, he is able to become morally removed from it, to put it in the past. It is a tendency that remains with Clemo, always emergent. It is the mark of one who suffers too much, as well as of one incorrigibly optimistic.

In *Confession*, it is Jack's intention to suggest that he hardly cared about the war at all, which was a bold posture in 1949. There is a passage in which he describes his immediate concern, after he had entered a writing competition with one of his novels:

> I had become very anxious about *Private Snow*. Daily news of the blitz on London was disturbing, and when I read of the great fire raid of December 29th I was horrified to learn that the premises of the publisher who held my novel had been burnt down. I entered 1941 with the paralysing fear, almost amounting to certainty, that my manuscript had been destroyed.

There was concern again in 1944, when 'Roche Snow' was with a London company at the time of the Doodlebug raids: 'Hitler's secret weapon, the ~~rocket~~ flying bomb – hundreds sent over without pilots [...]. Pray God He will keep R.S. safe, as during the [...] blitz.'[243]

In 1943, we find another moment when Jack's distance from the realities of the war is evident. In a detached mood he bemoaned the fact that he had 'never seen or heard a bomb fall'. It's a 'pity I've no first hand knowledge of the war'.[244] This idea of the war being to some degree a valuable spectacle is described in *Confession*, as people walk up to the higher moorland to watch Plymouth burn:

> During the blitz on Plymouth early in 1941 many people in mid-Cornwall climbed to ridges of the moors after nightfall and watched the lurid glare from the burning city, forty miles away to the east. Such a spectacle was inspiring to the imagination, and one would think it the very thing a sombre-minded novelist would wish to contemplate, seeing in it material for

a thrilling story. But I remained stolidly within the cottage at Goonamarris, cutting myself off from such external drama.

Clemo was exhibiting his lack of concern for worldly affairs, as he had so often done in the *Cornish Guardian*. But the diaries contradict this nonchalance. Jack received *The Daily Mail* every day to keep up with war news, and the *Cornish Guardian* weekly for the local news, paying very close attention to the epic story unravelling away from the dumps, and in his diaries he wrote his own daily commentary on the war's losses and victories, praying for Hitler and the Nazis to be defeated. He marked the battles, the bombings, the takings of certain cities across the world, counted our losses and rated the military leaders: 'cheered by news that [Douglas] MacArthur has taken control of the Pacific war zone. I believe more in him than in any other military leader'.[245] There was local celebration when Montgomery triumphed over Rommel in 1942, so much that a thanksgiving day was held, and the 'church bells ring for the first time since July, 1940'.[246]

Aside from very rare moments of cavalier selfishness, the diaries show Jack's strong concern for world affairs and Hitler's progress, a picture rather different from that of the *Cornish Guardian*, *Confession*, or indeed from subsequent publications. 'Still depressed – about the war' was a common entry, or else, 'Cheered by war news'. He reported on progress in the Solomon Islands, Egypt, Libya, Bulgaria and Greece: 'Nazis overrunning Greece and Yugoslavia'; 'Hitler has seized unoccupied France'; 'depression abt. war news – it looks hopeless again, Hitler announcing jubilantly that Russia is near collapse and will soon be at his mercy'; 'Grand news – Russia has launched a great offensive to trap the Nazis at Stalingrad – Hitler's whole plan crumbling at an amazing pace'; 'War news good – Tripoli captured'; 'Horrible details in paper about Belsen concentration camps – thousands tortured and killed there. Yet people still go on believing in the goodness of human nature!' He listed the horrors, the torture, starvation and death, and for a moment in 1942 his faith wobbled: 'And yet God has not said a word', he wrote, quoting Browning's 'Porphyria's Lover'.

Against this backdrop – the evacuees, the bombings, the slow malevolent encroachment of war – the Clemos had to navigate their poverty and illness. Jack was attending Truro hospital weekly for the latest course of arsenic injections, causing an abscess on his hip and preventing him from walking properly: 'those injections poisoning my blood again'.[247] Some sort of war was waging over his body, as well as over the world. In terms of his physical condition, the most frequent refrain from this period is: 'Hearing no better'. Nevertheless, Clemo retained the belief that he was going to recover, occasionally bolstered by perceived improvements: 'Cheerful – my hearing improved. Wondering much when it will be fully restored – this year?'[248] But rather than improvement, 1943 saw another physical effect of Jack's condition surface; the sudden greying and thinning of his hair. 'A bit worried about my hair', he notes. 'Have begun taking treatment [...] and pray it will restore it to normal.'[249] The treatment is curious, and there is no hint what it might have been, but after six weeks: 'Much cheered in the evening – Mother telling me my hair is turning quite black again. I do thank God for this renewal of youth.'[250]

A miracle was still expected, but in the meantime the trips to Truro would double as research expeditions for *Wilding Graft*. Jack made notes on the city's streets, gardens, cathedral and scenery, and bought books when he could afford them. Without these trips, he would not have been able to reproduce the Cornish capital so effectively. He is, however, 'sick of these visits' to the hospital, 'as they don't make my hearing better',[251] and often he uses having a headache or bad weather as an excuse not to go. Jack had started making these hospital visits on his own, his mother staying home to work and look after the girls. It was on one of these lone trips, when Jack was kept longer than usual at the hospital, that he missed the last bus back and had no option but to make the sixteen-mile journey by foot. He had not eaten and after four hours he was exhausted, when a man saw him struggling and invited him in to his home to rest. Jack followed, but was awkward and embarrassed about not being able to hear or communicate with the man and his wife. A replenishing tea was soon made for him and Jack recovered sufficiently to continue. He arrived in St Stephen two hours after dark and found his mother waiting there, distraught, along with 'Irene crying her heart out.' Irene's tears 'comforted me – the thought of coming home to someone who *cared*.'[252]

Another time, Jack believed that his course of treatment was over for good, after the hospital was bombed one August evening. Two bombs were dropped on Truro, one hitting the hospital and the other hitting Brucefield on Agar Road, along with machine gun fire. More than ten people were killed, but to Jack's disappointment the Germans missed his ward and his treatment had to continue.

The threat of bombing remained constant, but it was not until 1944 that the action closed in around Goonamarris. On 1 April: 'From today we're living in a military zone, cut off from parts of the country more than 10 miles inland. Invasion at hand, no doubt – God bring swift victory.' There is a sense of fear in this diary entry, landmarking a terrible development. Suddenly, war had arrived.

Americans were camped on Rostowrack Downs, Trethosa and Nanpean, 'many of them negroes', and 'it was impossible to move anywhere without being bawled at by drivers of Army vehicles or challenged by sentries.'[253] One Sunday, his mother was prevented from going to Trethosa Chapel by 'the Yankee guard at Stepaside', so had to work back and along to Nanpean instead. The stationed troops were preparing for the Normandy landings, and 'the roads became lined with camouflaged guns and other equipment destined for the front – a tempting target for Nazi bombers.'[254] After the troops had gone, their presence left some residual drama, such as the two women 'sent to prison [...] for neglecting their children who'd been left home with a soldier to look after them', and the 'Trethosa women fined for keeping a negro soldier in hiding' after the other troops had left.[255]

If the allied Americans were not welcome, the Italian prisoners of war, held at White Cross, were. Clemo recalls them affectionately. Harry's bus took the prisoners to work at the farms and clayworks, dropping them off and collecting them again from Vinegar Point:

> While awaiting their buses they would sit on the field hedge opposite our cottage and stare across at me as I lounged idly at my desk. There was much nodding and

whispering, and on one or two occasions, when my mother happened to be outside, they strolled over to her and courteously asked whether that young man in there was a poet? Mother was surprised at their insight, but they assured her that anyone could tell at a glance that I had the peculiar 'look' of a poetic or artistic type.

They were charming, and it is clear from some surviving notes that they were invited round to the Clemo house. In the 1946 diary there is a letter which has only been preserved because it was recycled and used for notepaper. It is addressed to Eveline Clemo from Sergeant Pierinio Serio, explaining that he is unable to come that day but would like to another time. This may well have been the same 'sergeant' mentioned in *Confession of a Rebel*, who told Eveline that Jack ought to be in Florence, his own home town. The Italians enjoyed a warm welcome, with a striking level of freedom around the villages and intimacy with the villagers. Indeed, the Italians were sometimes rather too warmly received: 'The Italian prisoners were the chief causes of scandal: with their feline grace and self-assurance they were irresistibly fascinating not only to the young girls but to many middle-aged women.' It all made Jack wonder 'how much I'm missing through my deafness – what a novel I could have made with an Italian hero if I knew their stories. Still, God knows it all and must have a true purpose in mind.'[256]

On the back of that letter from Sergeant Pierinio Serio is a series of notes from Eveline to Jack. This was how they communicated after Clemo had turned deaf, Eveline writing on scraps of paper and passing them over for Jack to see. These notes invite the reader to consider an alternative future for Clemo, apparently influenced by conversations with the visiting Italians:

> We ought to have been able to start on a fish and chips business somewhere, there is a good living in that. I can't see for the life of me why you should ever have started writing if it wasn't your job, we didn't either one choose it.

After all, she wrote, if the novels are rejected yet again 'it looks almost as if faith is a failure and that cannot be, or life would appear meaningless.' 'If [the manuscripts] do come back it will be a great blow to my faith. I shall feel lost in a bog'. Jack tried to tell her it was his destiny to write, but Eveline was having a moment of doubt: 'Then why have you been led on so long'. The exchange offers us the alternative image of Jack as a thwarted novelist living behind a village fish and chip shop.

The Italians had a practical reason for befriending Jack and Eveline. They could not freely receive or send letters from the prison camp without them being 'closely scrutinized', so they used the Clemo address. This way, they could write whatever they liked without fear of their correspondence being read. Clemo writes in *Confession* that they were all love letters, often to local girls, a fact he considered a bitter mockery of his own romantic failures.

Jack was also one of the only people nearby with a typewriter, which drew a new contact into the cottage who would prove influential to his poetry. Brenda Snell was a local girl who visited the house now and then, first with her sister Sheila and later with her friend Genevieve Jago. The initial reason for their visits was that Brenda's brother, Reg, had been taken prisoner at the fall of Singapore in 1942 and the Japanese would only allow prisoners to receive typed letters twice a year. When the time came, they would take their letter to the Clemo cottage and Jack would type it up. The Snell girls became friendly with some of the evacuees, and so also with Jack, and Brenda inspired the poems 'The Token', 'The Burnt Bush', 'Surrender', 'Shuttered', and 'Intimate Landscape'. In 1945, Brenda was the herald of good news: 'I opened the door late last evening to find Sheila and Brenda outside, come up to tell me the war was over'. It was 'VE-Day – at last!'[257]

Brenda was unaware of the scale of her influence on Clemo's poetry, and of his romantic consideration of her. She knew only that the poem 'The Token', printed in *Confession*, was about her. Of the five Brenda-inspired poems, 'The Burnt Bush' is the most striking, and the narrative was based on a real event. In interview, Brenda did not recall it, but it is mentioned in Clemo's diary. It was, in fact, David, the young brother of Pat and Doris, who set fire to a gorse bush one day in July 1947, though it was Brenda who 'set fire' to Clemo:

> She fired the gorse – fired too
> One gnarled old bush of Adam's seed
> Which in a cleft of naked need
> Within my soul had fouled indeed
> White purity, and as it grew
>   Spread doubts in scent and hue.

The boy, David, had arrived at the cottage in 1944 with Pat and their little sister Rita, following the Doodlebug threat. The cottage was now overfull, with Irene, Pat, Rita and David, as well as Bertha, Eveline and Jack, all together in the four-roomed cottage. But while Pat and Irene were favourites of Jack's, it was the more mature village girl, Brenda Snell, who had the real impact on the next phase of his life and work: poetry.

Most of the girls had felt the war keenly in the twelve months leading up to its end. Brenda and Sheila lost their brother Reg on 23 June 1945. He was imprisoned on Borneo, where he died, aged 24. The previous year, the Jaunceys, too, had been dealt a blow, when in August the Clemos received word that their mother had died. Their father had written to Eveline, telling her the news but asking that she not inform the girls. Instead, he wrote them a separate letter, pretending that their mother was 'in the country'. The Clemos did not approve of this deception: 'In the evening mother thought it best to tell the children the truth. They have taken it very badly'. A few months later and Irene's family were suffering: 'Today we've had news of tragedy [...] – V-bomb fell in their garden last Sat – her uncle killed, aunt and cousins in hospital.'[258]

Jack and Eveline had a difficult task with the girls, caring for them in an alien and uncertain environment away from their parents, raising them through their early teenage years, and being responsible for their discipline and education while their families were under fire in London. And Jack's role was an unusual one. Partly he was an over-sized playmate, but he was also an older brother and a kind of surrogate father-figure, concerning himself with their wellbeing:

> Troubled a bit about the girls. Mother and I have tried to get them interested in reading good story books instead of knitting every evening, but they don't seem able to grasp anything beyond fairy-tales.[259]

In particular, Jack worried about the girls when they were in London, or due to go back. He had read many stories in the newspapers about the city's depravity, and in a puritanical fashion aimed his concern again at the hazardous and abhorrent act of dancing. It remains unclear exactly why Clemo held this lifelong phobic moral revulsion, but here it resurfaces as he worries about the girls 'flocking to dances and contracting V.D.'[260] A year later:

> Ruffled too by the daily reports of a London murder trial – a prostitute sentenced to death – and a year or two ago she was an innocent girl in Wales ruined thro' dancing and the modern craze for glamour.[261]

Once more: 'Much discussion about dancing being allowed on Methodist premises. Nothing to be surprised at: the Churches have been spiritual brothels for years.'[262] Dancing and promiscuity were indivisible to Jack, and he worried that busy city life would lure the evacuee girls away from his faith and towards destruction. When the war was over and the girls were recalled by their parents, Jack was concerned for their moral resolve. He would also miss them personally, their company, play and the happiness he felt around them. The house would feel empty again – just Jack, Eveline and Bertha – and the village girls would stop visiting. There would be no contact with anyone prospectively marriageable.

Sorrowfully, Jack counted down the days before the girls had to leave, a sadness made more poignant by the progress of his writing. At the end of May 1945, *Wilding Graft* had been sent to the agent Raymond Savage, and by the time he had received Savage's note of receipt the evacuees were being removed. The diary shows Jack crying helplessly at the prospect of their leaving, until:

> I can hardly believe it, but they are gone and God has not delivered me in any way – went to Nanpean with the luggage – we all broke down out by the corner, mother crying first and then all the children – and I came back feeling the good news *must* come.[263]

Jack waited anxiously by the door for this good news to arrive, hoping daily for letters from publishers or news of the girls. The post held a signal importance in his life, and is recorded in the diaries with urgent frequency. It was Clemo's only interaction with the world beyond the cottage walls. He was friendless and detached from others by the enclosure of his deafness, his speaking voice reduced to a quiet, breathy sibilance. He could not overhear the village gossip and conversation, let alone partake in it. By post, on the other hand, he was able to speak with literary friends, the London girls, sympathetic Christian contacts, the *Cornish Guardian* and poetry journals. Later he would await post from fans and girlfriends, as well as from other artists and writers: Cecil Day Lewis, Charles Causley, Lionel Miskin, Frances Bellerby, A.L. Rowse, E.W. Martin and D.S. Savage. It was through the post that he was able to hold conversations and receive the world. It held an almost magical fascination, constantly remarked upon. It was through the mail that Jack's life was transformed.

As he waited for the agent's response to the novels, Clemo continued to read and write. He was now working on some of his most exciting poetry. 'Prisoner of God', 'Christ in the Clay-Pit', 'A Calvinist in Love' and 'New Creation' were written this year, as well as sufficient minor poems to compile a manuscript and a further seven thousand words to the autobiography. It was the period of Clemo's greatest output, written against the backdrop of war and an uncertain future.

War had suggested to Clemo the most natural and appropriate of metaphors, with threat and personal destruction being all-consuming symbols of his existence. The literary device of a fallen world, incidental to the real divine drama being lived within it, might have held a fourfold poignancy to Clemo, having matured and written so much of his work through a war that ravaged towns and country alike; having been raised on a land perpetually consumed by the clayworks; theologically believing in a warring Nature/God dichotomy; and having his own body and senses destroyed by syphilis. In the early and mid-1940s, these coincided with the increased work rate and maturity, the result of which will fill the following three chapters. The breakthrough began in August 1945, with Raymond Savage agreeing to represent Clemo and his latest novel.

Publication day. Clemo with *Wilding Graft*, 1948

VI
Wilding Graft

Today I begin my career as a public man. Nearly every day for the next few months people all over the country will be going into bookshops and libraries and coming out with Wilding Graft under their arms, reading it by firesides and in bed, in trains, buses and on seats in parks, discussing it with their husbands, sweethearts and friends. 'Fine book by that new writer Clemo' or else 'The most awful tripe – not a single divorce in it!' I'm quite satisfied about the book itself, looking back on the wonderful 'education' that led me step by step to the writing of it, and I do believe that the best is yet to be through my Irma . . . A thrilling morning, receiving the parcel of presentation copies, reading the blurb – 'great things expected' – God must vindicate all this promise and confidence. Sent off copies to Barbara and Savage – I trust God to guide now for it is an hour of destiny.

Diary, 4 March 1948

Clemo's debut novel, *Wilding Graft*, was released on 4 March 1948. In England it was published by Chatto & Windus, and in America by Macmillan. Soon after, it was also translated into Swedish and published as *Hon Kom Till Sist* ('She Came at Last') by J.A. Lindblads. Jack received a welcome advance of £40 for this Swedish issue and it sold 400 copies in the first few months, but it was not to be a sensational hit.

The title *Wilding Graft* immediately suggests some of the novel's influences and intentions. It was taken from Robert Browning's 'Prince Hohenstiel-Schwangau, Saviour of Society':

> The seed o' the apple tree
> Brings forth another tree which bears a crab:
> 'Tis the great gardener grafts the excellence
> On wildings where he will.

'Wildings' are self-sown crab apples, onto which fancier or better-tasting varieties are grafted. The grafting of a finer variety onto a sturdier one is intended to make the grafted tree hardier and stronger, and the 'great gardener' of Browning's poem is God, who chooses which rootstock to graft onto. The crude, rough crab apple is transformed into a fine and fruitful tree. This metaphor is given greater depth by the discussion of the grafting of wild olives in Karl Barth's *The Epistle to the Romans* – a favourite text of Clemo's at this time – especially the passages describing the nature of the hybrid olive, when a 'wild' branch is grafted onto a 'good' olive tree. The process is described as 'contrary to nature' in the passage Barth is illuminating, from Romans 11. God, Barth says, 'is the holy root of the tree', and the wild branches are cut from their natural, fallen olive tree and grafted on to the tree of God. Barth's discussion parallels Clemo's belief that there are two possible paths in life: the natural, fallen path of fate into which we are all born, and the sacred, salvaged path of predestination to which we may turn. Clemo's insertion of this theology into the crude setting and plot of *Wilding Graft* is one of its most potent curiosities; the epic story of God's involvement in the world and invasion of individuals narrated within such a small, bleak, cruel-spirited mining region:

> No one guessed that a hamlet on one of the most remote ridges of the district was now the scene of a spiritual drama whose grandeur, stain of bled sap and scars of grafting, would have shown them the proper use of crisis and the conditions of success in any appeal for Divine intervention.[264]

The narrative of *Wilding Graft* begins on 24 January 1940 at Meledor, with Garth Joslin, the hero, returning home to his four-roomed granite claywork cottage after burying his mother at Bodmin Asylum. Garth had previously been in a relationship with Edith Chirgwin, who had since married Seth Spragg. This relationship turned sour when Garth's mother showed signs of mental illness, but only ended after a scandal, in which Garth had been physically intimate with a fifteen year-old girl named Irma Stribley, whose character is loosely based on the evacuee Irene. Originally, Irma's family were from the area, but her father had embezzled money in St Stephen and they had run away to London for a fresh start. Both of Irma's parents were unfaithful, but especially her father, who had so many affairs that in the end he killed himself. The novel begins four years after Irma's encounter with Garth. Irma is believed to still be in London, and Garth is suffering from missing her, as well as from the malice of the villagers following the scandal. A man named Griffiths appears on the scene, delivering atheist and pacifist pamphlets and becoming romantically interested in Minnie Lagor, who has an illegitimate daughter by the scoundrel Ted Blewett, a man said to have 'carried on wi' the maidens once too often and gone and hanged hisself'. Griffiths was a Welshman who had lived in London and escaped to Cornwall after his wife killed herself following a bad extramarital relationship. By now, the quantity of suicides will seem staggering, and it shows the causal connection Clemo made between extra-marital sex and despair.

Griffiths is the antagonist, a Hardyesque fatalist and anti-theist, rather than a real atheist. He is the counterpart to Garth, who is based on Clemo and believes that suffering is a necessary part of the journey towards his God-ordained destiny, a belief proved correct by the end of the novel. When Minnie Lagor's illegitimate daughter is killed in an accident, it is Garth who finds the body, and while she is mourning for her daughter, Garth comforts her with his faith, which leads to her rejection of Griffiths. As Minnie is explaining to Griffiths how Garth had helped her, she learns that Garth's old love, Irma, has evacuated to Truro, so that Minnie, now converted to Garth's faith, becomes convinced that everything is working towards Irma and Garth meeting again. Griffiths is furious with Garth for turning Minnie against him, and envious that his faith appeared to be proving correct. Minnie tells Garth that Irma is back and Garth goes wandering the streets of Truro in search of her, at the same time as she is in search of him. She finally catches sight of him entering the Cathedral and follows, providing the climax of the story. But all is not yet resolved, as Griffiths becomes more and more menacing. There is a fear of threat to Irma, so Garth brings her and the evacuee children she was caring for to his cottage at Meledor. Griffiths arrives there in the night, has a heart attack in a claypit and is rescued in the morning by Garth.

The abundance of characters is intimidating at first, Clemo weaving around forty people into the narrative. But he draws them tighter and tighter together until it becomes clear that every seemingly unrelated detail and event was pressing Garth and Irma back to one another. It is neatly structured, and in terms of style and period difficult to pin down. With regard to speech and realism, the novel feels overwhelmingly modern, but it has an unusual supernatural pulse. The region's social dynamics are well observed, and

Clemo uses the intimacies, gossip and tensions of the rural-industrial hamlets and villages to drive the plot.

A natural comparison from the period might be Graham Greene's *The Heart of the Matter*, which was published the same year as *Wilding Graft*. Both Clemo and Greene were Christian novelists, although their styles, lives and religion were markedly different. Greene was a Catholic from a large family and wealthier background. He travelled extensively and undertook spy work in Africa with MI6. He had a wealth of experience, and this shows in the complexity of his characters and the ease of his descriptive writing. By contrast, Clemo's characters are confined, stiflingly held within a small, local setting, and Clemo's prose almost growls with tension and frustration. This is the potency of a limited setting, the intensity of isolation, that Clemo had admired in Hardy, Powys, Emily Brontë and in Besier's play.

Contrasting Greene and Clemo shows just how unique Clemo was. Even within the context of Christian writers, he was an outsider, practically solitary, overwhelmingly outnumbered by Catholics and Anglicans. The same was true of his optimism. The story of *Wilding Graft* is of two young people finding happiness and fulfilment. The story of *The Heart of the Matter* is of a couple falling apart, of 'the pain inevitable in any human relationship'. 'To be a human being', Greene wrote, 'one had to drink the cup'. As the hero tries to do good in a place of undisguised cruelty and malice, he only causes more pain, more guilt, more suffering, more responsibility, and, in the end, he kills himself. Greene's story opens with marriage and ends in despair. It is Clemo's narrative in reverse.

Wilding Graft emerged into a market largely defined by pessimism, misery and dirty realism. Camus, Sartre, Orwell, Hemingway, Norman Mailer and Gore Vidal were just a few of the major novelistic figures of this period. Clemo's optimism and nonconformism were breaking new ground, so that the novel appears at once contemporary and antiquated. It is Hardy with a happy ending, though it also shares some of the unfashionable qualities of cheap melodrama. There is much lip-biting, lurching, writhing and sharp intaking of breath. These betray Clemo's literary history; the immaturity and hyperbole of the 'Cuckoospit' sequence. They are relics of a youthful style and are relatively infrequent in *Wilding Graft*, though this only makes them stand out all the more starkly. The following passage is probably the worst offender. Garth, having discovered that Irma is in Cornwall again, walks out late at night, where his silhouette is observed by chance:

> Just after midnight Colly Snell got out of bed to fetch brandy for his wife, who was threatened with a heart attack. He drew aside the curtain and stepping close to the window he peered out, up towards the ridge of the downs. The sky was moonless but brilliant with stars scarcely filmed now by any cloud. Colly noted the familiar landmarks, and he saw too, with sudden astonishment, that on Meledor pyramid a human shape thickened the bar of the fence beside the tip platform. The figure stood like a sentinel, facing west, alone with the night wind, mysteriously remote in starshine. As Colly watched the young man half turned, wafting kisses out along the sky, then remained with both arms stretched in vehement yearning towards Truro.

The passage follows a chapter of straight realistic dialogue, so that the 'wafting kisses' and 'arms stretched in vehement yearning' seem almost comic. Such mawkish behavior sharply contradicts the picture of the tough, clayworking character Clemo had been building. And it is made worse by discovering Irma doing the same fifty pages later, 'wafting kisses up towards his home'. The genre of melodrama was populist and said to have been preferred by the working people of the clay country, and it may be that Clemo was influenced so heavily by the form because it, along with religious literature, provided the literary context of his youth. Certainly Eveline Clemo admitted to a misspent girlhood reading the Hockings.

If *Wilding Graft* stood out from other British novels of the time, how much more did it stand out within the Cornish literary scene? Clemo's brutal portrayal of the clay country's working people, his dark and vibrant evangelism, his cultural background and geography, were sharply contrasted against the other bestselling novels of the period, such as Winston Graham's *Poldark* series, or Daphne du Maurier's Cornish novels. While his Cornish contemporaries were writing about Celtic wildernesses or wealthy families in romantic landscapes, Clemo was writing about waste dumps and quarry roads, hardness and poverty, and writing about them with a surprising beauty.

The relationship between people – particularly men – and their environment stands out in Clemo's writing. People both define and are defined by the china clay mining landscape. It employs and houses them, and they wander along the industry-built paths and lanes to work, school or to chapel. They live in and by the clay country. Man and place are interdependent, even though that relationship is dynamic and destructive, as the moorland rocks are exploded, the pit-faces blasted, and kaolin extracted. On top of this 'natural' relationship, there is a third figure looming supernaturally over the countryside: God. 'Nature' and God stand in opposition, and man stands inbetween the two, a child of 'Nature' whose divinity needs to be forced upon him. Man's connectedness with the natural world is assumed in Clemo's picture, and it is at the heart of the problem. He is born natural – that is, fallen. The prose of *Wilding Graft* reflects this strange connection and boundary between the landscape, people and God, as they blur and interact:

> To Seth and Martin the landscape meant nothing at all, yet as they impressed themselves upon it, passing between the high hedges overhung here and there by stunted, misshapen trees, their figures blended with a mood, a pervasive power that dwarfed their humanity to a symbol.

The villages and houses do not stand apart from the clay pits and moorlands, but all fill the same space:

> St Stephen gleamed just opposite – church tower, trees, rows of houses thinning out north-east towards the vast pyramidal wedges of clay-dunes driven upward from the bleaker folds of moorland.

Village, clay and moor are the same environment, the same place, essentially connected. It is shown again in the following passage, where the liveliness of the landscape is diminished by the Easter holidays:

> The labourers had been on holiday since Thursday, and the huts, pit-workings and mica beds had taken on an aggrieved air of neglect. The waggon stood motionless on the track, a dull sullen shape about which the wind whistled and the rain poured, dripping from its frame, mingling with the tar of an underlying roller, and oozing slowly like black treacle into the cracks between the rotting sleepers.

Both the 'mood' of the landscape and the details of it are used to reflect the fallen state of man and his purgative suffering at God's invasive will. But behind this metaphor and symbolism is Clemo's own unique intimacy with the place, and the clay-miners' ecological relationship.

The destructive landscape symbolism will be seen in its strongest form when considering the poetry of *The Clay Verge*. In *Wilding Graft* it is slightly less imposing, though there is a chronological as well as a geographical setting to the story that heightens the symbolism and mirrors the jeopardy of the individual. That is, the war. Nevertheless, the horrors of war are secondary to the salvation of individuals, an observation that draws us back to Clemo and how his biography imposes on the novel.

Wilding Graft was begun when Jack was twenty-five, the same age as Garth. Indeed, most of the characters were based on real people, some to the extent that when it came to publication the libel lawyers asked him to change details, such as the names of Cora and Irving, who had to become Bella and Martin Stribley. In a letter to A.L. Rowse, soon after publication, Jack wrote:

> Incidentally, the woman I portrayed as Bella has read the book, knowing she is the original, yet instead of suing me for libel she tells my mother it's 'a wonderful

book, as gripping as *Wuthering Heights*' – which I lent her the other day. One must be prepared for paradoxes if one lives in contact with these folk.²⁶⁵

He was also asked to change details about Minnie Lagor, but he assured the lawyers and publishers that nobody else could be recognised. This was not quite true, as a letter from Barbara suggested, in which she tells Jack – perhaps intending to wound him – that she recognised everyone in the book except for Irma. Irma was a compound of Irene and Barbara, with aspects of the other evacuees. For instance, the name of Irma's stepfather was Slade, which was also the evacuee Joan's surname, and the heroine lived in Stoke Newington, from where both the Jauncey family and Irene came. The other London placename mentioned notably is Dulwich, Joan's evacuated home. Years later, in a letter to Ruth, Clemo listed the bases of some of the characters:

> Edith is Evelyn, Seth is her brother Harry, Bella is Irene's foster-mother, Sal is my grandmother Esther, Minnie is Gladys, Colly Snell an old man I knew in my youth – his real name was Sam Snell.²⁶⁶

It is the carpenter Garth, however, who is most relevant to the biography, being an idealised version of Jack himself, as well as inviting conscious comparisons with Christ and Job. Garth is described as 'sphinxish' in appearance, reflecting the religio-mystic aspect of his character, but also a physical description that Clemo applied to his own profile, along with 'leonine'. Garth is handsome and rugged, desired by women, favoured by God and freshly recovered from illness. He wins all his arguments, his enemies all fall, and he gets the girl. This is the happy ending Jack had been promised, free from disabilities and suffering, no longer living with his mother, and betrothed. Yet Garth is a complete character, 'one of the most underrated in Cornish fiction', according to the writer Alan Kent. Although Garth is an idealisation of Jack, his flaws were not omitted, but rather the novel shows how the flaws and setbacks were to be overcome. Aside from the hyperbolic emotional moments, the character is a well-conceived working-class hero. He is not a caricature of a simple villager, but a clearly realised individual.

Clemo believed the novel was 'given to me by God as a prophecy for my own life',[267] and as such it developed extra significance. He did not consider it to be a projection or fantasy, but rather his own future fictionalised: first healing and then marriage, with both imminent. He even began to interpret the world by holding it up against *Wilding Graft*, as though the novel had become a sacred text. Previously, his life had driven the fiction, but now the fiction was driving his life. Sometimes it was an innocuous comparison: 'Was upset last night to hear that J. has gone to France for a holiday. Felt like Garth when he heard Irma was enjoying herself in London'.[268] Or: 'I go out after dark and pour out my heart to God – like Garth.'[269] But when he came across a new romantic infatuation, he began to look for the novelistic pattern, the strange ways they might be drawing towards one another according to God's will. In turn he would refer to prospective lovers Barbara, Irene, June, Eileen and Susie each as his Irma.

Jack's disabilities, too, impose on and are solved by the novel. Garth is said to have been seriously ill just before the story begins, a statement with little narrative value, but with considerable personal meaning, as it afforded Jack the opportunity to heal himself in his writing. These disabilities might be evident in other aspects of the prose. In particular, it is tempting to question whether his poor sight is revealed in descriptive choices, especially the repetition of the word 'blob'. A group of walkers is hidden behind 'a blob of trees'; a strip of verdure in Truro is a 'foaming green blob'; cottages lining the road to Virginia were 'dark blobs'; and on Meledor dune was 'the dark blob of the thicket'. A reader is also shown the figure of Bella Stribley, 'superimposed upon the scene like a gliding blot'.

As well as an idealization of Clemo, Garth is similar to some of Thomas Hardy's characters, particularly to Yeobright from *The Return of the Native*, the high-thinking working man, as Jack observed in his 1944 diary. Chatto & Windus thought the similarity between Clemo's work and Hardy's marketable, which was why they invited the comparison in the blurb and on the jacket of the first edition. Yet in *Confession*, Clemo wrote:

> I was nearly thirty before I read any of Hardy's mature works. Those reviewers who thought I was deliberately imitating Hardy in *Wilding Graft* did not know that I had been writing in that vein for ten years before I felt the stimulus of Hardy's influence.[270]

This passage is misleading. *Wilding Graft* was begun in December 1941, following an intense reading of Thomas Hardy's later works. Clemo was twenty-five when he read both *Jude the Obscure* and *Tess of the D'Urbervilles*, and within just a few weeks he was writing in his diary about a new idea for a novel: 'Dull weather – nothing to do now but wait for the … growth of that "Wilding Graft".'[271] The intention of Clemo's deception is obvious; he wants to replace the idea of Hardy's influence on *Wilding Graft* with the suggestion that he and Hardy are temperamentally similar and supernaturally connected. The claim that he was 'nearly thirty' is vague enough for him to feel that he is not being dishonest, but it very obviously leads the reader to imagine that he was reading Hardy *after* the novel had been finished, submitted and accepted, rather than just weeks before it was begun. Not only was Jack deeply ensconced in Hardy's writing immediately before planning his latest novel, but he continued to read Hardy's novels and life throughout the writing process, beginning in the New Year of 1942 with *The Return of the Native* and the *Life* written by Florence and Thomas Hardy. He read and re-read these books and congratulated himself when he had written a passage similar to Hardy's: 'I've been so tickled today reading chap. VIII scene – very Hardyish in humour'; 'scene between Garth and Edith – very tense and gripping, like Hardy's Clym-Eustacia scene in "Ret. of the Native" when he charges her with murdering his mother.'[272] The scale of the influence is further suggested by a diary entry written immediately after Clemo had flicked through *Jude* and *Tess* in 1941: 'I feel my work will be the Christian counterpart of his'.[273] In 1944, he made a similar remark: 'dipping into Return of the Native, feeling how close it is to my own outlook and that my life-work *must* lie in the production of similar work from the Christian standpoint'.[274] Clemo saw himself as the optimistic mirror of Hardy.

Clemo and Hardy had the same rural and working-class concerns, and used the landscape, destructive gossip and propriety in similar ways. The difference was Hardy's anti-theism, which led him to propose a kind of fatalism. There seem to be two fatalistic drivers in the later works of Hardy, the 'nature' inherited from one's ancestors, and the 'irresistible law' of some 'sinister intelligence'.[275] The 'sinister intelligence' appears often like a God, although not a benevolent one. The deity suggested in *Jude* and *Tess* is a malicious torturer, plotting a course of destruction for those on whom he focuses his attention. There is also the suggestion in Hardy that one might be of a right or 'wrong breed for marriage',[276] which parallels Clemo's 'faith in my "election" for marriage'.[277] Fatalism, inherited characteristics, gossip, romance, marriage, landscape and symbolism – the comparison was inevitable. But the great difference was that Clemo did not believe that suffering and misery were the inevitable conclusions of life. There was the other way, the Christian path to joy and fulfilment, guided by God.

In 1942, when reading the Hardys' (auto)biography, Clemo reflected on their differences:

> Rather saddened – I've been much moved in reading Hardy's Life: there are such problems to face when one gets outside the rut in which most people live. I know I'm fundamentally of the same artistic type as Hardy, *compelled* to approach things from a new angle and be honest, ruthlessly honest with myself whatever religions perish for me thereby. And if Christ had not broken down the screen between my soul and His ultimate truth, I should not be able to help *not* believing any more than I can now help believing. I should then have been a Hardy – by whose fault? . . . I know he's wrong, yet I'm not shocked by his blasphemies: but for the force of God they are what *I* should have written.[278]

God battered down the wall between Clemo's soul and the 'truth' of God. In this way, God showed Clemo preference, but ignored Hardy.

There is a pleasing footnote to add to the contrast between

Hardy's perceived pessimism and Clemo's optimism, written into the margin of Jack's copy of *Jude*. Where Hardy quotes Browning's 'By the Fire-side', and describes Browning as 'the last of the optimists', Jack has scribbled: 'Slightly incorrect – but T.H. couldn't be expected to know who would be born in 1916.'

Hardy was not the only influence, of course. Another Dorset writer, T.F. Powys, was still a favourite, and Powys's portrayals of the village 'fallen woman' bear a marked similarity to Clemo's, in character and also in the writer's sympathies. Then, single phrases, such as the 'quenching of Shirley's clay' to indicate Shirley's death, owe something to Powys's *Unclay*. Other influences included Emily and Charlotte Brontë, and Thornton Wilder's *The Bridge of San Luis Rey*. For a better understanding of these influences there is a helpful series of charts in the 1943 diary showing all of Clemo's reading from 1943 to 1947 and marking it with scores out of a hundred. There are four columns to the charts. The first column shows the author and work read, while the other three show the qualities to be marked: 'General Interest', 'Artistic Quality' and 'Usefulness'. Predictably, Powys, Hardy and C.S. Lewis feature prominently and receive some of the best marks, with Powys's scores going up after Jack received a letter from him. Before then, *Soliloquies of a Hermit* had scored a poor 10-80-20, and his *Interpretation of Genesis* an awful 5-30-10. Only *The Left Leg* fared well in 1943, with a 90-90-30, giving an average score equalled and beaten only by a few obscure books, such as Osbert Burdett's biography of the Brownings (80-60-70), Nicholson's *Man and Literature* (90-60-80), and the unexpected top entry of the year, Beverley Nichols' *The Fool Hath Said* (90-70-95), a testimonial book of the sort Clemo keenly devoured. Occasionally, Clemo returned to a book and reconsidered its value. Burdett's high-scoring work on the Brownings, for instance, received a second score in 1947 of 30-10-20, while *The Life of Thomas Hardy*, once a favourite, was later given a dismal 10-10-10. Yet this is nothing to the 0-0-0 for popular novelist I.A.R. Wylie's *Prelude to Richard*. Robert Browning hardly appears on the charts at all, in the same way as the Bible does not. He was, nevertheless, read on an almost weekly basis, and Clemo elsewhere mentions that 'Pauline', 'By the Fire-Side' and 'Evelyn Hope' were strong influences on *Wilding Graft*.

Still, it was the inspiration of Hardy that set *Wilding Graft* in motion, and by 1942 Clemo had not only an outline for the novel, but plans for two sequels, to form a second trilogy. This would begin with *Wilding Graft* at the start of the war, then continue with 'Hired Razor' and finish with 'Mainmast'. Their titles came from familiar sources; the Book of Isaiah[279] and Browning's 'By the Fire-Side'. Not a great deal is known about the two novels, and only a few lines in the beginning of the 1942 diary offer any details. 'The Hired Razor' was to be set at Karslake, while 'Mainmast' was to be set in St Austell town and at the docks. In the same set of notes, Clemo shows that he already had some fairly clear ideas about *Wilding Graft*:

> Wilding Graft: Hero a clay labourer of Brighton or Meledor, heroine a London evacuee billeted at Truro. Story shaped round police-court case (newspaper cutting, Cornwall Gazette, Sept 17, 1941) – ~~parents~~ mother returns to London, this girl, 17, left in charge – her father a deserter from the army. She'd stayed near hero's home 4 yrs earlier when his girl got in trouble with another man. He lives with aunt, is artistic (one scene set in Truro Museum Art Gallery). His first girl ~~dies~~ (wife of the other man) at opening of book.

We learn in this diary that at one stage in the novel's conception Griffith's wife and Irma's father were going to gas themselves together, a death not fully explored in the finished novel. We also find that the heroine is intended to die: 'Should the end be tragic – Irene killed by Home Guard? There's risk of bathos and incongruity in a happy-ever-after theme in war time. Possibly Irma shot in the second book.'

Neither 'The Hired Razor' nor 'Mainmast' was written, but Clemo did make a start on 'The Hired Razor'. It was to be 'set during the Battle of Britain, showing God using the Nazis' "razor" to shave off the superfluous outgrowths of our national life'.[280] In May 1944: 'Today I've surprised myself by writing 2,000 words or more to – The Hired Razor – workmen's talk of Kurt, Garth and Bryan, for one of the early chapters'.[281] This was the only writing done to 'The

Hired Razor', and it has not survived. Within a few months, Jack was returning to the old manuscripts again. This was frustrating for Clemo's publisher, as it was unanimously agreed by the agents, readers and reviewers that the second book was bound to be better. Indeed, Robert Hale had stated that if Savage did not find a home for *Wilding Graft* then he would take it, on the belief 'that the next book this author writes may well be an exceptionally good novel'.[282] It has already been seen that instead of a new novel, Clemo sent Hale 'Unsunned Tarn', and Hale retracted his offer.

Wilding Graft had been written fairly quickly, with seventy-five thousand words ready by December 1942 and a good full draft completed on 27 April 1943:

> Today *Wilding Graft* stands complete in typescript – 481 pages – 105,000 words – my longest and strongest book to date. My next job will be the final revision of *Private Snow* before submitting it for the contest.

Several novels were sent to competitions, and Jack used the letter from Q as a reference in his cover letters. But success only came when Clemo stopped submitting the weak old typescripts and instead started to think more seriously about *Wilding Graft*. The epiphany came on 22 March 1945:

> CB have returned [Roche Snow] – no chance for it yet, and I feel it can't be God's will for me to start with that book. I've been spared weeks of suspense and didn't feel the blow as I know R. S. isn't outstanding. May God lead me – I feel drawn to venture with W. G. next – God can't have let me write that for nothing.

Clemo is showing great resilience persisting with this worldview. It has taken him ten years of rejection to conclude that it might not be God's will for 'Roche Snow' to be his first published novel. Added to this, he believes that God must have let him write *Wilding Graft* for a reason. It is unclear whether Clemo believed that God let him write 'Roche Snow' (or any of the other failed novels) 'for nothing', but presumably he did not hold this belief. He had two ways out. Firstly, he might imagine that 'Roche Snow' would be published after *Wilding Graft*, justifying it. When this does not happen, all the failed novels could then be considered preparation for the real thing, in the same way that, romantically speaking, Evelyn, Violet, Barbara, Irene, Brenda, Eileen, Susie, June, Rosine and Mary would be considered preparation for his eventual wife, Ruth.

It was a good decision, at any rate, and after only a couple of rejections, on 29 May 1945 the manuscript was sent to Raymond Savage, the well-respected literary agent whose clients had included T.E. Lawrence and George Bernard Shaw. The event was marked simply in the diary: 'To Newquay – and posted W.G. Spent most of the day on the beach.' The proof of postage was pasted in beside the entry.[283] This was his last outing with the evacuees, so it had special significance, and in the diary along with the proof of postage Jack kept a piece of seaweed from the Newquay beach.

Savage was not quick to reply, and Jack was not patient waiting. Although Clemo did not know it, Savage was exactly what a new writer needed, an honest and sympathetic agent who understood what the author was trying to achieve. He made a number of suggestions for changes, creating a list that was then augmented by various readers and publishers. He invited Clemo to send any other work he had, which included two novels and a few poems he had begun to write recently. Savage then sent all three novel manuscripts to a reader he considered 'one of the best in literary circles', Osyth Leeston. Her feedback was thorough and severe, and upset Jack. Leeston wrote that the three stories were too similar and the three heroes 'so much alike that they might well be different facets of the same person'. The dialogue, she said, 'should not consist entirely of scandal', and Clemo's 'too frequent insistence on the baser instincts of sex defeats its own end. Surely young girls may have a more sensible outlook on life than continual preoccupation with sex?'[284]

Clemo protested, but by this time Savage was beginning to understand his client and allowed himself to be a little firmer: 'I am afraid you will really have to take her and my view and get down to this or you will not get anywhere.'[285] After speaking again with Leeston, Savage wrote with further criticism:

> There is no question but that there is little justification for Garth's spiritual love for Irma as you have at present expressed it. There must be a stronger reason for this and you must show it. It does not read naturally for this great love to arise from the beginning, i.e. the incident with a girl of 12 in a tool shed. [...] There is no doubt that Irma should be a bit older, because the age of 12 is repellent. Make her 15, which is reasonable, and develop the growth of the spiritual love.[286]

With regard to Irma's age, Clemo made the necessary change 'with some reluctance, but no doubt the change made the novel more palatable to the general reader who knew nothing of the author's private life.'[287]

It was then that Clemo had his first major success. Savage had sent *Wilding Graft* along with some of Clemo's poetry to John Lehmann, a publisher involved with Hogarth Press, Penguin and, in 1946, his own company, John Lehmann Ltd. Lehmann took 'Christ in the Clay-Pit' for *Orion* magazine, and then 'A Calvinist in Love' for *Penguin New Writing*. This poetry was like nothing Clemo had written before, and the first of them, 'Christ in the Clay-Pit', remains his most important and influential poem:

> Why should I find Him here
> And not in a church, nor yet
> Where Nature heaves a breast like Olivet
> Against the stars? I peer
> Upon His footsteps in this quarried mud;
> I see His blood
> In rusty stains on pit-props, waggon-frames
> Bristling with nails, not leaves. There were no leaves
> Upon his chosen Tree,
> No parasitic flowering o'er the shames
> Of Eden's primal infidelity.
> Just splintered wood and nails
> Were fairest blossoming for Him Who speaks
> Where mica-silt outbreaks

> Like water from the side of His own clay
>   In that strange day
> When He was pierced. Here still the earth-face pales
> And rends in earthquake roarings of a blast
>   With tainted rock outcast,
> While fields and woods lie dreaming yet of peace
> 'Twixt God and His creation, of release
> From potent wrath — a faith that waxes bold
> In churches nestling snugly in the fold
> Of scented hillsides where mild shadows brood.
>   The dark and stubborn mood
> Of Him whose feet are bare upon this mire
>   And in the furnace fire
> Which hardens all the clay that has escaped,
>   Would not be understood
> By worshippers of beauty toned and shaped
> To flower or hymn. I know their facile praise
> False to the heart of me, which like this pit
> Must still be disembowelled of Nature's stain,
>   And rendered fit
> By violent mouldings through the tunnelled ways
>   Of all he would regain.[288]

Meanwhile, Lehmann remained uncertain about *Wilding Graft* because of its ending, which he said was more like a sermon than a novel. Both Savage and his partner at the firm, Stella Shattock (later Savage's wife), agreed. Lehmann offered Clemo a £20 advance, providing the last quarter of the novel was rewritten.

Jack was stunned. He did not know what Lehmann meant. How could he rewrite a quarter of the novel? In the original version, the ending does seem something of an anti-climax. Garth and Irma meet up in the Cathedral, aware that Griffiths has become violently unhinged. The couple remain in Truro with the evacuee children, staying up all night worrying and imagining that Griffiths is going to burst in at any moment. In the morning they discover that far from posing a threat, Griffiths has left Cornwall altogether and they had been worrying for nothing. Tension had been building through the book for some sort of grand conflict, and then it is all hopelessly dissipated.

Clemo wrote back to Savage and Lehmann. What was he meant to do? Cryptically, Lehmann told Jack that he should not have to spell it out. Clemo thinks Lehmann wants a violent ending, so considers killing off Griffiths, either by another suicide or in an act of heroism, 'rescuing Irma's brother or sister from the river at Truro'.[289] Then, at the end of August 1946, it came to him while out walking: 'hurried in from Slip in evening to finish writing it – the last phrases came to me out on the burrow – "We've both paid the price... and you've won, Garth."'. The new ending was better, Griffiths confessing that Garth had it right all along, but it was not the dramatic climax the publishers were hoping for. For Clemo the real climax was the romantic resolution rather than anything to do with Griffiths, but Lehmann was still unsatisfied and rejected the novel, suggesting they try the new senior editor at Chatto & Windus, Cecil Day Lewis. Almost immediately, Harold Raymond of Chatto & Windus (the man who invented book tokens) contacted Savage, and on 23 October 1946, Savage sent the following telegram to his client: 'Success has crowned all our efforts. stop chatto and windus accept wilding graft enthusiastically. stop Congratulations, writing: Raymond Savage.'

At last:

> V.G. DAY (Victory at Goonamarris)
> Tonight while I was on St. Dennis Downs – THE NEWS CAME. Telegram from S. – Chatto and W. God's chosen publisher for me as for Theodore [Powys]. At last after 15 years struggle which only God has enabled me to endure 'He has set my feet upon a rock and established my goings' [...]. I set it on record here and now that I am not beginning a worldly career but a witness for Christ [...]. It does awe me – who am I to figure in the same publishers' list as Aldous Huxley, Powys, HG Wells, Faulkner and such great intellectuals? It is the Lord's doing and marvellous in my eyes. And what joy for mother after all the tears and heartache – *her* work![290]

Knowing Clemo's poverty, Savage negotiated that an advance of £330 be paid to Clemo in instalments over the next two years. The idea was that this gave Clemo time and space to write, and it was contracted that his next two books would both have to be offered to Chatto & Windus. Terms arranged were for Jack to receive 10% of the published price up to 1500 copies, 12.5% from 1500-3000 copies sold, and 15% beyond that. Savage said he would not take any percentage until royalties were coming in. The book was dedicated 'To my mother whose faith prepared me for the grafting.'

Critically, *Wilding Graft* was considered a promising debut. The publisher's blurb invited comparisons with Hardy and Powys, and very few reviewers failed to acknowledge the similarities. Mary Ellen Chase, who had studied and published on Hardy, was especially attentive to the comparison in her review for *The New York Times*. The review was one of great support and praise for Clemo and his 'Hardian' *Wilding Graft*:

> Jack Clemo, a Cornish writer, should attract deserved attention both from those who like an excellent story and from those who are interested in the novel as a form of art […]. Mr Clemo's story possesses a certain stature seldom seen in distinctly modern fiction.[291]

Angela Milne, in the *Observer*, recognised the work as an 'act of faith':

> his sincerity is immense, his purpose, at any rate in his first book, so high as to make *Wilding Graft* most fairly described as an act of faith […]. [Jack Clemo] is a richly promising writer who should eventually distinguish himself.[292]

There were, of course, unsympathetic reviews. Orville Prescott, also writing for *The New York Times*, focused solely on the novel's flaws, such as the 'theatrical gestures' and 'picturesque' brooding of the hero. He recognised the autobiographical elements of the novel and suggested these made the lead character implausible.[293] The Cornwall-based Welsh writer, Howard Spring, shown the novel by A.L. Rowse, gave a criticism that was later echoed in Jack's correspondence with Helena Charles, although Charles wrote the problem most succinctly: 'a superficial reader might take the moral to be "if you believe in god, you get your girl. If you don't you don't."'[294] Clemo responded to this in *The Marriage of a Rebel*, where he explains the difference between desire and vocation:

> I knew that many frustrated bachelors had been theists, and some of them had prayed for a partner and never found one. But to pray for a certain pleasure because you want it was very different from receiving a divine 'grafting', a mystical sense of *vocation* which involved painful training and identified the seeker with the sufferings of Christ.

God has singled Clemo out to identify with Christ through a special desire for marriage and a course of suffering preparing him for it. By turning to Christ, Clemo handed the erotic desire over to Him, as though purifying it. In spite of false predictions, in spite of the strange messages with regard to young girls, and in spite of Clemo's prayers not being answered, he still believed in his own prophecies and interpretations of the patterns in his life. Those false starts were redefined as 'painful training', and he remained certain that the next prophecy would come true, that all his prayers and desires would be answered imminently – especially those relating to healing, fame and women.

This position naturally raises questions about the role of suffering in Clemo's life. C.S. Lewis, who influenced Clemo a great deal during the 1940s, wrote of suffering as a necessary possibility in a free world granted by God: 'We are not merely imperfect creatures who must be improved', Lewis wrote, but 'rebels who must lay down our arms.'[295] But the problem goes back to creation. How did God make the first beings capable of sinning? That is not to ask, 'How did He allow man the freedom to sin?', but how was it in man's nature to sin? This is a problem suggested by Lewis, and attempted by Niebuhr, another important influence on Clemo.

Clemo did not resolve the issue, but focused his writing more on the role of suffering in his own life, which was complicated by his personal experience. On the one hand, suffering to him was a 'test':

> there are times when God's hand is clenched, the promised blessing withheld and concealed. These are trying periods – until the believer dares to look above the clenched hand of God and catch the twinkle in His eye.[296]

The sense is of God having a benevolent purpose behind the clenched fist. It is an image borrowed from Powys's collection of stories, *God's Eyes A-Twinkle*. As well as a test, or a necessary delaying of joy, suffering might also be a punishment for the sins of his progenitors: 'The "ancestral mesh" was an indisputable fact. [...] My handicaps belonged to the world of my pagan forebears'.[297] Jack was suffering because of their mistakes, although he was also purifying the nature he inherited. The inherited syphilis from his father's sexual straying in Montana meant that Clemo's own path to God had to be sexual, curing the venereal sin and disease he inherited. And here we touch on one of the keys to understanding Clemo's writing. The redemption of sex was spiritual and physical, and the signal of full redemption would be marriage and healing.

While the suffering was beneficial, Clemo still wrote that it 'taught me nothing'. However, it 'created the conditions in which joy could teach me'.[298] He did not believe it was his destiny to suffer, yet he did suffer, and there is a conflict between his belief that he was intended to be happy and the observation of his perpetual suffering and frustration. To an outsider, God appeared either indifferent to the idea of Clemo's happiness, or hostile to it.

Expressions of faith in *Wilding Graft* caused a good deal of consternation to reviewers. Maurice Lane Richardson, writing in the *Times Literary Supplement*, gave a mixed review, praising Clemo for his depiction of the region and recognising his potential, but criticising him for including too much 'mystical religiosity' and not enough 'humanism'.[299] Such criticism would have thrilled Clemo, who identified himself as a mystic and loathed humanism, but it shows how the framework for receiving a novel such as his was not ubiquitously acknowledged.

Overwhelmingly the criticism was positive and *Wilding Graft* was considered an astonishing debut. So highly was it rated that the neighbours and villagers could not believe Jack had written it. He was to them a brooding misfit, an undesirable. In an interview with Radio 2, Eveline Clemo said: 'Some of them wouldn't believe that he wrote it [...]. They think his mother done it.'[300] This sentiment is still repeated occasionally in the villages today, a testament to both how little some people thought of Jack and how much of Eveline.

Financially and emotionally, this success was a relief. After having sat day after day hunched at his writing bureau, Clemo was now an international success, held up for comparison against his literary heroes and boasting UK sales of two thousand copies in the first week alone. Letters of approbation came in from A.L. Rowse and T.F. Powys, reviews were aired on the radio, congratulations given in the local press and announcements made on Clemo in the chapels. The praise gave him confidence, so that even when a rogue bad review arrived, such as that by the distinguished scholar Gorley Putt, he seemed hardly to care at all, joking idly in the corner of his 1948 diary:

> There was a bright critic called Gorley
> Who read Clemo's work and said 'Surely
> The critics are daft
> Who applaud Wilding Graft:
> – I think of it ever so poorly.'

But the excitement was short-lived. Within a few months, gloom and depression returned. Jack found himself just as lonely as before, and the absence of romantic achievement seemed to him a 'harsh mockery' of *Wilding Graft*'s message and success. It had been the same story when the novel was accepted and Chatto & Windus had forwarded a large cheque. Initially he had thanked God for relieving the lifelong burden of grim poverty from his mother, but the lustre of comparative wealth and sated ambition wore off within days. The Clemos had puritanical tastes, so once the bills could be met they had little use for money. They did not go out, drink or travel, and it was not really until 1956 that Clemo did something even close to extravagant:

> Today I've done what is from the standpoint of common sense one of the most foolish things I ever did – spent £13 on a gramophone in faith that I shall soon hear Renee's record.[301]

'Renee' was the American evangelical Renee Martz, who became famous in Britain in 1947, when at the age of seven she sang, preached and trumpeted her 'hot gospel' message to thousand-strong crowds. The recklessness of buying a record player was not so much the expense of the item, as the fact that a deaf man had bought it. It was, as so often, a blind act of faith (and one that paid off, as we shall see).

Clemo found himself bored and frustrated, 'the thrill past and the need of further uplift pressing'.[302] 'It's clearer every day that nothing but love will touch me', he wrote after receiving a large cheque from America.[303] Several days are described as 'the blackest' of the year, and the gloom only dissipated for fleeting moments when another review fell through the door or one of the village girls popped round. It is a solid illustration of the great pessimist Schopenhauer's formula: 'Man is a compound of needs and necessities hard to satisfy; and […] even when they are satisfied, all he obtains is a state of painlessness, where nothing remains to him but abandonment to boredom.'

Clemo suffered the pains of aspiration to a greater extent than he suffered the dullness of satiety, allowing him to remain optimistic. The key frustrations were his deafness, failing sight and the absence of a plausible love interest. He had become infatuated with Brenda, and at the same time he was still thinking of Barbara. When the book was accepted, contracts signed and payments posted, Jack sent Barbara a note, telling her how much he was earning, so that 'it looks as if I shall be really rich one day'. He promises to send her a copy when the book is released, as well as a copy of the Penguin volume featuring one of his poems, adding: 'I don't forget how much you helped me when you lived here'.[304]

Jack handed a copy of the novel to Brenda personally when she visited the cottage in November 1948. She stayed for five minutes, wrote Jack a note – 'I have to go home for tea' – and left. 'This is the way Brenda thanked me for her book', Clemo writes, pasting the note beside his diary entry. 'It's all so disappointing and makes my success a mockery'.[305]

Wilding Graft was written to show the way in which God works and triumphs over atheism, paganism and worldliness. Its publishing success was God finally honouring His promise to the Clemos. He gave Clemo celebrity so that he might continue to praise God through his writing, and He gave money, which had been a relentless cause for concern throughout their lives. Previously, they had known nothing but poverty, and God had relieved it. But this was only a fraction of a reward. What good was it all if his senses were still deteriorating and he was still so lonely? Healing and marriage, Clemo believed, were his destiny, and God's erotic favour was the very theme of *Wilding Graft*. Why had God confirmed the novel's message by allowing it to be published, but not granted the happy ending promised by the novel itself?

At home, Jack hung the photographs of Powys and Browning above his desk, 'the two writers who've meant most to me'. He considered hanging Hardy, as 'the style and atmosphere are nearer to Hardy, but he was an atheist and I don't think it fitting to hang an atheist's portrait in a Christian home'.[306] Jack had written to Powys in 1946, when the novel had been accepted: 'Now that success has at last come to me […] I am writing to thank you for all that your work has meant to me during the past 10 years'. To Jack's astonishment, Powys replied, with a 'letter I shall treasure all my life – a lovely appreciation'.[307] Now, Clemo wrote again, enclosing a copy of *Wilding Graft*. There was, it should be noted, another motive for this correspondence besides the literary, which has been omitted from the autobiographies and other biographical work on Clemo and will be discussed in Chapter X.

For now, he had two more novels to write for Chatto & Windus and no inclination to write anything but poetry: 'two new novels that I feel I can't write. Forced into a work which I can't do while I'm deaf and loveless – what can it mean?'[308] Pressure was building for him to show something new. He sent off the old failed manuscripts, which

Cecil Day Lewis quickly dismissed as a waste of time. He also sent 'The Lamb of the Green Bed', which was rejected as a self-conscious imitation of Powys. 'What that man wants to do', one reader for Chatto & Windus wrote, 'is to forget about Hardy and forget about Powys and write like Jack Clemo. He is good enough to travel under his own steam.'[309] Clemo was desperate. 'I feel sick and stunned,' he wrote in his diary, 'abandoned and hopeless. How can there be a future for me? And why was WG ever accepted to bring me into this terrible plight?'[310] 'Chatto want me to write a new novel instead of revising the old ones'.[311] This should not have been a surprise to Jack; it was in all of the letters. Indeed, it is more of a surprise that he should have submitted such tired juvenilia when he had been asked for two new books. At the end of 1946, after reading *Alice's Adventures in Wonderland*, Clemo at last has a new idea, a variation on his earlier plans for 'The Hired Razor', to be entitled 'Howling Fir':

> Kurt [Hardy] returned from war to live with grandmother at Karslake. His girl has become a school teacher, lodging at Coombe […] she is an atheist, finding her relief in poetry and nature and humanism.

The character was to be developed in exactly the same way as Edith in *Wilding Graft* and Marvran in *The Clay Kiln*, to be given up when 'another girl of uncultured type attracts Kurt and he yields to her'. When Kurt's grandmother dies, he is to move to Grampound. Kurt will do something to prove that 'dogma is really more human than the humanists' while 'the girl carries on with an artist'. To show what a sinner she is, she is to arrange a dance in one of the drys. The story was going to end near Terras Mine the day after Hiroshima. A 'Conflict between dogma […] and poetry […]. A subject exactly to my taste'. The book never got off the ground. Clemo wrote a few speeches and planned the locations, but he quickly lost interest.

The strain and disappointment were evident, so much so that Harold Raymond recommended that Jack take a break from writing. Cecil Day Lewis was going to look at the poetry, and then, he suggested, 'an autobiography might prove to you a useful stop-gap'.[312] It was clear to everyone that Jack had hit a rut. His eyesight had taken a turn for the worse, on top of which his supportive agent, Raymond Savage, had married and retired, recommending Cyrus Brooks of A.M. Heath as his successor. Heath was the agency that had seen promise in Clemo's early novels in the previous decade, and had requested to see more. Jack continued to write to Savage for help, and asked whether he might still read the autobiography. Savage agreed, offering his vulnerable and needy writer some welcome encouragement.

Jack's inability to write a new novel built into a personal crisis. Day after day the diaries filled with angst:

> Mother and I still struggling through what she nightly describes as an 'awfully contrary atmosphere' [...] as if the devil is pouring his full fury around us, a thick spiritual fog – it's strange, unlike anything we've known.[313]

Such was his state of mind until publication day.

Over in America, Harold Latham, the Vice-President of Macmillan, had heard about the novel and was looking for new talent. His search coincided with a visit to Oxford and a meeting with the St Austell academic A.L. Rowse. Latham was an energetic editor, whose work included a defining contribution and publication of Margaret Mitchell's *Gone with the Wind*, as well as procuring H.G. Wells and Vachel Lindsay for their books. He wanted to publish *Wilding Graft* and had already been in contact with Heath about it. Rowse was approached as a knowledgeable and celebrated Cornishman with a reputation across the Atlantic, who might be willing to promote Clemo's novel for them. Rowse wrote to Clemo:

> I have at last got hold of [*Wilding Graft*] and am enthralled by it. I am still in the midst of it, very much moved by it, especially by the character of Garth. That's quite right, isn't it? I am afraid I am a very unprofessional reader of novels and don't think much of most contemporary ones. But I love this one. There are all sorts of things I long to ask you about it – if you can bear to have a

meeting. Can you? I should very much like to meet you, if you are free one day this week.³¹⁴

This led to a lengthy correspondence between the two men, who were geographically neighbours, but a considerable distance from one another in outlook. Jack was keen to have his novel sold in America, a place he felt was responsible for his condition, but he was anxious about his disabilities as well as about meeting the 'atheist' academic Rowse. He told Rowse it would be 'impossible' for them to meet because of his deafness and poor sight: 'This unrelieved loneliness is part of the price I've had to pay for my independence and for any originality that may exist in my work.'³¹⁵

Clemo was surprised to read Rowse's praise, expecting him to have been 'repelled by the "mystical religiosity"', and he was deeply grateful, agreeing that any promotion by Rowse would be invaluable, since 'you are the only product of the clay district whose name carries any weight with the reading public.'³¹⁶ The Rowse-Clemo correspondence continued for several years, becoming more significant when they wrote about the next book, *Confession of a Rebel*. It was always a one-sided exchange. Clemo showed no interest in Rowse's work or life, and only discussed his own writing, beliefs and biography. Indeed, there was occasionally a hint of contempt in Clemo's letters, which Rowse either did not notice or overlooked. It was not until the end of 1949 that Rowse began to show any frustration, as Clemo only wrote to ask favours, primarily for help raising money: 'Chatto has advised me to approach the Royal Literary Fund for a grant. They suggest that you should be one of the two supporters required – the other being Cecil Day Lewis.'³¹⁷ Rowse agreed, and offered on top of this to read Clemo's latest novel, *The Shadowed Bed*. Two weeks later Clemo was chasing Rowse for the letter of recommendation. Rowse sent it shortly after and Clemo acknowledged receipt with perfunctory thanks. Then he wrote again, asking Rowse to help him apply for a £200 Civil List Pension: 'My handicaps will prevent me from being a prolific writer'.³¹⁸ And again, Rowse agreed, even though he was about to be caught up in the local elections. Clemo gave him a very brief reprieve while the elections were running, but as soon as they were over, waiting for Rowse was: 'Dear ALR, Now that the

Election is over I am wondering what steps are being taken about the Civil List pension. I hope a start has been made, for it looks as if I shall need it pretty badly.'[319]

This is the last correspondence from Clemo kept in Rowse's meticulously ordered collection of letters. Jack had become pushy, assuming that everyone had as much free time as he had, and it is a pattern repeated through later relationships. The reason for Jack's neediness was his vulnerability. His health was in dramatic decline and he was dependent upon his mother for everything. He was deaf, turning blind, Cornish and working-class. In the scramble for position, notice and preference in a London-dominated industry, Clemo was at a practically insurmountable disadvantage.

Rowse, like the poet Charles Causley – who would become of signal importance in Clemo's literary life – was unfailingly courteous and generous in his correspondence, assuring Clemo that he was not at all bothered by the 'pestering', although immediately following this latest barrage of demands, the correspondence was closed.

With the support of Rowse, Latham published *Wilding Graft* in October 1948. He had wanted to change the title to 'Clay of Meledor', to which Clemo would not agree. Nevertheless, Clemo was sent a substantial advance of $750 – 'far more than I expected'. It gave Jack hope of becoming better known and more widely read: 'I believe I'll be like Browning more fully appreciated in the US than in England.'[320] It was, then, with some pride, if not excitement, that Jack received his first fan letter from an American autograph hunter in November. Disappointingly, 'not a girl though'.[321]

Meanwhile, Clemo had been informed that Cecil Day Lewis was recommending him for an Atlantic Award. This was a scheme set up by the Rockefeller Foundation in 1946, 'to aid young British subjects whose work in creative writing or criticism has shown particular promise but has been interrupted by the war'. The fund was $50,000, to be allocated over three years by a team of adjudicators at Birmingham University, among which was Louis MacNeice. Clemo received an award of £100, paid to him at the end of July 1948.

The sales figures of *Wilding Graft* went down considerably after the first month. Through the whole of April only 280 copies were sold and Clemo was upset to learn that his advance had not yet been paid back by the royalties. He had not understood the nature of an advance, and had written to Heath complaining that no one had been forwarding his money. Still, overall *Wilding Graft* was a fair seller and went through a second impression, after which it was out of print for thirty-five years, until being picked up by Anthony Mott, a personable but disorganised publisher who had set up his own firm and intended to produce an ambitious series of Cornish classics, 'The Cornish Library'. 'It will be good to feel myself a novelist again', Clemo wrote to a correspondent in 1983; 'I only thought of poetry as incidental till my sight began to fail.'[322] *Wilding Graft* was the fifteenth title in the Mott series, and at different times in the early 1980s Mott told Jack he would also take *Confession of a Rebel*, *The Marriage of a Rebel*, *A Different Drummer*, and a 'Collected' volume. None of these materialised. Mott even advertised volumes of 'The Cornish Library' which not only were never published, but had not even been written, including E.V. Thompson's 'A Short History of Cornwall', a book discussed but never commissioned or drafted. The project, as the company, was unfortunately short-lived, a fact made doubly unhappy by the failure of a similar deal made with Chatto & Windus in 1982.

Wilding Graft is a unique novel in Cornwall, capturing in an idiosyncratic way the postwar realist zeitgeist, and it is an excellent depiction of the time, place, landscape and culture of mid-Cornwall's mining villages. It is an entertaining read, well-structured and controlled, tense and powerful, ambitious but populist, with a mix of approaches, theological, working-class, melodramatic and symbolist. It is also flawed and difficult to review. As popular working-class melodrama, it had too serious a message and too raw a realism, but as a work of literature there were too many moments of naivety and distracting melodrama. It was as though Clemo had been caught between the desires to write a popular potboiler and a literary work of artistic value. As it is, the novel stands alone, a unique and powerful gesture, a page-turning romance with an undercurrent of divine interference and a surface of realism uncommon in writing about Cornwall.

His next book was the autobiography *Confession of a Rebel*, which would return to some of the themes of the novel and show how these were manifest within Clemo's own life. There is a clear agenda to this *Confession*, a paradoxical self-regard and self-mutilation, but its strange confidence and strength of voice make it likely to be Clemo's prose work with the greatest longevity.

Jack, 1949

VIII
Confession of a Rebel

O thinke mee worth thine anger, punish mee,
Burne off my rusts, and my deformity,
Restore thine image, so much, by thy grace,
That thou may'st know mee, and I'll turne my face.

    John Donne, 'Goodfriday, 1613, Riding Westward'

Clemo's confession fell into two established markets, one Christian and one Cornish, but it was also an act of personal justification, stating the sins of the past and the way in which these could be burned away, forgiven and absolved. Clemo might have had the above lines from Donne's 'Good Friday, 1613, Riding Westward' in mind, lines he would use again in *The Invading Gospel*.

In *Confession*, Clemo writes:

> Only an undisciplined type can prompt the 'stain of fire' that burns out a man's natural faith, whether through remorse – as might happen in a case of prostitution or adultery – or through an agonized conviction of moral rightness beyond moral convention, as in the actual case of Garth Joslin.

Clemo identified with both the sexually remorseful and with the 'agonized' moral transcendent. He showed guilt for his semi-accidental ejaculation and for his behaviour towards Barbara, and even expressed concern for Irene in what is, frankly, a suspiciously worded passage:

> Thinking a lot of Irene and wondering how much she remembers – praying she may 'remember and understand' as I quote in *WG* and not feel ashamed of anything between us.[323]

Some moments Jack burned with shame, while others he was staunchly committed to his own goodness, righteousness and divinely approved exceptionalism, 'beyond moral convention'. The conflict between these feelings of guilt and election suggests the tension necessary for the genuinely confessional aspects of this autobiography. Clemo details his personal history partly to protect himself from prying biographers, but also to transform his guilt into an aspect of faith – indeed, a condition of it – an inevitable suffering and strain. In this way, guilt is turned into a virtue, a confession, with the idea that forgiveness will follow.

'Absolution is the indispensable goal of all confession', wrote JM Coetzee in 'Confession and Double Thought'.[324] It is an opportunity for the confessant to present himself and events on his own terms with a view to being able to put sins behind him. The act implies two people, the one confessing and the one absolving. For Clemo, the act of confession meant two audiences absolving him. The first is the reading public, the other himself. The reason for this is that his guilt involved both a public accusation with a feeling of shame, and a self-accusation of conscience or esteem. Clemo's senses of guilt and shame had several roots. He perceived a shame in his disabilities, the result of a sexually transmitted disease. He was locally persecuted for this, as well as for his self-imposed alienation and his romantic attachments. He was also aware that he would seem guiltier if his sexual arousal and ejaculations were known. So Jack had reasons for both a private confession and a public one, and both are attempts to turn the facts of his biography into an absolution. The public nature of Jack's confession gave him the special opportunity to feel validated nationally and internationally, transcending the malice and condemnation of the villagers. When he told his story to the public, he claimed that even his flaws and sins had been divinely arranged and were the conditions of his eventual submission to God. The 'Browning pattern', the 'vocation' for marriage, the idea of election, were all connected to this confessional instinct, the need for justification, forgiveness, absolution, and a restoration of esteem. On top of this, we see Jack taking revenge on his persecutors – on Q, on his school, his enemies in the *Cornish Guardian*, Daphne du Maurier, his father and the neighbours.

Western man has become a confessing animal, Michel Foucault told us. Foucault was interested in the polarity between power and servility, with power connected to freedom and truth, and servility to error and lie. The formula for a Catholic kind of confession ought to be that revealing the truth leads to freedom from sin and error, while witholding the truth leads to servility and post-mortem suffering. However, senses of guilt and inferiority tend not to be so easily dissipated, and there is a tension between the need to confess and the desire not to be condemned, a tension illustrated by psychodynamic psychological models, where the confession offered to the therapist has to be interpreted rather than taken at face value.[325]

The ultimate aim of confession is to find peace, though it seems unlikely this was achieved, since Jack was not able to tell the full story. He gave a mythologised, pattern-wrought interpretation and apology. The approbation and absolution of others may have been achieved on his own terms, but it was insufficient. By not telling the full story, the confession was incomplete, leading to further guilt and requiring further confession.

A perfect example of this and the complexity of the confession is Clemo's account of the Barbara affair. Of course, he did not have to mention Barbara at all, but there were conflicting reasons why he might. In the first instance, there was the hope that Barbara would read it, realise her importance and reciprocate Clemo's feelings. But to state it plainly would be a great risk, as Barbara could say she did not feel anything of the sort for Jack and did not know what he was talking about, which would undermine him and be a final rebuff. There was also the risk that stating his continued hope of marrying Barbara would make his youthful infatuation more sinister and less forgivable to the reader and to the villagers, not to mention putting off other marital possibilities, such as Brenda. So Clemo desired forgiveness, hoped for love, but did not want to compromise the posture of innocence or risk humiliation. We find here the desire to expose, to confess, to be absolved, but at the same time to conceal. It would be no good if instead of absolving guilt and shame, the confession augmented them. Yet, paradoxically, that is what happened. Clemo did not risk a full confession, so the confession was only partial, and a cause of further guilt, though lesser shame.

If Clemo had been unable to cope with the guilt, then the confession might have been of a different nature. However, it appears as though the confessional aspect of *Confession* is weighted more towards relief from shame. He attacks his enemies too often, over-justifies his actions and emotions, and compares himself flatteringly to other writers. Audience and absolution are both implied in the act of confession, but unlike, for example, Augustine's *Confessions*, it is not God whose approbation Clemo desires, but his readers'. Sensitivity to the gossip and contempt of the villagers drive this confession, and we see it again in the repeated fear of 'mockery' in both the diaries and the work. (The diaries themselves might be considered a form of confession, with subject and audience both the same.)

Clemo's habit of writing lengthy prefaces to the earlier manuscripts, explaining how difficult the writing was for him because of his extraordinary suffering, has been mentioned already. In spite of being dissuaded by publishers and readers, he needed to place himself within the work, to attach his history and personality to the justified novel or poetry collection, and he needed to be in charge of interpreting himself. *Confession of a Rebel*, it will be recalled, was begun before *Wilding Graft*. That is, even before Clemo had achieved any success with his work, he had an autobiography planned, to describe the lives of his father and mother, his inheritance, the plan God had for him, and how in spite of his suffering and the ill-will of others, he was and will remain triumphant. Clemo was interpreting himself confessionally for the public before he was a public figure.

A further confessional context is that of the testimonial. Testimonial literature is an attestation of one's personal experience of God. It can be the testimony of someone who has always been a Christian, or it can describe the conversion experience, either within an established Christian framework or moving from atheism to a position of faith. Jack loved the genre. Testimonials, confessions and biographies were all part of the same urge and support. They provided a link to others with extraordinary lives and outlooks, and he learnt that he was not as alone as he felt day to day. The apophenic impulse can be considered in this light too: if Clemo is like the people he is reading about – Browning, Hardy, Chatterton, Tolstoy or Rossetti – then he is not doomed to the life into which he was born, the turbulent withering in the shadows of the clay dumps. The patterns he found in both secular and faith-based biographies enabled him to place himself among the biographees and escape from the despair that now and then closed in on him. Particular favourites were Bunyan's *Grace Abounding* and Mary Fletcher's *Life*. In 1961, Jack was pleased to read Kenneth Allsop's review of *The Map of Clay*, in which he is described as the 'Bunyan of this century'. *Grace Abounding* was read several times during the writing of *Confession*, and was listed as a favourite book in 1943, as well as in 1938-39, when he first read it. Bunyan's testimonial begins, as Fletcher's and Tolstoy's, when 'I was without God in the world'. Clemo himself was never 'without God', although the God serving his teenage years was less considered than the God to Whom he converted at the end of the 1930s.

A third context of Clemo's *Confession* is that of the autobiography in Cornwall. The 1940s produced a number of regional classics, including A.L. Rowse's *A Cornish Childhood* (1942), Anne Treneer's *School House in the Wind* (1944) and J.C. Trewin's *Up from the Lizard* (1948). Clemo and Rowse produced the most extraordinary works, being native local working-class writers with no desire to romanticise or idealise their towns and villages. Clemo read *A Cornish Childhood* as soon as it appeared, hoping it might help with his own autobiography, and in a 1948 letter to Rowse, Jack made a comparison between them, writing that his own was

> as different from yours as it could possibly be, much more raw and elemental: no story of struggle for scholarships […] but a record of spiritual and emotional upheavals which drove me out of Methodism (I was reared in strict Nonconformity and never lost my respect for the best type of Nonconformist, the Sam Jacobs type: even you admired *him*), into various forms of pantheism and at last to my present faith, a mixture of sex mysticism and Barthian Theology. The whole development is related to my physical handicaps.[326]

It is a gentle but unnecessarily antagonistic letter, and it shows Clemo's wish to forcibly distance himself from the irreligious and academic. In fact, he would never succeed, and it might be observed that many of Clemo's decisive breaks in the world of literature were aided by people of rather different beliefs, including the atheist Rowse, the agnostic Cecil Day Lewis and the lapsed Catholic Lionel Miskin.

Perhaps it was the war that made people think nostalgically of their childhoods in the 1940s. The sense of a loss of innocence, as well as of friends and family – the violence, destruction and depression – might have led to periods of self-reflection and spiritual re-evaluation. Or perhaps a greater sense of social equality following the wars offered more opportunities for working-class people like Rowse and Clemo.

Among Cornish autobiographies, Clemo's stands out. His life experience and perspective remain alien and remote, even within Cornwall, where the literary scene is still eclipsed by the non-native talents of Daphne du Maurier, Winston Graham and E.V. Thompson, all of whom were drawn, one way or another, by the romance of the region. Clemo's style has not dated either, unlike that of Anne Treneer's autobiography, which seems overly sentimental now. The unusual centrality of God, the personal vendettas, the clayscape setting, the poverty, disabilities, and the misfit character of Clemo, make *Confession of a Rebel* a compelling work.

The writing of it was begun in 1941, and its first working title was 'Confession of a Calvinist', reflecting Clemo's latest theological affiliation and his readings of Spurgeon, Thomas De Witt Talmage and Karl Barth. The title was kept for three years, but by the time the manuscript was being submitted to publishers and agents, in 1948, it had been renamed 'Confession of a Misfit'. It was Cecil Day Lewis who told Jack that misfits were not very marketable and suggested he come up with a few better options. The book was, however, always intended to be a 'confession', rather than 'confessions'. The difference is subtle and often overlooked. The singularity of 'confession' suggests the singularity of the theme and narrative. All aspects of the biography, it is being said, are a part of the one story, the plot of a journey to God. It is the confession of a nonconformist, not the confessions of a Catholic. It is also a dogmatic declaration of faith, like the 'Apostles' Creed', also known as the 'Confession of the Apostles'.

The autobiography was worked on intermittently to begin with. It was first mentioned on Friday 13 June 1941: 'Have written 500 words or more to my autobiography!' Work on it was soon overshadowed by the progress of *Wilding Graft*, but even so, by 1943, he had written 30,000 words of his life. In *Confession* we read that Clemo did not write anything in 1943 and 1944 except to rework old manuscripts, but Clemo must mean that he wrote no new fiction, since he continued to work on the autobiography, completing the preface towards the end of July 1943, and writing 13,000 words in February 1944 alone. By the end of the year he had written somewhere in the region of 60,000 words to *Confession*. He continued sporadically through 1945, by which point he was almost writing the autobiography as events were unfolding. This accounts for the emphases on the girls living in or visiting the Clemo cottage at the time, as well as for the inclusion of 'The Token', a poem that was only published in *Confession* during Clemo's lifetime and was never included in any of his collections of verse:

> A shift of His mood brings an hour's relief
> From the cloudy pressure of grinding grief,
> This hammering grief that kills all worth
> In woman's bounty and gifts of earth.
>
> No woman again, no flesh mature,
> With the serpent rhythm in its tidal lure;
> But He drops amid my hermit pain
> The old thrill purged of creative stain.
>
> In a field on which the sand-dump spilt
> A vomit of gravel where grasses wilt
> My ice-world broke for an hour of flame
> With one who shared it in childish game.
>
> We romped in the sun, but the warmth I felt
> Came only from her as she tried to pelt

My face into smiles with orange-peel.
 She skinned the fruit with her teeth – would steal

Close up, undeterred by the threatened smack,
 Her hand curled tightly behind her back,
Her hand clenched warm on the missiles broken,
 Growing soft and moist with her blood's shy token.

She would pull and push till my face was free,
 Then snuggle closer and shower on me
Those trivial tools of her childish freak,
 Splintered from Nature mature and sleek.

No symbol here to adjust, adapt,
 Be fogged and bogged by: beauty lapped
So calm her childhood's nakedness,
 I needed not mask its frank caress.

She is the real: I taste and see
 Her girlish magic, unflinchingly:
Unstripped to Nature's evil core,
 She shows her bounty of sense the more.

Each scrap of yellow peel she flung
 Lay fierily on the turf, a tongue
Speaking of bliss I dared not name
 Till I saw in her the new way it came.

With hints like this I can bear His shade,
 Nor fear His jealousy's blasting blade
Back under the cloud: here His eye shall see
 I am purged at last of idolatry.

Shall I praise Him again when, as Nature's foe,
 I emerge to deride its creative flow,
Hating flesh and flower when ripe for seed,
 But for sex, bare rind, feeling love indeed?

The poem was written on 29 July 1946 and intended to be the 'counterpart of Francis Thompson's "Poppy"', as Clemo wrote in his diary. Both poems use an aabb rhyme scheme and sprung tetrameter, and both were influenced by children, Thompson's by a girl named Monica and Clemo's by Brenda. The poppy flower is loaded with meaning for the opium addict Thompson. It is handed to the poem's narrator by the little girl he is walking with, a 'token', a 'withering flower of dreams'. The withered dreams are also the verses, immortalising the dying moment. For Clemo, instead of a beautiful description of an early summer flower, the 'token' was orange peel tossed at him mockingly by the teenager Brenda. The story, as she tells it, was that still under food rationing, her mother had somehow procured a few Jaffa oranges and given one for Brenda to share with her friends. A small troupe of children took it up the burrow with Jack, where Brenda divided it between them into segments, or 'pasties', as she called them. Only, when it came Jack's turn to be given a piece, Brenda pretended that she had run out and instead threw the peel at him.

Clemo had come across Thompson in 1943 and did not like the poetry initially, though soon he was perceiving parallels, specifically in the inspiration received from girls:

> Rereading T.'s poems and am profoundly moved – I *feel* the agony of the great prophetic soul in him, childlike and divine gratitude. 'A Child's Kiss,' 'The Omen of the Child-Woman' are nearer to my own actual circumstance than anything I've ever read, even in Browning.[327]

In 1947, *Confession* was requested by the publishers. Clemo had been unable to finish any new novels, so he reverted to the autobiography and began reworking the manuscript and typing it up. He was surprised how good it was. Soon after submitting it to Chatto & Windus, a long encouraging letter arrived from Cecil Day Lewis: 'I think the autobiography may well turn out to be one of the most remarkable records of our time', he begins. He writes how much he loved the back story of the Polmounters and the Clemos, although

I must frankly put on record my own impression that, when you turn to religious experience and to comment based upon your own religious faith, rather often a note of rancour, intolerance, or of spiritual pride creeps in. The worst example of this seems to me the comments on your father's death [...]: to my ear this passage says in effect, 'My father was no loss to me or anyone else when he died, but, if his life and death had any value at all, it was that they exploded the humanist fallacy and enabled ME to see the light.' It is rather odd, a few lines further down, to read 'the smug hypocrisy and swagger of the crowds (on Armistice days) were too remote from the lonely pain, the massive dignity of our loss.' The reader asks himself, 'Are Clemo and his mother the only people capable of lonely pain and massive dignity? Is it really true that all the other people – the people who kept the two-minute silence – were just smug, or swaggering, or hypocrites? Were they unable to feel their own losses?'

Day Lewis went on to question whether the sense that Jack and God are on the same side and that no one else matters is the intended impression of the autobiography, and puts pressure on Clemo's use of 'facts' and statistics. Which biographers, he wonders, really do 'morbidly insist on' presenting addictions to masturbation and homosexuality? And when Jack writes of the abnormality of modern marriage, Day Lewis asks, does he mean 'Marriage in Polynesia? or Belgravia? or Cornwall?' These are, he writes,

> generalisations, unsupported by argument, revealing nothing but the writer's contempt for his readers: and sometimes, when I can check yours against my own experience, I feel convinced that you have not any arguments or facts to support them with.

Day Lewis had been a schoolmaster, and he tells Jack that what he claims in *Confession* a schoolmaster *should* have done is precisely what 'no schoolmaster *should have done*.' Lastly, he perceives 'the suggestion of a sneer, of a too facile dismissal of beliefs or opinions which run counter to your own', and 'a hint of self-righteousness'.[328]

Jack reports this long letter in his diary, removing the critical parts: 'Splendid report on my auto from Chatto – C.D.L. says it may well become "one of the most remarkable reads of our time."'[329]

By March 1948 Clemo thought the book was complete:

> Revised more of Confession and rounded it off as I feared I'd have to, with Mrs Phillips' funeral, it's a complete record of my spiritual and literary struggle and the ripening of my vision and I'd be satisfied with it as the *first instalment* of a confession with a second volume to follow about the real love and 'personal rewards' – I can't believe God would let me down.[330]

Note the plan for a second autobiography. Clemo expected this to follow very quickly after the first, expressing the realization of the happiness promised by God. As it happened, the sequel would not appear until 1980.

More immediately, many revisions were needed before *Confession* was ready, and Chatto & Windus's libel lawyers were again anxious. Cecil Day Lewis sent the verdict, along with many demands for changes, both litigious and aesthetic. Clemo's references to his own work being like Hardy's, Day Lewis wrote, sounded too much like boasting. This was true. They were, unquestionably, braggadocio, but Jack wanted them kept. Other suggestions and concerns included the following list: 'references to your own talents, spiritual and intellectual, will tend to alienate the reader'; 'comment about "Elizabeth Myers" is probably libellous'; 'Humanist philosophies [...] have never rejected the great art and literature which did not "prophecy smooth things"'; 'don't call the Hockings "superficial"'; 'Will you please cut out the reference to me by name'. And he was firm with Clemo on removing some of the stronger descriptions of John Cowper Powys: 'We suggest omitting the words "maniacal", "the appalling" and "in which that other 'Loony John' delighted"'.[331]

For a dedication, Jack was uncertain. He wanted to dedicate it to

Brenda, but by the end of October he was starting to doubt whether his feelings for her were really reciprocated. Brenda has since stated very plainly that they were not, and that there was no romantic feeling between her and Jack at all. It was never discussed or hinted at, and later in life she was a little annoyed by a newspaper article referring to her as one of Jack's early girlfriends. In her mind, they had been playmates. Nevertheless, after *Confession* was submitted, Jack wanted to include more on Brenda, so in November 1948 he posted an extra section to Chatto & Windus. He also added a very late mention of Eileen, a new correspondent and another promising marriage prospect. Eileen is introduced on the last page:

> the progressive grafting [...] was not yet complete, and those touches of it which involved Christian fellowship were still to come – through a Hertfordshire girl whom I first heard of a few weeks after Phillips' death.

In subsequent impressions, in 1975 and 1988, the 'Hertfordshire girl' was named as Eileen Funston. The enlightening correspondence from Eileen to Jack has survived and will be looked at more closely in Chapter X. By publication day, 16 September 1949, the Eileen affair had effectively already fallen apart, a further 'mockery' of the book's message.

Sales and reviews of *Confession* were not as good as *Wilding Graft*'s, and Macmillan chose not to publish it in America. In the UK they were sufficient for Chatto & Windus to publish a second edition in 1975. This was a striking glossy red hardback, with a few subtle alterations to the text, like the description of the evacuee Joan being changed from 'a pathetic little slum product from Dulwich', to 'a dark, shy orphan called Joan from Dulwich'. This second issue was not given as much attention as the first. The publishers did not even think to change the biographical details on the back cover, in spite of more than twenty-five years having passed. Norah Smallwood, who would become Managing Director of Chatto & Windus the same year, was Clemo's contact, but most of the letters from her are apologies. Not only did they forget to change the biographical information, but they forgot to send Clemo copies of the book, failed to send any review copies, and they forgot to pay him. The book was, as a result, scarcely noticed and sales were poor, so in 1977 Jack was able to buy fifty cheap copies when it was remaindered.

By 1982, Chatto & Windus seem to have been even less interested in Clemo and even more disorganised. This was the year that Norah Smallwood retired from her position, and Carmen Callil, the founder of Virago, took over as Managing Director. A representative of the publishers, Jill Rose, had spoken to Jack and offered to reprint both *Confession* and *Wilding Graft*, at the same time as the small publisher Anthony Mott was showing interest. Jack offered Mott the novel and accepted Chatto & Windus's offer to publish *Confession* at their associated company, the Hogarth Press. It was to be a paperback issue for mass publication. Their offer was better than Mott's, with a larger advance, wider distribution and an established company. Terms were agreed and a publication date set for 1985. But it turned out Rose had no authority to make the offer, and when Jack wrote in 1985 to find out when the book was going to print, the reply came that it was not. There was no record of the offer and Rose had left the company. No one at Hogarth or Chatto & Windus knew anything about it. Later the same year, Mott's company went into liquidation.

The latest issue of *Confession* was published by Spire, an imprint of Hodder & Stoughton, in 1988, which they reproduced along with the second volume of autobiography, *The Marriage of a Rebel*. At Spire, Juliet Newport was an admirer of Clemo's work and keen to publish him. For the cover, they used a watercolour landscape of the clay tips looking like angry volcanoes, by the artist Lionel Miskin, an influential painter and sculptor who befriended Clemo in 1956 when he drew a series of portraits of the poet and his mother. By 1988, Lionel had not been in touch with Jack for some time, and no one seemed sure where he was. They tracked him down in Cyprus, though he did not remember painting the watercolour. Nevertheless, Miskin said if they had it they could use it, and he even offered to pay for the image to be copied properly. Juliet Newport then suggested that Clemo write another book, more typically testimonial than the others, and more of a counterpart to *The Invading Gospel* of 1958. By this time, Jack felt too old to take on a project of such magnitude.

Response to *Confession*, from the very first edition, was unpredictable and exciting. On 28 October 1949, the *Times Literary Supplement* printed one of the strongest reviews, acknowledging what a unique writer Clemo was, when 'recent Cornish writers have been romantics' or 'passionate loyalists', and describing *Confession* as 'a surprising porcupine of a book to shoot its quills from Cornwall.' At the other end of the scale, a bad review from Australia caused Clemo to reconsider his literary position. 'It's all too true', wrote Clemo, 'that much of my suffering has been "mystical self-pity", and I can't be content for my witness to remain on the level of what's already published.'[332] This diary entry anticipates Clemo's next prose work, *The Invading Gospel*. Clemo wants to 'witness', to say more, and he wants his writing to be more positive and less focused on the turbulence of his upbringing. His confession was incomplete.

In other reviews, the *Evening Standard* called Jack 'A queer fish, a misfit, a man with a kink', and said he was 'coming up the hard way'.[333] The *Daily Mail* found *Confession* 'extraordinarily irritating yet oddly absorbing'. It was 'One of the queerest and most candid self-portraits that I have read for a long while'.[334] V.S. Pritchett, writing in the October *Bookman*, wrote sympathetically: 'At first he sounds crankish, obstinate, conceited, arrogant, but this is merely the shell of the solitude in which he has lived and which he makes so profoundly interesting [...]. His remarkable devotion to very young girls recalls the innocent mysticism of the Kilvert Diaries, his pictures of working-class life are faithful; his thought is grim, strong and candid.'

Clemo's fan mail became equally mixed and suitably weird. Most correspondents wrote to tell Jack their own life stories and to say that they, too, were misfits. One would begin, 'My own life has, in some ways, resembled yours'. Another, 'I too am a modern Calvinist'. One wrote in sympathy, saying that she, like Clemo, has always hated people. A surprising quantity responded to Clemo's relationships with children, sharing their own feelings and experiences, usually innocent.

Jack kept two lists of the people who sent him fan mail. The first was a list of critics and celebrities that included A.L. Rowse, John Rowland, Raymond Savage, Denys Val Baker, Lewis Wilshire, David Stribley, Monica Hutchings, Littleton Powys, E.W. Martin, H.J.

Wilmott and Frank Baron. The second was of mail from the general public, a list that included Helena Charles, who became a regular correspondent. Undoubtedly, the oddest letter came from Richard Lea, who declared that Clemo was a prophet of the Apocalypse destined to lead mankind after the imminent deluge. According to Lea, Clemo was the man to found 'the new religious basis that will be needed' following God's purge, instituting 'new religious conceptions and a new social system'.

One other letter stands out, written by a young man named Philip Callow in 1953. It is in most ways exactly like the others, being an account of his own working-class background and biography and stating that he intended to write his own 'Confession'. The difference was that Callow did go on to publish his life story in a number of successful autobiographical novels, as well as several lives of writers and artists, including D.H. Lawrence, Robert Louis Stevenson, Chekhov and Cézanne.

Through the continued media attention, Jack became a major figure in Cornwall. Causley, Rowse and Lionel Miskin befriended him, as did the editor and critic Derek Savage, who lived in Mevagissey. There was a tight community of artists and writers here at this time, which included W.S. Graham, Daphne du Maurier and Denys Val Baker. Clemo was well ensconced. Derek Savage was an especially important character, and it was Savage who introduced Jack to the poet Kenneth Rexroth. He also wrote a number of supportive and helpful letters and reviews for Clemo. Among them, relevant to *Confession of a Rebel*, is this note he passed to Jack from an unnamed man who he says is 'a mystic and philosopher'.[335] The unnamed man wrote about *Confession*:

> Greatness is too hackneyed a word to use in connection with this book; it belongs to the same category as Genesis and Exodus. I do not feel that I have been reading a book so much as sharing the vision of an elementally living humanity, similar in its basic character to that which is offered by the account of Moses before the burning bush; an experience which I shall not forget.

In spite of this support, *Confession*'s sales were not spectacular. A religious autobiography of a writer who has only written one book was never going to hit the charts, but at the end of 1949 Clemo says his literary hopes have been 'dashed by news of poor sales'. It was at this time that Cecil Day Lewis and A.L. Rowse submitted their support of Clemo's application for a Royal Literary Fund grant. The grant was awarded and Jack received £100 in January 1950. He also applied for a Civil List Pension on the grounds of his disabilities. This was supported by a number of eminent figures, among them Aldous Huxley, V.S. Pritchett, W. Somerset Maugham, Isaac Foot, J.C. Trewin, John Betjeman and T.F. Powys. 'How ironic is God's way still – probably half these supporters are agnostics or atheists', wrote Clemo in his diary.[336] The Civil List Pension was not granted, in spite of the eminent support, though in the rejection letter dated 7 April 1951 Clemo was offered a 'Royal Bounty Fund' grant worth £300. The Civil List Pension would be reconsidered in 1961.

Confession of a Rebel has informed many bad impressions of Clemo. Its author was emotionally immature and volatile, and the work can seem cruel, self-congratulatory, self-justifying and narcissistic. Clemo used public exposure to criticise the people around him, the girls who let him down, and several recently deceased literary figures. As a writer, however, Clemo was continuing to prove himself. The unrelenting tension remains, a threatening buzz of barely contained electricity within the prose, and there is a primitive ferocity and frustration to *Confession*, aided by the idea of God's immediate presence, His constant looming over Jack's shoulder. It gives the theological perspective considerable vitality.

Clemo had a stronger sense of intimacy with his readers than many might. It was, after all, how he had grown up, being mocked and assaulted in press controversies. His writing is a constantly extended hand, which we see most conspicuously in his autobiographies, although it is present in the fiction and poetry, the forewords and prefaces, and in the newspapers. He puts forward an idea of 'Jack Clemo', writer, mystic and elect lover, through a confident and self-aware alloy of sincerity and misdirection. The autobiography is him 'playing Jack Clemo', so to speak. He knows that the story he is putting forward is not the whole truth, but he believes the conclusions of his untruth are true – the presence of God in his life and God's proven election of him. With the story unfinished, the 'proof' has not materialised, and along with the guilt of untruth there is a self-perpetuating motive for self-concern and autobiography. It is a classic case of what Sartre, Clemo's contemporary, would call 'bad faith'. So when Clemo wrote that his work cannot be understood without studying those 'certain broken boundaries', it seems he did not mean he wished to be looked at as we are here, working behind the myth, but rather on his own terms and by his own confessions.

1941 saw Jack's letters to the *Cornish Guardian* all but cease, and conduits for his prose dried up as the almanacks suffered from paper rationing and ceased printing. *Wilding Graft* was the new outlet for his fictional prose, and *Confession of a Rebel* was the receptacle of Clemo's urge to public confession and self-appraisal. The third literary drive has hardly been considered yet, and emerged almost spontaneously in 1945, when *Wilding Graft* was all but finished and the back of *Confession* well broken. This was the poetry. Clemo was unable to write a new novel, but he still had one more book to produce to fulfil his contract with Chatto & Windus. It was at this point that Cecil Day Lewis suggested putting together a selection of verse. And it is on this poetry that Clemo's literary reputation and longevity depend.

IX
The Clay Verge

He had lost everything except his faith in God, and he was at the prayer meeting to lead the singing as usual! And, not noticing that from the fatigues of that awful financial panic he had fallen asleep, I arose and gave out the hymn [...]. His wife wakened him, and he started the hymn at too high a pitch, and stopped, saying, 'That is too high'; then started it at too low a pitch, and stopped, saying, 'That is too low.' It is the only mistake I ever heard him make. But the only wonder is that amid the circumstances of broken fortunes he could sing at all.

The Autobiography of Dr Talmage

It was never Clemo's intention to be a poet, although it is almost certainly for his poetry that he will be remembered. Novels, he thought, were his writerly meat, while poems were brief moments of vision and inspiration. In the preface for his proposed first collection, he wrote:

> These fifty poems are all that I care to preserve of my output in verse. It is very unlikely that I shall write anything further in the medium: the lyrical form of expression was natural to me only before my talent had found its true medium in novels.

After *The Clay Verge* he would get back to novels, the real urge to write poetry, he says, having left him as soon as he began 'Roche Snow' in 1937. The manuscript was intended to include most of the juvenile verse submitted to the *Cornish Guardian* as well as the new work emerging. He finished the preface in February 1945 – 'prefaces are so much easier to write than the books!'[337] – the same day that he finished the first of a new style of poem, 'Christ in the Clay-Pit'.

There are several drafts of the list of poems Jack wanted to publish, but he seems to have sent just over forty to Savage in February 1946, by which time the collection was bolstered by a handful of poems in a new and stark idiom, three of which would appear in *The Clay Verge*: 'Christ in the Clay-Pit', 'Prisoner of God', and 'A Calvinist in Love'. The original title of the collection was to be 'Poems Christian and Erotic', which was soon changed to 'Crucifix of Clay', and from 1948 became *The Clay Verge*.

Savage sent the manuscript to John Murray, who thought 'the author deserves – and probably needs – encouragement'. Murray suggested submitting to Faber, Macmillan, and the new magazine *Orion*. Savage tried *Orion* right away, the editors being Cecil Day Lewis, Rosamond Lehmann and D. Kilham Roberts. As a result, 'Christ in the Clay-Pit' appeared in the Autumn 1946 issue, alongside the work of Louis MacNeice, Laurie Lee, Day Lewis, Edith Sitwell, Frances Bellerby and the critic who wrote negatively of *Wilding Graft*, Gorley Putt, and Clemo was paid four guineas.[338] Of this money, he gave his tithe to charity, 'carrying out the Scriptural rule of giving a tenth of all earnings to God's cause.'[339]

Further poetic triumphs followed. 'A Calvinist in Love', written November 1945, appeared in Penguin's *New Writing* collection in 1947, edited again by John Lehmann. Then 'The Excavator', written September 1946, appeared in Reginald Moore's *Modern Reading 17*. Other poems were brought out in *Facet*, *West Country Magazine* and *West Country Life*, as Clemo put the finishing touches to his autobiography and wasted his time with the old novels. When it became clear that there would be no new novel, Day Lewis wrote:

> I look forward to reading more of your verse when you have enough to send in a collection of it. There are traces of Browning and Hardy in them – two of my favourite poets – and I think of Francis Thompson too. […] I particularly admire 'The Excavator': in this poem, except for a little fluffing […] at the start of the fourth stanza, you have carried the thought on, though you control your central image, with great power and momentum.[340]

The only poets Clemo was reading at this time were the Brownings, Hardy and Francis Thompson, with Clemo adopting the ode form he associated with the latter. Day Lewis had also picked as his favourite the poem Jack considered his best to date: 'The Excavator'.

In 1947, Clemo submitted more poems, and in 1950 the full

manuscript was requested. The future Laureate discarded the majority of these, selecting only twelve: 'Prisoner of God', 'Neutral Ground', 'Snowfall at Kernick', 'The Water-wheel', 'Quarry Snow', 'The Plundered Fuchsias', 'Christ in the Clay-Pit', 'The Excavator', 'The Irony of Election', 'The Clay-Tip Worker', 'Sufficiency', and 'A Calvinist in Love'. But Clemo was writing poetry quickly and easily now, and in May 1950 he noted in his diary: 'Have over 40 pages of my second book of poems done.' He posted these off for Day Lewis to consider with the others. Once again, almost all of them were rejected, Cecil Day Lewis and Ian Parsons thinking less of the second batch than the first. They accepted three: 'The Flooded Clay-Pit', 'Burnt Bush', and 'The Winds', the last of which was reworked from a poem written for the *Cornish Guardian* to commemorate the 1939 New Year. Clemo, disappointed, begged for 'The Child Traitor' to be included, which was agreed, and the final poem, 'The Cinder-Heap', was accepted in January 1951.

So, from two full collections, Cecil Day Lewis selected only seventeen poems. The rejected work would bleed into later volumes, and some of those considered unsuitable by both Clemo and his publishers were collected posthumously in *The Awakening*. Day Lewis was not interested in the poems to or about theologians or writers, such as were submitted on Spurgeon and Browning; nor was he interested in the purely observational landscape poems or the purely theological ones. Instead, from the ramshackle and undefined submissions, Day Lewis extracted a handful of tight, gritty, industrial clayscape pieces with a harsh fallen-world symbolism and theology, from which he constructed an impressive debut volume.

The collection opens with 'Prisoner of God', originally entitled 'De Profundis' (a popular working title used for several of Clemo's earliest poems), then retitled 'The Captive Lover', and then 'Revelations in the Clay-Pit'.[341] The final title, 'Prisoner of God', might be another reference to Karl Barth's *Epistle to the Romans*, which Clemo was reading at the time. In his introduction, Barth writes of the man of faith being a 'prisoner' in this fallen world, and his only way out is through God and the grace of God. The poem seems to date from the mid-1930s, as Andrew Symons suggests in his introduction to *The Awakening*. Clemo told Symons that the poem related to the breakdown of his relationship with the girl Evelyn, and there is a hint in it of one of his favourite poets from the 1930s, Edgar Allan Poe. As well as the imagery and abstraction, Clemo's line, 'When you were slamming, slamming all my doors', is reminiscent of Poe's raven 'gently rapping, rapping at my chamber door'.

The original title, 'De Profundis', was apt. The poem is a supplication 'out of the depths' of the narrator's painful experience. He is appealing directly to God, as in Psalm 130, and is waiting for the answer to his prayer and query: 'What grace do you confer / Through tricks like these? What love could shape such doom?' This is the collection's starting point, a statement of suffering and isolation, a question as to why it is allowed, and the narrator waiting for God's response, accusing Him who 'tore our fates apart and broke the shape / And pattern'. It shows the desire for a narrative running through Clemo's poetry collections. 'Prisoner of God' is not the strongest poem, but it is the natural starting point, the depth from which the narrator would emerge.

The second poem, 'Neutral Ground', introduces the collection's methodology in a more direct way:

> God's image was washed out of Nature
>   By the flood of the Fall:
> No symbol remains to inspire me,
>   And none to appal.

It ends:

> I have lost all the sensitive, tender,
>   Deep insights of man:
> I will look round a claywork in winter,
>   And note what I can.

If it were not for the need to have a strong emotional and erotic narrative, this should have been the opening poem. The clay scenery is set. The narrator is speaking from the clayworks, a fallen world of destruction and redemption, and he turns not to 'Nature or God', but to the 'ravaged' clayworks, where the 'derision of Nature / Is rigid and shrill'. In a very direct way the statement of intent is given. The next poem, 'Snowfall at Kernick', introduces us to the clayscape:

> Here with a burly flutter and sting
>   The snow-blast scampers winnowing,
> And dribble of foam-flakes seeps and bores
>   Through clay-dump thickets, under doors;
> While flurry of snow-mist rises where
>   The waggons tug till rails are bare.
> The smoke is battered round the stacks;
>   Soot falls with snow on trolley-tracks.
> Even the mica-channel planks
>   And narrow walls of settling-tanks
> Are frilled and ice-splashed there between
>   The frozen pools now sickly green.
> The pit-edge merges with the fields,
>   A softened gash the clay-bone shields;
> Beyond it in the valley's fold
>   Virginia woods loom taut and cold.[342]

The emotional turmoil, religious principles and the idiom of clay have all been introduced, and now the symbols begin to blend. In 'The Flooded Clay-Pit', the landscape slowly comes to life. It begins as though continuing the clayey language of 'Snowfall at Kernick':

>   These white crags
> Cup waves that rub more greedily
> Now half-way up the chasm; you see
>   Doomed foliage hang like rags;
>   The whole clay-belly sags

Soon we see the zoomorphic and anthropomorphic images develop: 'Those iron rails / Emerge like claws'. The poem ends:

>   Those thin tips
> Of massive pit-bed pillars – how
> They strain to scab the pool's face now,

> Pressing like famished lips
> Which dread the cold eclipse.

It is as though the clayworks are beginning to wake up.

The narrator of 'Neutral Ground' continues to cast his eye over the works, moving to 'The Water-Wheel', where the Christian symbolism creaks out, and 'The Cinder-Heap', where the erotic imagery is developed and the collection's over-used 'sap' is introduced. Both 'The Cinder-Heap' and 'The Flooded Clay-Pit' develop the picture of the mining machinery being grotesque and monstrous, with brambles 'pushing with live brown claws'. The sense of menace is palpable, although the image is perfected in the 1967 collection, *Cactus on Carmel*, with 'Crab Country', where the traditional grotesqueness of the crab is exaggerated, over-sized and inland, and instead of sand it scuttles across the bleached kaolin quarries:

> Pincer movement on the hills.
> Salty clay-crabs advance, edging sideways
> Or straight ahead over fields, lanes and thickets.
> The whole scarp slowly fills
> With vast crusted shells, gleaming like armour,
> And the gravelly claws
> Baulk the bus, stop the plough of the farmer.

These dynamic symbolic landscapes are immediately compelling, and the eroticism is unavoidable. In a 1977 statement for students at Exeter University, Clemo said:

> I had a strong erotic vision, and though the excavators and kiln-fires might be symbols of God at work on the human spirit, the white sand-cones and the curved rocks in the pits were symbols of woman.

The idea is developed in *The Marriage of a Rebel*:

> I often felt that my rarest talent was not a talent for writing, or (as solemnly pious people have said) a

talent for suffering, but a talent for the erotic, for being mystical and theological about it. I spent a lot of time trying to work out the ultimate religious meaning of the minor but vivid thrills which girls had given me.

The erotic influences evident in *The Clay Verge* are primarily the teenager Brenda and the girl Iris. Iris was the cousin of the evacuated Jauncey girls, who visited for long holidays after the war. For the short periods she was there, in 1946 and 1947, Iris offered the warm contact Clemo felt he needed for his poetry. He wrote 'Clay Fairy' for her, which was not accepted for publication in *The Clay Verge*, but also 'The Child Traitor', which was. The latter poem is 'about Iris picking foxgloves'[343] and the same fallen world:

> She has turned from God and me
> To pluck a foxglove tenderly,
> And pressing through the brambles snapped
> The thick green stem, fondling the purple bells
> [...]
> Each thorn among those blackberries
> Has pierced the Hand that made it, yet she loves,
> Most plainly loves each little tugging spike,
> And witlessly approves
> Its freak – unhooks it gently; and were I to strike,
> Cutting it dead, or wrest the foxglove flowers,
> Trampling them underfoot to thwart the bees
> That press old snares upon my mind,
> Nuzzling for nectar they could find
> In the white feathery womb beneath the velvet towers –
> Were I thus to make
> A gesture of the way my faith must take,
> Her eyes would turn in quick dark mutiny
> Of protest, loyal to the staining beauty
> And not to God's grey truth that spurred my act.

The language is sensuous, with a sexual suggestion in the loving observation, the sense of 'betrayal', the tenderness and 'fondling' and the physicality. It is an intimate language, exaggerated by the Lawrencian 'sap', 'blood' and 'seed'. These overused words depict the natural urge, potency, life, efflorescence and excess, and so they need sanctifying.

A more lasting influence than Iris was Brenda. Through 1947, for reasons unknown, Brenda was being kept away from the cottage by her mother, which led to Jack writing more poetry about her. In *The Clay Verge* the only poem reflecting her influence is the most highly charged, 'The Burnt Bush'. The other Brenda poems appear in *Confession of a Rebel* and in *The Map of Clay*. In *The Marriage of a Rebel* Clemo complained about reviewers reading 'unpleasant sexual implications' into 'The Burnt Bush' (a reference to a review in *Poetry Quarterly*), writing that the poem was 'really' about how

> 'a gnarled old bush of Adam's seed' had produced doubts about divine love because of the loneliness and frustration I had suffered since Irene left me. Brenda's tender gaiety had burnt up this sickly growth so that I could once more affirm God's goodness.[344]

It is not the clearest explanation and analysis, but the gist is that Clemo was doubting the possibility of finding a divinely approved love, and contact with Brenda changed that. The important part of the explanation would be *how* she did this, and saying that it was her 'gaiety' is not quite enough. It shows the explanatory gap which Jack too often fails to cross in his non-fictional, theological and explicatory pieces.

The language of 'The Burnt Bush' certainly is suggestive of sexuality, and the apparently ingenuous despair that it should be interpreted as such seems naïve, unless he thought the 'unpleasantness' of the interpretation was pederastic. Following *Wilding Graft*, in which the hero falls in love with a fifteen-year-old girl, and following *Confession of a Rebel*, in which Clemo describes some of his feelings for Barbara and also writes that the girl in *Wilding Graft* was intended to be twelve, it is not surprising that this biographical context is brought to the poetry. On the other hand, it might be a fault when reading Clemo's poetry to assume that the narrative voice is always the writer's. Jack encouraged this in *Confession of a Rebel*, suggesting that people should study his life alongside his work, but in the case of 'The Burnt Bush' we are not merely looking at a poetic confession. Sexuality bursts out of it; the bushes, thorns, stumps; the 'curl of crackling flame' and 'cleft of naked need'; the 'licked', 'flicked' and 'pricked' rhyme; 'Nature's vein' and the 'slow / Thin pulse of smoke'; and then the repeated language of ignition. 'Fresh too was my desire', opens the fifth stanza, 'desire' rhyming with the 'fire' of its final line, implying that their meanings are related, an idea supported by 'the flame' leaping when 'her hand held mine'. The poem seems to be of purification through the action, the 'hush / Of clay delivered from the push / Of Nature's sap: now in God's ken / I stand unsoiled again.' Note the connection between sexuality and the Biblical burning bush and one of Clemo's favourite reads of 1944, the Christian psychologist Leslie Weatherhead's *The Mastery of Sex*. Many of Clemo's more frank ideas of sex and sexuality derive from this book. Weatherhead states that 'understanding the facts of sex' – a phrase very close to Clemo's provocative outburst in the *Cornish Guardian* – is essential to a child's psychological wellbeing, and that the avoidance of sexual education 'is hardly less than criminal'. Weatherhead condemns the Church's silence on sexual matters and writes of common symptoms of unhealthy attitudes, which would have reminded Jack of his youthful self, and he talks of masturbation as masochistic self-abuse. The union of a truly loving marriage, Weatherhead argues, can make a (heterosexual) couple 'more like God than ever before'. Weatherhead also makes the observation that if the feeling does not bring you closer to God then it may be lust instead of love. However, all of Clemo's driftings into love made him feel closer to God. Weatherhead then uses the phrase 'divine spark' when describing the feeling of love. It is a phrase that appealed to Clemo, and flashes, sparks and fire-flakes become favourite images in the poetry.

Especially pertinent to Clemo's 'The Burnt Bush' is Weatherhead's reference to Havelock Ellis: 'Sex is an ever-living fire that nothing will extinguish. It is like that flame which Moses saw on Mount Horeb, burning the bush which yet was not consumed.' The idea, then, of Clemo's 'Burnt Bush', which fires fiercely, smokes and then is burnt into cathartic silence, is strongly suggestive of a sexual act.

Sex is reclaimed, redeemed, spiritualised and sanctified here. As yet it is still immature in Clemo, and the period of maturation continues until his hazy engagement to Mary Wiseman and his marriage to Ruth Peaty. It is the poetry to Mary, written in the early 1960s, that has the strongest erotic roots and imagery, although it will be seen when discussing the volume of that period, *Cactus on Carmel*, that the published poems were stripped of some of their more overtly sexual language.

In Christian terms, the message of *The Clay Verge* is ferociously nonconformist. The narrator 'needs no ritual voiced / In speech or earthly idiom to draw / My soul to His new law'. God is not in the churches and rituals. Neither is He in the leafing trees, bird song or budding flowers. Recall *Wilding Graft*'s final chapter, in which the suitability of the landscape as a symbol is explored:

> He shrank instinctively from the lush natural landscape lying towards Falmouth. [...] His mood was one for the desert, a stripped barren expanse suggesting the ultimate conflicts. And he realised through an imaginative, poetic nerve still keen at times amid the general cloudy flux, the fitness of the clay area as a setting for his desperate spiritual battle.

This image of 'man in a stripped clay desert' would be used again in 'The Excavator'. Clemo is saying that the symbols of Christ are here, in the industrial clayscape: 'I felt that human nature had to be purified just as the clay industry purified the tainted soil and turned it into material for beautiful pottery'.[345] These themes are used to great effect in 'Christ in the Clay-Pit':

>   I peer
> Upon His footsteps in this quarried mud;
>   I see His blood
> In rusty stains on pit-props, waggon-frames
> Bristling with nails, not leaves. There were no leaves
>   Upon His chosen Tree,
> No parasitic flowering o'er the shames

Of Eden's primal infidelity.
    Just splintered wood and nails
Were fairest blossoming for Him

And again, in the 'The Clay-Tip Worker', one of two monologues from a worker's perspective (along with 'The Excavator'):

    I love to see the sand I tip
Muzzle the grass and burst the daisy heads.
I watch the hard waves lapping out to still
The soil's rhythm for ever, and I thrill
With solitary song upon my lip,
    Exulting as the refuse spreads:
        'Praise God, the earth is maimed'

The landscape and its Christian symbolism allowed him once again to juxtapose the natural and divine in reference to love and relationships. In 'A Calvinist in Love', we catch a glimpse of the ideal. It is fitting as the final poem of the collection, having a message of optimism, if not consummation. It begins:

I will not kiss you, country fashion,
    By hedgesides where
    Weasel and hare
Claim kinship with our passion.

I care no more for fickle moonlight:
    Would rather see
    Your face touch me
Under a claywork dune-light.

Importantly for the collection's message, the poem ends:

Our love is full-grown Dogma's offspring,
    Election's child,
    Making the wild
Heats of our blood an offering.

By 'dogma', Clemo wrote to a friend, 'I mean the doctrines of the New Testament and the Church creeds'.[346]

In a BBC interview with Causley, Jack gives an account of how 'A Calvinist in Love' was inspired, which is an insight into his method of working:

> I wrote it at the end of 1945, our evacuee girls had gone back to London six months before and I'd been wandering about the clay works every day, thinking of the happy times when I'd rambled around with the girls. [...] Then one Sunday afternoon a local girl who'd been a friend of our evacuees and joined in our rambles and parties, called to get their address so that she could write to them. She only stayed a few minutes, but the young feminine atmosphere was back in the house again and during the next few days I knew a poem was on the way. I couldn't get it through into words – it seems the feminine influence wasn't quite strong enough. On the Saturday morning I was sitting at my desk, trying to get the poem started. As I looked out of the window I saw the milkmaid coming up the path. She was a pretty girl of 12. That extra bit of feminine beauty on my doorstep at that particular moment brought the poem through – it began to flow at once and within ½ hour it was finished. [...] a lot of my poems are written almost automatically – I don't give much conscious thought to them except in revision, and there isn't usually much of that.[347]

It is from *The Clay Verge* that Clemo first got his reputation as a bleak, nature-hating Calvinist. He did not really hate the natural world, of course, nor was he especially Calvinistic, and it is peculiar that he was not often challenged on his theological self-identification.

The influence of Calvinism – or rather, post-Calvinism – is evident in the themes of election and predestination, although even there the perspective is Neo-Orthodox rather than Calvinist. Jack had struggled through Niebuhr's *The Nature and Destiny of Man*, and afterwards it became an important influence, leading him in 1943 to the other celebrated Neo-Orthodox theologian, Karl Barth. But 'Calvinist' was a much stronger and more attractive appellation to Clemo than 'Neo-Calvinist' or 'Neo-Orthodox'. It was cleaner, more poetic, more radical. 'Neo-Calvinist' gave the sense of a broken theology, something tinkered with, manufactured. This desire to ally himself with the more radical statement – the more misfitting and rebellious – would prove a nuisance later in life, in the same way as his repeated emphases on his disabilities and hardships would prove a nuisance. These factors would obscure the critics' reading of his work in the future.

The basic picture we get from *The Clay Verge* is that the world is fallen, as is man. It is not fallen by God's will, but because of original sin. The claywork machine-monsters digging over the earth, destroying the natural world, are a metaphor for 'tough truth attacking sentimental falsehood', a response to 'the pagan slop of nature poets.'[348] Throughout *The Clay Verge*, Clemo makes it clear that he is attacking the 'nature poets' – the Romantics. Particularly, it would seem, Shelley and Wordsworth. He dismisses their landscape in 'Neutral Ground' when he states that God's 'Hand did not fashion the vistas / These poets admire', and again in 'The Excavator' when 'Nature' tempts the narrator with the 'doom of poetry'. If God is to be found, He will be here, in the pits, rejoicing in the destruction of sinful 'Nature'. This is not a theological argument, and the metaphor should not be pressed too hard, but it certainly suggests several possible tensions: between God and 'Nature' itself; between God and 'Nature' in man; between man and 'Nature'; and between man and himself. It naturally parallels Clemo's own 'broken boundaries', his degenerative syphilis and the assault of his bodily nature, the sense being that for Jack to be ready for God's work he first has to be chastened, purified, baptized 'under the dripping clay'. Whether it is God or the Christian narrator destroying the earth, it remains an act of Christian revolution against the natural world.

In spite of this straining subject-matter and the fact that Clemo himself grew tired of the theme, the poems were composed with remarkable ease:

> Wrote another poem [The Plundered Fuchsia], but feel this theme is worked out – it's time I wrote about something else instead of always attacking flowers and resisting creation. I don't know that I want any girl to share that mood, only it's nature-lovers who're always belittling dogma and I must get my own back somehow.[349]

Later that year he noted: 'Wrote a poem called "Sufficiency" – same old theme. I wish I could get beyond it'. The following year he is still being haunted: 'Wrote another poem – "The stones cry out, but the flames die dumb" – good, but it's always the same theme, my thought going round and round in a circle – Dogma vs Nature'.[350] So easy and absorbing was his poetising that he believed his talent for writing novels had left him altogether, and in 1947 he wrote that he was 'troubled by the way my talent has changed: it doesn't see a novelist any longer.'[351] Jack still wanted to write novels, but he was alert to the possibility that 'the novel-writing phase of my witness may be over'.[352]

Poetry had always been too easy for Clemo to take it seriously. He tried to contradict the poetic impulse and the ease of composition by suggesting there was a pattern to the inspiration, offering a sense of the poetry coming from somewhere other than his desire, writing in *Confession*: 'While I lived for poetry I wrote only doggerel; it was only after I turned my back upon poetry that I became a poet.' There is no sense in the autobiography, or in the diaries, that there was ever a period of living 'for poetry' in his youth. His ambition was always to write stories and novels, from that earliest, 'What about if I was to write stories like – like they 'Ockings?', through the correspondence with Meggy, the sentiments in the *Cornish Guardian*, numerous drafts and submissions, and into the 1940s, as he was planning his second trilogy. It is because of his ambitions as a novelist that the success of his poetry was unsettling, and for the rest of his life he would express regret that his novels were not published or paid the attention he felt they deserved, believing that his 'best work as an artist was in [the] novels.'[353] 'If I'd been able to go on as a novelist,' he wrote, 'how different everything would have been.'[354] In a BBC interview with Charles Causley, he went further:

> I have never thought of myself as a literary man at all in the professional sense. I'm just a free-lance witness to the transformation of life through Christian faith. I would have preferred to have continued as a novelist because in that way the challenge gets across to thousands who wouldn't dream of reading a theological book or collection of poems. My increasing handicaps forced me into the kind of writing which is least influential as far as the masses are concerned.

This adds a practical element to the desire to be a novelist: novels get a wider audience. The idea was echoed in 1976, when Clemo blamed the decline of interest in his work on his movement away from prose:

> When the word 'novelist' was replaced by 'poet' and then 'blind and deaf poet,' the public interest in me waned, and probably won't reach another peak level till more critical attention is given to my prose.[355]

Not only was the inspiration for poetry flowing freely while the novelistic urge had withered, but when his sight worsened again in 1947, remaining in constant decline, Jack lost the ability to write long works. Poems he could write in his head, but a novel was too big to remember. Later, after he had turned completely white-blind, he had no option. If he was to write, he would have to write poetry. In this way, disability defined Clemo's literary legacy, as he continued to produce these striking, lively and alien, alienating and appealing verses.

Clemo may have begun to hate his poetry, but his friends believed that it was the poetry that would survive. Writing to the Devonshire literary man E.W. Martin, Clemo's friend Derek Savage recalled talking to Jack's mother about his legacy:

> She asked me if I thought any of Jack's work would 'live', and I assured her emphatically that his work as a poet would ensure for him a permanent place in

English literature, while his 'Confession' would remain as a unique document, both of human, and of regional significance.[356]

Savage was at the centre of the Cornish literary scene, a poet and critic living in Mevagissey, friends with Causley, Miskin, Colin Wilson and Martin, as well as Clemo. Mrs Clemo told her son what Savage had said, and it is worth comparing Savage's account with Jack's in his diary: 'D.S. Savage called – said my work is immortal.' He continues: 'Yet there are times when I just want to forget it, it's so bound up with morbidity and tragedy. Mother feels I'm going too far now in belittling my own work.'[357]

In spite of such appreciation, *The Clay Verge* was a financial disaster, apparently only selling 180 copies in five years. Meanwhile, reviews were mixed. *The Scotsman, Time and Tide* and the local papers all reviewed it pleasantly, but *Poetry Quarterly*, the *TLS* and *The Spectator* gave it a horrible press. Writing for the latter, Ralph Abercrombie said: 'Mr Clemo's clogged and cumbrous verses [...] are full of shop-worn tropes and faded poeticisms – an unpleasant mixture of clay and dead flowers'.[358] The review went on to show just how far Abercrombie had missed the point, but he was not the only one. Anne Treneer praised Clemo's originality, defiance and force in the *Cornish Review*, but regretted that he did not write more about 'the singing of the larks'. Worse still was the *Poetry Quarterly* review, which Clemo considered so bad that the copy he kept of it in his scrapbook was defaced to hide the worst passages.

Nevertheless, it is to *The Clay Verge* that readers, editors and critics most frequently return. Those poems are the most popular and anthologised of Clemo's writing, appearing in collections such as Faber & Faber's *Book of Landscape Poetry*, Bloodaxe's *Poetry with an Edge*, Peter Redgrove's *Cornwall in Verse*, Charles Causley's *The Sun, Dancing*, Lions' *Book of Christian Poetry* and D.M. Thomas's *The Granite Kingdom*. In many ways, they represent the height of Clemo's fame. They express the greatest intimacy with his native landscape and they are the harshest and most awkward of his poetic output. Being so forceful, uncompromising and unique, it is no wonder that these poems made an impression and established Clemo's reputation.

At the same time, Clemo had found success with a second sequence of poems, 'The Wintry Priesthood', winning a prize in the Festival of Britain. These were then published by Penguin in *Poems 1951*, and they would be republished alongside *The Clay Verge* in *The Map of Clay* ten years later. 'The Wintry Priesthood' is comprised largely of biographical and tribute poems to Spurgeon, Lawrence, Kierkegaard, Barth and Powys, mostly written in February 1950 and owing much to the new enthusiasm he had discovered for Theodore Powys's work. The recurrent ideas of the hermit 'priest' and God's 'moods' are straight from Powys's *Soliloquies of a Hermit*. These poems had already been rejected by Day Lewis for *The Clay Verge* and Clemo regretted their omission, feeling 'the seventeen poems that remained in the collection did not give a true or fair picture of me or my beliefs'.[359] He wanted to 'do a series of "Poems in Tribute", entering into the hearts and minds of men who've influenced me',[360] and 'The Wintry Priesthood' was close to this intention. Biographical poems always remained a preoccupation, a response to Jack's habitual reading of lives and autobiographies. In these earliest poems they are as often tributes as admiringly hostile responses, but they will become more frequently the latter. As Rowan Williams wrote in his preface to the 2015 *Selected Poems*, Clemo needed 'to find in his interlocutors the question to which his poetry and his experience are in some sense an answer.'[361]

The Clay Verge marks the end of Cecil Day Lewis's personal influence over Jack's work, although Clemo would continue to follow his career. He began to read Day Lewis's poetry more seriously and objectively in 1970, writing in his diary: 'it's great art, with a wide range and deep feeling. I wonder what he thinks of my later work.'[362] Within two days of this entry, Clemo had written 'Smoke', 'using Day-Lewis verse form'. The poem was published in the 1971 *The Echoing Tip*, and was actually written 'to' the Irish playwright Sean O'Casey, Clemo having read a collection of O'Casey's work in Braille that year and having enjoyed *Juno and the Paycock* particularly, though regretting its gloomy ending:

> At length someone unlatched the window;
> I would creep out coughing, my eyes in pain,

> Stand beside the gooseberry tangle,
>   Welcome the night wind's keen
> Capers and watch the smoke-clouds fumble slowly
>   Into frost or rain.

This is the form Clemo would associate with Day Lewis, and he would use it again when he wrote the dedicative poem 'On the Burial of a Poet Laureate' in 1972, collected in *Broad Autumn*:

> Laureate, your heart rests, after a rainy Whitsun,
>   Close to grave Hardy's heart which bore
> Much the same toils: warrant of Western sunset,
> The church towers fading, the unransomed moor
> Thrusting the outcasts, stoic or Promethean,
>   To sea's verge and poet's core.

Almost certainly, Clemo found this rhyme structure in Day Lewis's 'Emily Brontë' monologue, in *Poems 1943-1947*, which began:

> All is the same still. Earth and heaven locked in
> A wrestling dream the seasons cannot break:
> Shrill the wind tormenting my obdurate thorn trees,
> Moss-rose and stone-chat silent in its wake.
> Time has not altered here the rhythms I was rocked in,
> Creation's throb and ache.

The connection between Brontë, Hardy and Day Lewis is striking. Clemo had thought of Day Lewis as one of the rare, good sorts of humanists and agnostics, placing him with Hardy, a man he thought sympathetic to faith and yearning for it. Similarly, Clemo perceived an unfulfilled religious temperament in Emily Brontë. Earlier, in *Confession of a Rebel*, he seemed to dismiss her with the line, 'Nor was I much interested in vague agnostic mysticism like Emily Brontë's', but Clemo returned over and over again to the Brontë sisters, with notable mentions of Emily in *The Echoing Tip*'s 'The Islets', dedicated to her, and in *Approach to Murano*'s 'Emily Brontë'.

Cecil Day Lewis, however, fell from grace, following the biography written by his eldest son Sean in 1986. Clemo had already read Cecil Day Lewis's autobiography, *The Buried Day*, in 1964, but when he read Sean Day Lewis's *An English Literary Life* his feelings changed: 'Troubled by the notorious […] life of Day-Lewis. It's ironic that such a godless man would be used to open the door for my work in 1946. But he soon dropped me in favour of Causley.'[363] In a letter to Michael Spinks, Clemo added: 'I had no idea he was such a lecherous and treacherous man'.[364]

The Clay Verge was the last of the three titles contracted by Chatto & Windus. A powerful but imperfect first novel, a striking autobiography, and a volume of some of the most unusual poetry, as well as freedom from the burden of extreme poverty, were Day Lewis's pivotally important legacy in Clemo's career, which, it is fair to say, was established and defined by this editor and poet. Had the volume of poetry come out in its entirety, it would have been a disaster; had *Wilding Graft* gone to print in its first draft, the reviews would almost certainly have been less favourable.

Instead, Jack had become a writer by profession, his reputation established, his worldview and manifesto introduced. Day Lewis would play no major role now, although a handful of other influences were being developed. It is to some of these we will turn in the following chapter; to Littleton, Susie and T.F. Powys, Eileen Funston, Helena Charles and June Trethewey. Within only a couple of years, Clemo would believe himself engaged to two women, with hopes for others, and he would establish one of the longest-lasting friendships of his life with one of Cornwall's best-loved poets, Charles Causley.

X
A Mystical-Erotic Quest

Deliver me, O my God, out of the hand of the wicked, out of the hand of the unrighteous and cruel man. For thou art my hope, O Lord God: thou art my trust from my youth. By thee have I been holden up from the womb: thou art he that took me out of my mother's bowels: my praise shall be continually of thee.

The Autobiography of Dr Talmage

As Clemo's literary star was rising, his body fell into decline. At the beginning of 1947, his eyes suffered another attack. By March he was unable to read. Eveline visited the doctor and was told to go to Truro where the specialist could prescribe penicillin, the newly available wonder-drug for syphilis that 'might act as a stimulant to my mind and possibly help my hearing.'³⁶⁵ Penicillin's application in the treatment of syphilis had not been discovered until 1943, and did not become available until 1946, by which time it was just too late for Jack.

After collecting the drug from Truro, the Clemos went to St Austell Hospital, where Jack was admitted on 3 April for an intensive and painful ten-day course of injections. Jack was optimistic about penicillin: 'I've got real faith in that stuff', he wrote in his diary.³⁶⁶

After a few days of adjustment to the hospital, unexpectedly Jack started to enjoy himself:

> Getting used to it and enjoying [...] fun with the nurses and especially the nursemaid who cleans my room and brings meals – a dark, solid girl who tells mother I'm 'such a good boy'. I lie very politely hour after hour and they all say I'm marvellous.³⁶⁷

He had never received attention quite like this and he found the constant interaction stimulating. Before long, he was asking his mother to bring in the copy of *Orion* with his poem to show everyone. There was 'a handyman', he notes, particularly impressed, who came in to ask whether this was *the* Jack Clemo. During these days Jack deeply regretted his inability to communicate directly, believing that if he had been able to speak he would have found a girlfriend among the nurses.

More strikingly, between these moments of amusement Clemo felt a weird depletion of joy. It was a sensation he would remark upon during every hospital stay throughout his life. Everything felt 'so empty', he wrote, and he could not feel God's presence 'at all vividly only the dull prayer "Lord help me" in my heart while the injections were actually going into my hip'.[368] The absence of God is a poignant moment in the diaries, carrying with it the impressive implication that usually Jack *could* feel God's presence.

He left the hospital on 12 April:

> Well, it's over – the last injection at 2:30 and then home at 3 – not much better than when I left but they say when the penicillin begins to work through I shall get better every day and in a few months the full effects will be felt.

His eyesight would never recover. Aside from a short-lived reprieve that followed hospitalization, it would now be in slow and constant decline.

Around this time, Clemo read Aldous Huxley's *The Art of Seeing*. Huxley had suffered with his eyesight since his teens and wrote of a method of making reading possible for a little longer, which Clemo adopted. In a piece of black card a slit was cut, large enough for a single line of text to be seen. This was placed over the page, apparently assisting the partially sighted to focus while reducing any glare. Although Jack would say that he did not go fully blind until 1955, his diaries better show the gradual deterioration, when even in 1948 he describes himself as 'semi-blind', likening his condition to that of James Joyce.

The effect of this worsening of health was that Jack became more in need of help, more disabled, a state that coincided with a series of domestic disasters that would put pressure on his desire to find someone able to look after him.

The same year in which Jack was hospitalised, his dog Flush died. Flush had been a source of constant light relief and companionship, sleeping every night on Jack's bed. He was a comic companion, and often Jack wrote in his diaries of his escapades: 'Flush came in at noon looking more like a little polar bear than a dog. He's fallen in a clay-tank somewhere'.[369] His death, apparently from a heart problem, brought out a brief period of dramatic expression in the diary:

> Wandered around Goonvean and the fields crying in agony, and could scarcely realise that he wasn't with me still – the rooms are terrible when I look around, almost expecting to see him, and then think of the grave. It's so sudden, I can't see the mercy of God in it at all.[370]

Flush, he says, 'was my only comfort'. Then: 'Brenda will always be associated with his last few weeks'. Brenda had been around a lot towards the end of July, with her friend Myrna, and Jack was finding the company of these teenage girls more rewarding than the earlier infatuations with younger girls. They signalled the move towards a more mature romantic vision.

Jack buried the Pomeranian in the garden, 'my heart full and the tears coursing – wondering what God will do to cheer me up after all this.'[371] It made him consider for a very brief time whether 'Flush will share in the resurrection of the Body of this household, as Lewis explains it. I feel my Heaven could never be complete without him.' It is a slight surprise to read of Clemo's emotional and spiritual connection with Flush. Elsewhere in his writing, he suggests that he 'was not the sort of man who could find deep comfort in pets'. Jack cut a clump of black and yellowish hair off the dead dog, which he slipped into an envelope and kept in his diary. A month later he went to Redruth and bought a third Pomeranian, Spark. Spark had a short life, dying in 1952 with 'kidneys bleeding', though he again meant enough for Jack to preserve a lock of his golden coat.

The deaths of these dogs were more significant to Jack than the death of his Aunt Bertha in 1949. There was no period of mourning for Bertha, and no record of tears. He had seen how much frailer she looked, and noted she was dying, but he only recorded the inconvenience of her death. It disrupted his revisions of *Confession* and filled the house distractingly with visitors. Jack 'had no wish to see a corpse', so did not go upstairs where the body was kept, and when the funeral came:

> Neither I nor my foster-sisters attended the funeral on the Wednesday afternoon. We went to a neighbour's house in Goonamarris hamlet for tea, then climbed into a field where Brenda and some other girls were playing ball games.

The arrival of the foster-sisters Frances and Violet Allen was again a symptom of this difficult period, when the Clemos needed help. After Eveline's critical illness in 1942, they were concerned for what would happen to Jack if she suddenly died. Eveline's health was frail, with heart and gastric problems, and Bertha had been deteriorating, while Jack showed no signs of improvement. Eveline made the bold decision to go to London, the first time she had been 'abroad', intending to talk to Irene and encourage her back to Cornwall. She had wanted to go just before Jack was admitted to hospital, but had been held up until July 1947. Jack hoped Irene might return with Eveline, but in her daily reports the news was bleak:

> Mother writes that neither Irene nor Iris can come this year, so all hope for help during the holidays is gone and it looks like being a *Black Year* to the end. Mother sends Lewis' book on Miracles to try to make up for the bad news – so pitiful it's heartbreaking, for she must know that books can never be my substitute for the friendship I've been pining for all the year.[372]

A few days later:

> One of the blackest weeks of the year this – and mother writes that all our old evacuees have got worldly – our

> influence and prayer seem thrown away on them – she says it's far better for me to look to Ba than any up there. How gladly I would if only she gave any sign of being ready!

It is likely that Eveline also spoke to the Jauncey family during this trip about adopting one or more of the children. Nothing much came of it, although Rita and Doris made a long visit a few weeks later.

One might imagine Eveline Clemo in the sprawling capital, where her husband had once lived and worked, looking for the office of Chatto & Windus where Clemo's manuscripts were being held, and visiting Browning's Westminster grave on her son's behalf. A description of her visit constitutes the first chapter of *The Marriage of a Rebel*, but in spite of visiting old friends and seeing the sites, her trip was a disappointment. When she returned home, she spoke candidly with Jack about the future, resolving that it should be their priority to find him a wife who would care for him and who would help Eveline with the housework. She had 'had enough of the extra strain and wants a girl here who'll look after *me* instead of more girls whom she has to look after in addition to me.' They were now both on the lookout for the 'real girl'.[373]

After the Jaunceys had gone back to London, Eveline began to enquire about adoption. They had a relative in Plymouth who ran a boarding home, and they found two girls there looking to be fostered, their parents for various reasons unable to take care of them. A placement officer came to inspect the Clemo cottage, and there were a few tense weeks waiting to hear the verdict.

Frances and Violet Allen were not exactly what the Clemos had intended when they began their search, as Jack wrote in 1948:

> The only girls they've got are two sisters, the eldest 12, and I don't see how that could help, only be an extra burden for mother, and for me too if they were off together in the evenings, leaving me lonely still. I can't understand why [...] God doesn't cut through all this muddle by sending 'love.'[374]

Once the Clemos had heard the story of the Allen girls, they could not leave them to their unhappy city life, and on 17 September 1948, Frances and Violet arrived at Goonamarris, tired and timid. Frances recalls her time at the cottage with great affection. She had only known the city, and among her earliest impressions she remembers her astonishment when she first saw a real-life cow. Of Eveline and Jack, she speaks of their warm, loving welcome. Eveline told the girls that they were to call her 'Mum', and that Jack was their brother. Frances is the source of a great many fond memories of the Clemos, including the following, which occurred soon after the girls' arrival. She had been upset because other children had china dolls and she had never owned one. Eveline said nothing, but after the girls had gone to school, she got to work. First, she went to St Austell to buy the doll's china parts. Then, back at home, she started to sew all its clothes. Frances returned in the evening, by which time the doll was sitting in the chair waiting for her.

When she was first introduced to Jack, Frances says he took her to see the clay dumps, while Violet, who was older and a little quieter, stayed at the cottage with Mrs Clemo. Jack's patience with them is recalled; how long he was willing to hold the skipping rope or to stay bent over for leapfrog. Frances also remembers how, once a week, the Clemos would save the girls from school dinners, meeting them halfway between school and home with Eveline's hot, freshly made pasties, which they ate together on the roadside.

Gossip surrounding Jack still lingered, undeterred by his success, and in the 1950 diary there is an episode described at some length, which threatened the relationship with his new sisters:

> A strange little jolt tonight. I was out in the sand playing with F. and V. when two police came along. They were very suspicious and told F. they thought I had assaulted her. She was bewildered and said we were all there playing 'jump-backs' and nothing wrong. But the police were unconvinced and came in to tell mother they must report me for indecent behaviour. They were rather shocked when she produced C[*onfession*] and showed them the part about Irene, but [...] the unimaginative official mind was adamant – I felt like

Lawrence at Zennor. But I pray and believe there be no fresh trouble and upheaval.[375]

The following day the welfare officer came over to tell Eveline that it had been a mistake, 'a mere misunderstanding of strangers who didn't know I was Jack Clemo!' There is no sense from any other source (including from Frances) that anything inappropriate had happened, but the idea that Clemo might be an exception to moral and legal rules because of a self-evaluation in his autobiography suggests the faith he had in the redemptive potency of his confessional writing. It is not said why the police officers interrupted Jack and the girls. What had they seen? Had they seen anything at all? Or was Clemo's reputation sufficient for their concern? The fact that the policemen were unaware of Clemo and his books might tell us that they had not heard of him and were not aware of his history. On the other hand, perhaps they knew Clemo's history but had not read any of his writing, until Eveline showed them *Confession*. Certainly, Jack was an oddity in the region. He had always stood out, always been a loner, and this episode indicates that he had yet to achieve the full public absolution he desired.

Frances and Violet were too young to help Eveline very much when they first arrived, but they remained devoted to the Clemos and would be a great relief in the years to come. For the time being, however, pressure was increased on their need to find help. The death of Bertha reminded Jack that his mother was not in good health: 'I feel the shadow of Bertha's death fall like a nightmare whenever mother is unwell. She's still all I have in the world, the only person I really know'.[376] Jack's concern for the future was so distressing that Eveline made a bold and unusual promise. She promised that she would not die until she saw Jack married and provided for.

The search for a wife continued, and between 1948 and 1951 a number of prospects emerged. One of the most notable of these was Eileen Funston, an eighteen-year-old student and 'the Hertfordshire girl' of *Confession*. She was expected to be the final part of the 'grafting' process, the 'Christian fellowship' Clemo longed for. He knew of Eileen from her writing in the *Christian Herald*, and even as early as 1946 Clemo had shown interest in her: 'If only a girl like this

Eileen Funston knew what I'm going through – how she could write in exactly the way I need'.[377]

Following a long piece of hers entitled 'What are the youth looking for?' in January 1949, Jack began to think about her again. 'Very restless with the urge to write to Eileen', he wrote. Then: 'I've been haunted by Eileen's article. Mother says I ought to write to her'.[378] He conceived a plan. He would write an essay for the *Christian Herald* in response to Eileen's, and if the paper was accepted, this would be a sign of divine approval. At the same time, it would give him a reason to write to her. His article was entitled 'Faith Brings the Victory', and it was quickly accepted. Two days later, Jack composed his letter. He waited for her response impatiently and he was at the end of his tether when, four days later, she had still not replied. It was incomprehensible to him that someone might be too busy to write immediately. 'If E. doesn't reply', he told his diary, 'I shall be flung back worse than ever, feeling that Christian girls let me down as badly as the rest'. Eileen did reply, and Jack's mood soared wonderfully: 'I still feel I must be dreaming [...] I feel like a different man already'.[379]

Eileen had not heard of Clemo or *Wilding Graft*, but she was confident talking about poetry, literature and the Bible in her three-page letter. Jack responded immediately and ecstatically, sending some of his poetry, including 'A Calvinist in Love'. Her next letter was thirteen pages long, with some promising sentiments: 'I feel we have something in common which the world would not understand; and I feel we each have a message for the other which God knew we needed.'[380]

The correspondence with Eileen shows a great deal of Jack's character at this period, although he is still limitingly naïve and immature, responding to criticism with unbridled ferocity. Eileen did not like either the poetry or prose without reservation. Of the poetry, she wrote:

> You are determined to drain your poetry of beauty, because you are afraid of the power and cunning of beauty. But there is a beauty which is not of this world. Why must you deprive yourself of this? [...] I cannot

like your poetry not because I do not appreciate the sensations which inspired it, but because it is not beautiful. It is beautiful as far as words, rhyme and rhythm are concerned, but because you are afraid of worshipping beauty, are you not worshipping something else instead? – apart from God, of course – are you not worshipping a sort of idol of philosophic emotions – largely, of course, because you are confined to living in the emotions and in the mind, and because yours is the only human condition you have the opportunity of studying. [...] I don't want you to misunderstand me. I am a child of 18. You are a man of experience; a man who has suffered [...]. Yet I feel that your magnificent gift should be used to glorify Him in a fuller sense.[381]

Wilding Graft was given the same treatment, Eileen telling Jack that had she not known him personally, she would have thought that he had not experienced conversion:

Poor chap [...]. If he knew Christ and had a passion for souls he would have learned the secret of sublimating his sexual instincts, which are obviously very much alive through starvation. Some of his characters aren't natural either. I expect he's cut off from other talk –, and his understanding of womanhood is pretty scant![382]

She even questions the faith of Clemo's idealised hero, Garth: 'He was more morbid than happy. And I always thought Christianity was supposed to be selfless, too. Garth didn't do much about sharing his beliefs except when he was asked to.' 'Why had he no deep concern for Edith's soul, for Sal's and Griffith's too? Surely they were just as precious to the Lord.'

This was not the sort of response Jack was expecting, and although all of his replies were destroyed (burned by Eileen's husband) it is clear from Eileen's letters that he was severe with her. He apparently questioned her about her lifestyle, so that she felt compelled to tell him:

> I wear no artificial make-up, and cannot understand Christians who fall in love with girls who do. As far as jewellery is concerned, I wear a wrist-watch, bracelet, brooches, necklaces, etc., but I wear nothing expensive or elaborate. I also wear simple, inexpressive clothes, though I have a definite taste in colour […] but I choose my clothes as I would choose my food, not to appeal to the opposite sex, but to suit my taste.[383]

Jack is thinking in terms of marriage, and brings it up too often and too soon. Eileen berates him, writing that he is too concerned with it. She tries to deflect his advances, quoting 1 Corinthians 7:27: 'Seek not a wife'. 'Would [Paul] say this if to find a wife meant to find completeness in Christ?' She returned several times to the theme in this exceptionally long letter:

> Forgive me for saying so, but I think it is wrong to *expect* things of God – other than the promises given in His word. It is like saying to Him 'I want a wife and it's your duty to send me one'. – almost like telling Him what His plan for your life is.

This letter is very revealing about the sorts of questions Clemo was asking Eileen:

> You asked me if I *ever* danced or flirted! As to the former, no I never did; though I have not always been a keen Christian, I have always had a reserved, self-conscious *nature*. […] Did I ever flirt? Of course! Do I have to go into details?[384]

It is difficult not to sympathise with Eileen. Her letters are full of Bible interpretations, literary criticism, friendship and candour, while Jack wants to know what she wears and whether she enjoys flirting. He explodes in response to her criticism, and Eileen has to reply with cool defensiveness:

> It is the baffling moods of the *male* that terrify me – the volcanoes and icebergs of *your* letters which make me tear them open with a chilly sense of apprehension. Little did I know that the warmth and sunlight of your last letter was to be 'numbed to poison' at my 'uncouth touch'.[385]

Eileen told me that she began dreading Jack's letters.

It was not until June 1949 that Jack asked her directly about whether they should marry. Eileen replied that she had been thinking about the possibility, but admitted that she always did when she met someone new:

> But, Jack, I don't want you in any way to build your hopes upon this possibility, because if you did and the Lord unmistakeably pointed me in another direction, then you know you would have to suffer for it. To be quite honest I will admit that at the moment I am very divided about my own feelings in this matter.[386]

Jack was not always certain either. On the one hand he was ridiculously excited that someone was interested in him as a potential spouse, and he wrote in his diary that God would have to be very cruel to have led him this far into a relationship if it was not His intention that they wed. On the other hand, he did not 'feel the miracle'.[387] (The exact same statement would be made about Ruth.)

Meanwhile, Jack's mother made a mistake. She had begun telling the neighbours, as Jack put it, 'that this girl whose photo is on my desk will probably be her daughter-in-law. I feel God wouldn't have let Mother speak thus openly if it was going to fall through – what laughing-stocks we should be then!'[388] Years later, Eileen wrote her own account of the brief affair in her book *Reaching for God*, in which she describes Eveline as 'saintly'. But this would not be the last time that Jack's mother intervened and put pressure on one of his romances. The same would happen with June Trethewey and again with Mary Wiseman. The Clemos' combined sense of urgency was pressed onto Eileen.

At the time, Eileen was studying at a Missionary Training College, and in the evenings she performed volunteer work, so she did not have much time for writing letters. Yet Jack continued to push her, berating her for responding too slowly and jealously asking about other 'eligible young men' in her village, while at home he was referring to as his 'girlfriend'. Eileen tried to slow Jack down, raising the obstacle of her parents, who were not keen on their daughter becoming engaged to a disabled man fifteen years her elder before she had even met him. Her mother told her:

> He's one of those men who wants a wife so badly he'd do anything to get one [...]. It isn't that he thinks more of you than anyone, but that he'd have *any*one. The trouble with you is that you pity people too easily and then you go too far.[389]

The mother went further, saying she would not attend any such wedding and her father would disown her. In *Reaching for God*, Eileen interpreted her feelings through her faith:

> Was this not a challenge to face the seemingly impossible with God, to fulfil a mission which maybe he had been preparing me for all these years? This man longed for love and companionship and understanding, if possible, even more than I did. He was asking me if I would be that companion, that lover. What if he was blind and deaf, almost gray, and fifteen years older than me? What did that have to do with love? But my heart cried out, *No, No, not that, Lord. Please, not that!*[390]

By 26 July, Eileen began expressing deeper doubts in her letters: 'I was tempted to grow a little weary of the thought that you expected God to use me as a mere answer to your prayers'. This is a telling remark and an astute observation, as this is precisely how he treated romantic prospects. She became angry again when he attacked her for having a friend come to visit. Eileen responded with a fourteen-page barrage of inspired emotional torture in response, and Jack immediately regretted his haste: 'My misreading of E.'s friendship with a man her mother wants her to marry produced an ugly mood, and when E. saw it reflected in my letter she almost broke off our affair.'[391]

Things were not going well. Jack felt certain of their mutual destiny, but Eileen was confused and could not cope. Her friends and family told her not to even contemplate marriage, and in the end she let God decide with a tokenistic ultimatum. She and Jack would not write to one another for a month, and if in that time God healed him then they would take it as a sign that they were, indeed, intended to marry. Of course, God did nothing, and when Eileen wrote again on 20 September, it was to confirm God's decision: 'God has given me His definite "No" concerning what was once our possibility.' She tells Jack not to write anymore, that this was final and he must leave her alone. A pastor friend helped her come to the decision, a man who described Jack as both 'eccentric' and 'egocentric'.[392]

God's silence was a great relief to Eileen: 'I cannot explain to you how I felt when I received His final decision. My heart was filled with a peace and a joy I had not felt for weeks.' But Jack was dreadfully upset, and he attacked. Eileen's 'revelation' must have come from the Devil, not from God, because God had told *him* the exact opposite. This reveals Clemo at his narcissistic worst. His faith revolves around his desires. Eileen repeated her earlier accusation:

> You seem to think that the revelation of His will must come through *you* and because it has come through me you call it the Devil. [...] I have reminded you over and over again that God's ways are not our ways, but you are determined that His way *shall* be your way – or rather that He shall work in the way you expect Him to.

And the final barb:

> You once tried to prove to me that the real prayer of faith always received 'Yes' for an answer. I agree. But the Word of God gives three exceptions: – Sin in the heart; selfishness at the base; and lack of importunity. Can

you honestly say your prayer for a wife – for me, if you like – is quite selfless?[393]

Their relationship and correspondence ended. Eileen would be married in little more than eighteen months and would go on to write under the name Eileen Mitson. Jack concluded that her purpose in his life – 'her message' – must have been 'connected with the two points that I had become worried about – my vilification of nature and my rejection of churches.'

> I realized what a drastic psychological change had taken place in me through this extraordinary friendship. For eight months I had been pouring out to a young woman my innermost thoughts and longings about God, sex, marriage, and the spreading of Christian truth through art. I could never be the same man again.[394]

Following the publication of *The Marriage of a Rebel* in 1980, Eileen wrote to Ruth, telling her that Jack's account of their correspondence was not quite fair. Clemo had retold the story as though he himself had not been a part of the problem:

> I'm sure he didn't realize it, but Jack put tremendous pressure on me at the time we were corresponding, so sure was he that we were ordained to meet! I began to dread his letters dropping on the mat, and finally said that I felt we must look for a definite sign from God before I could even agree to meet him. It may have been a foolish thing to say, but I *was* only eighteen, and I had been backed into a corner. When I suggested that we remain friends, and continue our correspondence, Jack would not hear of it. The reason, as we all know, was that his main objective was to find a wife![395]

With obvious irritation, Ruth annotated Eileen's letter, stating that it was Eileen who was wrong and that Jack's account was accurate.

Back in 1949, Jack dived immediately into another – albeit fleeting – fancy. Within a week of receiving Eileen's last letter, Helena Charles had written to say that she would be coming to visit. 'So strange that God is bringing yet another person into my life', he noted.[396] Helena was never a serious prospect, and her lasting significance was not romantic. By the time of *The Marriage of a Rebel* she had been thoroughly reduced, romantically speaking, to one of two 'older women' Clemo knew, along with Monica Hutchings.

Helena was a poet from Redruth, the first leader of the Cornish independence party Mebyon Kernow and an Anglo-Catholic with an influential interest in faith-healing. In *The Marriage of a Rebel* Clemo writes that Helena bought copies of his prose works to give to Catholic friends and reported that 'A nun friend of hers in an Anglican convent thought I still had much to learn from Catholic mystics.' Clemo says she was more interested in his prose than his poetry and that she 'was anxious that I should write more prose books'. In her summary of their meeting, Helena laments that Clemo 'is cut off from all human contact, but also from everything that might stimulate his creative faculties. At present he is not writing anything.'[397] She was introduced to Clemo's work by A.L. Rowse's radio review of *Wilding Graft* in 1948, and immediately went out to buy three copies before sitting down to read it in almost a single sitting. Her first letter had many characterful personal touches, as Charles explained how her own novel manuscript was bombed in the war, and that she could see his 'clay pyramids' from her cottage. Their correspondence was brief, but insightful, particularly with regard to Clemo's beliefs, as they discussed the differences between his nonconformism and her Anglo-Catholicism, Clemo writing:

> I have the deepest reverence for the early Church which compiled the Bible and the historic Creeds. It is difficult, however, to see much connection between that Church and the 'religious organization' we find around us to-day – except, of course, in the continuity of the Roman Catholic Church. And I am cut off from that by my temperamental aversion to ritual. The 'sanction' of the dogma is the Holy Spirit, who works wherever the

> doctrine is received, whether through Providence (for the elect – e.g. Garth and Irma) or through preaching and the voluntary response (of the non-elect). This is my modified form of Calvinism. I don't claim that it is the only interpretation that an orthodox Christian can accept, but it has helped me and it may help others.[398]

He also states his case with regard to other aspects of Catholicism:

> I don't accept the doctrine of transubstantiation, though I admit the validity of the Mystical aspect of obedience to Christ's command: 'This do in remembrance of me.' On baptism, I incline to the Baptist view that it should be a symbol of a consciously-chosen identification with the death and resurrection of Christ: infant baptism has degenerated into a formality with little religious significance for many parents [...] But though I like a general Free Church attitude to the Sacraments, I think the Roman Catholics are right in regarding Christian marriage as a sacrament.[399]

In a diary entry from around the same time, Clemo's feelings about Catholicism are more robust. He had been reading Coventry Patmore, leading him to a meditation on Catholicism and his own role as witness.

> The unwholesome luxuriousness of the Catholic atmosphere repels me. I'm more than ever convinced that 'the mystic sensuous ardour of the puritan' – as I called it in my Browning poem – is the New Testament [?vision?] of sex, and the R.C. softness and slushiness a perversion.

His calling, he concludes, is to confront with his work 'the Roman Catholics as well as the pagans'.[400]

Jack and Helena met at the cottage on 23 November 1949, when Jack was still in turmoil over Eileen. Helena wanted to write an article about him, some of which has been preserved almost accidentally. The Clemos had to be frugal and did not waste paper, Clemo using the backs of manuscripts and the spaces in between typed lines to write out new thoughts and poems. Some of the later poems of *The Clay Verge* manuscript were written on the back of Helena's unpublished paper, which is why it has survived. So we have both Clemo's account of the meeting in *The Marriage of a Rebel* and Helena Charles's. From Clemo's perspective:

> I rose to greet a tall, dark-haired lady, not fashionably dressed but with an air of refinement and a pleasant, serious face. She had a long discussion with my mother while I slumped at my desk, speaking only when queries were jotted down and handed to me. When she had gone my mother commented: 'A nice woman, but she eddn jolly – she dun't never what I call laugh.'[401]

Helena wrote:

> I visited Jack Clemo as arranged [...]. During the whole period of about an hour that I was in the cottage, he did not say six words. His hearing has now gone completely so that he hears nothing at all, and his sight has deteriorated gravely during the past two years. Reading is laborious and painful.

Jack looked quite pathetic that day, and while Helena seemed a little surprised at his unwillingness to talk with her, the Clemos wondered that she did not seem jollier. It may be that Eveline Clemo sometimes lacked an empathetic imagination, or did not always take temperaments different from her own into account. And Jack relied on his mother's opinions and interpretations. Both accounts show the social expectation that Jack would not participate in conversations when people came to see him. It was expected that his mother spoke for him. Helena was not annoyed, only disappointed and concerned for Clemo's severance from the world and for the fate of his future work. The article was never published, and Helena's real influence on Clemo's life was in the murky edgelands of faith-healing. She introduced him to healers across the county and beyond, driving him out to St Day and Redruth. Both Eveline and Jack had complete faith that such miracles not only could happen, but certainly would. They only had to keep pursuing, to keep believing, and God would reward them. More frequently now we read in the diaries of meetings in which Jack 'knelt in my pew while the vicar prayed over me with his hands on my head'.[402] He could hear almost nothing, and could see little more than shadows beyond a pale mist. Sometimes, following a meeting, Jack would feel as though it was working, as though God was freeing him from his isolation. But He never did and Helena was troubled, as Clemo noted: 'Heard from Miss C. She seems disappointed that there is no sign of healing, and almost wonders whether God may mean me to remain all my life a solitary mystic'.[403] This was not the last time Helena would express the opinion that God might want Jack to suffer.

The most spectacular attempt of Helena's to facilitate Jack's healing was when she paid and arranged for him and his mother to visit the celebrated blind healer Godfrey Mowatt in London. Mowatt was an Anglican who had lost his sight after stabbing himself in the eye with a knife during childhood. He, too, spent time as a boy sitting in darkened rooms with bandages over his eyes. Mowatt, like Clemo, paid considerable attention to meaningful patterns and 'coincidences'. Clemo recorded their meeting of 17 October 1951 in his diary:

> Mowatt was awaiting us at St Anne's House. Dean St., and mother [?talked?] with him while I drank some tea to brace myself. She told him about June and he confirmed our belief that it was God's work. Then we went through the [...] church to the little chapel and I knelt before the altar, broken and crying [...] while M. prayed. The laying on of hands steadied me, the sense of panic and darkness passed, and though still blind and unable to sleep much I had a comfortable night, knowing we couldn't have come across England in vain.

The memory is developed in *Marriage*:

> I closed my eyes and waited, unable to hear the blind man move up behind me. His assistant guided him, and suddenly his big bony hands grasped my head and began to vibrate. [...] An absurd spasm of guilt and remorse gripped me, due largely to physical exhaustion and the emotional upheaval of the past few weeks. [...] The blind man was wasting his time, fastening his fingers around my skull, pressing, attempting to transmit.... I started to cry, the tears splashing down on my sleeves, my slumped body convulsed with sobs.

The 'guilt' is a reference to June Trethewey, or 'T', as she is named in *Marriage*: 'God couldn't heal me for T because all my work had been inspired by other girls.'

June was a local girl living at Stepaside who went to study English at Exeter University, a 'clever but deeply religious [girl], solitary, with a dreamy far-away look in her dark eyes.' She had been taught in Sunday School by Eveline Clemo and often used to walk home with her after Chapel. When she went away to study, Eveline continued to ask after her and in 1950 June wrote to Mrs Clemo with news of university life. Both Mrs Clemo and Jack wrote in reply, and when June returned for Christmas she was invited to visit the cottage. She recalls her first impressions of Jack in a typical way:

> He sat at the window, a slight, rather gray, figure and said little as his mother showed us his manuscripts. I found it difficult to equate the writer, evidently a strong-minded, powerful person with the silent, withdrawn man I met that day but the memory of him, sitting in the window, remained with me and still does today.[404]

She was invited back and became aware of 'a strange, very powerful connection' developing between them, in spite of the silence. Eveline invited June to visit again one Sunday, and June had a sense of this meeting owning a higher significance than before:

Mrs Clemo was waiting for me and took me into the kitchen. She started to say at once that she believed that Jack and I were destined by God for each other. She believed that God had sent me to them and that if I were to marry Jack he would be miraculously healed of his sight and hearing problems.

Jack himself appears to have been unaware of Eveline's conversation in the kitchen. His diary entry for the day reads:

June came in and said God had spoken to her and told her I needed her. She kissed me and stayed with me all evening, holding my hands and anointing my eyes as a pledge of her faith.

'She wept for me', he says, which stunned him to silence. He was reminded of Elizabeth Barrett Browning, and the following two days' entries are filled with rapturous exclamations. However, the joy would be short-lived. Two days later, on 11 June, Jack wrote twice in his diary. The first time was to record June's visit, 'The most amazing day of my life'. The second was to report 'the most terrific spiritual angst I've ever known'. June had visited and sat on Jack's knee, conversing by writing notes, a few of which have survived. From June we find: 'I believe God has sent me. I know no other reason. So if it is Jesus' will I can help you. I was led here today'. Then: 'I believe my life has been guided for this moment'. But Eveline interfered. She was desperate for Jack to marry and aware of her promise that she would not die until he was wed. Prematurely, she snatched at this opportunity. As June recalls, Mrs Clemo left the cottage for the evening service at Trethosa Chapel, where 'she announced to my astounded parents and an equally astonished congregation that Jack and June were engaged to be married.'

Predictably, June's parents, previously unaware of any burgeoning relationship, were furious, and her father went straight to the cottage to bring her away. It was a knee-jerk reaction, which June feels might have been different had her father, 'a natural poet and philosopher', been given a chance to speak with Jack. It was, however, the end of their relationship, and of Jack's briefest romance, though he considered it his deepest to date: 'No other attachment has ever held me like this', he wrote months later, still holding the hope that healing would be achieved in London by Mowatt and the way for them might become clear again.

Tucked away among the letters from girlfriends there are also some notes from Eveline to Jack from this period, which show that she was not only pushing the young women too hard, but she was forcing the pattern for Jack, too. About June Trethewey, she wrote: 'I think she is prepared to give her life to you in love'; '[your disabilities] don't effect her the least'; 'you mustn't worry, you must be thankful the pattern is working out, its just like B & EB'; 'I think this is the beginning of full deliverance'.

The last of this cluster of romantic failures is the most intriguing and has been completely omitted in all published works on and by Clemo. For a time, it was considered the best prospect, and it was the most favoured by Jack himself, with a number of key connections supporting the apophenic necessity. The object of desire was the adopted daughter of Clemo's literary hero, Theodore Powys. Her real name was Theodora Gay, but she was known as Susie Powys, and it was largely with her in mind that Clemo eagerly accepted an invitation to visit Theodore and his older brother Littleton in Dorset. The Powys troupe consisted of ten surviving brothers and sisters, almost all of them writers or artists. Among the most notable were the four brothers, John Cowper, Theodore, Llewellyn and Littleton, although Gertrude was a well-established artist, Philippa a novelist, Marian an expert in lacework who wrote a popular book on the subject, and Albert an architect who again published several works within his field. It was only the youngest two who did not become public figures in some way, but there cannot have seemed much left for them to do in the wake of their mighty siblings. Will became a farmer in Kenya, who also painted landscapes, while the youngest, Lucy, appears not to have had any artistic ambitions, unlike her daughter, Mary Casey, who became a writer.

Jack had sent a copy of *Wilding Graft* to Theodore and hung his photograph above the writing desk, but it was that other 'older woman', the nature writer Monica Hutchings, who coordinated their introduction. Hutchings had written to Jack in an attractively forthright letter that began:

> Your 'Confessions of a Rebel' was among my Christmas presents, and I read it through completely absorbed, though I am not in agreement with you all the time!
> On New Year's Day I am going to Theodore Powys's at Mappowder [...] and I shall take the book with me. He is beyond praise of flattery, but I feel it may give him pleasure to remind him of the help he has been to you.
> But may we correct you on one point, Theodore has never been bed-ridden – he is indeed (at 74) the most active and hale of the remaining Powyses in England.[405]

Hutchings tells Jack that she does not want to start a correspondence with him because she already writes to too many people. But his reply intrigued her and she softened her position, telling Jack that if he must write then he could, but he would have to type from now on, his handwriting being too much of a struggle to bother reading.

Soon, Monica Hutchings had introduced Clemo to Littleton Powys through correspondence. Littleton's wife, Elizabeth Myers, had recently died, and he wished to correct Jack's assessment of her writing as it was expressed in *Confession*. Hutchings warned Jack to be gentle with Littleton, who was still grieving, adding that the two men were unlikely to agree about much. It was Elizabeth Myers who had won the 1943 Tom-Gallon award, which Jack had thought was a fix. In the published *Confession* any accusation of dishonesty had been removed, but Clemo still criticized her mysticism and her outlook as being too obscure for 'the average mind'. Elsewhere, he called her a 'pantheist', and it was this that Littleton wanted to correct when he wrote in January 1950.

Littleton's autobiographies show him to have been an almost pathological optimist. They are an education in looking on the bright side. This comes across, to a degree, in his correspondence with Clemo. He claims that his life had always been good and easy:

> Now as for me, Jack Clemo, it seems in my life I have stood for everything you condemn in your book: for I was the rarity – a conventional Powys. Had an easy time everywhere because I did what the rest did, could play games and consequently shone at them – just good enough at work to get a degree at Cambridge and to become a schoolmaster.[406]

When Monica proposed a meeting between Jack and Theodore, the Clemos were invited to stop off at Littleton's on their way. 'The best of all the Powyses', she told Jack, 'is that each one is completely different', a sentiment elaborated in her 1969 'Men of Wessex' article for *Wessex Life*.

Monica visited the Clemos in June 1950 and quickly became attached to the foster-girls. It was then that she proposed the trip to Dorset. Before long, she had drawn up an itinerary for the Clemos, including 'Tea with Theodore, Violet & Susan' and 'Supper with Littleton & Mrs. Myers at Quarry House, Sherborne'. ('Mrs Myers' was the mother of Elizabeth.) When Jack recorded the proposed visit, however, it was not for the fact that he was to be meeting his new friends or his only living literary idol, but for

> the opening of a door to Mappowder and there my Irma – Susie. M[onica] writes to invite mother and I to visit them all – and Susie [...] was there when Theodore talked about me last Thursday – so she knows all about me. What a wonderful thing the healing would be in this context! I do feel I shall not remain captive much longer.[407]

As the relationships of 1949 and 1950 dissolved, the Clemos put greater hope on their Dorset connection. Susie had first been considered openly in 1946, when Mrs Clemo told Jack: 'if none of the girls I've thought of prove suitable, God may lead [you] to Susan Powys as he led Browning to Ba'. Jack wrote: 'I think still of Susie Powys and know I need that sort of girl.'[408] By the end of 1949, Susie was the main contender for Jack's affections: 'she's the only girl left who has any link with the past, who was in my mind when I wrote *Wilding Graft*.' On New Year's Eve he performed the resilient *Wilding Graft* ritual: 'Climbed Bloomdale clay dump as dusk fell and stood on the ridge blowing kisses towards Dorset'.[409] He was enacting the scene as though invoking the narrative and the story's happy ending. By August 1950, the significance of Susie had swollen, as he claimed that she had been 'in the background of my mind since 1936'.

This was the year before the London visit to Godfrey Mowatt, so it was Clemo's first time out of Cornwall, excepting trips across the border to the Plymouth hospital. The plan was that on 22 August 1950, Eveline, Jack and Spark would set off on the train. Monica would meet them from the station and drive them to her farm, where they would spend the night, and the following day they would go on to Theodore's and then Littleton's. Hutchings wrote an article on Clemo and the Dorset trip for *West Country Magazine*, recalling how relaxed Eveline seemed stepping off the train, 'as if she had just stepped out to an hour's shopping'.[410] Monica had expected Eveline to find travelling alien and awkward, though for the life-toughened Eveline this was practically a holiday.

Everything had been done to make the Clemos welcome, although Jack did not settle away from the cottage as easily as his mother. Dust from the open windows on the train had irritated his eyes and he was feeling homesick: 'For walk with Spark on farm – all strange and remote – longed to be back – felt I couldn't live or write out of Cornwall'. The idea that he would be unable to write out of Cornwall remained with him until he was almost seventy years old and packing his bags for Weymouth.

Jack wrote about meeting the Powyses in his 1980 autobiography and in an essay for The Powys Society. In *The Marriage of a Rebel*, Clemo described the Dorset view – a view he was unable to see:

> [It] resembled south Cornwall except that there were more sheep and more thatched cottages here: it was the literary spell that made it all so unique and pregnant. Tess's Blackmore Vale . . . Mr Weston's Folly Down . . . . The car zigzagged amid a maze of chalky lanes and at last drew up close to the window of a small, bare,

single-storey building – the Rectory Lodge at Mappowder.

Theodore himself came out to greet them,

> his ruddy, clean-shaven face beaming with a true countryman's welcome. Although seventy-five,[411] he was erect and robust, like a farmer, dressed with casual tidiness in a dark suit. His curly white hair grew thick but not abnormally long on his massive skull.

Powys led the young poet inside by the hand, and in Jack's article, 'Pilgrimage to Mappowder', he writes:

> At the tea-table I learnt more about his unworldly and unselfconscious habits. He soaked his bread-and-butter in his tea, and when Monica playfully chided him he said with a quiet smile: 'Jesus did that, didn't he?'

Clemo did not see or hear any of this, but was told about it afterwards by his mother. Some of her notes still exist, all written exactly as she would have spoken them: 'Theodore don't say a lot, but when he do, it convey a lot, hes got the most happy peaceful face Ive ever look on since fathers'. It was Eveline who watched the bread-dunking episode that Clemo so loved. She wrote:

> Theodore was soaking his bread and butter in his tea, Monica wanted to know where he learnt his manners, he wife said I keep telling him but its no use Theodore look up so sweet and innocent and said 'Jesus did that didn't he' it was so simple but very touching.

When Jack first wrote his impressions to Monica, he had interpreted his mother's note as meaning that Monica had told Theodore off. In fact, there were several things incorrect about his mother's account, which Monica corrected:

> I fear me that I must correct or at least modify some of her statements passed on to you, Jack. First of all I never criticised Theodore's table manners – his manners (as all the Powys – even the most unconventional of them, like John) are quite above reproach. I believe I pulled his leg about taking a lot of sugar and various like manners. I ALWAYS pull Theodore's leg. It may seem slightly irreverent to you!! but none of the Powyses are sacred to me, I know them too well, they are all so human and so full of faults – and full of kindness too beyond most humans. [...] Your mother appears to have taken our gentle badinage too seriously.[412]

When Clemo wrote up his final account of the meeting, he took all of Monica's corrections on board, and prominent in each of these accounts is the bread-dunking. Even in 'Wessex and Lyonesse', a poem in the 1975 collection *Broad Autumn*, he wrote:

> An hour before I stood on Bulbarrow
> I watched the hermit Powys, ruddy and leonine,
> Puff pipe-smoke musingly
> Into a modest book-strewn room.
> He had just soaked bread-and-butter in his tea,
> Explaining that Jesus did
> Something like that. But there was no Judas, no
> Croak of fate's craft in the Dorset valley.
> As I waved farewell through the clear notching sunshine
> The Hardy-refuting peace was solid.

It was an idiosyncratic gesture of unaffected simplicity and Christ-like innocence that moved the Clemos.

In all published accounts of this meeting the significance of Susie has been completely removed. She is dismissed in a single sentence in both *Marriage* and 'Pilgrimage to Mappowder', and her importance is not even hinted at. It is the diaries that show the day's full significance:

No fluttering of heart, tho' still suspense – M[onica] not knowing whether S[usie] would be at home. Town of Blackmore Vale in morn. – deepening grip of scene, all so […] humble, not needing to be humiliated like the clay-land. […] M. writes notes for me – Hardy country. Picnic by fence. Home in heavy rain, but cleared brilliantly for the afternoon journey down to Mappowder. Felt buoyant, praying in the car. Twisting chalky lanes, soft green hills, little white signposts – scattered sheep in fields. Then Mappowder – the Lodge, the incredible dream-come-true as Theodore came out, taking my hand and leading me in to S. when M. had photographed us. T. hearty, more massive than I had expected, yet so gentle and Christlike. S. shyly shaking hands – quiet slim Tess, soberly dressed – white blouse and slacks for riding. Brunette too – newspaper report led me wrong again. She's short-sighted and wears glasses, but appealing. Said it was wonderful I'd succeeded. […] Old-fashioned country – he kissed mother's hand as she left – wish S. had kissed mine, but T. led me out ahead of the women, so warm and fatherly, keeping my hand in his. Last glimpse of them all waving goodbye outside the window – Theodore, Violet and Susie. So deeply moved, my heart in my mouth all the way back – too poignant, such joy and yet the questions 'Why?' and 'What now?' On Bulbarrow later and Sturminster Newton bridge, then back westward as the sun set, clear and cloudless the new land. Sherborne gleaming in valley, then down into its streets for supper with Littleton P. and Mrs Myers, Elizabeth's mother charming and sympathetic. Got prayer book which we'd phoned bookshop to deliver at L's. Thrill to think of marriage service yet still questioning – 'Is it she – down at Mappowder?' Moonlight at back of car over Dorset as we rode back to Barrow – unique, unforgettable journey. Lay awake so full of confused wonder and joy.

There are many strong images here. One is Jack's observation of the fatherliness of Theodore Powys. He remarks on it again when the photographs are developed, and the image shows 'Theodore and I holding hands like father and son'. Another is of this paternal figure leading Jack in to Susie. Slightly more unusual is that Clemo wanted a particular prayer book delivered so that he could think about the marriage service and Susie together.

It was a magical day for Jack, and could not be ruined even when Monica's car broke down on the way home.

For days, Clemo pressed his mother for more details about Susie. He loved that she did not enjoy Theodore's writing, which evidenced 'independent judgment', and he meditated on how at home he would feel with the Powys family if they were to marry. But the excitement of the Dorset trip soon turned to disappointment that he had not even established a pen friendship with her. At this point, he decided to push Monica for answers. In his diary, he wrote: 'All that's needed is the healing and financial provision, and the Mappowder door would be wide open – tragic Cornish phase over – fulfilment in Dorset. I shall pray on.'[413] The questions he asked Monica were exactly the same superficial ones he wanted to ask every girl, about flirting, dancing and make-up. Monica replied wearily:

> Susan uses make-up & likes dances & flirtations. She is in fact 'Normal' – no, as your mother says she isn't 'cheap' and 'towny' but then you wouldn't expect her to be, any more than you'd expect my daughter or yours.[414]

She is aware of the subtext in Jack's letter, but she might not have been aware of how the news would upset him: 'M. wrote to say S. likes dancing, make-up, etc and I feel chilled again with the sense of another collapse'.[415] Even when Jack later wrote to Ruth, the woman who would become his wife, to lay out the conditions of their coupling, it almost fell apart when Ruth had to theologically justify the wearing of jewellery.

Many signs had pointed to how appropriate and timely meeting Susie should be, but nothing came of it, and when Susie wrote her own autobiography, *A Cuckoo in the Powys Nest*, she did not mention Clemo at all. His private turmoil never drifted beyond the Goonamarris cottage and Susie never thought of him again.

The depression was dramatic. Several times in 1950 Clemo expressed self-destructive thoughts, wishing he had died instead of Bertha. It was a familiar misery. In 1947 he had written: 'feeling that it is better to die than to live under all these afflictions', and even in 1946, fed up with the record of suffering he was creating in his diaries, he announced: 'This Diary shall either record blessing or remain blank. I will not continue the monotonous entries of misery and failure and despair'. He lasted two months before the urge to record the pain overwhelmed him again. Perhaps Helena Charles was right, and it was God's intention that Jack should suffer, that all his 'life and faith were an expression of disease'.[416] The coming years would be a bleak descent into blindness and disappointment, and yet formally the position was still one of unyielding hope:

> I believe it will come yet and these tests make me realise how necessary it is that my girl should have the grafting which enables me to use this discipline. I can imagine an ordinary girl getting fed up at these periods of crisis and saying she'd never have married me if she'd known I should get into such a pickle. It's natural to be as sour as vinegar when you get in a pickle.[417]

T. F. Powys and Jack Clemo at Mappowder, Dorset, 1950

Clemo, Spark and Eveline at Stourton, 1950

Jack and Eveline with foster-girls Violet and Fran Allen, 1950

XI
'Beneath the ashes'

I have seen his ways and will lead him. I will lead him also and restore comforts unto him and to his mourners.

Isaiah 57:18

The 1950s started promisingly for Clemo's writing, if not for his love life. He published *The Clay Verge*, completing the trilogy of contracted books for Chatto & Windus, and he entered the Festival of Britain prize with 'The Wintry Priesthood'. More than two thousand poets entered this competition, and there were just eight winners, three for single poems and five for collections. Jack won £100 and his poems were used in the 1951 exhibition curated by Laurie Lee. They were also published with the other prize winners by Penguin as *Poems 1951*, which opened Clemo up to a broader readership. The new poems were not as grim as those of *The Clay Verge*: 'All the harshness has gone out of my work – the suffering of the past five months has purged out the old bitterness and toughness.' So Clemo wrote in 1950, adding that his new work has 'not a trace of the harshness of "Calvinist in Love" and "The Excavator"'.[418] However, four of the nine 'new' poems were taken from the group rejected by Cecil Day Lewis and had been written between 1947 and 1949. The other five poems were all written in 1950, four of them in the first week of February and one in May. These were the biographical poems already mentioned, responding to Spurgeon, Powys, Barth, Lawrence and Kierkegaard.

Sales of Clemo's other books were negligible by now, and over the coming decade Jack would see every one of them pulped. *Confession* was remaindered in 1953, *Wilding Graft* in 1955, and then, in 1957: 'Heard Chatto have remaindered "Clay Verge". I'm not sorry'.[419] Clemo was depressingly unproductive, writing only a dozen or so poems in these ten years – most of which appeared in magazines –

and publishing a single testimonial volume, *The Invading Gospel*. He reworked the old novels while he could still just about read them, desperately wanting 'The Dry Kiln' and *The Shadowed Bed* to be accepted, but the only piece of original prose he wrote was a short story, 'The Clay Dump', for Denys Val Baker's *One and All: Stories from Cornwall*. Val Baker was the editor of the *Cornish Review*, one of the most ambitious literary periodicals attempted in Cornwall. It ran from 1949-52 and again from 1966-74, during which time Val Baker published most of the leading local literati, including Causley, Rowse, Betjeman, Peter Lanyon, Frances Bellerby, W.S. Graham, D.M. Thomas, Dora Russell and Arthur Caddick. In 1950, he was putting together a volume of short stories by Cornish writers and asked whether Clemo might have something to contribute. At first, Clemo sent an old unpublished dialect tale about a man and his tortoise; an amusing piece, but inappropriate and too parochial to place alongside the likes of Quiller-Couch, Baring-Gould and Winston Graham. Somehow, Clemo was surprised that Val Baker rejected the story:

> Ruffled – heard from Baker that publishers don't like my dialect tale – if I can't do a serious story I shall be kicked out of the short story book. I know I can't – it all makes me feel punished. Yet as we went to bed mother said: 'Let's pray about it.'

The following day:

> Prayer answered! It seems impossible, but I've written a 3,000 word story, 'The Clay Dump', very like Theodore's – the plot adapted from Miss Pascoe's experience in S[hadowed] B[ed] but all knit afresh and in detail quite new.[420]

In a single day Clemo had written a story of fair length, which would promptly be accepted and published by Val Baker.

The story is about Lucy Gribble, a caretaker who lived in a village dominated by a great clay dump. Gribble's 'home stood nearest the dump – so near that one side of the white pyramid loomed up from the garden hedge'. It was a feature of strange fascination and significance to Gribble:

> All her hope of enjoyment had been like the flowers that pushed out so pitifully through the turf fringing the dump's base – soon to be burst and flattened and buried by the descending vomit of sand and stone. The wooden tip-structure under which the waggon appeared as it spilled its load two hundred feet above the cottage, looked like a fantastic window in heaven, and Lucy's thoughts would grow darkly religious as she watched the inexorable movements up there.

Lucy was not a happy woman. She had fallen in love with a man who was 'crushed by a skip-waggon' before she could tell him how she felt. The man had worked at Pengarth pit, and the school where she was caretaker was Pengarth School. Pengarth is not a real place in the clay country, but a reference to the hero of *Wilding Graft*, Garth Joslin. In Cornish 'pen-' means 'head' or 'summit', so we have a place-name meaning 'Garth's Head', in which all of this story's symbolic action takes place.

In the story, Lucy Gribble starts taking lodgers, but the villagers become jealous and take to gossiping about her. At length, people cease coming to stay. Meanwhile, day by day, the clay dump grows, drawing nearer, and Miss Gribble watches 'as the sand spilled down, a cold gritty crust, pouring as from the sky and blocking the field of her vision.' We see the old theme emerging:

> The dump edged closer and Miss Gribble more resentful, writhing under the vague menace. She rebelled against the fate it seemed to impose on her. In retaliation she ceased to attend chapel.

Soon, she was stealing fuel from the school, unable to afford to keep her own fire alight and too proud to gather charred gorse from the moor like the poorer families. When she is caught stealing by the headmaster, they both hear the 'crash of refuse slithering down the clay-tip', and the headmaster becomes suddenly aroused. He blames the clay dump:

> It towered above the school like an obscene dribbling breast, throwing upon the classrooms a dank, clammy shadow, or reflecting sunlight in sharp, dazzling splashes, unnaturally white and fervid. He felt stifled by it, his emotions pressed back upon the near-adolescent girls like a sort of refuse, a squashed, muddy awareness of young female bodies. This perverse emotion had not yet focussed on any particular girl, but he had known for some time that his wife alone could not release him from the vague infantile infatuation.

This is an unusual and grotesque passage, and ends with the headmaster inviting Lucy Gribble back to the classroom, telling her there's a way she can prevent him from going to the police about her stealing. The story ends with Lucy Gribble following him back through the schoolyard, glancing up at the clay dump and saying: 'Tipping more sand over me. [...] Thee be still tipping sand.'

Among other things, Clemo seems to be presenting his own predicament here, but without a resolution. Lucy is being brutalised by fate, while God continues piling more and more sand over her and her home, presumably until God's sand overwhelms her and she can no longer resist it, thus moving into the stream of predestination.

This was the last piece of fiction Clemo wrote, and although it was done in a single day it is his best-structured and paced short story. The understated suffering of Lucy suggests a control not evidenced in the longer, earlier works, even in *Wilding Graft*, and the message is allowed to reveal itself clearly but not stridently. When Cecil Day Lewis had commented on *The Shadowed Bed* manuscript a few years earlier, he had compared the novel unfavourably with the work of T.F. Powys. Powys, he had said, wrote his allegories with a strength and naturalness, while 'Clemo, on the other hand, seems to me to impose his allegory upon us, and very crudely for the most part.'[421] This is not true of 'The Clay Dump', which was written only weeks after visiting Powys at Mappowder, and perhaps we see here the more successfully derivative Powysian direction in which Clemo might have continued had he been able.

In the early 1950s, Clemo fiddled a little with *The Shadowed Bed*, but even in 1952 'my sight isn't quite good enough – mother trying to type and messing it'.[422] There had been another turn for the worse. The trouble was said to have announced itself seriously only a few days after 'The Wintry Priesthood' had been published, with 'a swirl of red sparks that left the sight clouded for a minute or two', as Clemo wrote in *Marriage*. In 1950, Clemo had described himself as fully blind for short periods, then 'nearly blind' for all of 1951 and 1952. By 1954, he was 'a blind deaf wreck'. The difference between Clemo's 'blind' and 'nearly blind' was not great. It was a white-blindness, a cloud that thickened, sunlight colouring the white with a little brown or yellow. In strong sunlight in the early 1950s, Clemo was able to read, very slowly, with his piece of black card covering the page. But even this had its drawbacks, because while bright sunlight was needed for Jack to be able to read, it also caused inflammation and discomfort to his eyes. He wrote to Charles Causley in 1953: 'It often takes me days to read a letter, as I have to pick out a few words at a time with long rests between.'[423]

Soon, his mother had ceased passing notes to communicate with him and began writing words out into the palm of his hand with her index finger in capital letters. From the mid-1950s until the end of his life, this was the only way of conversing with Jack. He would answer by speaking, although he was self-conscious about the noises he made. Welfare officers encouraged him to learn Braille, but he refused. 'I must practise what I preach', he wrote in his 1952 diary, adding in a letter to Causley: 'The Braille instructress, Miss Williams, tells us she has had a talk with you about me. These people are very kind, but I feel the normal methods don't fit the general pattern of my life'. In an uncollected poem, 'Words to the Blind', from 1960, he wrote:

> Why should I track my way
> To men's minds through clotted Braille
> Bold gooseflesh on the corpse of words?

> My song is the clear-eyed bird's
> As I blaze a trail
> Where earth lies normal in the blithe day.

He must wait to be healed. It would be a sign of faithless submission to his disabilities if he were to learn Braille, as though he did not believe God was going to return his sight. Instead, he would wait and pray.

One of the most useful portraits of Clemo at this period comes from a personal letter sent from Derek Savage to E.W. Martin in 1954. Martin was showing interest in Clemo, and Savage had been described by a mutual friend as one of the only people to understand Clemo properly. Derek and Jack would remain close friends as long as they lived:

> Jack himself is not in a condition to conduct a conversation; but he shook hands with me on my arrival, sat in silence during the hour and a half during which I talked to his mother; and when I left, shook hands again and said, in a soft mild voice: 'Thank you for coming.' Jack's appearance is not unpleasing – his expression is calm, almost serene, and he was neatly dressed; but he is almost totally blind and deaf and can communicate only with his mother. He can read, in a strong light, just a word at a time, very slowly; but cannot read books, nor write. His heart is very weak, the doctor can hold out no hopes for him – says his 'system is worn out'. He apparently told his mother that he feels as if he were slowly atrophying through lack of stimulus and impressions. He looks twice his real age, is quite grey-haired, and his head is bent down on his breast. He sat with his back half-turned to us, at a little bureau in the corner of the tiny room, and ate his tea separately. I felt an intense sympathy for him, which I tried ineffectually to convey in my handshake. His mother, a sensible sort of woman, is very much the ordinary village housewife, with a strong religious streak, but I would say without

> 'spirituality': that is, not an enlightened person. It is, I feel, somewhat the same with Jack. [...] To put it very briefly, I could see that they had staked everything on a wrong definition of Faith, which was related to a wrong understanding of God. I say this very humbly, but I am convinced that it is the case.[424]

Savage wrote a similar account to Causley, apparently to help ascertain how much financial support the Clemos might need and to recommend a further application for a Civil List Pension. To the above account is added:

> He cannot write; and this frustrates him, for he feels that people are expecting further work from him, and wants to write a book of his religious and philosophical ideas. Besides this, the doctor says that physically he is worn-out. His heart is damaged, and while he may hang on for a few more years of life, it may fail at any time.
> I asked Mrs Clemo, a stout, grey-haired woman of sixty, whether this meant that, medically speaking, her expectation of life was greater than Jack's, and she said that she thought this was so.[425]

The weakness of Jack's heart is an often-understated symptom, but Savage is right, and as Clemo himself noted in *Marriage*, 'doctors feared that I had not long to live'.

As Jack's health deteriorated and he felt his death imminent, his desire for a miracle increased anxiously. With Helena Charles, the Clemos coordinated Christian groups across the country to pray for his healing, with the expectation that their combined prayers would be more effective. As the groups in London or around Cornwall prayed, Jack would kneel in the cottage with his mother, her hand placed on his head. Clergy of all denominations tried to help, and the Clemos travelled back and forth across Cornwall, visiting various vicars and fathers for 'healing services' and the 'laying on of hands'. The result was the same wherever they went: 'The Mission people in London have been praying for my healing today; yet I'm not healed.'[426]

At Monica Hutchings' suggestion they contacted a Dorset healing centre, which appealed to Jack who was still wondering whether all his desires might be destined to arrive out of Dorset. In 1952 the Clemos and Spark the Pomeranian visited Monica's Church Farm a second time, so that Jack could attend a service in Malvern where the American Baptist, Pastor Brown, was to appear. After the service, Clemo was given a private audience. Brown held Jack's wrists, told him that 'a strong healing current was flowing into me', and said 'Give back sight to these eyes and hearing to these ears. That your servant may be set at liberty to do your will.'[427] The process was moving and Jack had faith in Brown. He told the pastor, 'I believe it will cure me'. 'Well done', said Pastor Brown. 'Keep believing and be patient.' Sometimes, Clemo was so sure about a healer that he would perceive signs of improvement. According to *The Marriage of a Rebel*, a few days after the Malvern meeting Clemo felt a change, and he wrote to Monica to tell her the good news. In the evenings, after dark, he could now go outside and look up towards the tips and see 'the white flare of the arc-lamps more clearly than I had done for months'. As with the relationships declared prematurely, the sense of progress with his healing was humiliatingly short-lived. Just as he announced the arrival of Eileen in *Confession of a Rebel* moments before she told him not to write anymore, so he announced the apparent improvements in his health to friends and local newspapers, which added pressure and urgency to the process. Each proclamation was followed by failure, but still he would write, 'I know physical healing is coming.'

In 1954 the Clemos wrote to the celebrated preacher and self-publicist Oral Roberts. In the mid-1950s Roberts was already filming his healing services professionally and had written an autobiography. He would hit the headlines again later in life with sensational claims that he had raised the dead, and more critically as the extravagances of his jewellery and the several homes in Beverly Hills and Palm Springs became known. Roberts features quite prominently in earlier versions of *The Invading Gospel*, but his importance would be reduced later, as Clemo came to doubt the healer on account of his emphatic appeals for more and more money. The method used by Roberts came to be called 'prosperity gospel'. In *The Invading Gospel*, Clemo describes Roberts and Billy Graham as 'the two most obviously elect men of my generation'. So the letter the Clemos received in reply to their enquiry was exciting. 'I pray definitely that this request will be granted completely', Roberts wrote, in his characteristically dynamic and slightly awkward idiom.[428] The request was not granted.

All the while, Jack, his mother and their friends were cutting out articles and adverts in the national press, both Christian and secular, detailing stories of the blind suddenly becoming able to see, the crippled throwing away their walking sticks, mental disorders soothed, cancers, tuberculosis, asthma – all healed. Why not Jack? What was he doing wrong?

In 1952 he visited a Roman Catholic healer, Father Guy Barnicoat, who lived in the St Agnes vicarage. He met Clemo many times for healing, although he also hoped to convert Jack to Catholicism. In a letter Jack kept, Barnicoat appealed to Clemo to offer a full confession:

> All I want is to make sure that there is nothing in the way of worry or sins known which might hinder the Grace of God working in you. After all, one must assist the healing by showing trust and faith in God, and an endeavour to live according to His will.[429]

Clemo acquiesced, an elaborate anointment was arranged, and again nothing happened. Jack enjoyed these meetings and this new sense of connection with the Catholic Church, but they were ultimately another disappointment. Week after week, month after month, prayer after prayer, service after service, the requests all failed. Whatever pattern Jack observed, whatever church attended, and whatever appeal or offer he made to God, the response was always the same: silence.

But the silence was not only God's response to Clemo's prayers for himself. It was also His response to Jack's prayers for others. In 1951 Jack was told of a young local woman, twenty-four years old, stricken with TB. He was moved by her suffering and for the next three days prayed deeply and intently for her, feeling strong power and hope in his prayers. On the fourth day, she died.

Pursuit of a medical miracle continued until 1978, with the same cycle of hope, expectation, anticipation and disappointment. Helena repeated her belief that Clemo was meant to suffer, to be cut off and alone with God. Suffering was his gift and vocation, not happiness and success. But Jack was certain that God had promised him the threefold happiness of healing, marriage and marvellous success with his writing. These are the three strands of a single rope of faith connecting Clemo with God, and they must arrive together. He had to keep faithful and keep searching if the miracle was to be achieved. In the face of God's silence, his increased poor health, blindness, deafness, heart problems, as well as the loss of any real hope of love and the remaindering of all his works, faith in the future sustained Jack.

Yet there were still a few embers of encouragement beneath the ashes. With regard to his work, though the books were pulped and Cecil Day Lewis no longer dealt with Clemo, a new and important champion of his work emerged, the Launceston poet Charles Causley. Causley was a new writer only a year younger than Clemo, with his first collection of poetry, *Farewell, Aggie Weston*, appearing the same year as *The Clay Verge*. Causley was gregarious and generous, made friends and contacts easily and became a popular man as well as a popular poet. He was known for writing deceptively simple verse, blurring the boundary between poems for children and poems for adults, often juxtaposing bouncy ballad forms with tragic or melancholic themes. In his first letter to Clemo, on 19 October 1951, Causley started by saying that he considered 'the "Confession" – with A.L. Rowse's autobiography – the two most important books to come out of the west of England ever.' He continued in a typically light-hearted and politely deferential manner:

> I simply tell you the truth when I say that in your books Cornwall wriggles and comes alive. That […] you are obviously a writer of genius: and a tremendous inspiration to writers such as myself – merely pecking away at the barbed wire around the goldmine. […] Your books

blow the bogus Cornwall of Quiller-Couch, dear Miss
Du Maurier and Uncle Tom Cobleigh and all [...] a
million miles higher than Stonehenge. I hope you go
on blowing 'em; strength to your guns.[430]

One of Causley's great impacts in the lives of many writers was
his introductions. He encouraged meetings between Colin Wilson
and Lionel Miskin, as well as introducing both Derek Savage and
Miskin to Clemo, two of Jack's longest and strongest friendships.
These three men – Causley, Savage and Miskin – brought many and
diverse writers and artists into Jack's life, the writer Colin MacInnes
being a notable example. Correspondence and friendship between
MacInnes and Clemo blossomed for two years towards the end of the
decade, and it was MacInnes who made the successful recommendation that Methuen should take *The Map of Clay*. Daniel Hoffman,
future United States Poet Laureate was taken to the Clemo cottage
by Causley in 1961, the result of which was 'Lines to Jack Clemo', a
poem published in *Transatlantic Review* then collected in Hoffman's
Hang-Gliding from Helicon:

> Echoes crack between glass mountains.
> All-seeing gulls hurl rebel screeds
> At Cornwall's skull-white cones of clay.
> In the pits, black pools evade the sun.
>
> I stand on gritty Goonamarris,
> The four elements assail me.
> How can my senses hold all Nature's
> Clarity and the soil of man?
>
> He, leonine before the firescreen, paces
> The kingdom of deprivation's borders
> Striking the stones to make them sing.
> No land's so bleak he cannot find those stones:
>
> His Adversary guards the glazed ground.
> They wrestle head to head and wound to wound,

> Then inward darkness burns away,
> Shards of silence frame the essential palm.

Through Savage, another unexpected meeting took place. Kenneth Rexroth, 'Founder of the Beats', visited Savage in Mevagissey, once in 1949 and again in July 1959, staying in a cottage Savage let out in the summer months. During the 1959 visit, Rexroth, who had an interest in erotic mysticism and the connection between eroticism and spirituality, went with Savage to visit Clemo. Frustratingly, Clemo was not aware of Rexroth's work at the time, and merely noted in his diary for 13 July: 'Savage called today with American poet Kenneth Rexroth.' That was all, and no further account of this meeting has emerged. According to Rexroth biographer Rachelle Lerner, the American poet had changed his habits as a diarist by this time and was not recording events as thoroughly as he had been previously.

Clemo's correspondence with Causley was buoyant, the Launceston man's natural playfulness and light-heartedness bringing out a similar response in Clemo. When Clemo was depressed about his work, Causley would write with steadying encouragement:

> I can assure you that the writing grapevine is very much aware of your existence – in some cases uncomfortably aware of your superb integrity, strength of imagination and uncompromising honesty, if I may say so.[431]

He supports all of Clemo's petitions and approaches, and for Jack's birthday in 1959, Causley sent a new typewriter, with the following note:

> The accompanying gift [...] is a token of the tremendous admiration and affection nine of your fellow-writers have for your creative work. Please do us the honour of accepting it, and our warmest good wishes to you as a man and as an artist.
>
> My fellows wish to remain anonymous: but I am delighted to tell you, dear Jack, that they include some

of the most illustrious names in present-day literature: and that *all* are prompted by the sincerest of regard for your poetry and prose, and for the unique contribution you are making to letters today.

Only one condition obtains: that the gift is strictly anonymous, strictly private – for we would like this to be a personal act of homage from a few of your friends and admirers.

Long may you bash this machine into a state of insensibility with your magnificently powerful images and ideas. We shall be delighted, in due course, to send a replacement for your 80th birthday.[432]

Clemo sent a generous thank you to Causley in reply, but privately his depression was in such a slump that he could only note to himself what 'a pitiful waste of money' the gift was. He could not see to type, and he had nothing to write anyway.

Such glooms were frequent, the descent of a 'dank joylessness', to use Styron's phrase. There does not always appear to have been a cause for the descent, but because of the way it seemed to alter his outlook and sense of purpose, it was given a religious slant and disturbed his faith. That is not to say that Clemo could have imagined a world without God – on the contrary, every time he attempted to write persuasively on science and against atheists or agnostics he consistently failed to grasp any non-theistic perspective. But there is a difference between believing in a materialistic world and doubting one's own religious beliefs about the world. The problem for Clemo was not that the truth of a materialistic cosmology had suddenly overwhelmed him, but that the promises of God and Christianity so often failed. For a man held together by faith, these doubts could have posed a serious threat. They are described as 'dark' or 'deathly shadows', or as attacks by the Devil, who is sometimes named Beale in the diaries, after the character of *The Shadowed Bed*, as in: 'Beale has counterattacked this week. Browning's darker mood, "What if all be error?"'[433] Clemo's choice of Browning quote is impeccable, taken from *Ferishtah's Fancies*:

> Only at heart's utmost joy and triumph, terror
>   Sudden turns the blood to ice: a chill wind disencharms
> All the late enchantment! What if all be error –
>   If the halo irised round my head were, Love, thine arms.

After the publication of *The Map of Clay* in 1961, with its introduction by Causley, the gloom to some extent lifted. This is reflected in the playfulness that developed between Charles Causley and Jack Clemo in their correspondence. In that introduction, Causley had referred to Jack's home as 'a slate-roofed granite box of a cottage', which amused Clemo, and instead of heading his letters with the address 'Goonamarris', he began heading them 'Granite Box'. Later, after the cottage had been modernised for Ruth, and Clemo had bought two new chairs, he wrote from the 'Granite Mansion', and when a visitor turned up for Clemo's opinion on a poem of Causley's, it became the 'Granite Information Centre'. So the joke continued, through 'Granite Floor', 'Granite Dome', 'Granite College', 'Granite Dais', 'Granite Castle' and 'Granite Cell'.

The substance of the Causley-Clemo correspondence is more rounded than the Clemo-Rowse correspondence, though still there is the tendency in Jack to only talk about himself and to exhaust his correspondent with demands for help. Causley's sensitivity to Clemo's disabilities and his admiration for his writing led him to champion and promote Clemo's work to his own friends and associates. He arranged for BBC film crews and interviewers to visit the Clemos and for poems to be read on the television and radio. When these programmes were aired, the Clemos would walk over to the house of a neighbour or cousin and everyone would sit around to listen or watch.

Following their early correspondence and before they had met, Causley wrote 'Homage to Jack Clemo', which would be published in the 1953 *Survivor's Leave*:

> In the deep wood dwells a demon
>   Taller than any tree –
> His prison bars are the sailing stars,
>   His jailer is the sea.

> With a brain and ten fingers
>   He ties Cornwall to his table –
> Imagination, at battle station,
>   Guards Pegasus in his stable.
>
> He walks the white hills of Egypt
>   Reading the map of clay –
> And through his night there moves the light
>   Artillery of day.
>
> Turn, Cornwall, turn and tear him!
>   Stamp him in the sod!
> He will not fear your cry so clear –
>   Only the cry of God.

Causley would remain a good friend to Clemo, even when their correspondence cooled in the 1970s. The occasion for this cooling was Clemo's feeling that his old friend's popularity and celebrity was eclipsing his own. Causley's ease, both conversationally and in the media, was something Clemo could never hope to achieve, and the awareness of this was frustrating. As well as receiving greater exposure, Causley's poetry was more immediately accessible than Clemo's and appealed to a broader audience. For this reason, in the early-1970s, we find Clemo playing with themes and forms derived from Causley's work. These will be observed and discussed when considering the 1975 volume, *Broad Autumn*.

This mild professional jealousy was further fuelled by Clemo's fear that Causley intended to 'drop' him as a friend. Clemo felt that this was what Cecil Day Lewis had done in 1951, after their contractual obligations had been fulfilled. The fear appeared to have been confirmed when, in 1976, Causley changed his mind about reading some of Clemo's poems at an event: 'Charles has refused to read my poems at Truro. I feel I've no literary friends left who can be relied on to help.'[434]

Causley never had any intention of 'dropping' Clemo, and he continued to be an active and generous force in Clemo's life, proofing his manuscripts, inviting anthology submissions, pushing others to meet Clemo and promoting his work. When considering the next poetry collection, *The Map of Clay*, the value of Causley's considerable input will be seen again.

Of those introduced to Clemo by Causley, the most exciting was the artist Lionel Miskin. Miskin was living in Mevagissey, friendly with Causley and Savage, as well as the new literary celebrity of the neighbourhood, Colin Wilson. He first visited the cottage on 15 January 1956 with Derek Savage, and returned a fortnight later to make preliminary drawings of Clemo for a series of paintings. By the end of the year, Miskin was on his sixth painting of Jack, and they had become close friends. By the end of the decade, there were thirteen portraits, with another of Eveline Clemo, and still more to follow. Miskin would also illustrate some of Clemo's poetry, including 'Christ in the Clay-Pit' and 'Crab Country'. The artist kept no record of when or to whom he gave his work, and the whereabouts of the majority of these paintings is unknown. Many of them are said to have gone missing when he went abroad and left his paintings with a neighbouring farmer, who, in Miskin's absence, sold his farm and the paintings with it. Those that remain, however, are striking. In Exeter's Fine Art Collection, for instance, there is a large painting in which Clemo is sat at his desk with an expression of terrible melancholy. Miskin has painted the slumped figure with the same palette as the writing desk, the root of the clay dumps and the mud banks outside the window behind him. The peaks of the dumps are the same vibrant blue and white as Clemo's shirt, the blue also dotted down the jacket. The only colour that really gives the impression of standing alone and aside, outside of Clemo's environment, is the green of the fields, the natural world. They are remarkable works.

Eveline hated them, as did the foster-children, Frances and Violet. 'Wait till Jack can see it,' Mrs Clemo said when Lionel showed her the first painting; 'You may be in for it then!' The exaggerated – to the point of grotesque – sadness of the Clemo figure did not reflect her own image of her beloved son. Similarly, Frances describes the portraits of Eveline Clemo as being 'too hard and cold'. They show Eveline strong, determined, unyielding and grim, aspects of her character that ensured her own survival, as well as that of her son.

They do not, however, especially reflect the loving mother Frances and Violet recalled. The portrait of Eveline and Jack together eating at table shows the same grim expression, and there is a gulf between mother and son represented, with Eveline looking directly at Jack, and Jack looking to one side, away from the scene. However, once again the colours suggest a connection beyond this physical gulf, with Jack and his mother painted with the same ochres, greens and blues.

From the very beginning, Lionel was able to write on Jack's hand to converse, just as Eveline did. He was less inhibited than many visitors, who found it uncomfortable to hold a man's hand and touch it in such a way. Lionel was more like the children, who felt no awkwardness or embarrassment with Jack at all.

Miskin was also a controversial figure, a tall bearded Catholic Bohemian, not only a painter, but a multi-media artist, potter and etcher, who invented a method of making images with a paraffin lamp, creating what he called 'smokes'. While in Mevagissey, Miskin taught at St Austell College and later moved to Falmouth to teach at the Art School. One of his more extraordinary artistic gestures was the sculpting of a large polystyrene Christ and a series of angels, which he filled with helium and set off over Falmouth from his garden. A similarly headline-grabbing spectacle was delivered at the beginning of 1961, the newspaper report of which was cut out and kept by Clemo in his diary. Miskin was attending the launch of his latest London exhibition, and was to travel up from Cornwall in his car with Colin Wilson. The newspaper report records:

> Strapped on to the top of Mr. Miskin's car was a 'coffin' containing a full-sized effigy of himself in Madeira cake. He will cut up the cake when Mr. Colin Wilson, the author, opens the exhibition and will distribute pieces to those present.
>
> Mr. Miskin said yesterday: 'I believe that what the critics and public really want is the life of an artist and not his work. Many artists are famous because they had led sensational lives and therefore I am offering those present at my exhibition pieces of myself.'[435]

Miskin complimented Jack on his skill as a portrait sitter, writing in a note his mother would relay:

> I must thank you for your great pacience in sitting for me. I cannot remember painting a portrait which at the time interested me more than this one I have been painting of yourself. You have a head and presence that fit your work, your vision, even the landscape about you. If it consoles you for having sat so long and still, I have already shown the portrait to a number of friends including Derek Savage, and they all aggree that it is one of my best paintings.[436]

The spelling here is characteristic of Miskin. He would always spell 'patience' with a 'c', and would always write 'agree' with a double 'g'.

Jack enjoyed sitting for these portraits, and would spend the hours singing hymns in his head. The experience is recorded in his poem 'The Veiled Sitter', written in March 1957 and dedicated to Miskin. Their friendship would last the span of Clemo's life, with Miskin intended to be Best Man at Clemo's projected wedding to Mary Wiseman in the early 1960s. When Jack married Ruth in 1968, Lionel was still present, but it was Causley who took the role of Best Man.

There were few prospects of romance in the 1950s, when Causley, Miskin, Savage and Clemo became friends. After the episodes with June and Susie, the only two possibilities came when a sculptor named Pat Jenkins visited to make a bust of Clemo, and when Rosine, a Lebanese woman from Egypt with psychological and physical problems wrote to Clemo with a cry for help. The Jenkins bust is now held in the Royal Cornwall Museum in Truro, a plaster piece painted bronze. It was sculpted over five days in the middle of April 1957 and given to the Clemos at the end of May. Jenkins was introduced to Jack through their mutual friend, the writer and pacifist E.W. Martin. She had been staying with Martin in Devon, but interrupted her visit when he introduced her to Clemo's work, abandoning her holiday to go to Cornwall and make the study. She visited with a friend, Shirley, who kept in touch with the Clemos for a while and typed out the manuscript of *The Invading Gospel*, which Jack had recently finished.

'Pat is a wonderful Christian girl – and so is her friend Shirley. This might be God's opening if the stones were rolled from the sepulchre', Clemo wrote in his diary on 17 April 1957. However, 'It's clear I can make no advance until I'm healed.' Three days later: 'Pat has told my mother several times that I have a "kind mouth". What does she feel when her fingers mould it? There may be some intimate thrill – I can't know, here behind my mask.'

While she visited, Pat went to chapel with the Clemos and flicked through the scrapbooks of criticism and reviews they had compiled, while Eveline tried to make her interested in Jack romantically, telling her about the previous disappointments. But Jenkins found it difficult to write on Jack's palm and found correspondence awkward, knowing that it was being read by Eveline first and then communicated to Jack through the palm-writing.

Jack's syphilis was still his main problem and Miskin now began driving the Clemos to alternative healing meetings in Truro. Even so, Jack had not completely given up on medicine. In 1959, the Clemos returned to the doctor to discuss the latest medical advances and treatments. Eveline had been reading about a new anti-ageing drug, Gerovital H3, which was a Hollywood fad. It made no claims of being able to cure syphilis, but it was advertised as capable of reversing the greying and balding processes that had begun for Clemo in the early 1940s. The Clemos inquired at the hospital, but the doctors held no hope of his symptoms reversing and said there was nothing that could be done. 'Without a miracle I'm finished', Jack said.[437]

Writing about his belief in faith-healing attracted a response from other sufferers, and in January 1959 Rosine, who is discussed in *The Marriage of a Rebel*, wrote to Jack, asking more about this form of healing. The depths of Rosine's troubles were revealed letter by letter, and Jack found himself in an awkward position. Rosine had a long list of physical and emotional complaints. She frequently stated that she was suicidal, and she had applied to be lobotomised. She was leaning on Clemo for support. For a brief moment, they wondered whether their sufferings and spiritual sustenance were drawing them together romantically and they planned to meet, but

Rosine would be too ill to travel to Cornwall. The poem 'Lebanese Harvest', from *Cactus on Carmel*, was written about her, in May 1959, and published in 1967, six years before Rosine's early death.

The one great hope and accomplishment of the 1950s, following Clemo's 1951 boom and the subsequent literary, physical and romantic decline, was *The Invading Gospel*, his 'Christian manifesto'. It followed a series of evangelical revelations rooted in the US. Three figures are singled out between 1954 and 1956 as special influences: Billy Graham (1954), Oral Roberts (1955) and Renee Martz (1956). Graham is the best known of these, and he was the most influential on Clemo's spiritual atmosphere. In 1954, Graham visited Britain for a twelve-week 'Crusade' at London's Harringay Arena. Seats were free and Graham is said to have preached to around two million. He was a media sensation, charismatic and energetic, with a schedule as demanding as John Wesley's. Crowds and choirs swarmed to greet him on arrival at Southampton, and thousands were said to have been converted. Enthralled by this movement, Clemo's 1954 diary became a Billy Graham scrapbook, filled with cutouts and photographs, articles and conversion stories following the Harringay crusade. Supportive evangelical rallies sprang up all around the country. Much later, in 1988, Clemo had the opportunity to attend a Graham rally. He marked it in his diary: 'Very moving – many responded. I still identify as in 1954 but am baffled by the anti-climax.' The 'anti-climax' for Clemo by this point, late in life, was that God's promises had not been fulfilled in the way he had expected them to be back in 1954. In 1954, the triumphant energy of Graham's mission incited Clemo to write, and within a few months the first draft of *The Invading Gospel* was finished.

The importance of Renee Martz is slightly more unusual. Martz was the singing evangelical who had inspired Clemo to buy a record player. She claimed, Clemo wrote in *The Invading Gospel*, 'to have been converted through a vision and the voice of Jesus in a Los Angeles street.' He added: 'I do not question such testimonies', although this was before he had discovered the scandal surrounding Oral Roberts, who had also claimed to have been suddenly healed by God and addressed directly. Martz's youth engaged Jack initially, and when she returned to England in 1956, aged 15, he was intrigued. 'The only girl I would want to meet in heaven would be Renee Martz', he remarked in his diary.[438] As an eligible young Christian woman, Jack associated Renee with healing, and in August 1956 he attempted to effect healing on himself by holding an Oral Roberts magazine over his eyes, pressing a Renee Martz photo to his ear and balancing a Plymouth Christian mission paper on his head simultaneously, while kneeling in prayer. In continuing faith, this month he bought his £13 record player and his mother went into St Austell for the 7" single of Martz's 'The Song that God Sings / The Large, Large House'. When the volume was turned up on the gramophone and Clemo had his head pressed against the machine, he could hear Renee's voice as 'a faint squeak'.[439] He could hear 'Shea' better, he notes, referring to the classical gospel baritone George Beverly Shea, who performed at Billy Graham's Crusades. The Clemos seem to have bought Shea's 'How Great Thou Art / America the Beautiful' 7" at the same time as the Martz record.

Eveline disliked the music of Martz, deeming it 'too jazzy'. 'I wonder how soon I shall be able to judge for myself', replied Jack on 9 September. Amazingly, he did not have to wait long, and on 19 November a near-miracle occurred:

> Thrilling this afternoon to find I could hear Renee's voice all thro' her record – fairly loud, tho' distorted. She is certainly God's instrument of blessing to me this year. This vindicates my faith in buying the gram and record to act as point of contact thro' her voice.

The event is described more vividly in *Marriage*:

> One day in November, when I had a cold, I blew my nose and felt a squelching sensation deep inside my ear – and I heard myself cough. I hurried to fetch Renee Martz's record, and a few minutes later stood spellbound, listening to her clear strong voice soaring amid a thunder of jazz.

'The Song that God Sings' is not thunderous jazz or ragtime. It is a pop song with gospel influences and a defining Christian theme, but it influenced some of the freer rhythms and lyrics of poems in the third sequence of *The Map of Clay*. In 'Lunar Pentecost' we read of 'God's jazz-drums' and 'The beating jazz-fire', and then in 'Homeland' we find 'Christ's ragtime sacrament'. They contain joyfulness and a musical, though hymnal, pulse.

The record player opened Jack up to a world of music, and year after year he would add to his collection, with new records by the American pop singer Jo Stafford, or the Christian 'hillbilly' Redd Harper, a friend of Billy Graham's who starred in the Graham-funded movie *Oiltown, USA*. But it was Martz who would remain associated with healing and fulfilment, and it was the broader atmosphere of the celebratory American revivalist movement that sustained Clemo through the 1950s, providing the motivation and context for *The Invading Gospel*. This was to be a joyful work, and a corrective of the confessional introspected self-absorption of his autobiography, which he had come to regret: 'Christian witness should be a song. Not a [...] record of suffering and contemplation. I want to start all over again'.[440] *The Invading Gospel* would be Clemo's song:

> The decade ends with a year in which I have had no red-letter days, no peak experiences, a year in which all major tides have ebbed out and even the blessings seem only shadows of the real thing. But it closed in prayer and song – played Renee's record after mother went to bed – 'In prayer there's hope....' I go forward undefeated.[441]

Clemo posing for artist Lionel Miskin, 1957

Clemo with sculptor Pat Jenkins, 1957

XII
The Invading Gospel

And it came to pass, that, as I made my journey, and was come nigh unto Damascus about noon, suddenly there shone from heaven a great light round about me. And I fell unto the ground, and heard a voice saying unto me, Saul, Saul, why persecutest thou me? […] And when I could not see for the glory of that light, being led by the hand of them that were with me, I came into Damascus.

The Conversion of Saul of Tarsus, Acts 22:6-11

Methodism is characterised by its appeal to feeling and emotion. It is rooted in rebellion and simple in its basic principles of a return to the Bible and sola fide. Salome Hocking, the sister of Silas and Joseph, in her *Some Old Cornish Folk*, wrote that the clay and country people of Cornwall found Methodism so attractive because of its primitivism, its observation of God in the everyday. Clemo's early poetry almost feels like a return to this Methodist inspiration, replacing religion in the landscape and preaching in a primitively appealing, uncompromising and forceful manner. But Clemo's everyday experience was quite different from that of those around him, with greater loss and uncertainty, a fiercely faithful familial foundation, and the constant failure of health. He also had a brilliantly retentive and creative mind, which was restricted by the continuing loss of his senses. His own vision of God's presence was likely to be more dynamic even than that of his neighbours. If God was present, then He had a good deal of explaining to do.

Ever since Clemo had determined to become a writer, he had wanted to write a book of his beliefs and experience. Some of this had been achieved by *Confession of a Rebel*, but he had inadvertently doomed that book. Not only did he not give a satisfactory confession, but by adding the passages about Eileen and over-emphasising his disabilities, his 'Calvinism' and his travail, Clemo had given a warped sense of his life and faith. He now wanted to write more buoyant work, and contrarily he achieved this during a period of bleak physical decline. It is the ever-present juxtaposition in Clemo's writing that the greater his suffering and deprivation, the more hopeful and joyful was his message. In a discussion of his work with Charles Causley and Howard Sergeant for the BBC, Sergeant referred to Clemo's philosophy of optimism, stating:

> There is no place, [Clemo] feels in the Christian way of life, for mere resignation or even obstinate courage in the face of suffering, in return for spiritual blessing in the next world. The blessing he says is in this world and one must have faith to grasp it with radiant frivolity.[442]

In *Confession*, Clemo had written about how his dialect tales would come when he was at his lowest:

> Often [...] when I was under the pressure of religious perversion a ludicrous phrase or incident would flash across my mind, and within five minutes I would be throwing off the stagnant gloom by writing something hilariously funny. Most of the stories so written were sold, and few who laughed over them could have guessed that they were such desperately defensive products.

The same was the case for *The Invading Gospel*. Clemo was cut off from 'all feminine inspiration' by his disabilities and he 'had to switch the emphasis to the theological side.' This, he said, 'produced the prose book *The Invading Gospel*'.[443] Jack had descended into blindness and his diaries are dismally sparse for these years. Through 1954, 1955 and 1956, he would write no poetry. The last verse he produced before the final descent into ashy whiteness seems to have been 'Clay Phoenix', in 1953. The title holds the great image and metaphor of Clemo's life:

> Let my peak be smitten, then, I offer still
> No sufferer's creed from a sealed gallery.
> My soul foreknows its destined thrill
> Beneath the ashes and the oncoming moon,
> My phoenix-vision rising from the scorched heart.

Further incentive to write up his religious beliefs came inadvertently from Derek Savage. On 10 February 1954, Clemo noted in his diary:

> Broadcast discussion of Clay Verge – D.S. Savage exaggerating my Calvinism – wish I hadn't put so much stress on that aspect – it enables critics to ignore my Christianity – there's never a hint that I believe in Christ's redemptive love for all mankind, with the elect as a nucleus of belief only. Long to write more and put my faith right before the public.

Within three months he had begun work on *The Invading Gospel*. For a short period, the book was entitled 'An Outsider's Testimony', but the full working title became 'Outsider's Odyssey: My Creed and Challenge'. By the beginning of June the first two chapters were written, 'so different from anything I've done before', and by September a first draft was completed. Revisions were then postponed at the end of 1954 when Clemo fell ill, with 'nervous prostration, biliousness, insomnia, and heart attacks at night.'[444] For a while, he believed he was going to die, and later wrote that he had been 'brought back from death's door'.[445]

Once Clemo had turned 'fully' blind, the writing process had to change. The 1954 draft had been handwritten by Clemo into a series of red A5 notebooks. It appears aphoristic, comprising short paragraphs and statements, with headings like 'Honesty', 'Sin & Death' and 'Unitarians'. When it came to producing a fuller draft for the publishers, Jack dictated to his mother, presumably with Mrs Clemo prompting him from his notes in the red booklets and in his 1953 diary. In this way, Jack says, on 28 July 1954, 'Mother's rheumaticky old hand has written nearly 20,000 words'. Then, 22 August 1957: 'Today The Invading Gospel lies complete in my drawer – in mother's handwriting.' This was the same year that Pat Jenkins and her friend Shirley visited to make the bust of Clemo. Their visit resulted in Shirley agreeing to type up Eveline's manuscript.

Clemo was pleased with *The Invading Gospel*, and there are signs of a greater maturation in the writing process. For example, although it is about Clemo's belief as revealed to him through his personal experience, in August 1955 he cut out the ninth chapter for being 'padded out with too much autobiography'. He added the Oral Roberts references, and then in 1956 the Renee Martz 'ragtime' passages, too. But the following year, 1957, shows a less expected and unacknowledged stimulus: Colin Wilson.

Wilson's hugely popular response to trends in existentialism and humanism, *The Outsider*, was published in 1956. It was an ambitious and precocious work, and it launched the twenty-four year-old Wilson to overnight fame. Wilson was a self-taught working-class man, who tackled some of the greatest modern artists, writers and philosophers, and his book came with an entertaining mythologized back story of the young broke writer sleeping rough on Hampstead Heath and spending his days writing in the British Museum. Wilson had been brought to Devon by one of Clemo's best reviewers, Kenneth Allsop, and after a vicious backlash in London and several tabloid scandals, in 1957 Wilson retreated to Cornwall. He stayed briefly with Derek Savage before moving into a rented cottage nearby. This outrageous figure, with his instant fame, wealth and sensation, landed right in the middle of Clemo's own circle of friends and landscape and he was an inevitable target for Clemo's disfavour. In his diary, Jack writes:

> [Added] a bit about the Life Force to chap.6 of Invading Gospel prompted by Colin Wilson's egoistic rubbish. It does hurt to see anti-Christian books best-sellers while *Confession* is remaindered, but my reward must come. Christ said the false prophets would flourish for a time.[446]

The 'Life Force' is mentioned in the current chapter five, 'The Thwarted Earth', where it is said that 'a corrupted Life Force produces the horrors of the jungle, the asylum, the hospital and the graveyard.' It is a 'heathen veneration' that 'extracts reverence from "serious-minded" people, then makes them its victims. Reverence turns to perplexity and dismay as the mask of benevolence and beauty is swept aside by some disaster.' This 'Life Force' was a pernicious presence, the object of nature worship, it would seem, although a force capable of binding a person to it.

In truth, Clemo had not read a word of Colin Wilson's, but had the gist of it interpreted by his mother into the palm of his hand after she had read a crass newspaper article in the *Daily Mail*. The article Eveline had read was that of 23 February 1957, which luxuriated in a misunderstanding that had led to a rather publicly witnessed invasion of Wilson's flat by his girlfriend's father, who was wielding a horsewhip and accusing Wilson of all sorts of depravity. According to Wilson's autobiography, *Dreaming to Some Purpose,* the confusion came about when a family member found a notebook for his serial killer novel *Ritual in the Dark,* and took it to be Wilson's personal diary.

After just a few rejections, the publisher Geoffrey Bles accepted *The Invading Gospel* in March 1958. Bles was the publisher of a number of C.S. Lewis titles, including *The Screwtape Letters* and *Till We Have Faces,* so the company's acceptance was considered an auspicious start for the book. Clemo had first read *The Screwtape Letters* in the Bles edition in 1943, and had even written a diary entry in imitation of Lewis when a girl had become disinterested in him:

> My dear Wormwood, I am delighted by your report. Having got the girl this far you will find the rest plain-sailing. Don't forget to remind all friends and relatives that she is now doing really useful work, employing her talents in good causes. These are always helpful to our Father. As long as they distract the humans' attention from the Enemy and his miserable Book we are sure of success. Keep it up, my boy. A cheat is as good as a murder, as I almost said in Mr Lewis's selection of my letters, as long as you 'edge your victim away from the light and out into the Nothing.' I presume the girl herself is ignorant of the Enemy's plan as revealed to that little wretch at Goonamarris. Not that you need fear any counter-attack from him now that they are safely kept apart. I think the Enemy too has abandoned the idea. A triumph indeed – and

our Father is not without hope of gaining the little Goonamarris vermin too by other means.[447]

The sort of academic background Lewis came from would usually have troubled Clemo, but he continued to read and enjoy both Lewis's fiction and non-fiction throughout his life. In 1958 Clemo asked Derek Savage for an introduction to Lewis, and although Savage knew no one in Lewis's circle, it was suggested a copy of *The Invading Gospel* should be posted to him. If C.S. Lewis did ever read Clemo, there appears to be no evidence of it.

Following this *Screwtape* tribute, it bears noting that Clemo believed in the existence of Satan and demons. The diaries show that he considered there to be a war underway for dominion over his body and life, the 'devil' (his wife would later try to obscure mentions of the Devil with Tipp-Ex or black marker) paying him more attention when things looked to be going too well, such as when a girl was interested in him or a book was accepted. 'The devil seems angry', Clemo might write when someone turned away from the church,[448] or, when he descended into what he described as 'Dark Shadows', he would write: 'The Devil doesn't like the way we've been blessed recently', or: 'The devil attacked again last night, but was driven off'.[449] When his eyesight began to fail, it was the Devil behind the decline.[450] Throughout the years, the Devil is a constant presence in Jack's life, raising doubts and fears, troubling his senses, attacking him in the night. The Devil was a perceptible force, as immediate as God. The influence of Lewis even led Clemo to occasionally refer to the Devil as 'Screwtape', especially through the 1940s.

The Invading Gospel was published 20 October 1958, with striking covers on both the UK and US editions. The UK issue was designed by Sheila Perry and praised by Causley: 'the white crucifix blazing behind the rough black print of the title – it's arresting, remarkably well done.'[451] The US edition was more garish and futuristic, in lime green and turquoise with bold black print shrinking from left to write, and the rather awkwardly produced tagline running along the bottom:

> A distinguished poet describes his journey from isolated self-involvement to the joy of Christian fellowship

The book was intended to be Clemo's most straightforward religious statement. In the preface, he called it his 'Christian manifesto'. It is a work of both theology and biography, with Clemo illustrating – or 'proving' – his ideas about God and Christ with evidence from his own life. It is a bold expression of his faith and beliefs, brashly coloured by the zealous enthusiasm of the American hot gospel movement. Remarkably, this least stylized of Clemo's works has gone through the most reprints. It was not only published in the UK in 1958, but also in Toronto, by Collins. It was printed again in London in 1972, by Marshall, Morgan and Scott, at the same time as Fleming H. Revell of New Jersey issued an American version. Marshall Pickering picked the work up in 1986, and Louis Hemmings' Samovar Press issued it once more in 2011. That is not to say that the work was very well reviewed or that it enjoyed good sales. Indeed, the poor sales and lack of impact would be a disappointment to Clemo, making him question the value of his literary calling.

The 'manifesto' was a book Clemo had been pondering for many years. In the 1930s, he had structured and begun 'Blood Creed', a book expressing his faith as it was. He had planned four chapters: 'The Limitations of Intellect', 'Dogma and Experience', 'The Senses and the Essential', and 'The Necessity of Blood'. Already the germs of Jack's philosophy are suggested there, although the Lawrencian bloodiness would be moderated in *The Invading Gospel*. Through the 1940s, while writing *Wilding Graft* and *Confession*, Clemo was also intermittently at work on what he called 'Religious Scraps', especially in 1945. In the back of this diary, he wrote out his religious influences and when completing *The Invading Gospel* he returned to the list, updating it to 1955 and grouping it tidily into 'phases':

> First Phase (1930-34, age 14-18)
> *The Christian Herald* sermons, especially Talmage, […]
> Spurgeon's *All of Grace*, Sankey hymns, Carlyle's *Sartor Resartus*.
>
> Second Phase (1934-38, age 18-22)
> Spurgeon's sermons, CT Studd's biography, Oxford Group books (*For Sinners Only*, etc), Browning's

religious poems, Moody's sermons, Torrey's *How to Pray*, SE Burrows' *Gleanings*, SD Gordon's *Sermons*.

Third Phase (1938-40, age 22-24)
Spurgeon's *Cheque-book of Faith*, Mrs Fletcher's *Journal*, Bunyan's *Grace Abounding*, Chesterton's poems and essays, Browning *Love-letters*, Sankey hymns.

Fourth Phase (1940-45, age 24-29)
CS Lewis' books, TF Powys's *Soliloquy* & *Mr. Weston*, Chesterton (more deeply), Talmage's work (much more deeply), *The Methodist Recorder* & Methodist Hymn-book, Spurgeon's *Cheque-book* & Studd's biography [...], Fletcher's *Journal* & Browning's *Paracelsus* and *Pauline* & (new) *Ferishtah*; *God in Business*; Francis Thompson's poems.

Fifth Phase (1945-50, age 29-34)
AJ Russell's books, TF Powys's *Bottle's Path*, *God's Eyes A-Twinkle*, *Unclay*, *Soliloquy*, Browning's *Sordello*, C.S Lewis' *The Great Divorce* & *Miracles*, Barth and Brunner (*Natural Theology*), Barth's *Epistle to the Romans*, Donne's works.

Sixth Phase (1950-55, age 34-39)
Spurgeon and Barth still dominating in theology – R.C. influence through Chesterton entirely faded despite discovery (1950) of Patmore's poetry.

Clemo's refusal to commit to a single denomination did not change in *The Invading Gospel*. He had been identifying himself as a Calvinist for more than a decade, though he was always very clear that his Calvinism did not have much to do with the teachings of Calvin, but rather to the nineteenth and twentieth century theologians who had built on Calvin's reforms. In *The Invading Gospel*, Clemo states his case clearly:

> The Press and radio comment on my earlier books has sometimes made me wish I had never called myself a Calvinist. My creed has not changed, but the term 'Calvinism' gives a distorted idea of it to those who are not well acquainted with theological movements.

By this point he had begun to consider himself a 'Neo-Calvinist', though rarely used the word. By 1990, in an interview with a student, he used it more freely and described his understanding of the term. Neo-Calvinism, he said, 'is the positive side of Calvin's teaching, without the negative distortions of Puritanism'.[452] The Neo-Calvinists, like Charles Spurgeon, tried to reconcile the apparent theological discrepancy between agency and predeterminism and worked considerably on Calvin's doctrine of election. Neo-Calvinism is a term commonly applied to a specific group of theologians and does not fit all of Clemo's influences or beliefs. For this reason, it might be better to use the phrase 'post-Calvinism', which acknowledges the lineage of the discussion and does not reduce it to a specific theological school. Clemo did not follow anyone completely, but the men who had the greatest impact on his theological development were Charles Spurgeon, Thomas DeWitt Talmage, Karl Barth and Kierkegaard.

An unnamed reviewer in the *Times Literary Supplement* on 5 December 1988 warned Clemo's readers against trying to decipher his theology:

> Clemo's Calvinism, based loosely on the Crisis Theology developed by Karl Barth in the 1930s and 40s, is so eccentric as to be almost useless in providing an intellectual structure for his work. Calvinism has traditionally attracted the hard-liners among Protestants and flourished best in the stony ground of opposition and dissent. This more general context has more relevance to Clemo's work.

Clemo's self-identity as a Calvinist is biographically, rather than theologically, important. It will be recalled that the working title of *Confession of a Rebel* was 'Confession of a Calvinist', and the term litters his introductions, non-fiction, diaries and letters. Calvinism had a reputation for being an austere, stark and foreboding system. Largely, this was due to its hardening of the doctrines of election, justification and predestination, themes central to Clemo's own beliefs. Clemo's Calvinistic self-identity was an expression of rebellion and devotion; rebellion against the villagers and their chapels, and a statement of devotion to a more fundamental, direct and uncompromising faith. *The Invading Gospel* worked to temper the impact of this earlier shock-tactic of self-identification and to contradict its austerity with the cheerful tone of revivalism, as well as stating the case for Clemo's own set of dogmas.

For a secular reader, or one desiring to be convinced of Christianity, the book is practically worthless. This was acknowledged by the publishers Eyre & Spottiswoode in 1957 and informed their rejection of the manuscript:

> What you say about the necessity for personal revelation is something that professing Christians might do well to ponder, but there is little in your argument that would be likely to influence an agnostic to consider the truth of Christian revelation.

The work was intended to be persuasive and evangelical, to inspire conversion, but Clemo was poor when applying logic and hostile to logic when it did not serve his purpose. Yet, of course, the book *was* a proposition, a statement about the world based on data drawn from his personal experience and from theological discourse. It attacks others and supports its own position with reason and argument. Its professed hostility to logic is, then, problematic.

Clemo's anti-reason, like most of his beliefs, can be traced back to the earliest writing. In 1935, for example, he wrote a piece in the local paper entitled 'Methodism and Modernism', in which he stated: 'Christ's whole outlook was at variance with that which asserts the superiority of an intellect and the benefits of scholarship.' It went on: 'Not by study or learning or the light of reason can the truth of Christianity be demonstrated or aided at all, only by the spirit of Truth, which is intuitive, born, as genius is'. In *The Invading Gospel* Clemo invokes the cricketer and missionary C.T. Studd to support his view, quoting: 'God wants not nibblers of the possible but grabbers of the impossible'. More poetically, Clemo writes that God 'cannot be contacted in the icy regions of the intellect, but only along the frontier of flamy vision.' It may be seen, even in that earliest statement of anti-intellectual faith published in the newspaper, how necessarily connected the key theological statements in *The Invading Gospel* are likely to be. By proposing that people are either born with the ability to conceive a faith in God or they are not born with it, Clemo is suggesting some sort of predeterminism or election. Why are only *some* people born with it, rather than everyone? And what implications are there concerning one's freedom or fate? When the clutter of words is cleared away from Clemo's theological statement, a more simplistic faith emerges. Our purpose here will be to elucidate this faith and outline the most relevant of Clemo's core beliefs to his biography.

To begin with, let us look at one of the most frequently recurring of Clemo's Christian proposals: election. It is inevitably bound to predestination, fate and the problem of freedom, and it begins at the beginning of creation. This is the doctrine of Clemo's that is most closely associated with Calvinism. Calvin's vision of election is not Clemo's, but they do share a vision of a post-lapsarian world. That is, of a natural world from which God has withdrawn following the temptation and the Fall of mankind. This is shared by almost all of Clemo's key theological influences, and the problem they want to solve is how one returns to God. This is the problem of soteriology, the philosophy of salvation, and Christ, of course, is at the centre of it.

For Calvin, only the elect are saved by Christ. The elect, in this system, are a small group of people predetermined by God for salvation. We cannot know which of us are of the elect; only God knows. The picture here is that God knew everything when he created man. There is no room for meaningful choice or freedom in this view, as 'men can effect nothing except by the secret will of God'.[453] The irreconcilable problem is that while God is happily and generously saving a few people, He simultaneously damns the rest to Hell. This is sometimes called 'double predestination' and leads to the criticism that God cannot be good and merciful if he damns the majority of people and they are impotent to change matters. Strict Calvinists argue that God's mercy is very clearly shown, as God did not have to choose *anybody* for salvation. Moreover, some argue, God knew from the beginning who was going to be sinful and who was going to be good, so it is not the case that good holy people would be damned, but only bad people. Of course, there remains a question mark over God's complicity in the Fall and the subsequent damnation in this picture, as God apparently knows, creates and dictates all that happens. Even before the Fall, when man is said by Calvin to have been free, it is difficult to make much sense of this picture of freedom. Freedom would, presumably, need to be acausal and chaotic; otherwise it was all known when it was all created. That is, if God created everything and knew everything when he was creating it, then there is little room for freedom anywhere. Moreover, if God knew from the point of creation which people were going to be good and which were not, then it is difficult to imagine Him as a benevolent creator. This problem was acknowledged by both Luther and Calvin, but never adequately resolved.

Calvin's is not a comforting doctrine, but it was not meant to be. He was trying to teach what he considered the truth about God, rather than comforting lies, and he was trying to build an alternative Christian political structure to that of the Roman Catholics.

Those who now follow Calvin and believe in his doctrine are often called Hyper-Calvinists. But other post-Calvinists, including Clemo, considered Calvin's story of the role of Christ belittling of His purpose, rendering Christ's sacrifice arbitrary or unnecessary when God is said to have made up his mind about who was to be saved and damned years before. Different stories about election and predestination emerged, trying to reconcile the ideas of freedom and determinism. Karl Barth, for example, was much more positive about the role of Christ and left more room for freedom. His picture was essentially universalist, meaning that all people are saved, whether they know it or not, because of the sacrifice of Christ. In Barth's picture of election, Christ is at the centre. However, some are closer to Christ than others, having been specially elected, and these people are used by God to spread the word and draw those further from Christ towards Him.

Clemo's picture is akin to both Spurgeon's and Barth's, while not identical with either. For Clemo all people *can* be saved, but they are not *necessarily* saved. They remain on a path of tragedy until they turn to Christ and are saved by grace. The elect are those who have no choice in the matter of salvation, being chosen by God and forced into service as the 'nucleus' of believers and a 'bridgehead' between God and the non-elect. This nucleus are the 'invaded' and the 'bludgeoned' that Clemo mentioned in *Confession*.

> I know some Christian teachers, orthodox in other respects, deny that God ever acts in this way, ever *forces* a soul into His service. But being concerned with logical theories and not raw experiences, they are mistaken. At times when there has been no special strain upon me I have freely chosen Christianity, whatever the cost. But at the turning points of my life, the crises that produced my novels and poems, God has never consulted my will. His providences have struck like thunderbolts.

Clemo continued, explaining how a person comes under the control of the divine, in the path of predestination:

> a man's spiritual life passes from the control of the general Mood of Providence, which operates only through the laws of Nature, to the control of the Galilean Mood, the Will of Christ which subdues or adapts the tendencies of Nature when they impede the purposes of grace.

Integral to Clemo's story of election and salvation is the idea that Christ is calling out to all people, and they must simply turn to Him, submit and believe. Clemo did not follow Barth's universalism, by which all people were saved whether they knew it or not. Everyone is offered salvation, but it is only confirmed when one is willing to accept God's offer.[454] Those who refuse the offer are fated to damnation. This is reminiscent of the passage in Clemo's favoured gospel, John 11:26: 'And whosoever liveth and believeth in me shall never die.' Grace itself is something that arrives from above. It is an invading force,[455] a 'power from on high'[456] that can strike one down, as it did Saul of Tarsus on the road to Damascus.

Clemo was trying to retain the language of Calvinism, but to re-deploy it in an essentially Arminian way. 'Arminian' refers to Jacobus Arminius. The life of Arminius immediately followed that of Calvin in the sixteenth century, and Arminius had trouble with the same issues. He, too, was a post-Calvinist and he reformed reformation theology to reinstate freedom and a justification for the arbitrary punishment Calvin asserted. Clemo used the language of both Calvinism and Arminianism, believing himself to have finally reconciled the great rift between them. And, indeed, Clemo does employ ideas from both sides. However, his conclusion is not as radical as it sounds, and the big issue remains unresolved. In *The Invading Gospel*, he summarised his picture of predestination: 'That every human being has a tragic destiny in nature and a (potential) triumphant one in Divine grace.' This view was illustrated in his novels, and also owes something to Thomas DeWitt Talmage. Talmage was an influential American preacher, friendly with a long sequence of presidents in the second half of the nineteenth century. He was a celebrity, able to turn up in London and expect to be introduced to Carlyle, Ruskin and whoever was in charge at the time. He had an enormous congregation in Brooklyn and a regular weekly readership, he claims, of 180,000,000. For his day, Talmage was progressive. He was against firearms and vivisection, and in favour of sexual equality in education. His autobiography suggests he was a tireless, kind and determined man, while his sermons show that he was a firebrand with an apocalyptic turn of phrase and thundering command:

> You are a sinner. The Bible says it, and your conscience affirms it. Not a small sinner, or a moderate sinner, or a tolerable sinner, but a great sinner, a protracted sinner, a vile sinner, an outrageous sinner, a condemned sinner. As God, with His all-scrutinizing gaze, looks upon you

> to-day, He can not find one sound spot in your soul. Sin has put scales on your eyes, and deadened your ear with an awful deafness, and palsied your right arm, and stunned your sensibilities, and blasted you with an infinite blasting.

Talmage was more temperamentally attractive to Clemo than either Spurgeon or Barth, and Clemo's unfair conviction that non-believers ended up in asylums while 'surrendered' Christians enjoy better health and longer lives, appears to trace back to him.[457] Jack's own copy of the autobiography of Talmage is heavily annotated, marking passages on the piety of Talmage's mother, the direct involvement of God in one's life, and passages about the afflicted, matrimony and Talmage's wife. Poignantly, Talmage's question to himself is specially highlighted: 'I wonder if there is any special mission for me to execute in this world?'

So, Clemo proposed two forms of determinism, and he added the ability to choose between them. He distinguished the two forms by calling one 'fate' and the other 'predestination'. In 'The Dry Kiln', Euan describes these two deterministic possibilities:

> We're all born in the stream of fate, which bears everything in it towards tragedy. But close beside it, or above it, is the other stream of Christian predestination which bears everything in it to ultimate triumph.

The default and natural position one finds oneself in is that of fate. We arrive in a fallen world ruled by causality, 'darkened by original sin', and this is our fate. It is also 'tragic', because fatalism is without God and leads to ruin. Fate is the natural order, as Clemo writes in *The Invading Gospel*:

> On the natural level fate is inexorable and relentless: the greatest geniuses have not been able to break its stranglehold with all their frantic efforts of mind and will. Only one thing ever has broken it, and that is the impact of Divine grace working through the forgiveness of sins.

Further than this, fate is associated with Satan as much as destiny is associated with God:

> There are two ultimate Beings, God and Satan; two ultimate worlds, heaven and hell; two ultimate wills, divine predestination and natural (i.e. Satanic) fate at work on the limited free-will of man. [...] It is true that since God is stronger than Satan His Providence overrules that which is not His will. But this does not alter the fact that the division and conflict exist.

Remaining in the path of fate, one arrives at destruction, death. But here Clemo shows the way out – accepting the grace of God offered to us through Christ. One is then propelled onto the path of 'predestination':

> Where there is a divine covenant ratified by creaturely obedience, its fulfilment is predestined. Where there is no faith there is no divine predestination, but only the natural sequence of cause and effect which derives from the Fall.

It may be suspected that although Clemo is using the language of causality, predestiny and fate, he is not really talking about them at all and at the heart there is a choice, a freedom for the majority to choose damnation or salvation. If one is free to choose between the two then one is not a slave to predestination.

Attached to these ideas of election and predestination is the question of whether one who has been saved can then apostate, changing paths back to fated and doomed naturalism. That is, once one has become a member of the elect, can one then become unelected? In a letter to Victor Perry in 1974 Clemo responded to this problem: 'If the elect can apostasise, there would seem to be no point in God's electing anybody.'[458] In *The Invading* Gospel, he writes:

> If all Christians were elect there could be no apostates, for the eternal security of the elect is guaranteed in

dozens of New Testament texts. Apostasy occurs only among non-elect believers.

So the elect cannot 'backslide' or 'apostasise', but some Christians can. These are the Christians drawn to God, but who are not of the elect. In the end, even this is tempered by the sentiment that 'only God knows absolutely who is eternally secure and who is not', a claim at odds with Clemo's frequent declarations in his diaries about which of his friends and contacts are of the elect and which are not.

Clemo's system of beliefs can seem very personal. Partly, this is his non-conformist inheritance, and partly it comes from a need to interpret his life of suffering. The value of the subjective experience is most evident in the historically loaded concept of mysticism. Clemo described himself as a sex mystic or erotic mystic. It is central to his self-perception and the interpretation of his own narrative, yet it is not always clear how the phrase is being used. Eveline Clemo used the word mysticism to mean something quite simple when she wrote of her 'mystical love for devotional reading' and of her own personality being 'introvert, sensitive, meditative, mystical and somewhat solitary'.[459] Clemo used the word to describe the 'wild mystical intuitions' of the Celts,[460] his early 'perverse mysticism',[461] Emily Brontë's 'agnostic mysticsm',[462] and to describe a Wordsworth-loving girlfriend as a 'nature mystic'.[463] In *Confession*, Clemo writes of his experiences being 'not simply mystical; they were Christian'. Mysticism, then, is not specifically Christian. The base meaning of mysticism is something beyond or behind the intelligible, rational and tangible experience. It is something extra that comes as though from outside the natural experience. Mysticism is not necessarily the touch of God – though Clemo considered his own mysticism to be so. In many ways, Clemo's basic mystical experience appears to be synonymous with unconscious and intuitive mental processes. The juxtaposition of mystical apprehension against intellectual apprehension is made many times, along the lines of: 'My talents were spiritual and mystical rather than intellectual.'[464] It is also evident in the character of Bryn, who was edited out of *The Clay Kiln* when the three novels were botched together. Bryn was the 'mystical' character who had not read anything but the Bible since leaving school, and he is portrayed as a simpleton inspired by something other than intellect.

As something that appears non-rationally and as though from outside, mysticism is easily associated with inspiration. Clemo described this himself in a letter to Ernest Martin:

> Being sealed off from so much external stimulus, I cannot be a prolific writer. In any case, mystical power is so different from a trained talent: there is the flash and then the darkness till the next flash.[465]

This basic understanding allows for mysticism to be a connection with God, as well as a connection with anything else supernatural, and so it is not contradictory or inconsistent of Clemo to be talking about Celtic mysticism, or of his pre-conversion 'lawless mysticism'.[466] He is referring to a dynamic non-rational intuitive faculty which he feels can contradict the intellect. That is, while reason and observation of the external world might not necessarily lead one to conclude that there was a benevolent creator and loving God behind it all, Clemo's intuitive mystical experience told him there had to be. This created what he considered a paradox, although a secular interpreter might think it merely an internal conflict.

The two people who have written and spoken most emphatically on Clemo's mysticism are Clemo's friend, the Russian Orthodox Archpriest Benedict Ramsden, and the academic Heather Martin of Principia College, Illinois, and they both concentrate on the erotic element of the story, the most pervasive and distinctive manifestation of Clemo's mysticism. Both put his mysticism into its non-rational context, with Ramsden drawing from classical mystical traditions and texts, quoting from *The Cloud of Unknowing*: '[God] may well be loved, but not thought. By love may He be gotten and holden, but by thought, never'.[467] Of the specifically erotic aspect, Ramsden draws a parallel between Clemo's experience and Bernini's *Transverberation of St Teresa of Avila*. He describes the sculpture:

> A nun in an evident state of orgasm is falling back on a cloud, while being repeatedly stabbed in the heart by

an angel with a red hot spear and what could, I think, be fairly if somewhat crudely described as a dirty grin.

Ramsden writes that Clemo constructed his own mystical symbolism in the 'Browning pattern', and that this developed into a sense of a promise or covenant. The connection perceived between himself and the Browning relationship, Ramsden wrote, is Clemo's version of Teresa and the stabbing angel. Ramsden's paper ends with a certainty and an uncertainty: was his friend creating an allegory of mysticism, like Dante, or was Ramsden in the presence of a real mystic? Ramsden's perception of Clemo's joy convinced him that he was in contact with a mystic. That joy was not counterfeit, he wrote, but a 'sustained, quiet, evident joy'.

But the extent to which sexuality comprised Clemo's connection with God goes beyond the 'Browning pattern' and into Clemo's personal revelations, his private sexual experience, his syphilis and disabilities. The result of these was Clemo's personal covenant with God, a covenant he saw realised in the relationship of Browning and Barrett. In *The Invading Gospel*, Clemo tried to describe what and where sanctified sex was:

> The holiness of sex exists only where the natural 'unclean' striving towards self-fulfilment has been cancelled by faith. [...] In actual fact it means cosmic revolution, foreshadowing a new earth and enabling men and women to enter, here and now, a realm of experience which is completely barred to the materialist.

There is much ambiguous language here, so to clarify, he illustrates with a description of attraction and marriage:

> A Christian man meets a girl whose approach to Christ has some unique kinship with his own. Something distinct about her faith – the yearning on her face or the passion in her voice as she bears witness to it – arrests him and fills him with a great longing to fuse himself

with the facet of Christ which she reflects. This longing is very difficult to define; it is not mere fellowship or friendship, and it is certainly not the result of sex appeal, for if the same girl were an atheist her face and voice would never show the spiritual intensity which fascinates him. It is not her physical beauty as such which moves him so deeply, but the suffusion of that beauty by a soul which is on fire with love for his Lord.

This sexual fusion, Clemo concludes, is 'a direct product of discipleship. The man is in love in a way the materialist can never understand.'

These passages might be helpful to a Christian looking to understand their sexuality better, but otherwise it is quite confusing. Clemo just falls short of making himself clear. He writes that the attraction is physical, but not merely physical, and it has something to do with fellowship in Christ, but it is not just that either. It is more than this, and he goes on to use the conviction of Studd as an illustration. Studd, he explains, did not accept the rejection of his proposal to Priscilla Stewart, but convinced her that the Lord intended them to marry and there was nothing much she could do about it. In the resultant marriage, Christ was expected to come first. Still the picture of what Christian love and sex might be is vague, and perhaps this vagueness comes from the fact that by 1958 Clemo had not experienced a loving sexual relationship of any kind, Christian or unchristian. A Christian marriage was clearly the sanctification of his sexual or erotic drive, but as yet he had no personal experience to draw from.

On publication day, Jack wrote: 'D-Day. The invasion launched with song', and he waited anxiously for the impact to be announced. Sales were not terrible, but they were certainly not scintillating and he became horribly disheartened. All the signs, including the Billy Graham missions and the international overspill of American evangelism, had pointed towards *The Invading Gospel* achieving a wide audience and confirming Clemo's literary vocation. In his diary, on 27 March 1959, he wrote: 'The blackest Good Friday of my life. News that my book has sold only 500 copies. My Gospel Crucified.' Jack and his mother were so upset that they did not go to chapel that evening. By 1960, the publishers were ready to pulp it. They were selling fewer copies than were being returned and Jocelyn Gibb wrote to the Clemos:

> I am sorry sales are not greater. I know that it is little consolation to you to hear that we have lost fairly heavily in publishing the book – though only in terms of money. I am still very pleased to have published it.[468]

But no sooner had they announced the remaindering than they changed their minds. Clemo's next volume of poetry had been announced and Bles hoped sales would improve as a result of the extra publicity surrounding Clemo. In fact, *The Map of Clay* had very little impact on *The Invading Gospel*; only 27 copies of the treatise were sold in 1961, including books sold abroad. Over the next three years, sales reduced further, but it was remaindered having sold a respectable 1,000 copies.

Clemo's claim that the book had been 'Crucified' did not only refer to sales. Jack was also disappointed with the reviews and the impact of his work. There were one or two good responses from the national press, including from the *British Weekly* on 27 November 1958:

> It does good to us all to be reminded by a flaming evangelist how jejune, tepid and un-Biblical is the religion by which most of us Christians live. [...] The power and importance of this book lie in this that the writer is aflame with the astonished awe of one upon whom the wonder of the grace of God has newly dawned.

More frequently there was a bemused brevity to publication notices, remarking on the writer's apparent sincerity but saying little more. Thankfully, Clemo had several friends he could rely on for reviews. The *Cornish Guardian* and *Western Morning News* were encouraging, of course, as was his old correspondent, John Rowland in the *Inquirer*. However, the major papers that bothered to engage with Clemo's work at all tended to be ambivalent at best. On 5 December 1958, the *Spectator* wrote:

> He is so intolerant of other forms of Christian experience and also so indiscriminate in his hero-worshipping (Aimée Semple Macpherson is put in the first class along with Robert Browning) that his message is calculated to repel rather than win those who are not already where he is himself.

A few days later, Michael Wharton in the *Daily Telegraph* noted 'a take-it-or-leave-it air of absolute conviction about Mr. Clemo's *The Invading Gospel* which makes it something of an impertinence to review it at all'. He concluded: 'But noise and bravado apart, [Clemo] has written out of deeply-held faith an impressive book in the soul-wrestling tradition of Bunyan and Mark Rutherford'. Wharton's sentiment that it was an awkward book to review was echoed by the *TLS* notice on 21 November:

> The book is written with so intense an excitement that it seems almost brutal to stand critically aloof from its thrill. But have we all somehow to get into the revivalist's world […] or remain in the darkness of the non-elect? Must it be Barth or nothing for us? Dare a reviewer, who acknowledges Mr. Clemo's fiery conviction, venture to suggest to him that he seems so far to have reached only a stage in his pilgrimage, that he has had the thrill of the revivalist's meeting, and that with all that behind him the business of soberly living the Christian life in the Church will remain to him?

In Clemo's writing, it has been observed, it is as though he is always emerging or has recently emerged from a worse state into a better one. This is partly how he managed to remain so optimistic in his writing. The sense of emergence matches to some extent the theology, so frequently concerning the end, hope for the future, or the imminent promise. The impression one gets is that Clemo is always on this 'pilgrimage' of hope and expectation.

It is also useful to note the *TLS* reviewer's prediction that Clemo would begin 'the business of soberly living the Christian life in the Church'. As it happens, Clemo did settle into a chapel routine, though never denominationally. In Cornwall, he attended Trethosa, the Methodist Chapel, but in older age he attended a variety of places of worship, most regularly the Baptist Chapel in Weymouth. He always rejected affiliations, and his only attempt of self-identity (as a Calvinist) ended up backfiring. In his 1962 diary, Clemo wrote how he had been 'drawn in so many directions – Presbyterian, Pentecostal, Baptist, Catholic,' but he still felt 'outside.'[469] For the rest of his life he would resist all attempts to pigeonhole his faith, identifying himself straightforwardly as a non-denominational Christian. 'My personal bias has remained Nonconformist', Clemo wrote in the preface to the 1985 edition of *The Invading Gospel*, having been invited to clarify his status by his publisher, but 'I have not yet been guided to join a denomination'. Again, in 1989, when asked the same question by a correspondent, Clemo responded clearly and succinctly:

> The new ecumenical spirit removes the old barriers and misgivings. Christ is with us in any church which acknowledges Him as the redeeming centre of the Trinity.
>
> Our loyalty should be to the mystical Body of Christ, not to some form of religious organisation.[470]

Immediately following the release of *The Invading Gospel*, there was one review which had a greater negative impact than any of the others. It was printed in the *Observer* on 9 November 1958 and written by Clemo's friend, E.W. Martin. Martin criticized Clemo's anti-rationalism and his preference for 'feeling' over 'intellect'. It was not a violent or cruel attack of the book, but the tone was unsympathetic and Clemo had expected better of his friend. There began a correspondence that quickly turned nasty, and when Martin praised Colin Wilson, Clemo felt the affront even more keenly. Comparing the review with Derek Savage's, Clemo wrote to Martin:

> Savage's script is more comprehensive than your review, full of praise for 'a compelling and disturbing book.' He agrees with my orthodoxy, as he is himself an orthodox Anglican, and gently chides my austere critics: 'This book will not interest the average intellectual'; who will find it naïve and crude. 'That is his loss.' You do indeed lose much by your prejudice against the vitality of the little child in the Kingdom: it will outlive all the theories of Jung.
>
> It is strange that you should resist the Gospel and then claim in your letter that the self is not anti-Christian. Nothing could be more anti-Christian than an outlook which applauds a misanthropic heathen like Wilson and disparages a Spirit-filled apostle like Graham. Wilson is a rebel, and rebels can have no place in the Church of Christ, which is the communion of surrendered personalities.[471]

There is a touch of jealousy in Clemo's language about Colin Wilson. Wilson had done nothing to harm Clemo, but to read Martin applauding the 'heathen' Wilson's work over his own was hurtful. Unfortunately, Martin's responses have been destroyed, but whatever his reply might have been, it is clear it had the effect of upsetting Clemo further, eliciting the following Christmas greeting:

> Dear Ernest, I have now had fourteen reviews of my book, and yours is the only one which doesn't praise either its spiritual power or its literary style. John Rowland disagrees with me as much as you do, but he wrote two generous notices […]. Even the 'Times Lit Supp' and the 'Daily Telegraph' were friendly to my revivalism […]. You are so much alone in striking these jarring notes about neurosis and 'resentment' that I feel you must have reacted to the book in a neurotic way.

It is a book which the reader should conclude with the 'Doxology,' not a book which should send the reader gloomily to Jung. [...] My remark about Wilson was very mild compared with the term which Christ, Paul, Peter and Jude applied to such men. Jude called them 'filthy dreamers ... brute beasts ... wandering stars, to whom is reserved the blackness of darkness for ever'. [...] If you want a religion that is all kindness and tolerance, you simply will not find it in the New Testament. [...] The fact that I cannot share the spiritual experience of heretics doesn't preclude me from quoting what the bible says about them. [...] Your attitude to my book and to evangelism in general, shows too much of the Laodician fear of Pentecost.

Best wishes for Christmas to you and Elisabeth from my mother and myself.[472]

Setting aside the argument of the letter, Clemo's response suggests a vulnerability to public opinion and criticism similar to that shown in his newspaper controversies. There is also a lack of restraint, reminiscent of those 'volcanic' letters sent to Eileen when she did not agree with him. It is easy to forget how protected Clemo still was and how unusual his route into adulthood had been. His writing had always been an equalizer for his social and physical fragility, and Martin's review felt threatening. The effect of Clemo's response was that Martin and Clemo did not speak for two years, and even then they would find themselves at loggerheads over Clemo's occasionally aggressive hyperbole and Martin's undogmatic approach to faith.

In 1959, another letter arrived in response to *The Invding Gospel*, but worded in such a way and from such a man that Clemo could not have taken offence. It came from Joseph Fison, a former canon at Truro Cathedral and a well-respected Bishop of Salisbury. Fison had visited the Clemos during his tenure at Truro and wrote his criticism in July with great tact and humility:

> If it isn't impertinent, I think you praise C.T. Studd too highly. I fear that, at the end, he was rather bigoted, very

> dogmatic and unreasonable, and quite out of touch with England, and rather an impossible husband! [...]
>
> I wonder whether your enthusiasm for evangelists of a revivalist character does not lead you to minimise the truth of the 1st Beatitude, 'Blessed are those who feel they are spiritually bankrupt, etc' in order to glory in the truth at the end of Romans 8, 'We are more than conquerors, etc'. Do you not think that there is a narrow way between cocksureness and unsureness, and that perhaps your presentation of the Evangelical truth of the Epistles needs to be balanced by the equally Evangelical truth of the Gospels? If it isn't impertinent, I think your use of scripture is highly selective, but then I know mine is too, so this is in no sense a condemnation of you that doesn't apply to me! [...]
>
> I believe you have a great vision and a deep insight into the meaning of the Gospel. But I wonder whether your interpretation of the faith is really your own. [...] I don't know whether any of that makes the slightest sense to you, but I had the feeling, as I read your book, that its magnificent insights were perhaps spoiled by being put within a framework which was not entirely your own.[473]

Fison's sense that the theology was not Jack's own suggests the rift in Clemo's theological argument, between scriptural and experiential material. The experiential material sometimes compromised the scriptural interpretation, leading Clemo to a more idiosyncratic stance and to the awkward fusion of various theologies in an attempt to bridge the gap. In a follow up letter, Fison questions literalism in Clemo's scriptural interpretation:

> I think my real difference with you is that I disagree about God's infallible revelation. It seems to me this is not the way God deals with those he wants to bring into free fellowship with himself. I do not see why we should impose infallibility as a corollary of inspiration

upon either Holy Scripture or upon the decisions of the Church or upon any personal individual experience. It seems to me that the inspiration remains when the infallibility is removed and, for me at any rate, the removal of the claim of infallibility was a great step forward into entering the liberty of the sons of God. However, I have much to learn and I am only hoping that this new job will not be entirely sterile if I am willing to go on learning.[474]

The 'new job' was as Vicar of St Mary the Great's in Cambridge.

Fison subtly questions a good deal of Clemo's convictions, and the foundations of his faith. He is not only querying the infallibility of scriptural revelation, but also the revelation of 'personal individual experience'. Such a thought would have undermined the sense of an individual's own divine covenant with God, and especially the Isaian 'promise' and subsequent apophenic interpretations of events. Had personal experience and interpretation not been so important to Clemo's hope and spiritual story, this idea could have been incorporated into Clemo's picture of post-lapsarian total depravity. That is, the 'inspiration' from God may be true, but as soon as the fallen man gets hold of it and interprets it, it becomes corrupt. But this would have been to refute the solipsistic certainty of Clemo's beliefs from personal experience, a certainty restated in 1989 in a letter to Derek Savage:

> My books show that I don't accept the Kierkegaardian negative approach, emphasising suffering, dread and dark mysteries and paradoxes in a concept of freedom. I stick to the simple surrender and personal covenant because this form of Christianity has worked so well in my own life. I don't need any hair-splitting between being and existence, revelation and truth, the Absolute and the Godhead. But of course I haven't a mind drilled and trained in what universities call abstract thought: my faith has always been practical, down-to-earth stuff.[475]

Clemo's vision is true because it has worked, he says, even though his own experience points to persistent fallibility in the interpretation of personal revelation. We might be reminded of the Clemo of the late 1930s, who used the day-to-day facticity of events as 'proof' of God's intention that they should happen. When an occurrence was in tune with Clemo's will, it was provided by God, but when it was dissonant with his will, it was of the Devil. Clemo's will is conflated with God's will, and this is a problematic stance that was never fully relinquished.

Clemo still believed that at least a part of the purpose of his inspiration for *The Invading Gospel* was to introduce him to his future bride. Being of the elect, drawing others to Christ, it was expected that one of those responding to the book would be Clemo's destined lover and wife. 'I've been publicly labelled a hot-gospeller, linked with Billy, Oral and Aimee, but where are the "signs following"?', Clemo wrote on 16 November 1958. The only person the book seemed to have helped was the Lebanese-Egyptian woman, Rosine, but 'What's the good of the book if it's only going to help one person?'[476] Ultimately, Clemo was not even able to help Rosine, and following the 1972 reissue he remarked to himself that the book had failed to help anyone – not only Rosine, but all his other friends: Pru and Lionel Miskin, Monica, Mary, Margaret, and all the girls from *Confession*. None of them had been helped by *The Invading Gospel*. So what was its purpose? Why had God led him to write it? Perhaps the answer was still to be revealed.

When reconsidering Clemo's Christian manifesto for the 1972 edition, only a few changes were made. Lines were added to the end of the preface, and again to the end of the final chapter, updating the latest burning of 'rust and deformity' in Clemo's life. There are also occasional changes of words. For example, at the end of the second chapter, Clemo had stated that the only 'basis of philosophy or speculation' for the book was 'the Gospel of invading grace in all its transfiguring naivety.' In subsequent editions 'transfiguring naivety' became 'transfiguring paradoxes'. It is a shift from a position of simplicity to a position of contradiction. He also took out the word 'Fundamentalism', partly on the advice of Derek Savage, who had written to Clemo just before *The Invading Gospel* went to print:

> There seems to me to be a confusion in your mind between Orthodoxy (to which I would subscribe) and Fundamentalism. [...] Orthodoxy, to me, signifies wholeness and integrity in the doctrinal and also in the psychological sense. Fundamentalism signifies, to me, a narrow exclusiveness and the taking up of an arbitrary, that is to say an un-free point of view. It implies a literal interpretation of scripture; and literal-mindness I regard as a curse.[477]

Clemo altered 'fundamentalist' to 'Evangelical witness' when used in a positive way, and to 'extreme conservatives' or 'conservative beliefs' when used in a more ambiguous way, thus splitting up the two senses that confused Savage. There is also a slight change in the sixth chapter. In the 1958 text, Clemo wrote: 'I myself am much more of a literalist today than I was ten years ago'. In the 1972 text, this became: 'I myself recognize allegory and hyperbole in the Old Testament, but I am a literalist about the Gospels'.

A more significant cut is obvious at the end of the fourth chapter, where Clemo has completely removed almost 200 words about Francis Thompson. This was the passage in which Clemo had conflated ideas of childhood, mysticism and sexuality and confessed that he had published poetry of his own 'under the stimulus of Thompson's verse', describing these poems as 'aberrations'. Clemo was referring to the sexually suggestive verses inspired by children; poems such as 'The Plundered Fuchsias' and 'The Child Traitor'. His decision to omit this passage is indicative of a determined shift away from such influences and inspirations.

The 1972 edition sold better than the 1958, with a print run of 1500 selling all but 100 copies. The 1986 edition performed very similarly to the 1958, selling just over 1,000. This version is identical to the 1972, though it was given a new preface. (This preface was originally intended to be the postscript, though the publishers thought the 1958 and 1972 prefaces were dated and ought to make way for new material.)

'My beliefs haven't changed at all since my early twenties. It's only the tone that has altered', Clemo wrote to Lionel Miskin in 1972. The 'tone' of *The Invading Gospel* was set by the Billy Graham rallies and the American revivalist movement, but the theology had a longer history, featuring Methodism, nineteenth century Neo-Calvinism, Neo-Orthodoxy and conviction from personal experience. This chapter has not attempted to dwell on some of the subtler points of Clemo's fusion of systems, but rather to underscore those elements most pertinent to his life and progression. In doing so it is possible to lose sight of the lighter touches of the book. *The Invading Gospel* was intended to be a bold but buoyant statement, and Clemo constantly reminds the reader of God's moods and sense of humour, His comedy, and the twinkle in His eye. Clemo's own humour can sometimes seem impish among the solemnity of the subject and the reader's frustration when forced to untangle meanings. But Clemo was caught up in the mood of the revival, the raw, garish cheerfulness of a 'Gospel which advances with the urban stridency of banners and trumpets, neon signs and advertising campaigns.' At the end of his 1956 diary, Clemo was fully blind and deaf, his 'manifesto' was drafted and no poetry was forthcoming. Yet idly, almost, he scribbled what appears to be a song:

> One truth has never failed me;
> One fact has shown me Love's control:
> The ragtime swing of the kingdom –
> The jazz of Jesus in my soul.

Charles Causley and Jack Clemo, 1961

Daniel Hoffmann and Jack Clemo, 1961

XIII
The Map of Clay

Jack Clemo once described himself as the oddest writer Cornwall ever produced. I would describe him as one of the greatest. Whether I have been with him in the cottage on Goonamarris Slip, or re-reading his poems in my own Cornish home on the other side of the great frozen sea of Bodmin Moor, I have never doubted that I am in the presence of a man whose make-up includes genius.

Charles Causley's Introduction to *The Map of Clay*

1961 saw the publication of Clemo's best-remembered volume of poetry, *The Map of Clay*. The title came from Charles Causley's poem 'Homage to Jack Clemo', and it announces Causley's considerable influence on the book. *The Map of Clay* is a 'Collected' edition comprising three parts. The first part is the Chatto & Windus pamphlet *The Clay Verge*, the second is Clemo's Festival of Britain entry, 'The Wintry Priesthood – A Poetic Sequence', and the third contains seventeen 'new' poems presented under the title 'Frontier Signals', though initially entitled 'The Summer Priesthood' when it was being considered for publication as an independent volume. As an independent collection 'Frontier Signals' had been rejected through 1958 and 1959, before Colin MacInnes took it on and recommended it to Methuen: 'I shall not let go my teeth from the publishers' backsides until they do themselves the honour of presenting you', MacInnes told Clemo.[478] Methuen, too, rejected it initially, but MacInnes and Causley together agreed a plan. They would put their influence behind a larger collected edition and take it back to Methuen. Clemo was sceptical:

> The difficulty about a collected edition is that the constant repetition of the same ideas and clay work images through 40 poems would be tedious, and there is no clear development. At the end of 'The Wintry Priesthood' I repudiate Cornish symbols, only to go back to them again in 'Frontier Signals' and repudiate them again in the Dorset poem. There are mature love

CORNISH NIGHT

Here the sandhills white on the downs are staring
And the ripped pits gape at the sky
With the feeble lights from the lanterns flaring
Where the workmen toil; and the cry
Of some night bird wheeling above them heightens
The pulse of a terror that slides
Into a dark which no streak of dawn glow brightens

Here the cottages cower in the gloom-wrapped valley,
    Silent and stark; creep like ghosts
Past each shuttered window cold shapes that dally
    And linger and slink - the hosts
Of dread things abroad in the blackness thickening
    On the hillsides where in fright
A phantom wind in a demon-quickening
    Screams in the womb of night.

MIDNIGHT OF THE FLESH

To lie awake and stretch tired, yearning arms
Where you, girl-phantom of my prison, glide;
And try and make love's wanton, secret charms
Turn shade to flesh for seed unsatisfied.

To call your name and woo the heedless air
To speak myself what your ripe voice should say,
And burrow to the craven help of prayer,
Imploring Him who sneers in this delay.

Is He afraid earth-sparks would foul His lip
In that great hour when we together cling
As I ascend the fountain steps to dip
My torch in waters whence the rainbows spring?

Torch that now sears my vitals: Nature still
Glares with the greedy glint of lecherous fire.
Your breasts are rounded into Calvaries,
And 'gainst the sky His Cross is on the pyre

poems in 'The Clay Verge', but 'Frontier Signals' shows me still moving towards love as a goal not yet attained. The three series don't make sense if read consecutively.[479]

But the editor of *Outposts*, Howard Sergeant, also encouraged Clemo towards this collected volume, and he soon acquiesced. MacInnes and Causley wrote persuasively to Methuen and their proposal was finally accepted.

Clemo wrote a preface for the collection, a draft of which has survived, even though it was never used. There are many gaps in the manuscript, unclear words and ellipses where he intended to develop ideas:

> The 3 groups of poems here collected in one vol. reflect the moods of a spiritual journey from sensual mysticism thro' a phase of purgatorial Calvinism to buoyant C. orthodoxy. They record some explorations on the Clay Verge of the frontier between nature and grace, and these explor. carried on in a Wintry climate for some years [...]. The clash between individualism and the hunger for fellowship was apparent very early in my career [...]. This explains the savage anti-eccles[iastical] tone of some of the early poems – e.g. Christ in C., Excavator and C. Anchorite. They were not prompted by disbelief, but by belief which was ~~forced~~ compelled to Christ in a wrong setting.   I felt, even in those days, that it is good . . . . . . tub-thumping.
> This has been my ideal ever since I shed the perverse mysticism of such poems as Prisoner and Child Traitor. All my mature poetry is a poetry of faith, and faith wrestling towards fellowship and beauty. If I sometimes seemed to scorn these things it was merely a defensive gesture, a protection against scepticism and idolatry.
>   The basic [?strand?] was optimism. I suppose I have suffered but my essential Creed has never been that of a sufferer.[480]

Fragmented as these thoughts are, the sense is of a more mature person moving away from the 'perverse mysticism' criticised by Eileen, and towards 'fellowship and beauty'. He is fed up of his reputation as a disabled, nature-hating hermit-mystic, and he restates his interest in reaching out to the world.

The preface was rejected on the suggestion of John Cullen, general editor at Methuen: 'I think it would be a good idea to ask Charles Causley to write an introduction'.[481] Causley's is an infallibly generous introduction, an overview of the biography and key themes of Clemo's work, with several pleasant personal details:

> Sitting in the Clemos' kitchen, by the china dogs and the honeysuckle tiles on the grate, the photographs of Billy Graham and T.F. Powys, the glass-fronted bookcase with its volumes of D.H. Lawrence, Karl Barth and Coventry Patmore, the Browning love-letters and Picasso reproductions, I have never found myself in a hermetically-sealed hermit's cell. Incredibly, to the outsider, it is a home of happiness and hope.

There was another observation cut out of Causley's introduction, seemingly by request of the Clemos. It was a description of Jack's father:

> His photograph – that of a thick-faced, sad-eyed, reluctant-looking seaman – stares out of a photograph on the cottage wall, directly opposite a bronze medal ('For Freedom and Honour') the size of a small pancake on the mantelpiece.

Causley's introduction solidified their friendship. Even Eveline Clemo felt moved to write personally to Charles, expressing her gratitude: 'my heart and eyes over-flowed together as I read it. I feel very proud that you now have a lasting link with Jack's work.'[482]

Clemo sent Cullen a number of possible titles for the volume, preferring either 'Selected Poems' or 'Clayland Poems',[483] to which Causley added his own suggestions, 'The Scarred Uplands' and 'The

Lunar Citadel'. In the end Cullen once again looked to Causley over Clemo, proposing a quotation from Causley's 'Homage': 'He walks the white hills of Egypt / Reading the map of clay'. Similarly, when it came to ordering the poems, Clemo made his will clear, Causley disagreed, and Cullen sided with Causley. 'The Wintry Priesthood' remained the same, but minor changes were made to 'Frontier Signals' and to *The Clay Verge*. Instead of opening with the turbulent 'Prisoner of God', *The Clay Verge* section would open with 'A Calvinist in Love', originally the final poem of the sequence. Rather than starting in gloom and working through to hope, the sequence would start in hope, descend through 'The Water-Wheel', and then arrive in the darkness of 'Prisoner of God' before clawing a way back out again. Although initially objecting to Causley's interference with the narrative, Clemo was quickly converted: 'the more I visualise the new opening of the poems the more I like it as it gives readers a flashing glimpse of my goal before showing them the bog I had to wade through on my pilgrimage to it.'[484]

Causley's involvement in *The Map of Clay*, then, is definitive, and there is a suggestion that Causley felt some sense of ownership or responsibility for it. When it came to thanking those involved in the book's production, such as the jacket designer Madeleine Dinker, it was not the Clemos who wrote to them, but Causley. With typical kindness and enthusiasm, he sent Dinker flowers and a letter of praise, telling her what an apt and sensitive job she had done. Dinker replied to Causley with surprised gratitude. How marvellous the cover was such a success, she said, especially as she had not even read the book.

The new poems of 'Frontier Signals' were mostly written in the early 1950s, as Clemo's sight was declining and his despair and hope were pulling him in opposite directions. One of them, 'Intimate Landscape', was written in 1947 but had been excluded from previous selections. In *The Marriage of a Rebel*, Clemo explains that the poem 'expresses the mature pang' of Brenda growing up and losing her freedom and innocence, and 'the effect of woman's frigidity within marriage'. In his diary he wrote that the poem is about the point at which sex 'becomes most intimate – where a man realises what a girl can do to him in such a mood'.[485] It was written shortly after it had become clear that Brenda was being kept away from the cottage by her parents. Brenda recalled that if she had to go to the Clemos', she was expected to be accompanied by her sister. Clemo's erotic response to Brenda in 'Intimate Landscape' was creative rather than physical, and the poem seems to be an extravagant dramatization of his feelings. The first two stanzas state the problem and religious context, grounding the dilemma in a landscape of erotic metaphors, while the final stanza introduces a Donne-like pleading for the beloved to look after him, to 'lead me safely' through this 'Intimate Landscape'. The poem is one of doubt and the threat of missed opportunity, addressed to the lover, while its combination of intimacy and the second-person subject is unique among the earliest mature poetry:

> Oh darling, lead me safely through the world:
> Make clear each sign lest my male clay be hurled
> To flame when it seeks cooling, or to ice
> When lava leaps in you, hot veins entice
> Beneath a white breast I misread,
> Thinking it cold, and pass unconscious of your need.
> Instruct my nerves in nuance of your smile
> Lest clay-springs of your body deep and pure
> Pulse out to consummating ardours while
> I track dry kiln-beds, miss the lure,
> And slink unpurged through stale dust-laden air,
> Kiln-rafters darkening on my nuptial night's despair.

The trace of Donne in this third stanza extends to the use of rhyming couplets and the line length, similar to poems such as 'His Parting from Her':

> Since she must go, and I must mourne, come night,
> Environ me with darkness, whilst I write:
> Shadow that hell unto me, which alone
> I am to suffer when my love is gone.

Clemo and Donne shared an emphasis on the metaphysical and physical aspects of love, the divine and erotic, as well as the form of the dramatic monologue, and it is not surprising to find Donne listed as an influence during this period.

The poems of 'Frontier Signals' can be split into two groups – those of the early 1950s, before blindness, and those of the later 1950s, following blindness. Contrarily, the more exuberant and positive work seems to be the latter, as though the imagining of intense hope and joy is the result of suffering and despair. The earlier poems continue naturally from the previous volumes. The God, sex and clayscape interaction continues, with references to the 'ancestral vomits' of his medical inheritance and three poems written about the June Trethewey affair: 'Meteorite', 'Reclaimed' and 'Beyond Trethosa Chapel'. There are more poems written to the celebrated, such as 'Tregerthen Shadow' written to D.H. Lawrence, and 'Max Gate' to Thomas Hardy ('I almost could conceive / That to blaspheme with tears is to believe'). The zoomorphic language of *The Clay Verge* is developed, with the 'white snout' or 'sodden snout' of the tips, dribbling and pouting, the 'fanged revulsions', 'fanged decrees', 'fanged pit' and 'scabrous flesh'.

The post-1953 poems begin with 'Modelled in Passion Week', an autobiographical piece based on Clemo's experience of modelling for Pat Jenkins' bust. It is a sexually evocative poem, opening: 'The wet cloth was folded back; / The unformed lump stood naked for her touch'. This tactile sensuality is possibly exaggerated because of the new blindness, but it is a strong image, the blind man enjoying being stared at and recreated in clay. The narrator imagines 'The terrible soft potency / Of female strength aroused, in full control / Of the image', which, coupled with the eroticism, implies that he desires a partner capable of being both wife and mother. At the same time there is the suggestion of an overcome fear of death, or of a death itself overcome:

> I touch the plastic head,
> Corpse-cold beneath the cloth, still damp
> On its little gibbet of wood.
> What matters it now, this stamp
> Of a capricious force I used to dread?

The overt message is again of sexuality sublimated or 'retrieved' through contact with Christ, the poem ending:

> If death lurks in the fertile mood,
> I have passed over it and kneel
> At my faith's Emmaus, in the cool of Easter Day.
> There is a tomb not far away,
> Burst open to reveal
> Fate's ultimate bonds outgrown and folded back.

The second half of 'Frontier Signals' exhibits the influence of hot-gospel revivalism. 'Lunar Pentecost' is dedicated to the 'fire-flake' of Renee Martz and her 'jazz-drums'. An early draft of this poem, entitled 'A Spark from the New World', gives a good sense of the way Clemo worked during this period:

A Spark from the New World

Mere brooding bone, the scarred stillness
In the slow wash of lunar light -
the frozen cosmos of the dreamer
Dead, [??] which a song must smite.

This was my prison, a ghostly land
Which it seemed no song could smite

Fire-flake of song, just a fire-flake
Burst a crater in my clay:
God's jazz-drums seem to thunder
Where His lava breaks away.

There's a roar in the lunar valley
Not a blast with cold rock stinging down:
It is faith's new vein, the molten life
Laughing against the brooder's frown

Grim ritual of the isolate self
Is doomed now, for the fire swings on
The beating jazz-fire mounts the white skull,
Buries the credal skeleton.

Cowers the knotted paths
Sweet lava song steams on the glacial clues:
 I shall not find the way back
To the crag's lip and the wintry hues.

A fire-flake has pierced my silence
And the soul responds, too deep
To be greyly solemn, too sure
Of faith's glowing heart to share the dreamer's sleep

The dreamer's image, the cold fang
In lunar shadow. Now I feel
God's gay volcano the bedrock truth,
Our silent sufferings would conceal.

Lunar Pentecost

Scarred stillness of the brooding bone
In the slow wash of lunar light:
Such was my ghostly kingdom, a dreamer's land
Which the real heaven had to smite.

This was my ghostly kingdom
Which the real heaven had to smite

It smote with song – just a fire-flake
That clove a crater in my clay:
God's jazz-drums seemed to thunder
Where His lava broke away.

There's a roar in the lunar valley –
No blast with hard rock thudding down:
This is faith's new vein, a molten joy
Stinging the brooder's frown.

Grim ritual of the isolate self
Is doomed now, for the flame laps on:
The beating jazz-fire mounts the white skull,
Enfolds the credal skeleton.

Hot ragtime stains the austere track,
Bubbles and burns among my glacial clues;
I shall not find the way back
To the crag's lip and the wintry bruise.

A fire-flake has pierced my silence,
a tongue responds – too deep
To be greyly solemn, too sure
Of heaven's glowing heart to let me sleep

With the sufferer's image, that cold fang
Of lunar mystery. Now I feel
God's gay eruption is bedrock truth
Our stoic solitudes conceal.

As the draft is revised, it may be seen how ideas and phrases are connected. For example, the 'stinging' rocks become 'thudding' rocks, and the 'stinging' is transferred to the effect joyful faith has on the 'brooder's frown' – a much happier image and description. But it is the change of rhythm that is most striking, Clemo choosing more staccato phrases, plosives and harder consonants in the finished version. 'Fire' becomes 'flame', 'wintry hues' becomes 'wintry bruise', and so on. He tightens up the rhythm to heighten the musicality of this poetry, inspired, no doubt, by the 'jazz-drums' of Martz's record, the bawdy rhythm of which replaces the 'doggerel of heaven' from Clemo's earlier verse.

One Martz-inspired poem from this sequence, 'Beyond Lourdes', is a remarkable contrast of St Bernadette and Clemo himself. Bernadette was the impoverished visionary mystic who encountered the mother of Christ, Mary, at Massabielle, an event that led to Lourdes becoming a popular Catholic pilgrimage. Bernadette suffered from crippling ill-health, dying from the combination of tuberculosis and asthma at the age of thirty-five in 1879. Clemo and Bernadette connect through her poverty, simplicity and suffering, and the poem might be considered a response to Helena Charles's claim that Clemo was 'an embodiment of the ascetic ideal of the suffering saint'.[486] Clemo, we have seen, rejected Helena's assertion. There was no room for this sort of negative faith in his system of beliefs. 'Beyond Lourdes' simultaneously corrects and negates Bernadette's Christian experience. It was a 'vision born of pain', which Clemo believed could only turn one 'morbid'. He himself knew better:

> Faith has schooled me further, brought me round
> To the secret you may have lost
> Through your suffering: heaven's vivacity
> In the child world lit by Pentecost.

'Beyond Lourdes' was originally entitled 'The Ultimate Shrine' and it was the last poem of *The Map of Clay* to be written. Bernadette is mentioned in both *The Invading Gospel* and in *The Marriage of a Rebel* in the context of Helena Charles's comparison with Clemo, and she appears in the next poetry collection, *Cactus on Carmel*, after Clemo had read Franz Werfel's *The Song of Bernadette*. Jack found the image of 'the ragged slum girl [...] kneeling in the grim slimy grotto' profoundly appealing,[487] and in a letter to Causley 'Beyond Lourdes' is described as Clemo's favourite poem of the collection.

The final two poems of *The Map of Clay* reinforce these themes. 'The Veiled Sitter', like 'Modelled in Passion Week', is about sitting for an artist, this time for Miskin. The narrator muses on the idea that he is sealed off in his remote cottage, 'marooned and fog-bound', while the artist is preparing a vibrant portrait of him for an elegant and 'distant gallery'. He considers his appearance, inheritance and the overcoming of fate:

> The snaky mist
> Has tunnelled down from a past so grim,
> A fate so drab, a painter could limn
> With Hogarth-smirch, Picasso-twist,
> Yet not belie the pervert brow,
> The humped will in the twilight. And what now?
> You paint a man reborn through creed.

With this joyful rebirth, Clemo invites the painter to

> Pile on flamboyant colour: show my soul
> Retrieved from the dead mask!
> Bring Van Gogh riot to the task:
> No wistful half-tones or granite glooms
> Transmit the winged control.
>
> It's bold rough bubbly light you need
> To catch my spirit, trace the swerve
> Away from the ego's fumes
> And the tense blackened nerve.
> The faithful lines will glow
> With the convert's passion: you'll create
> A hint of something shattered, and that's my fate.

It is clear from these final poems the direction in which Clemo is heading. His body continues to fail, he is cut off and remains alone, yet he sings in praise. This is the 'battle-torn frontier', the crisis point at which one must seemingly either submit to God or be destroyed. In the final poem, 'Homeland', Clemo concludes:

> We have reached the brittle pass
> Where sweet surrender alone stands clear,
> And God's judgment turns to jazz
> At the penitent's tear.
>
> This is the homeland privilege:
> The ponderous quest, the sceptic's pang, are spent.
> Our goal is gripped on a razor's edge –
> Christ's ragtime sacrament.

It is a wonderfully irreverent formula and quite unlike the brutal landscape poetry of *The Clay Verge*. Surprisingly, Clemo states that the persistence of joyfulness in his poetry was the result of his blindness. On the one hand: 'I know the descriptive power died out as my sight failed. Without healing I can never get back and move on.'[488] But on the other:

> After I went blind [...] my writings became more balanced. I could no longer see either the clayworks or pictures of war damage, and so my inner world was more peaceful. [...] I haven't found it more difficult to write poems since I went blind. They come quietly in the atmosphere of fulfilment.[489]

The movement from sombre meandering prayers in the sagging belly of the clay-pits to swinging trumpet tunes of praise marked a revolution in poetic outlook and a continuation of the exuberant affirmation of *The Invading Gospel*. This was Clemo's new message, his bold pronouncement to his readers. American revivalism had revitalised his faith, jubilantly and violently wrenching him from despair.

MacInnes sent out the press statement:

The mood and quality of Jack Clemo's vision of the world can only be felt by reading some of these. What is certain is that, in him, we have perhaps the last of the inspired, self-taught English working-class visionary writers, surviving splendidly and triumphantly into the television era, recovering old truths about our life, and revealing new ones.

The Map of Clay was exceptionally well received. Radio and television producers from the BBC and ITV sent letters and telegrams asking for interviews, recordings of the poems, permissions and short documentary programmes. One of these was to be an interview conducted by Causley. For this, Causley wrote out a series of questions and posted them to Eveline so that she could communicate them to Jack in advance. Clemo then spent several days considering his answers and memorising them, so that, when prompted by his mother, he could recite his responses into the microphone.

Methuen and MacInnes promoted the poetry well in advance of publication, with broadcasts beginning the previous year, in 1960. This attention was sustained throughout 1961 and it was exciting for Clemo: 'there is a definite quickening in the atmosphere'. Jack adored public attention and he courted it. Any slight change in circumstance would be announced to the newspapers. His wife would later question this desire for attention, considering it excessive and warning him about those who 'hanker after fame'.[490] But in 1961, Clemo had much to celebrate. Not only was he the author of a popular volume of poetry, but he had also gained financial relief when he was awarded a Civil List Pension worth £250 a year (equivalent to almost £5,000 today).[491] This would mean that following a lifetime of struggle and uncertainty, the Clemos need never worry about money again. Out of habit, Jack went straight to the press, treating the pension like a literary prize or royal investiture, and the local papers dutifully all ran it as a story – the *Cornish Guardian*, *West Briton*, *Cornishman*, *Cornish and Devon Post*, and the *Western Morning News*. The Civil List Pension led Clemo to feel 'linked with the Royal family' and to imagine further honours. He wrote the poem 'Patronage' in response:

A gleam from the crown, among the hot bamboos,
Heralds relief, security
For a son of England who never found
The patriotic song till now. The bruise
Of clay, the jungle din
Were too real as the light receded.
There was some courage in the darkness:
They tell me I did not flinch.
But the gaunt shapes prowled or lay waiting
Between me and the native ground
Where the ancestral pomp overshadowing
The little cottage door, safeguards the dream.[492]

In his diary, he wrote a slightly less formal verse:

I've got my Civil Pension
But still I mourn a lack:
Though I get Royal mention,
I'll never be Sir Jack.

MacInnes was less than impressed with the publicity Clemo raised over his pension, explaining that it was bad etiquette to release such details. But by then it was too late; the newspapers, radio and television were already announcing the particulars.

The Map of Clay was widely reviewed. Kenneth Allsop, writing for the *Daily Mail*, said that the poems,

> in their vision and philosophy are as strange, as troublesomely haunting, as the desolation in which they grew. [...] Clemo is about as easily digested as hot steel ingots; his power and importance cannot be much longer evaded.

More ambivalently, Walter Allen at the *New Statesman* wrote:

> At his best – and he is at his best, I think, in his early poems, the poems of *The Clay Verge* – he has rendered

an industrial landscape more completely and more successfully than any English poet except possibly Auden, and rendered it as the compelling image of his own bleak creed. In these early poems, where the quarrel is still with himself, the language is taut, strong and naked. His recent verse, written as it were from settled conviction, is disappointing. The quarrel is now with others and the verse has become rhetoric.

The Scottish poet, George MacBeth, writing for *The London Magazine* was encouraging: '[Clemo has] written the only religious poetry since the war worth reading, apart from R.S. Thomas's.' MacBeth liked Clemo's poetry and had included it when he produced the BBC's *Third Programme*.

Overwhelmingly, the response to *The Map of Clay* was positive and Clemo received many fan letters. He was now a well-known poet of good repute, almost a mainstream figure. In journals, he began to appear as one of the establishment, alongside celebrated figures like Day Lewis, Graham Greene, Auden, Sillitoe, Spark, Beckett, Pinter, Lessing and Burroughs. In terms of poetic fame, Clemo had arrived.

But in spite of this celebrity, publicity and good sales, Clemo was still not happy. Causley observed in his introduction to *The Map of Clay* that 'Clemo has a livid and lively horror of being regarded, because of his physical handicaps, as some kind of literary freak or as a pathetic wreck of a man deserving only pity'. The truth of Causley's statement is borne out by Clemo's response to the reviews. 'Still it's all tribute to the blind-and-deaf wreck and his devoted mother', he wrote in April 1961, followed by: 'I wish critics would take more account of my later work: they ignore my evangelism and quote "Confession" as if it expressed my present outlook'.[493] In June the following year: 'Sunday Times photographer here all afternoon [...] more publicity for the lonely wreck and his mother.' The *Times* article, written by Derek Parker, who had been instrumental in the successful bid for Clemo's Civil List Pension, also bothered him, 'dragging in handicaps and poverty again'. On top of this, when anthologies asked to use a poem, it was invariably one of the starker early pieces, and most often 'Christ in the Clay-Pit'. In some notes for a BBC interview from this period, Clemo explains his shunning of these earlier *de profundis* poems:

> I don't surrender to depressing experiences, I don't regard them as authentic. A poet is vitalized by the things he surrenders to. In my youth I let myself be inspired through misery and resentment, but for a dozen years now I've drawn all my inspiration from happiness. I can't stand this mood of pessimism in modern literature and I'm determined not to make any contribution to it.

Writing privately to Causley, Clemo summarised the problem in a different way. Not only did the emphasis on his hardship and disabilities limit the impact of the positive message, but it also deprived him of 'feminine admirers'.[494]

Success had distracted Jack for a short while, but the underlying pains remained. He was still unmarried and unhealed, and his prophecies were unfulfilled: 'Success is still shadowed by loneliness'.[495] A few personal events highlight what Clemo was missing. In 1962, his foster-sister Frances, having married and moved out, gave birth to her first child:

> It made me realise that this is what marriage means even for Christian young women. Without an intervention there's no hope of my getting normal love – and I can no longer produce art as a substitute or even a foreshadowing.[496]

There also appears to have been contact with Bernard Smith this year. Smith wrote poetry and was a fan of Clemo's. He had written to Jack back in 1952 and visited the cottage, telling Eveline that he had been converted through Jack's work. His pivotally important impact on the Clemo story will be shown in Chapter XV, but they appear here, in 1962, at a curious time, just before Jack is to form the two most important romantic attachments of his life.

Otherwise, personal events for 1962 were fairly parochial. Clemo bought a hearing aid, which meant he could listen to records in a new way:

> I either lean close with my ear cupped or I stand or sit at a distance, holding my hearing aid to my ear like a telephone. I never use the aid in public, so I don't hear singing at meetings except for faint vibrations if a large assembly joins in. [...] Talk is just the bark of a voice to me.[497]

The cottage was also visited by a cousin, Jean Willcox, and her daughter Maria from London, which meant lots of paddling and playing on beaches.

Throughout this year Eveline and Jack continued to pursue faith healing, attending services at Ladock and Truro. At one of these a collection was made for the Clemos and Eveline was sent £5. Miss Leaf, a Catholic who had visited the cottage with a reporter, also tried to help by inducing healing, sending Clemo Lourdes water from the site of Bernadette's visions. Clemo wrote that he used the water 'with a vivid sense of strangeness and wonder, feeling near Bernadette while still loyal to "healing vivacity" in Renee.'[498] On 21 July 1962, Clemo noted in a perfunctory way that a new 'spiritual healing centre' had opened and its members would be praying for him. This, of course, was welcomed and encouraged. Or it was until four days later, when Jack realised that there had been a spelling mistake. They were not 'spiritual healers', but 'spiritualist healers'. Spiritualism spooked the Clemos: 'It's horrible to think of a medium directing a ghost to transmit energy to me while I sleep, but I have no fears. [It] drives us closer to Christ for protection'.[499] Soon, however, Jack *was* afraid, and he wrote to their spiritualist contact telling him to stop whatever he was doing at once. No sooner had Clemo learned they were spiritualists than he became suddenly unable to sleep: 'The occult power is very apparent at night, keeping us awake for hours and making mother ill.'[500] As psychosomatic as this might sound, embedded in Clemo's concern was the belief in a very real and worldly war between God and the Devil, and a fear that a follower of Christ could be physically and spiritually harmed by the forces manipulated by spiritualists. Clemo's Devil is present and active, a daily threat, interfering in all aspects of inconvenience, and we catch glimpses of this quotidian elf throughout the diaries:

> the devil counter-attacks with a monstrous demand for £35 Income tax, based on false estimates. It's a bare-faced fraud and I fight with nightmare visions of summonses, fines and lifelong victimization.[501]

As with most issues of this nature, Clemo asked Causley to sort out the Devil's demand for income tax.

The Map of Clay was an enormous influence on Jack's life. It had a broad appeal and readership, remaining in print throughout the decade. It was also invited for translation into Braille in 1962, along with *The Invading Gospel*. In the US, the publisher John Knox produced it in 1968, after a copy of *Penguin Modern Poets* 6 had been chanced upon by the theological writer Keith Crim while travelling in the Far East. *The Map of Clay* did not sell well in America, but the generous forward of $200 was welcome enough. It was also published in Canada, by Toronto's Methodist press, Ryerson.

Clemo was a much better marriage prospect after this volume, with its resultant media work and the Civil List Pension. The book's success at Methuen meant that they would continue to publish Clemo's work until they dropped their list of poets in 1977, and it was *The Map of Clay* that led to Clemo's inclusion in the *Penguin Modern Poets* series, alongside George MacBeth and Edward Lucie-Smith, in 1964. This Penguin collection was mostly work from *The Map of Clay*, but it also included five new poems, which would appear again in *Cactus on Carmel*. In fact, Clemo had wanted Penguin to publish more of this new work, but when Richard Newnham had invited the contribution, Clemo submitted too much material and it had to be cut back. In response to Newnham's cuts, Clemo argued rather jealously that in *Penguin Modern Poets 3* Charles Causley had been given a full forty pages of space. The comparison with Causley had a larger context. In 1962, when Causley had sent a copy of the Penguin volume to his friend, Jack had noted not congratulations or pleasure, but disappointment: 'I've been excluded from the series and feel disheartened.'[502] Newnham explained that Clemo's poems were much longer than Causley's, so that his own submission of 25 poems far exceeded Causley's, tactfully adding: 'There will, of course, be no question of a reduction in the advance. It is as nice to have you there with 20 poems as with 25.'[503] The *Modern Poets* series was incredibly popular, and Clemo's volume sold ten thousand in the first year alone. The last time the figures were recorded, in 1979, the book had sold around seventy thousand copies – staggering figures for a volume of poetry.

Even more remarkably, by the time the Penguin volume had been released, Clemo was engaged to be married.

Jack & Mary, 1963

XIV
Cactus on Carmel

Who can find a virtuous woman? for her price is far above rubies. The heart of her husband doth safely trust in her, so that he shall have no need of spoil. She will do him good and not evil all the days of her life. […] She openeth her mouth with wisdom; and in her tongue is the law of kindness. She looketh well to the ways of her household, and eateth not the bread of idleness.

Proverbs 31:10-27

At the end of January 1963, Jack received a letter from a thirty-three-year-old art teacher in Dawlish named Mary and immediately he was 'swept into an amorous cloud'. Mary admired Clemo's writing and wasted no time inviting herself to the Goonamarris cottage. 'I'm praying in deep earnestness, not knowing whether this is God's greatest miracle or the devil's fiercest attack', Jack wrote in his diary.[504] In little more than a week, Mary was met by Eveline and Jack at St Austell station and taken back to the cottage. She wrote easily on Jack's palm and they spent their short time together cuddling and discussing the future. By the end of March, he was announcing their engagement and sending out photographs to his closest friends. In the surviving letter to Causley, he wrote:

> In recent years I've told people frankly that I could do nothing more until my vision was fulfilled – and at the darkest hour the light flashed, so that I am now able to give a few friends what Mary Wiseman and I call our betrothal photo.[505]

The engagement was swift, and their time together over Easter is described pleasantly in *Marriage of a Rebel*:

> The Easter fortnight was a mixture of bliss and uneasiness. Every morning I took breakfast upstairs to Mary and sat on the bed while she drank her tea. We had long discussions alone there until my mother suddenly

opened the door and handed me the mail, which Mary would copy on my palm. In the afternoons we went out for walks around Trethosa or Carloggas, and on Easter Sunday we attended the christening of Frances' baby, Mandy, at Nanpean chapel.

Jack was sleeping in the large bedroom with his mother, while Mary took the room of his childhood, which had also been occupied by the evacuees and foster-girls for the past twenty years. Perhaps there is a hint in this passage of the tension that developed between Mary and Eveline. Why did he write of his mother 'suddenly' entering the room? Was it the sense that she was trying to interrupt the couple or catch them out? Some tension is suggested again in a later passage:

> In practical matters [mother] saw Mary succeeding where she herself had failed. Mary insisted that I must amend my personal habits – clean my teeth daily, take more baths (standing in a zinc bath in the kitchen), wear pyjamas […] and learn Braille and typing.

Mrs Clemo was ambivalent, eager to find a wife for her son but worried about this flighty, exciting woman who was more comfortable in the Bohemian atmosphere of Lionel Miskin's Mevagissey home than the cramped and antiquated cottage at Vinegar Point. Jack, too, had some sobering concerns, which he recorded in his diary during the early months: 'Mary has no use for the Church or doctrine – she's a Lawrence type and might offer only a pagan counterfeit.'[506] Later, he would call her a 'nature mystic, a disciple of Ruskin',[507] and claim that she 'despises evangelists and wants me to abandon much of my faith. The irony deadens the pleasure.'[508] It was not a promising start, and things only got worse. Jack and Mary argued terribly, his mother did not like her, and he sometimes doubted whether she was really God's intended bride. The engagement was threatened a number of times over the year. Jack had found someone to love who seemed willing to love him, but they were hopelessly incompatible.

In spite of the evident uncertainty of their relationship, Clemo publicly announced his engagement. In August 1963, writing for

Cornish Magazine, the journalist and publisher Michael Williams concluded his article and interview with the declaration:

> It gives great pleasure to be able to conclude this article on a note of optimism. This year, an art teacher in her early thirties, has come into Jack Clemo's life. In the exceptional circumstances they do not wish to reveal her name, but both are anxious that he should no longer be projected as a pathetic, lonely man, whose writings about love and sex are merely day-dreams or compensation phantasies.

It was Mary who did not want her name publicised: 'She always insisted that her surname must never be disclosed, and though a local journalist found it out I hid the cutting from her, knowing that she might threaten libel action.' In a foul mood that same month, Mary took advantage of her fiancé's blindness and deafness: 'she searched my drawers while my mother was out and burnt all the letters she had sent me during the previous six months'.[509] These were the 'love letters' they had been exchanging twice a week, seemingly uninhibited by the awkward fact that Eveline had to read them first.

When Mary destroyed her letters to Jack in 1963, she also broke off the engagement and moved to the Lake District. Jack was devastated, but Mary's outbursts were always followed by ameliorating love letters, and by November she had even convinced him that her conversion was underway. He felt certain now that God was overseeing the relationship. Mary wrote intimately and lovingly from her new home in Wynlass Beck, near Windermere. Being so far away, she was no longer able to pop down to the cottage as she could from Devon, but wrote that she looked forward to a time when she would visit Goonamarris and 'stay for always'.

It is noted in the diary that Mary was unable to marry until 1965, which suggests that she had some other obligation, although what it might be is not stated. It was not a contractual arrangement with work or accommodation, since she left Dawlish at the end of the year to take a position in Cumbria. It was just another hindrance and confusion to the affair.

With all these problems, contradictions and emotional fluctuations, both Eveline and Jack grew tired of Mary, but as long as she seemed committed to the marriage there was hope: 'Surely if it were a false track God would have blocked it and switched me elsewhere before now'.[510] In warmer moods, Mary sent down vinyl recordings of her singing hymns – 'The Day Thou Gavest', 'King of Love', 'Abide with Me' – and reading Clemo's poetry for him to play back on the cottage gramophone. These recordings, though of poor quality, are an extraordinary document. They are intimate moments and Mary's voice is sweet, if vulnerable. She also wrote to tell Jack what sort of engagement ring she would like. She did not want gold or diamonds, but a ring of granite carved from the cottage walls. This was a wonderful idea and Jack wrote to Lionel Miskin asking for help in finding a craftsman capable of doing it.

Then followed more troubles. Mary reneged on her willingness to convert, apparently telling Jack 'she'll only believe in God if he restores my sight.'[511] And having once said she looked forward to the time when she would visit and stay forever, she then said that if they were to marry then he must leave Cornwall, an ultimatum he considered cruel, both to himself and to his mother. 'I can't pretend M[ary] is giving me much happiness', wrote Clemo in his diary, but he replied to Mary, proposing that she move to Cornwall – just until his mother died – after which time they could move to the Lake District together. But when Mary's mother bought a house in the Lake District in October 1964, Mary said she could not leave her mother either. It was a standoff. Both Mary's mother and Eveline were frail and neither could be abandoned. Among her troubles, Eveline's heart was showing signs of weakness again, and for a callous moment Jack thought this might be the answer to their problems. The doctor tarnished that silver lining: 'he says she may live 10 years yet. I couldn't expect M. to stay in Cornwall 10 years. How will God satisfy all three of us?' He added, 'I can't leave my mother and she can't leave hers. If we wait till we're "free" it may be a decade and mother *must* see me settled.'[512]

During the summer of 1964, Mary encouraged Jack to learn Braille. She wanted to be able to write to him directly, without the intermediary of his mother reading their love letters. They both learnt together, and at the same time Jack learnt to slowly touch type so that he could reply. This was a turning point in Clemo's life. Suddenly the world of literature opened up to him again. He ordered Braille copies of the Bible and T.S. Eliot, then of Gerard Manley Hopkins and Dylan Thomas, all favourite writers of Mary's with whom Clemo had not previously engaged. 'My verse-structure became more complex and mature from that time onward', he wrote.[513]

This new freedom to read and write on his own had the effect of excluding Eveline from Jack's relationship with Mary, a healthy thing for the couple, but it usurped Mrs Clemo's protective sense of control. While not necessarily a domineering woman, her strength and unconquerable determination had saved the family in the face of overwhelming opposition and hardship. Her assumption of power and control were a necessary habit. Mary, ridiculing Eveline's faith, criticising her lifestyle, troubling her son and trying to draw him away from Cornwall, was now taking away some of his dependence on her, and Mary was bound to meet some resistance. She had no intention of becoming the domestic housewife Jack's mother desired her to be, or of falling into line at the cottage. So the conflict between Mary and Eveline was multifaceted – practical, ideological and temperamental – and it reached a head when the Clemos accepted Mary's invitation to visit the Lake District.

'I can't tell you how I'm longing to take you back up North with me Jack, darling. It will be such fun in the train and there's so many lovely things waiting for us when we get there', wrote Mary.[514] The trip was to be a tour of the Lakes, introducing Clemo to the landscape, sites and literary history. They were to climb mountains, visit Keswick and Grasmere, where Coleridge and Wordsworth lived, passing Helvellyn and Ambleside, all places associated with Mary's favourite writers. 'I mused about Ruskin at Friar's Crag,' wrote Jack in *The Marriage of a Rebel*, 'enjoyed a launch trip on Derwentwater, and (less enjoyably) bumped my head against Hugh Walpole's tombstone.' They took a bus to Dungeon Ghyll in Great Langdale to go walking, although when they arrived Eveline complained that her foot was too painful to walk.

This trip, and the subsequent one the following Easter, provided much of the material for the 1967 collection, *Cactus on Carmel*, a more sophisticated and fuller selection of thirty poems reflecting the physical sexual element to their relationship.[515] God, sex, Mary, disease and the Lakes are the key themes. The erotic language and imagery is stronger in this collection than any other, although the drafts are more explicit than the published verses. Here, for instance, is 'Dungeon Ghyll', first in its published form:

> Rowans – tender, shy, elusive rowans,
> Swaying, summer-warm, as a symbol
> Of a woman's gift at her nocturnal base:
> Soft puffy leaves and sleek stems brushing
> Like shaken tresses or the first kiss;
> And, with the rowans' whisper, you hear the purl
> Of a mountain stream, the pure, blissful cascade.
>
> Here at the foot of Langdale all is guarded:
> A flat rocky gulch, a turfed bank for the shy embrace;
> But farther up there are rowans, berried so brilliantly
> Under the bold green peaks.
> And if you ascend to them there is danger;
> There might be death, and the resplendent rowans
> Would seem to shrug coldly as you fell,
> And the torrents would laugh in the moonlight.
>
> Why should there be beauty
> On the lip of the ledge where you're tempted?
> There could be nettles and a thorn hedge
> To keep you safe,
> Down at the base, at your innocent meeting-point.
> Is the awesome beauty there as a pledge
> Of a coronal beyond the shock and the sundering?
> Flesh against flesh may chafe
> When the wind swoops and blusters;
> But suppose you mount the nocturnal height
> Sure of a rapture, sensing her perfect seed,
> And never plundering?

Unberried rowans shadow the path
Where she clings to you still: you must go on
Up to the blood-red clusters.

And now, in its 1964 draft:

Swaying, summer-warm,
Like wisps of a woman at the nocturnal base:
Soft tethered leaves like foaming tresses,
Smooth puffed stems like a pouted nipple
Escaping the lips in love-play.
And with the whisper of rowans there's the burble
Of mountain streams, the pure blissful cascade.

Here at the base of Langdale all is secure:
But farther up there are rowans, berried more bounteously.
And the clear peaks have a lure,
And if you ascend there is danger;
There might be death, and the rowans
Would nod gaily as you fell,
And the streams would laugh in the sunset.

Why should there be beauty
On the lip of the ledge where you're tempted?
Oh, there should be nettles and a thorn-hedge
To keep you safe,
Down at the base, at your starting point.
Or is the beauty there as a pledge
Of something beyond the stab, beyond the fall,
Beyond the death of the dream image?
It is a great thing to mount the breast,
And the lips closing on the dry tense teat
Were near the living God,
The thirst for resurrection.

References to breasts repeat through *Cactus on Carmel* – as does the association of Mary with rowan trees – but we see a marked difference from the way breasts were treated in 'The Excavator'. Here they are kissed where once they were bitten. In 'The Excavator', Clemo had sympathized with the destructive clay machinery, borrowing imagery from a report on the murderer Neville Heath, who had almost bitten the nipples off one of his victims:

> That broken-mouthed gargoyle
> Whose iron jaws bite the soil,
> Snapping with sadist kisses in the soft
> White breasts of rocks.

The 'sex killer' is Christ and 'the action of grace is a complete act of dominance much like a sexual assault', as Heather Martin wrote.[516] This is repeated in the 1973 poetic monologue 'Herman Melville', in which 'I saw girls' naked brown breasts gnawed / By the ulcerous lips of our Whalemen.' In 'Dungeon Ghyll', the sexual metaphor is in the natural world – the rowan berries – rather than in the violent mining landscape, and it is less imposing. The poem is still about the redemption of sexuality and the temptation of nature, but in the published poem this is more conventional. There are many bare trees lining the way and easily approached – many natural sexual temptations – but it is only the berried tree with 'blood-red clusters' – the colour of Christ's suffering – which the narrator will approach. It is, as yet, 'unplundered'. This is a reference to marriage, to an erotic urge submitted to God, a redeemed Christian sexuality as opposed to the temptations of premarital, or merely natural, sex.

The notebooks and manuscripts for *Cactus on Carmel* are full of such alterations, as well as a number of unpublished pieces dedicated to Mary. The following is one of these. It is a more personal poem, possibly never intended for publication, entitled 'Heather Stems':

> You picked this in a Cornish lane
> When it was clogged by summer rain.
>
> This other, wrenched from Lakeland snow,
> Holds secrets Wordsworth could not know.

> Between Carloggas and the Lakes
> We felt the venom of the snakes.
>
> Love swooned into a cold abyss
> Beyond the last despairing kiss.
>
> You found in Lakeland a wild shrine
> And blent its magic Word with mine.
>
> Hills raped for copper or for clay
> Will flower alike on our wedding day.

There are a number of personal references here. The mention of 'Carloggas and the Lakes' and the 'venom of the snakes' is a reference to an impulsive moment when Jack and Mary were walking down Carloggas Lane and some local children began teasing Mary. She abandoned Jack in the road and ran back to the cottage, leaving him 'to grope home alone'.

The Lakeland holiday was unfortunately curtailed. Trouble began that day at Dungeon Ghyll, when Eveline's bad foot prevented the lovers from walking out together. Instead, they all went back to the hotel where Mary started talking to another man in the lounge about mountaineering. As she was speaking to this man, Eveline was writing in Jack's palm. He wrote in his diary what he believed Mary had been saying: 'She said she often sleeps out on the mountains. Shadows of suspicion hung around – didn't sleep well.'[517] Jack was a jealous man in his relationships, aware that he was not obviously attractive and embarrassed about his disabilities. He was sensitive to the idea that there were better, more marriageable men threatening his destiny.

The following day came the rift. Jack had no idea what was happening. Out of the darkness and silence, he received a message from Mary on his palm that Eveline was 'ill and we must all go back to Cornwall at once.' Eveline said nothing. They got on the train together, the three of them, but at Crewe Mary 'walked off the train and deserted us. Mother said what had made her ill was M.'s decision not to marry me. Slumped in the train for eight hours.

Sick and stunned.' Eveline and Mary had had an argument. It would be consistent to expect that Eveline was pushing Mary to commit finally to Jack, and that Mary was unwilling to become the domestic wife she was expected to be.

Two days later, a letter arrived from Mary, suggesting they remain friends rather than marrying. (In *Marriage of a Rebel*, Clemo says the letter was a refreshed statement of Mary's love and commitment to him.) Jack had only heard his mother's version of events at this stage, so concluded: 'M's contempt for mother has been shocking.'[518] The following two months of the diaries have been torn out, and it is in the surviving letters from friends such as Derek Savage that we learn that Clemo had announced the relationship's collapse. On the single remaining page of the diary is this:

> Damped by a morbid letter from M. about one of her men friends dropping dead at her feet on a mountain. Blind suspicion again – she never lets me get out into a clear, unambiguous, wholesome atmosphere.

Jack was suspicious of Mary rather than sympathetic, but even so this was the beginning of them patching the relationship up. Eveline remained the only problem and Mary would not forgive her. She stopped sending her 'love' or 'greetings' to the matriarch when she wrote to Jack, an omission observed by the Clemos.

Letters continued to be intimate and loving and spoke of the couple one day inheriting Mary's mother's lodge, but the irreparable damage done by Eveline's interference and Mary's volatility was too great: 'M. full of renewed fears and says she doesn't want to see Cornwall or mother again', he wrote on 14 January 1965. A week later: 'Now M. says she'll marry me this year and invites us to Lakeland for Easter.' Jack himself was becoming frustrated and torn between the obviousness of their incompatibility and his desire to wed. One day he will say: 'I've borne this "scratching and clawing" repeatedly for two years. I couldn't marry this terrible alter-ego – but what's the alternative?' The next: 'I loved her more than ever before when her true self shone out from the postbag this morning. This thing is Destiny.' Meanwhile, Eveline was trying to draw her son away from the unpredictable Mary: 'Mother still fears I've been sidetracked and almost trapped'. But Mary kept hold with exhibitions of affection: 'I just love you so. You fill all my thoughts and all my dreams, day after day. You make life seem so simple and good. [...] Oh, Jack, I can't rest for love of you.'[519]

All details of the second Lakeland trip have been erased from the letters and diaries, so we have to reply on *The Marriage of a Rebel* for an account. It is said to have been a much greater success than the first holiday. Clemo writes that they visited Wordsworth's Dove Cottage at Grasmere and Ruskin's grave in Coniston. They spoke of Ruskin's 'tragic passion for Rose La Touche: the spiritual split so like our own'. Poems from *Cactus on Carmel* written immediately after this trip include 'Grasmere Reflections', 'Summer Saga', 'Crab Country', 'Gwindra', and 'The Rider', which, aside from 'Grasmere Reflections', all show a return to the clay-pits and works of his native landscape.

Mary's impact on these poems was considerable. Not only had she encouraged Clemo to read Hopkins, Eliot and Thomas, but she also helped to edit Clemo's work to make it more 'objective', as he would say in 1969. It is tempting to see this process when comparing the intimate drafts with the published poems. For example, the poem 'The Leper' was originally written in the first person, opening: 'In my life thus far / Each miracle has had a knot in it'. When published, it became third person: 'In his crabbed patch of life / Even miracle has a knot in it, / And the greatest miracle had the biggest knot'. The poem was not originally about 'a leper', but about Clemo as a leper. In the draft he described himself as 'barren and brideless, / a weeping leper-stem', and the poem had extra lines inserted, more sexually suggestive and clearer than the 'objective' finished poem:

> And now, in wonder unbearable,
> Fearless, exultant, whole,
> The woman and I are defenceless,
> Our hands on the knot in prayer, soul to soul.
> Chill mists of nullity from sleek altars
> Would bar out the moon:
> A priest's glance would bind my fingers.
> But her thicket is moist. I feel warm sap on limb.

There is no 'woman and I' in the printed poem, and the strong sexual imagery of moist thickets and warm sap is obscured to such an extent that one is only vaguely aware of it. The story of the poem is a straight biography, charting the development of the diseased and outcast 'leper' through much suffering, borne 'always with a faith / That somewhere [...] A perfect love was planted'. After three stanzas of optimistic misery, 'moonlight surged in'. This was Mary, or 'woman'. It 'Cleansed him of the leper stain', a reference to the belief that healing and marriage were two parts of the same redemptive destiny. It was Clemo's whole body that required cleansing – his sexual desire *and* his syphilis. The published poem concludes with personal fulfilment:

> In the clear wave of moonlight,
> As heaven and woman fused,
> Weed patches were remote and dim,
> And ripe male touch, allowed as miracle,
> Brought dew to the straight limb.

The story of *Cactus on Carmel* is the story of Clemo's relationship with Mary, with heightened sexual imagery and suggestiveness, a concentration on disease and the imminent expectation of healing, which fluctuates between the landscapes of Cornwall and Lakeland. The ultimate message is of fulfilment and attainment, but the tumultuousness of the relationship is also reflected. 'Eros in Exile' was inspired by the couple's troubles: 'I wrote it when my Lakeland romance was getting strained by Mary's bouts of militant scepticism'.[520] It was written in February 1965, a period of difficulty and doubt, and was triggered by one of his new Braille books: 'Reading Eliot this week has touched off a Biblical-erotic poem, "Eros in Exile" [...] Easter present for M.' The original title was 'Babylon in Exile', and the interchangeability of Eros and Babylon is suggestive of Eros being commensurably sin-ridden as the fallen city of Revelation. So this is to be a piece about the problem of erotic love when it is independent of Christianity:

> By the rivers of Babylon
> We lay down but could not love.
> Text from the clear springs, the erect tower,
> The surging stem:
> If I forget thee, O Jerusalem,
> Let my right hand forget her cunning,
> Let my right hand forget,
> Feel only the deadened stream, dead dream.

The touch of Eliot might be imagined in the repetitions and language play introduced in the opening lines:

> Locked grove, lost grove.
> Heavy air from mouldering clay-hills
> Fills the arbour and threatens the embrace.
> Nuptial bud at the lips
> Slips back into the natural stream
> Which gyrates blindly in the tense wood,
> Offering no drink, taking no reflections:
> Opaque dull gloss of instinctive waters
> Suddenly untransmuted. Male tower, female flower,
> Cower in the grey light. Pride of the copse
> Drops as the timid hazel-stems
> Lift from the thickened brook their soiled catkins.

Clemo's key influences at this point were innovative and exciting, as well as more obscure. The repetitions are a new direction, rhythmically and phonetically, and Clemo will use these techniques, derived from Eliot and Thomas, for the rest of his career. He is developing the poems away from his established pattern of writing, and this is shown in the drafts. The first drafts tend to be more formal and straightforward than the finished poems, which are often allusive and abstruse. This began with *Cactus on Carmel*, and it becomes more pronounced as the poet ages. At its best, there is an injection of drama, narrative and a depth of association added to the already vivid symbolism, which itself is developed far beyond the clayscape. At its worst, many years later in Clemo's final volumes, sentences risk reading like cryptic crossword clues. Looking through the drafts and manuscripts, it is as though clarity and facility came too easily to Clemo. He could toss out tidy doggerel all morning, but later in the day he would deconstruct it, disrupt the rhythms and rhymes, and impose more sophisticated associations and consonance. A simple example of the process is the late poem 'Pascal', which began life in 1984, a fairly twee and bouncy rhyme:

> He graciously thinned his library
>   And died with two books in his home.
> Such paradox in a scholar
>   Kindles respect for Rome.

By the time it was published, first in the magazine *The Cut*, in 1984, then in Clemo's collection *Approach to Murano*, in 1993, the verse was freer, the rhythm interrupted, and the sense considerably deepened:

> He graciously thinned his library, a rare act
>   For a scholar, dying with only two
> Books in his home: nun-sister,
>   No wife, matched the ascetic martyrdom.

The influence of Mary had a sophisticating effect on Clemo's poetry, and Eliot to Clemo became the exemplar of poetic sophistication.

Thematically, *Cactus on Carmel* often covers familiar ground. 'The New Creation' is about the need for Clemo or the narrator to redeem sex from nature: 'If you were nature's child / I could not love you', it begins. It suggests, however, that the beloved is converted. She is

>   not of these,
> Not one with earth and nature's powers,
> For He Who fashioned creeds to shame the flowers
> Remade you through his stern theologies.
> Limbs, breasts and hair were naught to me
> Till cleansed by baptism

The poem ends with the fantasy: 'You are with child by me.' No doubt this is metaphorical, but it also belies the strong desire to have children of his own. Clemo would later criticise the poem: 'like most youthful poems it overstates the case. In order to exalt God as Redeemer it almost rejects Him as Creator.'[521] He calls it 'youthful' because it was written in 1945, so it is really one of his earliest mature poems, a contemporary of the *Clay Verge* sequence. 'Gulls Nesting Inland' is another from the period published in *Cactus on Carmel*. Written in 1948 it was always considered a minor poem, but here it offers pleasant respite from the heavier work surrounding it.

Syphilis – the great unredeemed sexual burden – is continued as a theme. There are hints in a great many of the poems, but most suggestive are 'Bunyan's Daughter', 'Frontier City', and 'The Leper'. In 'Bunyan's Daughter', Clemo seems to be attributing Mary Bunyan's blindness from birth to something sinful, contracted and inherited. It is a monologue, from the perspective of Mary. The following verses might be recognised from earlier:

> I owe to you all the leprous scars,
> Peeled down to slime that spat at the Cross;
> Fumes of the sunken furnace,
> Ice on the iron bars,
> As I staggered from loss to loss,
> Hawking laces, bearing the coarse jeer,
> Crying all night because you had made me one
> Whom pure men would shun.
> [...]
> You need not even feel shy,
> Dear guard-room Magdalene,
> Much less ashamed if we come face to face:
> A blight is cancelled, though the smoke of your thighs
> Remains till death upon your eyes.
>
> That soldier boy, that camp carouse ...
> My father dreams of pilgrims now, of grace
> So potent at life's core
> That he can write: 'I never touched a whore.'

It is a reworking of 'Montana Shade', the poem directed at the prostitute from whom Reggie Clemo contracted syphilis. It is a bold near-confession from Clemo, and a strange interweaving of his own narrative with that of Mary Bunyan.

Immediately following 'Bunyan's Daughter' is 'Frontier City', a title suggestive of the Wild West and reminiscent of the unpublished poem 'Inheritance' quoted in Chapter I. Initially, 'Frontier City' was entitled 'Truro', and Clemo was writing about his treatment at the hospital; the tests, the 'bandaging doom' and the onset of blindness. Connecting this with the 'Frontier' does two things. In the first instance, it connects the treatment of the disease with the cause of it in America. In the second, it reinforces the idea of being at the front of a battleground, on the edge between two territories – just as in his earliest collection he had been on the 'verge'. Clemo stands between the natural and the divine, and they are warring. It really is an erotic redemption, from the sin-based infection to the sex-saving conversion.

Many of this collection's titles are intended to evoke a broader landscape. The title *Cactus on Carmel* itself evokes the Holy Land and Elijah's display of God's power on Mount Carmel to the followers of Baal. This is reinforced by the first poem, 'Cactus', then the Greek reference in 'Eros in Exile', the Roman in 'Venus in Grace', and the American suggestions of 'Frontier City' and 'Prairie Song'. As the volume progresses, a pair of clayscape pieces interrupts the foreign climate – 'Exit' and 'Gulls Nesting Inland' – before we are edged out to Egypt, in 'Lebanese Harvest', the 1959 poem about Rosine. From here, the reader is taken to Massabielle for two poems, after which the imagery begins to fuse. 'Cactus in Clayscape', originally 'Elijah in Clayscape', blends Biblical geographies with Cornish, while 'The Rider' likens the clay-tips to 'white elephants / Saddled for the ride'. Following the other foreign landscapes, the introduction of elephants suggests a continuation of earlier themes, but the simile was introduced to Clemo by Mary, who thought elephants grotesque creatures. The following three poems, 'Confessional', 'The Leper' and 'Charlotte Nicholls', do not progress geographically, though they are relevant and worthy pieces for the collection. They create a pause in the subtle narrative before Clemo launches into the end sequence of Lakeland poems and the two geographically disparate closing pieces stating the book's moral.

The final two poems are 'Gwindra' and 'Carmel'. Gwindra is a place just over a mile south of the Clemo cottage, so the reader has been led back home. In the first draft, it was about Clemo and Mary out walking, when 'She led me to the clay-dry'. This version concludes by showing us where Clemo positions himself, as a 'priest' on the frontier between God and man, 'Fenced between dune and kiln'. The published version is twice the length, but Mary ('she') is no longer in it, and there is now no 'priest'. There is, though, a greater emphasis on marriage, a movement 'towards harbour' and a 'deep plashing bell of fusion'. We are nearing a happy ending. As the collection began with 'Cactus', it ends with 'Carmel', dedicated to Saint Thérèse of Liseaux, the sick and sensitive nineteenth-century Carmelite who died of consumption aged twenty-four. 'Carmel' uses diverse metaphors and symbols. Carmel itself is not only the site of Elijah's miracles, but a place associated with fertility, the Hebrew *Kerem* meaning vineyard. It is with equal relevance associated with the sixteenth century Carmelite mystic St John of the Cross and his *Ascent of Mount Carmel*, a commentary on asceticism. Both *Ascent of Mount Carmel* and *Dark Night of the Soul* begin with St John's celebrated poem and the remainder of both books is a detailed analysis of the verse. The 'Dark Night' of asceticism is a personal tribulation of suffering and deprivation necessary for approaching God. It is presented as a journey in the dark, ascending a stairway to the beloved one (God) in the turret. The moment of bliss is when the lover reaches the beloved, and John's language becomes almost sensual:

> I remained and I forgot,
> My face resting on the beloved;
> Everything stopped and I left me,
> Left my cares
> Among the lilies, forgotten.

It is the experience of these mystics Clemo cares for. As Heather Martin wrote, 'their individual witness matters more to him than their Catholic faith'. In 'Carmel', St Thérèse is considered an exception among them:

> the true child-bride,
> Burning among the passionless, cold-eyed,
> Uncomprehending species, bats or fish,
> Who glided in corridors,
> Clicked rosaries or tapped a refectory dish.

It has been seen how Clemo refused to acknowledge asceticism and suffering as his purpose or fate, so the imagery he is trying to evoke is of mystical experience through personal tribulation – of Christian joy felt by 'Spirits still chaste for Christ'. It is a purification of the body, once again, by submission to God. Having revealed his admiration for Thérèse, the poem concludes with the claim that the 'ultimate Carmel of the soul' is achieved by the 'doubly wedded' – those married not only to God, as the Carmelite mystics were, but those 'Flesh-fertile pilgrims, canonized at Cana'. The message is that 'Christian mysticism can lift married couples to a level beyond the ascetic.'[522]

The volume is jacketed in plain desert-yellow card, with only Clemo's name and the title on the front. Methuen made the unusual decision to produce the book as though half of the pages needed cutting. In some secondhand volumes, the decorative intentions of this feature have been ignored, and the pages have been forced open, revealing them to be completely blank. Clemo questioned this feature when writing to Causley, saying that the poems' 'prickles [are] nicely softened between a lot of uncut blank pages. This device seems weird, and I should think it would irritate some readers.'[523] Causley, of course, replied with nothing but praise for the collection:

> You've extended your range; the observation and sensibility and thought are all touched with real profundity; even more revealing light is cast on you and your philosophy. It contains, unquestionably, some of the finest poems you've ever written: and there isn't the faintest hint of staleness, tiredness, boring repetitious-

ness. The whole thing has great force, and freshness; a kind of driving clarity.[524]

Writing in the *Church Times*, the Cumbrian poet Norman Nicholson agreed with Clemo's concern for the peculiar production: 'why on earth have the publishers issued it with two out of every four pages left blank?'[525] It is a little confusing, but it bulks a fifty-page book out to a hundred pages, making it feel more substantial. (The next volume, *The Echoing Tip*, also published by Methuen, again tried to bulk the book out, by printing on heavier paper.)

The manuscript was submitted in February 1967. It was to be dedicated to Mary, and the preface referenced her personally. But through 1966 Mary was more volatile than ever. She 'still loathes the cottage, the district and the Cornish people and insists on my buying a house in Lakeland or Skye before we marry.'[526] Miskin advised Clemo that these were very dubious tactics, but Clemo would not stop telling the press every detail. The *Independent*, the *Western Morning News* and the *Cornish Guardian* each wrote similar articles, informed by the Clemos. They ran along the lines of this one in the *Western Morning News* of 31 January 1966:

> Miss Mary Wiseman, a brunette, aged 36, who teaches at a school at Windermere, Westmorland, is not keen to live in Cornwall [...]. But Mr. Clemo, whose roots are deep in the clay country, does not want to forsake his birthplace.

Perhaps these public pronouncements were defiant statements of Clemo's faith in his destiny. Certainly they were misguided. The relationship was a hopeless mismatch and everyone knew it. Mary was religiously and emotionally incompatible with Jack. She hated Cornwall, disliked much of his writing and did not care for his mother or their faith. She offered nothing but sexual contact and the conclusion of the 'Browning pattern'. It was a surprise only to Jack when on 15 September 1966 she wrote with a practical finality:

> The black minute M. says she loves and means to marry someone else. This is worse than I expected – felt stunned. Is this the end of 3 years of prayer and witness? It's crushing for mother. God help us.

Still, there is that innocence in the question, 'Is this the end?', as though there is some chance of things working out. For safety's sake, he changed the *Cactus on Carmel* preface and recalled the dedication, at the same time writing back to Mary and asking her to think again. 'I don't rule out a miracle here', he noted in his diary. 'Told her she's fickle, but a Christian can't be bitter and I'd forgive. Felt hopeful and very sure of God's help.' Mary told him she was to marry at Christmas but would allow Jack to keep in touch if he sent back the love letters she had given him. This was a ruse to destroy the evidence of their relationship, but Jack wanted to keep communications open. He offered to send the letters back a few at a time, accompanying them with new persuasive and ameliorating letters. Instead, Mary moved to Barrow-in-Furness and never wrote again.

She left in her wake a horribly miserable man, but one now capable of reading Braille and more socially acceptable, cleaner and tidier. He had been introduced to more modern and innovative poets and he was now able to read them. Clemo gained great pleasure in being able to order Braille versions of the books of the Bible, each volume huge and cumbersome, and only occasionally did he chastise himself: 'It's good to read Hosea and Joel again, but to fill the house with Braille duplicates seems pitiful after all my faith for healing.'[527] The volume of poems that Mary had inspired was one of his best. It was broader, more intelligent, but still urgent and 'prickly'. The *Telegraph* approved of it, though again the *TLS* did not. Elizabeth Jennings, writing for the *Catholic Herald*, was ambivalent, and seemed to consider Clemo's a form of 'nature mysticism':

> Generally speaking, I would say that I prefer my mysticism taken pure than when it is mingled with some other element. Thus it is that I am always slightly suspicious of nature mysticism. Jack Clemo does, I think, come in for these strictures.

> He writes much of Cornwall and its clay-pits but, almost against my will as it were, I find many of his poems very moving. I like their starkness and directness.[528]

Derek Parker, the writer and broadcaster, wrote to Clemo:

> There seem to be one or two poems [...] which are quite perfectly assured in a manner which you have not previously shown; the striving which has sometimes been a little too obvious in the past in your poetry has settled [...] into the most amazing perfection of form; they are like the later religious poems of Donne.

Parker was in correspondence with Clemo in the 1960s and vainly tried to sell Jack's old novel *The Shadowed Bed* to publishers for four years, eventually returning the manuscript in 1966. Parker told Clemo that Mary Wilson, the Prime Minister Harold Wilson's wife, was a fan of his, her favourite poem being 'Crab Country'.

Another literary man, the controversial poet and travel writer James Kirkup, also enjoyed the new work and published 'Exit' in his Tokyo magazine, *Orient/West*, sending with his appreciation a record of Japanese folk tales. 'My fame spreads, but "Exit" won't challenge the Buddhists and sun-worshippers', Jack noted grumpily.[529]

The atmosphere around the publication was not as exciting, Jack felt, as the buzz Causley had stimulated for *The Map of Clay*. There were television and radio appearances (including one in which his mother affects a more 'English' accent), as well as readings, and most of the major papers noticed the volume. But Clemo told his diary that it was 'the worst reception I've ever had for a book'. He was depressed when the *TLS* said they preferred the alienating clayscape poems, and again when the *Scotsman* perceived a 'Calvinist gloom' in *Cactus on Carmel*. They had not seemed to notice the new breadth of experience and the projection outside of himself. In *The Map of Clay*, Clemo's poems about other writers were written 'to' them, from his own point of view. Here, in *Cactus on Carmel*, Clemo had gone further, putting himself into the lives of Mary Bunyan, Elijah and Charlotte

Brontë, imagining himself as them, blurring new boundaries. Perversely, this broadening of perspective appears to have been the result of increased disabilities. Clemo lost his only personal contact with the landscape when his sight and hearing failed, so now his stimuli were books, news and correspondence, leading him out into the world.

In five years, *Cactus on Carmel* sold only 500 copies before it was remaindered. It was a book about fulfilment, though the truth was that Mary had left forever, sales were disappointing, both spiritual and medicinal healing continued to be useless, and Jack's mother was in decline. However, by October 1967, when the book was released, a new romantic prospect had emerged, a laundress from Weymouth named Ruth Peaty, who wrote to Jack on the auspicious date of 12 September – the wedding anniversary of Robert and Elizabeth Barrett Browning.

Jack and Eveline Clemo, 1966

Causley, Jack, Ruth and Bella at Clemo's wedding outside Trethosa Chapel, 1968

XV
Ruth and the 'Dorset Pull'

One woman will never find
   A deceiver's smirk behind a mask:
No amorous arts have spread
   A net while you fed:
Some brides have been tricked, made blind
   As they basked, but not where *you* bask.[530]

'God had destined me for marriage', Clemo wrote in *The Marriage of a Rebel*, and 'for this very reason the devil had tried to make me unmarriageable.' When Clemo committed himself to God he believed that the redemption of his body and fate had to be a redemption of his sexual being. The divine form of sexuality occurred within a Christian marriage, so this, he was certain, was his destiny. It was not just a *desire* to marry, but a promise between man and God that he should.

The story of the marriage is told many times: in *The Marriage of a Rebel*; in his mother's pamphlet *I Proved Thee at the Waters*; in Sally Magnusson's *Clemo: A Love Story*; and in his wife Ruth's notebooks. The story of how Ruth first came to write to Jack, and how the couple met and married is crucial to the sense of predestination and justification in this narrative. Yet a central aspect of this mythologised story is not quite as it has been presented by the Clemos.

Jack's account, given in *The Marriage of a Rebel*:

> [Ruth] wrote to me because a friend had told her about my books and she wanted further details; she also felt that I must be 'an interesting person'. I sent her a copy of *The Invading Gospel*, and its odd mixture of autobiography, polemics, evangelism, poetry and literary criticism seemed to meet her need of a more complex approach than that of the average religious book.

Another version, in Eveline's pamphlet:

> In 1967, a lady from Weymouth wrote him saying how much she admired his book, 'The Invading Gospel' […]. He was able to see from her letters that he was in touch with quite an unusual personality.

The discrepancy between Jack's and his mother's order of events is a mistake of the mother's. She says Ruth had read *The Invading Gospel* before writing to Jack, but Jack says she had not. In fact, she had not read any of Clemo's writing before approaching him. Sally Magnusson's version, told in *Clemo: A Love Story*, muddies the water further. Magnusson's book is the story of the courtship of Jack and Ruth, alternating their narratives chapter by chapter until the stories coincide, giving the sense of two streams inevitably converging. The importance of predestination in this account is strongly emphasised. Magnusson writes how in spite of events making Jack appear 'unmarriageable':

> It arrived, just like that out of the blue – a letter dated 12 September, the anniversary of Browning's marriage. 'Dear Jack,' it began chattily, as if they had known each other for years. It was signed 'Ruth (Peaty)'.

These features were clearly considered the most salient elements of the book's plot, being used as the hook for the back cover blurb. The idea of spontaneity, of the letter arriving 'out of the blue', is central to that sense of destiny, of God's fulfilment of his promise. Magnusson went on to say that when Ruth

> picked up her pen to write to Jack Clemo […] he was simply a name passed on by one of her many correspondents who knew she was on the look-out for challenging books and interesting people.

Magnusson received her information directly from the Clemos through Ruth, who put considerable effort into the project, filling several notebooks with information, ideas, directives and characters to include, as well as subjects for Magnusson to avoid. Ruth's skeleton of the above passage from *A Love Story* is in one of these notebooks:

> Heard of Jack through a correspondent Sept 1967 who informed me in a letter of a certain Jack Clemo (Blind & Deaf) who had written books on subjects I was interested in – The Cruelty of Nature – The Problem of Pain.

Another correspondent of the Clemos', Michael Spinks, wrote a similar story in an article for *London Cornish*, but added the name of Bernard Smith to it, stating that 'it was through him [Bernard Smith] and his wife Avril that a young disillusioned girl wrote Jack what she thought was to be a pen-letter from her home in Weymouth'. Spinks goes on to say that the subsequent correspondence of Jack and Ruth after 'that first unlikely approach', 'grew and moved towards romance'. Smith, then, is the 'correspondent' or 'friend' written about by Jack, Ruth and Eveline Clemo, and by Sally Magnusson. Smith's visits to the Clemos have already been noted and he maintained intermittent contact with Jack.

The story being propounded in these accounts is quite clear: gaining the address from a mutual friend, Ruth wrote a letter of spiritual admiration to Jack on an auspicious date and their correspondence developed into a romance. By divine contrivance, Ruth and Jack were pressed together, the element of unlikelihood and apparent chance evidencing predestination at every turn. However, this is not the full story. These mutual acquaintances ran what was called 'The Christian Introduction Bureau', essentially a dating agency for Christians. Both Jack and Ruth submitted forms to the 'Bureau', including personal details like height and income, with statements of what they were looking for in a relationship. In this section, both wrote 'Marriage' and enclosed their fees and photographs. Ruth considered this a last desperate attempt to find the relationship she was looking for. In correspondence with the 'Bureau' she wrote that 'the only way seems to resort to this', adding, 'one cannot expect God to work wonders for us while we just sit and wait.'[531]

These documents are important in a unique way. In the first instance, seeing Clemo describe himself and what he is looking for in such direct language is illuminating, and seeing him sell himself as a marriageable prospect is singular. In the second instance, there is the question of why the couple did not want to mention the 'Bureau'. Did they think that it harmed the mythopoeic quality of their marriage narrative, or did they fear it was in some sense culturally taboo?

In terms of details, the forms offer some otherwise uncertain information, such as both Ruth and Jack being 5' 6" tall. There is more to be found by comparing their different responses to the same questions. For example, under 'Ambitions', Jack has written: 'To continue Christian witness', while Ruth has: 'To be an interesting companion to someone.' The form then shows Clemo describing himself physically. Under 'General Health', he writes: 'Good. Blind and partially deaf – people write on my palm.' Under 'General Appearance': 'Medium build, grey-haired, large leonine head, rugged face.' Then there is this lovely summary of what he is looking for in a woman:

> Any age under 40. About my own height or only an inch or two shorter; good powerful figure. Not fashionable or expensive in dress – simple and plain and perhaps untidy with long hair tumbling around her shoulders. Strong personality, serious and reliable but not solemn and stuffy – keen sense of fun and humour desired. Some taste for Christian literature. Must not smoke, drink, gamble or go to dance after marriage.

Reading this, Ruth could have been concerned. She was 44 – too old for Jack – and in her photo she looks slim, rather than having 'a good powerful figure'. Her hair does not tumble anywhere, but is worn short, and her tidiness would certainly have been a disappointment.

Ruth was not the first woman to respond to Jack's profile. In April, he was corresponding with a 'Quaker Lady', who has since been edited out of the diaries by Ruth. Where exchanges took place, the pages are missing, and where her name was once written Ruth has scratched it out and Tipp-Exed over the scratchings, writing 'Quaker Lady' over the top. She was not a prospect for long, and the few remaining mentions of her are unilluminating. It is uncertain why the 'Quaker Lady' needed to be edited out, but it is possibly for her connection to the 'Bureau'.

In all this censorship, a generous interpretation of the couple's motives might be that they were willing to avoid telling a distracting truth in order to maintain a clearer view of what they considered a more general and important truth. If an issue was clouded by controversy so thickly that it was felt one could not perceive it with sufficient clarity, then the Clemos were willing to pretend that there was nothing to see anyway. Alternatively, perhaps it was thought that the real story took something away from the magic of Clemo's personal myth. Did the 'Browning pattern' allow room for dating agencies? At first glance, the agency seems to diminish the narrative's sense of 'chance'. In one way this is true, but in another it is beside the point. It is true in the sense that an attempt was always made to present the likelihood of Jack and Ruth meeting as implausible, and signing up to an agency significantly detracts from the conjured sense of the supernatural. On the other hand, it has already been mentioned that Clemo considered this election and destiny to marry as a vocation, not as a simple gift. It was not something that would just happen, but something that must be pursued.

Because of this formulation of destiny, a secular reader may well have trouble distinguishing Clemo's conception of destiny in this instance from the plainer observation that when one pursues something one is significantly more likely to achieve it. That Clemo found love and marriage after his relentless pursuit of them is seen by him as a 'proof' of God, and a 'proof' of his election for marriage. To the secular reader this is difficult to sympathise with, because the fact that one looks hard for something and as a consequence of considerable effort finds it – when that something is presumed to exist in the world – is an utterly mundane formula. Not only were they both looking for love and marriage, but they also employed help to find it. And, it must be said, Clemo was not fussy about whom he married. He did not rebuff any interested woman, but they always spurned him, whether 'pagan', irreligious, Methodist or Anglican.

To maintain the myth, Ruth undertook heavy editorial work after Jack died. The most extensive work has been done to their early correspondence and on the years 1967 and 1968. She has torn out diary entries she does not like, thrown away letters or cut them up, scratched out, blacked out or Tipp-exed over words and phrases she wanted to change, and she has annotated Clemo's words in a ludicrous way, messing up the punctuation, adding exclamation marks and arbitrarily underlining words. The 1967 diary is missing twelve whole weeks of entries, and the letters have been chopped about and sometimes re-dated. A part of this process seems to have been Ruth's desire to be close to Jack again after he had died, and to re-immerse herself in his life and in their life together. But it is also a crude attempt to obscure the real story.

Many of the remaining 1967 entries show Jack bemoaning poor reviews and re-evaluating the relationship with Mary. He began to blame supernatural forces: 'I know it wasn't just her own personality I had to fight: there was a sinister inhuman power trying to destroy us both!'[532] Among these entries, there remain some unedited hints at what is going on at the 'Bureau', such as 'Still waiting and wondering', and 'Got a new photo album for my birthday. How soon will my wife's photo be in it?', then 'Signed contract for *Cactus on Carmel*. I do pray my wife may be with me when it's published'.[533] He had always been optimistic of imminent success, but there is a definite sense in this diary that he is waiting for a new kind of response.

As she worked through the diaries, editing and spoiling them, Ruth added dramatic tension by entering into dialogue with the 'dark and fretted' diarist through this year of despondency. So, on 14 August 1967, Clemo writes: 'Reading an anthology of Victorian Verse. I note that a dozen of the poets died before they were 51. God must have some purpose in sparing me – may it be clear soon.' Against this, Ruth has written: 'God did have a purpose – he married Ruth and produced 4 poetry books and autobiographies'. Again, on the nineteenth of the same month, Jack writes of his 'awful loneliness […]. Yet there must be someone with a kindred stress'. Ruth responds: 'there was in the shape of Ruth who was a believer in God and loved poetry'. This continues throughout the year, a dialogue between the despairing bachelor Jack in 1967 and the widowed Ruth thirty years on. The drama is an interesting embellishment, creating a sense of the year as Jack's preparatory 'Dark Night' before the mystical consummation. It is possibly for this very effect that Ruth also steps out beyond her loving enthusiasm and makes deliberately misleading statements. The couple had entered into correspondence each aware that the other was looking for marriage from their relationship – they both stated this on the forms they submitted. Yet in the midst of correspondence with Ruth, Jack wrote in his diary, 'I have neither hopes nor fears at this stage. M. is still the only woman who has loved me, and as long as this is so I'm bound to shrink from the thought of marrying someone else. God will adjust my emotions if he wants me to marry Ruth!' This is a consistent and honest statement, but Ruth's commentary on it is not. She writes in the third person: 'Ruth was only writing about his work […]. It seems any contact with a woman caused J. to think of marriage!' This is dishonest, directly and deliberately. Ruth had entered into correspondence with the sole hope of becoming married. From the beginning, she was writing to Jack as a potential husband. Yet here she pretends she had not had any such thought, even gently mocking Jack in this marginalia.

It would be easy to think the worst of Ruth's motives for spoiling these documents, sabotaging future study, and for her dishonesty. She took considerable care not only to destroy offending sections, but also to rewrite the story against Jack's words in the diary and to give false information to Sally Magnusson about a pivotal moment of the narrative. But the motive appears to be mixed. It is, in part, the desire to seem less negatively odd and more positively odd. That is to say, Ruth perceived an impropriety in meeting through the 'Bureau'. It was, to her, an inferior way of finding a husband, or one that questioned the supernatural design of their coupling, so that she wished to hide it from her friends and the public. She wanted to appear a part of the cosmic plan, a wife chosen by God, the one elect lover of her mystic spouse. But there is also a sense in which the widow takes an intimate pleasure going back over these years and talking to her husband again, comforting him and promising him that things were going to turn out okay.

Ruth was born in 1923 into a Plymouth Brethren family in Plaistow, then a part of Essex. She was evacuated in the Second World War to Weymouth, along with her mother, sister Bella and schizophrenic brother Jacob (also known as Jack). She, like Clemo, had suffered. Her parents had lost two other children, and Ruth lost her father at the age of twelve. He had returned home from the First World War shell-shocked and had never recovered. Her brother was in care, where he would remain the rest of his life. Ruth also had a failed engagement with a Plymouth man named Ben Dawes, who was a musician in the Royal Marine Band. It was an affair that still affected her. She had met Ben when a friend had suggested he write to her in 1945, and they shared a long religious correspondence while he toured, before meeting in Easter 1946. Only a few months later, the couple were engaged. Much of their relationship was letter-based, and on 24 June 1947, Dawes wrote to break off the engagement, apparently having met another woman. It was eight years before Ruth recovered sufficiently to be interested in men again, when she enjoyed a brief flirtation with a minister in training. He is never mentioned in the published writings, and it is the marine who haunts the early letters to Clemo, with Ruth occasionally comparing Jack unfavourably to him in a deliberately provocative way:

> I do not know whether I *ought* to let the attachment between us develop any further. Supposing I could not 'cope' with the 'household' arrangements and looking after you, I always thought if ever I got married I would have liked the man to help me with the house, etc. That 'marine' I was going to marry was very handy, he would have helped me with everything.[534]

This was followed by: 'I like a man to be a man, I am very feminine. I like a man to take the lead in everything. You do not want me to feel sorry for you because you are blind and deaf do you?'[535]

When she first wrote to Clemo, she was working in South Dorset Laundries on the outskirts of Weymouth. That initial fateful letter, headed 12 September 1967, was simple, unremarkable, even a little stiff:

Dear Jack,
    I have been given your address so that I can contact you, you sound a very interesting person from what I have heard, I would like to know more about you, how you came to be like you are etc. What are your thoughts on God and the realities of life?
    I have not read your book: - 'The Invading Gospel' but would like to do so. I hear you write poetry now mostly, I should like very much to see some if I may.
    I suppose all your correspondence has to be read to you by somebody? Shall be pleased to hear from you soon.
  Yours sincerely
  In Christ
  Ruth (Peaty)

It did not overwhelm Clemo, but made a favourable enough impression:

> By an odd coincidence a Ruth Peaty writes to me on the anniversary of Browning's marriage. Last year this was the date on which M. wrote the stunning letter about her new romance. I like Ruth's letter and her name. And Dorset – fits into my past. May God overrule everything.

Several years after all hope of marrying Susie Powys had left him, he spoke of this special connection with Dorset: 'Mother heard broadcast tribute to Theodore – moved me, though the Dorset Pull is another enigma I shall never understand in this world.'[536]

Rather cruelly, in response, Clemo sent Ruth a photograph of himself with Mary, and the idea of the dynamic and unpredictable art teacher attracting Jack made her self-conscious. 'I am sure I must seem a real "sobersides" against Mary', she replied.

Conversation quickly turned to marriage. Ruth's editorship has made it impossible to date exactly when, though it was evidently discussed within the first few weeks of correspondence. When annotating the letters, Ruth numbered them, purportedly to give the correct order, date estimate and quantity to any future students browsing the archives. But it can be seen by comparing Clemo's remarks in his diaries and letters to other correspondents that this has been done with another motive. Clemo always noted when he received a letter, and often what the subject of the letter was, or what information Ruth gave him. In this way, it can be estimated that around half of the correspondence was destroyed by Ruth and the remainder mislabelled. In spite of this, enough remains to detect some of the details of their peculiar and hesitant courtship. For instance, it would not be a Clemo romance if the questions of dancing and jewellery did not emerge, and it was a subject they disagreed upon. In his letter, Jack argued that Adam and Eve did not have any need for mineral embellishments, to which Ruth replied that they did not exchange wedding rings either. If this was not convincing, she then quoted Billy Graham on the subject, who fell on her side. She concluded:

> [Jewellery] is artistic and beautiful and obtained by great effort and skill and a marvoulous illustration of 'eternal realities'. I am only sorry you cannot 'jump over' your childhood aversion.[537]

There is an impressive strength and steeliness about Ruth in these moments, and a knowing manipulativeness. Similarly, when Jack impatiently chastises her for being slow to respond to his letters, she writes:

> I am up at 6am every week day and out of the house for twelve hours doing my daily work. If you have never been out to work like that, you cannot possibly understand how restricted one is for time.

There were a few other small domestic details and disagreements, as when Ruth tells Jack she is no good at housework, and he notes in his diary: 'can't cook or wash clothes! Why is there always some snag?'[538] More troublesome was the idea that they would have to update the house. Ruth was not prepared to leave her comfortable modern townhouse to live in a cottage without water, toilet or television. 'I do wish ladies weren't so exacting', Jack said to himself.

As the tentative couple were hammering out the details of their future together with a mix of humour and frustration, *Cactus on Carmel* was published: 'Neither Mary nor Ruth know that I have a book out today.' 'Tears come as I put Cactus silently away among M.'s letters.'[539]

The soonest Ruth could plan a visit was June 1968. By then, the letters had become more settled and intimate. They were 'love letters', headed 'Dearest' and 'Darling'. For Jack, the correspondence was so frequent and demanding it became 'almost a full-time job'.

The date of their first meeting approached. Ruth and her sister Bella booked into a Porthpean guesthouse and on 23 June 1968 they took the bus to Nanpean. The sisters were excited, and not knowing the area they disembarked too early and had to walk farther through the industrial clay country. Eveline and Jack started out to meet them along the road, and half a mile up, at Fernleigh Terrace before the substation at Drinnick, Eveline spotted two women walking down towards them. There is a pleasant idealisation in Clemo's description of Ruth in *Marriage*. She was, he writes,

> a tall, slender young woman with a delicate oval face, long brown hair held loosely around her head by clips, and blue eyes which had a naturally vivacious sparkle but also showed pain and a momentary flash of rebellion when she lapsed into silent questioning.

On meeting, the party all shook hands and walked together back to the Clemo cottage, Ruth taking Jack's arm. It was an awkward beginning, made worse when Ruth was unable to communicate with him. She tried to write in his palm, but could not make herself understood. Nevertheless, they went to chapel together and spent what was left of the evening 'kissing' on the settee. To Jack, this was a familiar pattern and behaviour, but to Ruth it was all very weird. The following day was the same: 'She still can't converse with me and is worried about it – the lack of words and mental stimulus makes it so dead. She feels she may only find a nun's ecstasy. Yet she kissed me later.'[540]

On the third day, the stone was rolled away:

> A miracle day. […] [A] dark shadow fell as R. did not arrive by noon! I feared she'd never come again, but at 12.30 she walked in and kissed me. She'd missed the bus. [We] all prayed, and it was marvellous – how well she wrote on my hand! – God entered, I proposed and she said 'Yes,' sealing it with a long sweet quiet rapture on the settee.

The story is developed in *Marriage*:

> Next day we were still baulked in our attempts to converse, and Ruth went back to Porthpean depressed and doubtful. She prayed long and earnestly at the guest-house, and on the Tuesday she arrived at Goonamarris in a more confident mood and started writing on my palm quite legibly. In mid-afternoon, while we sat together on the settee and my mother prayed for us upstairs, I proposed and held out my hand for the verdict.

It was a dictate of the 'Browning pattern' that on their first meeting Clemo should propose, just as Browning had declared 'I love you' to Elizabeth Barrett in his opening correspondence. Jack gave her money to go out and buy an engagement ring and the following day she returned with it. They spent three days talking through plans and expectations, listening to records, looking through photos and taking some more of their own. The visit ended rapturously:

> A perfect close to our first happy miracle. We had a long spiritual talk after dinner, she copied poems on my hand, then had our sweetest and most ardent love-making. I really am in love with her now. […] R. has everything I want, and it's all in Christian light.

> She's so generous – she gave me a nylon shirt, bath salts and framed Epping picture.

Next to the phrase 'ardent love-making', Ruth added later: 'Keeping to the moral boundaries.'

Ruth named the wedding day, to be 26 October of the same year, and Jack and Eveline had only a few months to get the cottage in order. During this time the couple wrote dozens of letters, often three a week, with short intimate poems and trivial practical details, such as what Ruth would like Jack to wear in bed, or how long his hair was allowed to be (Ruth wanted Jack's hair shorter than Jack considered 'poetic'), and how normal married couples traverse such issues: 'Our immediate prospect is of hot water bottles. I don't know if married couples usually have one each.'[541] Sometimes a more serious problem was raised, such as the embarrassment Ruth said she would feel writing on Jack's palm: 'I could never make an exhibition of myself by writing on your palm in public'. In this sense, Ruth compared poorly with Mary, who was apparently 'not at all embarrassed', and Jack had to convince Ruth how much worse it would look if she just ignored him.

Work on the cottage was finished the month after the wedding, with alien devices newly installed – not only a television, but also a new bedroom suite (£57), bookcases (£11), an ironing board (£2), new clothes (£3), a refrigerator (£32) and a spin-drier (£8). Goonvean and Rostowrack, the clayworking company that owned the cottage, were commissioned to build a little extension for a fibreglass bathroom, and Jack kept accounts of every expense in his diary.

The wedding took place at Trethosa Chapel, with extended family and close friends attending. Jack memorized the vows, and his mother stood behind him in the chapel, prodding him when it was his turn to speak. He had wanted someone famous to be Best Man, and invited Charles Causley to fill the role, believing it unlikely he would accept. But Charles was honoured and delighted, which was a thrill for both Jack and Ruth. Lionel Miskin was to act as a stand-in for Albert White, who was giving Ruth away and was uncertain of making it. Causley wrote in advance: 'What would you like your gift from me to be? I've no idea, and would certainly appreciate your help. Shall it be an electric kettle or a 1st edn of Mrs Browning (I'd need good notice for this) or a pair of Hardy's socks or a coal scuttle? Or what?'[542]

On the day, Causley collected the Clemos in his car, gave them the electric kettle and drove them to the wedding. Melba Kessell was on the Brewer organ and they sang the hymns 'O God of Love, to Thee we bow' and 'O Father, all creating'. A photographer was arranged by the *Cornish Guardian* to capture the event, and after the service, twenty-nine guests went back to the Clemo cottage. 'All peace', Jack noted in his diary.

Clemo marked the event with a long poem, 'Wedding Eve', written on 27 September and gifted on the eve of their marriage:

> Chrysanthemums scent the empty chapel
> On this last night of my unpartnered bed:
> There, foam-like under the dark cliff
> Of the pulpit, they blend their stiff
> Thick tufts with an unseen swell,
> A tide absent when most men wed.

When writing his entry on Clemo for *Contemporary Poets of the English Language*, Charles Causley quoted this poem, but he had also drafted a poem of his own about the wedding, a poem he never satisfactorily completed. The first draft began by calling Clemo a 'granite Archbishop' and likening him to John Wesley. Some of this Cornish imagery was turned to Egyptian in Causley's second and fuller draft:

> I see you crouching like Aminhotep
> In your sarcophagi of granite stone
> Under the clay-white mountain.
>
> I hoped, that autumn in Trethosa Chapel,
> When, dressed to cure, I shakily shepherded you as your best man
> Before the altar, the brazen cross, in the metallic fragrance
> Of Chrysanthemums. And when, at a warning stab
> Of your mother's Methodist finger you recited your vows

As the poem they are, a profound silence fell
On the chapel, on the village, on Cornwall.
Even those cows, mooing with Cornish accents in the
    smearing mist and rain
In the chapel field made – for that moment –
No sound: and we emerged to where a clay dump
Spilt milky waste across the road and painted our
Shoes and the car-wheels the colour of sex as we addled
    towards
The wedding breakfast of sausage-rolls and Wincarnis.

Ah well, my old friend, I thought, you've made it at last
And good luck to you; though I must confess I wondered
If Wincarnis could be strong enough a brew
To repel the demons that for forty years pursued you
To the edge of a pouring grave that now, suddenly, put forth
    orange blossom.

You, honoured by having your book burned by a local
    preacher,
You, honoured by being dubbed village idiot as a child,
You, of whom it was said your poems were all written by
    your mother –
You having no brains nor gifts to do so.

The poem breaks down at this point, as Causley tests out a few lines about the minister who:

Gazed with a natural suspicion at his glass.
Old Mrs Clemo speaks reassuringly –
'You may drink it with impunity, minister,
'Tis only grapes.'

Causley wanted to finish the poem on a doubt about the future of Clemo's work, so we see several end couplets being played with. In the first draft the ending is:

> But as to what it's doing to your verse
> Ah well, my friend, is quite another matter

He tries again:

> My God, I thought, a prince could have done worse
> – and hoped the whole thing wouldn't stop your verse.

As he played with the couplet, he might have imagined how upset Clemo would be to read that his friend thought marriage would affect his poetry, and he changed the doubt from his own ('I thought') to that of the newspapers:

> How all the papers cried out at the news
> – And only wondered how it would affect your muse.

> And several papers, joyful at the news,
> Wondered just how it would affect your muse.

> And somewhat anxious at the joyful news...

In a hastier scrawl, Causley added, but did not integrate the line: 'Though, as it turned out, there was no cause to worry'.

Clemo had a last minute doubt of his own before the wedding, though it was of such a different and trivial nature that it is surprising it bothered him as much as it did: 'I wonder how marriage will affect my nights. If it spoils my sleep I shall wish I stayed single – I feel really ill if I don't have seven or eight hours sleep.'[543] Eveline Clemo also approached her son on the eve of his wedding, adding her own misgivings 'over R's lack of energy for housework'. It sounds another comically slight problem, but for years following their marriage Ruth felt she was bullied by Eveline over housework, and many years later, when Ruth bumped into the early love-interest, Eileen Funston, on a bus, she told Eileen how miserable she had been. 'You had a lucky escape,' Ruth said, with Jack seated beside her but unable to hear; 'His mother made life very difficult for us. [...] I could hardly bear it.' The amount of work demanded by Eveline and the amount of attention by Jack was strenuously difficult. 'I regretted the whole thing', she said.[544]

In *The Marriage of a Rebel*, Clemo suggests that it was not only the housework that was the problem, but some of the care work expected of her:

> The necessity of adapting herself to awkward and embarrassing practices, repeated every day, in public as well as private, was often a strain to her. […] If we had married to express a sociological ideal, requiring an environment congenial to both parties, the stark predicament at Goonamarris would have shattered our dreams and our relationship before we had spent the first winter together.

On top of these strains, Ruth did not like the landscape or the silence and isolation of the clay country, and she had no friends in Cornwall. In their first year of marriage, she went back to Weymouth twice, and it was agreed that she should be allowed to go every year. The letters from Jack to Ruth while she was away are all intensely loving and sweet, peppered with pet names and playful rhymes, yet 'I had to get away', Ruth told Eileen, and she would tell her own mother in Weymouth, 'It's all off I'm finishing with him.'[545]

Jack was aware of her unhappiness, mentioning some of the strain in his diary: 'Ruth has no zest for domesticity. I told her she mustn't be ladylike and she called me a dictator – reminded me of Mary – she softened though'.[546] In a margin to this, Ruth has written of herself in the third person again, stating that she 'felt she was taking on more than she could cope with at times – a blind and deaf husband'. Her misery developed as the months passed: 'R. was unhappy and dissatisfied last night, saying she'd sacrificed too much. It depressed me, but mother says God will overrule the future.'[547]

At their worst moments, Ruth told Jack that she did not want to remain with him. Eveline, Ruth believed, was declining in health, and whenever she was ill or away Ruth had to take over her duties. As well as being more work, Eveline not being around the house meant that Ruth had nobody to talk to normally. Clemo claims in his diary that he helped with the chores: 'R. and I had to do the washing, and the machine wouldn't work. A most unromantic morning, but we were very brave and heroic'. Ruth disagreed, adding in the margin: 'J. liked to think he was helping by carrying out the wet sheets, towels etc for R. to hang up.'[548] In a similar way, Clemo enjoyed trying to mow the grass and clear snowdrifts.

Neither of them were 'exactly fulfilled yet', Jack wrote in 1969, and his boredom with life becomes a frequent refrain in his diary. He says he feels 'dead', and notes how the time 'drags', stating that he is 'still stagnant' and 'still tested', in spite of marriage. He was feeling once again the dullness of satiation: 'We glide happily from day to day, with no sense of any goal except heaven. My earthly goal was marriage and now I've reached it so late in life there seems nothing left to achieve.'[549] He thought marriage would change everything, but he was still deaf and blind, still in the white silence, and he was bored. 'R. wishes we could feel more mystical about our love', wrote Jack. 'Yet she was elated tonight when I started wearing short summer pants which are anything but mystical.'[550]

Joking aside, this was not the relationship Clemo had foreseen. It was not the vibrant Browningesque honeymoon, but a dreary, domestic and conventional anti-climax. The comparison with Browning's relationship troubled him. How could this tedium be considered similar to the Browning marriage:

> There's been no drama, no flight to a foreign country, no epoch-making sensation. I share B.'s vision – 'Wedding Eve' might rank with 'By the Fireside' – but the fulfilment hasn't worldly dazzling splendour.[551]

Again, after attending a healing service at Par:

> People at Par told R. our marriage is a miracle. So it is, but not so clear-cut as the Brownings'. 'Why did I receive you and only you,' asked [Elizabeth Barrett]. I have to ask why so many miracles began and then twisted and broke – why marriage came so late so that I was still a bachelor at 50, at which age Browning was

already a widower. Yet it was a great act of faith for Ruth to come here, and God will reward it.[552]

Things might not be great now, the phoenix is saying, but they will be soon.

Moments of relief came when the Civil List Pension was raised, and when new poems announced themselves. By the end of 1969, Clemo had written the majority of his next collection, *The Echoing Tip*. At these times he was much cheerier: 'The BBC series I'm in started today with Donne and skunks. Good company.' Or, when Ruth was away: 'Missing R. but, like her, finding compensation in the old freedom – more sleep and less shaving'. He also believed for a short period that marriage was having a miraculous effect on his hair, turning it black again because Ruth was shampooing it every Friday. Bella and their mother Mabel visited occasionally, and Ruth enjoyed visits from Jack's literary friends, such as Derek and Connie Savage. (Clemo's celebrity was always a source of pride for Ruth.) It was in these early years that Ruth bought Jack his first beret, in February 1969. The beret and the dark glasses, which had been suggested by Mary, became the two most iconic features of Clemo's profile.

In their cards and letters to one another throughout the year, the couple remained intimate and Clemo began a ritual of marking events with a verse. For their first anniversary he composed the following:

> Today our hearts would celebrate
> The thrill that never comes but once –
> Life's deepest call and our response:
> The vows contrary to our fate
> Which lifted to the wedded state
> A wood nymph and her blighted prince
> Whose dreams had been so passionate.
>
> We look back now and mark the course:
> The frets and threats of wilding light
> That scoured the wintry anchorite

> Have been dispelled by gentler force.
> The fate that might have frozen worse
> Has turned to autumn colours bright
> As grace invades our universe.
>
> The days have passed in peaceful rank,
> We've walked on beacon, dump and beach;
> The treacherous bogs were out of reach.
> Our paths are safe and we would thank
> The Providence Who filled the blank
> And made our love rise, strong to teach,
> With pledge of spring buds on the bank.

In this way he would observe anniversaries, birthdays and Christmases. Later, the verses would become lighter, intimate pieces, reviewing the year and the couple's happiness together, and they would continue unfailingly throughout the marriage.

Pressures on the couple included their inability to have children and Clemo's frustration that it was still his earliest poetry that was receiving all the attention. His less isolated, more optimistic verse was being overlooked. In 1969, Clemo referred to *The Voice of Poetry*, an anthology edited by Hermann Peschmann, who had requested the use of 'Christ in the Clay-Pit' only to use the austerity of the poem to make a more general judgment about Clemo's harshness:

> His outlook is Calvinistic, and much of his poetry is harsh and denunciatory, but of considerable power. In some ways his work resembles that of R.S. Thomas, but he lacks the latter's deep, compassionate humanity.[553]

Clemo justifiably wonders why, if Peschmann wanted 'compassionate humanity', he had asked for the harshest and least compassionate example of his work. Of the comparison with R.S. Thomas, Clemo was not completely content either. He found Thomas 'too stiffly detached' and preferred Elizabeth Jennings.

He now hoped his next collection, still influenced by Eliot and Dylan Thomas, but with the ambitious message of genuine fulfilment through marriage, might convince his readership and critics that there was more to the poet than his old divinely ordained daisy-stomping.

XVI
The Echoing Tip and Broad Autumn

And when he was come into the house, the blind men came to him: and Jesus saith unto them, Believe ye that I am able to do this? They said unto him, Yea, Lord. Then touched he their eyes, saying, According to your faith be it unto you.

Matthew 9:28-9

Clemo completed three volumes of poetry in the 1970s: *The Echoing Tip*, *Broad Autumn* and *A Different Drummer*. Both *The Echoing Tip* and *Broad Autumn* were published by Methuen, or Eyre Methuen as they became, but the third collection was rejected. *A Different Drummer*, though finished in 1977, would not appear until 1986, when it was published by a small regional press, Tabb House. The two Methuen collections were released in the first half of the decade, *The Echoing Tip* in 1971 and *Broad Autumn* in 1975. *The Echoing Tip* was mostly written through the period of courtship with Ruth and in early marriage. The majority of the poems of *Broad Autumn* were written after 1971, as the couple had settled and grown to know one another. Instead of being a statement of faith, showing what marriage might look like in the future, these volumes are written from the perspective of one who believes the promises of God and the 'Browning pattern' to have been, to a large extent, fulfilled. 'I sit in the glow / Of June sun and my wife's smile', Clemo writes in 'Porthmeor cemetery', the opening poem of *The Echoing Tip*. In his brief preface, he informs the reader: 'Nearly all the poems in this collection were written after my marriage in 1968, and this may explain why the personal erotic element so familiar in my verse is less aggressive here, often replaced by objective portraiture.'

The cover of *The Echoing Tip* is an image of Clemo in front of a clay-dump. It was a black-and-white photograph, but the white has all been replaced with crepuscular blue, and the white flash of Clemo's collar becomes suggestive of priesthood. The themes of the collection are familiar – marriage, redemption and faith – but

Clemo and Lionel Miskin in Mevagissey, 1963

Ruth 'talking' to Jack, 1978

there is an imposing increase in poetic responses to the lives of other writers, artists and prominent figures. More than two-thirds of the thirty poems are biographical responses or monologues, which might indicate an absence of original imaginative material, as well as Clemo's broadening of interests. Jack was aware of this reactivity, and writes in his 1969 diary that this new body of work 'seems second-hand in material'.[554] The book was tentatively entitled 'Genevan Towers'.[555]

In terms of style, the influences of Eliot, Hopkins and Dylan Thomas remain prominent and are developed from *Cactus on Carmel*. A notable exception to this sophistication is 'The Brownings at Vallombrosa'. The story of this poem begins in 1946, when it was entitled 'Rebel Love', before being revised in 1960. The original poem read:

> Not in pagan quest or the old boarded rapture
>   Do we pierce this foamy glade:
> A bolder bliss than Greece could capture
>   Stirs us in the broken coppice shade.
>
> Heirs with Christ, her thrill is wilder
>   Than the dryads' swoon of revelry:
> My new sonship found and recovered her,
>   Waking the alien ecstasy.
>
> As we pause in adoration
>   The burning text prevails where trees were strong,
> And praise runs riot for sweet salvation,
>   Foreign to the woodland song.
>
> Let the earth deny and wallow:
>   We are risen in Him Whose feet may pass
> Even here, till our spirits follow
>   And our flesh blasphemes the grass.

When finalised in 1969, the last stanza was cut and the poem was developed, becoming twice as long again. There is another obvious difference between the early draft and the published poem, in that 'Rebel Love' is about 'we', the Clemo-like narrator and his lover, whereas 'The Brownings at Vallombrosa' is written about 'they', Robert and Elizabeth Barrett Browning, visiting the Tuscan monastery where Milton was believed to have stayed. This episode in the lives of the Brownings was known to Clemo through Elizabeth Barrett Browning's 'Casa Guidi Windows', in which Vallombrosa is described as a place of extraordinary beauty, where 'pinewoods ever climb and climb' up the 'breasts' of mountains. Barrett Browning imagines that the beauty of Vallombrosa suggested itself to Milton's vision of paradise:

> He sang of Adam's paradise and smiled,
>   Remembering Vallombrosa. Therefore is
> The place divine to English man and child,
>   And pilgrims leave their souls here in a kiss.

In Clemo's poem, he adds the disappointing conclusion to the Vallombrosa visit, which Elizabeth Barrett Browning omits. When the couple arrived at the monastery where they were expecting to stay, the Benedictine abbot would only allow Robert entry, as women were not permitted. In his own poem, Clemo allows himself a slight at the Church, showing that the married couple had a vision 'not that of the cowled'.

Redrafting the poem in this way, Clemo was placing the story of the Brownings over his own story of early Christian-erotic transcendence of the natural world. This was an important process for him, a symbolic gesture fusing the Clemo love story with that of the Brownings. Now he is married, the parallel between the couples is almost complete and the poem interweaves their narratives in a very personal way. It is never revealed to the reader that this had once been an idealised erotic poem about Clemo himself, so the fusion is private and intimate.

Another poem of progression is 'Torrey Canyon'. It is an attempt at engaging with current affairs, but also a corrective of the nature-baiting verse Clemo was still most famous for. HMS Torrey Canyon was an oil tanker shipwrecked off Land's End in 1967, devastating the wildlife and coastline. In his poem, Clemo writes of the death and destruction, but he puts it subtly into a personal context:

> Yet men have said, through bleared piety,
> That the wreck of our fuel-laden dreams
> Cleanses the soul's tides and beaches....
> Oh bright gulls smeared, sinking with grease-deadened screams,
> Unwinged in the crash-bred slough!
> Fuel-film rotting the seaweed, the smothered cockle;
> Rocks daubed, mere slime-heaps, though the rollers' sport
> Rinsed them while the tanker ploughed towards port.

Of course, this is not just a poem mourning the loss of wildlife. The oil slicks are also the natural disasters the poet has suffered. In his diary soon after the event of March 1967, Clemo wrote: 'Cornish beaches soaked with oil from a wrecked tanker this weekend. My life feels soiled and deadened like that. What is to clear the current?' It is a minor poem, but it shows a new way of thinking about the natural world as something innocent that has been spoiled by man, and Clemo identifying with a healthy landscape, instead of its despoliation.

There is a similar engagement with current affairs in 'William Blake Notes a Demonstration'. The original poem was written in 1962 and entitled 'Pagan Disarmers'. It was a response to the Aldermaston marches organised by the CND. Clemo's correspondent, Rosine, had been caught up in these by accident and hidden in a church to avoid the protesters. It is possibly her account of the marches that first interested him, although when he wrote 'Pagan Disarmers' it was also in the midst of the Cuban missile crisis, when the United States put up a military blockade to prevent the Soviet Union from placing strategic nuclear missiles in Cuba pointed at the US. It was a tense situation and nuclear war felt like a real threat, yet in 'Pagan Disarmers' the poem was aimed at the protesters. It opened:

> Those marchers ought to kneel, not glumly sit:
> The street they deaden is still unscarred.

> But a poisoned splintering world looks out
> Already through eyes that dread the bomb-burst.
> Radiations of pride, lust, doubt
> Were not banned in time, and the hard
> Revolving ego has been blighted first.
> Faith would proclaim a fact
> More shattering than the nuclear test:
> The angels guard the rocket sites.
> And megaton terror won't cremate the West
> Till the angels quit
> And the Judgment smites.

When the piece was reconsidered in 1969, it tripled in length and became a monologue of an elderly William Blake, who, walking home, stumbles into modern London and finds it very unlike his visions. 'Where's my Jerusalem?' he asks as he sees 'harlots abound / In street, school and pulpit' and the CND protesters marching 'where I once trod'. Blake is made to say that the protesters do not need to worry for the bomb, because angels are guarding the missile sites and 'would not quit while creators pray'. People should be praying, not protesting – their world is already 'poisoned, splintered'. Moreover, 'If men can't die praising God / They're not ripe for life, not fit / To protest against the means of exit'. Blake has been worked into an already established moral. His addition improves the narrative and dulls the didacticism of the original poem, but Blake is secondary to the message, a pleasant after-thought. Unlike 'The Brownings at Vallombrosa', there seems to be no biographical or persuasive value in Clemo's earlier sermonising verse being filtered through Blake. On the other hand, the poem certainly becomes more interesting, and we see Clemo approaching another poem and another important figure of the early Romantic movement in a similar way in 'Beethoven'.

The story of 'Beethoven' began in the 1940s clayscape with a poem entitled 'The Awakening'.[556] This was rejected for *The Clay Verge* and Clemo returned to it in April 1970. The original clay-based poem – nothing to do with Beethoven – has Clemo as the first person subject, rather than the composer. Below are the opening stanzas of both versions:

The Awakening

Fate meant that I should walk our earth
In derelict disguise,
Shuffling beneath these icy Cornish skies,
Aware of menace from some hidden sea,
The flicker and pulsation, magnetism
Of cold inhuman currents working schism
In the sharp thorn's shadow, sagging fast
In the flesh-dank shadow that slipped fast
Over the silent clay-world dearth,
The scabbed anomaly
On which the ironic stars look down
With baleful frown
To await the last
Convulsions of the smitten heart
When hopeless trust has failed,
Thorn pierced too deep and pull of the tide prevailed.

Beethoven

Fate tuned him for the abysmal soundings
Through Bonn's wine-dense disguise:
In penury at raping sunrise
The wizard was adrift, tossing to keys and strings
Those flickers and pulsations – magnetism
Of wild inhuman currents working schism
In the flesh-dank shadow that slipped fast
Over the tavern songs, the shafted laughter
Of glutted harpies playing their noble birth
On his moody shallows of vanity.

Clemo's dislike for Beethoven came from a biography he had read in 1969: 'I read about Beethoven – don't feel drawn to him. He had no Christian faith, and all those worldly love affairs repel me.'[557] As well as their shared deafness, the parallel of a damaging sexuality might be relevant. Clemo would have known of the hypothesis that

Beethoven's deafness had been caused by syphilis, and in this poem he goes on to damn the worldliness of Beethoven's 'rebellious strains' as the composer dies, 'His numb fist shaken at the lightning-fleer'. There is an ambiguity in the final stanza, suggestive of Beethoven's salvation as he dies:

> Wait till the *Kyrie* rises, then scan him again:
> See his face soften, clear of fate's pouring web,
> Laved with a glow of Luther's secret.
> This is faith's music, purged of the long fret,
> Moving to the *Gloria* which he can hear
> Forestall, outlive the marginal ambush –
> That final hush in which he lies
> On a ragged bed in Vienna,
> His numb fist shaken at the lightning-fleer.

While questioning his character, Clemo loved Beethoven's music, so the idea that God might have been speaking through him and that the composer had been rebellious but 'elect' could have appealed, and may account for the overlaying of Beethoven's narrative on top of Clemo's own.

Clemo appears to have dispensed with the idea of an overarching narrative in *The Echoing Tip*, as he developed the range of influences and subjects against which he could contrast his own ideology and experience. 'Harpoon' is an example of a poem that blends some seemingly incongruous components. It was originally drafted when Mary was on holiday in Skye in 1966 and wrote to cancel her August visit to Goonamarris. In its published version, the poem is more overtly concerned with the sixteenth century Scottish Calvinist John Knox, to whom it is dedicated, Clemo having received his information on Knox from Edwin Muir's biography, *John Knox: Portrait of a Calvinist* – a fairly unsympathetic account emphasizing Knox's egomania and cruelty. References to Melville's 'white whale' run through the poem, and it is perhaps the piece most stylistically influenced by Dylan Thomas. The hyphenated compounds and rich, rhythmic alliterated obscurity are exercised in the opening stanza:

> Knox, it was from your seal-sleek,
> Eagle-clawed coast that the harpoon winged,
> Stilling my fabulous white whale,
> Sperm-taut with its spout and plume
> Of hot texts, your texts, that scalded
> Cool modern currents and shook the minstrel winds
> Over untrafficked straits of my clay.

The obscurity in Clemo's poetry is increasing. If the reader was not aware of the letter from Mary, which is the 'harpoon' sent from Scotland, then the poem might be difficult to decode. The whale, presumably, is Clemo's faith or mystical belief damaged by the letter, while Knox himself is used in a fairly tokenistic way, as the lucky man enjoying a happy marriage in contrast to Clemo's failing affair with Mary:

> You the much-loved,
> Never-betrayed husband – how far removed,
> As man, from my white whale, speared near harbour,
> Harpooned from the pale sands of Skye.

Clemo did not like Knox, and said he was the 'wrong' sort of Calvinist. Nevertheless, he would reappear prominently in the poem 'Alive' and again in later collections.

For what ought to be a celebratory volume following marriage, *The Echoing Tip* is conspicuously critical. Clemo highlights his own approach to Christ (or a correct approach to Christ) by contrasting it with approaches he considers unsuccessful or lacking. It is difficult not to remember the Clemo of the newspaper controversies and autobiography, settling scores from a safe distance. This was more than the assertion and defence of his own position; there was an enjoyment in the process of elevating himself by diminishing others, achieving some sort of 'compensation in an imaginary revenge', or *ressentiment*, which Nietzsche had considered 'inevitable among the weak and the powerless'. Clemo's message remains one of personal redemption, but while asserting his own route he rather devalues the lives and beliefs of others, and this was not confined to his writing.

Around the same time, his unwillingness or inability to empathise is evidenced in an exchange with his old friend, Lionel Miskin.

Miskin had done much for Clemo, promoting him, compelling shops to stock his work, appealing to Goonvean and Rostowrack clay company when there was a problem with Jack's tenancy agreement, allowing his artwork to be used for free and driving Jack around Cornwall for healing services. Miskin had been exceptionally kind during the relationship with Mary, openly sharing the joys and loyally supportive when it finally broke down. It was Lionel who had first discovered the couple together, when he arrived unannounced at the cottage to find them 'playing blind man's buff', as Clemo put it. The friendship and admiration Lionel felt for Jack was the primary thing in their relationship, while their Christian affinities – Lionel was a Catholic – seemed secondary.

Relevant to the disagreement between Miskin and Clemo was the presence of the intriguing analytical psychologist and anthropologist John Layard. Layard was a fringe member of the Mevagissey circle that included Miskin, Savage and Colin Wilson. Layard had been in Berlin with Auden and Isherwood, and had been analysed by Jung. He was a man of considerable experience and adventurous spirit, who attracted and influenced poets and artists in the region, notably W.S. Graham and Peter Redgrove. Layard stayed with Miskin in Falmouth for periods through 1968 and 69, receiving clients there, and it was from Layard that Miskin learnt about Jungian symbolism, myth and dream interpretation. On his website, Miskin wrote: 'It was through [Layard's] influence I came to study over 5 years the art of schizophrenics, which in turn led to directing two Arts Council Films on Adolph Wollfli and Rolanda Polonsky.' These films are referenced in the correspondence below. It was after long exposure to Layard's analytical methods that Miskin wrote his rape-fantasy novel, *The Pantechnicon*, in 1969. Only a year later, just before the publication of *The Echoing Tip*, the Layard-Miskin alliance took a disastrous turn when Miskin found Layard in a compromising situation with his wife.[558] Lionel punched Layard and Layard sued Lionel. Miskin had learnt a lot about himself, but it had been at great personal cost. This is the context of Miskin's apostasy and personal turmoil, which was the chief point of contention between Jack and Lionel. Soon after *The Echoing Tip* was released, Miskin moved away from Catholicism and towards Buddhism, at the same time as the unfortunate (albeit temporary) split from his wife. Clemo met both Miskin's apostasy and marital breakdown with contempt and a correspondence of strongly worded letters ensued. Only a few of those written by Clemo have survived, with considerably more of Miskin's. Clemo's aggressive derision is clear from both. In the first instance, he dismissed Miskin's apostasy as childish and 'shallow', 'like the mystical individualism that bogged me in my teens.'[559] Sometimes Miskin's letters are headed with sketches and watercolours of landscapes or symbolic compound creatures, suggestive of the new psychodynamic influences, and Miskin remained generally jovial, enjoying the debate, if surprised by Clemo's invective.

Clemo took Miskin's loss of faith personally, and, as in his poetic attacks, he focused on the differences between the two men rather than the common ground. Miskin, on the other hand, was of a more liberal temperament and embraced their differences:

> I relished and gained from even your astonishing repudiation of Nature in your early work, although I passionately loved and lived in Nature. I detest dogmas as much as you love them. I detest the repressive and toxic pressures of moral systems accepted by rote, scriptural rote or otherwise, because I can see […] in the poor souls whose breakdowns bring them to either Pru or myself, that they form unendurable conflicts within them. […]
>
> When I was making my two films […] in the context of an asylum, I encountered patients and staff and again and again saw the degree to which faith and morality were supporting madness – the identification with Christ being a particularly common symptom – and the higher and more spiritual the ideal, the more total the alienation and dislocation.[560]

Clemo responded to the intimation that something should be

read into the frequent concurrence of psychological problems and religious identity:

> The fact that some schizophrenics have religious obsessions has no bearing on genuine conversion. [...] Van Gogh babbled about Christ, yet he lived with prostitutes and suffered the fate decreed by his pagan nature. [...] Christian morals would have saved Nietzsche, Van Gogh, John Clare and many other artists from a breakdown, but you don't even seem to wish that they had escaped disaster through conversion, as I did. I think you are too complacent about evil [...]. When you've felt the pressure of the enemy, as I've felt it on my eyes and ears for so long, you don't need any theologians to tell you what nature has fallen to.[561]

Clemo is claiming that the faithful thrive while the faithless wallow in anguish and insanity. This had already been stated in *The Invading Gospel* two decades prior to this exchange:

> I had noticed that while the instruments of creative nature (the poets and artists) were usually overwhelmed by catastrophe, the instruments of grace (the evangelists) were strangely immune from such horrors.

Clemo accused Miskin of complacency and generalisation, to which Miskin replied:

> But there are no aspects of thinking which show greater generalisation than your own dogmas. [...] You speak of Christian truth as an overcoat, a secure, warm covering I have discarded! [...] You attack Neitzsche very briskly and mock his madness. I would certainly not do that, myself. Nor did I mock that sculptor 27 years in a mental home and overwhelmed by imaginary guilts and shames. Neitzsche, as you know, contracted syphilis, the outcome of which was his madness.[562]

This was a barbed response; Miskin knew the cause of Clemo's disabilities. Clemo wrote: 'I don't "mock" these tragic figures. I simply imply that they built on sand instead of on the Christian rock'. He continued in a different vein, on beauty:

> The brief glimpses of finite beauty we get in this world are merely intended to whet our appetite for infinite and incorruptible beauties beyond nature. [...] I do think your present views are much shallower and narrower than your old Catholic vision.[563]

Clemo is emphasising the old theme of his work, relegating natural beauty to a shadow of true incorruptible beauty, which Miskin did not believe or welcome as a concept. Jack's conclusion that Miskin had become more superficial both entertained and infuriated the artist:

> What an interesting correspondence – certainly one of the most interesting I have ever had. [...] A pantheist is certainly not a person I despise. But it already intimates to me a division between gods and the rest. In monotheism it is between a god and the rest. For me, this division seems a very odd one, eccentric even. [...] When you suggest that I am indifferent to the 'Christian remedy' it is because I have yet to see it as a remedy, by rote, dogmatically. It seems in those senses astonishingly materialistic, full of judgements, appalingly uncharitable and insensately smug and self-satisfied. [...] You say my present views are shallower and narrower than my old Catholic vision. What did you know of my Catholic vision? Perhaps you had a fantasy about it. I don't remember projecting any very complex visions of a Catholic kind. I do know I upheld various views with extreme difficulty and in a cowardly way did not dare to challenge them over many, many years. How do you define shallow and narrow? You are quick to judge: too quick! Or do you take a man's uniform – his creed –

his dogma as the REAL thing; that which you can form judgements about. I don't accept such a notion. It is like mistaking a man's hat for his head.[564]

Clemo:

Yes, it's an interesting correspondence, though a sad contrast with the old ones in which we had so much common ground. [...] I would define a narrow and shallow outlook as a temporal, earth-bound outlook in which thoughts and feelings go round and round inside the little rut of nature, never breaking out to glimpse ultimate solutions.[565]

Miskin:

You are easily saddened. Perhaps because you formed a certain image of me and now it no longer fits. But all such images are untrue [...]. Moreover I begin to wonder from your comments if my regimental colours meant more to you than I did. At least I have no such feelings about you. You stand for grand, good, strong, positive, courageous things. Nor do I seek to comment on the religion which supports them, as I fear you continuously comment on those equally strong beliefs which I have. [...] I once wrote and congratulated you on an article Val Baker published, but which you later told me you no longer stood for; it represented writing ... and ideas of your youth. So change, development – into different feelings, beliefs – may be true of both of us.

Shallow is a word you use a lot. I take it that it means the opposite of depth. Or is it merely a critical term: mildly cantankerous?

Miskin then wrote about nature and how both their views had changed. He began: 'Our cerebral, polluting disregard for Nature is very much a consequence of "dualism"', and continued:

> You hint that I would wish in some way to repudiate my feelings about your work, while at the same time esteeming my 'tolerance' rather low. I have changed. I have changed my ideas. You have too. Even your poetry has changed a lot. I admire it; its strength is dynamic and its vision a real achievement which heartens all. I never accepted your Calvinism. Why should I? I never accepted your evaluation of Nature. It was my inspiration then, as now. I was in fact drawn to asceticism – as Simone Weil was – and I think we disagreed there. I found the Mariolatry of the Roman church impossible – my father was a Protestant! There we might have aggreed then: but now?[566]

The correspondence has been edited to some extent, probably by Ruth, but it evidently ceased in the New Year of 1973. In his last note, Clemo offhandedly dismissed Buddhism as 'boring because of its sleepy negation of dynamic life'. Miskin's response was the concluding one of interest:

> Your last letter seemed rather a cul-de-sac. Not sure what you intend by it. I am not really able to follow you in the particular lines you chose to establish. It seems to me your fundamentalism, which is your strength in one sense, is in another your weakness [...]. I am amazed at what you say about Buddhism. Whatever do you know about the subject that you can dismiss it in such a manner. [...] Easing a whole list of sins and guilts and moral duties from my back has not so far hurried me to the 'temple prostitutes' you mention or much altered my day-to-day attitudes to violence, or stealing, or other such actions. But certainly feeling no longer at odds with the 'dynamic life' you set against 'sleepy Buddhism', I am encouraged and strengthened and supported by my love for it – by its presence in me. This again you will find 'heart rendingly tragic.' But take care lest your pity be tainted with contempt.[567]

In this correspondence, Miskin has identified some central flaws in Clemo's character. Clemo had a lack of imagination outside of monotheistic Judaic statements about the world. His argument against Buddhism was not useful or convincing; it did not challenge or support a truth. It was a mere emotional preference – Buddhism bored him. The intention of this statement was to wound, rather than to persuade, and it suggests an intellectual limitation. Clemo was not philosophically disciplined and was argumentatively weak. The arguments in the letters to Miskin fall still-born, useless, incomplete, unpersuasive, unable to engage. When Clemo does engage with ideas, they are commonplace evangelical clichés, such as the notion that without faith one loses one's moral compass. And the assertion that Buddhism is 'sleepy' and 'boring' was a crude attack. Clemo's inability to engage intellectually with anyone outside of faith, and the way in which he lapsed into subjective abuse, supports the impression that if one did not agree with him then in his mind one simply did not understand the truth. Yet he does not offer any evidence that could convince another. This is Clemo's evangelical flaw. His 'proofs' of God do not prove anything to anyone outside the Christian faith. For those outside, his experiences appear to be an apophenic desire to make sense of a sequence of sufferings. It should not be forgotten that since the 1930s he had been expecting every year that he would get married, that he would be cured and physically healed, and that God would make a great evangelical success of his writing. The statistics were against him. It was about thirty years before he would marry, his disabilities would worsen, and because Clemo was unable to continue as a novelist, his work never had the evangelical reach he felt he was promised.

In this last letter, Miskin warns Clemo against becoming contemptuous. Clemo denied this, but he was aware of the negative impulse. In a letter to Causley during the composition of *The Echoing Tip*, he explained that he had been busy lately 'doing poems on ladies I don't like much – Simone Weil, Helen Keller and Sappho'.[568] It was a comment intended to be humorous, but it signals an unsympathisable extension of his broadening interests. Instead of being prickly about churches and nature, or about intimately personal influences like D.H. Lawrence, Hardy, or even Browning, Clemo was attacking beloved public figures without the provocation or urgency of intimacy. Figures like Beethoven, Mary Shelley, Helen Keller and Simone Weil. There was less obvious need for these sorts of attacks, and they can read like the author's crankiness rather than anything vital. Among his friends, it was the Simone Weil poem that was enjoyed least. Weil was a compassionate French intellectual heavyweight of the twentieth century who had become a Christian following mystical experiences. She took work as a labourer to understand the conditions and lives of the working classes, and she is said to have starved herself to death in sympathy with the suffering of wartime French workers. When Clemo read about her, he wrote in his diary: 'Feeling very lonely in my writing. O'Casey's anti-Christian materialism, Weil's anti-Christian mysticism – the devil seems to have it both ways!'[569] The following day he wrote the poem 'Simone Weil', adding: 'I still find S. Weil antipathetic – a tiresome blue stocking with no blue sky, a cold agnostic glacier with a bog of fake mysticism at its foot.' In the poem, he wrote:

> But among the reapers, day after day,
> There moves an intruder, a daemon spirit,
> A frail young woman, shabbily dressed,
> Sibylline and sinister,
> Tragic as a strutting Nazi,
> Though her steps waver and between her teeth
> A Greek prayer is forced out, groping and sour:
> 'Give us this day our daily bread.'
> She wrenches at a vine-bough, her mind gabbles on:
> 'Starvation is the true bread:
> Give us this day our
> Daily starvation till the soul itself is dead.'

It continues, repeating the 'gabble' and describing Weil as 'proud', 'agnostic', 'hungered for desolation'. It is a very difficult poem to feel any sympathy for. Ernest Martin certainly did not like it: 'I did not feel that a woman who had given her life to be at one with her people had much likeness to a Nazi, strutting or otherwise.'[570] Clemo's reply is revealing:

> I hardly expected you to agree with my Simone Weil poem, but I've no affinity with her in temperament or belief. I can't feel her to be a true mystic. She was essentially an agnostic, subjecting her spiritual experiences to relentless intellectual scrutiny and frankly admitting that they were probably illusion. A true mystic never does that. Blake was furious at the least suggestion that he might be self-deceived, and if you contrast his death with Simone Weil's you can see which of them was the real mystic. Blake died singing the praise of God, while Simone died in dumb defeat.[571]

The grounds for his public mockery of Weil were her self-consciousness and humility, and the fact that he has 'no affinity' with her. Distrust of her own experience precluded her from a genuine mystical event.

Empathetically intractable as a man, as a poet Clemo continued to mature, though this was not always noticed by reviewers, and the reception of *The Echoing Tip* was – as always for this divisive poet – mixed. Some appreciated a serious poet so staunchly advocating their faith, while some questioned the oddness of his beliefs and his attacks on others. Gilbert Thomas at the *Methodist Recorder*, for instance, wrote on 9 December 1971: 'Marriage has given Mr Clemo more than happiness; it has extended and deepened his vision. [His poetry] has become mellower and more lyrical', while the *Morning Star* wrote: 'Jack Clemo is at his best as a regional poet. [...] When he takes on larger themes, his writing becomes slovenly.'

Note the word 'mellow' in *The Methodist Recorder*'s review. It becomes a common label for Clemo's writing from this period onward, and it stems from the marketing of *The Echoing Tip*, the Methuen advert reading: 'The poems are endowed with a mellow lyricism and broader perspectives, reflecting his new mood and new perceptions.' When reviewers did not know what to write, they reverted to the advert. This is most plainly seen in *The Cork Examiner*, where the reviewer has lifted passages from both the advert and Clemo's preface to compose his 'review', using them as though the words were his own, acknowledging neither: 'the erotic element, so familiar in his verse, is less aggressive here, often replaced by objective portraiture […]. The poems, with their mellow lyricism and broader perspectives reflect his mood and perceptions'. More useful was Norman Nicholson's response in the *Church Times*: 'As example of the poet's craft Mr. Clemo's verses are still angular and sometimes awkward, but as autobiography, they are among the most impressive of the last decade.'[572]

In the *TLS* on 7 January 1972, an unnamed reviewer squeezed a cursory paragraph on *The Echoing Tip* between a long section on Kathleen Raine and another on a professional friend of Clemo's, James Kirkup:

> Mr Clemo's language merely mimes the muddled swarm of images which make up his private world. The result is an over-charged, over-heated poetry, a thrashing whirlpool of inflated, quirkily unpredictable metaphors which seem selected by no discernible pattern of imaginative logic.

The reviewer proffers a single stanza from 'Wedding Eve' to prove the point:

> To plant the cross in the nerves
> Intensifies the wedlock sun;
> Faith's ravaged fibre now revives
> Where the blood thrives,
> And I feel in your flushed curves,
> In your kiss, the world-renouncing nun.

To an extent, this is a reminder that former knowledge of Clemo can be essential for understanding his poetry. It is fairly clear that Clemo is writing on an old theme in the quoted poem – redemption through a marriage submitted to Christ. The 'world-renouncing nun' line might be a surprise, but Ruth, it has already been said, once feared that their love would always be more spiritual than physical – more duty than attraction. Ruth had considered becoming a nun or virginal ascetic of some sort before meeting Clemo, and in one of their early letters, we find an attractive appeal in response to the possibility of Ruth's asceticism:

> Your mother says Jesus may want you in heaven as a virgin, but your flesh-and-blood body will never be in heaven, and your soul can be as virginal for Him if you marry as if you stay single.[573]

The significance of the poetry was not lost on the poet Frances Bellerby. Bellerby was living at Goveton in Devon, and first wrote to Jack in 1971, after reading *The Echoing Tip*:

> Dear Jack Clemo,
> I have your most beautiful poems. At the moment, I am hardly able to speak, or to write, because of the strength with which they have battered me. So this is the moment in which I must send you that message.
> I would mention especially William Blake Notes a Demonstration; and Laika. And the poem to Dylan Thomas.
> There is much more that I could say, were I less deeply moved as I write. Were I not so burning with gratitude for these poems, and for having them here with me in my house.
> I have thought often of you lately, and of the letters in which you told me that your poems came to life through joy, through the peace of belief, not through sorrow and struggle.
> For what my opinion is worth – I think these poems the most powerful, the deepest and widest in vision, of any of yours that I have ever read. You've proved your point.
> You know how very highly I've thought of your work always. (I told you once what I found in *Wilding Graft*, which led me to the poems.) Now it's more than that. These poems batter me. Sometimes I've cried out as I read. Sometimes they've come from places where

my spirit has been, and has thought itself alone.
Bless you, Jack Clemo.
Frances Bellerby
(Don't feel any reply is needed.)[574]

Following the *TLS* review, she wrote again:

Dear Jack Clemo,
I don't expect you'll be too deeply perturbed by the T.L.S. specimen of words-by-the-yard, but knowing my own unconquerable vulnerability I just want to report my reactions. What struck me so forcibly about the whole article was the sheer impudence of anyone who writes so appallingly badly during the set up as a reviewer of poetry. (I can't guess who it is. It's too bad for any of those whom I might recognise.)

I myself, by the way, received the worst service I've ever had in my life, from the T.L.S. after the publication of my *The Stone Angel & The Stone Man*. Amongst other delicacies, the reviewer commented that there was no tolerable poem in the whole book, – I had, in fact, foisted 75 bad poems on the unfortunate public. This remark gave me ecstatic bliss, because the book contained fewer than 60 poems in all! I wrote, therefore, a brief and courteous letter to the editor, saying that although it was perfectly possible that every poem in my book was bad, it was *not* possible that I had published 75 bad poems, for the number contained in the book was only 56 (or whatever it was). This letter was duly printed!

(I guessed, and a more knowledgeable friend thought, that that reviewer was Christopher Logue.)

I may add that it was the only bad service I had, of that book.

It is rather nonsense about Kathleen Raine too [...] though this new book of hers I have not yet read. But I've read a lot of her poetry. (She told me in a letter her opinion of reviewers, not long ago!)

> Don't bother to answer this. It's just a spontaneous outburst!
>
> The best of good wishes to you – Frances Bellerby.[575]

For the first time, the production of one of Clemo's books was also in paperback: 'a small hard-bound edition for libraries and millionaires, paper-back copies for poor Beatniks and churchwardens'.[576] It was a sign of the change in markets, and so in publishing, and it worked. In five years *Cactus on Carmel* had sold around 500 copies, but almost instantly *The Echoing Tip* sold more, with 294 hardbacks and 361 paperbacks. It would go on to sell more than double. The order of the poems was finalised by Methuen and altered slightly from Clemo's original intentions so that the longer poems would each fit onto a single two-page spread. There was little narrative order to the collection, so it did not matter very much that 'Porthmeor Cemetery' was moved to the front of the book, in place of Clemo's projected 'I Go Gentle'.

It might have been expected that Clemo would dedicate this volume to Ruth, being the first book written and produced since their marriage, but instead it was dedicated to Causley. Causley, along with Savage, had proofed the manuscript, and was grateful for the dedication: 'no words of mine could thank you for this adequately enough'. Perhaps Clemo thought too many of the poems derived from the years before Ruth's arrival, including from the relationship with Mary. Ruth's influence is certainly still felt on the volume, most conspicuously in the subject matter:

> R talked about poetry last night. The jargon about iambic and sprung rhythm is new to her. I have to work alone with no technical help as I did before Mary came. But I often felt M. interfered too much, though some of her advice was sound. R. is more concerned about the message.[577]

It was after talking to Ruth about Dylan Thomas and death that Clemo wrote 'I Go Gentle', and it was Ruth's suggestion that he respond to Helen Keller. But she had no sensibility for poetry, she was more conservative than Clemo, and she was less literate. She did not like the clayscape work at all, did not like the 'coarseness' and references to sex in the novels, so that she resisted Clemo publishing his *The Shadowed Bed*, telling him that it was 'so crude and sexy that it would damage [his] Christian reputation',[578] and that 'it would repel everyone'.[579] Similarly, she disliked his short story, 'The Clay Dump', describing it as 'menacing' and 'hopeless'.[580] It made Clemo feel lonely to know that the writing he had been most ambitious about was so disliked by his wife. She could only approve the evangelical message, the merely Christian, so to speak. The significance of this is that the world was now filtered through Ruth and projected by her onto Clemo's palm. And when Eveline Clemo died, Ruth's version of the world would be the only one to which Clemo had access.

Life in the cottage became more bearable for Ruth in September 1970, when she made a friend, Gwen Pearce. They had met when Gwen was preaching at Trethosa Chapel one Sunday evening. Gwen owned The Good Book Shop in Newquay, a Christian outlet sympathetic to Clemo's work, and she had a car, so she could take Ruth out for day trips, to religious meets or blackberrying, leaving Jack at home with Eveline or one of the foster-girls. Gwen would become a part of the network of people the Clemos relied upon. When Clemo was reconsidering *The Shadowed Bed*, Gwen offered to type up the manuscript with his proposed corrections, which took the pressure off a swiftly ageing Eveline. And when the Clemos finally moved from the cottage, they would return annually to visit Gwen in Newquay for their 'perennial pasties', Gwen apparently making them almost as well as Eveline herself.

With Ruth for stability, Jack could enjoy trips to the beach again, paddling at Porth and Bedruthan Steps. He also had no more excuses for rejecting invitations from the Cornish Gorsedd to be considered for a bardship. In 1966 he had rejected the invitation because Mary would not attend with him, but in 1970 he noted in his diary: 'Now I'm married I may face the ceremony'.[581] He replied to the latest letter and waited anxiously for the Gorsedd's reply. He was torn between genuine excitement and the feeling that it was only a trivial, 'worldly' event. In his diaries he counted the days, while pretending not to care: 'The Gorsedd decide today about my bardship. It doesn't really matter.'[582]

An internationally acclaimed poet, born in Cornwall and using the Cornish landscape so originally and effectively, the Gorsedd naturally accepted him, but two days later Clemo was searching for excuses not to attend the ceremony: 'Bothered about bardship. I'd have to buy my own robe.' Then: 'Got draper's form about the bardic robe. We're pleased but it's only incidental and local.' Then he became worried about being associated publicly with the Gorsedd, and wrote to tell them that he was not a Cornish nationalist and to ask whether this precluded his admission. Jack had already raised this question with Causley a decade ago, Causley having been a bard since 1952. Causley replied: 'don't take the Cornish nationalism idea from anyone – don't think the gorsedd is bothered about it, either'.[583] The Gorsedd replied in confirmation of Causley's statement, saying that they were apolitical. They asked Jack to come up with some ideas for a bardic name, which they would then translate into Cornish and send back to him. Five were suggested: 'Poet of the Clay', 'Son of the Clay', 'Son of China Clay', 'Horn of Truth', and 'Trumpeter of the Faith'. The Gorsedd recommended the least religious: 'The Grand Bard has named me "Prydyth an Pry" (Poet of Clay). It sounds best in Cornish. And of course the bardship is for my service to Cornwall, not theology. I need that recognized elsewhere.'

The ceremony was held on 5 September 1970 at Perran Round. Ruth was allowed to lead her husband and to 'crown' him, and Clemo seemed more proud that Ruth got to do this than he was for the bardship itself, writing that it was a first in the Gorsedd's history:

> Ruth's action was, of course, allowed only because of my blindness, but I thought it beautifully symbolic, showing that we represented the mystical love I wrote about, and that I was not merely acknowledging myself to be a Cornishman.[584]

Here again, the importance of the public statement and the justification of Clemo's faith and beliefs is elevated.

Jack and Ruth had even greater personal ambitions. Both wanted to be parents, but Ruth was a little old and it is uncertain how plausible paternity was for Jack. They wistfully compiled a list of baby names, the favourites being Adrian John Clemo for a boy and Melanie Ruth Clemo for a girl. More practically, they applied to 'Müller Homes', the group of orphanage houses in Ashley Down, Bristol, founded by George Müller. They specifically wanted 'a teenage daughter' – perhaps to help around the cottage or because an older girl would be more independent and capable – though the orphanage reported that they had no openings and the plan was abandoned.

At home, a routine began to establish itself. The housework discord was slowly soothed, and warmer routines were established. Wednesday was the day that the bus to Truro passed and Ruth could go shopping, while on Saturdays Jack would take Ruth breakfast-in-bed. There were moments of novelty, too, such as the television documentary made by Tom Salmon, who interviewed Eveline and Ruth on camera. Carrie Oates (always 'Miss Oates' in Clemo's diaries) with her 'Odic force' visited with Miss Northey, both followers of the healer Brother Mandus. They practised the laying on of hands and prayed with the Clemos for healing while playing Mandus's audio cassettes. In 1971, Clemo explains their motivation for continuing this ineffectual treatment: 'R[uth] still feels she couldn't face life alone with me unless I was healed.'[585] Hope of healing was finally abandoned in 1978. Or, at least, this is when references in the diaries cease. Yet the ultimate failure of three decades of faith-healing and prayer appears to have had no impact on Jack's faith.

Meanwhile, Clemo was receiving attention from several students who wanted to work on him, most notably Victor Perry, Andrew Symons and Stephen Lane,[586] and he established a new Catholic contact through a warm correspondence with Sister Mary Agnes, the nun poet of Lynton's contemplative Poor Clare monastery in Devon. Her work is a remarkable contrast to Clemo's – peaceful and elegiac – and Clemo worried that his force and erotic poetry might upset her. 'I assure you', she told him, 'nothing offends me – either Catholic or Protestant. They are you, these poems, and I have a great admiration for you.'[587] Sister Mary Agnes was inspired to send Clemo a plaque of the Virgin Mary, which Jack used at bedtime together with the Lourdes water Miss Leaf had sent him as an aid to his prayers for healing.

Other visitors included the Australian poet Chris Wallace-Crabbe, a visiting fellow in Exeter at the time, who was taken to the cottage with Charles Causley in July 1973. Then, in 1975, George MacBeth visited with a girlfriend. In 1972, the Clemos received a surprise visit from the 'moral crusader' Mary Whitehouse. Whitehouse would go on to make one of Clemo's poet-friends, James Kirkup, notorious, when she took legal action against a newspaper for printing his poem 'The Love that Dares to Speak its Name'. This was a calculatedly provocative poem about a Roman centurion fellating and having sex with the corpse of Christ, and Whitehouse charged the paper with 'blasphemous libel'. The writer and barrister John Mortimer defended them, but lost the case. When Whitehouse visited Clemo in Goonamarris, she is said to have been 'very enthusiastic about my blend of Christian values and art', expressing her admiration for Clemo's work and suggesting that Malcolm Muggeridge would enjoy *The Invading Gospel*. After their meeting, Muggeridge was sent a copy, and Whitehouse was sent volumes of Clemo's poems, along with her coat, which she had left behind.

With new routines and new friends, married life became easier for Ruth, her only major cause of distress being the death of her mother on Bernadette's Day in 1973. In Clemo's next volume, *Broad Autumn*, he dedicated a poem to Mrs Peaty, entitled 'A Mother's Tragedy'.

Broad Autumn feels like a more generous collection than *The Echoing Tip*. It was completed in May 1974, accepted in July and published in May 1975. The same critical biographical tendency can be found, but to a lesser extent, and it would be possible to overlook most of these in favour of the striking new imagery and the return of Clemo's innovative play with old clay symbols. Before considering these stronger features, there is one biographical poem in *Broad Autumn* that deserves some attention, and which might have been expected earlier in Clemo's career. 'Helpston' is his evaluation of what went wrong with John Clare. The shared impoverished background and antithetical approaches to the natural world could have made Clare an even more attractive target than Wordsworth or Shelley, both 'Writers I've Never Liked and Still Find Uninteresting', as Jack wrote in the back of his 1943 diary. Yet Clemo, until now, had been silent on Clare. It was not that he was unaware of him; in the 1930s Jack had cut out a small biographical article on Clare from a newspaper and pasted it into one of his scrapbooks. It seems likely that the subject was suggested to Clemo by Causley's John Clare poem, also entitled 'Helpston', which appeared in *The New Statesman* in 1971. In less than a year from the appearance of Causley's verse, Clemo's own 'Helpston' was drafted, in May 1972. His conclusions on Clare are given in the final stanza:

> Merely instinctive, merely natural,
> Unchecked by limestone creed, the greed
> Grew: gay love pleaded too often
> And a rare beauty was hurt,
> Coarsened by tavern stench worse than the bog's.
> The white plough-horse trod too deep in the furrows
> Of his broken ideal, and his Helpston –
> Unlike mine, which choice of limestone saved –
> Dropped to the softening water
> Till High Beech madhouse hid the crater.

Clemo's critical poem undermines Causley's sympathetic response to Clare, just as Clemo would soon undermine the ballad form he associated with his old friend. Helpston is, in part, an illustration of Clemo's claim that madness could be prevented by adhering to a Christian faith. In a letter to Louis Hemmings, Jack offered a brief exposition:

> The white horse is a familiar sexual symbol, and Clare let his fantasy of an ideal 'dream-woman' become a sensual obsession that made his marriage to a humdrum village girl seem a cruel distortion. He tried to escape through vice, but found himself in a bog of insanity. The hard 'limestone' of Christian faith and morals would have saved him as it saved me.[588]

The idea that Clare's insanity was due to poor emotional and spiritual hygiene rather than mental health is not a kind one. It is essentially a folk belief, but Clemo was always able to respond to criticism with the evidence of himself, just as he had with Miskin. Elsewhere, Jack gave another, clearer, though contrasting, impression of his formal position on 'insanity' in a letter sent to Gwen Pearce:

> Insanity may be caused by chemical poisons in the brain or by psychological and emotional shock or strain. This is not demonic in origin, but when the mind is deranged it is easier for the dark 'principalities and powers' to enter.[589]

It is unclear what work the demons do in this explanation, and why they are proposed. They seem superfluous to the story of 'insanity' once the other causes are allowed. Likely, Clemo was being forced to reconsider insanity and mental health as Ruth visited her brother and reported on the progress of his mental illness.

Broad Autumn shows Clemo's mature responses to several figures central to his poetic Pantheon. John Donne, Wesley, Hopkins, Hardy and Powys stand out, with the addition of less obvious subjects, such as Herman Melville and feminist figures like Josephine Butler, Helen Roseveare and Mary Slessor. Butler is known for her social reform work. She campaigned against slavery and child prostitution and against the 1864 Contagious Diseases Act, as well as for educational and employment opportunities for women. Clemo's poem is a monologue focussing on her work with young prostitutes:

> While a million wives lie free, soothed with their husbands,
> Unhaunted by harlots' laughter, in a sweet swell
> Like that which cured my unstrung girlhood's
> Acid of questions, I am driven to docks and stews,
> To the soul's vicarious, bitterest black sands,
> Where the urge of rescue receives the bruise
> From the stony chattel, the cynical male stride,
> The trafficker's manipulation
> Of a State license to buy and sell.
> I lead my period's
> Christ-war on vice, on a vast betrayal – England's.

The impression is almost infernal, Butler descending into darkness to retrieve and save souls almost lost to pagan humanity. Clemo had always been more sympathetic to the prostitutes in his work than the men who visited them, and it is reminiscent of that desperate moment in his earliest diary when he fantasised about rescuing a girl from 'the ways of sin and prostitution', declaring how he would 'fall with her that we might rise together'. The women rescued by Butler are to be saved by Christ: 'Pure flame would gut cruel threads, / snap the last dark thrill'.

Similarly, Mary Slessor was a missionary in Nigeria, about whom Clemo wrote in the poem 'A Clash at Ikpe'. It 'isn't one of my best poems', Jack noted in his diary, but it repeats the theme of the Butler piece.[590] Slessor volunteered for another descent into Hell:

> Naked bodies catch drum-rhythm, writhe and sweat
> In the light of wagging torches, in the clawing fire-glow
> That glints on gin bottles drained at hut doors.
> Couples stamp to the offer and orgy
> With lips wrenched, gross and slobbering:
> Human hyena laughter, smothered
> In dung-dressed hair or hot greasy flesh,
> Cackles against the chaste hymn.

The native tribal people are associated with animals as Slessor attempts to save them from their 'Witchmen's dabbling, worship of phallus and skull, / Dread of poisonous *juju*, curse of the tree-god'. Salvation is achieved, and the moral is stated at the poem's end:

> Seed lapsed, adulterated, bad for the Word,
> Having lost the old ways of atonement,
> Needs the snapping dust, the explosion among the fruit.

Clemo loved biographies, especially evangelical biographies and stories of missionaries, and his information for these poems derives from such works, in this case from Brian O'Brien's *She Had a Magic*. The Slessor biography reminded Jack of another missionary, as he meditated: 'Most of what [Slessor] did could have been done by a plucky humanist. Prefer Helen Roseveare'.[591] Roseveare is the subject of a third Christian feminist poem, 'Wamba Convent 1964'. The poem is a reference to a horrific period of Roseveare's missionary life in Zaire, when she had been captured with other mission workers and imprisoned in a house in the jungle, where she was brutalised and raped. Her mission was founded by another Clemo influence, C.T. Studd, who had been one of Clemo's 'elect' influences since 1941, and Roseveare had a Cornish connection, with family from St Issey, near Padstow. From 'Wamba Convent 1964':

> Rebel soldiers! Oh Mary, here's Congo hell's
> Heat, denser than we dreamed, inside the cloisters.
> Brothel-glint, war custom, burst on our cells;
> The scars of black tusks deface the ivory
> When veil and habit are torn from us.
> *Turris eburnea,*
> *Ora pro nobis*

Sex, hell and women. The Latin at the end is from a Marian litany, the *Litaniae lauretanae*, and means 'Ivory tower, pray for us'. This litany begs the 'Mother', 'Virgin', 'Queen' and 'Tower' for mercy, and Clemo's choice of lines is an erotic reference. It derives from the *Song of Solomon*: 'Thy navel is like a round goblet, which wanteth not liquor: thy belly is like an heap of wheat set about with lilies. Thy two breasts are like two young roes that are twins. Thy neck is as a tower of ivory'. The line repeats through Clemo's poem at the end of each stanza, a device he found in Ezra Pound's 'Night Litany', with its repeated refrain, 'O Dieu, purifiez nos coeurs!' – 'Oh God, purify our hearts!' At the time, 'Night Litany' was the only one of Pound's poems Clemo liked: 'he writes in too many languages and has nothing much to say in any of them'.

'Wamba Convent 1964' focusses on Roseveare's rape and juxtaposes Mary's virginity against it. Both were interpreted as blessings, Roseveare believing that her violent abuse in the jungle brought her closer to the suffering and sacrifice of Christ. Clemo does not state his agreement with this, but represents Roseveare's questioning of God's purpose:

> We came coifed against Congo's drumming arts,
> Built our base, God's hidden forge in the forest.
> How far the armour, the mystic woman-parts,
> Cover us now is His secret, guessed
> Dimly through anguish of involved senses.
> *Turris eburnea,*
> *Ora pro nobis*

Mariology – particularly the apparitions of Mary – had become of greater interest to Clemo after reading Cardinal Léon-Joseph Suenens' *Mary the Mother of God* early in 1972. It was an extension of his interest in womanhood, mysticism and sexuality, and it might be useful to consider Mary among other representations of women in Clemo's work. Mary is the perfect and divine mother, a human woman chosen by God for the most special grace. She is the mother of God and the wife of God, and neither the role of mother or wife can be ignored in Clemo's life. For Clemo, the strongest and most admirable person he knew was his mother, and the relationship he most desired was with a similarly endowed wife.

Concerning the practicalities of the Marian apparitions, Clemo asked: 'why does the Virgin assert only non-Biblical Catholic dogma?'[592] And in a letter to his wife he mused idly on why Mary is seen so frequently. Why was she here? Why specifically Mary? He never questioned the literal truth of the visions, but he did wonder what they meant, and considered the possibility that Mary, as a privileged person, might have risen from death before everyone else for the end of days.

In contrast to *The Echoing Tip*'s three critical poems on Sappho, Helen Keller and Simone Weil, *Broad Autumn*'s trilogy on Christian women and activists reflected Clemo's own woman-wonder and worship. That they are Christians is central to Clemo's sympathy. In *The Marriage of a Rebel* he said *Broad Autumn* was largely 'about marriage and the natural alternatives of rape and prostitution.' This is an awkward phrase and open to misinterpretation. 'Natural' is being used in its fallen sense, rather than meaning something like 'necessary' or 'inevitable'. Nevertheless, if it was Clemo's intention to represent sex without Christ then to exclude all forms of sexual relations except for rape and prostitution is outrageously misleading. A poetic simplification perhaps, or otherwise a further sign of his dichotomizing simplicity. The fixation on morally rotten sex has surfaced in every collection and novel, and was a theme of his childhood, the squalid family history he is forced to come to terms with. We find brothels, disease and prostitutes, sex killers and rapists, and every form of sexual deviation, but no mention of the sexuality of normal people who are not Christians. He believed that there were good agnostics, such as Hardy and Day Lewis (though Day Lewis would be dropped from this list when Clemo learned of his extra-marital relationships), but they are treated as anomalies when they are treated at all.

The direct representation of depravity is increased in *Broad Autumn*. In *The Echoing Tip* there were Beethoven's 'harpies' and Blake's 'harlots', but in *Broad Autumn* are Clare's 'wild oats' and 'tavern stench', Josephine Butler's brothels, Donne's whores, then the 'worship of phallus' in 'A Clash at Ikpe'. However, instead of being condemnations of people, the *Broad Autumn* depravities are more frequently used to highlight redemptive potential, especially from the perspectives of the women. Even when they are 'worldly' victims, as in the Helen Roseveare poem, they redeem their experiences through faith. Clemo is representing the empowerment of women through Christian belief.

One poem in *Broad Autumn* gives an interesting insight into how Clemo developed his drafts. It started out as 'School of Clay' in 1969, when it was printed in a local exhibition brochure for *Kernow 70*. Five years later it was revised into 'The Harassed Preacher' and published in *Broad Autumn*. The two versions appear side by side overleaf:

School of Clay (May 1969)

Now summer has come to the clay lands,
The dunes gleam white in the sun,
And over the slag and the outcast crag
A tangle of green is spun.

Bushes have burst into blossom,
Flicked by the dancing sand;
There are milk white brooks in the valley nooks
And larks in a lunar land.

Our forefathers dug in the field here,
Built us a house of God,
So His truth might spread from the big clay bed
Deep in the spirit's sod.

A hundred summers have ripened
Around these village lanes
Since that hungry gang of children sang
Inside our window panes.

The seats were clumsy benches;
No piano struck the tunes;
The bare bleak room held a stuffy gloom
Even in those boiling Junes.

But grains from the Holy Scriptures
Were flicked by the winds of prayer;
In our sheltered nook these children took
New shape in Christian air.

Midsummer is the season
When the clay shines white on the hill;
Our tools advance, but we catch the glance
Of that shining Potter still.

The Harassed Preacher (1974)

Now that summer has brimmed on the uplands
    White mine-crusts seed in the sun,
And around each pit and its outcast grit
    A gabble of green is spun.
Soon silenced by bomb and gun.

Bushes have bragged into blossom,
    Flicked by the teasing sand;
Milk-wan streams vein the valley's dreams;
    Larks lilt where the tip-beams stand.
Faith's dream and song are banned.

Our forefathers dug in the field here,
    Built us a preaching place,
So that truth might spread from the ringing bed
    Ruled by the Galilee base.
Too distant now – no trace.

A hundred summers have panted
    Along our zigzag lanes
Since the first raw crowd of converts bowed
    Inside these window panes.
But the analyst explains. . . .

The seats were rough bare benches;
    No organ spun a tune;
The squeaky hymns and unwashed limbs
    Made a meagre mock of June.
The new age mocks the boon.

Grains from the towering scriptures
    Were flicked by the winds of prayer:
In our grit-ringed nook those drab lives took
    Fresh shape in Wesley's air.
Now shapeless atoms wear. . . .

(The Harassed Preacher continues...)

> We toil in a fevered season;
>   Soul-crusts lie hard on the hill.
> Do our tools ring true? Don't we signal through
>   To a ruling Potter still?
> *Our super-egos spill....*
>
> A plague on the heckling voices
>   That would check my sermon's flight!
> It's eleven o'clock and here's my flock –
>   Five villagers, old and bright,
> *Knowing their faith is right.*

The earlier poem is a straightforward ballad, a form Clemo associated with Causley. It is a simple, rousing, sing-song summery hymn. But when Clemo returned to it in 1974, the tone changed, becoming bleaker, and the heaps of alliteration and lengthening of vowels slowed the pace, giving the piece greater texture while making it more awkward to read out. The most obvious change Clemo made was the additional italicized line – the 'heckling voices' – at the end of each stanza. This is the voice of modernity, threatening the buoyant ballad of primitive faith. It seems a very simple idea, but it deepens the piece, dramatizes it and allows for the final stanza's triumph, where the form is reclaimed and the italics abandoned. Effectively, the innocent chapel setting of the original ballad is spoiled in 1974 by the creeping materialism of the 'new age', which is then, in the added stanza, silenced by the approach of the resolutely faithful few.

There remain in *Broad Autumn* a few assaults on predictable enemies. As well as John Clare, Nietzsche was an obvious choice; reputedly syphilitic, famously declaring 'God is dead', descending into madness and never marrying. More useful responses are those to Donne and Gerard Manley Hopkins, both men of faith and defining forces in Clemo's poetic development. 'A Night in Soho' makes a connection between the night Clemo spent in London, when he visited the blind healer Mowatt in 1951, and Donne's ministry as Dean of St Paul's:

> I had skirted bomb rubble, stumbling in
> From the street to that Catholic boarding-house:
> I felt the medieval terrors – sin,
> Judgment and the worms' distilled carouse.
> Only St Paul's, your intact stone
> Tongue, chimed a post-war grace.
> You hymned the whore's license and the rake's bone,
> Then blasted through to our time, to me in that place,
> The art of a coping penitence, renewing the race.

The church where Clemo met Mowatt was St Anne's, and Ann was also the name of the woman Donne married in secret. Ann Donne's death in 1617 marked the end of his love lyrics, and came just before his appointment at St Paul's. Clemo references her in the poem, stating that Ann was on his mind when he lay in bed that night. In his diary of 1971, Clemo added a summary of his feelings towards Donne: 'He was closer to me than modern poets, but he grew too much like Kierkegaard after Ann died.'[593] It was the positive fusion of love and faith that Clemo admired most.

This is the same point at which Clemo diverges from Hopkins. Hopkins was a great influence on Clemo at this time, greater now than Francis Thompson. There is a strong sense of sympathy in 'Wart and Pearl', written 'to Gerard Manley Hopkins', and Clemo forgives him almost everything. Hopkins' asceticism is not so heavily leaned upon, and his academic background – the 'cool Oxford halls' – is overlooked as a mere difference of approach. Clemo felt that Hopkins had suffered in a similar way: 'your Master […] wrung / Such tears from me too'. In his diary, the statement of sympathy goes further: 'Reading Hopkins. I have the same sense of failure, God's absence. I've only written one poem in six months, I've only one book of poems and one prose book in print, and both are flops.'[594] Hopkins had doubted the value of his own work and had destroyed it as a young man, but Clemo's sense of 'God's absence' here is more significant. This is the unpredictable loss of joy that occasionally struck Clemo. When Ruth annotated Jack's diaries, she sometimes referred to these moods as his 'depression', using emotional or medical language rather than his preferred demonic imputation.

'Wart and Pearl' is not a criticism of Hopkins, but an admiring poem showing similarities and differences, while introducing new ways of describing the clay landscape, the 'warts' of the title:

> White warts everywhere, a land's face never sleek,
> Never wholesome, but powerful, looked back at me
> As I strained for a ritual, oddly
> Like you in my youth: the art streak
> Feared fatal, an ego-bulge that blocked
> Soul's vows from true bend in the cell
> Which should honour Christ's Bride, no pagan Muse.
> The grey Body was felt, the midnight knell
> Knocked hard on our self-rhythms: we had to choose.

Clemo describes his own warty world, in contrast to that of Hopkins:

> I never heard a lecture, except the steam-babble
> From engine-house pipes when the squat walls
> Vibrated, iron rods and wheels flung
> Rasp and boom, explaining haulage,
> Pit-peelings dragged out where blasts still vex
> The warts' base, the sick slimed rock.
>
> A world you hated – machines, hot boilers,
> Smoke-snarl on the brick lip of stacks –
> Imaged an awe like that which your cassock
> Witnessed to. I found your torn language
> Haunt and echo through my desolate hollows,
> Between wart-face and grey-lapped beach.

The first stanza summarises the whole poem, but Clemo's personal response or progression following the 'tears' and doubts is added in the closing lines. After the weeping and suffering in Clemo's world,

> [...] there followed a ray,
> Beyond grey-lapped beach and wart-blight,
> Flashing where breast and blown hair mounted

Incredibly on the crest of my vow:
Touched, harboured, balancing now –
Christ-sanctioned Aphrodite.

This is the fusion Jack had pursued since the 1930s, sex and God, *eros* and *agape*.

There appears to be a subtle interaction with Hopkins' 'The Wreck of the Deutschland' in this poem – and indeed in the whole of *Broad Autumn*. The grey seas, wombs, flashes, the maritime metaphors, even the 'breast and blown hair' are suggestive of passages and phrases in Hopkins' poem. Such subtle reflections add to the symbolic and linguistic depth of these pieces, but they did not ease the concerns of reviewers who already considered Clemo too obscure. It was a charge that bothered Jack to some degree, and one he also encountered at home: 'R. and mother worried about my obscure images […]. Gwen can't grasp my poems till I "explain" them. It makes me feel so useless.'[595] In fairness to them, Clemo was blending specific events from some fairly niche biographies with personal events, Biblical allusions, diverse poetic references and the old clay symbols, while constructing a statement of his own uncommon beliefs and experiences. The ideal reader would be a rare person. Fred Pratt Green, writing in *Outposts* flagged up the obscurity, but still considered *Broad Autumn* 'beyond question Clemo's best book to date'. More common, however, was the sort of review Jack's long-time contact John Rowland offered in his paper *Unitarian*, which did not tackle the poems at all, but rather stated how remarkable Clemo is, being a Christian writer as well as disabled. It was only fellow poets who directly and openly praised the work, as George MacBeth did in a letter to Clemo:

> I particularly admire the way you've been able to relate foreign environments and other writers to your own vision and experience: this gives the book an underlying unity behind a surface of greater variety than ever before.[596]

Other than the supportive and insightful reports of fellow poets, such as MacBeth and Norman Nicholson, reviewers did not seem to know what to say about Clemo's work, and when this was combined with the publisher's disorganization and unwillingness to send out review copies, it is clear why the book did not sell half as well as *The Echoing Tip* before going out of print in 1977.

By this time, Clemo believed that all his work was out of print (although *The Echoing Tip* limped on unnoticed). As well as *Broad Autumn* being remaindered, new editions of *The Invading Gospel* and *Confession of a Rebel* had been withdrawn, while *The Shadowed Bed* was still being rejected. It was a cause to re-evaluate life, particularly the missing miracle of healing. The greatest blow to Clemo's faith in healers was probably his visit to the celebrated Trevor Dearing's sensationally reported services. In a 1976 Newquay service so many people were collapsing in trances that Ruth took Jack's breakables off in preparation for a salubrious tumble, but Clemo's disabilities were irreversible.

For sound, Jack had relied on his hearing aid and record player, which he could turn up loud enough to recognise some noises, but when he received a cassette player in the 1970s, he could have a healing service recorded and play it back to himself at volume. He could also record his wife's voice, and those of friends and relatives. And when he was eventually given a portable recorder, he could go out and record the sounds of the clayworks and the outside world again and play them back to himself. He would stand in the doorway recording the sound of a gale, or take it to the seaside and record the waves, or to Tregargus to capture the waterfall, and then return to the cottage and play it all back.

More worrying than the lack of change in Clemo's condition was the deterioration of his mother. Eveline was having trouble with her angina and had developed cataracts, requiring an operation. Then, Ruth hurt her knee and had her teeth removed in favour of false ones. She was in so much pain that the frail eighty-year-old Eveline had to look after both Ruth and Jack for a time. Amazingly, Jack was in better health than either of them.

Broad Autumn ends with a monologue from Ruth's perspective, in which she tells her own story of error and final fortune. As an ending it has some biographical significance. The book was dedicated to Ruth, and she always referred to it as hers. But this poem marks the end of Clemo's most successful poetic period, and *Broad Autumn* was the last collection Eveline would see published before she died. It was, then, a hopeful and aptly celebratory conclusion, with Ruth establishing herself in Clemo's life and poetry as though in her own words. The poem does not have any striking imagery, or develop any established themes, but it gives Ruth a voice in the Clemo narrative, with her own speech mirroring the message Clemo had been promulgating for years. It concludes with Ruth addressing Jack directly:

> Five years with your positive bright leaves!
> I, too, hear the rumour
> Scraped on the autumn vein: we meet
> Pain in a new context. Our earth grieves
> Within the golden humour
> Rayed from soul's heaven's unshifting heat.

Eveline Clemo, c.1975

XVII
The Marriage of a Rebel and The Bouncing Hills

And the third day there was a marriage in Cana of Galilee; and the mother of Jesus was there: And both Jesus was called, and his disciples, to the marriage. And when they wanted wine, the mother of Jesus saith unto him, They have no wine.

John 2:1-3

Bustling activity closed the decade. A new collection of poems was completed in 1977, a prose work written blisteringly quickly in 1978, and a BBC film proposed in 1977. Several further proposals for works were made, as well as many friendships, and in the early 1980s a collection of dialect tales and verse for children was compiled.

It all began with the surprise announcement that Eveline Clemo had written a book, a pamphlet of autobiography entitled *I Proved Thee at the Waters*. It was a terrific achievement for her, and aside from religious talks and sermons, it is her only surviving literary output – contrary to the village rumour that she had written all of Clemo's works. Eveline kept her writing a secret until the pamphlet was finished in 1974, and Jack was overjoyed as she read it out in the palm of his hand. She was eighty years old and would be eighty-two by the time it was published in 1976.

I Proved Thee at the Waters tells the story of her son from her own perspective, in very few words and with prominent religiosity. To help the volume sell, Jack donated some previously uncollected poems and sought advice from Causley about publishers. Not an easy book to market, most publishers would not touch it, but in the end it was agreed that with significant contributions Moorley's Bible & Bookshop would take it on. Several friends chipped in, notably Gwen and her husband, as well as the healer Carrie Oates. A small print run of 250 was made, and the booklets were sold at every poetry reading and celebratory event the Clemos attended. Miss Oates took fifty copies, as did their friend Shirley and the local butcher, who sold them at the shop. A second print of fifty copies was commissioned from 'Malthouse Duplicating' by Jack in 1983, costing him £49. It is now a rarity almost indistinguishable from the original.

The poems of *I Proved Thee* date as far back as the early 1930s and span Clemo's whole career. The earliest had been printed in the *Northern Weekly Gazette* on 4 February 1933, entitled 'A Homely Wife'. In 1975, for Eveline's booklet, the title was changed to 'A Homely Mother'. This version begins:

> Her lot lay in humdrum duties;
>   She sought no pleasures with the strung throng,
> But found a balm inside the cramped routine:
>   From its ache and grind came her bright song.
>
> Daily she labored for the household,
>   That their outreaching lives should be equipped,
> And never, amid the weary grapple,
>   Complained that her life seemed blanched and stripped.

It is remarkable that mother and wife are so easily interchangeable. When Clemo first wrote the poem, he used the word 'homely' frequently in his diaries. It was a desirable quality applicable to girls, indicating someone content with simplicity who is unambitious, affectionate and belonging, and who would dedicate her life to the household. Considering the difficulty Ruth had meeting Eveline's standards of housekeeping, the change of title might have been diplomatic. It makes a considerable difference, turning a piece that might have seemed cringingly old-fashioned into something nostalgically pleasant. When it was about a 'Wife' it was about Jack's desire for a domesticated woman, a traditional housewife, but when it was about a 'Mother', it became a tribute. The poem ends with a questioning reproach of the devaluation of such homely wife-mothers:

> Is there now no trumpet or crown for her values?
>   Will no-one pay tribute, raise hat, say
> Real goodness teems where such souls endure,
>   Content with life's simpler, purer way?

Some other verses collected in *I Proved Thee* have similarly long histories. 'Winter Scene in Cornwall' was a poem first published on 28 March 1935 in the *Cornish Guardian*, for which Clemo received praise from Frank Baron, who compared the young Clemo to Keats. Later, when Clemo was preparing *The Clay Verge* manuscript for Cecil Day Lewis and Chatto & Windus, this piece was reworked and retitled 'Clay Scene in Winter', and it was rejected. It was published a second time in 1949 as 'Frost Above Meledor' in J.C. Trewin's *The West Country Magazine*. For Eveline's collection it is again 'Winter Scene in Cornwall', but its history does not stop here. Working on the posthumous 2003 collection of 'poems newly found', Alan Kent, John Hurst and Andrew Symons were unable to decipher Clemo's handwritten edits, as a result of which they reverted to the typed 1935 version. The new title, 'Clay Scene in Winter', was written in capital letters and more legible than the other changes to the text, so the poem they published was a hybrid of drafts. The editors were probably unaware of the poem's inclusion in *I Proved Thee* due to the title discrepancy. In its completed version, 'Winter Scene in Cornwall' is a straight landscape piece:

> On windy slopes this evening gorse fires rise
>   In knots of licking flame through smoke that pours,
> Clipped into thread-like tatters as it flies
>   Along the stack-pierced skyline of the moors.
>
> The clay-streams tugging swiftly from the tanks
>   Strain under shivering bushes; hardened frost
> Pales wood and iron in quarries, whose mud banks
>   Keep hobnail prints where last week workmen crossed.
>
> The white sand-cones tower rigidly above
>   Each pit; smudged sunset hues glint icily
> On ruts and rails where laughing children rove,
>   Watching a bird or rabbit scurry by.

This is the sort of poem Clemo would call 'light' or 'incidental', by which he meant there was no religious message. That is not to say that he did not like the poem; after all, he submitted it for publication four times.

For the reader, such poems are insights into the language of the clay country. It is a landscape almost unique to Clemo, in literary terms, and the placedness of his writing has proved one of its most lasting and appealing features. Another strong example of such a descriptive clayscape poem is the contemporaneous uncollected work, 'The Clay-Dry':

> The wooden awnings swing
> Between the kiln-pan and the tanks
> Where slurry settles into banks
> Like ghostly stooks in rotting ranks
> Till shovels delve and trolleys bring
> Full mood of harvesting.

With only 250 copies available and a price of 30p, *I Proved Thee at the Waters* was not produced for fame or fortune. The purpose and the tone of the booklet are suggested in the full title: *I Proved Thee at the Waters: The Testimony of a Blind Writer's Mother*. Eveline is pushing her son to the foreground. The work is as much a 'testimony' to Eveline's commitment to him as it is to their commitment to God. Her faith is unshakably strong and primitive, her character fortitudinous, and the impression is of someone kind but toughened by battle. She passes easily over her eighty years of hardship in little more than twenty pages.

Eveline's health was in decline while she was writing. She was frailer and more frequently bedridden. In February 1977 she fell and had to go to the hospital for stitches. Meanwhile, Clemo was coming to the end of his latest collection. On 29 May 1977, he added the final piece, 'Blind Girl at a Service', and gave the manuscript to his mother to read through. This uncollected poem was the last thing Eveline Clemo would read.

> So the footsteps I've just heard
> Were those of nuns, two nuns walking
> Down the aisle of this Wesleyan chapel,

Their robes flicking stiff boots;
And the heavier tread, quick and firm on the matting,
Was that of the sister who carried a big cross.
I can fancy her soft warm hands
Tight on the barren wood or metal.

I wonder what they meant, bringing that here
To a blind person's service? Are we supposed
To feel solemn about a bit of mist,
Or sparks or funny black bubbles
Caused by measles or a car skid
Or something in the family? She understands
Better than that, I hope: her own clear
Eyes show the only crucifixion
That's being borne in this assembly.

Before a cross can gall
The eyes must see the charms that are renounced,
And the magnet of suffering, at faith's roots,
Must impress the vivid sense, call through, compete
Till the coloured feasts pall and the vow is spoken.

These nuns must have seen a convent gate,
A coif-sealed face looking placid,
Or pictures, statues of saints and the Virgin.
Their fingers, unguided by sight,
Would have missed the crucifix;
Blocked sense would have denied them their vocation.

As for us sightless – we're free
To riot (if we're that sort) in the carnal dream,
Fan passion's flicker, with no iron rules
To baulk us when a lover's hand is found.
I shall soon glow in the good normal bride-flush,
Lie curled and kissed, outside the nuns' secret,
The sacrificial meaning: just aware that life is kind,
My eyes closed, forgetting I'm blind.

On 4 June, Jack went in to wake his mother as usual, but 'this time her hand did not reach out to welcome me'. Eveline was still warm, but dead.

'Sustained in sudden darkness I found Mum has passed and was with the Lord. R. was given strength. God provide for us.'[597] The evening before, Eveline and Jack had gone out for a short walk on the Slip, but in the night she seems to have had a heart attack and she was found with her pills in her hand. By previous appointment, E.W. Martin turned up a few hours later, in the middle of this chaos. Jack was in 'spasms of grief', Frances had arrived and was arranging affairs, while Ruth was being hysterical and Eveline's body remained upstairs. It was an awful scene.

Over the week, some of Jack's feelings slowly emerged onto the diary pages. 'We feel stunned', he wrote; 'Can't believe Mum has gone'. 'We just want her back to tell her we love her.' But Eveline had kept her promise. She had not died until Jack was provided for.

Life was about to change. Ruth was in charge of Jack and the household, and the cottage was even more intolerably lonely for her, with no one else to talk to, no one to hear her voice. On the other hand, Eveline's death meant Ruth could press Jack to be more sociable, to consider moving, and to visit Weymouth. They went that very Autumn, Ruth's friends Maurice and Jean Gabb collecting them from the cottage, and they spent three weeks at the Peaty family home at 24 Southlands Road, in the Rodwell area, where the Peatys had lived since the war. Ruth and her sister Bella took Jack to tourist attractions – Chesil Beach, Portland, the Castle Gardens – then to Dorchester and Hardy's monument, to Weymouth Baptist church and to the prison, where Bella sometimes sang in the chapel and the Clemos sat among the convicts. The prison episode was of special significance to Clemo and was used to end *The Marriage of a Rebel*:

> I belonged to both worlds – the refinements of religion and culture, and the raw humanity for which redemption must be a crude flame. I knew what a depth of understanding and kinship I would feel if I could look into the faces of these men, all of whom had battled

with the dark sensual fires. When the guests were conducted out into the calm October night, I realized that I had reached a new level of liberty and resurgence.

Ruth recorded the episode, too, highlighting the sermon, which she described as a 'pungent message from [...] one convict, serving a life sentence'. As well as ending *Marriage*, the prison service appeared in the poem 'Chesil Beach':

> We were privileged guests with the singers,
> The guitar-throb in the prison chapel
> Where the convicts are rounded. Freak and chaos
> Were the criminals' heritage and mine,
> Since we were not of docile grain;
> Only, for some reason, I am free
> To come back here, taste human love's vivacity
> And innocently scramble
> From primeval pebbles to the brisk normal road.

Aside from the usual evangelical message and the acknowledgment that Clemo is in a better position than the criminals, there is also a questioning component to this piece; that throwaway phrase, 'for some reason'. Clemo seems to be emphasizing the element of chance or uncertainty in his fortune, and it will not be the last time.

Ruth enjoyed showing her husband the sights, no doubt hoping he might be seduced by town living and the seaside. Jack found the trip 'miraculous', but more important to him was the assurance that Ruth had not left him. He had been afraid that once his mother died, Ruth would find life too hard and would abandon him: 'Thankful to know absolutely that R. loves me and our marriage is secure.'[598] He had been living with that private fear for almost ten years.

Settling in at Weymouth for those weeks was easier than expected, and being surrounded by Ruth's friends, family, church contacts and children, Jack started to rethink his life. On their return, he began talking again about the long-considered second autobiography and he started writing it tentatively – against Ruth's will – in the winter of 1977. Serious work began in January 1978, and a clean draft was completed by May. The book is a contrast to *Confession* – more honest, less aggressive, less extraordinary, less frustrating and more kind. The potent tension and vitality has weakened, so it is a nicer but less exciting read. Several titles were considered in the early months of writing, including 'Burn off my Rust' and 'East of the Farm', and then 'Clay Phoenix'. 'Clay Phoenix' was the title Clemo settled upon until the publishers suggested the book would sell better if it referred back to *Confession of a Rebel*. They suggested *The Marriage of a Rebel*, and also asked that the subtitle be altered. It was submitted as 'The Record of a Mystical-Erotic Search' (in the first handwritten draft the full title is 'Clay Phoenix: The Record of a Strange Erotic Search), and reduced to *A Mystical-Erotic Quest* by the publisher.

This publisher, Victor Gollancz, was chosen in an unconventional way. Clemo had been submitting the manuscript for some time without any luck, the work being considered weak in comparison with *Confession of a Rebel*, or its market too limited. Then, one morning, Jack woke and wrote in his diary: 'I've had a strange dream in which I saw the words "Victor Gollancz" in big letters. Does this mean something?'[599] The manuscript was submitted to Gollancz as the dream dictated, on the anniversary of Browning's death, and it was quickly accepted, Livia Gollancz acknowledging that the market was small, but that she liked the book. Proofs were sent to Savage for correction, and he quickly gave his verdict:

> My first impression is that the book is as well-written as one expects from such a master of words as yourself. The narrative grips, and one wants to read on, as with the earlier work. I would not be at all surprised if this book were a popular success.[600]

Causley also appreciated it:

> the central theme is expressed and communicated very brilliantly and with a marvellous clarity […]. In intellectual matters I flounder about like a squid lost in a jelly factory.[601]

All Jack's old friends commented on the updated autobiography, although not always with unreserved praise. E.W. Martin's response was, once again, more direct than Clemo would have liked:

> I felt an editorial interference had touched the book in places, but my sense possibly of the decline of the rebel – into a 'Bard' of a 'nationalist' circus and at least a partial supporter of a harsh religious 'establishment' – did affect my judgment. The 'Confession' was a rougher diamond but it wore an original sheen.[602]

This was not quite fair, and it smacks of residual bitterness from their earlier exchanges. Yet it is true there might have been some 'editorial interference'. In the first instance, Jack was aware that Ruth would read it and that she would want to make changes: 'I've no freedom to say just what I want to without scrutiny', he complained to himself as he wrote.[603] There were subjects Ruth did not want raised – children, former loves, syphilis, their courtship – which restrained Clemo's writing. After she had seen the draft, he complained: 'Thought I'd finished the book but R. was doubtful about some bits and I got depressed.' Ruth would add further pressure by telling Jack that they would lose friends if he published it as it was, and he was forced to make a number of changes: 'R. fears it will alienate her Weymouth friends and upset our prospects of moving.'[604]

There were also editorial changes suggested by Livia Gollancz, who was worried about libel, just as Cecil Day Lewis had been. June Trethewey's identity should be hidden better, she suggested, changing the initial from 'J' to 'T', and Clemo would have to make sure that physical descriptions of individuals were not too obvious. The book focused almost exclusively on Clemo's 'quest' for a wife, and included many of the women he had loved prior to Ruth. *Confession* was the book of a young man who believed the world had been promised him, one who was hopeful and expectant of the great 'rewards' he would receive. *Marriage*, on the other hand, is the book of a man 'scarred, yet singing', to borrow a phrase from 'Wedding Eve'. It is not the record of an Isaian promise kept, of agate windows, carbuncle doors and borders of pleasant stones, and Clemo had lost many of his 'fair colours'. Yet the book is not a document of failings, but of triumph. It could easily have been a sustained lament, or a withdrawal of faith, the promise of marriage being the only promise even vaguely fulfilled. But instead of recording the failures, the decline, the disappointments and the loneliness, he writes in uplifting satisfaction and delight. He explains how he only wrote poetry in this mood: 'I was determined to be inspired only by happiness and therefore wrote nothing when I felt depressed'.

The importance of this message was lost on the reviewers. They, like the *Bookbuyer* of 7 February 1980, found *Marriage* 'heartwarming' but 'putdownable'. The statement of 'mellowing' was again ubiquitous. Clemo acknowledged that the earlier work might have *appeared* more urgent, but he denied the validity of the appearance:

> The whole situation [of financial and personal contentment] proved the fallacy of the popular idea that poverty, loneliness and frustration are good stimulants for an artist. I had always found them cramping, suffocating and distorting. While a poet is fighting desperately to make his vision work, he will mis-state or overstate his case and present a faith bleared by the smoke of battle. This may give his writings a strange originality, but it makes him less reliable as a guide and teacher.

Reliability 'as a guide and teacher' is more important than poetic force and originality now. Here again, the border between a secular and evangelical reader appears hostile. The evangelical reader might agree that it does not matter whether the work is painfully or strangely original when the message happens to be true. On the other hand, when all that is left is the message, the secular reader loses an important route into the writing and may find he now shares little with Clemo. This causes a further problem, being that if religious poetry is only accepted by or attractive to the converted, then what is its evangelical value? How are people to be saved? In an interview with David Porter in 1975 Clemo had said: 'I'm an evangelist first, artist second, and then I'm an evangelist third.' But take out the artistry and much of the evangelical value disappears with it.

Clemo's life story gained him a new audience in 1980, when the BBC aired a film using the same title proposed for his next poetry collection, *A Different Drummer*. Contact was made in 1977, and Steve Turner visited to conduct interviews and to photograph the landscape. The following year, Turner returned, bringing a young director named Norman Stone with him. Stone would become a friend of the Clemos and several years later would invite Ruth to take part in his 1983 film on Martin Luther, throwing cabbages at the pope. He would marry the television broadcaster and writer Sally Magnusson (daughter of Magnus Magnusson), who wrote the 1986 *Clemo: A Love Story*. *A Different Drummer* was Stone's first attempt at a full length film, although he would go on to win many awards, notably for *Shadowlands*, the C.S. Lewis biopic written by William Nicholson and starring Joss Ackland. The script was only later picked up by Richard Attenborough and Anthony Hopkins.

Stone and Turner drove the Clemos around the St Austell area, looking at potential filming locations and discovering many of the old places demolished or altered by the deepening, broadening, merging clayworks. The film was to cover the early years of Clemo's life, before he achieved success. It was approved by the BBC and Norman returned in May 1979 to interview Jack. This interview lasted almost the whole week, a gruelling schedule for Clemo and one that made Ruth concerned 'about the exposure of my teenage "oddities". What a queer fish she married.'[605]

The impact of the film on Clemo's life and work was varied. In a very obvious way, it was evidence that although sales of books were not very good and Clemo was having trouble placing his latest poetry collection, he had not been forgotten and was still being celebrated. More than this, the production and shooting period was great fun, bustling and entertaining, as well as being surreal for Clemo as he was introduced to the children playing himself and his old 'girlfriends'. Filming inspired several poems, including 'Filming at Gunheath', which would become the final poem of *A Different Drummer*, taking the place of 'Blind Girl at a Service'. The Clemos had done radio and television interviews in the past, but this was a much grander and more popular production. It would be aired on Good

Friday to a large audience and positive reviews. It also had an impact on the local community, the budget being so small that volunteers from the villages were needed, and it might not be an exaggeration to say that the filming probably had a greater positive impact on Clemo's reputation within the community than any of his books.

As well as professional importance, the film brought the Clemos into contact with a new group of friends, such as Marjorie James, who was instrumental in the casting of the film's children. James had been selling programmes on the evening of 3 May 1979 for a local theatre company in St Austell. It was the day of the general election, the year that Margaret Thatcher was first voted into power, and no one turned up for the play. Mrs James sold just one programme that night – to the odd group of Norman Stone, Jack Clemo and his wife Ruth, who had been hoping to find talented acting children for the film. As it happened, Marjorie was also the drama teacher at Penrice School in St Austell, so they cancelled the performance, closed up and Marjorie took the poet and the director home with her.

Filming began in September, and there are at least four accounts of the schedule. One is presented in an additional chapter of *The Marriage of a Rebel*, appended to the text for Spire's 1988 reprint. Another is in the diaries, a third in the poem 'Filming at Gunheath', and the fourth is the account given by Shirley Ball, the mother of one of the child actors who played Jack Clemo in the film. Mrs Ball kept a day-by-day diary of filming, written from the perspective of her son. It does not reveal much about Clemo, but it does document in a charming way how meaningful the film was to people in the area, bringing with the crew, actors and cameras a moment of glamour and excitement.

Instead of using the Clemo cottage, they shot at Gunheath in a roughly similar worker's cottage. Clemo wrote his own version of the script, adapting *Confession of a Rebel*, which Stone then completely reworked, to the mild annoyance of the Cornishman. Filming was done in two exhausting weeks. St Austell-born actor Robert Duncan (best known for his role as Gus Hedges in *Drop the Dead Donkey*) played Jack from the age of twelve into adulthood. Duncan was twenty-eight at the time and perfectly apt for Clemo as an adult, though in the pre-teen schoolroom scenes he does appear a little advanced. Since filming, Duncan has said that his own Christian conversion was in part due to Clemo's support.

In the diaries for these weeks, Jack begins by noting how weird the process is, but as the days pass he becomes only concerned with the children, specifically Cerris, Kate and Zoe. Cerris Morgan-Moyer was playing Barbara and went on to become a professional actress. She was the daughter of Patricia Moyer and James Morgan, new friends of the Clemos who were connected with the University of Exeter. Dr Moyer had been in touch with them since 1977, when she arranged an event based on Clemo and his work in St Austell, with fellow Exeter academic John Hurst. The relationship they developed paved the way for all contemporary study, introducing Clemo formally to academic audiences and encouraging the deposition of literary and personal material, a process soon negotiated with the help of the poet Ron Tamplin. For Jack, the most bizarre effect of this relationship came in 1980:

> An official envelope was delivered to our home one morning. I opened it and passed the letter to Ruth. A minute later she grabbed my hand and I could sense the startled dismay in her fingertip as she scribbled on my palm: 'They want to make you a doctor!'

On 9 July 1981, the working-class, self-educated clayland poet was conferred with an honorary doctorate. After initial concerns about what duties he might be expected to perform, Clemo accepted, recording the day simply in his diary: 'Thundery rain then fine for our day at Exeter. I drank 3 glasses of sherry and kept singing in my heart "Praise to the Holiest".'

The jollity continued when they returned home. Before the day had begun, Ruth had made space in a photo album for the pictures she was going to capture of Jack in his gown. Unfortunately, due to the weather or schedule, she could not get the precise shots she was looking for. She returned home disappointed but still determined. What she wanted was a good close up of Jack in his robes. The Clemos no longer had the gown, but Ruth had held on to the cap and hood, so she dressed Jack up in one of her red blouses, in lieu of the university's scarlet robes, then put the cap and hood on him and went to a neighbour's garden to take the photo. When they were developed, Ruth noticed something missing. She had forgotten the blue facings of the original gown. She had already developed many copies of the image to give to friends and to the press, but they would not do without the blue facings. Undeterred, Ruth cut a length of blue masking tape into thin strips, trimming them down to the rough shape of the facings, and she stuck these onto each printed photograph. Even now, this improvised and crudely doctored image is one of the stock Jack Clemo photographs used by the local papers. This episode appealed to Jack's sense of humour, and there are other images of him laughing through the photo shoot.

A few months prior to the conferment letter, the Clemos were in London to watch a preview of the film at Broadcasting House. It was the first time Jack had been to the capital since 1951. He took with him a troupe of friends, including the James family and Cerris with her parents. The trip was given added significance by a visit to Wimpole Street, the scene of the Browning romance. Stone happened to know the occupants of the Barrett house and arranged for Clemo to have a tour. The director recalls Jack being led to the mantelpiece and placing his hands on it. In a subsequent letter, the owners of the Wimpole Street house confirmed that the mantelpiece was the original, and told the Clemos more about a girl who haunts the place, singing and playing a spinet. It was, Jack said, 'an incredible day', and they returned to Weymouth in the evening, another piece of the 'Browning pattern' set in place.

The Clemos were spending longer in Weymouth now – six or eight weeks at a time – and there was much discussion over whether they should move there permanently. Friendships and 'child contacts' were among the more important factors in the decision, though also the question of whether it would harm Jack's work or reputation to move. He remarked that on television 'I was mentioned [...] today as one of Cornwall's famous poets. Would I be ignored if I moved to Weymouth?'[606] To aggravate the problem further, while *The Marriage of a Rebel* was selling poorly and *A Different Drummer* was being rejected by every major poetry publisher, some of the smaller regional presses were showing interest. Donald Rawe of Padstow's

Lodenek Press had been considering publishing Clemo for several years. In 1976 he had been enthusiastic about reissuing *Wilding Graft*, and they had spoken about a collection of poetry. In 1981, Clemo sent Rawe a new manuscript of rhymes for children, which Clemo called his 'comics', entitled *The Bouncing Hills* after the lines in Dylan Thomas's 'Poem on his Birthday': 'I hear the bouncing hills / Grow larked and greener at berry brown'. Thomas's is a poem about death, and how the closer Thomas finds himself to it, 'The louder the sun blooms / And the tusked, ramshackling sea exults'. It gives the impression of being triumphant, anxiety transformed by faith. By using the quotation, Clemo seems to be highlighting the epic gaiety of a life lived in Christ.

Rawe was enthusiastic but non-committal, finally abandoning his plans for Clemo's work and passing *The Bouncing Hills* on to Len Truran of Dyllansow Truran in Redruth. Throughout the eighties local publishers would jump at the chance of adding Jack Clemo to their lists, and three collections of original material were released with regional interest presses, *The Bouncing Hills*, *A Different Drummer* and *Banner Poems*. Yet smaller publishing had its problems. In this instance, the finished product was a mix of nine dialect tales from Clemo's youth and thirty-two rhymes for children, both targeting slightly different audiences and as a result appealing to neither. More awkwardly, the humour of the poetry frequently depends on knowledge of certain facts about Clemo. For example, the poem 'It's Only Acting', which begins:

> We're grouped in a lane
> In a smudge of rain
> That fits the scene we are shooting.
> Young Liz plays the part
> Of my first sweetheart,
> Who nearly gave me a booting.

The reader would probably need to know about Clemo and about the film for this poem to make sense and seem relevant. These verses were written to entertain *specific* children, and it might be considered that the children involved were the volume's real audience. At any rate, the book was practically unmarketable and performed dreadfully. Len Truran believed the mistakes were his own, writing that the failure was largely down to his inexperience of publishing poetry as well as the general public's 'abysmal lack of interest in poetry': 'I will never see back the money I laid out on its publication.'[607]

It is possible to imagine that Clemo's poetry for children was influenced by Causley's success writing for children, and perhaps in turn Causley's had been influenced by that of his close friend, Ted Hughes. For Clemo, it was an amusing stopgap while he waited for more mature verse to announce itself. He presents the problem he was having in his diary: 'President Regan has been shot. A nightmare world ... and I just write comic rhymes. I feel so useless.'[608] 'I long to write Christian poetry again', he adds. Clemo let his old friend, Charles Causley, know about the collection, writing: 'This book should end the legend about my being an austere and humourless dogmatist'.[609] In a letter to Derek Savage, he develops this thought a little:

> [*The Bouncing Hills*] is at least typical of me in being hybrid – part prose and part verse, part dialect and part normal English, partly for adults and partly for children. It has little value as art, but it throws light on my psychology, showing that all my hardships and frustrations failed to turn my humour sour or cynical.[610]

The Bouncing Hills is valuable, Clemo believed, because it corrected the tenacious public perception of him derived from the early work. What Clemo did not appear to see was that his later poetry required knowledge of his life and previous writing. It was more diffuse and abstract than the earlier poetry, and less accessible to new readers.

The Norman Stone film focused on the poet's youthful struggle, and when it came to a shot of Clemo working on a poem at his typewriter, they disagreed about which poem he should be filmed 'writing'. Stone wanted one of the old clayscape poems, more inkeeping with the period being portrayed, but Clemo insisted on using 'Weymouth', one of several recent poems about his Dorset fulfilment:

> Shingle and mist weave no morbid spell
> Between Wyke and Upwey wishing-well.
> If a raven croaked on the crumbling cliff-fort,
> I would heed only the laughing children
> Who trust the song-bird, the poet unhurt.
> Fate's dark dice drowns here, a bright ball is thrown,
> Caught, like my kingdom, from love alone.

The significance of Weymouth had not been fully realized yet, but it had the symbolic meaning of relief, success, justification and proof. Clemo believed in a 'Dorset Pull' and he was married to a Dorset woman. They were spending many weeks of the year in Weymouth now, and were discussing whether to move there permanently. Clemo had settled into the Peaty home easily during their first visit, and he enjoyed descriptions of the scenery and the stimulus of new contacts. For many years they had spoken of moving out of Goonamarris, looking at cottages nearby or at Porth Beach, which would have been closer to Gwen and Frances. Ruth was eager to leave. She was miserable in the isolated Clemo cottage and would rather be almost anywhere else. Weymouth was her obvious first choice, with a home already established and live-in help in the form of her sister Bella. After Eveline died, the talk about moving became more serious. Jack was uncertain. He did not want to leave friends and family, and his worry about the impact on his writing was exacerbated by Charles Causley, who thought moving would be a mistake.

Year after year, the Clemos fluctuated between wanting to move and wanting to stay. In the late 1970s, one of the most distasteful aspects of the cottage was the new 'plague of mice', attracted by the neighbours' chickens. Clemo thought this might be a divine message, writing in December 1978: 'It might seem that God wants us to move but we can't till I'm 65.'[611] Only a few weeks prior to this he had said the opposite: 'R. depressed about conditions here – damp walls, mice, dumps blocking out the view. We can't see a way out. I couldn't be happy in Weymouth with my work frustrated.' Then, for a moment in 1980, Jack was again itching to leave: 'We've discussed the Weymouth move. She says it can't be arranged till 1982. These heartbreaking delays.'[612] The delays appear to have been financial, Clemo unable to claim a state pension until he was sixty-five.

After years of deliberation, indecision and vacillation, in 1984 they reached a resolution. At the beginning of the year their rent was increased by the clay company. This was the push they needed, and when they went to Weymouth on holiday in July, they took Jack's books with them, as though the decision had already been made. On their return, after a long summer in Weymouth, Jack noted gloomily in his diary: 'Back to Goona for the last time. The cottage seemed dead – no mail awaiting us in the doorbag, and the TV wouldn't work.'[613] The cottage had not felt the same since his mother had died:

> From my infancy onward she had provided the aura of security from which I looked out on the gloomy clayscape, the chapel, the sea to which she took me in summer. Now that she had vanished all this was stripped of a private, reassuring idiom.[614]

Some people believed that Ruth forced Jack to move and manipulated him by giving a dishonest impression of her hometown. Certainly, it is a surprise that Jack believed Weymouth to be some sort of 'Promised Land' full of spiritual sunshine and exotic paradisal palm trees, a place in stark contradiction with his grim Cornwall. Sophie Bateman, one of Father Benedict Ramsden's daughters, believed that 'Jack had been conned' into moving by Ruth and Ruth's annotations in the diaries show that she was aware of this common perception and that she wished to contradict it. When editing the papers in the mid-1990s, she underlined the passages in which Jack showed some attraction to Weymouth, as though to give greater weight to the notion that it was his idea to move rather than hers. And when he wrote of his disinclination, as in the 1981 question, 'Why should we have to leave all this?', Ruth responded in the margin, 'We did not have to – just we were isolated and lonely.' Similarly, in 1985, when Clemo wrote about his 'captivity' in the new Weymouth house, Ruth responded in the margin for future readers: 'by "captivity" Jack means about his work being stuck.' She is implying that he was talking about writer's block or a lack of publishing success, though this was not what he meant at all. Jack was referring to his physical restrictions and the increased confinement imposed by moving to an unfamiliar town suburb. That Ruth was so sensitive to these suggestions of manipulation gives greater credence to later criticisms of her. Many found her overbearing, demanding or manipulative, sometimes in a comic way, such as the Cornish writer Alan Kent described. When Kent went to see Jack, Ruth unfailingly pressed him to perform chores about the house. Rather than interviewing the famous poet, academics and writers found themselves mowing the lawn, changing bulbs and fixing cupboard doors. When one was in closer contact with the Clemos, this quality could be less entertaining, as their friend Patricia Moyer recalled: 'The more you gave, the more they wanted.' The same sentiment was expressed by Frances and Ray Brown, Clemo's foster-sister and her husband, who were frequently Ruth's first port of call for favours.

After a farewell tea and service at the chapel, during which one of Clemo's favourite hymns was played, 'Breathe on me, breath of God' – a hymn Jack would sing to himself as he climbed the stairs at Browning's Florentine home in 1993, and which would, soon after, be sung at his funeral – on 20 October 1984 James Morgan hired a van and drove Jack away from his birthplace; the claustrophobic lifelong home and landscape of his juvenile Jacob-like claypit wrestling, misdirected love, turmoil, physical decline and unyielding, inexorable hope. The poet of the clay was displaced to chalk and shingle in a pantechnicon.

> For nearly seventy years the slate roof
> Has slanted above my sleep or my empty bed,
> But the man I am, the fulfilled believer,
> Needs palms, sweet modest hills and gentle
> Cleansing ripples on the unhacked beach,
> Not the rubble-wreckage of defiled meadows,
> Or the iron teeth of an outgrown rejected cradle.

XVIII
A Different Drummer and The Shadowed Bed

Therefore, if any man be in Christ, he is a new creature: old things are passed away; behold, all things are become new. And all things are of God.

2 Corinthians 5:17-18

Weymouth bay is a thumb of sea prodding into coral-rich limestone and clay along the Jurassic coast, with a thick plug of sand the colour of golden sugar beneath its neglected fingernail. The beach has carousels and shrieking mechanical entertainments, donkeys, food stalls, a sand sculpture of the Last Supper, and carrion crows and herring gulls fighting for scraps in front of canvas deckchairs decorated with cartoon fish and lengths of rope. A front of restaurants, hotels and guest houses with bay windows gazing out to sea clings to the coastline, and on the knuckle of the town centre's isolated balled fist is Weymouth Baptist Chapel, which Jack, Ruth and Bella attended.

The Clemos and Bella lived in a suburb of Weymouth, on Southlands Road, a housing estate up the hill to the south and just off the main road out of town. They gave their address as '24 Southlands Road, Rodwell, Weymouth', Rodwell having once been a hamlet distinguishable from the seaside sprawl. By the time the Peaty family had moved in, Rodwell was a suburb of Weymouth, with Southlands Road a small new estate on its outskirts, an exploratory finger extending out and bothering the farmland south towards Wyke Regis. When Jack arrived, the farmland had given way to new housing, along with the allotments and reservoir.

Number 24 was one of the red brick semi-detached homes with a tiny square of grass to the front and a small garden to the back. A functional house, unremarkable, more modernised than the Goonamarris cottage, but not more obviously practical. Bella had arthritis and Ruth suffered from uncomfortable recurring urticaria, or hives, so there were few places they could visit without a lift or getting the bus. Really, the only place within walking distance was Sandsfoot Castle and Gardens, a five minute walk from Southlands Road through the estate and onto the more verdant Old Castle Road. This became their favourite and most frequent walk, where they would take visiting friends and admirers, and when Clemo wrote his early impressions of Weymouth in *A Different Drummer*, he included a poem on Sandsfoot:

> Damp-haired in the stone memorial shelter,
> We wait while a shower veils Portland harbour
> And the palms look strange, marking no oasis,
> Rejecting the desert image, since their fruits,
> Like the buds of the neighbouring rose-bowers, swell
> Between the cove and suburban Rodwell.

The image of the palms is continued:

> Soft Channel rain glides, too, from the slim green banners
> Hoisted by sap on the live ringed pillars,
> The palm trunks. You watch the leaves dance,
> While I recall white crystals and the red
> Fanatic tinge on humped hills as dawn broke,
> Etching a scraggy thorn-clump. How different here, instead,
> Is the push of the delicate palm-roots,
> Strong and confident through dense English earth,
> With no shift and cackle of dry grains,
> No whirlwind on a scorching horizon.

'Sandsfoot Castle Gardens' was written after Clemo's second Weymouth visit, in 1978. The palms are symbols of the exotic and are reminiscent of Christ's triumphant return to Jerusalem before crucifixion. But the poem is also an introduction to this favourite site and to its intimate association with Ruth and their marriage.

The Peaty sisters had a small network of friends in the area, which they augmented by socialising at the Baptist Chapel. They met for extra services with Portland's Sailors Rest at an Aggie Weston's, and Ruth took them to neighbours in Rodwell for Bible meetings. Among these neighbours was the writer Elsa Corbluth and her husband, renowned psychotherapist David Boadella. The couple had recently lost their daughter Eilidh in tragic circumstances. Eilidh, only eighteen years old, had committed herself to following Mother Teresa in Calcutta, and she began working for one of Teresa's London organisations in a hostel for homeless women. She left her parents one March day, and that very night her hostel caught fire and Eilidh was killed. She left behind a number of poems, which her parents bound in the volume *I Won't Paint Any Tears*, for which Clemo wrote a foreword. In *A Different Drummer*, he added a biographical poem about Eilidh and her call to service:

> Her poet-fibre withstands
> Briefly, clinging to beauty.
> 'Bright star, enchant my Dorset still . . .
> No, I am beyond, I am dedicated.
> Bright star, would I were constant as
> Mother Teresa's helpers in Calcutta.
>
> 'The foul streets sweat, the creeping shadows are callous.
> Lift the dustbin lid: there's a baby inside,
> Its brown skin smelling of scabs.
> We'll snatch and rescue . . . My hands
> Must do more than stroke these Chesil slabs:
> So few get the vision – so few.'

Another Dorset literary friendship was developed accidentally in 1978, when Ruth was introducing Jack to the attractions of the county. They journeyed out to Mappowder, where Clemo had visited T.F. Powys almost thirty years before, and as they wandered around the churchyard, he and Ruth got talking to 'a farmer who knows my work'. This farmer seemed to know all the Powys gossip and Jack noted to himself that Susan had never married. It turned out the 'farmer' was the writer Gerard Casey, husband of Mary Casey whose mother, Lucy Powys, was Theodore's younger sister. The following day, Gerard collected the Clemos from Weymouth so that they could meet Mary and Lucy. It was to Gerard Casey that the poem 'Mappowder Revisited' was dedicated in *A Different Drummer*. Mary died not long after their first meeting, in 1980, but the Clemos would continue to visit Mappowder almost annually until Jack died, driven either by Gerard or by a Weymouth friend. Around this time, Jack compiled a long list of the people for whom he prayed daily, a list of old friends and correspondents, to which he added Lucy and Gerard.

Missing from their Weymouth social circle were children. Ruth was aware that Jack always liked having children around, and they both still regretted that they were unable to have one of their own. The couple's sense of absence, or lack, led them to place an unusual advert in the *Christian Herald* at the beginning of 1984, asking for a 'foster granddaughter'. Surprisingly, two families answered, the Labdons and the Hortons, with their respective daughters Cathy and Lucy. Jack and Ruth maintained contact with both, although it was Cathy who became the official 'granddaughter'. Neither family lived in Dorset, but both would visit regularly, when the Clemos might stay with them in Torquay, making trips to Paignton Zoo together. Such trips were enormous fun for Clemo, who loved both children and animals, keeping not only his Pomeranians as a boy, but also rabbits and cats. As an adult, he had fewer opportunities to interact with the 'beasts of the earth', but one such chance presented itself when a friend, John Hughes, invited Clemo to his animal sanctuary. In a letter to Savage, Clemo described the experience:

> The previous Saturday we were at John Hughes's R.S.P.C.A. centre at Taunton, where I stroked a seal, was playfully bitten by a badger, and allowed inside the pen of Pepi, the famous monkey whose career, chiefly criminal and alarming, John described in a book.[615]

In the photographic archives at Exeter, this series of images is a perfectly comic interlude. First there is Jack stroking a swan, then Jack with a little owl, with a magpie, patting a badger, stroking a deer, driving a tractor, touching a seal, and then nervously edging towards Pepi the 'criminal' Macaque.

A few years earlier, Clemo had taken the opportunity to help animals in his capacity as a writer, when he was invited to add his name to a list of literary figures against vivisection, a list that included R.S. Thomas, Anthony Powell, Margaret Drabble, Philip Larkin, Iris Murdoch, Richard Ryder and Spike Milligan. The general letter was published in *The Times* on 25 July 1975, but Clemo's personal contribution to the cause was more strongly worded and specific to his faith. He wrote:

> I have always regarded the torture of animals in scientific experiments as one of the most perverse and unpleasant proofs of man's depravity. When a stronger creature with a moral conscience inflicts cruelty on a weaker creature which has not moral conscience but only the capacity to enjoy or suffer what comes to it, there is evidence of the corrupting effect of power. [When the] object of the experiments is not even human health but only feminine glamour and housewives' convenience in the kitchen, the question is placed beyond controversy and the practice stands unmasked as an outrage and a disgrace to civilised humanity.

On other outings, the Clemos would visit Liverpool, where the Labdons lived, and stay with the family, sometimes for New Year's Eve. Jack often wrote in his diaries for these years that such contacts 'restored' him 'spiritually', while prolonged absences from the girls troubled him. The strongest example of this sort of emotional dependence was his relationship with a girl named Naomi, one of his favourite contacts from the late eighties and early nineties, who attended the same chapel as the Clemos, though not as consistently as Jack would have liked. Naomi was in her later teens when Clemo was most influenced by her, and it might be said that she infatuated him. In his diaries, Jack records how many times Naomi has kissed him, and if she speaks to someone else instead of him after Sunday service, he would be thrown into a gloom and might not write in his diary for the rest of the week. On occasion, someone would question his habit of kissing girls at church. When Dublin correspondent Louis Hemmings visited with his new wife Liz, Jack noted: 'We all went to chapel, and suddenly Liz asked, "Who's that kissing Jack?" Naomi isn't daunted by strangers.'[616] And when Vicki Horton, the mother of Lucy, attended chapel with the Clemos, Ruth is asked to explain why there is a little girl kissing Jack. Apparently Ruth 'explained about Bouncing Hills' and it was all okay. The event of Naomi's baptism became a moment of extraordinary importance to Clemo, and he referred to it many times in his diaries and in his poetry, most obviously in 'Baptism', published in *The Cut* magazine in 1987.

Father Benedict Ramsden was another important new friend to Jack. As well as being an Archpriest, Father Benedict was the founder of The Community of St Antony and St Elias for people with mental health conditions, often from criminal backgrounds, who are to be reintegrated into society. The community began in Father Benedict's own house, shared with his wife Lilah and their many children. Ramsden met the Clemos in 1985, having admired the relentless joy in Clemo's work (an admiration Clemo told his diary he felt unable to live up to). The Clemos visited the family several times, Jack writing about Sortridge Manor in *Approach to Murano*, a volume dedicated to the Ramsdens for their role in helping Jack to conclude his 'Browning pattern':

As well as new friendships, Weymouth produced a series of exciting literary prospects. The *Dorset Year Book* became a frequent outlet for Clemo's poetry, and the Dorset poet Paul Hyland lived nearby. Hyland became a friendly contact and would read Jack's work at festivals and poetry evenings. At the same time, a series of books were suddenly accepted. In 1986, along with a reprint of *The Invading Gospel*, there was Magnusson's *Clemo: A Love Story*. The up and coming poetry publisher Bloodaxe was making positive noises about a collected edition, and two of Clemo's seemingly ill-fated publications were finally placed. The 1938 novel, *The Shadowed Bed*, was accepted by Lion for a paperback issue, and the poetry collection, *A Different Drummer*, which Clemo had been submitting since his mother's death in 1977, was accepted by the small local firm

Tabb House on the recommendation of James Morgan and Donald Rawe. 'If there was no room for the book in the big "inn" it must be born in a lowly shed', Clemo wrote to Gwen.[617] In total, four books were published in 1986: one reprint, one study of Clemo and two original works.

Poetry publishing appears to have been changing through the 1970s. Clemo's regular publishers, Methuen, had become increasingly chaotic, forgetting to send out review copies, author's copies and payments, until in 1977 they told Clemo that they were no longer going to publish poetry. Methuen had supported Jack since Colin MacInnes had approached them in 1959, and they produced his finest four volumes, *The Map of Clay*, *Cactus on Carmel*, *The Echoing Tip* and *Broad Autumn*. By 1977, Clemo was an older man and the publishing business was changing. Methuen was not the only publisher dropping poetry and poets, as Clemo discovered when he began posting off the manuscript. 'We are publishing very little poetry at present', said Cape; 'Alas, our poetry list is closed', wrote John Murray; 'We are no longer publishing poetry', Sidgwick & Jackson told him; 'We do not publish any poetry at all', said Thames and Hudson. Faber, Chatto & Windus, MacMillan, Routledge, Carcanet, Anvil, Oxford University Press, WW Norton, Heinemann, Secker & Warburg – among many others – all rejected the latest Clemo collection. Many of those who had closed their doors to poetry expressed considerable regret at having to turn Clemo away, while others offered more tangible reasons for their rejections. Peter Jay of Anvil Press wrote:

> I think there is a core of poems in 'A Different Drummer' which are markedly better than the rest, which seem to me to suffer from a diffuse kind of wordiness. The title poem, Unearthed, Poem at Sixty, In Roche Church, Drought on a Clay Ridge, Salvaged, Private Pompeii, La Salette, Juan Diego, and the poems on Gill and Hunt seem to me the best, most achieved poems. [...] I really don't think the collection as a whole is satisfactory – but my own doubts may well reflect more on the difficulty I have with the uncompromising approach than on

the poems. I may simply be the wrong person to judge your writing.[618]

Craig Raine, who was the poetry editor for Faber & Faber, also replied with a lengthy and insightful review. To begin with, Raine writes that the 'poems which deal with historical figures' are in fashion, but:

> The genre, it seems to me, has an in-built tendency to diffuseness which you don't sufficiently combat. The formula is to tell the life and draw the moral or illuminate some conflict or aspect which speaks to you directly. [...] 'Gladys Aylward' is the best illustration of my reservations. You point out that her missionary work was a way of avoiding the spinster's fate – including the 'Goblin-damps of fancy'. I have to say that I find this phrase uncomfortably archaic. [...] In 'Holman Hunt', I was puzzled by the lines: 'Beauty itself, its wild intoxications, / Blinded us to the snake's fang in the mist.' In every case, I was unsure of the diction's status. Is the poet speaking in dramatic character or not? When I turned to 'Drought on a Clay Ridge', the phrase 'Wizard weather brought wizened stillbirths' compounded the problem, since in this poem you are definitely speaking as yourself. The poeticism here is repeated in a poem like 'A Taste of Scilly': on the one hand, there is the crisp precision of 'the small scars / Out there on the grey-blue skyline'; on the other hand, there is the flamboyant romanticism of your assertion that the native island girls are uncorrupted and special, 'Their mermaid hair loose, tossed over their backs, / Their faces stark, moulded by remote tidal mystery.' While this may be true, I find the use of mermaids rather too easy a comparison.
>
> Overall, then, it seems that, in terms of diction, we are evidently out of sympathy. Let me just say, in conclusion and by way of mitigation, that the poems in which your wife appears are unfailingly touching.[619]

This hurt Clemo very much. Both Raine and Jay had found a 'diffuseness' in the latest poetry, an effect heightened by the fact that the biographical poems did not progress on ideas from previous volumes, and the message was less clearly stated.

Some of the decoding of *A Different Drummer* can be done by following Clemo's reading, as he has written several more biographical pieces, which, on first sight, appear fairly abstract. For example, the poem 'Juan Diego' opens:

> Morning Mass would make me forget the desert,
> Even the heart's desert, cold bed, my squaw
> Gone under sand, away from cactus, totem,
> And the strange Spanish faces we used to hate.

The following stanza:

> A dark red hand above me had dissolved:
> Aztec mother-goddess, cruel weaver,
> Leaving the coarse *tilma* blank of meaning,
> And the bare body more blank, meaning only lust.
> I felt her melt in the candle-flame
> My white brothers lit: our Mexican dust,
> Our feathered serpent, no longer shuffled
> Glinting in my blood's bowed dream.

It was written 2 December 1976, and the source of Clemo's information was *A Woman Clothed with the Sun*, edited by John Delaney. This is a collection of essays on eight classic mystical visions of Mary. The first study in Delaney's collection is of Juan Diego's 1531 vision, entitled 'Our Lady of Guadalupe in Mexico', written by Ethel Cook Eliot, and read by Clemo on 1 December 1976. Diego was, according to Eliot, a 'poor-as-poverty Aztec Indian', who, with his uncle, had been 'among the first Indians to be converted to Christianity by Franciscan missionaries'. Diego was running across the hills to get to Mass, when he was 'halted in his tracks by what he took for a burst of bird song'. Then, from the top of Tepeyac Hill, where previously a temple to the 'Mother-goddess of the Aztecs' had stood, in the frosty mist a woman called urgently down to him, declaring herself 'the ever-virgin Mary, Mother of the true God' and stating that a church ought to be built where she stood. Diego was told to inform the Bishop of Mexico City of Mary's presence and to repeat what she had told him. He successfully gained an audience with the Bishop, but proof was required before the Bishop was willing to act. As is typical in Marian visions, roses were seen blooming from the Tepeyac hilltop, and as a sign, Mary tied some of the flowers up in Diego's 'tilma' which he was to take back to the Bishop. This Diego did, and when he dropped the flowers at the Bishop's feet, an impression of the virgin had been imprinted by them onto his tilma, which was accepted as sufficient proof, and the tilma is today still displayed in the Basilica of Our Lady of Guadalupe. The 'feathered serpent' of Clemo's poem is the god Quetzalcoatl, 'to whom countless men had been excruciatingly sacrificed', and by an apparent error of pronunciation, it was believed that Mary had announced herself as Quetzalcoatl's successor. Clemo's account is simply a poetic rendering of Eliot's chapter, with an occasional stereotype, such as Diego's dead wife being described as his 'squaw', an Algonquian derivative with no place in Mexico, the Aztec people or Nahuatl. Another slight error is the name of the hill on which Mary appeared, Clemo calling it 'Tepenac' instead of 'Tepeyac'. This error might easily be accounted for by recalling that Clemo would have been reading Delaney's work in Braille, where the letters Y (⠽) and N (⠝) are very similar.

Having written 'Juan Diego', the following day Jack read up to the third chapter of Delaney's collection and wrote another poem, 'La Salette', after John Kennedy's essay, 'The Lady in Tears', describing the apparition of Mary to two young cattle herders in 1846. A few days later, Clemo wrote 'Medals', a poem summarising the second chapter, 'The Lady of the Miraculous Medal', by Joseph Dirvin. This was the story of Catherine Labouré and it was never published:

> You reached the Paris cell, tears raining
> On the grim iron bed.
> O Mary of the Immaculate heart,
> O Mary of the seven-times wounded heart!
> Eclipse now, detachment and swaying. . . .

Thrust farther. Touch. The flood comes
In the weird chapel at midnight,
Your hands in the Mother's lap.
Wrench the soul from dream-traffic.
A host of broken lives implore you
To be convinced that this was more than a dream.

These poems are fine and well-wrought, but they are only poetic reductions of the chapters, and as Norman Nicholson observed in the *Church Times*, reviewing *A Different Drummer*: 'Such pieces seem often to be written when a poet can't think of anything special to write about. Even Auden, who was especially good at the genre, was sometimes guilty of this.' They do not add to the accounts in Delaney's book, or lend a new perspective, but reduce, obscure and repeat them. They read like writing exercises rather than purposeful and considered poems. This sequence marked the end of Clemo's heightened interest in Mariology and the mystical experiences of Mary. It was a period that spanned the middle years of the 1970s, from around 1972 until 1977. But the problem with the biographical poems continued, often offering nothing more than a condensed and obfuscated review of a life or book. No more was this the case than in the later poem, 'Salieri', the story of which was lifted straight from Peter Shaffer's *Amadeus*.

When Tabb House invited the manuscript, Clemo was asked to add biographical notes to the poems. A few of these were less than generous at first and had to be changed. The note about Virginia Woolf and her father was altered, to describe them as 'agnostics' rather than 'nihilists', while the more dismissive description of the poet Charlotte Mew was allowed to stand: 'Charlotte Mew was a dwarf who wrote poetry'.

There are a handful of poems that stand out, however, seeming to do something different. And, indeed, when Elizabeth Jennings reviewed the book, she was able to find a great deal to praise (even though the title of the volume was mistakenly given as 'A Different Summer' in her review). Jennings, writing in *The Tablet* on 22 November 1986, said: 'When we read Jack Clemo's work we can forget blindness and deafness. [...] There is an aural and visual beauty'.

She continued: 'We can truly call him a visionary poet. His book is irradiated with this bounteous and hardly-won gift.' It is a common compliment of Clemo's writing that it remains so sensuous, though reviewers usually added something like, 'in spite of his disabilities'. The poem 'In a Truro Garden' stands out from Clemo's other work as being from a deaf-blind perspective, the sensual imagery coming through touch and feel as he holds 'flower-shapes at my finger-ends', nudges his head against an apple in the orchard, or feels which way they are turning by the 'hot slant' of the sun on his face.

'Drought on a Clay Ridge', on the other hand, is a good example of the sensuality Clemo retained. It describes an extreme period of heat in the clay district, and picks gently at ideas of a person feeling connected with the land. It was written in May 1977, before Eveline had died and before Ruth and Jack were seriously thinking about moving to Weymouth, although it is difficult to read it out of this context. The following are the final four stanzas:

> I loved to tilt the strong foxglove cups,
> So sleek amid the rough leaves, here in summer.
> But this year they did not open:
> Small deformed skins tried to thicken,
> But were scorched dry, shrunk like tissue-paper
> And dropped in shreds from dead, rigid stems.
>
> Almost daily, in lanes that sweat tar,
> A fire-engine clangs and rattles through dust-clouds,
> Through odours from over-heated walls and wood,
> Racing to a field or down-patch
> Where something that should drip sap is ablaze.
>
> The smoke does not rise or spread fast
> In the compressed atmosphere:
> It huddles and thins around the commotion
> Till the weary, exasperated firemen
> Are back on the road again, heading for more trouble
> From the bland incendiary sun,
> Leaving another black sore where the soot's

> A shameful substitute for bloom and berry.
>
> Weird and desolate in a new way
> Are the mine-scarred hills, the pyramid-shadowed valleys:
> The native feels himself a foreigner
> When the climate disregards his roots.

As well as the sense of feeling like 'a foreigner', there is the statement that the thing missing is the voluptuousness of flowers and berries, which marks an obvious progression. But the language is overwhelmingly negative: words like 'shameful', 'disregards', 'unlike', 'deformed', 'over-heated', and phrases such as 'I can't recognize my own garden hedge', 'drained and old', 'The smoke does not rise', 'bland incendiary sun' and 'black sore'. It is reminiscent of those moments of absence and disappointment Clemo occasionally felt. There is no triumphant resolution or ecstasy here. Rather, it seems that this 'Drought', along with the following poem, 'Coppice Tarn', edges into a private pastoralism, with a landscape in need of salvation. 'The old coppice tarn' of the poem was at Tregargus, a spot with a little waterfall that Clemo enjoyed and wrote about in *Broad Autumn*. It was also where he used to go out and cut down the family Christmas tree. In 'Coppice Tarn' the narrator is looking at a lost landscape and expressing regret that its absence means it cannot be saved:

> The old coppice tarn – were it still here,
> I could expunge or exorcise the cringe of fear
> Which made my child eyes dilate in that hollow.

The method of recovery would be through Ruth, 'Under a grown love-spell'. The poem allows a few wonderfully indulgent descriptive lines:

> The witches' den's dark Sabbath of sagging elder,
> Elm, nettle-tooth, puffed thumb of toadstool,
> Curdled green slime on the slow,
> Rarely ruffled eye of veiled water.

It is a strange sort of nostalgia, as though he wished the place could be just as horrid as he remembered it, in order that it might be salvaged:

> A rotten fence at the coppice tail
> Would have given us exit to fields and the hand-rail
> Plank bridge across the stream. Good to get clear,
> You would agree, of that eerie spot
> Where my favourite cat
> Was drowned by a ragged old village man
> While I watched and shivered... Well,
> It's all lost in clay-waste now – nothing here
> But white dumps and tanks: no pool-green or tree-green.[620]

These are poems of loss and regret, implying an ambivalent emotional response to place, and in both there is a strong sense of dislocation. Of particular thematic importance is this idea that the place requires saving, and the superstitious belief that hallowing could be achieved by visiting it again as a fulfilled and faithful spouse. Clemo is reclaiming his youthful experiences, which are marked in the land, by exposing them to his divinely determined love of Ruth. Throughout the rest of his life, Clemo would feel this desire to reclaim. Not only would they visit the old haunts of Cornwall, but they would go to Mappowder and to the Lake District, saving them all from their earlier associations with other loves. In his 1988 diary, Clemo notes how their trip to Keswick and the Lakes was so different from his visit in 1965 with Mary, and he made a fairly full account of it in the poem 'Keswick Revisited' (in *Approach to Murano*), which Clemo completed in his head before they had returned to Weymouth. In 'Keswick Revisited', Mary is invoked again as a Valkyrie – 'Icelandic, Scandinavian, pagan anyway' – and her sexual association with rowan berries is continued, as 'Red rowan berries could turn sinister'. Visiting with Ruth, 'in my wife's orbit', the Lakes are reclaimed: 'The whole scene's purged / Of pagan threats.'

The idea that the nature of a place could be changed in a moment is the latest incarnation of the apophenic impulse, and is consistent with the confessional need and the recurrent phoenix-like rebirth. In the diaries, Jack would mark weekly, monthly and annual anniversaries, and claim that from *that* new moment the world was in some way refreshed. The same was true of his relationships, his work and his disabilities, and it seems to have been a way of remaining optimistic when all other senses of potency had been removed, as well as a way of coping with guilt. As the confession wipes the slate clean, so too did Clemo's recurrent moment-marking.

'The Restored See' suggests another form of reclamation through reconciliation. The poem was written on the request of Bishop Graham Leonard to mark the diocese of Truro's centenary. Clemo considered the invitation, the writing and the recital of the poem in the Cathedral's chapter house a resolution of the rift between himself and the higher churches.

With this theme of salvaging the past and the landscape, the original intended final poem 'Blind Girl at a Service' no longer made sense, so it was replaced by 'Filming at Gunheath'. Stone's film, referenced in the poem, is a part of the reclamation process, as the narrative of Clemo's grimy youth is revisited, reenacted and justified with Ruth at his side. Yet, 'Filming at Gunheath' is most remarkable for its statement on suffering: 'Let others ask / Why the pain had to be: I merely bless each mask.' This sentiment is present in the Sandsfoot poem, too:

> I have questioned often, questioned the worth
> Of the long pain and mirage, the rotten clay-fields,
> Or the cruel fate distorting clay-fields and me.

Clemo is allowing us to question why God acquiesced to his intense and protracted suffering. There is a suggestion that the suffering might not have been necessary. It is passively stated, but present nonetheless, implying that although once Clemo had been confident about God's plan, now he will let other's ask what the purpose of his pain might have been. It is not a theological departure, but a personal one, indicating a more considered and objective reflection on an issue which, as a younger man, he had thought would be resolved by the clearing of his senses, imminent marriage and popular success as a novelist.

The second book of 1986, *The Shadowed Bed*, is another visitation of the past, and to the period of Clemo's first achievements as a writer. Cecil Day Lewis and Harold Raymond at Chatto & Windus invited Clemo to write a new novel for them, but instead of a new work from their maturing investment, they received his old manuscripts. The last of these was 'The Lamb of the Green Bed', its title a reference to Christ the Lamb and to a passage from *The Song of Solomon*: 'Behold, thou art fair, my beloved, yea, pleasant: also our bed is green' (1:16).

In 1946, Raymond Savage had rejoiced after reading the story, briefly considering it the best thing Clemo had produced, but in spite of Savage's enthusiasm, the book was not nearly good enough. It was a self-conscious imitation of T.F. Powys. When he had first drafted it as a short story in 1938, under the title 'Potter's Lane', Clemo admitted the influence, writing in his diary his determination to write:

> a story [...] in the style of Powys' 'Mr Weston's Good Wine' [...] God and the devil struggling for the possession of sex – God [...] as Mr. Potter, the devil as Mr. Beale – Christ the Lamb, who changes things.[621]

The summary given to Louis Hemmings in 1987 suggests that not much changed over the intervening half-century: 'Potter is God, Beale is Satan, Potter's Lane is Christianity and the magnetic and mediating *Rock* is *Christ*.' The original lamb, sitting and bleating in Potter's field in the earlier drafts, has become a 'Rock'. Both are accepted metaphors of Christ. The rock is mentioned in 1 Corinthians 10:2-4:

> And were all baptized unto Moses in the cloud and in the sea;
> And did all eat the same spiritual meat;
> And did all drink the same spiritual drink: for they drank of that spiritual Rock that followed them: and that Rock was Christ.

This is a reference to a much earlier episode in Exodus 17, when Moses proves his God by drawing water from a rock to slake his thirsty followers. Moses names the place of this miracle 'Massah, and Meribah' (17:7), and we are reminded of Eveline Clemo's pamphlet, *I Proved Thee at the Waters*, which was also a reference to the Mosaic miracle recounted in Psalm 81:7: 'Thou calledst in trouble, and I delivered thee; I answered thee in the secret place of thunder: I proved thee at the waters of Meribah.'

The synopsis of *The Shadowed Bed* is fairly simple, but there is no real plot. It is framed as though a love story tracing the romantic vicissitudes of Bronwen and Joe – the Jack character who is recovering from an illness and trying to find work. Bronwen came to be based on Brenda Snell. Although the Joe/Bronwen story opens and closes the novel, they are largely absent from the rest of it. Really, the story is a simple fight for allegiance, a fight between Potter and Beale. Potter once came to the clayland village of Carn Veor, but he has now retreated across the river, and although he is the protagonist he does not appear in person in the novel. His power in the village comes from the Rock at the end of Potter's Lane; the lane representing the sexual-mystical approach to Christ. It is by approaching the Rock that one becomes 'born again' or 'baptized'. The antagonist Beale, meanwhile, lives in the clays, though he came from a deep pit, Helburn, which was worked by the 'inmates' of an asylum. Beale and Potter are fighting for the claylands around Carn Veor, a community representing the wider world – squalid, treacherous and ruled by lust. As the story opens, Beale controls most of the clay works, which he rules through the carnality of his adopted daughters Florrie and Rosa. Florrie was born 'within the walls of the clay-pit, amid the hot white slime' of Helburn, her mother and father both 'inmates' at the asylum. Florrie is said to be the 'Infernal Venus of the claylands', a seductress since the age of twelve. (Twelve, it will be recalled, was the projected age of Irma in the first draft of *Wilding Graft*.) Rosa had been a normal girl until she was caught by Beale on her way down Potter's Lane and seemingly raped, again at the age of twelve. Soon after, she became a prostitute. (Curiously, Clemo told his wife that Rosa was based on the child Barbara.) At length, Rosa begins courting the drunkard and boxer, Bert Truscott, after they have both made their way to the Rock and returned 'born again'. Bert gives a sermon to the villagers, his testimony a catalyst to their baptismal awakening. He tells them: 'Go down to that lane. Feel the stab o' they thorn trees. Fight through to the Rock. That's where Potter's grip begins'. Rosa is described as the 'Terrestrial Venus' when she is a temptress, which suggests that the sin of sex is a temptation with its origins in two separate forces, one born in Hell, the other on earth. The first appears to be an objective principle, the second contingent. Once Rosa is purified and the terrestrial temptation eliminated, there is yet the character Florrie, spawned in hell, who cannot be saved. It appears as though Clemo might be stating that sins can be forgiven, but the temptation of sexual deviation will always be present and will always have to be fought. The risk of succumbing to worldly lustful temptation is destruction, indicated by the suicide of another girl 'touched' by Beale, and by the decomposing horse cadaver discovered by Bronwen when she was chased into a lane adjacent to Potter's. It may be recalled that Clemo symbolically connected the horse with sexuality, and the message is that pursuing sex outside of the 'shadow' of Christ leads to death and ruin.

As well as Beale and Florrie, the other baddie is Mr Reed, the Church of England vicar arrived from Saffron Walden (notably, the Essex town from which Eileen Funston had written). He teams up with Beale to promote religious complacency and progressive natural theology, rather than the primitive orthodoxy of simple uncompromising faith. Considering Jack had only recently announced his reconciliation with the Church of England, his decision to retain this expression of contempt suggests how much of this book derives from an earlier period, and also confirms the influence of Powys, who enjoyed mocking the clergy in his similarly geographically enclosed allegorical novels.

The problem for Chatto & Windus in the 1940s was that they were also Theodore Powys's publishers and could not print anything so flagrantly derivative of one of their established authors. In the first instance, it would invite comparison, which Cecil Day Lewis felt would not favour Clemo:

> Instead of lucidity we get naiveté; instead of simplicity, a dogmatic division into black and white. I feel that

> Clemo is not interested in his characters at all, except as vehicles of his beliefs, and in consequence they appear much more like vehicles for prejudice than for belief.[622]

Lionel Miskin, on the other hand, liked the 'dogmatic division into black and white':

> That novel is remarkable! I meant to write you about it long ago. It is so starkly a contrast of black and white, good and evil and operating against that demented lunar landscape with its blazing engine house and dour village seething with aggression and sexuality. [...] But it is so very well written, poetic, passionate. Must owe a little to Lawrence [...]. You know it must curiously be the closest to German Expressionist writing that an English novel ever got, for they too cut out the naturalism in favour of savage symbolism.[623]

Miskin's perception of the connection with Lawrence was a keen one and had been highlighted in a letter from Clemo to Ernest Martin in 1954:

> [*The Shadowed Bed*] is quite different from *Wilding Graft* – no Hardyesque gloom but more of Lawrencean primitivism and revivalist fervour – the elements of grace and nature presented through symbols with no direct reference to God.[624]

In this instance, 'primitivism' appears to be an unquestioning, emotion-led simplicity. This is consistent with the 'supernatural magnetism' said to be a quality of the Christ symbol in the novel, and is reminiscent of Clemo's youthful response to Parkyn in the *Cornish Guardian*: 'The mind can only serve God while it is the servant of emotion, religious instinct, passion, impulse.'

Day Lewis called for the project to be abandoned:

No patching or tinkering with it would redeem its primal error – the artistic error of hammering out a story with the will as a hammer and the characters as a mere anvil, instead of allowing the imagination to mould it and tempering 'mystical fantasy' with human sympathy.[625]

The novel is an intriguing and entertaining read, all the more striking for being finally published and read when Powys himself was no longer a household name. It shows better control than *Wilding Graft*, although it does not have the same seething quality that made *Wilding Graft* so emotionally potent and readable. The obvious difference is that *Wilding Graft* is a plot-driven novel and a romance, with a raw religious principle guiding the outcome, whereas *The Shadowed Bed* is primarily a theological exposition, repeating the theme of fallen 'Nature' and redemption through conversion in a very direct and unnatural way. The landscape encasing the allegory is well evoked, as it was in *Wilding Graft*, again in tense and intimate prose:

> The moorland was harsh, reduced to a shrivelled passivity in the hour of moonrise. It stretched as a dried skin, wrinkled and scarred, between the gravel heaps and the grim buildings of clayworks. A few of these works were still active; the clank of waggons echoed from the pyramids, and at their tips, under the arc-lights, the refuse spilled out in little jets of white foam – tiny and derisive vomits that fanned out over the slopes.

The story was revised through the 1940s, becoming *The Shadowed Bed* in 1949. This was the year Clemo was writing to Eileen Funston, and the manuscript bears a dedication to her, as well as a lengthy preface. The revisions did not alter the key features of the book, but Jack believed the theology had been bent to align with that of Karl Barth.

Further, lighter, revisions were made in 1952 and in 1971, when Gwen Pearce finished typing the manuscript for Jack, and an inscription to his father was added:

In tribute to

MY FATHER

You snatched the opposing shovel
Near the orchard, under the pit-waste cone:
My life soon followed and had to be sane.
Clay-dust on the cancelled apple
Bade me close your foreign mine.

Sunken now is the farm's lap
Where my journey was jolted;
The shadowing headstocks have decayed.
But you hand me tools on a green lip
Somehow cleansed for my art and creed

Clemo's father is almost always spoken of in terms of Jack's inheritance; his syphilis and sexuality. This dedication is an allusion to the novel's overt sexual theme and the need for purification.

In all versions of the novel, the story and moral remain the same, and the similarity to Powys is unmistakable. However, by the time of publication, in 1986, Clemo no longer liked Powys and in the new briefer preface he failed to mention Theodore at all, inviting instead a comparison with the allegories of C.S. Lewis, Clemo having recently read Lewis's Narnia books. Nevertheless, *The Shadowed Bed* was written under the influence of Powys just as plainly as *Wilding Graft* had been written under the influence of Hardy. The attempt to ignore Powys in later editions did not fool his most supportive critic, Norman Nicholson. Reviewing the 1986 publications *A Different Drummer*, *Clemo: A Love Story* and *The Shadowed Bed* together in the *Church Times*, Nicholson wrote: 'T.F. Powys, in his curious brand of devout, fatalistic atheism, is perhaps the one writer who might have been able to make a success of *The Shadowed Bed*'. He marked an anomaly in the publication: 'Since Clemo himself has expressed a wish that critics should not concentrate on his "clay-pit" period […], I am rather surprised that he has chosen to print this immature work.' Nicholson's preference has consistently been for the poetry, and *The Shadowed Bed* was a disappointment: 'I hope that no one will read it without having read the poems first.'

Derek Savage offered his own private criticism, recognising the novel's strengths and veiling his own issues with it as though predicting a mixed response from the press:

> Sophisticated critics could go nit-picking through the chapters and point out inconsistencies and improbabilities; but the quality of the prose simply insists that one take all these in his stride and let the novel do its work on the inner intelligence.[626]

As it happened, there were few insightful reviews. Some minor publications showed their support, like the Christian journal *Reform* and the *Librarians' Christian Fellowship Newsletter*, but more often approbation was banal, summarising the plot and saying that they liked the book, while failing to engage with it. It could be that this critical failure was due to the unfashionableness and awkwardness of the novel, or a sign of disinterest in Clemo's prose, or even of a more general disinterest. Since *Broad Autumn*, Clemo had not published anything striking or attractive, and the audience may have cooled. Still, critical cooling did not seem to prevent sales. *The Shadowed Bed* had an ambitious print run of 5,000, of which around 3,000 sold; a very respectable figure for Lion Publishing, whose founder and director David Alexander had taken a risk publishing the novel. Initially, Alexander had been uncertain about accepting Clemo's old book, writing: 'I am not sure we could do justice to it'.[627] The Commissioning editor, Simon Jenkins, was also hesitant, but ultimately agreeable: 'Although it is unusual for us to publish works of this kind, we do like the manuscript very much and would like to see it in print'.[628]

The pulping of 2,000 volumes upset Jack, and in 1992 he considered both of the Lion titles – Sally Magnusson's and his own – to be failures. By now, it will have been noticed that Clemo was never satisfied with sales figures. This is not necessarily because they were dreadful, but because popular success had always been a part of Clemo's divine covenant, and he did not ever perceive this success arriving.

Sally Magnusson's *Clemo: A Love Story* had first been proposed in 1982, after Norman Stone had introduced Magnusson to the poet. Stone and the Clemos had remained in close contact, with Norman bringing back relics from Jerusalem for Jack. Ruth prepared the material for Sally's book, recording extracts from her husband's diaries onto tapes and filling notebooks with episodes and characters. Informed by Jack, Ruth even suggested titles, such as 'Impassioned Clay', 'The Best is yet to be', 'How do I Love Thee', 'A Bud that Dares not Disallow the Claim', and 'Beyond the Clay-Bound Scars'. Other than the clay titles, these were all references to the Brownings. The picture developing is of a throttlingly strong editorial grip held by the Clemos.

The couple were flattered and glad to welcome Sally into their home, and Jack enjoyed the long sessions of interviews and questions; sometimes six hours at a time. The problem was that Jack had written everything he wanted to write about himself and Ruth, and had omitted information they did not want public. Magnusson would have to come up with a new angle, and the Clemos exercised their editorial control immediately. In 1983, Magnusson gave the Clemos a fragment of her projected book, which they were not happy with, and throughout the year Jack records concerns and disgruntlement. 'We're worried about Sally's work', he begins early in the year, which is soon followed by: 'Dark pressures this week. R. upset by extravagances in Sally's narrative.' Even worse: 'It looks as if Sally's book will have to be dropped, as she won't make the alterations we insisted on.'[629] Sally, at last, did agree to the changes, and she remarks in the acknowledgements section of her book that 'there were a few areas where my journalistic curiosity had to be sacrificed to their request for privacy.' In the end, the book was a lightweight piece of warm-hearted journalistic prose. It was not intended to be ground-breaking biography, as Magnusson acknowledged, but rather 'to chronicle an extraordinary love story.' Clemo's final verdict fell short of enthusiastic: 'It's not deep but it's much better than her 1983 fragment.'

While Jack and Ruth worried needlessly about Sally's book, a more concerning review of Clemo's work appeared in the Christian journal, *The Third Way*, written by Margaret Brearley and entitled

'Scarred yet Singing.' Brearley closely analysed the new novel and she did not like it. It was 'bad art', 'repellent', 'melodramatic and oppressive'. She encouraged a diagnostic approach, and read into the work a medical confession, concluding as obvious the fact that Clemo had contracted congenital syphilis from his parents. Her conclusion was correct, but it was an astonishingly bold imaginative leap to make – bolder still to put into print. But Brearley denies the suggestion that she had been told about Clemo's syphilis by a third party:

> I had heard no rumours about him at all. Never having heard of Clemo, I was asked by Third Way to review The Shadowed Bed out of the blue, and was deeply puzzled by it – and by Clemo's curious facial profile and blindness. I felt sure that the Shadowed Bed held symbolic clues to some enigma – and suddenly realised what the solution must be – congenital syphilis. My husband is a surgeon and confirmed that Clemo's profile and blindness could indeed be explained by tertiary syphilis – and all became clear.[630]

Brearley goes on to say that when she discussed her hypothesis with the editor, Tim Dean, Dean told her that he had heard something to this effect before, and that friends of Clemo had been urging Jack to talk about it publicly.

The Clemos responded to the magazine directly:

> I'm afraid my wife has been very upset by the needless personal discussion and clinical guesswork about my father. She feels that this irresponsible probing into private matters – some of it quite inaccurate – is damaging to us and might lose us friends. We strongly object to such defamatory statements and feel that we should have been consulted before they were rushed into print.[631]

There was nothing 'defamatory' about Brearley's article in the legal sense, of course, her 'diagnosis' being correct, but the worry was for their public reputation, their 'good name' and their friendships. In spite of the strongly worded initial response, the only correction Clemo actually offered was that he had no idea the word 'gumma' was 'medical jargon' relating to syphilis, as Brearley had stated in her review, and in a second letter to the editor, he is fairly positive about the piece, restating that his only worry was that they might lose friends, who were not 'sophisticated arty Christians'.[632] This sounds more like Ruth's concern than Jack's, and is a repetition of the fears she expressed about the publication of Clemo's prose fiction and the early drafts of his second autobiography.

It might have been more troubling that reviewers seemed to have a new disregard for privacy. The fact of Clemo's congenital syphilis had been as obvious in the 1950s as it was in 1986, with *Confession*, the poetry and *The Invading Gospel* all suggestive of an inherited condition, and Clemo's profile already profoundly altered, quarried and undermined by the disease. Yet it is not until 1986 that any reviewer thought to mention it. It would be wrong to suggest any salaciously sensationalist motive behind Brearley's *Third Way* article, but it is worth observing that this was a period swamped with tabloid scandal-mongering, with readers and writers more desensitized than ever. Rupert Murdoch was gaining influence, his tabloid *The Sun* dominating the market and lighting a murky way with its intensifying focus on sensation, sex and celebrity.

The following year showed just how little Clemo's friends were deterred from their relationships, as Father Benedict offered one of the most substantial and symbolic signs of admiration Clemo ever received. It had first been suggested only weeks after the books were released, in December 1986. It was a spectacular idea and seemed to Jack just too fanciful: 'Talk of a possible Italian honeymoon trip!'

Ramsden proposed taking Jack, Ruth and Bella, along with his own wife and three children to Venice to pursue or conclude the 'Browning pattern', just as the Browning story had ended with Robert's 1889 death at the palazzo Ca' Rezzonico on the Grand Canal. The Brownings had run away to Italy after their secret wedding, and nothing could seem more romantic and poignant to Jack than following them on his own wedding anniversary in October. Just the thought and expectation of the trip inspired Clemo to write about Venice, and Italian poems would conclude his next collection, *Approach to Murano*, published in 1993, a volume that would be the last produced in Clemo's lifetime. 'Centre', 'Parallel' and 'Palazzo Rezzonico' were all Italian poems written in the months *before* the trip, though only the latter would make it to the collection. It predicts the wonder of flying, 'Teaching a trick of levitation, / Air-flight at seventy-one', and blends this boyish enthusiasm with the trip's deeper significance:

> Back in Cornwall, remote from these flowing streets,
> My Bridge of Sighs was an unfenced plank
> Above the clay-slime. I felt giddy,
> But even in my hermit-bonds prepared to thank
> God for what native wit called mirage.
>
> I clung, by stubborn grace, to the alien
> Glitter of the Browning pattern
> Which closed here, noble and clean,
> Near the reserved church, in a frescoed palace.
>
> Wedding allegory on a ceiling
> Spills clues to the room of homage,
> High over the nodding gondolas
> And the whispering water's affirmation
> Of outreach, the ultimate glad bridge.

The party flew from Heathrow on 25 October 1987:

> An unjolted glide across Europe
> With sandwiches eaten above the Alps
> And my air-sickness bag unused
> When the bump came, the neat landing
> On a Venice runway.

In a poem for *The Cornish Banner*, Clemo draws the image of the snowy Alps below them into his personal landscape, describing them as 'white peaks / Sprawled like clay-tips at Rostowrack', as though no landscape could be imagined without a clay country contextualisation.

The following day after their flight was their wedding anniversary, and Father Benedict had obtained special permission for the Clemos to visit Ca' Rezzonico and the room in which Browning had died. It was run-down inside, Ramsden recalls, the room a mere shell, with mud for floors and planks to walk over, but Clemo never saw this. Instead, he touched the walls, just as he had touched the fireplace at Wimpole Street, and he felt wonderfully moved. In the afternoon, 'came our romantic gondola trip along the Grand Canal.' Jack had promised Ruth a gondola ride, and although she was not quite as keen as he was, this was the honeymoon adventure always intended. In the chapter added to the 1988 reprint of *The Marriage of a Rebel*, Clemo described the moment:

> There was a curious romantic rhythm in the movement of the craft as the gondolier began dipping his oar in traditional style. Ruth pressed closer to me, sometimes holding my hand or playfully poking me to make me feel how inevitable this enchanted odyssey was. […] It was all soft and dreamlike, aglow with history, linking us with the days when Doges had sailed here to drop wedding rings into the Adriatic. Our focal point was nearer, in the gondola excursions the Brownings must have enjoyed during holidays when Elizabeth was alive.

In the following days, the group visited St Lucy's shrine, the Armenian monastery and St Mark's tomb. They 'climbed innumerable steps to the Doge's palace' and 'crossed the Bridge of Sighs without adding any.' On the Sunday, Father Benedict took them to a service at St Mark's Basilica, the opulent cathedral across the Bridge of Sighs, 'where I survived the incense and prayed spontaneous Evangelical prayers when the whole congregation knelt.'[633]

Various perspectives of the trip have wonderfully differing foci. Sophie, Father Benedict's daughter, recalls being frustrated at having to walk so slowly, and remembers with distaste the constant bickering of Ruth and Bella, which the children used to privately mimic.

Father Benedict, meanwhile, was amazed at Jack's observations of the places they visited, and when several details the priest had not himself observed appeared in Clemo's poetry, Benedict determined to return to the same sites and verify them, discovering all of Clemo's observations to be correct. Jack was in a private rapture, a delightful mix of being profoundly moved and childishly gleeful, insensible to anything other than the delights of his Venice.

With the same attention that he might have recounted a service at St Mark's or a gondola ride with his wife, Jack recalled the lighter moments that amused him: 'Fed the pigeons in St Mark's Square, standing still with birds perched on our heads, shoulders and outstretched arms.'[634] Perhaps there were local Venetians on the piazza, looking on and shaking their heads – much as Cornish locals curse tourists tossing pasty crumbs to gulls on the quay – as Clemo, obliviously happy, handfed the 'fluttering avalanche of pigeons'. In 'Late Honeymoon' he civilizes the pigeons, transforming them to a softer symbol:

> Doves make my raised arm a loaded branch;
>   Eager beaks peck seeds off my palm:
> All's a flutter from shoulder to finger-tip –
>   And she feasts through the seeds in a psalm.

He glorifies this perturbation of feral pigeons fighting for crumbs into a superb vision of divine and physical intimacy, of hope and faith realised, perhaps of the Holy Spirit itself. It is an incredible purification of his experience, and we see it again when he picks up a piece of tourist tat, a little model gondola with a brash yellow base made of 'real Murano glass'. Clemo is oblivious to the ubiquity of these trinkets, the cheap haggling and predation of merchants. The ornament to him was a symbol of clarity – the very opposite of opaque clay – and it became a central symbol in *Approach to Murano*, with its opening poem, 'The Model', dedicated to it:

> Modestly harboured where my pen glides,
> Near the uncut western Channel,
> A Venetian souvenir glitters, high and apart –

A gondola, swan-smooth in Murano glass,
Gold-edged, recalling the guided waters.

It's my symbol of unsplintered clarity,
Perfected vision, owing nothing
To the blast-thuds of diseased rock,
Or the muddy, snarling iron tooth.

As the party flew home on 1 November, Clemo prayed on the plane in praise of the trip and the Ramsden family's uncommon kindness. Every correspondent of the couple must have received a personal account: 'It was an incredible adventure', he wrote to Savage; 'It all seemed a miracle', to Causley; and to Victor Perry, it was 'the most spectacular event in our lives.'

Jack and Ruth on the balcony of Robert Browning's death-place, the Ca' Rezzonico, 1993

XVIII
Greeting the Unseen

But we have this treasure in earthen vessels, that the excellency of the power may be of God, and not of us. We are troubled on every side, yet not distressed; we are perplexed, but not in despair; persecuted, but not forsaken; cast down, but not destroyed.

2 Corinthians 4:7-9

The 'miracle' continued when the Clemos returned home. Not only had Juliet Newport, the new editor for Hodder & Stoughton's Spire imprint, contacted them to say that they would like to reissue the two autobiographies, *Confession* and *Marriage*, but Neil Astley at Bloodaxe had agreed to publish a volume of *Selected Poems*. The poems for the Bloodaxe volume were chosen in the first instance by Clemo himself, who sent a list of sixty-six possible pieces, each annotated with reasons for inclusion. 'A Calvinist in Love' was said to be the 'most popular of my stark 1945-50 theological love poems'. 'Beyond Lourdes' was the 'deepest poem of my "jazz" phase'. 'Bunyan's Daughter', however, had a plea for inclusion attached to it, as Clemo described it as, 'My most moving dramatic monologue in the "historical" genre'.

Astley approved the list then forwarded it to Paul Hyland. Hyland preferred the poetry from Clemo's earlier periods and thought this was being underrepresented in the selection. Pieces such as 'Neutral Ground', 'Clay-Land Moods' and 'Clay Phoenix' had been omitted, and Hyland recommended the inclusion of a further eight poems to the *Map of Clay* sections, as well as several more to the subsequent sections, all of which Astley approved. Only one poem had to be culled, 'Coppice Tarn', when they had run out of space. Eighty-eight poems remained, and the only work obviously omitted is that inspired by children; poems like 'The Burnt Bush', 'The Plundered Fuchsias' and 'The Child Traitor'. The connection between childhood and sexuality was being edited out of Clemo's life and work. The omitted poems are not by any means bad, and back in 1954

Clemo had begged Cecil Day Lewis to include 'The Child Traitor' in *The Clay Verge*. In the 1980s, a sense of shame surrounded them, exacerbated by Ruth. There are also notably few poems from the latest collection, Tabb House's *A Different Drummer*. Jack himself had suggested using only six.

Bloodaxe's *Selected Poems* was published in 1988, with a June launch in Truro, and Jack considered it 'my last peak as a poet', an uncharacteristically pessimistic statement, which shows the importance of the volume to him.[635] Clemo had wanted to produce a 'selected' or 'collected' volume since the 1970s, and had written introductions to them already in anticipation. The Bloodaxe book sold more in its first few months than *A Different Drummer* sold in three years. The idea that this would be his 'last peak' came mostly from a sense of failing health. He had suffered blackouts a few years previously, as well as what Ruth thought might have been a stroke, in 1984, but which Jack described as, 'an unexpected physical attack – I felt numb and nearly collapsed several times.'[636] These were not symptoms of the end – those would not appear until 1992 – but Jack was seventy-two when he returned home from Venice, and Ruth sixty-four. They were ageing quickly and Ruth's health in particular was poor. The late 1980s saw her endure a series of painful afflictions, beginning in 1988. Her hives continued to be bothersome, and she had tonsillitis at the beginning of the year. Then she broke her wrist at a friend's house after tripping over a child, so that her arm was in plaster when they were taken to Oxford by Norman Stone to see where his film *Shadowlands* had been shot. The Stones and Clemos wandered around Magdalene College and then visited C.S. Lewis's former home, 'The Kilns', built on the edge of a clay pit. Clemo's long-held personal interest in Lewis and the clay parallel invited poetic comparison:

> I feel the scorching irony
> In this quiet room as I stroke the hollow
> Your shifting bulk wore in a big arm-chair.
> The house-name prods faint images
> Of my Cornish gut: hot kiln, steam, bubbling clay,
> Thick suffocating dust that muffled rails

> Where a tank-waggon vomited. It's a way
> Of refining: some such jargon
> I recall dimly. Not a trace
> Of its truth in my wedded life. I salute
> Your faith's hard test, but I am past my furnace.

The following year, 1989, while walking in the Lake District with the Labdons, 'Ruth broke her leg at Dungeon Ghyll. A nightmare of ambulances and hospital. We left her at Kendal and had a boat trip on Windermere. I felt stunned.'[637] When Ruth was incapacitated, Bella took over caring for Jack, to such an extent that she would sleep next to him in Ruth's place; an unconventional but practical arrangement.

Regardless of their health, the Clemos were impressively active. Amid preparations for the new volumes and reissues, and the writing up of post-Venice poems, the Clemos spent the end of 1987 in St Helen's, near Liverpool, with their foster-granddaughter Cathy. There, they were taken to see the Disney film, *Benji the Hunted*, which was possibly the first time Jack ever sat through a film in the cinema after the aborted viewing of that 'wanton, glamorous affair' back in 1928. Clemo wrote of this visit as soon as he got back to Weymouth in the New Year:

> We're steering towards a vicarage, having touched
> Roots, precious to us, at Birkenhead,
> Birth-place of the sweet fish-dreamer.
> Her dancing eyes await the bright shoals
> Of Liverpool shops, toy-decked,
> Holly beyond the common cargo,
> And then the mystery in the vicarage
> Epilogue before supper. There she'll keep
> My hand on her tambourine and the swing
> Of the high carol will mean heavenly traffic
> No sorrow's sullen flood can reach.

The Clemos and the Labdons visited one another throughout the year, and Lakeland poems appear in both *Approach to Murano* and the posthumously published *The Cured Arno*.

On top of these visits and their socializing with Weymouth church friends, the Clemos would holiday in Cornwall annually, staying with Frances or Gwen and meeting Derek Savage in Mevagissey, occasionally revisiting the old Goonamarris cottage and the new family living there. Cornish connections remained loyal to Clemo and his work, and in 1989 there came a further expression of this loyalty from the Cornish Nationalist journal, *The Cornish Banner*. The journal has now moved away from its nationalist roots and is more a celebration of Cornish arts and history, but when Savage introduced the editor James Whetter to Clemo in 1979, Whetter had only recently founded both the *Banner* and the Cornish Nationalist Party itself. Savage had been talking to Whetter – who lived a couple of miles along the coast, in Gorran – about a pacifist paper on 'Amnesty in Cornwall' and had raised Clemo's name: 'We talked about you, and he said that he would welcome poetical contributions from you'.[638] Clemo submitted a piece for almost every subsequent issue until his death. By 1989, Whetter had printed some thirty-six poems, and he wrote to Jack informing him of his intention to publish these in a single volume to be entitled *Banner Poems*. It happened very quickly. The collection was proposed in March 1989, the proofs arrived in Weymouth in May, and the volume launched in August, in Gorran, at an event led by Derek Savage with intervals of Whetter's daughters reading and playing the flute.

The volume itself Clemo considered unimportant. Even in his short preface, he described the contents as 'simple descriptive pieces', and he did not attend the launch, writing to Savage that 'the little booklet of about 30 short descriptive poems hardly seems to justify the expensive journey.'[639] It is easy to see why Clemo might have been disappointed. In the first instance, he had not put the poems together himself and did not have a very strong sense of ownership of them. Also, they were not intended to be collected. They were individual pieces, independent of one another, rather than parts of a whole. There is no sense of progression, no thematic movement or grouping, and the poems were published in plain chronological order. More than this, it was cheaply produced, typed on a typewriter and then photocopied on thin paper, folded and staple bound, all of which belies the fact that much of the work here is just as good as the collected poetry from the same period, and the cover is a delightfully appropriate clayscape drawing by Lionel Miskin.

The poems continue the theme of revisiting sites from Jack's childhood and upbringing – Mevagissey, Nanpean, Foxhole Beacon, the north coast – and reclaiming them, re-mapping the landscape, wiping clean the shame-shaded private geography and replacing it with a romantically and spiritually salvaged map. 'Nanpean' is a good example of the process:

> The inn-railings where the road dipped
> Sharply downhill, looked sinister
> At dusk or in moonlight, fifty years ago.
> I passed them on foot, always alone,
> Haunted by the creak of a dream,
> Listening for a crash on the bridge,
> In the stream, on the wharf and trucks
> Just outside the village.
>
> All's different now; I never turn that corner
> Except with my wife, in a friendly car,
> In clear daylight. How atmospheres
> Change, places are purged
> Of bristling omens, ghost-taps, leers!
> I feel the spread of summer
> Within the creative mind –
> Sun-sparkle on railings, the clay-tips refined
> By a kind of foreign climate, just like my marriage.

In 'Porthpean', meanwhile, Clemo comes close to a more typical ecopoeticism, concerned with change and negative impact on the landscape:

> Very thin, relatively harmless,
> The stains of oil on my wet legs:
> They wouldn't smother a gull
> Or poison a fish above minnow size.
> But I sigh, recalling

> The pure waves in which I danced and sported,
> With my young mother's eyes
> Never needing to search
> Each lifted ripple for the darting,
> Tanker-dropped, trade-reeking smirch.

Other notable poems include 'Arsenal', in which the poet-narrator recalls wandering past the 'claywork dynamite store', a 'sullen square of concrete / In a clearing where starved hazels screwed / Raggedly round the dune-trapped path', and 'Well at Bloomdale', where he recalls spending a day filling up an old well with stones. He had found the well 'quite near / Where the vast white clay-pit face / Dropped sheer to the flood-water'. It evokes the loneliness and isolation of that landscape, as well as the change and the absence of any sense of permanence. The well was no longer useful, but an impotent relic, or even a hazard to passersby.

The descriptions of place and landscape might not have been profound enough for Clemo, but they are evocative of a period and place that changed swiftly, with few reliable literary representatives. It is a landscape of destructive intimacy between man and the moorlands, a place inhabited by a rural working-class facilitating the eradication of the 'natural world'. The mining profession does not have the ambiguity of farm work, in which livestock or crops are perpetually nurtured and encouraged to grow and breed, while attention is paid to the seasons and weather. There is an easily implied wholesomeness to farming which is less evident in the pit work of clay quarries. Before Clemo, the clayscape had never inspired a significant native poet. Clemo's writing stands alone in representing the period, identity, class and rural industry of a substantial regional group, and *Banner Poems* is a useful addition to the Clemo canon.

A second unexpected publication, *Clay Cuts*, was proposed at the end of 1990. *Clay Cuts* was the inspiration of Dennis Hall of Hanborough Parrots, an Oxford-based publisher who had made a similar volume with Anne Stevenson. It is a beautifully produced artistic book of some of Clemo's clay poetry with woodcuts by Stan Dobbin. Only 186 copies were printed, each signed by both Dobbin and Clemo, with a small number of them hand-coloured. Initially,

Hall says, he approached Charles Causley, but Causley declined and recommended his friend Jack Clemo. In the Spring of 1991, Dobbin was on his way to Cornwall to make some drawings. While there, he could not resist making cuts of Falmouth Dockyards, which appear anomalously in the book.

In his diary, Clemo had been excited by the prospect of *Clay Cuts*, considering the selection of poems to be good, with material from every one of his works, but later, when writing to Michael Spinks, he dismissed it as 'just an incidental reprint'.

Clay Cuts was published in 1991 and launched at Sterts Theatre on Bodmin Moor on 14 January 1992, as part of the 'Festival of Poetry'. The festival was running all week and included Kneehigh Theatre's performance of Nick Darke's *Ting Tang Mine* and the folk band Show of Hands. Clemo stayed with Father Benedict Ramsden in Devon the night before, and Ramsden drove them to the event, where he read Clemo's poetry. In spite of Clemo's reservations, the event was a success. Ramsden gave a terrific performance, there were twice the expected number of attendees and the books sold well. Clemo 'enjoyed the launch more than I expected to.' Indeed, the launch and the book were such a success that Dennis Hall wrote enthusiastically soon afterwards, suggesting they make another book together, with Father Benedict writing the introduction. The theme would be 'Women and Weymouth'. Hall hastily threw together a dummy copy, which would include some Cornish themes, nudes and later some Weymouth cuts. Unfortunately, the nudes bothered the Clemos, and Jack wrote in reply with the statement: 'in these days nude art is associated in the public mind with pagan values'. Instead of the nudes, perhaps Hall would consider 'a veiled figure kneeling at a church altar.'[640] Clemo sent a list of fifteen poems he would want to comprise the volume, though half of these were biographical or Italian and would not suit the idea of place-based poetry, which was Hall's speciality. The volume Hall wanted to make, Clemo did not, and the volume Clemo wanted to make, Hall did not. Politely and carefully, Hall backed away.

At the same time, Bloodaxe accepted Clemo's latest collection, *Approach to Murano*. Clemo had completed it in October 1990 and written to Neil Astley, but did not get a reply until Ruth chased him on the telephone the following year. Astley was enthusiastic, accepting the manuscript but warning that the publication date depended on funding. The book was further delayed by a series of court cases, in which Bloodaxe were suing distributors and marketers, and *Approach to Murano* did not appear until 1993. As the book was accepted, Clemo wrote sadly and candidly to himself that *Murano* 'isn't major Christian witness, but it's infinitely better than that nothing ahead'.[641] Clemo doubted the quality and importance of this latest collection. He apparently did not share these doubts with his friends, but kept his sense of disappointment and bleakness about the future private. The diaries in these years are sparser, with brief scratchy entries of a single line or two, as Clemo's moods are dulled, and the feeling is of more frequent 'blank days' passing.

The material for *Approach to Murano* came from a broad period, incorporating poems from three decades, the earliest seeming to be 'Hudson Taylor to Maria', written in 1975, and the latest 'Perennial', written in the middle of 1990. The forty-two poems are grouped into five sections: the first introduces Italy, Weymouth and the move from Cornwall; the second is biographical; the third is about friendships in England, generally speaking outside of Weymouth and Cornwall; the fourth is biographical again; and the fifth is about Venice. Of the biographical poems, there is little to add from earlier accounts. They cover familiar subjects, including Emily Brontë, Hardy and C.S. Lewis, and add to these a couple of new subjects, such as the nineteenth century Cornish miner-poet John Harris, and the Dorset writer and dialect poet William Barnes.

The richness and tightness of form and narrative are no longer as obvious as earlier collections, but there are still some strong and exact images. A fair example of the new, looser style working might be 'Perennial':

> Modern lights in Venice
> Do not annul, or even distort,
> Tradition's dowry. When the trespassing glow
> Saps the haunting moon-flutter on St Mark's,
> On quaint shops, canal craft, statues in squares,
> The classic soul still breathes uncheapened.

> At night-drop in English cities the fagged crowds
> Sharpen in illusion, seeing the cold
> Steady white wave teem with traffic,
> But here no vehicle, no jolt of brakes,
> Shakes the ancient road. There are only footsteps,
> Footsteps and low voices: you think of lanterns
> And torches bobbing a thousand years ago.
>
> Fancy the relevant dream-drawn walkers'
> Plod across bridges and islands
> To a church rite or a lovers' rendezvous!
> Modern light, falling on roads unbruised
> By dubious transport, cannot distort,
> Much less annul, our primal trysts.

It is not Clemo's most exciting poem, but it is an evocative and perceptive touristic meditation. The obscurity that sometimes results from the use of personal experience and perspective is not present here. Or, rather, the experience is more fully presented.

In twelve years, *Approach to Murano* sold four hundred copies, most of these in the first few months, with smaller peaks of sales when subsequent works about Clemo were produced. Critically, reviewers were kind. In July 1993, Alwyn Marriage, a friendly contact of the Clemos, wrote in her magazine, *Christian*: 'It is refreshing to find a poet celebrating the increased happiness of age, rather than looking back nostalgically to lost youth.' Adam Thorpe, in the *Observer*, added: 'The book has an extraordinary integrity to it, cupped in a style both conversationally tender and glisteningly etched, with the transparent weight of crystal.'[642] A review in the *Times*, on the other hand, compared Clemo's latest efforts quite unfavourably with his earlier work. Robert Nye had written, on 28 October 1993, that the volume

> requires some acquaintance with the harsher vision of his early work, if it is not to seem benign to the point of banality. [...] The trouble is that the Clemo of the clay-pit days had a fierceness to his thought and feeling which is quite absent from his present lucubrations.

Father Benedict Ramsden responded to this review in a 2002 article that was never published, entitled 'More than a Poet':

> *The Times* lamented the loss of fierceness in Clemo's later work. As with Eliot, the critics who had loved *The Waste Land* did not want to follow him out of it. Hell and clay-pits are to the critic far more exciting than heaven, which is very difficult to write about.

Ramsden continued: 'If we find his late poetry less satisfying than the awesome early stuff, it is perhaps because we find sustained joy no less a castigation of our own joylessness.' This seems true, but it is not only 'a castigation of our own joylessness' that is the problem. It is not just that the reader 'did not want to follow' Clemo out of hell, but that they could not follow. They were not convinced by Jack's route out of the clay-pit. The pain, isolation, turmoil and anxiety of the earlier work people could understand, believe in and follow, but Clemo's route out was unfamiliar, unexperienced. The earlier position was more universally plausible and sympathisable, but when Clemo began writing about his evangelical triumph in an exotically palm-laden Weymouth, he was appealing to a reduced readership.

The collection's joy and fulfilment is now contrasted against the grim, distant clay-land past, so clay means something different in these later volumes. It is no longer the purifying slurry that baptized the clay-worker in 'The Excavator', but the thing in need of purification, a 'clay-blight'. Murano glass is the new model of perfection and lucidity here, while later, in *The Cured Arno*, the preferred metaphor is the murky Florentine river being clarified.

Approach to Murano had several promotional launches, first in Exeter and Bude, and then with a reading at Torrington. Paul Hyland and Ramsden read the poetry, with many of Clemo's friends and fans attending, including Ron Tamplin and Alan Kent. But the clear skies of the collection, the poetry and the public attention, were clouded by sickness; early signs of a terminal problem. These started in 1992. At the beginning of the year, both Ruth and Jack were ill, and '1992 opened darkly', as Clemo wrote in the New Year. But it was in the summer, in August, that serious problems began.

'Sudden crisis', Jack wrote in his diary, elaborating in a letter to Derek Savage: 'I was taken to hospital in great pain through a blockage, and stayed trussed with tubes for five days'. The immediate trouble was thought to be his prostate, and he spent several nights in the hospital, with Ruth in the chair at his bedside. A memory he relayed to Savage was of lying in bed on the Sunday, with the hospital television on and Ruth beating time to the hymns of *Songs of Praise* on the back of his hand. But in hospital, all the joy sapped out of him. His faith, Clemo wrote to himself, 'struggled against a nightmare of isolation, bewilderment and panic.'[643] Jack always responded to hospitals in this way, with this feeling of joy lost and of being abandoned by God, and he would feel it more often now, as the sickness progressed and hospital visits became more frequent. Jack was discharged in September and told to return for tests later in the month, possibly for an operation. He received a Get Well card signed by many of the Cornish literary establishment, including D.M. Thomas, Philip Payton, Bert Biscoe and Donald Rawe, but the pain persisted and as soon as Jack had left Dorchester Hospital new symptoms developed, including fever, vomiting and non-stop hiccups. He could not think or sleep and he had to return to the ward, where he stayed for twelve more days, 'Drugged and confused'. They performed tests and determined to operate in October, but the symptoms and another 'blockage' meant he spent little time away from hospital.

His diary describes the feeling of being anaesthetized for the operation:

> Ruth was with me at the beginning and end of the ordeal. I felt I was sinking into a deep freeze, dead from the waist down for four hours shivering while the surgeon worked on me. No pain, but a frightening loss of identity.[644]

Clemo did respond poetically to his stay in Dorchester Hospital, a piece that stands in stark contradiction to the diary accounts. Rather than confusion and panic, the poet describes a buoyant state of mind, contrasting his happiness with the misery of other men on the ward:

> My soul breathed a more genial air
> Than that of average sufferers: I was nourished
> Only by joy and the years of exemption
> When no ill-wind cut to the heart. My faith
> Pulled clear of plausible doubts
> And honest wintry surmises. I grasped
> Always the pledge of unfailing spring,
> Even here with Hardy's statue forbidding.

The moral is forced – almost dutiful – and the poem was written in November, a little while after the event. It appears to be a re-telling of the story as it ought to have been, rather than how it was. The 'last optimist' Jack Clemo could not be seen to falter in sickness.

During the operation, the surgeon removed an 'enlargement [...] as big as an apple', Clemo told Savage, and 'by some medical marvel it was sucked out in tiny fragments through my catheter tube'. The operation was a short-term success, and it sounds like Clemo had kidney stones, though the letters and diaries suggest further symptoms and a deeper issue belying Clemo's condition, perhaps prostatitis or prostate cancer. There were more troubles in the New Year, which meant that Jack had to undergo scans of his bladder in February after what he describes as a 'relapse' of his symptoms. His 'blackouts' returned in April. These were fainting spells or absences usually attributed to his irregular pulse and problems with his heart. Silently, beneath the distracting surface of symptoms, a cancer grew and spread undiagnosed. Tests and scans were administered almost monthly, Clemo grew weak and felt sluggish, and the blackouts became more frequent. In 1994, the pains in his stomach were almost unbearable, even with strong medication.

Jack became uneasy about his faith, life and work. His now nearly bare diary shows a concern for the absence of answered prayer and the need for something to 'save me from fear of rejection.'[645] It appears that the cancer was undiscovered until the month of Clemo's death in July 1994. In April, Clemo reports that the doctor was still 'puzzled by my symptoms and worried because I don't recover.'

Most remarkable about this period of deterioration, spiritual doubt and the loss of inspired joy, is the fate-defying activity of the

Clemos. Immediately after that initial operation in 1992, Jack did not go home for a period of recuperation, but within the week was staying with Alwyn Marriage to attend a Donald Davie lecture on Clemo's poetry at the University of Surrey in Guildford. One result of the event was a series of portraits drawn by the artist Heather Spears, best known for her sketches of terminally ill children. Spears drew both Clemo and Davie quickly and effectively, with a focus on the movement of fingers writing in the palm of Jack's hand – that pinpoint through which the outside world entered.

Back home the following day, Jack, Ruth and Bella settled in for a quiet Christmas before the Labdons came down to celebrate New Year. None of them were well. Jack was in and out of hospital, Bella was suffering from arthritis and bleeding varicose veins, while Ruth also had arthritis and cataracts. Nevertheless, they all went along to the Plough Arts Centre in Torrington to hear Paul Hyland read, and they still went down to Cornwall. Earlier in the year, they were forced to cancel a trip while Jack was in hospital, so they missed a celebratory evening in Clemo's honour and an exhibition at Wheal Martyn Museum of newly acquired manuscripts and furniture from the Goonamarris cottage.

Most astounding of all is that in August 1993 the Clemos decided to make another Italian journey, more demanding than the previous one, to celebrate their silver wedding anniversary and the publication of *Approach to Murano*. Again, Father Benedict and his family acted as guides – especially the oldest daughter Sara, to whom *The Cured Arno* was dedicated. (All dedications in *The Cured Arno*, it should be noted, were added by Ruth later, rather than by Jack.) With the knowledge that they were all in foul health, with Jack's fainting and sickness and the Peaty sisters' inhibited mobility, this trip was a bizarre leap of faith.

When Robert and Elizabeth Barrett Browning ran away to Italy, they first arrived in Pisa, where they spent the winter before travelling to Florence in April 1847. The Clemos followed their route. On 15 September, the party flew in to Pisa, from where they took a train inland to Florence. 'Very tired, but the sun shone on the Arno', Jack noted. They stayed four days in Florence, wandering the streets and bridges, having lunch under the replica of Michelangelo's 'David' in the Piazza della Signoria, and pursuing the 'Browning pattern', receiving special permission to enter the Browning apartment in Casa Guidi. In a letter to Victor Perry, Clemo wrote how they were admitted into these closed apartments:

> The highlight of the tour was our visit to the Brownings' old home – Casa Guidi, in Florence – in a sad state of neglect now unfurnished and closed to the public. We were admitted only after Benedict showed the curator my Browning poems in Murano. I was thrilled to stand in the study where he wrote *Christmas Eve and Easter Day*, and had soon written a poem about the experience when we got back to Weymouth.[646]

This poem was dedicated to Father Benedict and entitled 'Casa Guidi'.

> I step to a window ornate but shuttered,
> And imagine San Felice church
> In the palace shade, where regular chanting voices
> Jarred on him somewhat, yet attuned him
> (Though less than Elizabeth's plumed kiss)
> To the blue sky of a robust summer faith.

It draws the required comparison, the impact on Clemo's romance:

> His tangle of key meanings, clues to God,
> Led straight to the heart of my marriage.

The poem ends with Jack and Ruth physically fusing the connection, standing on the same balcony paced by the Brownings:

> Soon I shall stand on the balcony,
> My wife's hand and mine on a roughly-carved cherub.
> The same sun burnished Via Maggio
> When that pair slowly paced the terrace,
> Discussing Euripides or Cavour,

Or merely recalling Wimpole Street
And their life of wonders unfolding.

In his diary, Jack records this moment, the holiday's peak:

> An unforgettable morning. We were shown over Casa Guidi. Walked on the balcony where R and E often strolled. And in the bedroom, sitting room, and Browning's study. I gave the curator a copy of Murano.

In an annotated note to the 1976 diary, Ruth had written how Jack 'often hummed tunes to himself when he was very happy', and in Casa Guidi the hymn 'Breathe on me, breath of God' rose in him.

They pursued the Brownings by taxi to Vallombrosa: 'Climbed to the monk's church and the monastery from which EBB was barred. Such heat and peace among the chestnut woods.' Or, at least, Clemo *believed* this is what happened. According to the Ramsdens, they never went as far as the Abbey. It was a long way for Ruth and Bella to go with their arthritis, and a long way to lead Jack. The Ramsdens believe that Ruth misinformed her husband, telling him they had arrived at Vallombrosa when they were still some distance away.

Following this, the group fought their way onto the only train running during a rail-strike, taking a long ride among Tuscan hills and groves to Venice, 'our dream city'. For another three days, the Clemos revisited St Mark's Cathedral (where former Soviet president Mikhail Gorbachev happened to be in the congregation with them) as well as the Bridge of Sighs. They took photos of themselves outside a Murano glass factory and went back to the Palazzo Rezzonico. They were very active, though there were signs that Jack was not altogether well. He was incredibly slow getting about and several times he mentioned how exhausted he was.

The majority of the poems in *The Cured Arno* were written after the pains that hospitalised Jack in the summer of 1992. There are forty-one poems, with only two from an earlier period: 'Cloud over Bugle', from 1980, about proposals for a nuclear power station in the clay country, and 'Growing in Grace', a poem that deserves consideration.

'Growing in Grace' was begun in July 1949, and it was one of two poems written about the prospect of leaving Cornwall to live with Eileen Funston, along with 'Priest out of Bondage'. In 1950, following Jack's trip to the Powyses in Mappowder, the location of the poem was moved from Cornwall to Dorset and it was published as 'Dorset Mood' in the spring 1952 edition of *West Country Magazine*. Later, in 1975, Clemo revisited 'Dorset Mood', pruning it back almost unrecognisably. This new version was published as 'Growing in Grace' in Eveline Clemo's *I Proved Thee at the Waters*. The 1975 edit is identical to that of *The Cured Arno* (save for one possessive apostrophe and orthodox ellipses), and is something of an oddity in Clemo's last collection.

The poem as it appeared in *West Country Magazine* was about fulfilment in Dorset. The first of its nine stanzas states its intent:

> Fantastic Cornish clay-land – how
> Shall its idiom satisfy me now
> I have stood and dreamed on Bulbarrow's brow?

There follows a descriptive section of jarring images and sounds from the industrial clayscape – a 'deafening clang', 'scarred entrails' – and the statement that those old clay images had failed him:

> Purgation's landscape failed to purge,
> But left me with each human urge
> Fouled by the fear of slapping surge
>
> From hose-jets, gore of pouncing tool;
> Rotted by stagnant water, cruel
> Mauling micas. Dogma's rule
>
> Was here but travestied by coarse
> Bleared symbols […]

The original version, written for Eileen in 1949, was seventeen stanzas long and entitled 'Dubiety at Dawn'. It can be found in handwritten form in the original *The Clay Verge* manuscript. When Clemo typed this up for submission, he cut off the final four stanzas, though otherwise left it very much the same, altering the title to 'Moment of Dubiety'.[647] In the earlier versions, the poet had denounced his homeland, declaring: 'I am tired of Cornwall, tired of clay'. In the 1950 Dorset version, Clemo pushed beyond this stormy clayland angst and firmly towards fulfilment, when marriage and physical healing were to coincide and Jack and Susie Clemo would be looking out of their windows of agates over the unravaged downs around Mappowder and Bulbarrow. 'Dorset Mood' ended prophetically:

> By wood-fanned Stour my sight's restored:
> Those crouched claywork thorns accord
> Only with soul that never soared.

He has emerged from the depths and is beginning a new phase. The poet is again on the cusp of contentment. It has begun. He raises his head out of the clay-pits, the old symbols and suffering are over, his eyes are clearing, the 'clay-world stain' has been washed away, and a new set of 'soaring' symbols become visible.

But by 1975, Clemo's eyes were not clear, and neither Eileen nor Susie had proved his intended bride and saviour. He was married to Ruth and still living in the clays. 'Growing in Grace', then, is boiled down to three truncated stanzas, reproduced in full here:

> My native clay
> Symbols grow unreal.
> Blunt clanging tools
> Corroded rock
> Kiln-scorching…
> O shepherd
> Of green pastures!
>
> Purgation's landscape
> Fails to purge,
> Makes us afraid.
> Slap of hose-jets
> Blinding
> Deafening blast

Rattle on bleared dunes
Scoops' and sirens'
Howl over stagnant mud.

Waters of Meribah.
I proved thee at the…
I proved thee.
Baptised into the death…
O shepherd
Of green pastures!

The minimal punctuation causes the ellipses and the final exclamation mark to stand out. Vestigial lines and impressionistic descriptive fragments mark an experiment in form found nowhere else in Clemo's work. As a whole, it might even seem a weary piece, the lines never forming and some of them trailing off, if it were not for the emphatic end. Note how the clay landscape 'failed' to purge in the 1950 version. The failure is in the past. In the 1975 version, however, the failure is current and continuous; it 'fails'. This was, of course, because Clemo believed he was turning his back on the clayscape in the earlier version, though in 1975 he was settled again, still in the cottage but now with his wife.

Viewed in another way, as a poem with a half-century of history, the first two stanzas of 'Growing in Grace' look like a mosaic of 'Dorset Mood' – 'corroded rock', 'slap of hose-jets', 'Purgation's landscape', 'blunt', 'bleared'. The old narrative poem of emergence has been chopped up, the parts that do not apply discarded. But instead of creating a new narrative sort of poem, which was his usual method of reworking, Clemo left the charred fragments on the page where they fell, remnants of that anticlimactic squib. But then in the final stanza is a new mosaic, salvaging the scorched remains. It is biblical. The 'waters of Meribah' return, only inverted, no longer 'I proved thee at the waters of Meribah', but: 'Waters of Meribah. / I proved thee at the…' A reason for this might be the double meaning of 'proof' in the Bible, as discussed by Spurgeon in his exposition of Psalm 81, where a proof is a test. In 'Growing in Grace', the 'Waters of Meribah' represent the tests Clemo has undergone and passed. The repeated phrase, 'I proved thee', seems to be dramatic and emphatic. The next piece of the biblical mosaic is the line 'Baptised into the death', which is from Paul's Epistle to the Romans 6:3-4:

> Know ye not, that so many of us as were baptized into Jesus Christ were baptized into his death?
> Therefore we are buried with him by baptism into death: that like as Christ was raised up from the dead by the glory of the Father, even so we also should walk in newness of life.

The narrator has been tested and proved, and as a result comes the promise of 'newness of life'. The narrator's reward in 'Growing in Grace' is his salvation, and the final part of the poem is the moment of praise: 'O Shepherd / Of green pastures'. This is from Psalm 23:

> The LORD *is* my shepherd; I shall not want.
> He maketh me to lie down in green pastures: he leadeth me beside the still waters.
> He restoreth my soul: he leadeth me in the paths of righteousness for his name's sake.
> Yea, though I walk through the valley of the shadow of death, I will fear no evil: for thou *art* with me; thy rod and thy staff they comfort me.
> Thou preparest a table before me in the presence of mine enemies: thou anointest my head with oil; my cup runneth over.
> Surely goodness and mercy shall follow me all the days of my life: and I will dwell in the house of the LORD for ever

The testing, the saving, and the praise.

The biographical elements chopped about in the first two stanzas are completely absent in this final one. The poet has relinquished his ego, handed himself over to God full-bloodedly, and become purified. There is nothing of him left, only what is in Christ. It is an intelligent and original poem of triumph, and one of the most noteworthy pieces of *The Cured Arno*.

But perhaps the most obviously impressive poem of the collection was the last Clemo ever wrote, and it was not certainly intended for inclusion in the volume. It was found by Ruth written upside down near the back of a red Silvine notebook. This is the only booklet in the archives that is not crammed full of drafts and corrections. It has only three poems in the front – 'Lulworth', 'Fever Zone' and 'Fitting In' – while right in the back is the order in which the *Cured Arno* poems are intended to appear. Clemo died before the collection could be submitted to a publisher, but his ordering was adhered to. However, 'Quenched' hangs in the back of the notebook alone, and there is some discrepancy between its various drafts. There are three versions available. The earliest is written on blue notepaper, from a travelling notebook, as they were away from home, and it was labelled by Ruth, 'First Rough Draft'. It shows the usual pages of corrections, although some pages are clearly missing. The second version is the one in the red notebook and appears to be the poem as Clemo wished it. The third version is the one published in *The Cured Arno*. So we have the blue, the red and the published versions, and no two are identical. Here is the poem as it was published:

> I have returned in fitful spring rain
> To the knot of hills that will never untwist
> In trick lighting again, as it did while I lived here.
> The hill-knot fantasy has been abolished:
> Its switches are stiff and unused, ignoring the sunsets.
> No current jabs at the clotting shadows
> With strange hints of industrial magic.
>
> Tip-flare, pit-spurt, tank-twinkle –
> They thrilled me for years, but they have gone.
> The hamlet dwellers are dismayed
> By the sudden plunge into wartime blackout,
> A daily trauma, the final sting
> Of failure in trade bargaining.

> I'm glad I escaped this blow:
> The clay fantasy blazed around my cottage
> When I last slept there. I had watched it, drawn
> Into a glow of mystery, not costs and markets.
> But I avoid the house now:
> Its dark night has no message for me.

The published and the red versions are very similar. In the first stanza, there are only minor variations, a few punctuation alterations and two minor word changes. The second stanza is identical, but the final stanza shows one or two variations. The red version has the line 'When I last slept here', which the published version alters to 'When I last slept there'. The change from 'here' to 'there' is probably an error, since in the first stanza the narrator has already located himself as 'here', at the site of the cottage, and it might be inconsistent to then distance himself without any narrative development. But more importantly, in the published version the final line reads: 'Its dark night has no message for me.' The 'dark night' references St John of the Cross again, and his painful process of ascetic separation from the world before being drawn to God. It also echoes the poet's observation of the old arc-lights of the clay works that used to shine at night having been extinguished. In the red version, however, there is no 'dark night', but only a 'dark hour'. The darkness is just a moment, bereft of the symbolism of asceticism. It is a more informal, colloquial and less allusive phrase. The old cottage is not a symbol of the process of detachment from the world that might lead to God's gathering up of the mystic, but more simply an image of misery. The changes appear to have been made after Clemo's death, and most probably in the typing up of the poem, which was done by Ruth.

The plot thickens when looking at the earliest draft of the poem, the blue version. The blue version shows Clemo's first attempt, followed by a few pages of alterations. These alterations were applied when Clemo came to write the poem up into the red notebook. The problem is that in this blue version, the final line has that published phrase, 'dark night':

> I am glad I escaped this blow:
> The clay fantasy blazed around my cottage
> During my last sleep here…
> But I turn away now
> Its dark night has no message for me.

So, in the earliest (blue) version it is 'dark night', in the updated (red) version it is 'dark hour', and in the published version it is 'dark night' again. Why was 'dark night' reinstated, and by whom? Could there be another draft between the red version and the published? Or did Ruth compound the drafts to include it? If she did, then it is the only reversion to the blue draft she made. In any event, there appears to be no evidence that the published version, the 'dark night', was Clemo's intention.

Perhaps, with a heightened sense of his own mortality, the 'dark hour' was a reference back to 'Prisoner of God', the painful opening poem of Clemo's first collection, and that early anxious question 'from the depths':

> Why elate
> Upon that Easter turret of Your power
> When I am buried still in His dark hour
> And *her* heaven mocks us both?

Might the last line of Clemo's final poem be a return to the first – the last and greatest reclamation?

When Paul Hyland presented the manuscript of *The Cured Arno* to Neil Astley, he included a note expressing regret at the overall quality: 'You're good, doing *The Cured Arno*, and finding the right cover painting. I do wish it was a better book'.[648] The response of reviewers justified Hyland's concerns. Friends tended to be supportive, but otherwise, critics were underwhelmed, and when they bothered to review the book at all it was mostly negative. In 1996, Anna Adams, writing in *Acumen*, stated:

> The late poems seem egocentric and self-congratulatory. Perhaps Clemo was entitled to be complacent after

so difficult a life, but cruising about in the sheltered waters of his seventies he seems to be writing the journal of a Saga tourist.

Mario Petrucci put the same point into a more sympathetic and entertaining phrase for *Ambit* 149: 'The Cured Arno is a master craftsman's Anglo-Italianate Cook's-tour cum hagiography in verse.' The awkward diction was again frequently referenced, and the overall sense was of a sad decline of power. 'Quenched' was singled out as the most successful and complete poem of the collection, a poignant return to the clay country and to the old language of the works.

'Quenched' had been drafted at Gwen's house in Newquay during their last visit, on 21 May 1994. This trip was an unnecessary strain on Clemo. Diary entries in the weeks preceding it are filled with discomfort and unease. Yet, on 19 May: 'Went to Cornwall in faith, as I don't feel in holiday trim. Ruth and Bella need a rest and change.' Clemo was so ill, with nausea and spinal pain, that he had to be pushed around in a wheelchair, and it is difficult to see how the Peaty sisters could justify their decision to go on holiday when he was so unmistakably sick.

Within a week of returning home, 'Things have grown rather worse', and Jack makes an effort to find a solicitor to rewrite his will. He only writes four more diary entries after this, the first remarking on having found a solicitor; the second mistakenly believing that Exeter had refused to take the remainder of his manuscripts; the third, on 18 June, 'Worried about bleeding ulcers in stomach'. The final entry is difficult to read, but appears to say: 'Some Christian white "Africans" called here. I gave them *I.G* and *S.B.* My influence spreads unlike my work is.' This was 23 June 1994, and Ruth has filled in the following month's entries. It is sad reading:

> 27 June: Doctor came – tried to get Jack into hospital
> 28 June: Hospital – Bleeding Internally
> Very weak
> 29 June: They tried to give Jack an x-ray – But he was too ill to co-operate
> 30 June: Dr had a look into Jack's stomach

> 1 July: The awful day we had the verdict on Jack's tests –
> He has inoperable growth in top of his stomach
> 2 July: In hospital
> 3 July: In hospital
> 4 July: In hospital
> Trying to stabilize him so he can come home for a while.

Father Benedict Ramsden's personal diaries continue the narrative from a different perspective. They begin where Ruth ends, on 4 July:

> Ruth rang me today to say that he is dying. He has a cancer somewhere in his oesophagus – Can't take food and is nourished by intravenous drip. Ruth won't have him told he is dying – which I think is insulting to such a man – the author of three volumes of frank, objective autobiography, sheltered from the final facts – so sad.

Two days later, 6 July, the priest visits his friend in hospital:

> The visit itself was very strange; the usual mixture of sheer horror and fraughtness from Ruth, and, to a slightly lesser extent, Bella. But the other ingredient was Jack, looking far beyond all that – a man of dignity – a mystic and a poet and one of the great influences on my life. I looked back at him as I left. He was lying in bed in a blue nightshirt and he looked remarkably fine, and even beautiful.
>
> There is a strange tidying up of things as someone dies, and a rounding off. The story is done and now it can begin to be sorted out. When Jack is dead, perhaps I can sort out what I really think of his work as distinct from all the frass of his marriage […].
>
> At his house, where we dropped off Ruth and Bella, I looked at two photographs – one of Jack as a quite young child, bright-eyed and intelligent, in the

arms of a rather gaunt looking young mother – the other of him as a young man in a boat. So much mist, such thwartings, and out of it comes what? Is it inspiration or compensation? Is there a God or do we kid ourselves? I must say, that when marriage is the great sign of Covenant, it seems to me to mean something a little more idyllic than the awfulness of Ruth.

Yet there was one special moment – just as I was leaving the ward, the dignified, silver-haired poet-prophet, puckered his lips to kiss Ruth and I saw for a moment, the lover – the faith Cana-vindicated.

This vision of Jack as a lover, rather than a dying man, was important to Father Benedict. Later, another moment struck him, told to Benedict by Ruth. Apparently, during this period of hospitalization between 28 June and 14 July, that familiar hospital feeling overwhelmed Jack again, and he asked his wife, 'Where has all the joy gone?'[649] It moved Ramsden that Clemo admitted with surprise and regret when this joy left him. It implied that usually within the quiet and sunken husk of Clemo's body there echoed that music, part hymnal, part ragtime.

On 14 July, Jack was sent home to be cared for by Ruth and Bella with the help of Macmillan nurses. There is a photo of him at this time, sitting in a deckchair in the garden with an ice cream. He would not eat much else. They tried giving him high-protein drinks, but he was dying, growing weak and confused and worrying about his work. On one day, the Hortons visited, and the decision was made to drive him out to Portland, the last trip Jack would make.

A week later, on 24 July, Jack took a sudden and violent turn for the worse, vomiting great amounts of blood. He was rushed into Weymouth and District Hospital suffering a massive hemorrhage. Ruth and Bella stayed with him through the night as they tried to draw out the blood, but in the morning, at 6:30am on 25 July, he died.

In a letter to a friend who had also lost a family member, Ruth described the end movingly:

My experience at Jack's death was nowhere near so wonderful as yours, no feeling of Joy just terrible loss and sadness. I felt Jack was meant to live at least two more years, he was prayed over and anointed with oil etc and we all felt God was going to get a wonderful victory and Jack was going to be healed! I did however feel the rapid heartbeat just before he died the same as you did […] I had been with Jack all night in hospital lying quite close to him […]. He did not say any last words I could not whisper in his ear because he was deaf! I was trying to get through to him by writing on his palm which is how we communicated, but he was too weak to take it in as it needs a lot of concentration and he was being given morphia. The last words that passed his lips in this world were 'no pain' after I ask him on his hand the day before if he had pain after the morphia injection that was his answer.[650]

The funeral was held at Weymouth Baptist Church a week later, with a memorial service in Cornwall in September, where Father Benedict Ramsden, Andrew Symons, Paul Hyland, Norman Stone and Robert Duncan spoke in tribute of their old friend. Jack had chosen the hymns 'O Love that will not let me go', 'Breathe on me, Breath of God' and 'When I survey the Wondrous Cross'. The main reading was to be 2 Timothy 4:7: 'For I am now ready to be offered, and the time of my departure is at hand. I have fought a good fight, I have finished my course, I have kept the faith…'

Jack and Ruth, 1980

Postscript

After Clemo's death, the decline of interest in his work steepened. Cornish scholars rifled through the archives, in search of new material, and what they used and published were old, rejected manuscripts and abandoned verse. It was not until 2015 that any of his published poetry was brought back into print, when Enitharmon produced their *Selected Poems*, introduced by Rowan Williams. To date, no 'Collected Poems' has appeared, no reissue of *Confession of a Rebel* or *Wilding Graft*. The only works of Clemo's to have been made available since his death and *The Cured Arno* have been the failed novels and juvenilia, such as *The Clay Kiln*, discussed in Chapter V, and *The Awakening*. *The Awakening* is typical of the rushed approach to Clemo scholarship in recent years, suffering from a lack of definition and including some significant mistakes and questionable decisions. The most unfortunate of the obvious errors is the poem 'Clay Fairy', which has been published incomplete for the simple reason that the researchers did not turn the manuscript page, where they would have found the second half of the poem. It is also worth noting that as a tentative attempt at an 'Uncollected' edition, *The Awakening* is gapingly incomplete. In the *Cornish Guardian* archive alone a further forty poems might be retrieved – a quantity of verse exceeding that represented in the book. This is before considering the poems contributed to the Torch Trust newsletters, or the poems in the diaries, letters, literary magazines and other early verses scattered throughout the archives. There is still much work to be done.

Of the most notable people working on Clemo, Alan Kent has

probably published the greatest volume, including chapters in many of his studies of Cornish literature and history, such as *The Literature of Cornwall*, *Pulp Methodism* and *Wives, Mothers and Sisters*. Kent was born in the clay country and is a sympathetic critic and champion of Clemo's work. John Hurst, meanwhile, is probably the most rigorous and notable of the Clemo scholars in Cornwall. Hurst worked through a limited archive at the University of Exeter, producing a very useful paper for *Cornish Studies Three* in 1995. This was before some of the hefty biographical material, such as the diaries, had been donated to the collection.

In terms of poetic and literary influence, Clemo's legacy can be difficult to trace. He appears overtly in some very small publications, such as Brian Louis Pearce's *Clemo the Poet*, Alan Kent's sequence in *Modern Cornish Poets* and David Woolley's *Written on our Hands*, as well as occasionally in a volume like Toby Martinez de las Rivas's 2014 *Terror*, a dense and daunting Faber & Faber debut that included the poem 'Jack Clemo' in its 'Triptych for the Disused Non-Conformist Chapel, Wildhern'. Clemo has made cameo appearances in a number of prominent ecoliterary settings, including Jeremy Hooker's *Openings* and Paul Farley and Michael Symmons Roberts' *Edgelands*, and he was granted a chapter in Philip Marsden's *Rising Ground*.

Within the clay community around St Austell, Clemo's legacy has been threatened, undermined and then lovingly salvaged in a number of ways. In 2009, he was included in a large trompe l'oeil by Janet Shearer on what was once The General Wolfe pub at the west end of Fore Street. The mural is of prominent St Austell figures sitting outside a café, and includes A.L. Rowse, John Nettles, William Cookworthy, Daphne du Maurier and Bishop Colenso among many others. Jack is sitting to the right of the painting, next to the aviator Captain Percival Phillips.

In Trethosa Chapel, a 'Jack Clemo Memorial Room' was founded in 2001, opened by Ruth Clemo and the novelist E.V. Thompson. It was assembled by the remaining chapel-goers and overseen by a Stepaside man, Alan Sanders. The material held here was threatened in 2013, when the chapel was forced to close. Its reduced congregation, however loyal and resolute, could not afford to keep Trethosa open any longer. Wheal Martyn Museum rescued the chapel collection, restoring Clemo's humble writing desk for permanent exhibition and relocating the material to the safety of their exhibitions and archives. Among this material was a replica of the Clemo cottage made by Andy Hawken of Indian Queens. This is a huge model, built in part as a response to the demolition of the Clemo cottage by Goonvean China Clay Company. The demolition was a fiercely emotive issue, frequently reported in the local press through 2000 and 2001. The cottage had been boarded up by Goonvean due to vandalism, and they told newspapers they needed to build a laboratory complex on the site. Proposals were made to dismantle the cottage and rebuild it brick by brick at Wheal Martyn, which proved a prohibitively costly plan. By 2005, Goonvean had grown impatient and they tore down the cottage. As Alan Sanders said in *Roots of my Story*:

> They had every right to knock it down. They owned the building, it wasn't habitable, the council had condemned it for human occupation, so they were quite entitled […]. On the other side, we've now knocked down a part of Cornish heritage.

The site today retains the old stone wall, but there is still no laboratory. Behind the wall, over the rubble and levelled ground is an overgrown scrub of bramble, gorse and hawthorn on the edge of a car park surrounded by recently constructed corrugated buildings. Although Andy Hawken denies the suggestion, it is generally believed that his model of the cottage was built using granite from the original walls and slate from the roof retrieved from the demolition site.

The year following Clemo's death, the Arts Centre Group founded a 'Jack Clemo Poetry Competition', organized by Christian music journalist Tony Jasper. It was started after Clemo left a bequest to the ACG in his will and has run ever since.

There has been, then, a continuous loyal group of readers within Christian poetics and Cornish literary studies, but the absence of publications of his work outside of these minority groups has had the effect of reducing, or containing, his general readership. This trajectory might be traced back to the late 1970s, when Clemo's loosening of form and tension coincided with Methuen's decision to drop their poetry list. The kind of poem the Clemo reader had previously enjoyed was no longer being written, so Jack was left trying to entice a new publisher with a less attractive volume of verse. *A Different Drummer*, *The Shadowed Bed*, *Clemo: A Love Story*, *The Bouncing Hills* and the reissues of *The Invading Gospel*, *Confession of a Rebel* and *The Marriage of a Rebel* were all published by Cornish or Christian-interest companies. It was not until Bloodaxe published *Selected Poems* in 1988 and then compassionately printed Clemo's last two volumes that he regained anything like a national audience. The loyalty of those Cornish and Christian demographics that sustained Clemo in his later years, and their impact on his spiritual and emotional wellbeing is indisputable. On the other hand, neither 'group' has shown much enthusiasm for presenting Clemo outside of their own interests, and as a result his reputation as an important feature of the twentieth century's literary landscape has been largely forgotten. In specific fields of study, Clemo's work has continued to be anthologized, such as Kenneth Baker's *Faber Book of Landscape Poetry*, which included 'The Clay-Tip Worker', and Wendy Bardsley's book of poetry on the Brontës, *An Enduring Flame*, which included 'Charlotte Nicholls'.

Ruth's impact on her husband's literary reputation should not be ignored, either. She dissuaded Clemo from writing his tenser clayscape and sexually symbolic work, and his outside world was now filtered through her. She described the land around them, fed him the news, relayed conversations, reflected moods and interpreted events, etching it all into the palm of his hand. In Clemo's non-fictional prose, she comes across as saintly, but this is an impression in stark contrast to that gathered from the archives and interviews. Here, she appears interfering, dishonest and overbearing. In truth, Ruth was deeply conflicted. She had married a famous poet, and she was proud of him – she wanted people to work on him, to remember him – but she could not overcome her fear or relinquish control. She knew her husband's kinks and oddities and she did not want them to emerge.

In later years, Ruth's mental health weakened and this affected her work on the manuscripts. She died in residential care in 2007. Financially, Jack had provided for her adequately. Their simple and frugal lifestyle allowed them to save a considerable amount, and this did not change after Jack died. Ruth continued to live sparingly, her pension and the royalties from books proving substantially more income than she was able to spend.

With questions hanging over Ruth's ethical treatment of Jack and his material, one is almost inevitably led to wonder about the nature of Clemo's joy and his happiness. For a start, there can be little doubt that Clemo was misled about Weymouth. Had he been able to see and hear, and had he been free to wander the seaside town as he had the tips and pits of his native clayscape, Weymouth surely could not still be considered the rich, exotic, palm-laden paradise he imagined. And, were he aware of Ruth's manipulation and cosseting, her distortion of facts, her embarrassment and frustration, would she still be his 'pixie', his redemption and fulfilment? That is, Jack's happiness seems grounded in a lie. His joy was genuine, of course, but it relied on his inexperience and his inability to see what was going on. Is it possible, then, that his happiness depended on his disabilities? And what are the implications of this? Was this the best that could be done for Clemo in the end? Did God consider it better that he remain disabled, manipulated and warped? Was God unable to heal him? Or unwilling to interfere? Clemo did not believe so, but it is difficult to make sense of Clemo's life by his own beliefs.

We *can* say that Jack was, in however limited a way, a happy man, and we can say that his happiness with Ruth in Weymouth was dependent on a unique interpretation of his situation and suffering. The feeling of joy is certainly authentic, but if there was a point of contact with the divine, then it was hidden behind the dark curtains of disability and privation. Another possibility is that God was forcibly showing Jack the way through an imposed dark night, but Jack misinterpreted God's intentions and favours, unwilling to let go of his idea of worldly fulfilment and divine promises. The joy was grafted onto Clemo in spite of him. A more desperate interpretation might be that God did indeed show Jack favour, invading his fallen world like a scalding sliver of light trained on the individual and burning the world away, taking away his sight and hearing. And this very burning is the touch of God, His favour. The sights and sounds of a revolting world gouged out.

However we interpret Jack's beliefs about the role of God in his life, they seem wrong. Over and over again, his statements and expectations were disproved; the signs and patterns perceived were incorrect; God's promises were broken. It would be possible to construct a picture of a divinity working through Jack's life, but it would require a complete renegotiation of the terms, and its only evidence is the conviction of one man, one witness, who consistently misinterpreted the information he claims to have been given; a man who had a firmly inculcated grounding in that belief system, and who had a profound personal motive for not deviating from it. Put another way, we have a demonstrably unreliable witness to an interpretative perception of a contested belief, in which the witness had a high-stake vested interest. While categorically unfalsifiable, Clemo's theology, derived from personal experience, seems improbable.

This is different from his basic faith, however. Clemo had a simple faith, a primitive pulse, of the sort Tolstoy admired. Tolstoy's method of approaching God was a stripping back of the argument and sophistry, the accoutrements of religious practise. But in one sense Clemo went in the opposite direction. He built up and away from this plain primitive faith with his apophenic interpretations of events. These were theories, non-canonical undogmatic pronouncements about God and the world, based on an interpretation of both explicit and implicit evidence. There can be little doubt that the hope Jack and his mother received through their faith saved their lives, but equally there can be little doubt that Jack's faith was warped by the pressure of his need. His soul, if you like, remained close to his foundational primitive pulse, and it is something to which he repeatedly returned, but Clemo had urgently imposing problems and strong ambitions, and these complicated his beliefs. They caused a confusion and tension that led to the unpersuasive logic and anti-logic of *The Invading Gospel*, and a confessional self-interpretative solipsistic impulse. But these anxiously opposing forces, of faith, syphilis, ambition and interpretation sometimes – especially in the poetry – beat a divine rhythm.

Jack Clemo has left a body of work remarkable for many reasons. Reviewers comment on the fact that he produced such poetry 'in spite of' his disabilities, which is a way of overlooking the work itself. Clemo's poetry shows a value system antagonistic to materialism, modernity and to nostalgic pastoralism. It is, on one level, landscape poetry, though it is not elegiac or pantheistic. It holds a unique and rebellious position. Clemo's work is equally unique in portraying a geography and culture otherwise silent. The twentieth-century clay country and clayscape, the rural-industrial communities, the potent Methodism now almost unrecognisably faded, the language and dialect, the roads and fields, the tips and pits, are given a gaily growling voice. His prose, too, is unique, *Wilding Graft* the unlikely admixture of a realist body with a strongly throbbing supernatural vein, of Hardy, Lawrence, Spurgeon and Browning. Then there is the autobiography, *Confession of a Rebel*, possibly the most original piece of life-writing to have come out of Cornwall, at once exciting, frustrating, peculiar, strained, alien and intimate. It seems Clemo was incapable of doing anything in a predictable way. He was a misfit, a rebel and, indeed, a phoenix.

This theme of triumphant phoenix-like emergence was sustained in Clemo's life and writing. He was constantly either due to rise or had recently risen from a worse state. Recall how, in his earlier poetry, Clemo repeatedly used the working title 'De Profundis'. He was calling – then emerging – from the depths. It is his underpinning optimism, his faith in the happy ending, in progression, and it is present in all his work and private writing. We find it in the very first surviving diary fragments of 1934, already quoted, in which the teenage Clemo writes exultantly of the possibility of a girl – any girl – rising with him out of squalor, sin and prostitution. And it is in the drafts of those earliest novels, in the title and repeated theme of 'Travail', as well as the narrative.

'Clay Phoenix' was both a poem written in 1953 and the proposed title for the 1980 autobiography. The theme never tired. In later collections, Clemo looked back again, now at the clay country, the 'dark night' from which he had emerged triumphantly. Always, Clemo is emerging or due to emerge, so always, in the face of physical deterioration, disappointment and failure, the poet preaches in rapture. His life is a record of extraordinary suffering and resilience, but more than this, it is a record of implausible – even unsympathisable – triumph and joy.

Bibliography

The following is an attempt at a comprehensive bibliography of Clemo's work, as well as of some useful writing about him. There will inevitably be a few errors and omissions. One problem has been that a small number of the publications are difficult to confirm, being magazines or newsletters with short lives or small print runs. In these instances, when I have not been able to view a copy myself, I have trusted references in Clemo's diaries or letters.

Major Works by Clemo

Wilding Graft. London: Chatto & Windus, 1948.
Confession of a Rebel. London: Chatto & Windus, 1949.
The Clay Verge. London: Chatto & Windus, 1951.
'The Wintry Priesthood', in *Poems 1951*. London: Penguin, 1951.
The Invading Gospel. London: Geoffrey Bles, 1958.
The Map of Clay. London: Methuen, 1961.
Cactus on Carmel. London: Methuen, 1967.
The Echoing Tip. London: Methuen, 1971.
Broad Autumn. London: Eyre Methuen, 1975.
The Marriage of a Rebel. London: Victor Gollancz, 1980.
The Bouncing Hills. Redruth: Dyllansow Truran, 1983.
The Shadowed Bed. Tring: Lion Publishing, 1986.
A Different Drummer. Padstow: Tabb House, 1986.
Selected Poems. Newcastle upon Tyne: Bloodaxe, 1988.
Banner Poems. Gorran: Cornish NPP, 1989.
Clay Cuts. Oxford: Previous Parrot Press, 1991.
Approach to Murano. Newcastle upon Tyne: Bloodaxe, 1993.
The Cured Arno. Newcastle upon Tyne: Blooadaxe, 1995.

Foreign Editions and Reprints

Wilding Graft. New York: MacMillan, 1948.
Wilding Graft. London: Anthony Mott, 1983.
Hon Kom Till Sist. Trans. Elisabet Akesson. Uppsala: J.A. Lindblads, 1949.
Confession of a Rebel. Toronto: Clarke Irwin, 1949.

Confession of a Rebel. London: Chatto & Windus, 1975.
Confession of a Rebel. London: Spire, 1988.
The Invading Gospel. Toronto: Collins, 1958.
The Invading Gospel. London: Marshall, Morgan and Scott, 1972.
The Invading Gospel. New Jersey: Fleming H. Revell Co., 1972.
The Invading Gospel. London: Marshall Pickering, 1986.
The Invading Gospel. Dublin: Samovar, 2011.
The Map of Clay. Toronto: Ryerson Press. [Unconfirmed]
The Map of Clay. Richmond: John Knox Press, 1968.
The Marriage of a Rebel. London: Spire, 1988.

Posthumously Collected Works

The Clay Kiln. St Austell: Cornish Hillside Publications, 2000.
The Awakening. Ed. Alan Kent, John Hurst and Andrew Symons. London: Francis Boutle, 2003.
Selected Poems. Ed. Luke Thompson. London: Enitharmon, 2015.
A Proper Mizz-Maze. Ed. Luke Thompson. London: Francis Boutle, 2016.

Poems and Stories by Clemo

[Unknown poem.] *Christian Herald*, November 1930.
'"Gyp" and the Cats.' *Tail-Wagger Magazine*, January 1931.
'Bond of the Past'. *Cornish Guardian*, 17 September 1931.
'Benjy an' his Sweetheart.' *Netherton's Cornish Almanack*, Winter 1930/1.
'Beef, Taaties an' Luv.' *Netherton's Cornish Almanack*, 1931/2.
'The Return.' *St Austell Hospital Handbook*, 1932.
'The Legend of the Doom Bar.' *Doidge's Annual*, 1932.
Vital Sayings of the Year 1933. London: Shaw Publishing Co. Ltd., 1933.
'Night's Power', 'The Homely Wife', 'The Lover's Cry', 'Memory'. *Northern Weekly Gazette*, 4 February 1933.
'The Letter.' *St Austell Hospital Handbook*, 1933.
'The Old Hill', 'This Will Remain'. *Northern Weekly Gazette*, 16 December 1933.
'Love Comes to Bethlehem.' *Cornish Guardian*, 21 December 1933.
'Jemmy Trenowth An' Tha Capn's Dafter.' *Netherton's Cornish Almanack*, 1933/4.

'Plums for Evelyn.' *St Austell Hospital Handbook*, 1934.
'A Child's Prayer.' *Children's Weekly*, 31 May 1934.
'Shrine of Springtime.' *Cornish Guardian*, 14 June 1934.
'The Legend of Hellenclose.' *Doidge's Annual*, 1934.
'Summer.' *Cornish Guardian*, 2 August 1934.
'Perranporth.' *Cornish Guardian*, 23 August 1934.
'Goonamarris.' *Cornish Guardian*, 6 September 1934.
'Autumn Desire.' *Cornish Guardian*, 20 September 1934.
'The Cenotaph of God.' *Cornish Guardian*, 8 November 1934.
'Marcel's Christmas Gift.' *Doidge's Annual*, 1935.
'Birth in January.' *Cornish Guardian*, 10 January 1935
'Postman Treziz Vinds Out', 'Jemima Trebilcock's Tom Cat', 'Med-Zadler's Mawther-Law'. *Saundry's Almanack*, 1935.
'A Genius in the World.' *Cornish Guardian*, 14 February 1935.
'Johnny Sowsa An' Tha Barber's Sister', 'Pantry Winda'. *Netherton's Cornish Almanack*, 1934/5.
'Winter Scene in Cornwall.' *Cornish Guardian*, 28 March 1935.
'Cornish Night.' *Cornish Guardian*, 4 April 1935.
'As Winter Departs.' *Cornish Guardian*, 11 April 1935.
'Love's Easter.' *Cornish Guardian*, 18 April 1935.
'Spring Storm.' *Cornish Guardian*, 30 May 1935.
'Spring Night.' *Cornish Guardian*, 6 June 1935.
'The Comer.' *Cornish Guardian*, 18 July 1935.
'Magic Touch.' *Cornish Guardian*, 1 August 1935.
'Love in a Wood.' *Cornish Guardian*, 3 October 1935.
'War.' *Cornish Guardian*, 21 November 1935.
'New Year's Garden.' *Cornish Guardian*, 9 January 1936.
'Oblong Gits his awn back.' *Saundry's Almanack*, 1936.
'Charlie, the Smutties an' The Baaby.' *Netherton's Cornish Almanack*, 1935/6.
'Joe Tonkin's Visitors.' *One and All Almanack*, 1936.
'Summer in Love', 'The Bright Side', 'Through Common Days'. *Northern Weekly Gazette*, 1936.
'Porthpean.' *Cornish Guardian*, 20 August 1936.
'Jim Currah's Match-Making.' *Saundry's Almanack*, 1937.
'Tommy, The Gurl an' the Currls.' *Netherton's Cornish Almanack*, 1936/7.
'Maria an' The Milkman.' *One and All Almanack*, 1937.
'Watch-Night Reflections.' *Cornish Guardian*, 1937.

'Crucifixion.' *Cornish Guardian*, 25 March 1937.
'Advice.' *Cornish Guardian*, 21 October 1937.
'Teddy's Terboggin.' *Saundry's Almanack*, 1938.
'Mrs Craddock's Cloas-Line.' *Netherton's Cornish Almanack*, 1937/8.
'Bert's Delivery.' *One and All Almanack*, 1938.
'The True Optimsim.' *Cornish Guardian*, 6 January 1938.
'Barney's Tricks.' *Saundry's Almanack*, 1939.
'Mrs Strout's Match-Making.' *One and All Almanack*, 1939.
'Perce Trezidder's Revenge.' *Netherton's Cornish Almanack*, 1938/9.
'The Winds.' *Cornish Guardian*, 5 January 1939.
'S.E. Burrow: A Tribute.' *Cornish Guardian*, 27 July 1939.
'An Exciting Wash-Day.' *One and All Almanack*, 1940.
'Christ in the Clay-Pit'. *Orion III*, 1946.
'A Calvinist in Love'. *New Writing*. London: Penguin, 1947.
'The Excavator.' *Modern Reading 17*, May 1948.
'Snowfall at Kernick.' *Facet*, Winter 1948-9.
'Intimate Landscape.' *The Cornish Review* no. 1, Spring 1949.
'Night Shift, Goonvean Claywork', 'Gulls Nesting Inland', 'Quarry Snow'. *West Country Magazine* thirteen vol. 4 no. 2, Summer 1949.
'Alien Grain.' *Cornish Review* 4 spring 1950.
'Water-Wheel near Goonamarris', 'Frost above Meledor.' *West Country Magazine*, Winter 1949.
'Plundered Fuchsias in a Cornish Garden.' *Westcountry Life*, May 1950.
'Flooded Clay-Pit.' *West Country Magazine* vol. 5 no. 2 spring 1950.
'A Day in Dorset', 'The Cinder-Heap', 'The Clay-dry'. *West Country Magazine* nineteen vol. 5 no. 4, Winter 1950-51.
'The Clay-Dump.' *One and All: A Selection of Stories from Cornwall*. Ed. Denys Val Baker. London: Museum Press, 1951.
'The Shadow' (poem). *The Cornish Review* no. 7, Spring 1951.
'The Awakening.' *The Cornish Review* no. 9, Winter 1951.
'Meteorite.' *Devon and Cornwall Journal*, Winter 1951.
'Reclaimed.' *Modern Reading 20*, Winter 1951-2.
'Dorset Mood' (also Charles Causley's 'Homage to Jack Clemo'). *West Country Magazine*, Spring 1952.
'Impregnation', 'Initiated'. *The Cornish Review* no. 10, Summer 1952.
'Clay-Peak.' *John O'London's Weekly*, 18 July 1952.
'Trethosa Chapel.' *The London Magazine* vol. 1 no. 7, August 1954.

'Clay Phoenix'. *The London Magazine* vol. 2 no. 9, September 1955.

'The Water Wheel', 'A Calvinist in Love'. *The Chatto Book of Modern Poetry 1915-1955*. Ed. Cecil Day Lewis and John Lehmann. London: Chatto and Windus, 1956.

'Neutral Ground', 'Snowfall at Kernick', 'Christ in the Clay-Pit', 'The Winds', 'Sufficiency', 'A Calvinist in Love', 'Clay Phoenix'. *Western Review* vol. 20, Winter 1956.

'Clay Phoenix', 'Reclaimed'. *New Poems 1957: A P.E.N. Anthology*. Ed. Cecil Day Lewis, Kathleen Nott and Thomas Blackburn. London: Michael Joseph, 1957.

'Truro', 'Shallow Yield'. [Unknown][651]

'The Veiled Sitter.' *The London Magazine* vol. 4 no. 12, December 1957.

'Beyond Lourdes.' *The London Magazine* vol. 5 no. 11, November 1958.

'Modelled in Passion Week.' *The Painter & Sculptor* vol. 3 no. 1, Spring 1960.

'Prairie Song' (also 'The World of Jack Clemo' by Charles Causley). *The London Magazine* vol. 7 no. 10, October 1960.

'Lebanese Harvest.' *Outposts* 45, Summer 1960.

'Frontier City', 'Priestess and Lover'. *The New Beacon*, December 1960.

'Shuttered.' *Unicorn*, Winter 1960-61.

'Frontier City' (also a review by Michael Curtis). *Unicorn*, Summer 1961.

'Rebel Love',[652] 'Laika', 'Service to England', 'Outsider'. *Unicorn*, Winter 1961.

'Lines to the Blind'. *Outposts* 47, Winter 1961.

'Max Gate.' *The Guinness Book of Poetry 5*. London: Putnam, 1962.

'Exit' *Orient/West* vol. 8 no.3, 1963.

'Bedrock.' *Outposts* 57, Summer 1963.

'The Cinder-Heap.' *Poems of Today*, 1963.

'A Calvinist in Love', 'The Water-Wheel', 'Christ in the Clay-Pit', 'The Excavator',

'Sufficiency', 'Clay-Land Moods', 'A Kindred Battlefield', 'The Two Beds', 'Thorn in the Flesh', 'Reclaimed', 'Intimate Landscape', 'Clay Phoenix', 'Lunar Pentecost', 'Beyond Lourdes', 'The Veiled Sitter', 'Outsider', 'Service to England', 'Confessional', 'The Leper', 'The New Creation'. *Penguin Modern Poets 6*. London: Penguin, 1964.

'Venus in Grace', 'Betrothal'. *The Poetry Review*, Summer 1964.

'The Burnt Bush.' *Faber Book of Twentieth Century Verse*. Ed. John Heath-Stubbs and David Wright. London: Faber & Faber, 1965.

'Border Raid'. *Tantalus* 6, 1965.
'Friar's Crag', 'Dungeon Ghyll'. *The Poetry Review*, Spring 1965.
'Summer Saga', 'Lines to Wordsworth'. *The Poetry Review*, Winter 1965.
'Christ in the Clay-Pit'. *Palgrave's Golden Treasury*, 1964.
'The Pierced Valley.' *The Cornish Review* no. 1, Spring 1966.
'Eros in Exile.' *The Transatlantic Review* 21, Summer 1966.
'Crab Country.' *The Poetry Review*, Autumn 1966.
'The Rider.' *New Measure* 2, Winter 1966.
'Carmel.' *Poetry Book Society: Christmas Poetry Supplement*, 1966.
'Cactus in Clayscape.' *The Cornish Review* no. 4, New Year 1967.
'Massabielle' (also Lionel Miskin article 'Jack Clemo'). [653] *The Aylesford Review* vol. VIII no. 3, Winter 1966/Spring 1967.
'Cactus.' *Transatlantic Review* 24, Spring 1967.
'Frontier City', 'Gwindra', 'The River Niche' [sic], 'Line to Wordsworth'. *The Cornish Review* no. 5, Spring 1967.
'Grasmere Reflections', 'Charlotte Nichols'. *The Poetry Review*, Summer 1967.
'Death of a Student.' *Cornish Review* no. 8, Spring 1968.
'St Gudule.' [Unknown] December 1968.
'Christ in the clay-pit.' *Let There Be God*. Ed. F. J. Teskey and T. H. Parker. Oxford: Religious Education Press, 1968.
'Transfer.' *Chirimo* no. 2, October 1968.
'The Islets.' *The Poetry Review*, Spring 1968.
'Alfred Wallis.' *The Poetry Review*, Autumn 1968.
'Christ in the clay-pit.' *The Voice of Poetry*. Ed. Hermann Peschmann. London: Evans Brothers Ltd., 1969.
'Wedding Eve.' *The Cornish Review* no. 11, Spring 1969.
'In contrast', 'Mould of Castile'. *The Poetry Review*, Summer 1969.
'Mr Barrett in Cornwall', 'Genevan Towers'. *The Poetry Review*, Winter 1969.
'After Billy Bray.' *The Cornish Review* no. 13, Winter 1969.
'On the Death of Karl Barth.' *Candelabrum* vol. 1 no. 1, April 1970.
'Katherine Luther.' *The Poetry Review*, Summer 1970.
'Clay-Dams.' *The Cornish Review* no. 15, Summer 1970.
'Torrey Canyon.' *Cornish Nation*, Autumn 1970.
'Porthmeor.' *Cornish Nation*, Winter 1970.
'Christ in the Clay-Pit', 'Snowfall at Kernick', 'The Water-Wheel', 'Sufficiency', 'A Calvinist in Love'. *The Granite Kingdom*. Ed. D. M. Thomas. Truro: D. Bradford Barton Ltd, 1970.

'Harpoon.' *Transatlantic Review* 37 & 38, Autumn/Winter 1970-71.
'A Couple at Fowey.' *Poetry Review*, Winter 1970/71.
'I go Gentle'. *Twentieth Century Magazine*, 1971.
'Simone Weil.' *Antigonish Review* issue 3 volume 1, 1971.
'Gulls Nesting Inland.' *Horizons*, 1971.
'St Just-in-Roseland' *Cornish Review* no. 17, Spring 1971.
'Beethoven', 'Virgin Harbour'. *Candelabrum* vol. 1 no. 3, Spring 1971.
'Tregargus.' *Cornish Review* no. 20, Spring 1972.
"Seer and Warrior". Nietzsche Symposium at University of Victoria, 1972.
'Broad Autumn.' *Aquarius* 5, 1972.
'On the Burial of a Poet Laureate.' *Cornish Review* no. 22, Winter 1972.
'Broad Autumn.' *Counter / Measures* 2, 1973.
'Asian Girl in Mid-Cornwall', 'Helpston'. *Workshop New Poetry* no. 20, April 1973.
'Frosted Image'. *The House that Jack Built*. Ed. Brian Patten and Pat Krett. London: George Allen and Unwin, 1973.
'In Harlyn Museum.' *The Cornish Review*, Summer 1973.
'The Testament.' *The Cornish Review* no. 25. Winter 1973/4.
'Royal Wedding.' *Aquarius* 7, 1974.
'Wart and Pearl', 'A Wife on an Autumn Anniversary'. *Meridian* vol. 1 no. 1, Autumn 1973.
Christ in the Clay-Pit.' *Moorlands Message*, Summer 1974.
'Porth Beach', *Meridian* vol. 1 no. 4, Summer 1974.
'The Rift'. *Candelabrum* vol. 2 no. 4, Autumn-Winter 1974.
'Whispers.' *Cornish Review* no. 27, Winter 1974.
'A Different Drummer.' *Pennine Platform* no. 1, 1977.
'Vistas Within Marriage.' *Outposts* 104, Spring 1975.
'Affirmative Way.' *Candelabrum* vol 2 no. 5, April 1975.
'A Rendering.' *Outposts* 105, Summer 1975.
'Launched.' *Unitarian*, Winter 1975.
'Caradoc Evans.' *The Anglo-Welsh Review* vol. 26 no. 57, Autumn 1976.
'Poem at Sixty.' *Outposts* 111, Winter 1976.
'Charlotte Mew.' *Meridian* no. 9, Summer 1976.
'Thankful Shepherd.' *Deafblind*, December 1976.
'The Clay-Dump.' *Cornish Short Stories*. Ed. Denys Val Baker. London: Penguin, 1976.
'Bethel Centenary.' *Trethosa Methodist Church 1876-1976*. Ed. Rev. P. D.

Williams. Wadebridge: Quintrell & Co, 1976.
'The Restored See.' *Truro Diocesan Centenary Pamphlet*, January 1977.
'Unearthed.' *New Poetry* no. 38, 1977.
'Holman Hunt.' *Meridian* no. 12, Spring 1977.
'A Choice About Art', 'Salvaged'. *Third Way*, 30 June 1977.
'Dietrich Bonhoeffer.' *Outposts*, Summer 1977.
'Virginia Woolf Remembers St Ives.' *South West Review* no. 2, October 1977.
'Coppice Tarn.' *Pennine Platform* no. 1, 1978.
'Chesil Beach.' *Third Way*, February 1978.
'Private Pompeii.' *Anglo-Welsh Review* vol. 27 no. 60, Spring 1978.
'Drought on a Clay-Ridge.' *Meridian* no. 14, 1978.
'Eric Gill.' *Meridian*, Autumn 1978.
'The Winds', 'Broad Autumn', 'Priest out of Bondage', 'Harpoon', 'Josephine Butler', 'Tested'. *The Country of the Risen King*. Ed. Merle Meter. Grand Rapids: Baker Books, 1978.
'Francis Thompson.' *Third Way*, 26 March 1979.
'Mill Rods at Barrakellis.' *The Cornish Banner* no. 8, September 1979.
'Chesil Beach.' *Dorset Year Book*, 1980.
'Cloud over Bugle.' *Cornish Guardian*, 20 March 1980.
'Mappowder Revisited.' *The Powys Review* no. 6, Summer 1980.
'St Juliot's.' *The Cornish Banner* no. 21, August 1980.
'Dawn Threat.' *The Cornish Banner* no. 22, November 1980.
'Transplant.' *The Cornish Banner* no. 23, February 1981.
'Gulls Nesting Inland.' *Symphony* no. 11, Spring/Summer 1981.
'Nursery.' *The Cornish Banner* no. 24, May 1981.
'Francis Thompson', 'La Salette', 'Coppice Tarn'. *PN Review* 22, 1981.
'The Winds', 'Christ in the Clay-pit'. *The Lion Book of Christian Poetry*. Ed. Pat Alexander. Herts: Lion, 1981.
'Weymouth.' *Dorset Year Book*, 1981.
'Isle of Slingers.' *Resurgence*, January 1981.
'Dark Reaping.' *Resurgence* no. 88, September/October 1981.
'Asian Girl in Mid-Cornwall', 'Henry Martyn.' *The Journal of Indian Writing in English* vol. 9, July 1981.
'Neither Shadow of Turning', 'Mould of Castile', 'Growing in Grace', 'On the Death of Karl Barth'. *Oxford Book of Christian Verse*. Ed. Donald Davie. Oxford: Oxford University Press, 1981.
'The Crest.' *The Cornish Banner* no. 26, November 1981.

'Sandsfoot Castle Gardens.' *Dorset Year Book*, 1982.
'The Blacksmith.' *The Cornish Banner* no. 27, February 1982.
'Lamorna Cove.' *The Cornish Banner* no. 28, May 1982.
'Contrasts in a Corner.' *The Cornish Banner* no. 29, August 1982.
'The Winds.' *The Sun, Dancing.* Ed. Charles Causley, Charles. Middlesex: Kestrel Books, 1982.
'The Water-Wheel', 'The Flooded Clay-Pit', 'Snowfall at Kernick', 'Tregargus'. *Cornwall in Verse* Ed. Peter Redgrove. London: Secker and Warburg, 1982.
'Meeting-Points.' *Poems for Charles Causley.* Ed. Michael Hanke. London: Enitharmon Press, 1982.
'Porthpean.' *The Cornish Banner* no. 30, November 1982.
'Whispers', 'Eros in Exile', 'Broad Autumn'. *100 Contemporary Christian Poets.* Ed. Gordon Bailey. Herts: Lion, 1983.
'Christ in the Clay-Pit.' *The Cool Web*, 1983.
'At Hardy's Birthplace.' *Dorset Year Book*, 1983.
'Display at Truro.' *The Cornish Banner* no. 31, February 1983.
'Mevagissey.' *The Cornish Banner* no. 32, May 1983.
'Safeguard.' *The Cornish Banner* no. 33, August 1983.
'Arrival.' *Resurgence,* January 1984.
'Via Carhayes.' *The Cornish Banner* no.34, November 1983.
'At Cerne.' *Dorset Year Book,* 1984.
'Leaps and Bounds.' *Torch Newsletter,* 1984.
'Portholland.' *The Cornish Banner* no. 35, February 1984.
'The Minack Theatre.' *The Cornish Banner* no. 36, May 1984.
'Roche Rock.' *Christian Woman,* September 1984.
'Nanpean.' *The Cornish Banner* no. 37, August 1984.
'Pascal.' *The Cut,* September 1984.
'In Roche Church.' *Christian Woman,* September 1984.
'Baldhu.' *The Cornish Banner* no. 38, November 1984.
'Tryphena.' *Dorset Year Book,* 1985.
'Well at Bloomdale.' *The Cornish Banner* no. 39, February 1985.
'Foxhole Beacon.' *The Cornish Banner* no. 40, May 1985.
'Downpark Field.' *The Cornish Banner* no. 41, August 1985.
'Marie Stopes.' *Tears in the Fence* 3, 1985.
'On the Prospect of Leaving my Birthplace.' *South West Review* no. 24, February 1985.

'John Harris.' *The Cut*, September 1985.
'Eilidh Boadella.' *Christian Woman*, October 1985.
'Jonathan Swift: June 1723.' *Poetry Ireland Review* no. 14, Autumn 1985.
'St Dennis Church.' *The Cornish Banner* no. 42, November 1985.
'William Barnes.' *Dorset Yearbook*, 1986.
'After a Removal.' *The Cornish Banner* no. 43, February 1986.
'Longships and Portholland.' *The Cornish Banner* no. 44, May 1986.
'Jean-Pierre De Caussade.' *The Cut*, May 1986.
'Coast Watch.' *The Cornish Banner* no. 45, August 1986.
'At the Cottage.' *The Cornish Banner* no. 46, November 1986.
'Barbecue' *Nexus*, November 1986.
'Windsor.' *Christian Woman*, 1986.
'Near the Race', 'Sunset in Dorset'. *Dorset Year Book*, 1987.
'Chimney.' *The Cornish Banner* no. 47, February 1987.
'Emigrant.' *Acumen* 5, April 1987.
'Arsenal.' *The Cornish Banner* no. 48, May 1987.
'Baptism.' *The Cut*, June 1987.
'Bank Holiday Storm.' *The Cornish Banner* no. 49, August 1987.
'Katharine Luther.' *Das Deutschlandbild in der englischen Literatur*. Ed. Gunther Blaicher, 1987.
'Open Waters.' *Christian Woman*, November 1987.
'Trerice House.' *The Cornish Banner* no. 50, November 1987.
'Palazzo Rezzonico.' *The Cut*, January 1988.
'Carmel.' *Thirty Years of the Poetry Book Society*. London, 1988.
'Parallel.' *The Cornish Banner* no. 51, February 1988.
'Festal Magnet.' *Orbis* no. 68, Spring 1988.
'Nightfall at Veryan.' *The Cornish Banner* no. 52, May 1988.
'Centre.' *Symphony* no. 1, 1988.
'First Flight.' *The Cornish Banner* no. 54, November 1988.
'Late Honeymoon.' *Acumen* 7, April 1988.
'Frostbite.' *Dorset Year Book*, 1988.
'Clay-Land Moods', 'Open Waters', 'The Water Wheel'. *Poetry with an Edge*. Ed. Neil Astley. Northumberland: Bloodaxe, 1988.
'Venice.' *Outposts* 157, Summer 1988.
'Abbotsbury Gardens', 'Daybreak in Dorset'. *Dorset Year Book*, 1989.
'Tunnel.' *The Cut*, January 1989.
'Keswick Revisited.' *Christian Woman*, February 1989.

'Cultures.' *The Cornish Banner* no. 55, February 1989.
'San Lazzaro.' *Westwords* no. 9, April 1989.
'At the Kilns.' *The Cornish Banner* no. 56, May 1989.
'Cliff Garden.' *The Cornish Banner* no. 57, August 1989.
'Moving Clay-Tips.' *The Cornish Banner* no. 59, February 1990.
'Haworth Keys, 1840.' *Symphony*, 1990.
'Link at Oxford.' *The Rialto* 16, Spring 1990.
'Island Contrasts.' *Acumen* 11, April 1990.
'Corfe and Poole.' *Dorset Year Book*, 1990.
'Cooling Down.' *The Cornish Banner* no. 60, May 1990.
'In Wales.' *The Cornish Banner* no. 61, August 1990.
'Market-House.' *The Cornish Banner* no. 62, November 1990.
'Sanctuary.' *Symphony*, November 1990.
'Perennial.' *Orbis* no. 79, Winter 1990.
'The Kilns.' *New Christian Poetry*. Ed. Alwyn Marriage. London: Collins Flame, 1990.
'Fleet.' *Dorset Year Book*, 1991.
'Devon Abbey.' *The Cut*, January 1991.
'Bohago.' *The Cornish Banner* no. 63, February 1991.
'Triple Tug.' *The Cornish Banner* no. 64, May 1991.
'Hensafraen.' *The Cornish Banner* no. 65, August 1991.
'Beach Ritual.' *The Cut*, August 1991.
'Values.' *Symphony*, October 1991.
'Padstow.' *The Cornish Banner* no. 66, November 1991.
'Kirkstone Pass.' *The Cut*, December 1991.
'Milton Abbey.' *Dorset Year Book*, 1992.
'Sortridge Manor'. *Christian Magazine*, January 1992.
'Parks.' *The Cornish Banner* no. 67, February 1992.
'Lake Paddle.' *Acumen* 15, April 1992.
'Salieri.' *The Cut*, April 1992.
'Drinnick.' *The Cornish Banner* no. 68, May 1992.
'Clay Riddle.' *The Cornish Banner* no. 69, August 1992.
'Voyage.' *The Cornish Banner* no. 70, November 1992.
'Heard at Sandsfoot.' *Dorset Year Book*, 1993.
'Ward View.' *The Cornish Banner* no. 71, February 1993.
'Ashley Down.' *Symphony*, April 1993.
'Grampound Road.' *The Cornish Banner* no. 72, May 1993.

'Wheal Martyn.' 'Salvage'. *Cornish Links*, June 1993.
'Village Carnival.' *The Cornish Banner* no. 73, August 1993.
'T. E. Lawrence.' *Acumen* 18, October 1993.
'The Moor Hunt.' *The Cornish Banner* no. 74, November 1993.
'Silver Wedding.' *Dorset Year Book*, 1994.
'Wadebridge.' *The Cornish Banner* no. 75, February 1994.
'Newman.' *Rhubarb*, April 1994.
'Delabole.' *The Cornish Banner* no. 76, May 1994.
'Casa Guidi.' *The Rialto* no. 29, Summer 1994.
'Fever Zone.' *The Haiku Quarterly* nos. 11 & 12, August 1994.
'George Muller' (also 'Household' by Heather Spears). *The Christian*, September 1994.
'Jack London.' *Rhubarb, Rhubarb*, Christmas 1994.
'Dorchester Ward.' *Outposts* 180-181, Winter 1994-5.
'Anne Bronte.' *Rhubarb, Rhubarb*, 1995.
'Stourhead.' *Dorset Year Book*, 1995.
'Heretic in Florence.' *Acumen* 21, January 1995.
'Fitting In.' *The Cornish Banner* no. 79, February 1995.
'Delabole Quarry.' *Independent*, 1 November 1995.
'The Plundered Fuchsias', 'Moor Hunt', 'Beatific Vision', 'T.E. Lawrence'. *Completing the Picture* Ed. William Oxley. Devon: Stride,1995.
'Salvaged', 'Wheal Martyn'. *Cornish Links*. Ed. Bill Headon. Tunbridge Wells: Kernow Poets Press, 1995.
'Daybreak in Dorset.' *Poet's England 19: Dorset*, 1996.
'Lulworth.' *Dorset Year Book*, 1996.
'Salieri.' *The Herald*, 12 February 1997.
'Charlotte Nicholls.' *An Enduring Flame*. Ed. Wendy Bardsley. Yorkshire: Smith Settle, 1998.
'Alfred Wallis.' Lanyon, Andrew. *Old Iron*. St Ives: St Ives Printing and Publishing, 1998.
'In Roche Church', 'St Just in Roseland'. Hall, Dennis. *A Choice of Churches*. Oxford: Previous Parrot Press, 2000.
'The Veiled Sitter.' *Prayers from the Edge*. Ed. Catherine von Ruhland. Middlesex: Society for Promoting Christian Knowledge, 2000.
'The Clay-Tip Worker.' *The Faber Book of Landscape Poetry*. London: Faber & Faber, 2000.
'A Calvinist in Love', 'The Water-Wheel', 'The Flooded Cay-Pit', 'Christ in

the Clay-Pit', 'The Excavator', 'Clay Land Moods', 'Lunar Pentecost', 'Gulls Nesting Inland', 'St Just-in-Roseland', 'After Billy Bray', 'Testament', 'Tregargus', In Roche Church', Windsor'. *The Dreamt* Sea. Ed. Alan Kent. London: Francis Boutle, 2005.

'Maria and the Milkman.' Kent, Alan and Williams, Derek R., eds. *The Francis Boutle Book of Cornish Short Stories*. London: Francis Boutle Publishers, 2010.

'Barney's Tricks'. *The Clearing*, 7 March 2014.

'Blind Girl at a Service.' *PN Review* 217, May/June 2014.

'The Clay Dry.' *Archipelago* 9, 2014.

'At a Devon Abbey.' *The Guardian*, 29 August 2015.

Articles by Clemo

'Faith Brings the Victory.' *Christian Herald*, 19 February 1949.

'Creed and some Modern Christians.' *Christian Leader*, March 1949.

'The Hocking Brothers'. *The Cornish Review* no. 7, Spring 1951.

'Lines to the Blind.' *Outposts*, Winter 1961.

'Jack Clemo states his case.' *Unicorn*, Winter 1961.

'The China Clay Country.' Williams, Michael, ed. *My Cornwall*. Bodmin: Bossiney Books, 1973.

'My Life in the Clay World.' *The Cornish Review* 14, Spring 1970.

'Letter.' *The Rainbow*, September 1972.

'Pilgrimage to Mappowder.' Humfrey, Belinda, ed. *Recollections of the Powys Brothers*. London: Peter Owen, 1980.

'Towards Christian Balance.' *Moorlands Message*, Summer 1974.

Introduction. *I Won't Paint any Tears*. By Boadella, Eilidh. Surrey: Outposts, 1981.

'A Dorset Legacy'. *Dorset Yearbook*, 1982.

Introduction to fragment of Browning's 'Pippa Passes.' Shewell, Christina, and Dean, Virginia, eds. *A Way with Words: Favourite Pieces Chosen by Famous People*. London: Sinclair Browne, 1982.

'Peaks in Venice.' *Christian Woman*, January 1990.

Works on Clemo

Allen, Walter. 'A Calvinist Poet.' *New Statesman*, 24 February 1961.

Apichella, Michael. 'Interview with a Rebel.' *Christian Writer*, January 1985.
Apichella, Michael. 'Third Person Singular. Interview with a Rebel.' *Eternity*, April 1985.
Boadella, Elsa. 'Jack Clemo in Dorset.' *Dorset Year Book*, 1986.
Bold, Alan. 'The Amorous Christian Quest.' *The Weekend Scotsman*, 1 March 1980.
Brearley, Margaret. 'Scarred Yet Singing.' *Third Way* vol. 9, no. 10, October 1986.
Burville, Julia. 'Clemo Country'.*Cornish Links*. Ed. Bill Headon. Tunbridge Wells: Kernow Poets Press, 1995.
Causley, Charles. 'Jack Clemo.' *Contemporary Poets of the English Language*. Ed. Rosalie Murphy. London: St James Press, 1970.
Causley, Charles. 'The World of Jack Clemo.' *The London Magazine* vol. 7 no. 10, October 1960.
Chase, Mary Ellen. 'Dunes, Moors and Tors.' *New York Times*, 7 November 1948.
Chedzoy, Alan. 'A Poet Come to Dorset.' *The Dorset Year Book*, 1987.
Church, Richard, 'The Melodic Line.' *Essays by Divers Hands Volume XXXVI*. Ed. Mary Stocks. London: Oxford University Press, 1970.
Clemo, Eveline. *I Proved Thee at the Waters*. Ilkeston: Moorley's Bible and Bookshop, 1976.
Corbluth, Elsa. 'A Living Land... Jack Clemo in Dorset.' *The Dorset Year Book*, 1986.
Davie, Donald. 'A Calvinist in Politics.' *Poetry Nation Review* vol. 6 no. 1, 1979.
Drabble, Margaret. *A Writer's Britain*. London: Thames & Hudson, 1979.
Fairchild, Hoxie Neale. *Religious Trends in English Poetry* vol. VI, 1920-1965. New York: Columbia University Press, 1968.
Foot, Sarah, ed. *Methodist Celebration*. Redruth: Dyllansow Truran, 1988.
Goodman, Gemma. 'Seeing the Clay Country.' *Cornish Studies* 17, 2009.
Goodman, Gemma. 'Cornwall: an alternative construction of place.' Diss. Warwick University, 2010.
Headdon, Bill. 'Jack Clemo Cornish Giant', 'On His Blindness and Deafness'. *Cornish Banner* no. 78, November 1994.
Hemmings, Louis. 'The Road to Goonamarris Slip.' *Strait Magazine*, 1981.
Hemmings, Louis. 'The Word is Clay, How I Met Jack Clemo.' *Cowbird*, 16 February 2012.
Hemmings, Louis. Personal correspondence with Clemo.

Hill, Brian Merriken. 'Not Golden Beaches but Clay-Pits.' *New Hope International*, 1982.
Hoffman, Daniel. 'Lines for Jack Clemo.' *Transatlantic Review*, April 1965.
Hong, Edna. *The Downward Ascent*. Minneapolis: Augsburg Press, 1979.
Hummer, T.R. *Available Surfaces*. Michigan: University of Michigan Press, 2012.
Thurley, Geoffrey. *The Ironic Harvest*. London: Edward Arnold, 1974.
Hurst, John. 'Literature in Cornwall.' *Cornwall since the War*. Ed. Philip Payton. Redruth: Dyllansow Truran, 1993.
Hurst, John. 'Voice from a White Silence.' *Cornish Studies* 3, 1995
Hurst, John. 'An Awkward Blessing: the Poetry of Jack Clemo.' *Expository Times* vol. 103 no. 9, June 1992.
Hurst, John. 'Cyprus Well to Goonamarris Slip.' *The Charles Causley Society Newsletter* 13, Winter 2013.
Hurst, John. Personal correspondence with Clemo.
Hutchings, Monica. 'The Cornish Rebel.' *West Country Magazine*, Summer 1951.
Hyland, Paul. 'Quest for Love.' *Third Way* vol. 4 no. 6, 1980.
James, Marjorie. 'Personal Memories of Jack Clemo.' *Acumen 75*, January 2013.
Jones, H. L. 'Clay Prophet.' *New Beacon*, December 1960.
Isaac, Peter. *A History of Evangelical Christianity in Cornwall*. Buckinghamshire: WEC Press, 1999.
Kendall, Ena. 'A Vocation for Marriage ' *Observer Magazine*, 17 February 1980.
Ena Kendall 'A Vocation for Marriage' *New Beacon* vol. LXIV no. 755, March 1980.
Kent, Alan. *The Literature of Cornwall*. Bristol: Redcliffe Press, 2000.
Kent, Alan. *Pulp Methodism*. St Austell: Cornish Hillside Publications, 2002.
Kent, Alan. 'Jack Clemo, Cornish Rebel.' *Book and Magazine Collector*, July 2004.
Kent, Alan. 'A Sustainable Literature?' *Cornish Studies* 17, 2009.
Kent, Alan. '*Wives, Mothers and Sisters*': Feminism, Literature and Women Writers in Cornwall. Penzance: The Hypatia Trust, 1998.
Laird, Stephen. 'Fellow-Feeling for a Scarred Landscape.' *Church Times*, 5 September 2014.
Jones, Leslie. 'Jack Clemo Prydyth an Pry: Poet of the Clay.' *Harvester*

Magazine vol. LXI no.3, 1982.

Lamb, R.E.T. *The Poetry of Jack Clemo*. London: BBC, 1972.

Lane, Stephen. *Dictionary of Literary Biography*, 1983/4.

Lane, Stephen. 'A Reading of the Manuscripts of Jack Clemo.' *PN Review* 22 vol. 8 no. 2, November/December 1981.

Lane, Stephen John. 'Jack Clemo: Cartographer of Grace.' Diss. Newcastle University, 1989.

Lowman, Peter. `Supernaturalistic Causality and Christian Theism in the Modern English Novel.` Diss. University of Cardiff, 1983.

Magnusson, Sally. *Clemo: A Love Story*. Herts: Lion Publishing, 1986.

Martin, E.W. 'The Loneliness of Jack Clemo.' *Cornish Review* no. 5, 1967.

Martin, Heather. 'Jack Clemo's Vocation to Evangelical Poetry and Erotic Marriage: an Examination of his Poems of Personal Tribute and Critique.' Diss. Baylor University, 2010.

Martinez de las Rivas, Toby. 'Different Gods: Conflict and Change in the Poetic Theologies of C. H. Sisson and Jack Clemo.' *PN Review 217*, May/June 2014.

Martinez de las Rivas, Toby. 'Jack Clemo.' *Terror*. London: Faber & Faber, 2014.

Middlebro', Tom, 'The Spirit and the Clay: the Poetry of Jack Clemo.' *Queen's Quarterly*, 1973.

Milne, Angela. 'Clay Country.' *The Observer*, 14 March 1948.

Miskin, Lionel. 'Jack Clemo.' *Aylesford Review* vol. VIII no. 3, Winter 1966/Spring 1967.

Mitson, Eileen. *Reaching for God*. New York: Christian Herald Books, 1978.

Morgan, Kathleen E. *Christian Themes in Contemporary Poets*. London: SCM Press, 1965.

Mudd, David. *Cornishmen and True*. Newcastle upon Tyne: Frank Graham, 1971.

Murphy, Rosalie, ed. *Contemporary Poets of the English Language*. London: St James Press, 1970.

Newman, Paul. 'The Long Voyage out of Loneliness.' *Cornish Scene*, June/July 1986.

Parker, Derek. 'The Lonely Inspiration of Jack Clemo.' *Sunday Times Magazine Supplement*, 19 August 1962.

Parker, Derek. *The West Country*. London: Batsford, 1973.

Pearce, Brian Louis. *Clemo The Poet*. Middlesex: Magwood, 2002.

Porter, David. 'Scarred yet Singing.' *Salt*, Summer 1975.
Porter, David. 'A Blind Poet Sees.' *Crusade*, April 1980.
Press, John. *Rule and Energy: Trends in British Poetry Since the Second World War.* London: Oxford University Press, 1963.
Press, John. *The Lengthening Shadows: observations on poetry and its enemies.* London: Oxford University Press, 1971.
Rafferty, Jean. 'Love Story.' *Telegraph Sunday Magazine*, 11 January 1987.
Rawe, Donald. 'In Memoriam Jack Clemo.' *Cornish Banner* 78, 1994.
Rawe, Donald. *Cornish Villages*. London: Robert Hale, 1978.
Rowland, John. *One Man's Mind: an autobiographical record.* London: SCM Press, 1952.
Rowland, John. 'A Visit to Goonamarris.' *Cornish Review*, Winter 1974.
Rumney, Sylvia. 'The Poet of Vinegar Point.' *Cornish Life*, April 1989.
Rylance, Rick, and Featherstone, Simon. 'The Poetry of Jack Clemo and the Way We Read Today.' *Ideas and Production* IX-X, 1989.
Sandford, Rosemary. 'Poet in White Silence, A Critical Analysis, & Stripping the Cadaver, A Collection of Poems.' University of Newcastle, 2011.
Savage, D.S. 'Jack R. Clemo: an introductory essay.' *Western Review* vol. 20, Winter 1956.
Savage, D.S. Personal correspondence with Clemo.
Sergeant, Howard. 'The Discovery of God's Jazz.' *English* vol. 14 no. 83, Summer 1963.
Smelt, Maurice. *101 Cornish Lives*. Penzance: Alison Hodge, 2006.
Smith, John. 'Jack Clemo, Clay Phoenix.' *Cornish Life*, February 1985.
Spinks, Michael. 'Jack Clemo: Poet of Sight and Sound.' *Cornish Banner* no. 109, 2002.
Spinks, Michael. 'Jack Clemo: Poet of Time and Space.' *The Cornish Banner* no. 110, 2002.
Spinks, Michael. 'The Poet and the Vision.' *Talking Sense*, Spring 2003. Web.
Spinks, Michael. 'Jack Clemo's London.' *London Cornish Association Newsletter*, Spring/Summer 2009.
Spinks, Michael. 'The Developing Image in the Poetry of Jack Clemo.' *Poetry Salzburg*, Autumn 2009.
Spinks, Michael. 'The Poets of the China Clay Country.' *Cornish Banner* no. 149, August 2012.
Stone, Norman. 'A Different Drummer'. *ACG Magazine*, July/August 1999.
Symons, Andrew. 'Jack Clemo, Poet of Cornwall.' *Nexus*, November 1986.

Symons, Andrew. 'The Spiritual Achievement of Jack Clemo.' *Christian*, July/August 1989.
Symons, Andrew. 'A Visit to Jack Clemo.' *Acumen*, May 2008.
Symons, Andrew. 'Clemo, Kent and Clay.' *Cornish Banner* 74, 1993.
Symons, Andrew. 'Clemo: The Authentic Voice.' *Cornish Banner* 78, 1994.
Symons, Andrew. 'The Vision of Jack Clemo.' *Artyfact* 12, 1999.
Symons, Andrew. 'Jack Clemo's Italian Holiday.' *Journal of the Royal Institute of Cornwall* 3, 2000.
Symons, Andrew. 'Clemo's Clay Inferno.' *Cornish Banner* 104, 2001.
Symons, Andrew. 'Jack Clemo's Mystical-Erotic Quest.' *Cornish Studies* 13, 2005.
Symons, Andrew. 'Jack Clemo: Poet, Novelist and Autobiographer' *Expository Times* 121 (5), 2010.
Thompson, Luke. 'The Cornish Bond.' *The Cornish Banner*, August 2013.
Thompson, Luke. 'The Happy Chance of Jack Clemo.' *Cornish Studies* 21, 2013.
Thompson, Luke. 'The Fulfilled Believer.' *Dorset Year Book*, Winter 2013/14.
Thompson, Luke. 'Blind Girl at a Service.' *PN Review* 217, May/June. 2014.
Thompson, Luke. 'Chalk Heart and Clay Heart.' *The Powys Journal*, 2014.
Thompson, Luke. 'Clay Country.' *Archipelago* 9, 2014.
Thompson, Luke. 'The Correspondence of Jack Clemo and A.L. Rowse.' *The Cornish Banner*, February 2015.
Thompson, Luke. 'Dear Dorset.' *Dorset Year Book*, Winter 2015/16.
Tolley, A. T. *Poetry of the Forties*. Manchester: Manchester University Press, 1986.
Trewin, J.C. and Willmott, H.J. *London-Bodmin*. London: Westaway Books, 1950.
Trower, Shelley. 'Clayscapes.' *Cornish Studies* 17, 2009.
Uncredited. 'Jack Clemo and TFP (1950).' *The Powys Society Newsletter*, April 2002.
Val Baker, Denys. *The Spirit of Cornwall*. London: W H Allen, 1980.
Val Baker, Denys. *Britain Discovers Herself*. London: Christopher Johnson, 1950.
Wakefield, Gordon S. 'God and Some British Poets.' *The Expository Times* vol. 109 no. 4, January 1998.
Walsh, Chad. 'The Refined Fire.' *Christianity Today*, 11 October 1974.
Warner, Felicity. 'Jack Clemo – Poet of Clay.' *Peninsula Review*, 1981.

Warren, Richard. 'The Invading Gospel of Jack Clemo.' richardwarren.wordpress.com, 16 January 2012.

Westland, Ella. *Cornwall: A Cultural Construction of Place*. Penzance: Patten Press,1997.

Williams, Derek. 'Writing of Cornwall.' *Cornish Banner* no. 59, 1990.

Williams, Katie. 'Jack Clemo'. *Cornish Banner* no. 70, 1992.

Williams, Michael. 'The World of Jack Clemo.' *Cornish Magazine*, vol.6 no. 4, August 1963.

Williams, Rowan. 'Bonhoeffer and the Poets.' *Travelling with Resilience: Essays for Alastair Haggart*. Edinburgh: Scottish Episcopal Church, 2002.

Wintle, Frank. 'A Seeker of Light in a World of Darkness.' *Western Morning News*, 7 September 1973.

Woolley, David. 'Written on our Hands.' *Written on our Hands*. Denbighshire: Headland, 2006.

Woolsey, Stephen. 'The Awkward Blessing.' *Mars Hill Review* 13, 1999.

Woolsey, Stephen. '"Naming Wholeness in a Sick Climate": Landscape, Nature and Grace in Jack Clemo's Poetry.' *Stonework* 4, April 2007.

Endnotes

1. Diary, 24 February 1994.
2. DS to JC, 26 February 1986.
3. *The Marriage of a Rebel*, pg. 12.
4. R.M. Barton, *A History of the China-Clay Industry*. Truro: D. Bradford Barton Ltd., 1966. Pg. 19.
5. *Confession of a Rebel*, pg. 36.
6. In *Confession of a Rebel*, Clemo would write that the annual Tea Treat was 'a bustling, noisy affair that was torture to me, all the more incomprehensible because it was inflicted in the name of religion' (pg. 51). For a brief collection of clay country traditions, see Alison and Merv Davey's *Snail Creeps and Tea Treats*. Bodmin: An Daras, 2008.
7. A pamphlet was written by Reverend Williams in 1976 to mark the centenary of Trethosa Chapel, for which Clemo wrote the poem 'Bethel Centenary'.
8. See Thomas Shaw's *A History of Cornish Methodism*. Truro: D. Bradford Barton, 1967.
9. Quoted in John Pearce's *The Wesleys in Cornwall*. Truro: D. Bradford Barton, 1964. Pg. 131.
10. *Confession of a Rebel*, pg. 102, and 'Hocking', pg. 53.
11. Diary, 1 April 1944.
12. *The Marriage of a Rebel*, pgs. 94-5.
13. Ibid.
14. *Confession of a Rebel*, 1975 edition, pg.2.
15. *The Marriage of a Rebel*, pg. 95.
16. Sally Magnusson, *Clemo: A Love Story*. Herts: Lion Publishing, 1986. Pg. 14.
17. There is a photograph of Reggie aboard the Majestic in the photographic archive at the University of Exeter, though it is mistakenly dated 1909.
18. A relative of Eveline's, Maria Willcox, said that most marriages came about in this way, though it was a surprise to her that it happened to such a religiously moral woman as Eveline. Throughout the remainder of her life, Eveline developed a strong reputation in the community for her puritanism and moral rectitude.
19. *Confession of a Rebel*, pg. 9.
20. This conversation is recorded by Clemo in his diary, 9 March 1941.
21. *I Proved Thee at the Waters*, pg. 8, and *Confession of a Rebel*, pg. 18.
22. *The Marriage of a Rebel*, pg. 21.

23 *Pause for Thought*, BBC Radio 2, 13-17 December 1976.
24 *Confession of a Rebel*, pg 15.
25 Ibid. pgs. 18-19.
26 In the original handwritten manuscript of Charles Causley's introduction to Clemo's volume of poetry *The Map of Clay*, Causley included the detail Eveline Clemo had informed him of, that the Tornado was sunk 'bringing back butter or margarine'. This is one of several details edited out of Causley's final draft that suggest a sense of the war's absurd waste of life.
27 *Confession of a Rebel*, pg. 20.
28 This may have been the wreck of the French trawler, *Philomene*, and the last launch of the traditional lifeboat in 1920.
29 *I Proved Thee at the Waters*, pgs. 7-8.
30 *Confession of a Rebel*, pg. 22.
31 Ibid. pgs. 24-5.
32 *I Proved Thee at the Waters*, pg. 9.
33 'Montana Shade' was removed and set aside by Clemo's wife, Ruth, and the diary entry referring back to it was also cut out and set aside. It appears as though Ruth was intending to destroy the poem and all references to it, though she adored it so much she changed her mind. It was written 20-21 October 1962.
34 *Confession of a Rebel*, pg. 28.
35 *Cornish Guardian*, 19 November 1936.
36 *Confession of a Rebel*, pg. 30.
37 Ibid. pg. 90.
38 Ibid. pg. 92.
39 Ibid. pg. 29.
40 *I Proved Thee at the Waters*, pg. 12.
41 Michael Williams, 'The World of Jack Clemo.' *Cornish Magazine*, vol.6 no. 4, August 1963.
42 *Confession of a Rebel*, pg. 36.
43 *The Marriage of a Rebel*, pg. 39-40.
44 Several books of accounts and minutes of meetings were held at Trethosa Chapel, where I viewed them on 15 July 2013, but since closing their whereabouts are uncertain. The current information came from a book marked 'Statement of Accounts Trethosa Bible Christian Sunday School Jan 1905 – Dec 1998.'
45 Eileen appears in *Confession of a Rebel* and wrote her own account of the romantic correspondence in her book *Reaching for God* (New York: Christian Herald Books, 1978). Their correspondence will be

46 *I Proved Thee at the Waters*, pg. 6.
47 *Confession of a Rebel*, pg. 6.
48 Ibid. pg. 26.
49 Ibid. pg. 52.
50 Ibid. pg. 48.
51 Ibid. pg. 62.
52 Speaking more literally, there were indeed glittering gems among the kaolin dust, and whenever Eveline found any bright crystals in the rocks around the clayworks she would add them to the garden wall at the front so that they would sparkle in the morning sun.
53 *Confession of a Rebel*, pg. 59.
54 Ibid. pg. 62.
55 Diary, 1 October 1935.
56 *Confession of a Rebel*, pg. 69.
57 *Pause for Thought*.
58 Diary, 10 February 1936.
59 Diary, 10 June 1936.
60 Diary, 21 November 1934.
61 JC to Mr. Sands, 31 May 1980.
62 Mr Phillips is amusingly represented in Norman Stone's 1980 film *A Different Drummer*, where he is called 'Mr Thomas'.
63 *Confession of a Rebel*, pg. 83.
64 JC to Stephen John Lane, 14 November 1976.
65 *Confession of a Rebel*, pg. 84.
66 Ibid. pg. 83.
67 Ibid. pg. 64.
68 Ibid. pg. 83.
69 Ibid. pg. 109.
70 Diary, 1 July 1936.
71 Diary, 21 May 1935.
72 Charlotte Brontë, *Jane Eyre*. London: Penguin, 2006. Pg. 336.
73 Diary, 26 November 1942.
74 JC to Louis Hemmings, 13 December 1982. The Browning quotation is from 'Giuseppe Caponsacchi', *The Ring and the Book*, ll. 2085 and 2096-7.
75 Diary, 7 May 1937.
76 Although this quotation is from the diary entry for 30 December 1934, it is an example of Clemo marking the anniversaries of notable events and is in fact a comment on the previous Christmas and New

Year period.

77 *Confession of a Rebel*, pg. 108. Carlyle's *Sartor Resartus* had a great influence on Clemo, though it is rarely acknowledged. 'Teufelsdrockh' was the name of the fictional philosopher who was the subject of Carlyle's novel.
78 Ibid. pg. 107.
79 Diary, 3 February 1945.
80 Diary, 16 November 1934.
81 Diary, 25 January 1936.
82 Diary, 3 July 1936.
83 Diary, 8 April 1935.
84 *Confession of a Rebel*, pg. 90.
85 Ibid. pgs. 90-91.
86 The pleasure of a girl's smile is recurrent in the diaries, as in this entry from 24 March 1936: 'I went into Smith's for the *Author's Handbook* and typing paper, and the girl smiled, smiled as she handed me the parcel. Life is worth while while there's one girl who looks at me and smiles'.
87 Diary, 28 May 1935.
88 Diary, 9 December 1934.
89 Diary, 23 September 1935.
90 Much of this essay may be found on the backs of drafts of poems in the manuscript of *The Clay Verge* at The University of Exeter.
91 Diaries, 25 May 1944, and 26 August 1949.
92 Diary, 20 November 1934.
93 Diary, 3 July 1936.
94 Diary, 19 November 1934.
95 Diary, 16 January 1937.
96 *Confession of a Rebel*, pgs. 128-9.
97 Rudolf Besier, *The Barretts of Wimpole Street*. New York: Dramatists Play Service, 1957. Pg. 39.
98 G. K. Chesterton, *Robert Browning*. Cornwall: House of Stratus, 2008. Pg. 35.
99 *The Invading Gospel*, pg. 29.
100 Robert Browning, *Poems and Plays*. London: J.M. Dent, 1936. Pg. 10.
101 *Confession of a Rebel*, pgs. 128-9.
102 Diary, 25 December 1937.
103 Diary, 4 April 1944.
104 *Confession of a Rebel*, pg. 236.
105 Diary, 27 October 1937.

106 Diary, 9 October 1935.
107 Diary, 6 February 1936.
108 Diary, 27 June 1936.
109 Diary, 3 February 1936.
110 Diary, 9 March 1935.
111 Diary, 15 September 1936.
112 Diary, 27 August 1936.
113 Diary, 18 February 1936.
114 Diary, 7 June 1935.
115 Diary, 25 October 1936.
116 Diary, 29 January 1936.
117 Diary, 30 January 1937.
118 Diary, 11 March 1937.
119 Diary, 22 March 1938.
120 JC to Andrew Symons, 16 May 1975.
121 Diary, 9 September 1937.
122 Diary, 12 July 1837.
123 Diary, 8 March 1938.
124 *Confession of a Rebel*, pg. 71.
125 This was declared 'my life motto' in 1942.
126 This simple hymn is indicative of the decade's development. One day he kept singing the chorus of it in his head, and Clemo remarks poignantly of God: 'I love Him and His love is breaking my heart into utter surrender'. Diary, 5 June 1936.
127 *Confession of a Rebel*, pg. 74.
128 Diary, 29 October 1937.
129 Diary, 8 April 1936.
130 Paramount Music to JC, 11 August 1936.
131 Diary, 24 October 1941.
132 *Cornish Guardian*, 23 October 1930.
133 *Cornish Guardian*, 25 December 1930.
134 *Cornish Guardian*, 24 December 1931.
135 *Cornish Guardian*, 31 December 1931.
136 *Cornish Guardian*, 7 January 1932.
137 Originally, The St Austell Picture Theatre. There seem to have been three cinemas in St Austell in 1928, The Savoy, The Picturedrome (in the Town Hall), and The Capitol. All three had adverts for films in the *Cornish Guardian*. It has been suggested by David Stark and Mark Williams, historians of St Austell and of Cornish cinema, that the Truro Road cinema was the most likely venue.

138 *Cornish Guardian*, 5 May 1932.
139 Diary, 15 February 1944.
140 *Cornish Guardian*, 12 September 1936.
141 SB to JC, 4 February 1935.
142 SB to JC, 20 February 1935.
143 *Cornish Guardian*, 21 July 1932.
144 *Cornish Guardian*, 19 September 1935.
145 *John O'London*, 3 October 1936.
146 Ibid. It is unclear whether Clemo intends 'gambles' or 'gambols'.
147 *Cornish Guardian*, 23 September 1937.
148 DH Lawrence, *Fantasia of the Unconscious* and *Psychoanalysis and the Unconscious*. London: Penguin, 1971. Pg. 51.
149 *Cornish Guardian*, 14 October 1937.
150 Clemo appears not to have read any of these at this time. In 1980, however, he did request a Braille version of Euripides' *Alcestis*, following his friendship with the academic Patricia Moyer.
151 Diary, 29 December 1934.
152 Diary, 4 October 1943.
153 *Cornish Guardian*, 1 June 1933.
154 *Cornish Guardian*, 29 June 1933.
155 *Cornish Guardian*, 6 July 1933.
156 *Cornish Guardian*, 15 June 1933.
157 *Cornish Guardian*, 19 July 1934.
158 Diary, 29 June 1943.
159 Diary, 9 November 1984.
160 *Cornish Guardian*, 24 January 1935.
161 *Cornish Guardian*, 31 August 1933.
162 Diary, 2 November 1961.
163 *Cornish Guardian*, 3 October 1935.
164 Ena Kendall, 'A Vocation for Marriage ', *Observer Magazine*, 17 February 1980.
165 *Cornish Guardian*, 10 October 1935.
166 *Cornish Guardian*, 17 October 1935.
167 *Cornish Guardian*, 24 October 1935.
168 Frank Baron to JC, 16 Jan 1950.
169 *Confession of a Rebel*, pg. 134.
170 A brief description of Martin is given in the front of Clemo's 1941 diary, where Clemo has written out a list of inspirational and motivational quotations from his literary friends and contacts.
171 *Confession of a Rebel*, pg. 133.

172 Martin to JC, 14 April 1937.
173 Martin to JC, 8 February 1937.
174 Ibid.
175 *Confession of a Rebel*, pg. 134.
176 Martin to JC, 23 February 1937.
177 *Cornish Guardian*, 20 April 1939.
178 Rowse diary, 29 October 1939.
179 *Cornish Guardian*, 14 April 1938.
180 *Cornish Guardian*, 7 May 1936.
181 *PN Review*, vol. 6 no. 1, 1979.
182 *Confession of a Rebel*, pg. 150.
183 *Cornish Guardian*, 7 May 1936.
184 *Cornish Guardian*, 21 May 1936.
185 *Cornish Guardian*, 30 November 1933.
186 Hocking to JC, 1930. Jack pasted this letter into his copy of *Confession of a Rebel*, along with others from Sir Arthur Quiller-Couch and T.F. Powys, and photographs of Browning and Powys.
187 Rowse, pg. 119.
188 Meggy to JC, 16 July 1931.
189 Gordon Meggy to JC, 22 May 1931.
190 GM to JC, 16 July 1931.
191 GM to JC, 23 July 1931.
192 Ibid.
193 GM to JC, 27 November 1931.
194 GM to JC, 11 February 1932.
195 GM to JC, 12 August 1931.
196 GM to JC, 16 July 1931 and 12 September 1932.
197 GM to JC, 26 July 1932.
198 Diary, 17 May 1937.
199 ALR to JC, 2 April 1948.
200 GM to JC, 13 June 1933.
201 GM to JC, 13 June 1933.
202 GM to JC, 4 November 1931.
203 John T. Nettleship, *Robert Browning: Essays and Thoughts*. London: Elkin Matthews, 1890.
204 Diary, 20 September 1935.
205 John Green to JC, 2 March 1936.
206 P. Ross for Heath to JC, 14 October 1936.
207 Diary, 22 July 1936.
208 Raymond Savage to JC, 7 and 10 August 1945.

209 Harmony Press to JC, 26 July 1939.
210 Q to JC, 6 January 1940.
211 *Confession of a Rebel*, pgs. 169-70.
212 Diary, 5 November 1941.
213 Diary, 11 September 1943.
214 Quoted in a letter from Raymond Savage to JC, 5 February 1946.
215 RS to JC, 8 March 1946.
216 Forwarded by Harold Raymond to JC, 17 February 1947.
217 Diary, 18 February 1947.
218 RS to JC, 22 March 1946.
219 For reference, in 'Penance of the Seed' the ending is very similar, with Bryn and Lory honeymooning at Hugh Town, and the light like a 'sword' in the final phrase.
220 JC to FW, 5 November 1990.
221 RS to JC, 19 November 1945.
222 Diary, 14 September 1946.
223 John Calvin, *Institutes of the Christian Religion*. Trans. John Allen. Philadelphia: Presbyterian Board of Publication, book III, chapter XXI, 1816.
224 Many of Spurgeon's sermons can be found at spurgeon.org.
225 Charles Spurgeon, *Spurgeon's Sermons*. 10 volumes. Massachusetts: Hendrickson Publishers, vol. 2. Pg. 75.
226 *Confession of a Rebel*, pg. 191.
227 Diary, 27 September 1941.
228 *Confession of a Rebel*, pg. 191.
229 Dr Stanley Maurice Coleman was then Medical Superintendent at St Lawrence's Mental Hospital, Bodmin. He was clearly interested in artistic temperaments and a few years later wrote a paper on Peter Warlock, entitled 'The Dual Personality of Philip Heseltine'.
230 JC to A.L. Rowse, 4 April 1948.
231 Diary, 8 October 1941.
232 *Confession of a Rebel*, pg. 193.
233 Ibid.
234 Ibid.
235 Diary, 22 September 1944.
236 Diary, 22 April 1943.
237 Diary, 26 October 1942.
238 Diary, 12 April 1944.
239 Diary, 1 January 1945.
240 Diary, 30 April 1944.

241 *Confession of a Rebel*, pg. 171.
242 Ibid.
243 Diary, 17 April 1944.
244 Diary, 12 April 1943.
245 Diary, 18 March 1942.
246 Diary, 15 November 1942.
247 Diary, 24 June 1942.
248 Diary, 29 January 1943.
249 Diary, 6 September 1943.
250 Diary, 23 October 1943.
251 Diary, 26 May 1943.
252 Diary, 28 April 1943.
253 *Confession of a Rebel*, pg. 218.
254 Ibid. pgs. 218-9.
255 Diary, 1 May 1944.
256 Diary, 18 June 1946.
257 Diary, 8 May 1945.
258 Diary, 9 March 1945.
259 Diary, 12 January 1944.
260 Diary, 4 May 1943.
261 Diary, 25 January 1945.
262 Diary, 13 July 1943.
263 Diary, 25 June 1945.
264 *Wilding Graft*, pg. 274.
265 JC to ALR, 4 April 1948.
266 JC to Ruth, 7 April 1969.
267 Diary, 14 April 1952.
268 Ibid.
269 Diary, 2 October 1952.
270 *Confession of a Rebel*, pg. 102.
271 Diary, 4 December 1941.
272 Diary, 4 June and 5 October 1942.
273 Diary, 5 November 1941.
274 Diary, 8 May 1944.
275 In *Tess of the Durbervilles* and *The Mayor of Casterbridge*.
276 See *Jude the Obscure*.
277 JC to Charles Causley, 6 May 1969.
278 Diary, 13 December 1942.
279 The theologian Thomas DeWitt Talmage, one of Clemo's key influences during this period, gave a famous sermon on this section

of Isaiah, entitled 'The Lord's Razor'.
280 Diary, 12 April 1943.
281 Diary, 4 May 1944.
282 Quoted in a letter from RS to JC, 6 November 1945.
283 Diary, 29 May 1945.
284 Quoted in a letter from RS to JC, 22 March 1946.
285 Ibid.
286 RS to JC, 27 March 1946.
287 *Confession of a Rebel*, pg. 204.
288 This version is the earliest published, taken from *Orion III*, autumn 1946.
289 Diary, 19 August 1946.
290 Diary, 23 October 1946.
291 *NYT*, 7 November 1948.
292 *Observer*, 14 March 1948.
293 *NYT*, 27 October 1948.
294 Helena Charles to JC, 24 November 1948
295 C. S. Lewis, *The Problem of Pain*. London: Collins, 2012. Pg. 88.
296 *The Invading Gospel*, pg. 101.
297 *The Marriage of a Rebel*, pgs. 95-6.
298 *The Invading Gospel*, pg. 125.
299 *TLS*, 27 March 1948.
300 A recording of this is held by the University of Exeter's Special Collections archives, although at the time of writing it is without a reference number. The recording is of an interview with Eveline Clemo, broadcast daily from 13-17 November 1976.
301 Diary, 28 August 1956.
302 Diary, 29 October 1946.
303 Diary, 13 April 1948.
304 JC to BR, 9 November 1946.
305 Diary, 19 November 1948.
306 Diary, 25 October 1946.
307 Diary, 16 November 1946.
308 Diary, 1 November 1946.
309 Forwarded by Harold Raymond to JC, 17 February 1947.
310 Diary, 18 February 1947.
311 Diary, 10 July 1948.
312 HR to JC, 25 February 1947.
313 Diary, 5 November 1946.
314 ALR to JC, 31 March 1948.

315　JC to ALR, 1 April 1948.
316　Ibid.
317　JC to ALR, 17 November 1949.
318　JC to ALR, 19 December 1949.
319　JC to ALR, 27 March 1950.
320　Diary, 8 May 1948.
321　Diary, 22 November 1948.
322　JC to Michael Spinks, 1 February 1983.
323　Diary, 21 August 1945.
324　JM Coetzee, 'Confession and Double Thoughts', in *Doubling the Point*. Ed. David Attwell. Massachusetts: Harvard University Press, 1992. Pgs. 251-293.
325　As well as Coetzee's 'Confession and Double Thoughts', much of the discussion here was influenced by Peter Brooks' *Troubling Confessions: Speaking Guilt in Law and Literature*. Chicago: Chicago University Press, 2000.
326　JC to ALR, 4 April 1948.
327　Diary, 2 December 1943.
328　CDL to JC, 21 April 1947.
329　Diary, 24 April 1947.
330　Diary, 29 March 1948.
331　CDL to JC, 26 August 1948.
332　Diary, 24 May 1950. The review was in the *Sydney Morning Herald* at the beginning of March 1950, entitled 'Warped Soul from Cornwall'.
333　*Evening Standard*, 20 September 1949.
334　*Daily Mail*, 8 October 1949.
335　It is just possible that this man is Rexroth himself. Rexroth first visited Savage at the same time as *Confession of a Rebel* was published, and has been described in similar terms by Savage.
336　Diary, 3 October 1950.
337　Diary, 9 January 1945.
338　In *Confession*, Clemo states that *Orion III* was published in January 1947. This is incorrect. The confusion seems to derive from the delay to the contributor's copies being sent out. Clemo's copy arrived on 24 January 1947.
339　Diary, 23 April 1946.
340　CDL to JC, 19 March 1947.
341　Inexplicably, this poem was included in *The Awakening: Poems Newly Found*, in 2003 (25). It is word-for-word identical with the published version, only missing some of the correct punctuation and using the

old title 'Revelations in the Clay Pit'.
342 In *The Clay Verge* 'clay-bone' is misprinted as 'clay-cone'. This is corrected in *The Map of Clay*.
343 Diary, 30 September 1946.
344 *The Marriage of a Rebel*, pg. 28.
345 Statement to Exeter students, 18 June 1977.
346 JC to Sara Ramsden, 29 June 1990.
347 Quotation from the typed manuscript of the interview, which Clemo wrote to help memorize it in preparation of the recording.
348 *The Marriage of a Rebel*, pg. 26.
349 Diary, 9 February 1947.
350 Diary, 30 January 1948.
351 Diary, 13 January 1947.
352 Diary, 15 September 1951.
353 Diary, 4 January 1971.
354 Diary, 13 August 1959.
355 JC to Andrew Symons, 13 May 1976.
356 DS to EM, 15 November 1954.
357 Diary, 13 February 1954.
358 *Spectator*, 18 April 1952.
359 *The Marriage of a Rebel*, pg. 66.
360 Diary, 4 February 1950.
361 *Selected Poems*. Ed. Luke Thompson. London: Enitharmon, 2015. Pg. 6.
362 Diary, 20 July 1970.
363 Diary, 29 October 1986.
364 JC to Michael Spinks, 4 December 1986.
365 Diary, 14 January 1947.
366 Diary, 2 April 1947.
367 Diary, 7 April 1947.
368 Diary, 15 April 1947.
369 Diary, 11 April 1943.
370 Diary, 9 August 1947.
371 Diary, 8 August 1947.
372 Diary, 5 July 1947.
373 Diary, 17 April 1948.
374 Diary, 11 August 1948.
375 Diary, 12 May 1950.
376 Diary, 24 March 1950.
377 Diary, 30 December 1946.
378 Diary, 13 January 1949.

379 Diary, 5 and 8 February 1949.
380 Eileen Funston to JC, 17 February 1949.
381 Ibid.
382 EF to JC, 28 March 1949.
383 EF to JC, 8 April 1949.
384 EF to JC, 26 May 1949.
385 EF to JC, 2 June 1949.
386 EF to JC, 12 June 1949.
387 Diary, 3 July 1949.
388 Diary, 17 July 1949.
389 EF to JC, 17 July 1949.
390 Eileen Mitson, *Reaching for God*. New York: Christian Herald Books, 1979. Pgs. 87-8.
391 Diary, 15 August 1949.
392 Mitson, pg. 88.
393 EF to JC, 26 October 1949.
394 *The Marriage of a Rebel*, pgs. 43 and 50.
395 EF to the Clemos, 23 July 1987.
396 Diary, 5 November 1949.
397 Helena Charles wrote a very brief account of her meeting with Clemo on 24 November 1949, the day after she visited Goonamarris. It was discovered, along with Clemo's letters to Helena, by the artist Tony Martin in the back of a secondhand copy of *The Map of Clay* he bought from a Canadian bookseller.
398 JC to HC, 31 October 1949.
399 JC to HC, 7 November 1949.
400 Diary, 20 March 1950.
401 *The Marriage of a Rebel*, pg. 53.
402 Diary, 15 March 1951.
403 Diary, 26 March 1951.
404 June Trethewey, or Morcom, has written an account of her time with Clemo and has shared it with those working on his life. At the time of writing, it is yet to be published, though Trethewey has written many useful historical reminiscences about the Trethosa area for *The Cornish Banner*.
405 MH to JC, 30 December 1949.
406 LP to JC, 22 January 1950.
407 Diary, 24 July 1950.
408 Diary, 8 May and 4 August 1946.
409 Diary, 31 December 1949.

410 Monica Hutchings, 'The Cornish Rebel.' *West Country Magazine* summer 1951.
411 He was seventy-four.
412 MH to JC, 30 August 1950.
413 Diary, 16 September 1950.
414 MH to JC, 18 September 1950.
415 Diary, 20 September 1950.
416 A sentiment expressed in his diary, 6 October 1941, after visiting Dr Coleman for psychological evaluation.
417 Diary, 27 November 1948.
418 Diary, 6 February 1950.
419 Diary, 13 April 1957.
420 Diary, 29 and 30 April 1950.
421 Quoted in a letter from Harold Raymond to JC, 17 February 1947.
422 Diary, 10 April 1952.
423 JC to CC, 1 September 1953.
424 DS to EM, 15 November 1954.
425 DS to CC, 15 February 1954.
426 Diary, 25 May 1950.
427 *The Marriage of a Rebel*, pg. 78, and Diary, 11 March 1952.
428 Oral Roberts to Eveline Clemo, 2 November 1954. In his note, Roberts misspelled the name, addressing Eveline as 'Sister Clenie'.
429 GB to JC, 26 March 1952.
430 CC to JC, 19 October 1951.
431 CC to JC, 26 August 1953.
432 CC to JC, 10 March 1959.
433 Diary, 19 March 1988.
434 Diary, 18 August 1976.
435 This article was cut out from an unspecified newspaper and glued into Clemo's diary for 17-20 January 1961.
436 LM to JC, 22 February 1956.
437 Diary, 25 November 1959.
438 Diary, 6 November 1956.
439 Diary, 4 November 1956.
440 Diary, 15 April 1954.
441 Diary, 31 December 1959.
442 The transcription of this can be found in Exeter's Special Collections Library, reference EUL MS 50a/PROF/6/1/2/14
443 These quotations are taken from an undated transcript, dictated by Clemo to his mother in preparation for a BBC radio interview. They

would have been written December 1961 for a 1962 broadcast.
444 Diary, 17 November 1954.
445 Diary, 14 June 1958.
446 Diary, 25 February 1957.
447 Diary, 27 December 1943.
448 Diary, 24 February 1985.
449 Diary, 28 February and 16 March 1975.
450 See diary, 13 September and 3 November 1951.
451 CC to JC, 22 October 1958.
452 JC to Sara Ramsden, 21 June 1990.
453 Calvin, Book I, pg. 211.
454 See *The Invading Gospel* pgs. 138, 140-1 and 146.
455 Ibid. pg. 106.
456 Ibid. pg. 92, as well as Luke 24:49.
457 See, for example, Talmage's sermon 'Ransomless', as well as his autobiography.
458 JC to VP, 30 October 1974.
459 *I Proved Thee at the Waters*, pgs. 4-6.
460 *The Marriage of a Rebel*, pg. 94.
461 Mentioned in the unpublished preface Clemo wrote for *The Map of Clay*.
462 *Confession of a Rebel*, pg. 126.
463 JC to Stephen John Lane, 14 November 1976.
464 *Confession of a Rebel*, pg. 31.
465 JC to EM, 17 December 1949.
466 *Confession of a Rebel*, pg. 71.
467 Ramsden's paper, 'The Mysticism of an Erotic Mystic', was given at the 2013 Jack Clemo conference *Kindling the Scarp*.
468 JG to JC, 30 March 1960.
469 Diary, 7 January 1962.
470 JC to Prior, 23 January 1989.
471 JC to EM, 12 November 1958.
472 JC to EM, 18 December 1958.
473 JF to JC, 9 July 1959.
474 JF to JC, 20 July 1959.
475 JC to DS, 27 May 1989.
476 Diary, 9 December 1959.
477 DS to JC, 13 December 1957.
478 CM to JC, 22 May 1959.
479 JC to CC, 18 March 1959.

480 The preface has been inserted, along with a proposed order of the poems, in the front of Clemo's 1957 diary.
481 Cullen to JC, 19 February 1960.
482 EC to CC, 29 March 1960.
483 Prior to publication, some local newspapers, including the *Western Morning News* and *Cornish Guardian*, advertised the forthcoming volume as 'Clayland Poems', and it was titled as such on the original contract with Methuen.
484 JC to CC, 4 October 1960.
485 Diary, 16 September 1947.
486 See *The Marriage of a Rebel*, pg. 82 and *IG*, pg. 127.
487 JC to AS, 5 September 1977.
488 Diary, 11 April 1962.
489 From an address intended to be read at a Newlyn reading, 20 April 1978.
490 Diary, 24 April 1969.
491 This amount would be raised over the years, going up to £300 in 1966, £400 in 1969, £500 in 1970, and so on. By 1981 the amount had been raised to £1,000, and by 1991 to £1,600.
492 A version of this poem was published as 'Border Raid' in *Tantalus*, though it is otherwise uncollected.
493 Diary, 29 April and 7 January 1961.
494 JC to CC, 3 May 1962.
495 Diary, 1 February 1960.
496 Diary, 11 November 1962.
497 JC to Ruth Peaty, 16 December 1967.
498 Diary, 24 April 1961.
499 Diary, 25 July 1962.
500 Diary, 29 July 1962.
501 Diary, 9 December 1961.
502 Diary, 19 December 1962.
503 RN to JC, 27 November 1963.
504 Diary, 8 February 1963.
505 JC to CC, 30 March 1963.
506 Diary, 4 February 1963.
507 JC to SJL, 14 November 1976.
508 Diary, 9 February 1963.
509 JC to SJL, 14 November 1976.
510 Diary, 6 February 1965.
511 Diary, 2 January 1966.

512 Diary, 8 June 1966.
513 JC to SJL, 15 July 1977.
514 Mary to JC, 10 August 1964.
515 As an aside, it might be worth mentioning that Clemo states in a 1991 letter that although he showed 'tenderness' before marriage, he did not 'grab marital passion before marriage'. That is to say, he did not have sex with Mary.
516 Heather Martin wrote probably the most useful academic work on Clemo to date, entitled 'Jack Clemo's Vocation to Evangelical Poetry and Erotic Marriage: an Examination of his Poems of Personal Tribute and Critique.' Baylor University, 2010.
517 Diary, 20 August 1964.
518 Diary, 22 August 1964.
519 Mary to JC, 1965. The exact date is not given, though is probably late June or early July.
520 This is taken from a list of notes Clemo wrote on a handful of individual poems which Charles Causley was due to read at the Poetry Society, 28 September 1973.
521 JC to David Porter, 14 April 1975.
522 Also from the notes written by Clemo for Causley's 1973 reading of Clemo's work at the Poetry Society.
523 JC to CC, 5 October 1967.
524 CC to JC, 20 October 1967.
525 *Church Times*, 23 February 1968.
526 Diary, 1 January 1966.
527 Diary, 15 December 1964.
528 *Catholic Herald*, 1 December 1967.
529 Diary, 18 December 1963.
530 This poem was sent in the last correspondence between Jack and Ruth before they married, 11 October 1968.
531 Ruth to CIB, 23 July 1967.
532 Diary, 10 January 1967.
533 Diary, 3 February, 13 February and 7 March 1967.
534 Ruth to JC, 5 November 1967.
535 Ruth to JC, 15 October 1967. In later correspondence on this subject of domesticity, Clemo wrote the following rhyme as a joke:
Hanging clothes is a feminine feat
   In sunshine or blizzards or fogs:
If a husband pegs up the sheet
   The marriage will go to the dogs.

536 Diary, 18 February 1954.
537 Date destroyed.
538 Diary, 5 February 1968.
539 Diary, 26 and 8 October 1968.
540 Diary, 24 June 1968.
541 JC to Ruth, 4 October 1968.
542 CC to JC, 17 October 1968.
543 Diary, 7 August 1968.
544 This is from a conversation with Eileen Mitson, 2 March 2014.
545 From notes given to Sally Magnusson for her book.
546 Diary, 23 October 1968.
547 Diary, 23 July 1969.
548 Diary, 6 January 1969.
549 Diary, 7 January 1969.
550 Diary, 6 June 1969.
551 Diary, 13 June 1969.
552 Diary, 27 May 1969.
553 Hermann Peschmann, *The Voice of Poetry*. London: Evans Brothers, 1969. Pg. 24.
554 Diary, 9 November 1969.
555 Other titles considered for the collection included: 'Wesleyan Towers', 'The Bleached Cone', 'Towers in Clayscape', 'Outreach from Geneva', 'Towers in Halcyon', 'The Vibrant Cone', 'The White Cone', 'Skyline from West Trethosa', and 'The Scarred Tip'.
556 The title will be recognised as that of the posthumous selection of Clemo's early verse, *The Awakening*, published in 2003 by Alan Kent, John Hurst and Andrew Symons.
557 Diary, 19 July 1969.
558 Newman, pg. 134
559 JC to LM, 6 November 1972.
560 LM to JC, 8 October 1972.
561 JC to LM, 6 November 1972.
562 LM to JC, 29 October 1972.
563 JC to LM, 20 November 1972.
564 LM to JC, 2 December 1972.
565 JC to LM, 11 December 1972.
566 LM to JC, 12 December 1972.
567 LM to JC, 27 December 1972.
568 JC to CC, 24 June 1970.
569 Diary, 24 April 1970.

570 EM to JC, 12 July 1971.
571 JC to EM, 14 July 1971.
572 Clemo appears not to have read Heaney until 1981, when Louis Hemmings sent him a copy of *Selected Poems*, to which Clemo responded with little interest, suggesting it would have been better if Christian writers spoke more of 'conversion experiences'.
573 Diary, 25 January 1968.
574 FB to JC, 12 December 1971.
575 FB to JC, 8 January 1972.
576 JC to CC, 14 December 1970.
577 Diary, 14 May 1969.
578 Diary, 27 April 1975.
579 Diary, 7 January 1971.
580 Diary, 7 July 1976.
581 Diary, 9 June 1970.
582 Diary, 11 July 1970.
583 CC to JC, 7 November 1961.
584 *The Marriage of a Rebel*, pg. 140.
585 Diary, 21 March 1971.
586 Perry composed a bibliography for a librarian qualification, Andrew Symons produced an undergraduate thesis, and Lane a doctoral thesis.
587 SMA to JC, 21 March 1975.
588 JC to LH, 10 January 1981.
589 JC to GP, 28 January 1971.
590 Diary, 13 December 1973.
591 Diary, 25 November 1973.
592 Diary, 1 December 1976.
593 Diary, 4 July 1971.
594 Diary, 2 November 1973.
595 Diary, 23 May 1973.
596 GM to JC, 28 July 1975.
597 Diary, 4 June 1977.
598 Diary, 24 July 1977.
599 Diary, 19 October 1978.
600 DS to JC, 2 September 1979.
601 CC to JC, 19 February 1980.
602 EM to JC, 9 March 1980.
603 Diary, 11 Apirl 1978.
604 Diary, 12 May 1978 and 7 February 1980.

605 Diary, 11 May 1979.
606 Diary, 22 May 1981.
607 LT to JC, 9 August 1984.
608 Diary, 31 March 1981.
609 JC to CC, 1 March 1982.
610 JC to DS, 12 January 1983.
611 Diary, 29 December 1978.
612 Diary, 10 November 1980.
613 Diary, 4 October 1984.
614 *The Marriage of a Rebel*, 2nd edition, pg. 160.
615 JC to DS, 21 July 1982.
616 Diary, 5 July 1987.
617 JC to GP, 3 January 1986.
618 Peter Jay to JC, 22 February 1979.
619 Craig Raine to JC, 17 November 1981.
620 The killing of pets and the theme of drowning echo through Clemo's work and may well be connected in his mind to the drowning of his father. As well as in 'Coppice Tarn', there is a cat-drowning scene in *The Clay Kiln*, where the hero's father smashes a cat against the wall and throws it in the river. It will also be recalled that Jack questioned his father's character over his inability to shoot a dog in *Confession of a Rebel*.
621 Diary, 24 February 1938.
622 Inserted in letter from Harold Raymond to JC, 17 February 1947.
623 LM to JC, 18 February 1989.
624 JC to EM, 19 February 1954.
625 Quoted in letter from Harold Raymond to JC, 17 Februry 1947.
626 DS to JC, 21 February 1986.
627 DA to JC, 30 May 1985.
628 SJ to JC, 16 August 1985.
629 Diary, 28 September and 13 October 1983.
630 MB to Luke Thompson, 11 February 2012.
631 This letter survives in handwritten form, drafted by Ruth. It is unclear whether the words are hers, whether they were dictated to her, or whether they are a copy of the original letter sent. It is dated 'Oct 1986'.
632 The Clemos to *Third Way*, 14 November 1986.
633 JC to LH, 17 November 1987.
634 This fragment is taken from a long article intended for *Christian Woman* magazine. In the end they published a second and much

shorter version.
635 Diary, 15 June 1988.
636 Diary, 9 March 1984.
637 Diary, 1 August 1989.
638 DS to JC, 15 January 1979.
639 JC to DS, 27 May 1989.
640 JC to DH, 11 April 1992.
641 Diary, 1 May 1981.
642 *Observer*, 20 June 1993.
643 Diary, 2 September 1992.
644 Diary, 14 October 1992.
645 Diary, 7 April 1994.
646 JC to VP, 2 December 1993.
647 Editors of *The Awakening* reverted to the first typed draft, 'Moment of Dubiety', probably because they were unaware of the *West Country Magazine* publication and could not read the handwritten corrections on the manuscript.
648 PH to NA, 10 July 1995.
649 This has been dramatized by the Clemo scholar Andrew Symons, who wrote in an article for *The Expository Times*: 'immediately before his demise he suddenly shouted out "Where has the joy gone?"' Symons is attempting to draw a parallel between Clemo's appeal and Christ's 'Why hast Thou forsaken me?' and in doing so deviated from the facts. It was not on Clemo's deathbed that he asked his wife this, and not 'immediately before his demise', but almost a month prior to his death.
650 Ruth Clemo to Mark Shallis, date uncertain.
651 In the 1957 diary, Clemo writes that these appeared in 'a west country anthology'. The poem 'Truro' would also be published in *Cactus on Carmel* as 'Frontier City'.
652 'Rebel Love' became 'The Brownings at Vallombrosa' and appeared in *The Echoing Tip*.
653 A different draft of this poem, bearing the same title, appeared in *Cactus on Carmel*.

Index

There are a handful of people I thought it better not to name in full. They will appear in the index by their first names only, including Irene, Iris, Naomi, Rosine and Violet.

Abercrombie, Ralph, 263
Agnes, Sister Mary, 448
Alexander, David, 507
Alice's Adventures in Wonderland (Lewis Carroll), 222
Allen, Frances (foster-sister), 17, 271, 272, 273, 274, 315-6, 372, 379, 471, 482, 484, 519
Allen, Violet (foster-sister), 271, 272, 273, 274, 315-6,
Allen, Walter, 370
Allsop, Kenneth, 234, 327, 370
A.M. Heath (literary agency), 154, 155, 223, 226
Angilley, Brenda *see* Snell, Brenda,
Arminius, Jacobus, 337
Astley, Neil, 516, 523, 537
A Woman Clothed with the Sun (John Delaney), 494, 495, 496

Ball, Shirley, 477
Barnes, William, 523
Barnicoat, Father Guy, 308
Baron Frank, 88, 112, 130, 134, 172, 244, 468
Barth, Karl, 127, 170, 199, 235, 250, 260, 264, 300, 331, 332, 335, 336, 338, 345, 359, 505; *The Epistle to the Romans*, 198-9, 250, 331; *Natural Theology* (with Emil Brunner), 331
Bateman, Sophie, 483, 512
Beecher Stowe, Harriet, 60
Beethoven, Ludwig van, 429, 431, 440, 455
Bellerby, Frances, 17, 194, 249, 301, 443, 445
Bernadette of Lourdes, 366-7, 373, 449
Besier, Rudolf, 96, 201
Best, Richard, 39-40, 41
Betjeman, John, 245, 301
Biscoe, Bert, 526
Blake, William, 126, 138, 428, 429, 441, 443, 445
Bloodaxe publishers, 263, 491, 516, 517, 522, 523, 547
Boadella, Eilidh, 488

Bodmin Asylum, 30, 180, 199
Bray, Billy, 120
Brearley, Margaret, 508-9, 510
The Bridge of San Luis Rey (Thornton Wilder), 209
Brontë, Charlotte; 209, 393, 398, 547; *Jane Eyre*, 79-80, 96-7, 125, 167, 209
Brontë, Emily, 201, 209, 265, 340, 523; *Wuthering Heights*, 205
Brown, Frances (see Allen, Frances)
Brown, Pastor, 307
Browning, Robert, 75, 80, 96-8, 123, 124, 153, 155, 158, 168, 184, 187, 198, 209, 210, 221, 225, 231, 233, 238, 249, 250, 272, 283, 290, 312, 330, 331, 342, 345, 359, 396, 403, 406, 410, 413, 419, 426, 427, 429, 439, 473, 479, 484, 508, 510, 512, 514, 528-9, 530, 550; *The Browning Love Letters*, 96, 123, 124, 331, 359; 'Evelyn Hope', 209; 'Ferishtah's Fancies', 312, 331; 'Fifine at the Fair, 153; 'Ixion', 168; 'Paracelsus', 158, 331; 'Pauline', 97, 209, 331; 'Porphyria's Lover', 187; 'Prince Hohenstiel-Schwangau, Saviour of Society', 198; 'A Soul's Tragedy', 153; 'The Statue and the Bust', 168
Browning, Elizabeth Barrett, 75, 96-8, 126, 184, 287, 399, 413, 419, 427, 512, 528, 529
Bryant, William, 25
Bullen, George, 27, 29
Bunyan, John, 54, 234, 331, 345; *Grace Abounding*, 234, 331
Bunyan, Mary, 54, 392, 393, 398
Butler, Josephine, 451-2, 455
Burdett, Osbert, 209
Burrow, S.E., 112, 114-5, 116-9, 125, 129, 331; *Gleanings*, 331

Caine, Hall, 60, 124, 180
Calvin, John, 126-7, 139, 168, 170, 331-2, 334, 335, 337
Carlyle, Thomas, 120, 125, 126, 330, 337; *Sartor Resartus*, 330
Casey, Gerard, 488-9
Casey, Mary, 288, 488-9
Catholic Herald, 397
Causley, Charles, 17, 194, 225, 244, 259, 261, 263, 266, 301, 304, 306, 309-15, 317, 325, 329, 355, 356, 358, 359-60, 367, 369, 371, 372, 374, 375, 378, 395, 398, 400, 414-7, 439, 445, 449, 450, 458, 466, 473, 481, 482, 514, 522; as Best Man, 317; *Farewell, Aggie Weston*, 309; 'Helpston', 450; 'Homage to Jack Clemo', 313, 356, 360; introduction to *The Map of Clay*, 355, 359; *Penguin Modern Poets*, 374-5; *Survivor's Leave*, 313
Chase, Mary Ellen, 216
Charles, Helena, 90, 217, 244, 266, 282-5, 296

Chatterton, Thomas, 125, 233
Chatto & Windus, 161, 163, 198, 206, 215-6, 219, 221, 222, 224, 226, 238, 240, 241, 242, 246, 266, 272, 300, 356, 468, 492, 501, 503
Chesterton, G.K., 124, 331
Christian Herald, 77, 110, 274, 275, 330, 489, 306, 309, 366
Church Times, 396, 442, 496, 506
Clare, John, 435, 449-50, 458
Clemo, Esther (grandmother), 31, 172, 205
Clemo, Eveline, 26, 29, 36, 37, 41, 48, 51-3, 64, 65, 111, 136, 183, 219, 271-2, 274, 287, 291, 340, 359, 382, 387, 417, 462; birth, 28; death, 471; *I Proved Thee at the Waters*, 466-9, 502, 531; marriage, 38
Clemo, Horatio, 30
Clemo, Jack, life
Atlantic Award, 225; birth, 44; blindness, 12, 13, 52, 53, 57, 67, 68, 80, 185, 262, 269, 285, 304, 305, 325, 368, 392-3; Braille, 304-5, 379, 381-2, 397, 495; Buddhism, 398, 438, 439; the 'Browning Pattern' and 'Wimpole Street Miracle', 75, 96-7, 231, 342, 396, 413, 479, 491, 510, 511, 529; Calvinism, 15, 61, 126-7, 168-72, 259-60, 282-3, 326, 331-3, 334-40, 353, 358, 438; the Christian Introduction Bureau, 404-6, 407, 408; cinema, 71, 115-6, 518; Civil List Pension, 224-5, 245, 306, 369, 371, 374, 420; Cornish dialect, 17, 42, 59, 66, 106, 108-9, 117, 119, 129, 130, 131, 134, 147, 301, 325, 480, 481; the Cornish Gorsedh, 131-4, 446-7, 474; on dancing, 116, 172, 193, 200, 222, 277, 295, 405, 411; deafness, 54, 88, 89, 90, 144-5, 185, 190, 220, 221, 224, 304, 305, 388, 409, 497; death, 538-41; Darwin and evolution, 140-1; faith-healing, 54, 77, 206, 217, 282, 285-6, 288, 290, 306-9, 318, 320-1, 373, 389, 397, 419, 433, 448, 449; honorary doctorate, 478; hospitals and joylessness, 13, 269, 526, 540; Isaiah, 21, 43, 52-3, 153, 210, 299, 350, 474; Italy, 510-514, 528-30; the Lake District, 380, 381, 382, 383, 385, 386, 387, 388, 389, 394, 396, 499, 518; on marriage, 54, 75-6, 79, 96, 123, 166, 172, 206, 208, 217, 218, 221, 231, 256, 277, 283, 342-3, 386, 389, 394, 400, 402ff. 442, 520, 529; move to Weymouth, 471, 474, 479, 482, 483, 484; mysticism, 28, 32, 61, 81, 83, 87, 103, 172, 234, 254, 283, 340-2, 419, 440, 441, 447, 496; on nature, 15-16, 69, 85, 119, 120, 140, 171, 199, 203, 214, 237, 251, 260-1, 336, 391, 404, 435, 504; predestination, 31, 158, 159, 166, 168-71, 199, 334-5, 336, 337, 338, 339; spiritualists, 47, 373-4; syphilis, 53-7, 59, 67-8, 89, 124, 218, 268-9, 392, 509-10;
Clemo, Jack, works
'A Homely Mother' (and 'A Homely Wife'), 467; 'Alive', 432; *Approach to Murano*, 265, 391, 511, 513, 522-5; 'Arsenal', 521; *The Awakening* (posthumous collection), 250, 544; 'The Awakening' (poem), 429-30; *Banner*

Poems, 480, 519-21; 'Baptism', 491; 'Beethoven', 429-31; 'Beyond Lourdes', 366-7, 516; 'Beyond Trethosa Chapel', 362; *The Bouncing Hills*, 109, 480, 481; *Broad Autumn*, 293, 424, 449ff, 498; 'The Brownings at Vallombrosa', 426-7; 'Blind Girl at a Service', 469-70, 476, 500; 'Bunyan's Daughter', 54, 392-3, 516; 'The Burnt Bush', 191, 255, 256; 'Cactus', 393, 394; 'Cactus in Clayscape', 393; *Cactus on Carmel*, 257, 366-7, 383ff, 412; 'A Calvinist in Love', 120, 194, 213, 249, 258-9, 275, 360, 516; 'Carmel', 394-5; 'Casa Guidi', 529; 'Centre', 511; 'Charlie, the Smutties and the Baaby', 66; 'Charlotte Nicholls', 393, 547; 'Chesil Beach', 472; 'Christ in the Clay-Pit', 194, 213, 248, 249, 257-8, 315, 421; 'The Cinder-Heap', 250, 253; 'A Clash at Ikpe', 452, 455; *Clay Cuts*, 521-2; 'The Clay-Dry', 469; 'The Clay-Dump', 301-4, 446; 'Clay Fairy', 254, 544; *The Clay-Kiln*, 31, 132, 144ff, 222, 340; 'Clay-Land Moods', 516; 'Clay Phoenix' (poem), 325, 516, 550; 'The Clay-tip Worker', 250, 258, 547; *The Clay Verge*, 85, 161, 175, 248ff, 309, 356, 357, 358, 360, 370; 'Cloud Over Bugle', 531; *Confession of a Rebel*, 29, 61, 76, 92-3, 94, 108, 113, 145, 182, 230ff, 255, 263, 274, 289, 300, 309, 324, 327, 371, 473, 474, 516, 550; 'Confessional', 393; 'Coppice Tarn', 498-9, 516; 'Crab Country', 253, 315, 388, 398; *The Cured Arno*, 519, 525, 528, 530ff; *A Different Drummer*, 226, 424, 476, 479, 480, 487-8, 491ff, 517; 'Dorchester Ward'. 527; 'Dreams of Yesterday', 111, 112; 'Drought on a Clay Ridge', 492, 493, 497; 'Dungeon Ghyll', 383-5; *The Echoing Tip*, 396, 424-32, 439, 441-6, 454, 462; 'Eros in Exile', 389-90; 'The Excavator', 16, 249, 250, 257, 260, 385; 'Exit', 393, 398; 'Filming at Gunheath', 476, 477, 500; 'Flower of the Vale', 111-2; 'The Flooded Clay-Pit', 250, 252-3; 'Frontier City', 392, 393; 'Frontier Signals', 356-8, 360, 362-8; 'Gladys Aylward', 493; 'Goonvean Claywork Farm', 28; 'Grasmere Reflections', 388; 'Growing in Grace', 531-4; 'Gulls Nesting Inland', 392, 393; 'Gwindra', 388, 394; '"Gyp" and the Cats', 108; 'The Harassed Preacher', 455-8; 'Harpoon', 431-2; 'Heather Stems', 385-6; 'Heaven Number Eight', 111, 112; 'Helpston', 449-50; 'Herman Melville', 385; 'Holman Hunt', 493; 'Homeland', 321, 368; 'Hudson Taylor to Maria', 523; 'I Go Gentle', 137-8, 445; 'In a Truro Garden', 497; 'Inheritance', 35-6; 'Intimate Landscape', 191, 360-1; *The Invading Gospel*, 243, 307, 318, 319, 321, 324ff, 402-3, 410, 449, 491; 'The Irony of Election', 250; 'It's Only Acting', 480; 'Josephine Butler', 451-2; 'Juan Diego', 494-5; 'Keswick Revisited', 499; 'The Kilns', 517-8; 'La Salette', 495; 'Late Honeymoon', 513; 'Lebanese Harvest', 319, 393; 'The Legend of the Doom Bar', 109-10; 'The Leper', 388-9, 392; 'Lunar Pentecost', 321, 363; *The Map of Clay*, 234, 264, 310, 313, 356ff, 398; 'Mappowder Revisited', 489; *The Marriage of a Rebel*, 226, 242, 272, 281, 291, 402, 471-6, 547; 'Medals', 495; 'Mersey Tunnel', 518; 'Meteorite', 362;

'Midnight of the Flesh', 84; 'Midnight Longing', 83-4; 'The Model', 513-4; 'Modelled in Passion Week', 362; 'Montana Shade', 54-6, 393; 'A Mother's Tragedy', 449; 'Nanpean', 520; 'Neutral Ground', 250, 251, 260, 516; 'New Creation', 194; 'A Night in Soho', 458-9; 'Pagan Disarmers', 428-9; 'Palazzo Rezzonico', 511; 'Parallel', 511; 'Pascal', 391; 'Patronage', 369-70; 'Perennial', 523-4; 'Pilgrimage to Mappowder', 292, 293; 'The Plundered Fuchsias', 250, 252, 516; *Poems 1951*, 264, 300; 'Porthmeor Cemetery', 424, 445; 'Porthpean', 520-1; 'Prairie Song', 393; 'Prisoner of God', 194, 248, 250, 251, 360, 537; 'Quarry Snow', 250; 'Rebel Love', 426, 427; 'Reclaimed', 362; 'The Restored See', 500; 'The Rider', 388, 393; 'Salieri', 496; 'Sandsfoot Castle Gardens', 487; 'School of Clay', 455-6; *Selected Poems* (Bloodaxe), 516, 517, 547; *Selected Poems* (Enitharmon), 264; *The Shadowed Bed*, 144, 158, 224, 303, 304, 312, 398, 446, 491, 501-7, 509; 'Shuttered', 191; 'Simone Weil', 440-1; 'Snowfall at Kernick', 250, 252; 'Sufficiency', 250; 'Summer Saga', 388; 'Surrender', 191; 'A Taste of Scilly', 493; 'The Token', 191, 236-7; 'Torrey Canyon', 427-8; 'Tregerthen Shadow', 362; 'Twilight Where God Dwells', 83-4; 'The Veiled Sitter', 367; 'Venus in Grace', 393; 'Wamba Convent 1964', 453; 'Wart and Pearl', 459-60; 'The Water-Wheel', 250, 253, 360; 'Wedding Eve', 415, 419, 452, 474; 'Well at Bloomdale', 521; 'Wessex and Lyonesse', 293; 'Weymouth', 481-2; *Wilding Graft*, 31, 80, 135, 144, 145, 155, 159, 160, 161, 162, 177, 182, 188, 197ff, 242, 257, 276, 282, 288, 290, 291, 443; 'William Blake Notes a Demonstration', 138, 428-9, 443; 'The Winds', 250; 'Winter Scene in Cornwall', 468-9; 'The Wintry Priesthood', 264, 300, 356, 360

Clemo, John (grandfather), 31, 172

Clemo, Reginald (father), 24, 27, 28, 30, 31, 33, 34, 35-40, 41, 44, 45, 46-8, 51, 53, 54, 56, 57, 58, 62, 65, 88, 393, 506, 509; America, 33, 34, 35-40, 41, 62, 218; death, 47-8; London, 40; Plymouth, 40, 46;

Clemo, Ruth (nee Peaty), 18, 80, 400, 402-8, 409, 410-11, 417-9, 462, 472, 476, 479, 499, 508, 526, 539, 541, 547; birth, 409; death, 548; editing the archives, 18, 101, 281, 405-6, 407, 411, 483-4; meeting Jack for the first time, 412-3;

The Cloud of Unknowing, 341

CNP Publications, 519

Coleman, Dr. Stanley Maurice, 180-1, 182

Coleridge, Samuel Taylor, 382

Cookworthy, William, 22-3, 545

Cornish Guardian, 14, 58, 74, 77, 81, 91, 106, 108ff, 149, 174, 175, 187, 194, 231, 246, 248, 250, 261, 344, 369, 396, 415, 468, 504, 544

Crim, Keith, 374

Cullen, John, 359, 359-60

Daily Mail, 187, 243, 328, 370
Dartnell, Peter, 120-3
Daudet, Alphonse, 124
Davie, Donald, 138-9, 528
Day Lewis, Cecil, 29, 117, 161-2, 167, 173, 194, 215, 222, 224, 225, 235, 238-40, 245, 246, 249-50, 264, 265, 266, 300, 303, 309, 314, 371, 455, 468, 474, 501, 503, 504, 517
Diego, Juan, 492, 494-5
Dinker, Madeleine, 360
Dobbin, Stan, 521, 522
Donne, John, 126, 229, 230, 331, 361, 362, 398, 420, 451, 455, 458, 459; 'Goodfriday, 1613, Riding Westward', 229, 230
Dorset Year Book, 491
Drabble, Margaret, 490
Du Maurier, Daphne, 127-9, 203, 231, 235, 244, 310, 545
Dyllansow Truran publishers, 480

Election, 83, 168-70, 282-3, 326, 332, 335-6, 339-40
Eliot, T.S., 382, 388, 389, 390, 391, 421, 426, 525
Ellis, Havelock, 256
Epstein, Jacob, 125
Evening Standard, 243

Faber & Faber, 249, 263, 492, 493, 545, 547
Fison, Joseph, 348-50
Fleming H. Revell publishers, 330
Fletcher, Mary, 234, 331
Florence, Italy, 190, 529
The Fool Hath Said (Beverley Nichols), 209
Foot, Isaac, 245
Freud, Sigmund, 126, 155
Funston, Eileen, 64, 77, 87, 241, 274-82, 283, 307, 324, 348, 359, 417-8, 503, 505, 531, 532; *Reaching for God*, 278, 279

Gabb, Jean and Maurice, 471
Galsworthy, John, 119, 124, 125, 180; *The Forsyte Saga*, 119, 125
Gay, Theodora – see Powys, Susie
Geoffrey Bles publishers, 328, 344

God in Business (author unknown), 331
Gollancz, Livia, 473, 474
Graham, Billy, 139, 308, 319, 320, 321, 343, 347, 353, 359, 411
Graham, Winston, 203, 235, 301
Graham, W.S., 244, 301, 433
Greene, Graham, 201, 371
Green, John, 154
Gribble, Grace, 64
Gribble, Preston, 65

Hale, Robert, 160, 211
Hall, Dennis, 521-2
Hardy, Thomas, 124, 125, 151, 157, 182, 200, 201, 206-9, 210, 216, 221, 222, 233, 240, 249, 265, 293, 294, 362, 415, 439, 451, 455, 471, 523, 527, 550; (auto)biography, 208, 209; *Desperate Remedies*, 151; *Jude the Obscure*, 157, 182, 207, 208, 209; *Return of the Native*, 157, 206, 207; *Tess of the d'Urbervilles*, 157, 182, 207, 208, 291, 294
Harper, Redd, 321
Harris, John, 523
Hawken, A.J.G., 127, 129
Hawken, Andy, 546
Hemmings, Louis, 80, 330, 450, 491, 501; Samovar Press, 330
Hitler, Adolph, 136, 137, 139, 177, 186, 187
Hoffman, Daniel, 310, 354; 'Lines to Jack Clemo', 310-1
Hocking, Joseph, 14, 29-30, 146
Hocking, Salomé, 29-30, 324
Hocking, Silas, 29-30
Hopkins, Gerard Manley, 382, 388, 426, 451, 458, 459-60, 461
Horton family, 489, 491, 540
Hughes, John, 489
Hugo, Victor, 125, 126
Hummer, T.R., 152
Hurst, John, 468, 478, 545
Hutchings, Monica, 243, 282, 288-9, 290, 291, 292, 293, 295, 307
Huxley, Aldous, 148, 215, 245, 269; *The Art of Seeing*, 269
Huxley, Julian, 130
Hyland, Paul, 491, 516, 525, 528, 537, 541

Irene, 179, 180-1, 182, 183, 189, 192, 199, 205, 230, 255, 271, 273
Iris, 80, 254, 271

Jacobs, Sam, 146, 147, 234
J.A. Linblads, Swedish publishers, 198
James, Marjorie, 477
Jasper, Tony, 546
Jauncey, David, 179, 191, 192
Jauncey, Doris, 179, 182, 191, 272
Jauncey, Pat, 179, 182, 191, 192
Jauncey, Rita, 179, 192
Jay, Peter, 492-3
Jenkins, Patricia, 317-8, 322, 326, 362
Jenkins, Simon, 507
Jennings, Elizabeth, 397, 421, 496
John of the Cross, 394, 536; *Ascent of Mount Carmel*, 394; *Dark Night of the Soul*, 394, 408, 536-7;
John Knox: Portrait of a Calvinist (Edwin Muir), 431
John Knox publisher, 374
Joyce, James, 124, 269

Keats, John, 15, 468
Keller, Helen, 439, 440, 445, 454
Kent, Alan, 205, 468, 484, 525, 544-5
Kessell, Melba, 415
Kierkegaard, Søren, 264, 300, 332, 350, 459
Kirkup, James, 398, 442, 449
Knox, John, 431, 432

Labdon family, 489, 490, 518, 528
Lane, Stephen, 39, 448
Latham, Harold, 223, 225
Lawrence, D.H., 74, 121, 124, 149, 172, 244, 264, 274, 300, 359, 362, 379, 439, 504, 550; ; *Fantasia of the Unconscious*, 121-2; *Kangaroo*, 149
Lawrence, T.E., 212
Layard, John, 433
Lee, Laurie, 249, 300
Leeston, Osyth, 161, 212
Lehmann, John, 213, 214-5, 249
Lehmann, Rosamond, 249
Lewis, C. S., 87, 209, 217, 270, 271, 328-9, 331, 476, 506, 517-8, 523; *The Great Divorce*, 331; *Miracles*, 271, 331; the Narnia books, 506; *The Screwtape*

Letters, 328-9; *Till We Have Faces*, 328
Lion publishers, 491, 507
Loti, Pierre, 126
Lucie-Smith, Edward, 374
Luther, Martin, 335, 431, 476

MacBeth, George, 371, 374, 449, 461, 462
MacInnes, Colin, 310, 356, 358, 368-9, 370, 492
Macmillan publishers, 198, 223, 241, 249, 540
MacNeice, Louis, 225, 249
Macpherson, Aimée Semple, 345
Magnusson, Sally, 15, 403, 404, 408, 476, 507, 508; *Clemo: A Love Story*, 15, 37, 402, 403, 491, 507, 508
Mandus, Brother, 448
Marriage, Alwyn, 524, 528
Marshall, Morgan and Scott publishers, 330
Marshall Pickering publishers, 330
Martin, Ernest (E. W.), 17, 194, 243, 262, 263, 305, 317, 341, 346-7, 348, 440, 471, 474, 504
Martin, Heather, 17, 341, 385, 394
Martin, William, 135-6
Martinez de las Rivas, Toby, 15, 545
Mary the Mother of God (Cardinal Léon-Joseph Suenens), 454
The Mastery of Sex (Leslie Weatherhead), 256
Maugham, W. Somerset, 245
Martz, Renee, 220, 319-21, 327, 363, 366
Meggy, Gordon, 125, 142, 147-9, 150-2, 261
Methodism, 25, 26, 27, 28, 69, 83, 172-3, 193, 234, 324, 353, 550
Methuen, 154, 310, 356, 358, 359, 369, 374, 395, 396, 424, 441, 445, 492, 547
Mew, Charlotte, 496
Milton, John, 427
Miskin, Lionel, 10, 194, 235, 242, 244, 263, 310, 315-7, 318, 322, 351, 353, 367, 379, 381, 396, 414, 425, 433-9, 451, 504, 520
Mitson, Eileen (see Funston)
Moody, D.L., 331
Morgan, James, 478, 484, 492
Mott, Anthony, 226, 242
Mowatt, Godfrey, 285-6, 288, 291, 458-9
Moyer, Patricia, 478, 484

Muggeridge, Malcolm, 449
Mussolini, Benito, 71, 136, 137, 138, 139-40
Myers, Elizabeth, 157-8, 240, 289, 290

Nance, Robert Morton, 133-4
Naomi, 490-1
Newnham, Richard, 374-5
Nicholson, James, 107
Nicholson, Norman, 209, 396, 442, 462, 496, 506
Niebuhr, Reinhold, 127, 217, 259
Nietzsche, Friedrich, 138, 432, 435, 458
Nye, Robert, 524

O'Casey Sean, 264, 440

Parker, Derek, 371, 398
Parkyn, Rev. 120, 127, 129, 504
Patmore, Coventry, 283, 331
Payton, Philip, 150, 526
Pearce, Gwen, 446, 451, 505
Peaty, Bella, 5, 400, 409, 412, 420, 471, 482, 486, 510, 512, 518, 528, 530, 538, 539, 540
Peaty, Ruth – See Clemo, Ruth
Pellymounter, W.S., 61
Penguin Books, 213, 220, 249, 264, 300, 374-5
Perry, Victor, 339, 448, 514, 529
Petrucci, Mario, 538
Phillips, Evelyn, 68-9, 75, 76-7, 78-9, 80-3, 85, 86, 87, 91, 92, 93, 98, 102, 104, 105, 106, 110, 123, 131, 146, 148, 154, 172, 185, 205, 251
Phillips, Harry, 67, 68, 69, 77, 78, 79, 175, 189, 205
Pitt, William, 125
Poe, Edgar Allan, 251
Polmounter, Bertha (aunt), 27, 39, 41, 63-5, 66, 95, 104, 179, 192, 193, 270-1, 274, 296
Polmounter, (Elizabeth) Jane (grandmother), 26-7, 39, 41, 48, 64
Polmounter, John (grandfather), 26, 27, 39, 40, 120
Porter, David, 475
Pound, Ezra, 453
Powys, John Cowper, 240
Powys, Littleton, 158, 243, 288, 289

Powys, Lucy, 288, 488, 489
Powys, Susie, 266, 288, 290-1, 293, 294, 295-6, 410, 532; *A Cuckoo in the Powys Nest*, 296
Powys, T. F., 14, 124, 130, 167, 180, 201, 215, 216, 218, 219, 221, 222, 245, 264, 288-95, 297, 303, 304, 331, 451, 488, 501, 503, 505, 506, 531; *Bottle's Path*, 331; *Goat Green (The Better Gift)*, 167; *God's Eyes A-Twinkle*, 218, 331; *Interpretation of Genesis*, 201; *The Left Leg*, 201; *Mr. Weston's Good Wine*, 130-1, 331; *Soliloquies of a Hermit*, 201, 264, 331; *Unclay*, 201, 331;
Prelude to Richard (I.A.R. Wylie), 209
Prescott, Orville, 216
Previous Parrot Press, 521
Pritchett, V. S., 243, 245
Putt, Gorley, 219, 249

Quiller-Couch, Sir Arthur, 14, 128, 156-7, 211, 301, 310

Raine, Craig, 493-4
Raine, Kathleen, 442, 444
Ramsden, Fr. Benedict, 95, 341-2, 483, 491, 510, 512, 513, 514, 522, 525, 529, 530, 539-40, 541
Ramsden, Sara, 159, 528
Rawe, Donald, 163, 164-5, 479, 480, 492, 526
Raymond, Harold, 215, 222, 501
Redgrove, Peter, 263, 433
Rexroth, Kenneth, 244, 311
Richardson, Maurice Lane, 218
Roberts, Oral, 249, 307-8, 319, 320, 327
Roseveare, Helen, 451, 453, 455
Rossetti, Dante Gabriel, 234
Rosine, 317, 318-9, 351, 393, 428
Rowland, John, 112, 130-1, 243, 345, 347, 461
Rowse, A.L., 14, 17, 36, 137, 146, 150, 156, 157, 204-5, 217, 219, 223-5, 234, 235, 243, 244, 245, 282, 309, 545
Rowse, Barbara, 19, 75, 76-7, 79, 85, 92-6, 97-105, 116, 179, 180, 182, 183, 184, 197, 205, 220, 230, 232, 255, 502
Ruskin, John, 337, 379, 382, 388
Russell, Arthur J., 331
Rutherford, Mark, 345
Ryerson publisher, 374

Sanders, Alan, 66, 545, 546
Sankey, Ira, 35, 82, 111, 330, 331
Sappho, 439, 454
Savage, Derek (D. S.), 17, 194, 244, 262-3, 305-6, 310, 311, 315, 317, 326, 327, 329, 347, 350, 351-2, 387, 420, 445, 473, 481, 489, 507, 514, 519, 526, 527
Savage, Raymond, 155, 160, 161, 162-3, 167, 193, 195, 197, 212, 213, 214, 215, 216, 223 243, 248, 249, 501
Sergeant, Howard, 325, 358; *Outposts*, 358, 461
Shaw, George Bernard, 130, 212
Shearer, Janet, 545
She Had a Magic (Brian O'Brien), 452
Shea, George Beverley, 320
Shelley, Mary, 440
Shelley, Percy Bysshe, 69, 260, 449
Skemp, A.R., 96
Slade, Joan, 162, 182, 205, 241
Slessor, Mary, 451, 452
Smallwood, Norah, 241, 242
Smith, Bernard, 372, 404
Snell, Brenda, 6, 77, 191-2, 212, 220, 221, 232, 238, 241, 254, 255, 271, 360, 361, 502
The Song of Bernadette (Franz Werfel), 367
The Spectator, 263, 345
Spears, Heather, 528
Spinks, Michael, 266, 404, 522
Spire publishers, 242, 477, 516
Spring, Howard, 216
Spurgeon, Charles, 69, 124, 127, 153, 154-5, 158, 168-70, 235, 264, 330, 331, 332, 336, 338, 534; *All of Grace*, 330; *Check Book of the Bank of Faith*, 331
Stafford, Jo, 321
Stevenson, Anne, 521
Stevenson, Robert Louis, 244
Stone, Norman, 476, 477, 481, 508, 517, 541; *A Different Drummer*, 44, 76, 476, 481
Studd, C. T., 124, 330, 331, 334, 343, 348, 453
Symons, Andrew, 250, 448, 468, 541

Tabb House publishers, 424, 492, 496, 517
Talmage, Thomas DeWitt, 69, 235, 247, 267, 330, 331, 332, 337-8

Tamplin, Ronald, 19, 478, 525
Thérèse of Liseaux, 394, 395
Thomas, D.M., 263, 301, 526
Thomas, Dylan, 137-8, 382, 421, 426, 431, 443, 445, 480
Thomas, R.S., 371, 421, 490
Thompson, E.V., 226, 235, 545
Thompson, Francis, 160, 238, 249, 331, 352, 459; 'Ode to Easter', 160; 'The Poppy', 238
Thurlow, Charles, 163, 164
Times Literary Supplement, 218, 243, 263, 332, 345, 346, 397, 398, 442, 444
Tolstoy, Leo, 120, 125, 233, 234, 549
Torrey, R.A., 331
Treneer, Anne, 234, 235
Trethewey, June, 77, 278, 285, 286-8, 362, 474
Trethosa Chapel, 14, 25, 26, 28, 64, 179, 189, 287, 346, 362, 400, 414, 415, 446, 545
Trewin, J.C., 234, 245, 468
Truran, Len, 480, 481
Turner, Steve, 476

Val Baker, Denys, 29, 243, 244, 301, 437, 530; *The Cornish Review*, 29, 263, 301; *One & All*, 301
Van Gogh, Vincent, 124, 367
Venice, Italy, 510-4, 518, 523
Victor Gollancz publishers, 129, 473, 435
Villari, Pasquale, 126
Violet, 75, 76, 92

Wallace-Crabbe, Chris, 449
Weil, Simone, 438, 439, 440-1, 454
Wells, H.G., 130, 141, 215, 223
Wesley, John, 25, 26, 319, 415, 451, 457
West Country Magazine, 249, 291, 468, 531
Western Morning News, 344, 369, 396
Wheal Martyn Museum, 14, 163, 528, 546
Whetter, James, 519
Willcox, Jean, 373
Willcox, Maria, 38, 54, 373
Williams, Michael, 380
Williams, Rowan, 264, 544

Wilmott, H.J., 136, 244
Wilshire, Lewis, 243
Wilson, Colin , 263, 310, 315, 316, 327-8, 346-8
Wilson, Harold and Mary, 398
Whitehouse, Mary, 449
Wiseman, Mary, 77, 257, 278, 317, 376, 378-91, 393, 394, 396-7, 399, 407, 410, 412, 414, 418, 420, 431, 432, 433, 445, 446, 499
Woolf, Virginia, 496
Wordsworth, William, 15, 69, 260, 340, 382, 385, 388, 449

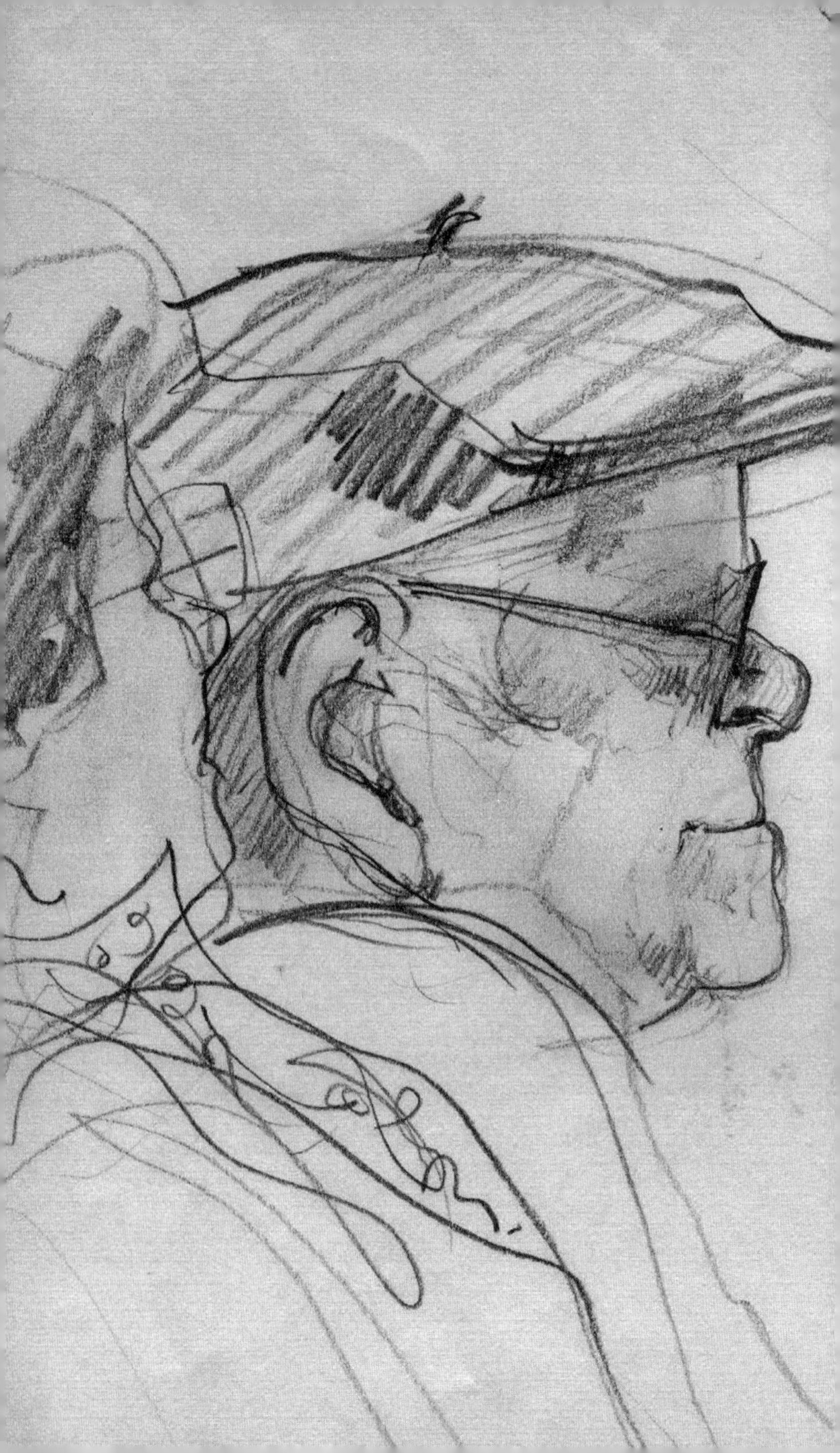

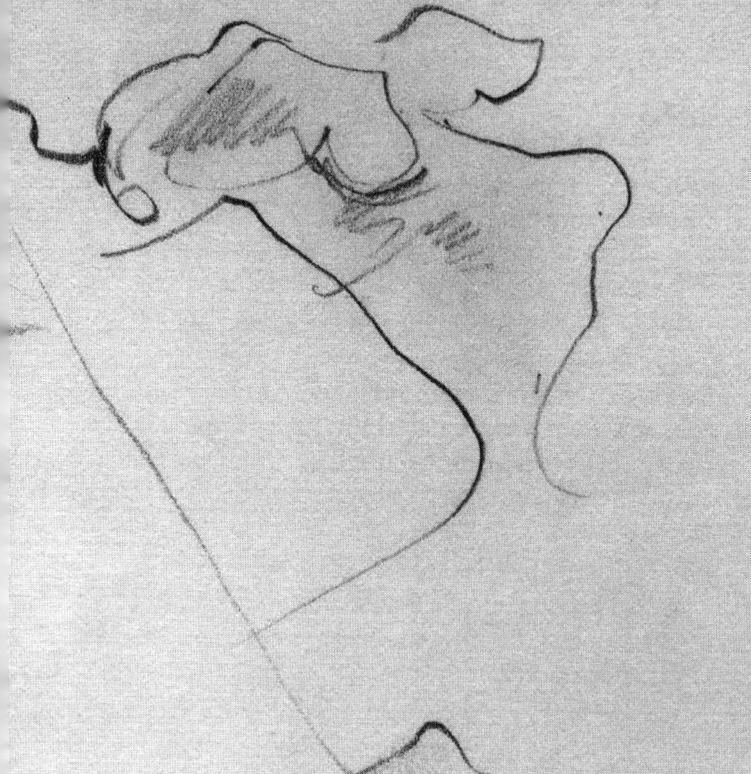

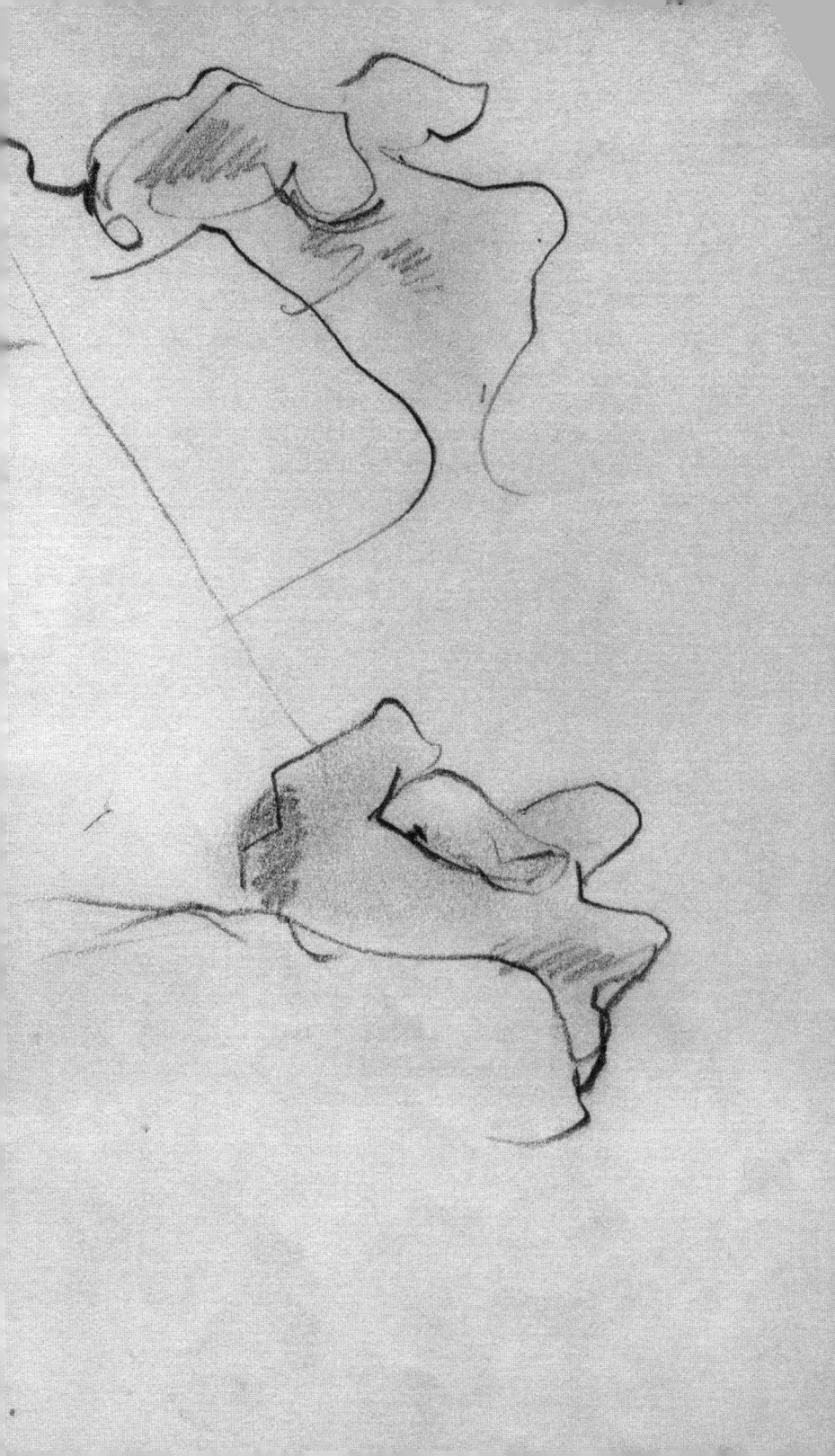

List of Illustrations

Frontis portrait by RL Knight

8-9	Clemo Country Map, by Jennie Murt
11	Diary page, courtesy of the University of Exeter's Special Collections
20	Trethosa Pit, courtesy of the China Clay History Society
33	Reggie and John Clemo, Montana, c.1910
34	Reggie Clemo and friend 'on a ranch', 1911
45	Eveline, Reggie and the baby Jack, 1917
49	(top) Jack, Eveline and Reggie, doctored image
49	(bottom) Eveline and Jack Clemo, c.1920
50	Jack, 1926
72	Jack with early novel manuscript, 1935
176	Evacuees playing outside the Clemo cottage, 1940
196	Publication day. Clemo with *Wilding Graft*, 1948
228	Clemo portrait, 1949
297	T.F. Powys and Clemo at Mappowder, 1950
298	(top) Clemo, Spark and Eveline at Stourton, 1950
298	(bottom) Clemo and Eveline with Frances and Violet Allen, 1950
322	(top) Clemo posing for Lionel Miskin, 1957
322	(bottom) Clemo and sculptor Pat Jenkins, 1957
354	(top) Charles Causley and Clemo, 1961
354	(bottom) Daniel Hoffmann and Clemo, 1961
357	*The Clay Verge* manuscript
376	Jack and Mary, 1963
400	(top) Jack and Eveline, by Ander Gunn, 1966
400	(bottom) Causley, Jack, Ruth and Bella at Clemo's wedding, by GWF Ellis, 1968
425	(top) Jack and Lionel Miskin, 1963
425	(bottom) Ruth 'talking' to Jack, by John Chard, 1978
464	Eveline Clemo, 1975
514	Jack and Ruth on the balcony of Robert Browning's death-place, Ca'Rezzonico, 1993
542	Ruth and Jack, by Paul Broadhurst, 1980